ON STATE, MARGINALIZATION, AND ORIGINS OF REBELLION

ON STATE, MARGINALIZATION, AND ORIGINS OF REBELLION:

THE FORMATION OF INSURGENCIES IN SOUTHERN SUDAN

Aleksi Ylönen

AFRICA WORLD PRESS

TRENTON | LONDON | CAPE TOWN | NAIROBI | ADDIS ABABA | ASMARA | IBADAN | NEW DELHI

AFRICA WORLD PRESS
541 West Ingham Avenue | Suite B
Trenton, New Jersey 08638

Book design: Dawid Kahts
Cover design: Ashraful Haque

Library of Congress Cataloging-in-Publication Data
Names: Ylönen, Aleksi, author.
Title: On state, marginalization, and origins of rebellion : the formation of insurgencies in Southern Sudan / Aleksi Ylönen.
Description: Trenton : Africa World Press, 2016. | Includes bibliographical references and index.
Identi iers: LCCN 2016023148| ISBN 9781569024225 (hb : alk. paper) | ISBN 9781569024232 (pb : alk. paper)
Subjects: LCSH: Insurgency--Sudan. | Internal security--Sudan. | Sudan--Politics and government.
Classi ication: LCC DT157.5 Y56 2016 | DDC 962.4--dc23
LC record available at https://lccn.loc.gov/2016023148

*It is wisdom to seek knowledge about the World
even though the process may be traumatizing*

In memory of Ann-Lis, Martta, and Suvi

Thank you for your abundant love and support

ACKNOWLEDGEMENTS

This book is inspired by my research endeavors on state and conflicts in Africa, particularly Sudan and South Sudan, since 2004. I would like to express my gratitude to many people and institutions for their support during the research and writing process. First and foremost I would like to thank my late grandmothers and my parents. Without your help, support, and inspiration this project could not have been successfully completed.

Secondly, I would like to extend my gratitude to Itziar, Eric, colleagues, friends in the Sudans and diaspora, and other friends in Africa and elsewhere. Your advice, guidance, and comments were paramount for the materialization of this book.

Thirdly, the contribution of a number of individuals and institutions which enabled me to pursue field and literary research has been important. I am particularly thankful to María Elvira at the now defunct Bancaja International Center for Peace and Development, Professor Christopher Cramer and Angelica Baschiera at School of Oriental and African Studies of University of London, and Associate Professor Ibrahim Elnur at Department of Political Science of American University of Cairo, for hosting me in their respective institutions.

Moreover, I was able to count on the help of various institutions and organizations operating in Sudan. Of these, I would like to thank particularly the universities of Juba and Khartoum, ministries and public and private figures in northern and southern Sudan, the United Nations, the Danish Demining Group, and various other non-governmental and religious organizations.

Finally, completing the project would not have been possible without the assistance of a number of funding institutions, mainly the Center for International Mobility (CIMO), *Kansan Sivistysrahasto*, *Oskar Öflunds Stiftelse*, Asociación Española de Cooperación Internacional, Ministerio de Educación y Ciencia, and Fundación Universidad Autónoma de Madrid, which all provided financing at different stages of the research and writing process.

I owe all the abovementioned individuals and organizations deep gratitude for their belief in me and this project. All errors remain my own.

In Valencia, Spain

April 2015

TABLE OF CONTENTS

Maps

Main Abbreviations and Acronyms

AACC	All African Council of Churches
ACNS	Advisory Council for Northern Sudan
ALF	Azania Liberation Front
APF	Anya Nya Patriotic Front
CAC	Constitutional Amendment Commission
CAR	Central African Republic
CPA	Comprehensive Peace Agreement
CUSS	Council for the Unity of the Southern Sudan
DRC	Democratic Republic of the Congo
ELF	Eritrean Liberation Front
FOM	Free Officers' Movement
GC	Graduates' General Congress
HEC	High Executive Council
KFAED	Kuwaiti Fund for Arab Economic Development
LFA	Land Freedom Army
NF	National Front
NGO	Non-Governmental Organization
NPG	Nile Provisional Government
NUP	National Unionist Party
OAU	Organization of African Unity
OPEC	Organization of Petroleum Exporting Countries
PDP	People's Democratic Party

SAC	Sudan Administrative Conference
SACDNU	Sudan African Closed Districts National Union
SANU	Sudan African National Union (former SACDNU)
SCP	Sudan Communist Party
SEC	Southern Equatoria Corps
SF	Southern Front
SPLM/A	Sudan People's Liberation Movement/Army
SRRG	Sue River Revolutionary Government of the Suer Republic
SSLM	Southern Sudan Liberation Movement
SSO	State Security Organ
SSWA	Southern Sudan Welfare Association
TRG	Transitional Regional Government
U.N.	United Nations
UNHCR	United Nations High Commissioner for Refugees
U.S.	United States
U.S.S.R.	Union of Soviet Socialist Republics (Soviet Union)
WCC	World Council of Churches
WFL	White Flag League

A. Sudan Political Map (Pre-2011)

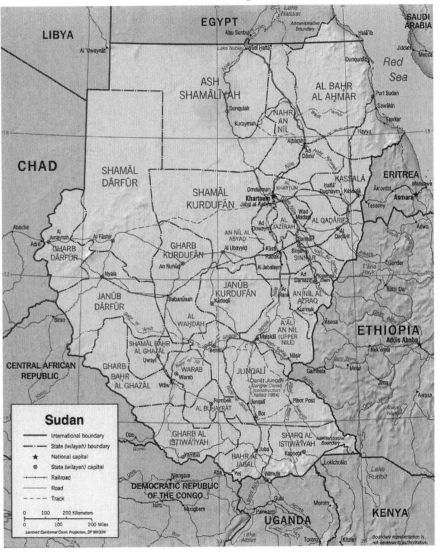

CHAPTER I

INTRODUCTION:
Theoretical Interpretations of Causes of African Insurgencies

Insurgencies are a complex phenomenon involving a variety of actors and forces. They contain historically embedded political, economic, and social dynamics that intertwine local, domestic, regional, and international arenas. Many of these conflicts, mainly manifested by armed violence within the state, have involved actors from neighboring countries and been influenced by international players and forces. In order to try to understand how insurgencies in Africa materialize, this study focuses on their formational processes in southern Sudan, which underwent the longest two-stage war on the continent until its formal end with the Comprehensive Peace Agreement (CPA) in January 2015.

The roots of war in Sudan are complex. Although insurgencies first took place in southern Sudan, other areas, mainly Darfur, Red Sea region, Blue Nile, and Southern Kordofan, have also witnessed armed opposition. This has led to an understanding of war in Sudan as a wider conflict between the center and the marginalized state peripheries,[1] which initially manifested itself with violent confrontation between sections of the state's governing elite and sectors of southern leadership. This study provides a historical analysis on insurgency formation in southern Sudan where the first and longest rebellions in Sudan took place, although similar processes of state marginalization and organization of armed opposition have since occurred elsewhere in the periphery of the Sudanese state. However, the study's in-depth focus on southern Sudan and its complex relationship with the state, as well as limited time, have not allowed the author to conduct similar detailed investigation on insurgency formation in Sudan's other peripheries.

Southern Sudanese armed struggles took place within one of the most elaborate and complex state crises in the contemporary world.[2] The incalculable human toll of its first two large-scale conflicts since the 1950s reached millions of conflict-related deaths. The first insurgency in southern Sudan, the initial violent manifestation of the so-called "Southern Problem",[3] erupted through violent disturbances in August 1955 only months before Sudan gained its independence. In the early 1960s the conflict accelerated and it took approximately 17 years and more than 500,000 lives before Addis Ababa Peace Agreement[4] ended the large-scale hostilities between the government and the southern insurgents in February 1972.[5]

However, a number of southern factions were unhappy about the peace treaty. Some engaged in residual guerrilla warfare and others became increasingly discontented in the course of the 1970s. In May 1983 the second rebellion broke out in southern Sudan, which ended almost 22 years later after more than 2 million people had perished and 4 to 6 million had become displaced.[6] From the signing of the CPA and other subsequent peace treaties[7] Sudan's future continued to be highly uncertain, and the CPA implementation finally led to a secession and the establishment of a new state of South Sudan on 9 July 2011.

In the political context of the war in southern Sudan, armed opposition emerged also in other areas of the periphery of the Sudanese state. Rebels took up arms in the Nuba Mountains of Southern Kordofan and the southern part of the Blue Nile region where the local guerrilla forces formed part of the broader southern insurgency, while other insurgent groups emerged later in Darfur and the Red Sea region in northern Sudan.[8]

Insurgencies in Sudan, and their causes, have been debated for a long time. As in the case of most of Africa, the predominant media image projected to wider audiences has often portrayed the Sudanese crisis as originating either from a new form of barbarism, a resurgence of ancient hatreds drawing on primordial religious, racial, and cultural differences, or from violent competition over resources (a resource war) with exaggerated emphasis on the importance of a war economy based on looting, or controlling and selling, Sudan's high value natural endowments.

Yet, the attempts to present causes of insurgencies in Sudan in a simplified manner have led to a large number of studies with incomplete analyses that allow potential misinterpretations of these conflicts. For instance, although a number of scholars have claimed that apparently unchanging and regionally manifested identity differences and incompatibilities are a major, if not the main, source of war,[9] this view has been largely discredited by deeper analyses on identity formation.[10] Secondly, following the focus on analyzing rebellions through economic factors, a tendency credited to Paul Collier and Anke Hoeffler,[11] some authors have pulled particularly the

second insurgency in southern Sudan out of its historical context and argued that it was provoked mainly by economic greed,[12] the mere existence
of natural resources,[13] or simply petroleum.[14] Thirdly, while the so-called
"failed state" analyses have been applied to the case of Sudan,[15] they have
not been convincing in explaining the processes of insurgency formation.
Fourthly, a large part of the current historical literature on insurgencies in
southern Sudan has an endogenous, or domestic, focus, and there tends to
be a lack of deeper analysis of the intertwined local-regional-international
causes and the wider context in which rebellions have taken place. Finally,
when analyzing causes of insurgencies in southern Sudan, an influential part
of the Anglo-Saxon historical literature has been largely deterministic and
at times presented Victorian overtures.[16] Thus, it is argued in this work that
closer observation of historical analyses and interdisciplinary literature on
Sudanese conflicts reveals that studies focusing on a single cause, or solely
the domestic sphere, are not fully reflective of the formation processes of
insurgencies in southern Sudan.

Although a number of the abovementioned interpretations hold explanatory power, there are other more immediate factors that contribute to the
underlying political and economic crises and their escalation into insurgencies. An in-depth examination in the interdisciplinary literature on the roots
of conflict in Sudan reveals, for instance, the importance of the discourse that
argues that armed conflicts within states take place in conditions of extreme
inequality and uneven development.[17] This is recognized here, and it is therefore argued that the dynamics of state marginalization, generating perceptions of injustices through political, economic, and social exclusion between
the state's center and the periphery, are among the principal preconditions
for the establishment of armed opposition against the highly exclusive, narrowly representative, and predominantly authoritarian state.[18] This consideration not only helps to gain a more complete understanding of the causes of
insurgencies, but also highlights the limitations of interpretations pursuing
unidisciplinary or unifocal analyses restricted by boundaries of specific academic methods and disciplines.

The contemporary literature on insurgencies tends to utilize terms
such as "civil", "internal" or "regionalized" war, but in this study the in-
ter-changeable use of insurgency and rebellion, and conflict and war, is preferred. This decision has been made on the basis that it is misleading to call
any war "civil" or strictly "internal", since war can hardly be characterized
as a "civil" affair and because regional and/or international actors and forces
are always somehow present in the making, driving, and ending of insurgencies.[19] The attempt to avoid such qualifiers has motivated the adoption

of part of O'Neill's[20] definition of an insurgency " . . . as a struggle between a nonruling group and the ruling authorities in which the former consciously employs political resources (organizational skills, propaganda, and/or demonstrations) and instruments of violence . . ." as the guiding thread for the study. This definition provides a flexible foundation for examining insurgency formation.

Insurgencies are complex and involve a variety of actors and forces. This work explores the process of insurgency formation in southern Sudan by investigating the processes that led to politically, economically, and socially inspired large-scale violence. It therefore attempts to remedy the ". . . dearth of analysis linking colonial international relations with the post-colonial world . . . ",[21] which is necessary for any attempt for a comprehensive understanding of the intractable rebellions in southern Sudan. The investigation is guided by a theoretical approach based on the notion of state marginalization, which incorporates regional and international factors in the historical analysis and allows deeper and more comprehensive interdisciplinarily informed explanation of the process of insurgency formation than political or economic approaches based on "failed state" and "new wars" paradigms, or "rational choice", "greed", and "opportunity" of *Homo Economicus*.[22]

First, the research presented here adopts a historically anchored concept of state marginalization. This is an approach that draws from state exclusiveness, weakness, and illegitimacy in the peripheries, elite theory, identity politics, and center-periphery approach (concepts of "uneven development" and "internal colonialism") to explore the origins of insurgencies in southern Sudan. Second, unlike most literature on Sudanese conflicts, the study highlights the agency of specific sections of particular elites in the process of insurgencies formation in southern Sudan. This takes place in the context of a process of persisting violence and socioculturally derived political and economic domination to which southern Sudan and its peoples have been historically and contemporarily subjected.[23] These dynamics and structural conditions owe largely to the exclusive governance by the culturally Arabized ruling elite that has exercised a monopoly on political and economic power since decolonization. Whereas historically this domination has taken the form of colonialism, arguably from the time of decolonization it has become characterized by "internal colonialism".[24] This is a somewhat controversial term[25] but one which can usefully illustrate the colonist mentality of the northern Arabized elite towards southern Sudan, underscoring similarities with the mentality of the preceding European and Ottoman colonizers. In the case of southern Sudan, these dynamics are easily perceived but not significantly substantiated in scholarly literature.

4

Finally, by incorporating Bayart's concept of "extraversion"[26] along with literature on social networks, this work proposes unveiling interconnections linking actors and influences as a useful approach. It allows exploring insurgency formation in southern Sudan in a more comprehensive manner (including local, regional, and international context). In other words, rather than focusing strictly on unidisciplinary explanations of causes of war, an attempt is made here to provide an analysis which is historically founded, interdisciplinary, and overarching.

Summary and Organization of the Study

This monograph provides an attempt to respond to the need of a comprehensive account on how state marginalization and elite agency influence the processes of insurgency formation in Africa. It begins by reviewing the major theoretical currents used to explain the origins of civil wars and then analyzes the first and second rebellion in Sudan, which are among the longest and most complex in Africa. The chosen cases not only help to understand the historical continuities contributing to the origins of such wars, but also provide excellent examples of how the processes of insurgency formation are integrally bound to the state and its policies as well as to the regional and international context. These dimensions have not been emphasized in a holistic manner in the literature on the causes of civil wars in Africa, which tends to focus on internal societal dynamics in the origins of rebellions without fully integrating regional and international dimensions. As a result, the current literature often fails to improve the understanding of the role of relevant regional and international actors and forces.

This study begins with a review and analysis of major theoretical approaches used to understand the causes of civil wars in Africa (Chapter I), pointing out some of their strengths and weaknesses. In Chapter II, the theoretical propositions that guide this study are presented and contextualized in the historical and contemporary foundations of insurgency formation in southern Sudan. The empirical part of the analysis begins in Chapter III, which provides a concise background to the emergence of a regional elite and the formation of the Sudanese polity. It deals with controversial issues, such as slavery, representations and memory of which were an important mobilizing factor for rebellion in southern Sudan. Chapter IV is dedicated to the colonial experience, with an explicit emphasis on the emergence of nationalism in northern Sudan as an elite project, which became contrasted by the embryonic contemporary southern elite that surfaced shortly before Sudan's independence. The process of decolonization during which the first insurgency broke out is discussed in Chapter V. It highlights the state elite's strategy of portraying southern Sudan as a "problem" in response to which a selection of southern leaders engaged in political mobilization, as well as the importance of the regional and international actors and forces in the process of decolonization leading up to the insurgency.

Chapter VI details the failed efforts to find a solution to the southern rebellion and the establishment of authoritarian rule that put a formal end to the insurgency through the peace agreement in Addis Ababa. However, as Chapter VII explains, the conflict lingered on largely due to the incomplete incorporation of southern Sudan into the Sudanese state and the continued interest of the northern state elite to marginalize the region. The processes that led to the deterioration of the situation are then analyzed in Chapter VIII, including the regional and international context of Islamicization and the Cold War environment which facilitated the end of the limited southern autonomy and led to southern Sudan's renewed marginalization that in turn favored re-militarization. Chapter IX then details the conspiracy leading to the second rebellion in southern Sudan, and explains the complex landscape of the early struggle. Finally Chapter X, the epilogue, engages in the debate of seeking comprehensive understanding of the formation of insurgencies in southern Sudan, while summing up the major findings of the study and discussing its capacity to explain origins of rebellions in Africa.

Major Analytical Trends Seeking to Understand Causes of Insurgencies

During the Cold War, a number of major explicative narratives were used to analyze insurgencies. The Cold War rebellions tended to involve the competing superpowers and their allies in the client states of the opposing party, which frequently converted peripheries of post-colonial states in the global South into war zones.[27] A common feature of Cold War conflict studies was to describe insurgencies as internal. It is true that these conflicts owed much to the systemic contradictions of states, which involved the processes of identity polarization and hybrid forms of social organization, including amalgamations of imposed colonial and indigenous institutions. However, it is important to recognize that these realities are a product of a combination of intertwined local, regional, and international actors and forces, and that their origins often include heavy influence of external players and dynamics. In the case of African states, where penetration of external influences has been particularly salient, colonial history and the process of decolonization are particularly relevant. Here, for instance political boundaries are an important factor because many ethnic groups have been perpetually divided by borders drawn during colonialism.[28] These borders have provided a significant element in inspiring "reciprocal separatism" particularly when the leading cadres of a politically mobilized ethnic or regional group have been excluded from state power.[29] They have often also contributed to regionalization and internationalization of conflicts,[30] especially when boundary claims have involved various actors.

Explanations that grow out of these analytical foundations to interpret insurgencies in Africa, particularly after their proliferation in the 1990s, can be organized in a number of broad and interrelated categories according to their theoretical base.[31] Firstly, identity-based essentialist analyses drawing from primordialism and "ancient hatreds" could be said to have crystallized in the "new barbarism" argument, which attempts to explain the emergence of insurgencies due to population pressures or historically incompatible identities that have been let loose by the weakening of states after the Cold War. Secondly, a discourse emphasizing economic and material factors, such as resource scarcity and underdevelopment, has explained the origins of conflicts through related pathologies, focusing the contest over natural resources, greed, violent economic opportunity, and poverty. Thirdly, controversies over the preponderance of economic explanations generated new focus on grievance-based analyses in part to re-emphasize the importance of identity and to highlight perceptions of injustices as opposed to *Homo Economicus* explanations derived from material self-interest. What could be considered as a fourth parallel current, but strongly linked to comparative Political Science and Sociology, is analyzing insurgencies through the crisis of the post-colonial state, or state failure, which became increasingly apparent in the 1980s due to the economic crisis and culminated in the increasing internal political strife after the end of the Cold War. This latter literature, out of which the "new war" paradigm could be said to have emerged, laid the basis for later analyses explaining state weakness, failure, and collapse.

Identity Centered Analyses

Identities have played an important role in social sciences in explaining collective mobilization for protest and armed resistance.[32] According to social identity theory,[33] individuals attempt to achieve a positive social identity that allows them to participate in an in-group with which they share values and emotional significance.[34] They do this by defining the out-group (the categorical "other") through social comparisons.[35] It is also considered that such self-categorization is based on shared social identity that de-personalizes behavior in collective action,[36] and allows groups to engage in more radical behavior than the individuals would themselves. According to Jean Piaget,[37] the processes of accommodation and assimilation are of paramount importance as new information is weighed, shaped, and interpreted according to already established background, which results in an individual's decision to participate in, or reject joining, an insurgency. In the case of analyzing the causes of conflict in Africa, essentialist, constructivist, and instrumentalist approaches to identities have been put forward.

Essentialist Interpretations

In the early 1990s a trend in literature emerged which perceived insurgencies as increasingly "new" and "uncivil".[38] From these studies the essentialist "new barbarism" thesis surfaced, which explains civil wars as a new form of savagery with the primary victims being civilians.[39] Kaplan and Peters put forward the idea of "new barbarism" as senseless violence, with Kaplan[40] claiming that the prevalence of violence and insurgencies in the 1990s resulted largely from Malthusian population pressures and accelerating urbanization.

Perhaps the most famous work to lend support to argumentation along the abovementioned lines has been Huntington's *The Clash of Civilizations and Remaking of World Order* (1997), which portrays international politics as an extension of a "tribal"[41] conflict between competing civilizations. This argument also gained momentum through ill-explained media images, given that " . . . many anthropologists, NGO activists, and journalists tend to perceive violence as an outcome rather than a process . . .".[42] This trend resulted in violence in Africa being largely portrayed as irrational, inhumane, and tribal, in the midst of misery and poverty.

Inherent to the discourse based on primordial identities is the "ancient hatreds" argument. For instance, Garnett claims that because of the ancient hatreds which had retaken the arena of ethnic politics in a number of developing countries after the Cold War, political structures dwindled or collapsed, resulting in anarchy and conflict.[43] The idea that ancient hatreds or incompatible identities were bound to clash in given opportune conditions was used to explain ethnic and tribal conflicts.

However, any close observation of the essentialist current should discredit some of its major claims. The catastrophism projected through the overpopulation argument as the cause of insurgencies, for instance, is largely flawed since a number of states experiencing insurgencies are in fact sparsely populated relative to their large geographic extensions and extensive natural endowments.

In addition, many academics have found primordialist argumentation insufficient in explaining why insurgencies take place.[44] As a result, the idea of violence in Africa based on incompatible and unchanging identities has been largely discredited. While some have argued that there exist inherent ethnic incompatibilities, this is often not the case. For instance, although it has been argued that such insurmountable differences exist between the "Arabs" and the "Africans" in Sudan,[45] prominent scholars, such as Ali Mazrui, have shown that intermixing through marriage and reproduction " . . . has saved the Arab-Negro division in Africa from being a dichotomous gulf – and converted it instead into a racial continuum of merging relationships".[46]

Moreover, Kalyvas has asserted that the focus of the ancient hatred arguments ". . . is on instances of violence rather than the complex, and often invisible, non violent actions and mechanisms that precede and follow them. Often, the description of very recent acts of violence is accompanied by references to ancient historical events, with no reference to the period in between".[47] This has led him to argue that discovering the real cause and effect relationships related to the origins of insurgencies should oblige us to consider violence as a process, and, to assert that it also requires a contextualized analysis.[48] Such an approach defies strict categorization of causes of conflict because narrowing down the determinants at one point in time through classification and qualification is likely to exclude relevant elements that affect the process.

In other words, despite the popular and sensationalist appeal of the "new barbarism" and "ancient hatreds" argumentation, the essentialist discourse appears to have limited explanatory power on how mobilization for armed violence takes place. This is because it rather simplistically assumes that state decay and collapse (re)activate hatreds that automatically lead to violent conflict.

Constructivism and Instrumentalism

Constructivism opposes essentialism and argues for the importance of social context in shaping the development of identity of an individual through the continuous process of socialization.[49] According to the constructivist approach, identities are built and shaped.[50] Thus, they change gradually over time. Constructivists believe that political decisions are to an extent founded upon innate beliefs acquired via cultural context, upbringing, and education of the individual.[51] This approach for understanding identities is advocated by many africanists.[52] In the African political context, the constructivist approach opposes the essentialist discourse and points to the ability of the

9

elites, or political strongmen ("big men") who draw large part of their legitimacy from their prominent role as "nodes of resource distribution",[53] to channel resources to their constituents in exchange for loyalty and readiness for sacrifice along (neo)patrimonial patron-client networks. This endows such strongmen with a variable degree of capacity to mobilize followers for personal or group objectives in pursuit of their own personal agendas, but it also constrains them because these big men depend on their ability to allocate resources to maintain their constituents who expect material returns for their loyalty. Thus, many constructivists would agree that political decisions by elites that lead to action are neither inherently instrumental nor merely manipulative and self-interested, but that they inescapably reflect, to a certain degree, the leading individuals' convictions and social background as well as the interests of at least some of their constituents.

A number of influential studies showing how national identities are constructed exist,[54] and arguments concerning how constructed identities relate to societal conflict have been put forward by various scholars. For instance, the main argument of *Invention of Tradition* (1992) edited by Hobsbawm and Ranger is that many of the public traditions recognized by masses are well-designed inventions of 18th and 19th centuries to facilitate control and manipulate opinions of large populations. Ranger demonstrates how in Africa the colonial authorities imported Western, and invented new local, traditions, which were later used by ethnic and nationalist movements.[55] In a similar vein, Ignatieff points out that rebellions largely owe to what he calls the "narcissism of minor difference", having to do with elites manipulating the political discourse and ethnic differences to gain or preserve power.[56] A similar thesis is advanced in a number of chapters in *Armed Conflict in Africa* (2003) edited by Pumphrey and Schwartz-Barcott.

These and other works subscribe to an instrumentalist view in which roots of armed conflict include mobilization using instrumentalizable identity elements such as religion, ideology, customs, and ethnicity. For ethnopolitical constituencies such elements are the foundation of a "collective sense of identity and heritage", and, at times, they can be used to deliberately provoke inter-ethnic conflict and armed violence.[57] Indeed, reconstruction, reinforcement, and manipulation of the continuous process of shaping ethnic identity by the elites for political mobilization and conflict is widely demonstrated.[58] For Chabal and Daloz, motivations for political strife are often linked to the shrinking of the financial patrimonial base of political strongmen, turning clients into enemies, and other strongmen challenging those in power, or excluding minorities from accessing national resources.[59]

The wide acceptance of both constructivist and instrumentalist explanations among scholars points to the importance of considering a mixed approach in an attempt to pinpoint identity causes of armed conflicts. After all, identity (re)construction and manipulation plays a crucial role in generating inter-group cleavages that may escalate into armed violence and eventually major wars.

Identity Analyses and Southern Sudan

Identity discourses provide a number of useful aspects for the analysis of insurgency formation in southern Sudan. In particular, the constructivist and instrumentalist approaches appear relevant. This is because in order to maintain power exclusively, the governing sections of the Arabized elite have developed a long history of justifying their paramount role in Sudanese social hierarchy, politics, and economy, through their self-proclaimed Arab-Muslim identity. While this is partly a feature of searching identity within the larger Arab world/cultural sphere, it has also been used to justify the instrumentalization of culture and religion, e.g. Arabization and Islamicization, as political tools. At times these tools have been imposed repressively, demonizing local populations in the periphery and holding them responsible for creating instability, most notably in the case of the largely non-"Arab" and non-"Muslim" southern Sudan. This way the southern Sudanese have been portrayed as the most extreme "other" against which the particular type of Arab culture and Islam promoted by the leading state elites has been reflected, while depicting the state elite's particular interpretation of Arab culture and Islam as superior identity and personal status elements.[60] This outlook has also justified the dismissal of the political opposition from the peripheral marginalized regions by portraying their "regional" demands as a security threat to the state, and permitted continued marginalization and exclusion of such regions by denying them the possibility of building effective representation at the center of the political system. Arguably, this has been the case in Sudan since decolonization when sectors of the Arabized Muslim elite assumed exclusive political power from the British, and consequently faced strong political opposition from sections of the southern Sudanese leadership demanding federalism.

Such strategies benefit immediately mainly the narrow sectors of the governing elite and tend to exclude others. This is why competition over control of the state and political and economic power is intense even among the factions of the Arabized elite itself. Yet, the promotion of an Arab-Muslim dominated social hierarchy also benefits the Arabized elite's constituencies particularly in north-central Sudan, as it generally provides them with a

11

socially privileged position relative to the non-Arabized and/or non-Muslim peoples from the state periphery in terms of social status and economic opportunities distributed along ethnic and family lines.

Conversely, especially during the Anglo-Egyptian Condominium, influential sectors of local elites in southern Sudan received Western education. This to an extent maintained the memory of slavery, which served to demonize the northern Sudanese "Arabs". Together with personal experiences, and local histories of slave trade and oppression, education has been instrumental in shaping the views of contemporary southern elites. According to constructivists, such socialization through education would in turn condition political decision-making of individuals. Indeed, it appears that this has often been the case in terms of political orientations, sentiments, and actions of Sudanese elites. For instance, many authors mention collective sentiments of fear, anxiety, and mistrust as being relevant to conflict formation in southern Sudan,[61] and others also emphasize the local leaders' use and encouragement of such feelings which has served to fuel the existing sense of insecurity towards "the other".[62]

Although "African" and "Arab" are not identities that in principle prevent coexistence in Sudan, their instrumentalization and use as tools for exclusive political and economic power have had polarizing effects between groups subscribing to these constructed categories. This has led to varying degrees of differentiation based on ethnic and cultural lines (e.g. instrumentalization of differences of religion and language) through time, and in some situations resulted in political strife and armed violence. Such identity approaches also point out the divisive politics of fragmented ethnic communities, including their crucial regional and international dimensions. This is highly relevant to the case of Sudan where many groups maintain links and networks with their ethnic kin in the neighboring countries and the diaspora, while a number of states and other external actors tend to sympathize with groups they are linked to through cultural, ethnic, kin, or other ties. Moreover, Berman and Lonsdale's and Lonsdale's claim regarding political interest groups, or parties, reinforcing divisive politics and local dynamics of ethnic exclusion appears to apply in the case of Sudan in terms of the significant use of ethnic and religious identity politics to enforce the sense of difference leading to political factionalism and "tribalism".[63] In this, the personal agency of prominent individuals, not only structural conditions, is important, along with people's reactions to changing circumstances which may differ considerably. Although often rational, such reactions do not always follow the individual's own beliefs or moral frame since they can be heavily influenced by other factors (e.g. fear, repression, and violence).

12

Therefore, both constructivism and instrumentalism can be considered important in insurgency formation in Sudan. Posner has adopted a mixed identity-based view in interpreting political behavior in Africa, as for him ethnic identity is (re)constructed and at times instrumentalized. To Posner identities are also situational, with both leaders and followers selecting aspects of their identity for group belonging. This guides their decision-making depending on the particularities of each situation. He further claims that leaders have a variety of identity elements to choose from, among which they select the most appropriate to exploit for their purposes, while sharing a degree of genuine belief in any such identity component with their followers.[64]

The usefulness of constructivist-instrumentalist approach to explain political mobilization based on identities has resulted in a similar position adopted in this study. The analysis here considers ethnic identity not only as constructed but also at times instrumentalized, depending on the situation. This means that individuals hold various layered identity aspects which are innate and which they truly believe in. Depending on the situation, such as times of perceived extreme insecurity, they choose among them either consciously or being less aware. It is considered here that this mixed identity-based approach is the most appropriate manner to analyze insurgency formation in southern Sudan. Neither instrumentalist nor constructivist approach can be considered exclusive of the other.

Economic and Material Explanations

The second group of narratives explaining insurgencies concentrates on economic and material factors. In the early 1990s these evolved into a discourse perhaps best exemplified by the work of Homer-Dixon,[65] which argues that underdevelopment related to environmental scarcity creates conflict between societal groups to the extent of causing inter-ethnic feuds and even rebellions. While Kaplan used this as part of his argument for "new barbarism"[66] in the course of the late 1990s, the terms development and underdevelopment (Western concepts that had emerged after World War II)[67] became increasingly tied to explaining armed conflicts. Considering African conflicts to result from increasing poverty, environmental degradation, population explosion, social exclusion, marginalization, elite corruption, and inherent militarism of African societies became popular.[68]

The underdevelopment discourse has argued for the importance of development in curbing conflict. Three major variants of the underdevelopment discourse are the neoliberal, dependency, and Marxist, of which the latter two focus mainly on distorting effects of capitalist economic and trade relations on developing countries. For instance, Duffield has shown that the neoliberal discourse uses underdevelopment to explain why conflict happens in the poorest parts of the world and uses it to justify the moral obligation for aid and development cooperation.[69] Some authors highlighted the economic aspects of insurgencies, arguing that these had become increasingly important, particularly in the case of "internal wars"[70] that had become the most common form of large-scale armed conflict.[71]

By the mid-1990s analyses founded on neoclassical economic theory gained momentum, although traditionally the study of war has not been central to the economic inquiry. Some influential studies laid the basis for the emphasis on economic causes of civil wars.[72] These studies coincided with more descriptive historical analyses, some of which described state-making process as organized crime perpetrated by violent entrepreneurs.[73]

The Collier-Hoeffler framework,[74] which was highly publicized and vigorously debated,[75] became probably the most influential economic theory paradigm to grow out of this discourse. Academically, it initiated and dominated the "greed versus grievance" debate, developing a research current based on economic rational choice logic (according to neoclassical economics), while generating highly debatable results.[76] The Collier-Hoeffler discourse claimed that insurgencies take place in poor regions of the world mostly because of economic greed, or opportunity, of anti-government leaders seeking to extract wealth through armed violence by looting or controlling natural resources.[77] As such, it presents a normative approach siding with governments and de-legitimizing armed opposition, which is appealing to states and international organizations. In conjunction with Collier-Hoeffler framework, a discourse depicting post-colonial conflicts as "resource wars" became increasingly popular.[78]

However, although it appears that contemporary insurgencies are characterized by a more visible economic logic relative to rebellions during the Cold War, many scholars disagree with the most economicist arguments of the causes of civil wars. For instance, Bowles, Franzini, and Pagano[79] and Fine[80] demonstrate that the idea of supremacy of economics has often been used to justify the subordination of other academic disciplines that have long explained armed conflict. Yet, the empirical record of insurgencies defies the simple economic analysis. It suggests that rebel motivations and operations are complex, and likely to be less founded on greed than what economic theory based on material rational choice logic and profit maximization would appear to indicate.[81]

Various scholars have further questioned the methodology employed in the economicist studies.[82] In their criticism, they have mainly targeted the statistical approach, simplicity, inaccuracy, and dichotomy of "greed versus grievance".[83] In addition, Berdal points out that the absence of historical foundations, and portraying only single-intent motivation, provides a distorted image.[84] Indeed, the approach tends to criminalize insurgencies and buttress policies to restore state authority,[85] preventing objective evaluation of the state which may itself be authoritarian and criminal. Apart from ignoring the degree of state legitimacy, the economicist studies have often lacked variables or recognition of repression, regional or group-based (horizontal) inequality,[86] and coercive capacity in the context of state peripheries where insurgencies tend to occur.[87]

Moreover, the Collier-Hoeffler approach emphasizes material poverty, the existence of natural resource wealth, and unemployed urban youth as determinant factors of insurgencies, while dismissing anything but material motivations.[88] Yet, others have argued that the political process through which resources are distributed is paramount, and that its relationship with insurgency formation needs more emphasis,[89] while according to Richards the strategies of poor young men (likely recruits) in search of material rewards are complex and in many cases do not result in them becoming rebels.[90]

Another questionable claim by Collier-Hoeffler is the motivation to loot as one major initiator of insurgencies. Although looting exists in almost every armed conflict, empirical record goes against the argument that looting is generally the principal cause of rebellions. Rather, resistance to looting or other types of violence and repression may lead to armed conflict, as has arguably been the case in Sudan.[91]

Indeed, largely because of the complexity of the war in Sudan the economicist analyses of civil wars have rarely been applied to this case. However, some attempt to this end was made in the World Bank publications, *Understanding Civil War, volume I* (2005a) and *II* (2005b), which were used to solidify the Collier-Hoeffler analysis of economics of civil wars. The first book, *Understanding Civil War: Evidence and Analysis* (2005a), includes a chapter called "Sudan's Civil War: Why Has It Prevailed for So Long?" by Ali, Elbadawi, and El-Batahani. The authors begin the chapter with two quotes of which the second is a statement of late John Garang, founder and leader of the SPLM/A, the main rebel group of the second southern Sudanese insurgency. In an interview on 3 March 1984 Garang stated that

> The burden and incidence of neglect and oppression by successive Khartoum clique regimes has traditionally fallen more on the South than on other parts of the country. Under these circumstances, the marginal cost of rebellion in the South became very small, zero or negative; that is, in the South it pays to rebel.[92]

15

Gadir Ali, Elbadawi, and El-Batahani use the quote in an effort to draw the Sudan case study closer to the Collier-Hoeffler framework, but they take Garang's statement out of the context of state oppression and erroneously portray the decision to start the war as purely economic and opportunistic.[93]

In fact, the multiple causes of Sudanese insurgencies cannot be appreciated through simple economic modeling. Rather, the economic motivations behind the rebellion should not be seen as paramount, but as part of the sociopolitical context influenced by local (national), regional, and international actors and forces. Restricting the causes to economic logic only does not explain how economic and social factors (e.g. marginalization and exclusion) create grievances that generate exploitable political opportunities for mobilization, and how such mobilization takes place. It therefore downplays political and social grievances, such as perceptions of subjugation, injustices, and marginalization (exclusion), to which a variety of economic determinants, including lack of jobs, uneven development, unequal distribution of wealth, and poverty, are inherent. It also disregards the role of elites and the political objectives they pursue. Thus, for instance, Garang's abovementioned statement equally refers to the poor economic conditions in southern Sudan, social subjugation of the southerners, socioeconomic inequality, political marginalization and repression, and the lack of regional economic development, all of which are inherent to the political dynamics of the Sudanese state.

Finally, Gadir Ali, Elbadawi, and El-Batahani subscribe to the largely discredited essentialist argument for primordial identities. They conclude that the civil war in Sudan could not have been avoided due to the social polarization ("Arab" vs. "African"), which they claim to be the "key explanatory variable".[94] Yet, the claim regarding the inevitability of war due to identity distinctions is highly questionable because social polarization is a product of a process of deepening identity differentiation. Identities are subject to continuous (re)construction and manipulation, and transform over time. Thus, identity differences are not fixed and it is too simplistic to argue that they automatically cause armed violence.

Economic Approaches and Southern Sudan

Among the most important contribution of the economic analysis of insurgencies has been the finding that material motivations interact with political conflicts. This has been explored from Economics and a Political perspectives in the UNU-WIDER volume *War, Hunger, and* [...] (2000) edited by Nafziger, Stewart, and Väyrynen. Defying [...] of Collier-Hoeffler framework, the study demonstrates that contextualized economic factors in their political frame (grievances rather than greed), founded on rational choice, are relevant to the origins of insurgencies particularly when economics is viewed in the context of the distribution of political and socioeconomic power. These aspects are significant in the mobilization for insurgencies, which cannot be reduced simply to economicist argumentation.[95]

Researchers differ in their focus and opinion on to how and to which degree economics, material motivations, and well-being/deprivation are related to armed conflict.[96] However, the economic focus has made clear that the role of the material in conflicts is probably more eminent than many previous analyses have recognized. As a result, comprehensive conflict analyses should include economic aspects. These are useful, for instance, in mapping economic motivations and activities of relevant actors and forces among other non-economic motivations and within the broader social and political context of insurgency formation, duration, and termination. Yet, there are many possible explanations of how economic factors relate to civil wars,[97] and unfortunately comprehensive studies, considering economic and material aspects as one facet of motivations in the social and political context of insurgencies, are seldom undertaken. This study seeks inclusive analysis to highlight the complexity of factors in the processes of insurgency formation in Sudan.

Grievances-Focused Interpretations

The trend to highlight "grievances" in insurgencies gained renewed strength in response to the growth of the economic and material explanations in the late 1990s. For Richards and Johnson, most material explanations lack sufficient emphasis on social context and attention to construction, transformation and manipulation of collective identities by the elites.[98] In this sense, they have fallen short of challenging those identity explanations that are able to also incorporate economic agendas.[99]

Indeed, it is the politics of economic exclusion that appear generally to be at the heart of insurgencies. For instance, Ballentine explains that grievances are " . . . bred by systematic exclusion of ethnic minorities and from political power and an equitable share of economic opportunities and benefits".[100] According to Ross, exclusionary politics is a central factor to the formation of grievances based on a perception of inequitable distribution of resources, which in turn fuels armed mobilization and reinforced a deeply founded sense of ethnic exclusion.[101] Although in terms of violence Kalyvas states that " . . . it does not matter if civil wars begin because of grievances or opportunities . . . ",[102] what is common to insurgencies, at least in the case of Sudan, is that their material origins often lie in local grievances. These are often caused by broken government promises, unanswered expectations involving drastically disparate levels of regional economic development, expropriation of property or resources, and violent dispossession of economic assets.[103]

Insurgencies are also directly related to grievances caused by state policies. For instance, Ballentine and Nitzsche have argued that conflict formation ". . . is mediated by critical governance failures by the state. Systemic corruption and economic mismanagement, patrimonial rule, and political and socio-economic exclusion of ethnic or other minority groups may create conditions conducive to the onset . . .".[104] Ballentine has further noted that "In all cases, political motivations appear to have been dominant factors in the origin of insurgent and ethnoseparatist movements . . . [and] combatant motivations appear to have been shaped by a mix of continuing aspirations for political power or independent statehood as well as desire to capture resources".[105] It appears therefore that grievances, as well as greed, are motivational factors behind insurgencies, but that the processes of insurgencies formation cannot be reduced to these two alone.

Specifically pinpointing the exact "grievances" is sometimes difficult. For instance, grievances narratives (as well as the "greed" narratives) often fail to consider that the leaders behind governments or rebel groups seldom constitute homogeneous groups that can be treated as unitary entities. Instead, these are often amalgamations of a number of interests and individual and/or collective power centers with specific constituencies.[106] In these power centers, leading individuals, at times referred to as "big men",[107] tend to mobilize constituents to a significant degree based on material self-interest despite also at times having a certain level of belief in perceived injustices and other "grievances" indicators.

Combatants and civilians have varied motivations that guide their responses to situations of personal physical insecurity and an emerging insurgency. These decisions are based on a wide variety of factors and rationalities which are not always strictly founded on "grievances" or "greed". For instance, Nordstrom has argued that combatants are affected ". . . by everything from local grievances through foreign military advisors to global media and music".[108] Indeed, there are many motivational factors for rebel recruits to join an insurgency, including political reasons, personal ambitions, the need of belonging and survival, enrichment, or any combination of these factors.[109] Social pressure, as in the case of Nilotic warrior cultures in Sudan in which militarism and deterioration of family structures has become more pronounced after prolonged wars, can also be an important determinant in recruitment. Moreover, it is plausible to argue that some may rebel due to emotional factors such as fear or belief in the rebel "cause", involuntary conscripting, or as a form of cultural, community, and family allegiance or survival strategy.[110]

It should also be mentioned that grievances do not automatically result in mobilization for violent action, but can be answered in non-confrontational and non-violent ways. For instance, some members of southern elites in Khartoum who occupy lower social standing have deliberately "Arabized" themselves as a coping strategy to facilitate coexistence with the local "Arabs". This conforming with the persisting Arab-Muslim dominated social hierarchy in north-central Sudan in which "the southerner" is viewed as "black", "African", and the source of slave, and a provider of low level labor, shows that social inequality itself is not necessarily a source of conflict. However, it may be *utilized* as a source of grievance and as a powerful mobilization tool for armed violence in certain situations.[111] Therefore, the fact that grievances can be answered in a number of ways is often ignored by the more general analyses that portray them as a source of rebellion. Indeed, even in the presence of grievances, the responses and strategies of accommodation and/or resistance may be distinct depending on each individual or group.

Finally, Utas argues that the social structure formed around elite power centers, or "big men", tends to guide social behavior of their followers.[112] Particularly in the times of hardship, and physical insecurity and uncertainty, the belonging to a certain "group" is often emphasized. Through this belonging individuals tend to seek physical protection and material and social security. Many grievance-based studies fail to highlight this pattern.

Grievances Analyses and Southern Sudan

Grievances narratives contain a variety of useful elements for analyzing insurgencies in southern Sudan. Among perhaps the most important features are the notions of marginalization, poverty, social hierarchy, and exclusion, which often create structural and proximate conditions conducive to political instability and armed conflict. In addition, although grievances are normally structural conditions and not necessarily directly cause conflict, the elite strategies to maintain or gain power, and respond to repressive politics, linked with the overall state legitimacy and economic marginalization along ethnic lines, are crucial to the formation of insurgencies. Moreover, any analysis of insurgencies formation should consider political practices and conduct, such as the use of authoritarian ruling methods and military interventions, as well as conditioning factors such as collective sentiments and the availability of tools to perpetrate violent action (e.g. small arms and available recruits).

As is widely recognized, the grievances in southern Sudan stem from the history of slavery, inequality, and marginalization.[113] In southern Sudan, "Arab domination", "subjection", and "lack of development", among other factors, provide the major grievances deemed "general" or "regional". These are often portrayed as inherent, unchanging or "traditional" (cultural or other) incompatibilities between southern Sudan and the governing factions of the Sudanese state. It is useful to be able to recognize these grievances, but also to perceive how they have been (re)constructed through major narratives and interpretations of history. They are also picked up as political tools by those elite sections that are interested in organizing opposition and armed violence, while projecting southern "regional" identity as opposed to that presented as "northern Arab".[114] This reasoning justifies and legitimizes political action, and recognizing it is useful for the analysis of insurgency formation in southern Sudan.

"New" Wars and State-Centric Analyses

By the end of the 1990s, a paradigm coined "new wars" emerged.[115] Drawing upon Clausewitzian description of war, Anthropology, Development Studies, and Political Science, this paradigm laid emphasis on a perception of transformation of warfare, seeing wars essentially as manifestations of complex networks.[116] Kaldor has claimed that wars have become illegitimate and criminalized with emphasis on economic opportunism, expansion of informal networks, and systematic victimization of civilians as an end itself, while ideological factors apparent during the Cold War have disappeared.[117] This analysis claims that state weakness in developing countries and an increasing role for economic factors are major determinants causing "new wars". According to this discourse, post-Cold War state failure, which was related to inadequate social and cultural integration, resulted in inescapable "new" type of wars of state disintegration with intense external involvement (as opposed to the state-building wars of post-medieval Europe).[118]

Others, associated with the literature explaining "new" aspects of wars, have pointed out the importance of more apparent external influences and links between local, regional, and international spheres. According to Duffield, " . . . market deregulation has deepened all forms of parallel and transborder trade and allowed the warring parties to forge local-global networks and shadow economies as a means of asset realisation and self-provision-ing".[119] Moreover, many argue that such networks result in the emergence of "new" local non-state sociopolitical and economic authorities in conflict areas.[120]

This paradigm has stimulated state-centered analyses focusing on the strength, governance, and post-colonial and post-Cold War crises. The de-bate was divided early on between the authors who emphasized dysfunc-tional character of the state in Africa, and those who refused such a negative assessment.[121] It highlighted the low capacity of post-colonial states to de-velop formal institutions comparable to those found in the West, but argued that they were expected to do so to form part of the international commu-nity of states.[122] This generated a discourse for the need for post-colonial states to be "adjusted" or "corrected" to function more "properly" through economic, political, and/or military interventions. The debate pointed to the main elements of incapacity of the post-colonial states, which include in-heritance of imported colonial institutions that organized governance and resources resulting in ineffective regimes functioning through patron-client networks and personalized ruling methods. This buttressed "big man" logic, artificial borders dividing ethnic communities, economic and administrative structures to serve the metropolis, external dependency, and authoritarian politics aimed at "tribalizing" society along structures designed for "divide and rule".[123] According to a number of prominent authors, many of these elements linked to the "failure of monopoly statehood"[124] constitute causes of armed conflicts in Africa.[125]

Thus, the discourse centered on the state has underlined the structural conditions and the crisis of the post-colonial governance. It has linked the state crisis to chronic underdevelopment, poverty, and armed conflict. For various scholars,[126] it was largely the decline of superpower financing after the Cold War that conditioned many African states to political instability and war because their capacity to maintain state functions and coercive power over their territories lowered significantly and in some cases led to wars of disintegration. As a result, it is argued from the state-centric perspective that armed conflicts in Africa take place largely due to the financial crisis of neo-patrimonial political systems, poor governance, and weak state insti-tutions, creating conditions for increased elite competition for the spoils of the state.[127] For instance, Reno (various) has further pointed out the material sources for state weakening and increasing political conflict in the midst of deepening economic crisis due to the combination of international envi-ronment, state financial austerity, and the persisting neo-patrimonial ruling dynamics, resulting in elite competition over diminishing state resources.[128]

21

In other words, the proponents of state "failure" and "collapse"[129] causing insurgencies have suggested that the context of the decay of the African state is the main determinant for intensified resource competition and large-scale violence. In this, neo-patrimonial clientelist governance practices through personal rule and rent-seeking are highlighted, which has led scholars to call such states as "criminal",[130] "predatory",[131] and "vampire".[132] Indeed, despite the rather moralistic overtones, these analyses show that although being internationally and organizationally considered as states, many African polities fail to fulfill the basic requirements for being a state. These include empirical legitimacy, monopoly of coercion, civic order, and the capacity of extracting resources for public good,[133] and having limited capability to function autonomously from the populace.[134] As a result, some authors have claimed that the causes of insurgencies are linked to weakened inherently authoritarian rule which is unable to maintain monopoly of violence.[135]

Scholars further argue that patrimonial politics that consolidated at the national level in most African states after independence resulted in a number of regimes becoming "neo-patrimonial" and increasingly exploitative.[136] From the crisis of the post-colonial state emerged the theoretical categorization of states according to their strength and weakness,[137] which has heavily influenced policymaking until today. Some have taken the position that particularly Africa's big states (Angola, DRC, Ethiopia, Nigeria, South Africa, and Sudan) are especially dysfunctional and regionally destabilizing, suffering from structural problems and extending their problems to the neighboring states.[138] Moreover, some analyses have focused specifically on structures and dynamics of governance,[139] while others have emphasized the importance of "good governance"[140] and subnational governance[141] in Africa as a way of strengthening state through increased legitimacy. This may add to the state's ability to curb political instability and the emergence of armed opposition.

However, various aspects of the analyses depicting wars as "new" and centering on the state can be questioned. Kaldor has argued that insurgencies that broke out since the 1990s are "new" because they are characterized by looting and the lack of political objectives, as well as the parties to the conflict deliberately targeting civilians.[142] Yet, it is important to note that wars have always contained these characteristics to a variable degree, and that these economic, political, or strategic features may be more pronounced in some cases than others. Kaldor has further defended the "new war" paradigm by stating that it is intended to sway policymakers away from antiquated Cold War thinking, and that in the post-Cold War international environment the destructive potential of arms has grown and intersected with globalization, transforming wars.[143] Again, however, although there may be aspects of war that are more pronounced in some cases, this does not make them inherently "new". Also, although without doubt new ways of conflict resolution should be encouraged, simply viewing wars in a "new" way hardly results in an increased capacity to resolve armed conflict.

In addition, most insurgencies today remain as low-intensity conflicts. They therefore resemble the ones during the Cold War, particularly in terms of the prevalence of unsophisticated infantry weaponry, communications aspects, and extensive political, economic, social, and cultural networks (globalization) that facilitate the interlinking of local with regional and international dimensions.[144] This reality has continued to foster regional conflict complexes in Africa in which the causes of insurgencies have more to do with regional and international actors and forces than argued by those who continue to insist on their local origins.[145] Thus, although, as Kalyvas argues, the role of external non-state actors in the "internal" wars has been increasingly recognized only relatively recently,[146] one can convincingly argue that regional and international dimensions of contemporary wars are not "new".[147]

Moreover, the emerging socioeconomic and political authorities and networks during war are not novel, although some present them as a new post-Cold War phenomenon. This is the case of the insurgencies in southern Sudan, for instance, where such orders and networks emerged in the rebel held areas long before the end of Cold War. Arguably, this was a common characteristic throughout both insurgencies in southern Sudan and possibly in other cases as well.

Furthermore, it appears that the "new war" paradigm harbors Western theoretical reinterpretation of African history for and via Western discourses. This tendency, in turn, can be claimed to generate efforts to correct Africa's "problems" by means of state-building or other strategies that appear to serve Western interests.[148] Chabal has argued that such analyses bring about "scientific" misinterpretations of Africa based on misguided historical records.[149] This also entails the lack of cultural analysis related to social behavior that differs from the Western experience. Indeed, Chabal and Daloz show that the branch of scholars that focuses on the incapacity of African states to modernize and develop suffers from a degree of determinism, which obscures the observation and analysis of non-conventional modernization and development different from that experienced in the West.[150] In fact, too meticulous modernization dictated by the Western expertise,[151] may result in state crisis over modernization and heighten the politics of exclusion. For instance, Reno emphasizes the historical foundations and institutionalization of neo-patrimonialism and nepotism in the social fabric of African societies,[152] which is often forgotten in the Western state-centric analyses, while Erdmann and Engel emphasize the importance to refine the study on neo-patrimonialism to recognize various forms of patron-client systems in Africa.[153] Indeed, comparative political analysis suggests that the crisis of the post-colonial state should be explained in its social context to carefully analyze the complex causes of insurgencies.[154]

Finally, the state-based analyses have been criticized as being biased. They are said to serve the imposition of neo-imperialist policies from outside, or exaggerating the security threat of the weak states for the Western countries.[155] Such studies can also be damaging because they lead to the categorization of states based on their strength and may penalize the so-called weak states. They may justify the cutting back of foreign aid and investment if a state does not adhere to externally imposed conditions, which reduces the state's external resources that could be vital for maintaining peace and security.[156]

"New" Wars, State-Centric Analyses, and Southern Sudan

The "new wars" paradigm has pointed to the fact that conflicts take place in their specific regional and international contexts, and that the nature of war may change through time. It also highlights the importance of regional and international actors and forces, as well as the emerging politico-economic orders as alternatives to the state. Although not necessarily "new", the abovementioned considerations highlighted by the "new wars" literature are relevant to contemporary insurgencies.

Moreover, the narratives dealing with the crisis of the post-colonial state also have useful attributes for explaining the favorable conditions for political strife and armed conflict. Evidently one of the strengths of the state-centric analyses is that they often capture the interplay of political and economic forces in the process of conflict formation, and provide evidence for politically embedded factors in the causes of conflict.

In the following chapter, theoretical considerations of this study are introduced. They aim at constructing an analytical framework capable of overcoming some of the limitations of the analyses used to study origins of insurgencies that have been outlined in this chapter.

Endnotes

1   See e.g. Ylönen (2005a, 2005b, 2008, 2009).

2   This center-periphery confrontation has involved armed opposition not only in southern Sudan, but in the North-South transitional areas in Abyei, the Nuba Mountains of Southern Kordofan, Blue Nile, Darfur, and eastern region. These conflicts have pitted rebel organizations originating from state peripheries against the government in control of central Sudan. As such, in general terms the war in Sudan can be described as an armed conflict between the state center and the marginalized peripheries. Military confrontations have continued even after the independence of South Sudan on 9 July 2011.

3   Disorder in southern Sudan became commonly known as the 'Southern Problem' among the northern Sudanese political elite.

4   See AAA (1972).

5   O'Ballance (1977: 13, 158).

6   Collins (2008: 258).

7   See CPA (2005). In 2006 the regime also signed peace agreements with sections of Darfur rebels and the Eastern Front opposition movement.

8   Ylönen (2005a, 2005b).

9   Ruay (1994), Batahani (2005), and Poggo (2008).

10   There is a multitude of historical or political science analyses that portray Arab-African cleavage in Sudan as inherently incompatible, and northern and southern Sudan as homogeneous entities. However, it is argued here that these identities are not primordial *per se*, but have been historically constructed, maintained, and reshaped. Elites have played a fundamental role in shaping these processes.

11   Collier and Hoeffler (1998, 2002a, 2002b, 2004).

12   Batahani (2005).

13   Ross (2004).

14   Hernandez Zubizarreta (2009).

15   Prunier and Gisselquist (2003).

16   Some works showing these characteristics, such as Daly (1991), Ruay (1994), and to a certain degree Johnson (2003), have all been used in this work because the author recognizes their otherwise high scholarly value.

17   See e.g. Stewart (2000, 2001) and Cramer (2003, 2006).

18   Ylönen (2005a, 2005b, 2008, 2009).

19   For instance, Cramer (2006: 66-70) points out that civil wars are never strictly internal phenomena, but include regional and international involvement and influences.

20   O'Neill (1980: 1).

21   Nicolaïdis, Sèbe, and Maas (2015: 2).

22   See e.g. Cramer (2002).

23   de Waal (2007a, 2007b).

24   Bodley (1988, 1999).

25   The concept was applied to a number of cases in European countries during the 1970s. See e.g. Kirkinen (1972) and Salvi (1973).

26   See Bayart (1993, 2000).

27   Vast literature exists on these "proxy wars". See e.g. Henderson and Singer (2000: 2).

28   See e.g. Asiwaju (1985) and Clapham (1996).

29   Horowitz (1985: 278-9).

30   See e.g. Ryan (1995) and Lobell and Mauceri (2004).

31   See e.g. Ruiz-Giménez Arrieta (2002: 31-34), which offers an excellent overview of a number of explicative narratives since the Cold War.

32   Opp (2009) provides a broad study on theories of mobilization. On identity, see chapters 7, 9, and 11.

33   The formalization of social identity theory owes largely to social psychologists. See Tajfel and Turner (1979, 1986).

34   Tajfel (1978: 63).

35   Taylor and Moghaddam (1994: 61).

36   Turner (1990: x-xi).

37   Piaget (1971, 1985).

38   See e.g. Snow (1996).

39   See e.g. Kaplan (1994; 2000) and Peters (1994).

40   Kaplan (1994, 2000).

41   Stereotypical Western views of tribe are often related to traditional, stagnated, societies that lack progress and modernization. However, Chabal and Daloz (1999) argue that generally these are misconceptions in the case of Africa where colonialists manipulated the preceding social order to create and shape ethnic communities through "tribalism". They established competing group categories as a political weapon, coinciding with a peculiar type of modernization in part imposed by the colonial powers.

42   Kalyvas (2006: 21).

43   Garnett (2002).

44   See e.g. Geffray (1990), Deng (1995a, 1995b), Richards (1996), and Lesch (1998).

45   This has been part of politically charged rhetoric by the warring parties during the insurgencies, and part of the socialization and indoctrination processes to portray the conflict as a confrontation between "Arabs" and "Africans". Highly polarized dynamics of political and economic inclusion and exclusion have fed such perceptions, as has the media that has often been used as a propaganda tool by elites interested in extending such views. For instance Turner (1998: 203) has claimed, "The roots of the conflict are not only political but also religious and cultural, pitting the Muslim Arab north against the Christian and Animist African south".

46   Mazrui (1973: 56).

47   Kalyvas (2006: 21).

48   See also Richards (2005) and in the case of Sudan, Johnson (2006).

49 See e.g. George Herbert Mead's theory on identity and self. Carreira da Silva (2011) provides a good overview on this.
50 See e.g. Mitchell (1956), Epstein (1958), Barth (1969), and Castells (1997).
51 See e.g. Ruiz-Giménez Arrieta (2002).
52 See e.g. Mazrui (1973), Bates (1983), and Brass (1991).
53 Utas (2012: 1).
54 See e.g. Deutsch (1953), Anderson (1983), Gellner (1983), and Hobsbawm (1992).
55 See Ranger (1992).
56 See Ignatieff (1997).
57 See e.g. Bates (1983), Brass (1991), Chabal and Daloz (1999, 2005), Lemarchand (2003), and Pumphrey (2003: 9-10).
58 See e.g. Castells (1997), Romanucci-Ross and DeVos (1998), and Fearon and Laitin (2000).
59 Chabal and Daloz (1999). A number of these authors take a normative stance, considering mobilization for violence a criminal attempt by prominent individuals to use popular grievances for self-interest in order to assert themselves politically and materially. However in their *Culture Troubles: Politics and the Interpretation of Meaning* (2005), Chabal and Daloz revise their position by pointing out that politics is not only instrumentalization to achieve objectives but often founded upon identity and cultural connections between leaders and their constituents.
60 See e.g. Deng (1995a, 1995b), Lesch (1998), and Jok (2001, 2007).
61 Eprile (1974), Holt and Daly (2000), Collins (2005), and Wassara (2007).
62 Arfi (1998), Buzan, Wæver, and de Wilde (1998), and McSweeney (1999).
63 Berman and Lonsdale's (1992) and Lonsdale (1994).
64 Posner (2005).
65 Homer-Dixon (1991, 1994, 1999).
66 Kaplan (1994, 2000).
67 Munene (1995), Handelman (1996), and Rist (1997).
68 Ruiz-Giménez Arrieta (2002).
69 Duffield (2001).
70 The term "internal war" is used here to refer to wars that are fought in a territory of one state, pitting the government against non-state actors. According to the protagonists of this perspective the term "internal" is not meant to exclude regional or international dimension. According to one of the proponents of this analytical trend, Gadir Ali (2000: 242), "The economic core of the causes of African conflicts expresses itself in various guises: the high risk of dependence on natural resources; uneven development; and the capture and sharing of rents of the state machinery".
71 UCDP (2008).
72 Hirshleifer (1987, 1994, 1995) and Grossman (1991, 1995).
73 Tilly (1985, 1992).

27

74 See e.g. Collier (2000b, 2003a, 2003b), Collier and Hoeffler (1998, 2002a, 2002b, 2004), and Collier and Sambanis (2005a, 2005b). This led to de-legitimization and criminalization of rebellion and to a general assumption that any governments' counter-insurgency measures are justified, legitimate, and acceptable.

75 Advocating neoliberal economic tradition, backed by the World Bank with generous funding, publishing, and advertising support, it sought to explain causes, duration, and termination of civil wars since the Cold War. The Collier-Hoeffler framework became famous not only because of its findings, but also because it established a general cause and effect relationship based on rational choice that was popular and easily adopted by both policymakers (Herbst, 2000: 287) and the donor community.

76 The studies by Paul Collier and Anke Hoeffler established the greed versus grievance debate by claiming that rebellions are caused predominantly by the economic greed of the insurgents. See e.g. Collier and Hoeffler (2004). The authors use the basic concepts of orthodox neoclassical economic theory in their framework, and have inspired a growing literature since other authors have built upon their analyses. Some examples of econometric work inspired by Collier-Hoeffler paradigm are Elbadawi and Sambanis (2000), Reynal-Querol (2002), and Anyanwu (2004), while Latif Mohammed (1999), Herbst (2000), and Sherman (2000) are examples of qualitative studies associated with the rational choice theory in the African context.

77 Cater (2003: 20-1). See also Collier (2000a, 2000b, 2003a, 2003b), Collier and Hoeffler (1998, 2002a, 2002b, 2004), and Collier and Sambanis (2005a, 2005b).

78 See e.g. Markakis (1998), Klare (2002), and Clayton (2003).

79 Bowles, Franzini, and Pagano (1999).

80 Fine (1999, 2001).

81 See e.g. Herbst (2000) and Richards (2007).

82 See Cramer (2002, 2006), Herbst (2000), Mkandawire (2002), and Pearce (2005).

83 See e.g. Collier (2000a, 2000b).

84 Berdal (2003).

85 See Collier (2000a) and Collier and Hoeffler (2004).

86 Stewart (2000, 2001).

87 Some analyses, such as Betléhemy, Kauffman, Renard and Wegner (2002), have attempted to fill such gaps by comparing the impact of repressive and non-repressive state policies, while others, such as Elbadawi and Sambanis (2000), have analyzed the impact of governance in minimizing armed conflict. Yet others, like Buhaug and Gates (2002), deal with the geographic features of insurgencies.

88 Collier and Hoeffler (1998, 2002a, 2002b, 2004).

89 Reno (various) and Matturi (2007).

90 Richards (1996, 2005: 10).

91 For instance, southern Sudan, the Nuba Mountains, and Darfur can be seen as excellent examples of this.

92 Garang (1987: 21) and Gadir Ali, Elbadawi, and El-Batahani (2005: 193).

93 Gadir Ali, Elbadawi, and El-Batahani (2005).

94 Gadir Ali, Elbadawi, and El-Batahani (2005: 213).

95 On Sudan see Ylönen (2005a, 2008).

96 Gurr (1970, 1993) famously argues for the importance of "relative deprivation" between population groups as a key factor. For Richards (1996, 2005), motivations to join rebellion are contextually linked to culture and society, with frustrations over unemployment and poverty often motivating violent behavior. Meanwhile, Stewart (2000, 2001) has demonstrated the importance of "horizontal", or group-based, economic inequality, which is principally a political grievance. Moreover, Ballentine (2003) points out that sections of the Revolutionary United Front in Sierra Leone, and some insurgent sections in the eastern Democratic Republic of the Congo (DRC), were quick to invade the state capital rather than settling to loot and control the resource-rich areas in the state periphery, which shows that political grievances constitute a significant part of rebel motivations. This points to the crucial role of the state in alleviating grievances, while it may also be that the central government policy to attempt to exploit natural resources from the territory belonging to the regional government jurisdiction can provoke conflict in the periphery, as has been the case in southern Sudan. See e.g. Ylönen (2005a, 2008, 2009).

97 Humphreys (2003).

98 Richards (2005: 4) and Johnson (2006: 93).

99 Deng (1995a, 1995b), Ignatieff (1997), and Fearon and Laitin (2000).

100 Ballentine (2003: 260).

101 Ross (2003: 65-6).

102 Kalyvas (2006: 20).

103 See e.g. Ylönen (2005a, 2008).

104 Ballentine and Nitzsche (2003: 17).

105 Ballentine (2003: 262).

106 Ylönen (2015).

107 Utas (2012).

108 Nordstrom (2004: 13).

109 See e.g. Nyaba (2000) on the second insurgency in southern Sudan.

110 Nyaba (2000), Leonardi (2007), and author's field notes.

111 Akok and Schultz (2009) provide evidence of situational ethnic identities in southern Sudan. They show that, for instance, a southern Sudanese living in diaspora may choose to abide by an aspect of his/her ethnic identity that sees "Arabs" as the collective "other" and an enemy, while sections of southerners living in southern Sudan in distinct circumstances may opt to emphasize "otherness" towards other local groups for self-definition and mobilization.

112 Utas (2012: 6-9).

113 See e.g. Alier (1990), Holt and Daly (2000), Johnson (2003), and Collins (2005, 2008).

114 "Arab" here merely refers to categorization by the southern Sudanese of northern Sudanese as "the other" against whom identity politics discourse in southern Sudan has been generally oriented.

115 This has been generally attributed to Kaldor (1999).

116 Kaldor (2003: 119-23).

117 Kaldor (1999; 2003).

118 Münkler (2004: 7-10). It inspired an academic focus on state capacity, state-building, and consolidation, which has become emphasized in Western academic and policy circles.

119 Duffield (2001: 14).

120 See Callaghy, Kassimir, and Latham (2001), Nordstrom (2004), and Vlassenroot and Raeymaekers (2004).

121 See e.g. Ruiz-Giménez Arrieta (2000) on an excellent review of this literature.

122 ackson (1990).

123 There exists an extensive literature emphasizing these elements. See e.g. Bayart (1991, 1993), Chabal and Daloz (1999), Clapham (1996), Hyden (1983), Mamdani (1997), Sørensen (1998), and van de Walle (2001).

124 Clapham (1996: 209).

125 See e.g. Pumphrey and Schwartz-Barcott (2003).

126 Clapham (1996), van de Walle (2001), and Münkler (2004).

127 See Chabal and Daloz (1999), Reno (1997, 1998), and Bates (2008).

128 He has shown how this can lead to elite and state legitimacy becoming dependent on the elite's control of the markets, which in conditions of scarcity may lead to a severe competition and culmination of organized violence and state disintegration. According to Reno (2005: 132-3), weak rulers tend to buy out opposition and divert resources to other groups only when under extreme political pressure or threat.

129 This includes, among others, Doornbos (1994), Zartman, (1995), Chabal and Daloz (1999), van de Walle (2001), Milliken and Krause (2002), and Rotberg (2003a, 2003b, 2004). Englebert (2000) and Ayoob (2001) further emphasize the lack of state legitimacy and consistency.

130 Bayart, Ellis and Hibou (1999).

131 Frimpong-Ansah (1991) and Fatton (1992).

132 Ayittey (1999).

133 Cater (2003: 27).

134 Kopstein and Lichbach (2005: 27).

135 See e.g. Azam (2001) and Mueller (2002). Azam (2001: 442) also claims that " . . . the occurrence of civil conflict in Africa is intimately related to the failure of governments to deliver the type of public expenditure that people want, i.e., with a strong redistributive component such as in health and education".

136 An ample literature on the topic exists. For instance, see Reno (1997, 2001, 2002, 2003, 2004, 2005) and Chabal (2007) on "neo-patrimonial" state.

137 For instance, Rotberg (2003a, 2003b) puts troubled states into three categories: weak, failed, and collapsed. According to Zartman (1995: 1-11), Rotberg
(2003a: 9-10, 2003b: 4-5), and Aguirre (2006: 1), collapsed states such as Chad
and Uganda in the 1980s, and Somalia, Bosnia, Lebanon, Afghanistan, Nigeria, Liberia, and Sierra Leone in the 1990s, constitute the ultimate, but not permanent, manifestation of state failure created by a vacuum of authority filled
by the strongest private (elite) entrepreneur. Failed states, such as Angola, Bu-
rundi, and Sudan, are deeply contested, factional, and conflictive, experiencing
enduring political violence characterized by ethnic, religious, linguistic and
inter-communal antagonisms. They are unable to control their borders, prey on
their own people, cannot check increasing criminality, have flawed institutions,
are rife with corruption, suffer from deterioration of infrastructure, and provide
only limited political goods, emergency response, and state services for the selected few. This leads to the erosion of the social contract and legitimacy of the
state among the general population. Finally, weak states, such as Iraq, Belarus,
Libya, Turkmenistan, and North Korea, are feeble because of geographical,
physical or economic constraints, internal conflicts, management problems,
greed, despotism or external encroachment, intercommunal tensions, elevated
crime, diminishing state services, and corruption. They are possibly on their
way to failure. See Rotberg (2003a: 4, 5-9, 2003b: 3-4).

138 See e.g. Ottaway, Herbst, and Mills (2004) and Clapham, Herbst, and Mills
(2006).

139 See e.g. Pierre and Peters (2000).

140 See e.g. Abrahamsen (2001), Bekoe (2005), and Noman, Botchwey, Stein, and
Stiglitz (2012).

141 Here the debate on decentralization has been central. See e.g. Olowu and
Wunsch (2003) and Oxhorn, Tulchin, and Selee (2004). On Sudan, see Fegley
(2010).

142 Kaldor (1999, 2003).

143 Kaldor (2009: 16).

144 Kalyvas (2009: 20).

145 On the argument for the prominence of local sources of conflict see e.g.
Clapham (1996), and Chabal and Daloz (1999).

146 Kalyvas (2009: 18).

147 Cramer (2006).

148 Chandler (2006).

149 Chabal (2009).

150 Chabal and Daloz (1999).

151 See e.g. Currea-Lugo (2008) in the case of Sudan.

152 Reno (1997, 1998).

153 Erdmann and Engel (2007).

154 Chabal and Daloz (1999: 4-16).

155 Patrick (2006: 27-53).

156 Woodward (2005), and Pureza, Duffield, Woodward, and Sogge (2006).

CHAPTER II

THEORETICAL PROPOSITIONS:
State Marginalization, Elites, and Insurgency Formation

The review of major theoretical currents used to explain armed conflicts in Africa in the previous chapter shows that African insurgencies are composed of a complex combination of political, economic, social, and cultural factors.[1] Apart from internal dynamics, such as political instability related to state weakness and inter-group (ethnic) animosities, insurgencies in Africa involve a number of crucial external factors and dynamics, which intertwine with the internal realities. These include (among other aspects): economic considerations; historical variables, such as decolonization and Cold War; external social, cultural and religious actors and forces; and concrete actions and influence of external actors.[2]

Considering the shortcomings of the discipline-specific theoretical currents to comprehensively explain causes of civil wars, this study seeks to offer an inclusive interdisciplinary approach that highlights the more neglected aspects of insurgency formation. It aims to construct an overarching theoretical framework for an extensive understanding of insurgency formation, particularly in southern Sudan. The study draws principally from theoretical concepts associated with the state and political leadership, elites, and intersecting external actors and forces. More specifically, theoretical elements that are used include state marginalization, the concept of power, elite theory, construction and instrumentalization of political identity, and extraversion and networks linking local, regional, and international dimensions. These theoretical components are all considered important for more complete understanding of the processes of insurgency formation, and the case of Sudan in particular. The main contribution of the approach introduced here is the focus on state marginalization along center-periphery dynamics as an overarching theoretical umbrella. It incorporates the abovementioned theoretical aspects as well as emotional elements, such as sentiment of fear of perceived "internal colonialism", relevant for mobilization for armed struggle, while considering insurgency formation as a process in which political organization and mobilization together with collective (and individual) emotional and sentimental factors are crucial. The study is undertaken in an attempt to add to the understanding of the processes of insurgency formation, including the role played by local elites and external actors and forces.

State Marginalization

A growing number of studies claim that state as a coherent institutional structure hardly exists in Africa and should therefore not constitute the core of any socially founded analysis.[3] However, this assertion neglects the role of the state and provides little new to the study of African politics, especially because it contradicts the long-recognized fact that the state in Africa is an institutionalized social reality which orientates behavior and is itself conditioned by formal and informal channels. Although relevant, the competing political orders, for instance in state's peripheries, all consider the state in some way and are often able to exist due to the limited capacity of the state. Thus, even when such orders function as largely independent systems, they still necessarily relate and adjust their actions with respect to the central administration and other states with which they need to co-exist. In fact, despite the occasional existence of competing social, political, and economic orders at the local level, the dominant actors in them are all aware of the existence of the central state, and the neighboring and other states, to the extent that these are relevant in their decision-making and actions.

It is therefore argued here that the state is an important element of understanding societal dynamics in Africa. For instance in southern Sudan, the recognition of the existence of a state (at least by name) and its policies by the locally dominant political actors (e.g. elites and high level leadership) has historically affected their actions and responses. This is particularly the case during mobilization against the state. The fact that state is captured and controlled by actors that are perceived to promote "Arab" domination, forced Islamicization, and "internal colonialism", has motivated anti-state sentiments and action. In this manner, the presence and policies of a particular kind of state may justify social action especially in its periphery where it is weakest. This is one of the major reasons why considering the state and its strength is crucial to any analysis dealing with insurgency formation. Although this study seeks to avoid any strict categories of state strength, its theoretical framework draws heavily from state-focused analyses. It adheres to Aguirre's assertion that the state is central to almost all political, social, and economic questions in Africa.[4]

Rather than simply compartmentalizing states into broad categories, this study argues that when analyzing insurgency formation it is more useful to design a theoretical framework that explains the social (historical, cultural, and ethnic) foundations and leadership dynamics of the state. Thus, instead of considering Sudan simply as a failed state[5] one should analyze its formational process, leadership, and governance, which cause group-based and regionally projected marginalization of its peripheries.[6] The Sudanese state has become institutionalized through historical processes. Its formational trajectory has drawn (and currently draws) from pre-existing social dynamics, relationships, and hierarchies between societal groups, and from external actors and influences. The Sudanese post-colonial state is a product of historical dynamics and contemporary forces, which largely explains its particular political structures, governance, and ruling methods and strategies. In the case of Sudan, this process has resulted in a type of marginalization that has become an established (institutionalized) attitude, logic, and a state of mind, conditioning political decision-making of the governing elites. The state itself and its policies have also influenced the decisions and strategies of local and regional elites from state peripheries.

The type of state marginalization experienced in Sudan, manifested as a type of political culture in the governance practices of the governing elite, is a product of particular historical processes. These include the formation of an exclusive, self-proclaimed, culturally Arabized-Muslim minority state elite, exerting its influence over the widely heterogeneous polity. This draws largely from pre-colonial legacies and *Turkiyyah*, *Mahdiyyah*, and Anglo-Egyptian co-dominium periods. In the case of Sudan it is an established form of marginalization that has excluded effective representation from all but narrow sectors of the dominant Arabized sociocultural elite group, which is defined in terms of cultural attributes (including language, customs, and religion) that have justified its monopolization of political and economic power.[7]

During the colonial period, the narrow patterns of economic accumulation, distribution, development, and services facilitated the socioeconomic emergence of the Arabized elite and the concentration of political power to it. The continued concentration of economic power to these leaders buttressed their exclusive political prominence and allowed them to continue to justify their position through the exclusive view on culture and race. The Arabized elite's domination then extended the constructed perception of a narrow view on Arab culture and Islam as the dominant identity compo-

35

nents that justify the particular kind of distribution of political and economic power and opportunities in Sudan. The persistence of the particular kind of political and economic dominance, which developed through historical processes, was legitimized through self-perceived sociocultural superiority. It was buttressed by ethnic constituencies, leading to institutionalized claims to power and to a position that defies sharing power. A direct result was the Arabized elite's monopolization and privatization of economic and political power, and contestation of this power among its distinct sections.

In post-colonial Sudan, the marginalizing logic of the state has been to a large extent characterized by the continuation of the colonial form of governance through "divide and rule". This, combined with a highly stratified and exclusive view of Arab-Muslim dominated social hierarchy, has been used for creation of dependency and poverty (prevention of material accumulation) among the marginalized subjects particularly in the state peripheries. This is in part because in such regions local communities are less connected to the Arabized ruling elite, and often do not share its view on the nation and the society. While marginalization has to an extent a debilitating effect on state legitimacy among the majority, the neo-patrimonial logic, in which nepotism in patron-client relations is significant, has ensured the Arabized governing elite ethnic constituencies along ethnic and family lines in north-central Sudan. These constituencies have been the key for portraying legitimacy and justifying the exclusive rule. They have not only helped the Arabized elite to maintain power and survive challenges to its control of the state, but also backed the view of the nation based on Arab culture and Islam that it has sought to extend to the peripheries both by peaceful and violent means. Behind the common group agenda of the Arabized elite, however, also lays an intense competition for power among its sections, parties, and organizations, which also extends to individual power centers within such groups and leads to exclusion of those not collaborating with the particular governing clique in power.

It is pointed out in the following chapter that before the 19th century the region that became the contemporary Sudanese state was divided into small kingdoms and sultanates. Those societies located in the territory of today's northern Sudan gradually experienced an Arab-Muslim dominated, culturally defined, social hierarchy in which "social race"[8] largely dictated the distribution of political and economic power. This resulted in the marginalization, or mere exclusion, of the perceived lower societal cadres from access to wealth and power, the most extreme case being southern "blacks" who largely occupied the lowest position and the status of a slave.

The formation of a unified administration and polity in the 19th century served the purposes of (re)construction and extension of the pre-existing socioculturally defined marginalization and exclusion. It buttressed the social and economic predominance of Arabized Muslims from central region and led to the institutionalization of their version of the Arab-Muslim dominated social hierarchy which was justified by the self-perceived sociocultural superiority. After decolonization this institutionalized social reality, and related attitudes, has continued to guide the politics, ruling methods, and practices of the Arabized elite dominated state administration, as well as promoting exclusive economic accumulation concentrated on the prominent members of particular dominant Arab-Muslim social groupings.[9] In the process others within the Arabized Muslim elite benefited less, but often maintained a prominent societal position from which to contest political power. Still, it was the highly heterogeneous majority population, composed mainly of other ethnicities, religions, and cultures in the territories that constitute contemporary northern Sudan, which was largely marginalized because it failed to subscribe to the north-central Arabized elite definition of "Arab" and "Muslim" identity.[10]

Over time, a highly educated and prominent section of the ruling elite linked to the powerful Sufi orders in northern Sudan developed a philosophy of predestined predominance of the *awlad al-balad* (worthy sons of the land) relative to other social groups. It projected this view by constructing and promoting language and literature of cultural superiority,[11] based on a narrative that has continued to portray non-Arab and non-Muslim groups as inferior, and provided an exclusionary view of inter-group relations while stereotyping (and at times de-humanizing) those perceived as "the other".[12] A documented aspect of this particular type of social hierarchy is the general feeling of inferiority by the Sudanese "Arabs" in relation to Arabs abroad, who tend to view the northern Sudanese as "Arabized" Africans and often refer to them as *abd*.[13] Moreover, historically Europeans and North Americans tended to classify Sudanese "Arabs" as "black". As Sharkey has shown, these perceptions influenced the Arabized elite in Sudan, and it has sought to deflect such views to southern Sudan by projecting similar attitude that it has been subjected to towards the southerners in order to establish a justification for its privileged social status.[14] These societal dynamics have led O'Fahey to assert further that "Northern Sudanese society is profoundly racist and colour-conscious",[15] and Jok to add that "South Sudanese continue to be referred to as *abeed* (slaves) by North Sudanese, whose privileged position today has much to do with their history as slave masters in the past".[16] Finally, the prevalent narratives glorifying Arab culture and conquest of Sudan, together with the political ideology and policies of forced assimilation by the minority governing elite, continue to encourage attitudes of superiority in northern Sudan.[17] This transforms the relatively peaceful historical processes of Arabization and Islamicization into contentious and repressive political tools.

To contrast this perception, and in response to the resulting state marginalization, sectors of regional elites from the marginalized peripheries have promoted alternative narratives and political identities. One such identity has been based on the view of the highly ethnically diverse southern Sudan as a "regional" entity. It first emerged among the narrow Western-educated elites in southern Sudan in the 1940s and 1950s, and since then constitutes an identity layer in addition to the stronger "tribal" and family identities. It was constructed in opposition to the perceived "northern" and "Arab" domination. Despite being composed of a vast number of heterogeneous ethnic communities with ethnicity being the paramount determinant of group identity, the southern leaders generally opposed "northern Arab" domination and the hegemonic project of Arabization and Islamicization.[18] It was perceived as the reason for marginalization and "internal colonialism" southern Sudan was subjected to. In this view there is an important element of self-preservation, as the successful imposition of Islam and Arab culture would undermine the position of southern elites, their effort to contest the "Arab" elite, and profoundly transform southern cultures and identities. As a result, despite existing inter-ethnic animosity and occasional conflicts at the local level, prominent southerners have developed a relatively uniform view of rejecting the northern imposed social hierarchy in which they occupy the lowest level.[19] The relative cohesion, drawing from a perception of northerners as "Arabs" and "traditional" enemies, was a unifying force that was partially cemented during the *Turkiyyah* and *Mahdiyyah* (in the 19th century), and has since been periodically reinforced by sectors of the southern elite.[20]

In the process of decolonization, members of the southern elite became increasingly frustrated by the lack of access to political and economic power relative to the "Arab" elite in northern Sudan. For instance, being excluded from top civil service and military jobs, or from participating in shaping national culture and objectives,[21] gave rise to southern regional consciousness, characterized by frustration, resentment, suspicion, and fear, all of which became common elements in the widely extended attitudes towards the "Arab northerners".[22] These frustrations were further accentuated due to unemployment, northern individuals occupying superior positions, suspicion of Arabization and Islamicization among students, and adverse perceptions of northern merchants, the *jallaba*. All played into a general view of a northern conspiracy to dominate, or internally colonize, southern Sudan.[23]

The grievances of the southern elite also had other features. Many prominent southerners were frustrated by their numerical inferiority in the decision-making organs at the national level, lack of Arabic skills, internal differences, and northern attitudes of superiority. These sentiments were channeled to their constituencies in southern Sudan, where individuals from rural areas, initially mostly in Equatoria, responded with their support, which extended regional consciousness and federalist and separatist political agenda advocated by sections of the southern elite. Thus, attitudes rising from these social relations and dynamics related to political and economic power, and control of the state, inspired southern political opposition and separatism. The struggle for economic and political power crystallized in the state was at the core of the ensuing political strife and masked by the dynamics of the imposition and extension of cultural assimilation based on Islam and Arab culture.[24]

However, the emergence of southern resistance in contemporary Sudan was heavily influenced by the colonial context. The colonial state policies provided favorable conditions for disaffection among the contemporary southern elite regarding the political and economic order dictated by the "Arab" elite. By seeking to educate young members of the southern elite and socialize them to assume leading roles in the southern Sudanese society to protect it from northern Sudanese influences, the colonial educators emphasized the difference between southerners and the "Arab". The colonial administration sought mainly to curb nationalist threats to the colonial rule emanating from northern Sudan, and also aspired to safeguard local southern cultures. Thus, through historical processes, cultural identities related to the perceived "social race" and the Arabized Muslim dominated social hierarchy became an integral part of general attitudes between "northerners" and "southerners" in the post-colonial state.[25] This owed much to the structural dynamics of state marginalization, a colonial creation emanating from the 19th century, and was buttressed by the British through "divide and rule" and nepotism, fomenting ethnic politics along highly exclusive group identities. During decolonization, the ruling elite, claiming specifically select cultural "Arab" and "Muslim" status, and with experience of the workings of colonial administration, readily adopted this ruling logic and mechanisms, adapting them in order to consolidate its own claim to exclusive economic and political power.

Indeed, in Sudan the attitudes drawn from social reality that (re)produces and (re)shapes the inter-group social relations and dynamics are a defining part of political and economic power (e.g. participation, opportunities, wealth). Since colonialism, they have become increasingly politicized and an important factor in mobilizing challenges to the Arabized elite dominated state, particularly from southern Sudan.[26] The state has been challenged from elsewhere in the periphery as well, particularly due to the center-periphery marginalization and exclusion of local groups.

This adheres to Sørensen's affirmation that main cultural identifications in Africa are not only localist and "tribal".[27] Rather, they are also bound to political and economic power, social hierarchies, and formal and informal governance, which themselves are all shaped by the local context as well as its relation with external actors and forces. In this way, political manifestations of such identifications are an integral part of politicized regional or local nationalisms.[28] Moreover, examining Sudan from this perspective shows that the armed and non-armed challenges to the state are elite responses from the peripheries to a dynamic of forced assimilation and deliberately incomplete inclusion in the state system. This excludes the periphery elites from power as long as they continue to reject the imposed hierarchy and promote the political and economic interests of their constituents in the periphery. The assimilation also directly threatens the survival of local ways of life. The organized resistance to assimilation, in turn, has inspired the Arabized state elite to perceive periphery elites' political demands as a "problem", and to securitize them as a threat to the Sudanese state. As a result, the state elite has presented southern demands as a threat to the political unity of the state, although they have mainly sought to break the pattern of the narrow and exclusive rule by advocating more extensive redistribution of economic and political power.

In the course of the 19th and 20th century colonial age, marginalization and exclusion based on identity became socially institutionalized as part of state and governance in Sudan. This was dictated by the social hierarchy that determined economic and political power from the inception of the centralized state extending over most territories of contemporary Sudan. During the Anglo-Egyptian period, differential treatment of the northern "Arabs" and southern "Africans" by the colonial elite was reflected in the social foundations, structures, and policies of the state marginalization. The imposed indirect rule forced implementation of subjection as part of the prevailing societal structure,[29] being inherently linked to the creation of poverty in the peripheries and their dependence on the center as a method of control.[30] In Sudan underdevelopment and poverty became part of establishing a dynamic of periphery dependence on the more developed north-central Nile region, systematically enforcing the economic prominence of those Arabized Muslim groups best positioned to take advantage of economic opportunities and services concentrated in the north-central core areas. The impact of such policies in the marginalized regions was manifested particularly in the process of decolonization, which enabled prominent sections of the Arabized elite to inherit, monopolize, and to an extent privatize political power and buttress its economic prominence.

In Sudan, the perceived "Arabs" from the core of the state became the exclusive rulers of those peripheral areas considered to be populated by "Africans" or "blacks". The marginalized peripheries were governed from afar and only loosely integrated to state structures. They lacked economic development and services, while the shortage of resources at their disposition -owing largely to dependence on the center- hindered the emergence of powerful and coherent political representation capable of advancing the interests of the peripheries at the core. In north-central Sudan, financial resources,[31] education, and external interventions encouraged such development. Essentially this became a structural condition cemented by historical processes,[32] ultimately leading to the Arabized elite factions' control of the state.

Furthermore, the structures and dynamics of marginalization were carried over to the era of independence. For instance, Thompson demonstrates the persisting nature of the postcolonial state as interventionist, authoritarian, non-representative, and imposing coercion and cooptation.[33] This owes to the newly established political elite having collaborated with the colonizer and acquired experience in managing colonial state's political processes.[34] Such sociopolitical and socioeconomic organization stems from persisting historical cultural legacies (e.g. social inequality, political cultures, and patrimonialism) manifested in the political regimes and policies dictated by their formal institutions.[35] But it also draws on institutional dynamics deriving from traditional or cultural authority that are not formally incorporated to the state.[36]

In Sudan this has resulted in the structural condition of state marginalization, which is manifested socioculturally especially between the center and the periphery. This marginalization is ethnically based and regional, and justifies the persistence of exclusive power of the prominent members of the Arabized elite. Arguably the state's attempt to control and the structural condition of marginalization of periphery results in internal colonization of the state's fringe areas. It maintains exclusive power at the center and promotes regional inequality manifested in the extraction of resources, unemployment, lack of services, poverty and emigration from the periphery to the center of the polity.[37] In the case of Sudan, these dynamics have been accompanied by policies of various governments to forcefully assimilate periphery populations to Arab culture and Islam, and the imposition of the Arabized elite-dictated administrative, economic, and social order in the state peripheries.

In other words, it is argued here that the complex dynamics of state marginalization are the key to a comprehensive understanding of insurgency formation. This marginalization has to be understood not as an independent force distinct from society, but rather as an inherent feature of inter-group social relations drawing from prevalent exclusivist perceptions and logic of group identities. State marginalization therefore is a product of historical social processes of gradual but continuous (re)configuration of political and economic power, and domination within and between groups, which is affected by (f)actors that are both internal and external to the polity.

Thus, a historically founded analysis of state marginalization is fundamental not only to state formation but to the understanding of the structural and motivational origins of armed opposition. As pointed out above, the processes grouped together and designated here as state marginalization are manifested in contemporary Sudan in socioculturally and regionally defined political and economic exclusion, which has its roots in the 19th century state formation and the colonial period. Drawing from attitudes, values, norms, beliefs, and informal practices, the state marginalization is embedded mainly in the governance, ruling methods, and policies, shaped to work together to sustain the privileged position of the state elite. The political and economic power of the governing sections of this elite are connected to its control of the state, and also founded on defined constituencies. The concentration of power and marginalization articulate through institutions and policies, through both formal and informal channels, excluding representatives of other sections of the population from power (including those in the opposition within the Arabized elite itself). Above all this affects the population in the state peripheries, which is generally portrayed exclusively as "the other" and largely deprived from the state's political, economic, and social goods.

Power and Elites

On Power in Sudan

Because power is intimately linked to conflict formation in southern Sudan, the social sciences notion of power is a crucial part of the theoretical framework introduced here. Weber defines power as every opportunity/possibility,[38] which allows one to carry out one's own will in a social relationship, even against resistance.[39] Russell has defined it as "the production of intended effects".[40] Moreover, Weber's notion of power includes an attempt to further differentiate between overlapping economic power, in which a particular social group controls the means of production and the most profitable economic activity, and political power. Political power, in turn, enables the group to wield formal and informal influence in the society that enables it to elevate itself over other groups. Foucault contends that these forms of power are embedded in social structures.[41] This, including the relevance of institutionalized social hierarchies, is particularly relevant to the exclusive configuration of power in central Sudan, and grievances and insurgencies in the peripheries. Mills further argued that "All politics is a struggle for power; the ultimate kind of power is violence",[42] and Walter pointed out that "Power may be experienced as inspiring, wholesome, tolerable, or oppressive, depending on the circumstances . . . [and] . . . it may stimulate conflict and rebellion".[43] Arguably this has been the case in armed conflict formation in southern Sudan where state has used force and violent coercion extensively in the context that lacks of central government authority and legitimacy.[44]

The above description of power is intimately linked to the (re)construction and use of collective identities. These are sources of group formation and tend to provide legitimacy to the elites. This means that the elites, who share an identity layer/component with their constituents, may seek to instrumentalize these for political or material goals, often founded upon the collective desires of their followers.[45] An example of this in the case of Sudan is the state's use of "Arab" identity to extravert external support from the Arab states, or sections of the southern elite using "southern" identity against "northern Arab" for political mobilization and outside assistance while seeking to look past local "tribalism".

However, although group identities are often instrumentalized for political purposes, their (re)construction is a slow process. Castells proposes that such identities form along "legitimizing", "resistance", or "project".[46] He defines project identity construction as "when social actors, on the basis of whichever cultural materials are available to them, build a new identity that redefines their position in society and, by so doing, seek the transformation of overall social structure".[47] In the case of Sudan, this applies particularly to the dominant Arabized state elite's nationbuilding, but also to the contemporary southern elite seeking to build a "regional" identity. In addition, arguably the "resistance" identity is relevant to the groups in the peripheral areas in Sudan because according to Castells it is ". . . generated by those actors that are in positions/conditions devalued and/or stigmatized by the logic of domination . . . It constructs forms of collective resistance against otherwise unbearable oppression, usually on the basis of identities that were, apparently, clearly defined by history, geography, or biology, making it easier to essentialize the boundaries of resistance . . .".[48]

On Elites and Their Relation to Power

Hunter, Mills, and Putnam all analyzed elites and their relation to power. They demonstrated how elites are a result of economic and political forces within a social structure and become the *de facto* dominant forces behind political representation for groups and socially constructed entities.[49] However, in the case of Africa, it has been established that when resources in the disposition of the political elite diminish, this undermines the neo-patrimonial patron-client redistributive networks through which political leaders, or strongmen, acquire their legitimacy from their constituents.[50] Moreover, Reno has shown that power of the governing elite in Africa is intimately linked to its ability to control markets, which owes in part to its power over formal and informal institutions regulating social behavior.[51] This demonstrates the elite's desire to monopolize power to control the political and economic spheres inseparably. Yet, power can be considered to depend on perception and circumstances and be fundamentally contested,[52] which leads to what Bayart characterizes as internal circulation of elites within the governing class.[53]

When state power becomes contested, it often becomes a source of competition within and between elites. The excluded strongmen may turn to anti-state activities to claim their perceived share of political power and resources. This is often particularly the case in African states when such "big men" are deprived of spoils of the state and excluded from the circles of the governing elite. This deprives them from benefits such as lucrative political positions through which to channel public and private resources. Such leaders may also be pressured by their constituencies to challenge the state elite and claim resources perceived to belong to a certain region or a group. Consequently, Zartman proposes that in the process of organizing insurgencies, need (relative deprivation,[54] unfulfilled expectations, etc.), creed (identity based factors), and greed (elite's greed to obtain and control resources), become crucial.[55] Perceptions of group-based relative deprivation[56] and unmet expectations concerning social or political relationships linked to material well-being or extraction of local resources and labor (including forced labor), as in the case of sections of the southern elite in Sudan, may cause instability conducive to insurgencies. Thus, highlighting the elite agency behind domination and insurgency formation allows deeper analysis on the center-periphery dynamics beyond the broad categorizations of "northerners" and "southerners" widely used in the existing literature on Sudanese insurgencies.

In elite action the connection between power and identity becomes highlighted. For instance in Sudan, various historians, ideologues, and policymakers associated with the Arabized elite have sought to promote and instrumentalize the cultural elements they themselves adhere to (e.g. ethnicity, religion, and language). They have presented their view of Arab culture as superior in order to uphold the particular perception of "social race" prevalent in northern parts of Sudan. This is an integral component of identity politics as it provides the foundation for the Arabized elite's effort to maintain exclusive power, and the core to its political ambition of consolidating its self-proclaimed "Arab" and Muslim identity nationally. The political project that has been built around this aspiration seeks to maintain the *status quo* of state power concentrated in the sections of the Arabized elite. The state and its policies provides the vehicle for realizing the political project in which marginalization of non-Arabized state peripheries plays a crucial role in the attempt to forcefully assimilate the groups perceived as "the other". The peripheries are differentiated through mainly cultural claims, especially religion and language, which is even the case with some Muslim areas in northern Sudan perceived as not being doctrinally "pure" Muslim. This allows the use of identity (e.g. "Arab-Muslim" vs. "Darfurian", "Arab-Muslim" vs. "Beja", "Arab-Muslim" vs. "southerner") to justify the concentration of resources in the state's center and the systematically created dependence and poverty in the peripheries.

One face of these dynamics is presenting peripheries as a threat to the state order. This not only provides further justification for marginalization, but it allows securitization of the peripheries. In particular, political and economic demands from periphery opposition forces are presented as a menace which legitimizes repressive policies and the use of violence against those categorical "others" who are considered culturally non-"Arab" and/or unpure or non-Muslim. The creation of insecurity through inequality, deprivation, and injustice has allowed the use of disorder and armed conflict in the peripheries as a political instrument, and to uphold the power of the governing elite. It has also encouraged militarization in the peripheries. These dynamics maintained by governments composed of sections of the Arabized elite indicate solidarity and common interests among this elite against challenges to its exclusive socioeconomic and sociopolitical position. It allows to limit political competition within the ranks of the Arabized elite and to exclude effective representation of interests of the peripheries by regional and local elites. This, and the effective control of the state, has secured the longevity of power of the Arabized elite, even though within itself it has been divided by various political and ideological orientations ranging anywhere from Islamism to Communism.

Therefore, the "social race" is a significant component of understanding the concentration of economic and political power, and opposition grievances, in Sudan. Idris has described Sudan as a "racialized state".[57] It is deeply affected by the legacy of slavery, together with differential treatment during colonialism, with the British perceiving Sudanese "Arabs" as "semi-civilized" and "blacks" as "savages". Jok argues that due to persisting racism, the black southerners remain without the possibility of becoming full members of the "Arab" group and exercise equal rights despite adopting its cultural prerequisites such as language and religion.[58] Indeed, the legacy of slavery, and the fear of its return as a violent form of extreme marginalization, exclusion, and exploitation, contributed to the radicalization of opposition and insurgency formation in southern Sudan. Relevant to grievances involved in the second insurgency, Collins has noted that

> Unlike the relatively few missionary-educated Southerners who had dominated Southern political life since independence . . . new young men were politically and socially educated, and being at the lowest economic and social scale they became strongly militant as well as knowledgeable of the outside world. They returned regularly to their homes in the South, bringing with them a pent-up hostility and militancy that they developed while working as laborers on construction projects in the North.[59]

This unveils the constructed and persisting social marginalization in Sudan based on skin color, which has been pointed out by a number of authors.[60] It also shows the potentiality of the related frustrations to create animosity. However, this animosity does not automatically cause political violence since formation of armed opposition requires leadership and organized mobilization. Indeed, the conflicting identity categories in Sudan are a product of historical processes, (re)constructed and largely situational, and their role dictating social conduct depends largely, but not solely, on circumstances and political agency.

Thus, since assuming power in the 1950s, the governing elite in Sudan has consistently portrayed political opposition emerging from the marginalized areas as a security threat to the state. However, threat it poses is mainly to the continuity of the *status quo* of exclusive power of the "Arab" governing elite and the persistence of Arab-Muslim dominated social hierarchy. As a result, the situation in Sudan resembles to an extent that of Algeria and Egypt where the Muslim governing elites have politicized, extended, and used their own interpretation of religious doctrines and group identities to consolidate their claim on state power.

As explained above, in Sudan elite representatives from the peripheral regions have generally been excluded from claims to political and economic power at the national level. Perceivably, they and their regions of origin have been victims of deliberate marginalization and deprivation, which buttresses the relative power of the centralized state and the governing elite. In peripheries, such a southern Sudan, the exclusive and marginalizing state is commonly perceived as alien and hostile. This reality draws to an extent from the colonial era that encouraged certain cultural values, characterized either as "civilizing" or "African" in southern Sudan, in an attempt to limit the influence of the "Arab" culture from the northern provinces. It has favored the creation of a collective narrative of political identity in southern Sudan that contrasts the "Arab" and the state seen as an extension of the attempt to forcefully extend the hegemony of the governing elite through the imposition of Arabization and a particular type of Islamicization. This identity is often portrayed as primordially different from northern "Arabs" and inherently incompatible with the imposed Arab-Muslim state. Although the legacies of slavery, resistance, and cultural survival have become key pillars of this discourse, it should be recognized that the use of such identity politics is variable and situational in that these identities have been emphasized particularly in times of oppression. Thus, since decolonization the southern political leadership has played an important role in emphasizing difference between southern Sudan(ese) and the governing state elites. The southern leaders have linked these distinctions to the construction of a southern regional identity, as opposed to the "Arab", and some have engaged in effective organization of insurgencies.

Furthermore, this analysis draws from a center-periphery approach alluded to in a number of studies.[61] It is adopted here because such approach sheds light on the sentiments of marginalization, exclusion, and deprivation involved in conflict formation. The center-periphery approach is related to "growth pole" policies which tend to promote uneven development patterns by concentrating economic development and services near the metropolitan area where they are firmly under state authority, easily accessed, and provide job opportunities for urban dwellers and constituents of the national elite. This was the case in many European colonies in Africa in which the state did not consolidate itself in the peripheries, but maintained unequal relations of resource extraction without the social contract and service provision. The concentration of political power and economic activities in the state center also enabled the minimization of the cost of developing infrastructure in the peripheries. These development patterns are related to perceptions of relative deprivation[62] and group-based (regional) horizontal inequalities.[63] Due to their distribution along the lines of regional and group identity, these grievances generate perceptions of injustice and social subjugation, which local and regional elites may harness for political mobilization for protest and opposition. This, in the case of southern Sudan, has been particularly evident due to the attempts of some southern leaders' to capitalize on the perceived injustices arising in part from the pattern of uneven development and the legacy of slavery.

Finally, it is argued here that the legacy of differential treatment of sociocultural groups through racist perceptions, and the history of slavery arising from the colonial period and beyond, have affected the configuration of power, the state, and its policies. This, in turn, has maintained a pattern of exclusive and unequal distribution of wealth and political power, and generated regionally uneven development between the center and the peripheries of the Sudanese state. The unequal relationship between the center and the peripheries has then generated perceptions of relative deprivation and injustices in the less developed territories. Such aspects are useful in the attempt to highlight the role of exclusive elite power and state marginalization in the processes of insurgency formation.

Extraversion and Networks

The emphasis on local roots of conflicts in much of Africanist literature shies away from recognizing the role, impact, and responsibility of external actors and forces. It should therefore be emphasized that any holistic examination of processes of insurgency formation requires the understanding of interplay of local, regional, and international actors and forces. Indeed, some scholars argue that such separation between civil (local-national) and interstate (regional-international) wars analytically is likely to result in less telling results than more comprehensive and empirically founded conceptualizations of conflict.[64] However, such analyses require a wider internationalized dimension,[65] and should be conducted in their historical context taking into account the national political scene.[66] Murshed has argued that

> The actual outbreak of civil war, however, requires triggers that are usually both internal and external; these are not predictable and must arise in the context of the failure of state and society to manage conflict. Internal triggers are events that actually push potential belligerents over the brink into warfare. External triggers consist of actions and signals by outsiders, neighbouring countries and great powers that make the prospect of fighting or secession more attractive.[67]

It is also important to examine how local political realities have been constructed and transformed historically, and how they are affected by national, regional, and international influences.[68]

48

In the case of historical literature that deals with the causes of insurgencies in southern Sudan there is an emphasis on local causes of conflict. This is particularly the case with many prominent works of the Anglo-Saxon academic tradition, which tend to give little emphasis to external actors and forces that have greatly influenced Sudan's local and national reality.[69] Generally, these works tend to conform principally to local political, economic, and social factors to explain insurgency formation. However, this study seeks improved incorporation of regional and international dimensions to the historical analysis of formation of insurgencies in southern Sudan, and, as shown later, incorporates external actors and influences and goes beyond considering their role only as secondary.

Extraversion

It has been established that weak *de facto* statehood leads African leaders to use the recognized *de jure* status of the state to consolidate their rule. Bayart has called this "extraversion", describing it as rulers' attempts to build relationships with external actors, such as non-African states, multinational corporations, and international organizations, to acquire recognition and resources to strengthen their position and maintain domestic *status quo*.[70] Bayart further introduces cultural extraversion which " . . . consists in espousing foreign cultural elements and putting them in the service of autochtonous objectives".[71] In some cases, this may have inhibited state formation and the strengthening of weak or dysfunctional states.[72] In Sudan, such strategies have been manifested at least since the formation of centralized state in the 19th century, as prominent local social actors have collaborated with both colonial masters and external actors to confront domestic and regional adversaries.

However, extraversion linking the domestic and international spheres has also been used by non-state actors to engage in confrontation against the state. In situations where decrease in the state's ability to exercise monopoly of violence in parts of its territory facilitates an armed challenge,[73] extraversion may result in the birth and consolidation of alternative forms of authority. These can include, for instance, unofficial local administrations or transboundary orders, which may be characterized by violence and economic extraction or alternative forms of governance accepted by the local populations. Such formations emerged in southern Sudan during the war in the late 1960s, and again from the mid-1980s to 2005, in the form of rebel governance and administration. Indeed, Keen reminds that war " . . . is not simply a breakdown in a particular system, but a way of creating an alternative system of profit, power and even protection".[74] Reno argues that informal political and economic entities such as transboundary formations may help to determine winners in times of factional struggles or insurgencies because they facilitate resources to leaders.[75] The case of Sudan shows that the important role of such alternative authorities and politico-economic orders often goes unnoticed in analyses on insurgencies, even though they have been present in wars and are hardly "new".

Networks

While social networks (e.g. cultural, economic, and political) have existed historically, Castells argues that they are increasingly important as a social reality in the globalized contemporary world.[76] Kaldor defines such networks as " . . . flexible, fluid . . . forms of communication and information exchange; mutual discussion and debate transform the way issues are understood and the language within which they are expressed. They represent a two-way street . . . ".[77] The view on investigating networks adopted here draws from the work of Knoke and Burmeister-May who consider network analysis to consist of examining interactions of political power relations, influences, and domination among social actors, which can involve economic, social, cultural, or ideological, two-directional flows influencing those involved.[78] In such networks, " . . . the relations are treated as expressing the linkages which run between agents . . . [through] . . . qualitative measures of network structure".[79] Inherent to this approach is Wright's assertion that states should be viewed as complex networks of institutions,[80] and considering "big men" in Africa as nodes in such networks exercising formal and informal power by distributing resources.[81]

Moreover, when focusing on the analysis of regional and global (f)actors in Africa from this perspective, the concept of state marginalization provides an excellent starting point. Contemporarily, according to Callaghy, Kassimir, and Latham, the kind of states found in Africa have become sites of overlapping interests manifested in armed conflict, refugee management, external intervention, political manipulation, and economic extraction.[82] This is partly due to their juridic sovereignty, which can be used for multiple purposes in the context of their weak empirical sovereignty characterized by deep penetration of internal and external influences. However, it must be remembered that despite legal and institutional structures, African states contain patrimonial networks, and communal allegiances and leadership, that may be more significant for social and political organization than the formal institutional framework. Furthermore, transboundary formations and other alternative forms of authority may coexist with the legally established forms of order, as in the rebel-held areas and borderlands of southern Sudan that host ethnic communities closely connected to the territories of DRC, Ethiopia, Kenya, and Uganda. For Nordstrom, such formations, similarly to states, require social institutions to function, and are therefore inherently social constructions organizing political and economic activities.[83]

The network approach entails a study to contain the interacting spheres of local, regional, and international. Callaghy, Kassimir, and Latham engage in such analysis through structures, networks, and discourses, having an impact on Africa as well as the international community, while claiming that "Above all, they play a major role in creating, transforming, and destroying forms of order and authority".[84] This is due to the inter-connections between formal and informal institutions, including powerful individuals and hybrid formations that exercise political and economic power. Such links include relationships between institutions and networks that transit commodities (such as arms, natural resources, or foreign aid) and ideas (such as human rights, neo-liberal economics, development, or security). This form of networks are relevant to insurgency formation because they may transport material and non-material resources that facilitate organization and mobilization for rebellion. The concepts of extraversion and networks are therefore useful as they highlight the external dimensions of the processes of insurgency formation.

The Processes of Insurgency Formation

A number of studies have differentiated between types of causes of conflicts to understand locally, regionally, and internationally founded social, economic, and political actors and forces responsible for their outbreak. Scholars have argued that there are three causal clusters related to armed conflicts; root or structural factors, proximate factors, and triggers.[85] Grey-Johnson has further claimed that such ingredients relate to the operability of the state, governance, legitimacy, provision of services, and the state/citizenry relationship.[86]

However, this study views violence as a process.[87] It also underlines that insurgencies need to be organized and that they take place in opportune conditions in which adequate social and material support is ensured. Such circumstances include local conditions, such as relative lack of development and services, persisting violence and insecurity, emotional factors, sentiments and rumors, and regional and international elements, including social, political, and economic extraversion and networks. Weinstein argues that insurgencies are organized either around material resources, resulting in less control, more atrocities, and less conviction, or center on social resources in which certain norms and justice-seeking cause more control and less atrocities.[88] Indeed, in the case of insurgency formation processes in southern Sudan, social resources have been fundamental, although individual motivations to rebel vary greatly. In addition, as this study will show, minimum material resources have been necessary -mainly troops and their personal weaponry- but these have played a much lesser role in the mobilization for armed opposition.

Furthermore, academic literature has the tendency of classifying insurgencies by type[89] but such categorization is possibly less useful than often considered. This is because the objectives and nature of insurgencies are conditioned by local, regional, and international factors and realities which change over time. For instance, leaderships of rebel groups are often not clear and the leading figures may have different agendas and objectives. The case of southern Sudan demonstrates this eloquently since the objectives of rebel factions there have varied between secession, revolution, and reform, and have included different material motivations in various degrees. This study seeks to avoid such classifications that may blind the discovery of true agendas and motivations of insurgents.

Finally, recognizing emotional factors linked to local conditions and social inequalities as significant mobilizing forces in the process of insurgency formation is important. As Gurr posits, frustrations are likely to turn into aggression in the conditions of perceived relative deprivation when the state and/or its leadership are considered illegitimate.[90] As will be shown in later chapters of this study, such emotional factors have been relevant in the case of southern Sudan. For instance, Wassara has argued that "Many conflicts arise from what parties think may happen, from their anxiety, prejudice, fear, and uncertainties, rather than from any phenomenon that is actually threatening".[91] As this study will show, politics that emerge from cultural and ethnic identity perceptions[92] are significant in stimulating sentimental elements that have been crucial for mobilization for insurgencies in southern Sudan.

From State Marginalization to Insurgencies

Under certain conditions state marginalization may start a process that provokes armed violence and escalation into insurgencies. However, this process is not automatic and requires opportune circumstances, political actors, and social and material resources that allow engaging in organized armed opposition. Here below a theoretical model is introduced that draws from earlier scholarship and seeks to address the continuing weaknesses in literature, including single-factor explanations of insurgencies, the lack of identifying triggers of rebellions, and understanding the role of elites and leaders in provoking violence.[93] It provides an attempt to explain how state marginalization may generate circumstances that result in processes of group polarization, violence, and insurgencies.

As noted above, under certain conditions state marginalization generates grievances based largely on perceived injustices. The perception of intensification of state marginalization of one collective, e.g. on class, regional, cultural or ethnic grounds, and exclusion of its prominent members or representatives from access to economic and/or political power, may result in a view of state being dominated by actors potentially hostile to the group and its leadership. Consequently, access to the state, and having influence over its policies, is generally associated with any group's attempt to ensure self-preservation within any particular state political system.[94] Under certain circumstances of marginalization, the exclusion from influence at the state level intensifies the sentiments of fear, mistrust, and increasing physical, economic, and social insecurity, which drive individuals to grip harder on their group. Belonging to the group tends to be associated with higher individual security particularly when the state is unable or unwilling to provide such security. Heightening state marginalization can therefore function according to the logic of Posen's "ethnic security dilemma"[95] in which the state's inability to guarantee security of ethnic (minority) groups results in their mobilization and militarization for self-protection. In the case of intensifying state marginalization the heightening grievances are largely oriented towards the state, which may result in a particularly alien government to lose its legitimacy and authority among those it has marginalized.

The change in political environment caused by the intensification of state marginalization towards a group may result in its leading cadres to promote identity differences. This may occur due to individual aspirations for (re)gaining political and/or economic power, an attempt to ensure the security of the leader's own narrower constituency from which he draws his prestige and power, or aspirations to secure a larger identity group. It may then lead to polarization of cleavages between groups, in this case the one in command of the state and the other in which individuals perceive themselves to have been marginalized. As a result, the leadership, namely political elites or ethnic activists, of the marginalized group is affected by the changing political environment that drives some of its members to seek to secure their own and their constituents' interests by challenging the power of the state leadership.[96] The mobilization of constituents, in turn, draws from the perception of relative deprivation.[97] Thus, mobilization for opposition is a process that involves and requires both top-down (elite) and bottom-up (follower) action. In this process the leadership's role in organization and mobilization is crucial.

In addition, generating group differentiation on ethnic or other grounds requires collective sentiments, beliefs, attitudes, and values that define the in-group. In the process of mobilization, a key group of radical individuals, or hardliners, is necessary to expand the group size through example and re-cruitment,[98] while social networks, from the leadership (patrons) down to the level of individuals (clients), facilitate mobilization among those adhering to group norms, contracts, and conventions[99] against the perceived "other".

When political mobilization against the state meets violent repressive measures from the authorities, a violent response may result. This may hap-pen especially in circumstances in which the state has lost its legitimacy and authority, and has little capacity to combat dissent. If the state does not exercise full monopoly of violence or extensive control of its population, vi-olent response by the marginalized in areas where the state is weak becomes increasingly possible.[100] This is largely because the state's violent response heightens grievances, and sentiments of fear and mistrust, among those it represses, resulting in further polarization between it and those it targets. If the measures taken against dissent are oppressive, but unable to suppress the opposition, they are likely to lead to its radicalization, increasing the possi-bility of wider mobilization for violent resistance.

According to some scholars, state repression allows the overcoming of the free-rider problem of individual contribution to a rebellion because pos-sible recruits may face additional hardship by not joining a rebel group.[101] In the conditions of growing uncertainty and violence the role of the social net-works[102] along ethnic or other group identity lines, and the associated con-tracts, conventions,[103] norms,[104] and group solidarity,[105] become highlighted. Such networks generate assurance that encourages bandwagoning behavior (following the choice of others) among members of the group.[106] If the lead-ership is able to convince individuals of the importance of their personal contribution to the group's "cause" or survival,[107] and is therefore able to build a common perception through a successful frame alignment,[108] it may be able to eliminate the problem of having followers who do not significant-ly contribute to the struggle while benefitting from it (free-rider problem). Responsiveness of potential recruits to "the cause" is therefore largely de-termined by the social networks that connect clients to their patrons, and the resonance of mobilization to the wider communities mainly through friend-ship, family, kinship, ethnic, or cultural (religious and language) ties.

In other words, social contracts and conventions of a group play an im-portant role in convincing individuals to follow others in joining armed op-position. This is particularly the case in circumstances of growing instability and violence. When social group norms and practices (such as warrior traditions or experience in violent behavior) geared towards engaging in violence come together with attitudes, beliefs, and values, which justify the support for armed opposition, they may result in the recruitment of motivated individuals. When the number of hardline recruits increases, it can lead to a growing number of those who feel repressed also to join the armed opposition even beyond the most immediate social networks. This is especially likely to occur in circumstances of growing instability and violence in which individuals are increasingly forced to choose sides, while in extreme situations many attempt to flee and seek refuge in safer areas or countries. Yet, as mentioned above, the process just described is not automatic, since undertaking mobilization and armed struggle requires opportune political circumstances, elite organization, and available social and material resources.

But the process may also work in reverse. During more extended periods of peace, and circumstances favoring lesser strife between elites, the political cleavages among them and their constituencies tend to converge and facilitate cooperation instead of confrontation. As a result, the perceived lessening of state marginalization, and lessening exclusion of periphery elites from power at the national level, is linked to diminishing grievances in the peripheries. Therefore, gaining or maintaining access to political and economic power through state is likely to lower the interest of peripheral elites to confront the state and orchestrate armed opposition. Furthermore, elite strongmen's access to state is likely to satisfy their constituencies' demands for resources and lower their interest in engaging in armed opposition activities.

Thus, both the process of polarization and convergence are inherently linked to the actions, strategies, and positions adopted by the elites. These politicians and ethnic entrepreneurs seek to instrumentalize particular layers of ethnic identities for guiding the political behavior of their constituencies towards confrontation or cooperation. In the long-term, this may lead to reconfiguration and reconstruction of some self-defining identity elements as well as the general perception of the constructed "other".

The empirical part of this study seeks to demonstrate that insurgency formation process similar to what has been described here took place in the making of the southern rebellions in Sudan. The later chapters of this study seek to highlight aspects of this process, while also underlining the importance of the interaction between the domestic and the external in shaping local and national political, economic, and social trajectories, conditions, and circumstances. These provided the context for the formation of insurgencies.

Main Objective, Arguments, and Contributions of the Study

This study seeks to explain the relationship between state marginalization and insurgency formation with a particular focus on southern Sudan. It demonstrates how inclusion and exclusion of periphery elites from the state, and the accompanying political and economic power, is related to societal peace and armed conflicts. The study highlights that marginalization is not only determined by domestic factors, but is heavily influenced by external actors and forces.

This study argues that a broad and historically founded analysis is necessary in an attempt to extensively analyze insurgency formation in Africa and southern Sudan. It seeks to answer a number of questions related to the causes and timing of the rebellion(s), many of which continue to generate debate. The analysis also unveils less known but significant dimensions of the emergence of insurgencies. In the process, it considers how state, leadership, identities, mobilization, political and economic agendas, resources, and external actors and forces relate to insurgency formation.

The study offers a theoretical framework based on the broad and historically founded concept of state marginalization which provides a wide and inclusive basis for analysis. It allows identifying and highlighting the main actors, forces, and dynamics in the process of insurgency formation. The analysis shows how the history of marginalization and exclusion, based on exclusive view of identities and associated with racial and sociocultural subjugation (e.g. slavery and social hierarchy), has played a crucial role behind perceptions of "internal colonialism", relative deprivation, dependency, and poverty, and threat to physical and cultural survival. This intractable dynamic is paramount to the understanding of the emergence of insurgencies in southern Sudan.

From a constructivist-instrumentalist perspective, the study argues that identity categories[109] in Sudan result from historical processes. They are founded, on the one hand, on elite propagation of a perceived superiority of Arab culture and Islam, and, on the other hand, on the resistance to the legacy of slavery and/or Arab-Muslim elite dominated social hierarchy orchestrated by other, marginalized, elites. Periodic highlighting and instrumentalization of certain identity categories by political elites has at times deepened cleavages between social groups and led to their reinforcement or (re)construction. This has particularly been the case during periods of political instability and insecurity, while in more peaceful times identity categories have been less divisive. The crucial role of political elites in manipulating and (re)con-

56

structing identity differences disproves the idea of inherently incompatible, static, primordial, and inherently conflictive identities that has been used in part of the literature on insurgencies in southern Sudan.[110]

It is also imporant to note that a complex mix of internal and external (international and regional) actors, forces, and dynamics contributed to state formation and the emergence of insurgencies in southern Sudan. This assertion challenges the claim that the origins of insurgencies in Africa are internal and that regional and international actors and forces come into play only *after* a rebellion has begun. In fact, the focus on the domestic explanations has resulted in the role of the regional and international context been left with less emphasis in the historical literature on southern Sudanese insurgencies.

This study underlines that historical record of southern Sudan and its peoples' relations with the Arabized and Islamized north-central region differs to a degree from that of other peripheries in Sudan. These relations, characterized by the prevailing social hierarchy and generally the highest level of racial and sociocultural subjugation within Sudan, largely explain the emergence of periphery insurgencies against the Arabized Muslim dominated state primarily in southern Sudan. Furthermore, the timing of the insurgencies remains under debate. Some scholars argue that the the first rebellion began in the 1955 southern disturbances[111] and others consider the insurgency as being a result of the formal establishment of the Anya Nya armed opposition in the early 1960s.[112] Although there is less controversy on the starting date of the second insurgency, it can be considered as a continuation of the first rebellion since its causes cannot be fully understood without comprehending the earlier struggle and its aftermath. To this extent the second insurgency relates to the first. Finally, some prominent historians have deemed the first southern insurgency as inevitable,[113] but this assertion appears to favor the discredited primordial accounts of identities and obscures the key role played by the rapid decolonization process.

In addition, the study further shows that the insurgencies in southern Sudan were a result of a combination of particular historical processes. Southern territories were marginally incorporated to the state as peripheral areas, and their relationship with the centralized authority was characterized by deeper violent domination and subjugation than in other peripheral territories. These dynamics, along with the colonial policy of separation, gave rise to a politically conscious "southern" elite, projecting a regional political identity to counter the perceived hegemony and domination from northern Sudan. The analysis here explains how state formation in Sudan led to the established practice of state marginalization in the hands of a narrow and exclusive elite, and how colonial legacy and elite projects promoted the construction of the "Arab-Muslim North" and the "African South" as regional identities-entities despite the extensive heterogeneity of each region. Thus, it is shown that it was the periodic reinforcement of identity cleavages, not primordial and fixed identity categories of "Arab northerner" and "African southerner", which were important factors in the origins and development of the insurgencies in southern Sudan.

Moreover, this analysis on insurgency formation highlights state domination and the institutionalization of marginalization. It shows the importance of government policies in delegitimizing the state and provoking resistance in southern Sudan. The study points out how the decolonization process dictated by external (regional and international) (f)actors generated rising antagonism in terms of identity polarization along the constructed "Arab" vs. "African" differentiation, which led to the first southern insurgency. The study also shows how the second insurgency incubated in the course of the 1970s in conditions of rising Islamism and economic deterioration, and then became a rebellion in which the onset was again heavily influenced by external factors. The analysis therefore demonstrates that regional and international actors and forces played an important role in the processes of insurgency formation in southern Sudan.

Furthermore, this work contributes to the debate on the timing and inevitability of the insurgencies, and highlights the emotional elements (collective attitudes, sentiments, and feelings) in their formation. Although the military casualty accounts prior to the early 1960s might not have been very high, the antagonism of many southerners had resulted in low level violence that had a destabilizing effect already after 1955. Thus, it is argued here that the first insurgency in southern Sudan could be considered to have begun already in the late 1950s. In the case of the second insurgency, the deteriorating conditions in southern Sudan in the mid-1970s gave impetus to residual armed opposition activity that contributed to the making of the rebellion. This could be considered to have marked the beginning of the second insurgency that to an extent was a continuation of the preceding rebellion. Although many prominent authors claim that the insurgencies in southern Sudan were inevitable due to primordial "North-South" identity incompatibilities, it is argued here that the processes of conflict formation were heavily influenced by the periodically deepening identity cleavages. These were linked to external forces, intensifying exclusionary and repressive state policies, driven by the logic of marginalization and securitization of the "southern problem", as well as to the orchestrated resistance in southern Sudan in which perceptions of injustices and deprivation, along with sentiments of insecurity and fear towards the state, were significant.

Finally, the analysis here shows that state construction and insurgency formation in southern Sudan consisted of a complex interplay of factors. Historical, political, economic, social, and cultural determinants in the domestic and external (regional and international) context provided conditions conducive to the rebellions. However, the study recognizes limitations of the historical literature that uses broad identity-based categorizations and deterministic explanations on causes of war in southern Sudan, and seeks to deconstruct them to highlight the elite agency in the process of insurgency formation. Although the two insurgencies took place in slightly different political and economic circumstances, the emotional factors responding to exclusive governance, marginalization, and oppressive policies, and demonstrating general antagonism towards the state and its ruling elite, were similar in both occasions.

Endnotes

1   Fawole (2004).
2   See Clapham (1996), Chaigneau (2002), and Pumphrey (2003) for some of these factors.
3   See e.g. Bratton (2004), Kraushaar and Lambach (2009), and Hagmann and Péclard (2011).
4   Aguirre (2006: 2).
5   Prunier and Gisselquist (2003), Rotberg (2004: 13), and Mayall (2005: 51-2) view pre-independence Southern Sudan as a failed state.
6   See e.g. Ylönen (2005a, 2005b, 2008, and 2009).
7   Idris (2001, 2005) has argued that historical processes have shaped these into a type of "racialized state". However, it is emphasized here that this itself is not enough to explain insurgency formation in Sudan. Rather, analyzing insurgencies also requires the consideration of changing and situational identities, emotional and sentimental determinants of group mobilization, and regional and international (f)actors.
8   Deng (1995a: 369-400, 484-5).
9   As Abbink (2004: 4) claims, attitudes of superiority and inferiority based on this hierarchy continue to dictate the distribution of political and economic power and opportunities, which is significant because
     Northern Sudanese, also many of those opposed to the policies of the GoS [Government of Sudan], still largely think that most Southerners of various ethnic origins 'have no culture or religion', are 'primitive' and are in need of 'development', usually in the guise of Islamization. The entire political and economic programme of the GoS and its supporters, in slowly annexing the South and exploiting its labour force and natural assets, has been cloaked in a 'civilizational project' of Islamization.

10   For instance, the Rashaida who have relatively recently arrived in Sudan from Saudi Arabia are largely excluded from politics although they are genetically more "Arab" than the members of the Sudanese governing elite. Indeed, the Arabized groups holding power in Sudan share a long history of slavery and intermixing with other peoples, and their "racial" and "cultural" distinction from other groups in Sudan can be considered as a social construction of an invented tradition.

11   See e.g. Ezza and Libis (2009).

12   For evidence on this process see e.g. Eltahir (2009) and Adam, Bartlett, and Nour (2009).

13   Word "*abd*" has a connotation of inferiority as it refers to black peoples associated historically with the status of a slave.

14   Sharkey (2007).

15   O'Fahey (2002: 55).

16   Jok (2001: 21).

17   See Sharkey (2007) for an excellent analysis.

18   Badal (1976).

19   Badal (1976: 467-8) and Jok (2001, 2007).

20   According to Howell (1973, 1978b), such perception became common among the southern leadership in the 1950s and 1960s, particularly after it realized the privileged position of the central riverine northern elites manifested through wealth, social prestige, education, Arabic language skills, lighter-skin, and the way of dressing. Arguably, this perception was reinforced again during the second insurgency. It should be noted though that some prominent southerners have embraced Arab culture and Islam for status reasons although this tends to render them second class.

21   Badal (1976: 466-7, 469), de Chand (2000), and Johnson (2003).

22   Badal (1976: 469-70).

23   See Badal (1976: 470) and Woodward (1995: 92).

24   This is evident in Badal (1976: 465, 466, 470-1). According to Mamdani (1997), in Africa such imposition by the dominant groups is conducive to inter-ethnic violence.

25   Gray (1961), Adams (1991), and Woodward (1995).

26   See Deng (1995a, 1995b) and Young (2000).

27   Sørensen (1998).

28   Milliken and Krause (2002).

29   Mamdani (1997).

30   Munene (2001).

31   Woodward (1995: 95).

32   de Waal (2007a, 2007b).

33   Thompson (2004).

34   Ake (2000: 36) has further argued that

   Independence changed the composition of the managers of the state but not the character of the state, which remained much as it was in the colonial era. Its scope continued to be totalistic and its economic orientation statist. It presented itself often as an apparatus of violence, its base in social forces remained extremely narrow and it relied for compliance unduly on coercion rather than authority. With few exceptions, the elite who came to power decided to inherit and exploit the colonial system to their own benefit rather than transforming it democratically as had been expected. This alienated them from the masses whom they now had to contain with force.

35 See Bratton and van de Walle (1997).
36 Kaarsholm (2006: 14).
37 Kirkinen (1972).
38 Weber (1968).
39 The author is aware of the limitations of Weberian thought which emerged in a European context to interpret political systems and culture in Africa. However, he finds Weber's definition of power useful for the analysis.
40 Russell (1962: 25).
41 Dreyfus and Rabinow (1982: 208).
42 Mills (1956: 171).
43 Walter (1969: 32).
44 See e.g. MacIver (1947: 16).
45 Chabal and Daloz (2005).
46 Castells (1997).
47 Castells (1997: 8).
48 Castells (1997: 8).
49 Hunter (1953), Mills (1956), and Putnam (1976).
50 See e.g. Reno (various). While in many parts of Africa there is a long tradition of personalized patrimonial rule, the state order has added formal institutions to the patrimonial ruling logic and produced neo-patrimonialism. According to Bratton and van de Walle (1997: 62) "[…] neopatrimonialism is the incorporation of patrimonial logic into bureaucratic institutions". However, the concept of neo-patrimonialism remains blurry and debated among scholars.
51 Reno (2005: 128).
52 Lukes (2005: 14).
53 Bayart (1993).
54 Gurr (1970; 1993) used relative deprivation as a major factor in explaining motivations to rebel.
55 Zartman (2005).
56 See e.g. Schaefer (2008: 69) for a definition of group-based relative deprivation.
57 Idris (2001, 2005).
58 Jok (2007).
59 Collins (1985: 138).
60 Idris (2001, 2005), Sharkey (2003), and author's field notes.
61 See e.g. Roden (1974) and Badal (1976), and more generally Kok (1996) and Cobham (2005).

62   Gurr (1970, 1993).

63   Stewart (2000, 2001).

64   See Elbadawi and Sambanis (2000) and Henderson and Singer (2000).

65   Gleditsh (2006).

66   Mkandawire (2002: 208).

67   Murshed (2002: 392-3).

68   Appandurai (1996) and Hart (2002).

69   See e.g. the otherwise excellent accounts of Daly (1991), Holt and Daly (2000), Johnson (2003), and Collins (2005, 2008).

70   Bayart (1993, 2000). For instance, according to Reno (2001: 198), controlling economic transactions as part of international networks provides state leaders with economic resources to justify political power that extends beyond their juridical territorial authority, and enables them to use non-formal economic ties to face opponents.

71   Bayart (2005: 71).

72   Herbst (1990: 117-39).

73   Kalyvas (2006: 18).

74   Keen (1998: 11).

75   Reno (2001: 205-8). This is precisely why the leader of the first Anya Nya rebellion in southern Sudan, Joseph Lagu, was able to centralize power within the southern opposition in the late 1960s, and gave the SPLM/A of John Garang an upper hand against other factions in the mid-1980s. See also Utas (2012) on leaders as resource allocators.

76   Castells (1996, 1998).

77   Kaldor (2003: 95).

78   Knoke (1994), and Knoke and Burmeister-May (1990).

79   Scott (1991: 3).

80   Wright (1978).

81   Utas (2012: 1).

82   Callaghy, Kassimir, and Latham (2001: 5).

83   Nordstrom (2001: 227-9).

84   Callaghy, Kassimir, and Latham (2001: 5).

85   See e.g. Sriram and Nielsen (2004), and Alexander and Smith (2004).

86   Grey-Johnson (2006).

87   In this sense it follows Kalyvas (2006).

88   Weinstein (2005).

89   See e.g. O'Neill (1980, 1990) and Clapham (1996, 1998).

90   Gurr (1970, 1993).

91   Wassara (2007: 7).

92   Chabal and Daloz (2005).

93   Brown (1996: 13, 22) points out these shortcomings.

94   This was, for instance, the case of Nigeria before the Biafran rebellion as competition over the control of the state between regional elites resulted in those deprived of state power calling for secession. See Horowitz (1985: 278-9).

95   Posen (1993).
96   See Tilly (1978).
97   Gurr (1970, 1993).
98   Kuran (1998a: 41-2, 1998b: 654-7).
99   See e.g. Fireman and Gamson (1979), Hardin (1982), Coleman (1990), and Moore (1995). In the case of southern Sudan, warrior traditions among the main local groups, the militarization of society due to perpetual instability and violence, and the military organization (e.g. army and police) which bound the military leadership tightly to its soldier clients in terms of loyalty, are central in understanding the success of mobilization for armed opposition.
100 In the case of Africa, most insurgencies take place in the state peripheries where the central government's legitimacy and authority tends to be weak and its control over the territory subjected easier to contestation.
101 See DeNardo (1985), Mason (1989), and Mason and Krane (1989).
102 Tilly (1978) and Popkin (1979).
103 Hardin (1982).
104 Fireman and Gamson (1979).
105 Coleman (1990).
106 Moore (1995).
107 Frohlich, Oppenheimer, and Young (1971).
108 Opp (2009: 234-74, 292-3).
109 In the case of "northern-southern" relationship in Sudan these categories have included "northern", "Arab", "Muslim" as well as "southern", "black", "African", "slave". Similar categories have been used to make class, ethnic, and regional distinctions in eastern and western Sudan as well.
110 See e.g. Ruay (1994) on one such account.
111 Eprile (1974).
112 Chan, and Zuor (2006).
113 See Holt (1961), Daly (1991, 1993), and Collins (2005, 2008).

CHAPTER III

FORGING CONTEMPORARY SUDAN:
A Historical Background

Sudan is a land of paradoxes where the multiple pasts of a conquest state joust for acknowledgment against a hegemonic perspective that privileges one of the many constituent parts of the contemporary polity.[1]

Highlighting the importance of historical political, economic, and social trajectories is important for any comprehensive conflict analysis. This chapter demonstrates how the long-term foundations of marginalization, manifested in hierarchical social status expressed culturally, politically, and economically, was a product of historical processes and became a significant factor in perceptions of injustices and deprivation at the core of insurgency formation in southern Sudan. This particular history underlines how political identities are constructed in the local context and how they relate to the institutionalization of marginalization. In this, the legacy of slavery[2] is important. It is argued here that the emergence of a marginalizing polity took place as a result of an early state formation process in which previously dominant social legacies prevailed. In this way, during the course of the 19th century, the prevailing ethnically and culturally founded "Arab"-Muslim[3] elite-dominated social hierarchy was adopted as a major force in organizing the newly founded polity, based on conquest of a number of smaller pre-existing political entities. This hierarchy continued to serve dominant elites over time, and heavily influenced the construction of ethnic and regional political identities. Indeed, the domination of the leading sectors of the north-central "Arab"-Muslim elite played an important part in the construction of the "center" and the "periphery", and "northern" and "southern" Sudan,[4] extending ethno-cultural societal hierarchy. Over time, this hierarchy continued to deprive many of the peoples in the margins of northern Sudan of access to political power and resources, and those from

65

southern Sudan of equal social standing and treatment largely due to the legacy of slavery. It is shown in this chapter that identity-based marginalization became institutionalized as a structural force of the Sudanese state, and has served as a significant determinant of the discord between the "Arab"-Muslim state elite and dominant sectors of leadership in the peripheries, above all in southern Sudan. Yet despite its institutionalization, the marginalization it is not unchanging but (re)constructed and manipulated through historical and political discourses that gradually transform identities.

Social legacies that derive from historical trajectories are significant in shaping identities. Deng and Lesch among others argue that the origins of insurgencies in southern Sudan are embedded in the construction of local identities in the long-term.[5] These draw from responses to social institutions aimed at maintaining the political power of the Arab-Muslim elite by upholding the historically, culturally, and racially defined social hierarchies of the stratified society. In a similar tone, de Chand and Jok have pointed out that slavery, as a particular age-old institution predating Islam, provided historically founded legitimacy to create the structural conditions needed for enduring domination and subjugation in the process of creating the contemporary polity in Sudan.[6] However, what the literature fails to emphasize is that the dynamics involved in these processes were not only local but also regional and international, which fomented social, political, and economic marginalization in Sudan. These dynamics are important particularly in the case of southern Sudan because they explain how the sentiment of fear and resistance to domination became important elements in response to perceived intensification of institutionalized marginalization. They also partly explain the emergence of "southern" regional political identity that developed in response to the perceived northern "Arab" elite domination.

Arabization and Islamicization in the Region

Historical processes have been essential in shaping social organization of the heterogeneous populations of *bilad as-Sudan* (the land of the blacks). In this section reference is made to those social processes that the author considers as being significantly linked to the emerging identities and socially defined power related to Arab culture and Islam, and consequently dictating the social organization of the marginalizing polity. This power is associated with the perception of cultural superiority and the establishment of a particular social hierarchy dominated by sectors of elites of the self-proclaimed *awlad al-balad* (worthy sons of the land)[7], who claim superior Arab ancestry that entails prominent social standing.[8] Emphasis here is put on how Arabization and Islamicization affected social relations and organization and what took place southwards of its sphere of influence in the area of contemporary southern Sudan.

Arabization and Islamicization

The historical processes of Arabization and Islamicization have been essential in the formation of the social fabric of the Nile riverine region. This way, they have been relevant to the construction of "northern" Sudan,[9] a highly heterogeneous region in terms of population with Islam and Arab culture as its major homogenizing forces. They dictate the distribution of power, and form essential building blocks for social organization. Both are aggrandized through ideologies that fabricate historical narratives founded largely on the Arab conquest of Egypt and the following Arab migrations and takeover of Sudan.[10] However, not all populations in northern Sudan have been fully Arabized or Islamicized, which makes northern Sudan highly diverse with a number of different cultural traditions that have been affected by the two forces in various degrees.[11]

One generation after the death of Prophet Muhammad, Muslim armies invaded Africa. The area that later came to be known as northern Sudan was slowly annexed to Islam's sphere of influence through the gradual movement of nomadic Arab groups southwards in search of more fertile environment. This resulted in frequent intermarriage with local Nubians, and gradually produced mixed, to an extent culturally Arabized, frontier communities that at times were obliged to pay tribute to the dominant local groups before slowly being absorbed into local societies.[12] Over time, sectors of the Arabized part of the population gained prominence in the local communities, often due to their position as traders and by engaging in propagation of the self-perceived superiority of their religious culture. This gradually transmitted to other sectors of the population, particularly after the increasing wealth of part of the Arabized sections converted them into desired source of husbands for Nubian and other local women, while at the same time the culturally Arabized Muslim women were unable to marry non-Muslims.[13] The patriarchal system dictated by religion contrasted the Nubian matriarchal structure and fostered prominence of the Arabized stock, which based its claims for social adherence to Islam.[14] While the influence of the Arabized nomads continued moving southwards along the Nile, another migratory movement arrived in the eastern Red Sea region, gradually fusing the institutions of local Beja peoples with the increasingly Arabized communities and giving further impetus to Arabization.[15]

67

However, some of the culturally Arabized peoples also adopted aspects of Nilotic cultures. This was particularly the case in further south, in the fringes of Arab and Islamic influence, where they encountered fierce resistance. This suggests that the self-perception of cultural superiority varied extensively and was conditioned by social dynamics within and between communities. For instance, Arabized Baggara cattle-herding nomads, inhabiting mainly areas in current southern Darfur and Kordofan, became semi-sedentary, and mixing with the neighboring Nilotic populations replaced the camel with the bull as their main livelihood following Nilotic tradition.[16] Yet, they continued to use Arabic, " . . . a conquering language . . . in its very pride tending towards ultimate triumph".[17] In northern Sudan overall there was a gradually growing significance in claiming "Arab" identity as an indicator of social prominence.

Military campaigns occasionally accompanied migration. This, together with the intermixing, facilitated the gradual submission of Nubian Christian kingdoms to a social order dominated by claims to "Arabhood".[18] Southwards from the Nubian territories was the Funj kingdom, with its capital founded in 1504 in Sennar, which despite early opposition to incoming influences adopted Arab language, customs, Islam, and status of a sultanate over time.[19] From 15th century onwards the Funj kingdom became the largest political entity in the central Nile valley of contemporary Sudan, but was never able to subdue the neighboring Darfur in the west, or smaller neighboring groups north of it, and had faced sharp decline by the 19th century when Muhammad Ali's Turco-Egyptian army invaded lands south of Egypt.[20] The Funj society was organized mainly through customary laws, certain legal and property rights, and marriage, while its social order was based hierarchically on three classes, the nobility, the subjects, and the slaves, with the latter two groups providing tribute and labor to the nobility.[21] Smaller chieftaincies along the Nile, such as the *Jaaliyyin* in Shendi, Nubians in Dongola, and in the course of 16th century the *Shaigiyyah* around Kurti, resisted the Funj, and the latter gradually carved away its territories.[22]

Similarly, Darfur had experienced attempts at centralized administration by the 13th century. From the 17th century, the Keira dynasty of the Fur clan had claimed Arab ancestry and become prominent force for Islamicization of the region.[23] During the golden age of the sultanate in the latter 18th century, the centuries old caravan trade route, *Darb al-arba'in* (forty days' road), was revived. It linked the Fur territories with the Ottoman Empire and generated prosperity, while the strength of the Keira dynasty allowed it to annex the neighboring Kordofan. However by the 19th century the dynasty was in decline, which allowed Muhammad Ali's Ottoman forces to invade Kordofan in 1821 and conquer Darfur in 1874.[24] In the 1880s, the Keira dynasty re-emerged in Darfur, but it was deposed permanently in 1916 by the Anglo-Egyptian conquerors.

The conquests of the sultanates in the abovementioned northern areas of contemporary Sudan buttressed the social organization centered on the adherence to Arab culture and Islam as identity pillars of the conqueror and those deemed superior. Thus, Arabism was increasingly identified with social superiority and Islamicization, providing a further pretext for the conquest of perceivably "inferior" societies. As a result, "Arabization produced hybrid communities that identified more with the Arab culture and social structures and relegated their African/indigenous identities to a secondary tier".[25] Claims to Arab origins, despite the genetically mixed ancestry, meant one being a socially prominent descendent of Prophet Muhammad, which in turn emphasized the role of religion.[26] Thus, Islamicization accompanied Arabization, and linked Islamicized, but less Arabized, populations loosely to the Arabized stock.

Sudan also became an area of competing Islamic missionary activity. This divided northern Sudan into zones of influence between a number of distinct Sufi[27] orders, giving rise to a particular type of sectarian social stratification.[28] Originating during the Funj dynasty, Sufi leaders exploited differences between each other to establish their own followings and extend their influence. This converted Sufism into a mass movement under the patronage of distinct headmen, and created "A new transethnic and transterritorial identity . . . that countered the geographically and ethnically based kinship systems that guided the rules and norms of economic and political exchanges".[29] The strategies of conquest and peaceful propagation can be considered to have promoted a degree of perceived cultural similarity in these northern areas, as opposed to regions where the influence of Arab culture and Islam was minimal.

Gradually, in the sultanates and chieftaincies of northern Sudan, as elsewhere in the Sahelian belt,[30] claims to Arab identity linked to Islam became inextricably associated with societal power. As a result, "Arab" and Muslim identity became increasingly inseparable manifestation of identity among the central Nile riverine groups, linking the fabrication of genealogic Arab origins and adherence to Islam with political and economic power.[31] This led to a highly hierarchical and exclusionary form of social organization, arguably based on the "social race",[32] which defines peoples adhering to Arabic culture, language, and Islam superior to non-Arabized and/or non-Islamicized groups. It has made exclusion in terms of access to power in the society "almost a racial issue" for those deemed as non-Arabs.[33] The processes of Arabization and Islamicization continue to be of relevance in today's northern Sudan, as the most powerful sections of the governing elite have used them deliberately as part of their coercive nation-building project.[34] This became a significant factor in the insurgency formation in southern Sudan, because sectors of the southern elites who felt excluded from political presentation and power challenged the state elite's perception of Sudan as a nation of Arab-Muslims.

Indeed, given that many peoples in the contemporary Sudanese peripheries do not consider themselves as Arab, they often find politically induced efforts of Arabization offensive.[35] Historically, local elites in the peripheries who perceive themselves as culturally different have reinforced and utilized opposition to foreign influences of Arabization and Islamicization to mobilize resistance. This has often been left out of the analyses of causes of insurgencies in Sudan, although it has been crucial in leading to the Arabized Muslim elite controlled state's marginalization of culturally resistant populations in the context of contemporary Sudanese polity.

B. Approximate Extent of Arabic Culture in Sudan

Source: *The Author*

70

Finally, Arab identity has strong appeal due to its association with social prominence and political and economic power. It is therefore not uncommon that many from the margins of the "Arab" and Islamic influence in Sudan have praised and adopted these cultural features. However, such accommodation applies only partially to the peripheries of northern Sudan and is particularly scarce in southern Sudan where most people reject "Arab" and Islamic influences partly due to the historic resistance to Arabization and Islamicization.

Southern Fringes of Arabic and Islamic Cultural Influence

In Sudan, the southward expansion Arabization and Islamicization reached roughly the 10th parallel.[36] For instance, over the centuries Arabic-speaking cattle-keeping peoples gradually spread to the area, and during the Funj dynasty, Arabized and Islamicized mixed Arab-Nubian peoples from northern Sudan, mainly *Juhayna* and *Jaaliyyin* of which many were traders, extended Arab culture and Islam to today's Kordofan. However, peoples of such frontier areas often preserved an array of traits of preceding cultures. This is because in many such areas Arab culture and Islam were considered inferior to the local cultures, and were resisted by powerful sections of the local societies. According to Woodward, "the areas later known as southern Sudan proved geographically inhospitable and populated by resistant communities".[37] Only some northern sections of this area came in contact with Islam in the 19th century, and there was interest in seeing the local populations as cultureless and "pagan" so that they could be legitimately subjected to slavery.[38] For instance, in approximately 1750-1850, the area currently known as South Kordofan in the southern margins of contemporary "northern" Sudan was one of the main origins of slaves.[39] According to Spaulding, the slave-raiding " . . . generated in South Kordofan a permanent state of institutionalized insecurity that distinguished all southern regions from other provinces . . . ",[40] since their connection with the north-central Sudan was through resource extraction concentrating on slaves, cattle, ivory, and other trading articles.[41] Such persisting state of variable insecurity and violence since the 19th century shaped traditional social organization and traditions of the affected societies.

Further south of Kordofan lies the area that during the later Anglo-Egyptian colonial period became known as "southern" Sudan. In this ethnically highly heterogeneous territory the Nilotic Dinka, Nuer, Shilluk, and the Sudanic Azande, grew dominant after the great migratory currents that took place in Central Africa in the course of earlier centuries. Beswick has shown that their northernmost populations had been only marginally influenced by

Islamicization and Arabization, and that resistance to these cultural influences was championed through claims of own cultural superiority.[42] For the most part, the main Nilotic groups had entered today's southern Sudan by the 10th century, except the Azande, who are estimated to have arrived in the area as late as the 18th century.[43] The Azande, prevalent in the west of the southernmost Equatoria region in southern Sudan, created a loose confederation of smaller populations based on homesteads and adaptable agriculture. This provided the basis for tax collection and legal structures to support administrative cohesiveness, cooperation in warfare, and the Azande warrior culture,[44] while using " . . . slavery and slave-like institutions to incorporate local populations".[45]

On the other hand, the Nilotic Dinka, Shilluk, and Nuer peoples generally settled in more northern areas, from today's Bahr al-Ghazal to the White Nile. Therefore they maintained contacts with the neighboring Funj and Keira sultanates to the north, and the Abyssinian kingdom to the east. In general, the Nilotics have strong cultural traditions and social institutions that enable them to absorb individuals of other populations through naturalization. Generally, they account for a patrilineal system, as does the Arab culture, coupled with a warrior tradition that regards military activities as prestigious.[46]

The Dinka and Nuer are predominantly pastoral peoples, and adapted to the geographical particularities of Bahr al-Ghazal. Their most important possessions are cattle that play an overwhelming part in their economic, social, and religious life.[47] While the Dinka are mostly found in the center and west of southern Sudan, the Nuer inhabit mainly lands from the contemporary eastern southern Sudan to western Ethiopia.[48] The Shilluk, living near Malakal, are traditionally more sedentary, with agriculture and fishing forming a significant part of their livelihoods. The sedentary lifestyle facilitated the construction of the hierarchically structured centralized kingdom in Fashoda, which was based on social organization consisting of royalty, nobles, commoners, and slaves. However, the kingdom gradually deteriorated with the Shilluk putting more emphasis on cattle-raising. The once powerful Shilluk kingdom was located in the vicinity of the Funj sultanate, and influenced it, before having to give way to the actors and forces from northern territories.[49]

Despite their common Nilotic origin, distinct ethnic traditions emerged among the diverse southern populations. This was due to three major migrations, overpopulation, overstocking, and external factors. Each group divided into distinct subgroups and chieftaincies, forming loose confederations of a number of smaller populations that managed to uphold common culture, language, and religion despite foreign influences and occasional feuds between the subgroups.[50] Beswick has argued that the strength of the Nilotic cultures and belief systems is manifested in their resistance to Islamicization despite its geographic proximity.[51]

It is important to consider the extent of success of this resistance as part of identity formation. It was largely the Nilotic cultural traditions and effective military power, which allowed it to become the main source of ethnicity in the area of today's southern Sudan. This is significant because it contributes to the competition between the Arabization and Islamicization influences from northern Sudan, and the Nilotic and other local cultures that can be emphasized in contrast to the influences from the north.

Over the centuries, the main groups of Nilotics became increasingly dominant in the areas south of the Funj and Keira sultanates. Equatoria marked the southern limit of their influence, with the numerous Bari living around Gondokoro-Rejaf-Juba area and the Azande extending into today's DRC and the CAR. However, local communities remained largely divided along ethnic and clan affiliations, which external actors from the north exploited to expand their influence and gain a foothold in southern Sudan.[52]

Historically, a number of these local societies interacted with those in Kordofan, Darfur, and southwest Ethiopia. For instance, the Shilluk influence on the Funj sultanate was of such magnitude that it has affected the scholarly debate concerning the mystical origins of the Funj. Hasan asserts that what seems most likely is that many of the Funj were a mix of Arab, Nilotic, and local ancestry, with cultural and linguistic affinities with the Shilluk.[53] Although the Shilluk often raided the Funj communities, they also collaborated when faced with a common enemy such as powerful Dinka societies which sought to expand to the region surrounding White Nile.[54]

The historical inter-ethnic and sectional group relations provide evidence of cooperation and accommodation between distinct groups in southern Sudan. This tended to happen in the face of common threats, but the groups seeking cooperation to combat a common enemy also shifted alliances which in turn opened space for external forces to take hold in the region.

The Region in International Slave Economy

The role of regional and international context is important in the origin of the type of state marginalization that emerged in Sudan. Founded on the processes that led to the institutionalization and consolidation of the marginalizing socioeconomic organization, partly emanating from conquest and slavery, the marginalization became cemented and politicized in the logic and structures of the Sudanese polity. Slavery and its enduring memory were particularly important in the type of marginalization experienced in southern Sudan and linked to the incomplete annexation to the Sudanese polity. Therefore, the legacy of slavery was relevant to the later emergence of armed opposition in the region.

Slave Economy Prior to the 19th Century

Agriculture and commerce were the principal economic activities in the territories that came to constitute contemporary Sudan and still occupy an important role in its economy today. This is because apart from the sedentary agriculturalists of the Nile valley, the remaining nomadic and semi-nomadic population generally depended on trade, hunting, gathering, and selling natural products to traders and caravan-owners.[55] Long distance trade to Egypt was conducted through three principal trade routes. Caravans, which reached up to 5,000 travelers, transported slaves, ivory feathers, gold, vegetables, and minerals for textiles, metals, hardware, beads, semi-precious materials, and firearms, as they made their way to Asyut in Egypt.[56]

In the 16th and 17th centuries the local kingdoms exercised administered trade monopolized around the ruler. During this time slaves became a thriving export article.[57] *Darb al-arba'in* was among the main caravan routes connecting southern Sahelian Africa to North Africa, and the southern frontier of Arabized territory of what is contemporary Sudan to Egypt through Darfur. Most caravans were destined to Ottoman Egypt. For instance, the Funj sultanate exported gold and slaves captured from its southern peripheries, along with other articles, and the Keira sultanate exported slaves together with other products.[58]

Economic activity in the southern frontiers of the two sultanates was marked by the raiding of slaves, and the extraction of other commodities. Slave trade gradually depleted populations from the Nuba Mountains to the Ethiopian borderlands,[59] which required a southward expansion of raiding by the 19th century. This led to new areas to be subjected to extraction. The raids had a devastating effect on some of the local communities in which the prolonged sentiment of animosity became an important element of resistance.

Indeed, economic extraction in southern Sudan was often not conducted in equal terms. Rather, much like the Europeans in the Americas, the northern Sudanese merchants bribed locals by introducing locally unknown items (such as mirrors) in exchange for slaves and other articles. The relationship was largely limited to commercial exchanges with the foreign merchants primarily interested in the local resources. It did not promote general cultural understanding and accommodation in either side partly due to the exclusive and socially hierarchic categorical perceptions of the "other".

Slavery had existed in Sudan long before the arrival of Islam. The frontier of "Arab" slave extraction shifted southwards throughout the centuries when first the Nubians raided central Sudan, then the Funj sultanate in central Sudan enslaved Nilotic peoples around Gezira, and finally certain Arabized riverine groups and the Baggara engaged in slave-raiding in the northern margins of the territories of contemporary southern Sudan.[60] Baggara groups played an important role in organizing the trade which connected southern margins of today's northern Sudan with Middle Eastern economy.[61] In this context Islam brought with it another social context in which slavery was institutionalized, and which subjected all non-Muslim peoples potentially to slavery.[62] This was a crucial factor in consolidating a social hierarchy in which group-based marginalization formed an inextricable part.

Commercial networks extended between what was to become contemporary southern Sudan and the areas north of it. For instance the Shilluk established trade ties with the Funj through the Nuba Mountains, while sectors of some Dinka groups supplied slaves for the Funj markets.[63] In the course of the 18th century, commercial contacts between Keira sultanate and the communities southwards appear to have also grown in importance. At the time, some Arabized semi-nomadic groups and Nilotic herders had settled in southern Kordofan and Darfur. However, in part due to the ecological conditions, but also because of Nilotic cultural influences, the groups originating in the north substituted camel herding for cattle breeding and became mixed Arabized peoples known as the Baggara, "the cow herders". The near proximity between Baggara and Dinka facilitated exchange and coexistence, but also caused periodic competition for grazing areas which led to occasional hostility.[64] Over time, reparatory conflict resolution mechanisms emerged in response to the periodic feuds similarly to other parts of Sudan where occasional inter-group conflicts had occurred for centuries. By the 19th century, the Nilotic expansion menaced Arabized fringe territories, particularly around the southern frontier of the declining Funj sultanate. It was largely Nilotic influence that minimized the impact of Islam and Arabization south of the 10th parallel until the 19th century.[65]

Effect of the 19th Century Slave Economy

During the 19th century the Turco-Egyptian conquest brought centralized administration to the territory that covered most of contemporary northern Sudan.[66] This brought distinct groups under common rule, which stimulated trade and facilitated construction of enhanced communications infrastructure. These developments, including port of Sawakin and railroad connecting Wadi Halfa with Lower Egypt, encouraged increasing commercial ac-

75

tivity along the Nile.[67] By mid-19th century a waterway through the Nile to areas lying in the south was discovered. This opened the southern frontier for exploration and commerce, and enabled an increasing movement of merchandise, ideas, and cultural influences.

Moreover, reinvigorated traditional trade routes served as commercial networks connecting the southern borderlands with regional and international markets. According to Alier, " . . . military and commercial networks were expanded throughout the South by both Northern Sudanese and Turco-Egyptian officials, sometimes working in competition, but often working in conjunction with each other".[68] Particularly in Western Bahr al-Ghazal and Darfur, old slave caravan routes re-flourished momentarily, while the areas they penetrated were virtually controlled by slave lords as private entrepreneurs acting outside the government control.[69] This situation continued despite the administration's efforts to suppress slave trade in the 1870s.[70]

Progressively, during more than a decade in 1825-38, a government monopoly that dictated the exportation of a wide array of commodities to Egypt was put in place. It extended to products such as indigo, gum arabic, ivory, and feathers, and coincided with the increasing trade in slaves, cattle, and hides.[71] Although this regulated exports to Egypt, internal trade flourished, contributing to the growth of Khartoum as a commercial center by 1860 with over 30,000 inhabitants.[72] This led to economic opportunities in the central areas of the polity, of which people of periphery territories were largely deprived.

When the Egyptian government monopoly was loosened in 1838-41 under pressure from the European powers with interest in the region, local traders found increasingly ways to collaborate with the administration. Some gradually established themselves as the powerful merchant class, the *jallaba*.[73] The *jallaba* were a mix of largely north-central Nile riverine peoples who abandoned agriculture in an attempt to escape heavy taxation, and made their way increasingly to the southern frontier to engage in trade. Rumors of southern riches stimulated such migration since slaves and ivory were viewed as highly profitable trade articles.[74] Meanwhile, the perpetuation of slave trade maintained racial subjugation of southern peoples.[75] However, the loosening of the government monopoly resulted also in an influx of European traders who brought commercial enterprises with them and assumed a paramount role in local and import-export trade, while European administrators, consuls, and adventurers also arrived.[76] The increasing number of foreigners engaging in violent extractive commercial activities had far-reaching effects on attitudes of those southern communities they interacted with, reinforcing the construction of historical narratives of slavery and violence.

After the end of the government monopoly, commercial slave and ivory raiding parties took over from state-organized violent extraction. Despite the 1854 ban on selling slaves to Egypt, pushed through by the abolitionist movement in Europe, and counter raids by local groups on Arabized frontier communities, the trade continued to flourish and slaves were exported to the Arabian Peninsula where demand remained.[77] Referring to the southern frontier, Gray asserts that

> It was the decision and actions of European traders which inaugurated and intensified conflict, and although the search for ivory continued to be the dominant purpose of their activity, it became ever more closely bound to the extension of violence and the capture of slaves.[78]

European merchants remained prominent in trade in Sudan until the 1870s when the Egyptian regime sought to minimize external influence in the territory. The subsequent departure of most European traders allowed the *jallaba* to expand their control of commercial space.

Slave Economy and Consolidation of Stratified Social Hierarchy

During the 19th century captives from the southern frontier became one of the most important trade articles in Sudan. As with Arabized and Islamicized areas of northern Sudan, and other areas of the Ottoman Empire, slave owning became a privilege of the affluent. But in the 19th century there was an increase in Egyptian, Libyan, and Arabian demand for slaves. The consequent expansion of slave trade caused the number of slaves to rise dramatically also in the central and northern Sudan to satisfy the demand for manual labor.[79] This fed the established view of social hierarchy, and points to the self-perception of superiority by prominent sectors of the society, which permitted further institutionalization of the stratified social order dominated by Arab culture and Islam.

In what constitutes contemporary northern Sudan, slaves tended to remain in the hands of the north-central riverine groups. These included above all *Jaaliyyin* and *Danaqla* who constituted the majority of the *jallaba* merchants in the slave extracting areas. Warburg asserts that, "The ownership of land and slaves was a precondition for prospering in nineteenth century Sudan and the emerging middle class, consisting mainly of riverain tribes, achieved this by collaborating with the Turkish ruling élite".[80] Both access to land and slaves provided economic advantage for the riverine groups, which as a result became increasingly prominent.[81] Thus, hierarchical social structure was increasingly consolidated as part of prevailing attitudes in northern Sudan, while the centralized Arab-Muslim dominated polity, established following the 19th century Ottoman conquest, cemented this view as part of political organization. In this view, southern frontier was constructed as a subordinate territory and subjected to violent extraction for resources.

As a result, slavery became one of the principal factors in the origins of marginalization of southern peoples and their territories in contemporary Sudan. The word *abeed* (slave) came to describe black southerners generally in northern Sudan,[82] which demonstrates the importance of the perceived social hierarchy. Although it was to an extent rooted in socioeconomic perceptions in some pre-existing Arabized societies, the rampant slave economy contributed considerably to the widespread extension and consolidation of the perceived social hierarchy. The powerful sectors of the Arabized elites in the north-central Nile valley area, promoting their perception of the society, buttressed the view, and linked it to the safeguarding of their own socioeconomic and sociopolitical prominence.

In addition, external actors and forces contributed to the prevailing social hierarchy and marginalization. The Ottoman rulers' official endorsement of slave trade in Sudan due to the high demand in the neighboring territories, along with the European view that assumed the racial superiority over local peoples, complemented the local perceptions. This was integral in justifying racial and cultural distinctions used to define social status according to the general attitudes of the Arabized elites and their constituencies. Such perception became dominant in the northern parts and institutionalized the societal role of the southerner, hindering his social mobility and personal development within the Arabized-Muslim dominated social organization. Thus, both internal and external actors and forces contributed to the linking of social hierarchy with the highly exclusive political and economic power within the centralized polity in Sudan.

Finally, in northern parts of contemporary Sudan the legacy of slavery has served to justify the continuity of Arab-Muslim dominated social hierarchy. This has continued to portray marginalization of southern Sudan and its inhabitants as "natural". From the opposing perspective, the memory of 19th century slave-raiding has served sections of contemporary elites in southern territories to justify political mobilization against what is portrayed as northern riverine "Arab" domination and oppression. This, in turn, has contributed to the polarization of identities and facilitated the construction of narratives of "Arabs" versus "Africans" that consolidated further in the violent context of war.

The Turco-Egyptian Period

In the course of the 19th century the area covering most of contemporary Sudan fell under Ottoman rule. After its conquest by Muhammad Ali, the Ottoman Viceroy of Egypt, northern Sudan became as one centrally administered political entity, the *Turkiyyah*.[83] The discussion below highlights continuities from colonial to post-colonial period, emphasizing the institutionalization of marginalization, and the formation of political identities in response to the *Turkiyyah*.

External Conquest

In the beginning of the 19th century Egypt formed part of the Ottoman Empire. It was governed through an oligarchy of Turkish speaking governors, Mamluks, who drew from a class of slaves that had previously fought for the Ottomans. When the failed Napoleonic invasion left Egypt under British and Ottoman domination, a struggle to control it ensued. By May 1805, Muhammad Ali, an Albanian mercenary, had ascended, and was subsequently appointed as the Viceroy of the Ottoman Sultan and the Governor of Egypt.[84] Ali consolidated his rule by massacring many of his leading Mamluk opponents in Cairo in 1811, while those escaping took refuge in Dongola beyond Egypt's border in the south.[85]

In 1820, Ali's troops invaded territories south of Egypt in what was essentially a private venture by the autonomous viceroy of the Ottoman Sultan. As a result, in the course of the 19th century, most of today's northern Sudan[86] was annexed to Egypt and came to be known as the *Turkiyyah*.[87] The areas south of it remained as a frontier land for extraction of commodities where regime authority was largely absent, except in the fortified and heavily manned military-trading posts called the *zeriba*.[88] After the discovery of a navigation route through the Nile marshes during 1839-41 by Salim Qapudan, a Turkish frigate captain ordered by Ali to search for the sources of the White Nile, increasing contacts with the local groups south of the 10th parallel took place. This discovery of a waterway through the vast marshes of the *Sudd* (barrier or obstacle in Arabic) that extend hundreds of kilometers[89] gradually opened up the southern areas to northern influences by permitting the entering of government forces and private northern traders in the area. The new waterway provided a communication link between northern and southern areas beyond the White Nile, penetrating the natural boundary that had formed a geographical barrier for centuries.[90]

Muhammad Ali's expansionism, which resulted in the annexation of lands south of Egypt to his dominion, was largely motivated by economic and military considerations. However, after the rebellion that ended Egyptian domination of Sudan, coinciding with the 1884-5 Berlin Conference for partition of Africa, the European powers became particularly interested in Sudan. Viewed as "unoccupied" territory, geopolitical interests drove them to compete for the control of the sources of the Nile.[91] Great Britain emerged as the dominant European power in the region, warding off both French and Belgian threats. Britain's geopolitical aspirations in Sudan had mostly to do with controlling the Nile River, and ensuring the integrity of Egypt (including the Suez Canal) where the British maintained a strong presence.

Incorporation and Establishment of Centralized Administration

Ali's conquest forged together the territory of contemporary northern Sudan by centralizing power to colonial administration. Laying emphasis on commercial exploitation, the new rulers sought to extract local resources systematically. New commercial and criminal codes were implemented, which promoted stability and generated an attractive trading environment. Trade flourished, particularly after the abolition of government monopoly over commerce, allowing European and North American merchants, companies, missionaries, residents, and administrative officials to exploit the newly discovered opportunities.[92]

The *Turkiyyah* was administered by seizing power from the pre-existing and subjected sultanates and kingdoms through conquest and concentrating it in a central government. In order to do this, a geographically and economically central capital was needed. Consequently, Ali made the town of Khartoum the capital in 1833, which in continuation developed rapidly and became a prominent urban center.[93] Because of vast geographical extensions of Sudan, the governing system relied heavily on local actors for administration. Rather than collaborating in more equal terms with the "tribal"[94] shaykhs or the heads of established Sufi orders, seen as potentially threatening to the regime due to their local influence, the new rulers allied themselves with one of the northern riverine groups, the *Shaigiyyah*,[95] to impose a hierarchical top-down system of power. This system of centralized administration was not only used by the *Turkiyyah*, but it laid the foundation for governance during the later Mahdist and Anglo-Egyptian Condominium periods.[96]

In addition, the new conquerors brought cultural influences which were politicized with an aim to transform the local social order to consolidate the new administration. An orthodox religious doctrine was imposed together with exclusive economic and social development in favor of the collaborating groups in central territories of the colony.[97] These policies resulted in privileged treatment of selected central riverine groups, whose cultural affinity and willingness to cooperate also permitted the new rulers to train collaborators. This advanced cohesion further, although mainly with the population at the center of the polity. The periphery populations in particular tended to maintain an uneasy, and at times conflictive, relationship with the state, largely due to its tax regime and policies. Since many periphery groups received little recompense for their material contributions and sacrifices, and had little contact with the administration, their relationship with the state and incorporation into the centralized polity remained incomplete.

The new rulers recognized the need to collaborate with the prominent local actors, but also to maintain them weak enough to minimize challenges to their dominion. According to the model applied in Egypt, Ali and his successors encouraged a system in which religious institutions influenced by the regime played a significant role. The imposition of orthodox Sunni Islam as the official religion was used to exert control over traditionally powerful holy families and Sufi orders, and consolidate centralized power.[98] Accordingly, the authorities brought Islamic scholars, *ulama*,[99] educated in al-Azhar, to organize the employment of young local recruits in government offices and the official *sharia* (Islamic law) courts, while establishing a mosque-building program along with construction of religious schools and courts.[100] These efforts were undertaken to encourage the new administrative order, and they demonstrate the extent of Ali's attempt to control the newly acquired territories.

Hence, in the process of centralization, the power of communal leaders became increasingly emphasized at the local level. Local elites had for long used tribal logic to organize communities and monopolize trade and resources around the rulers and/or Sufi headmen. The Ottoman administration took advantage of this by prioritizing the traditional tribal formations under communal leaders as a form of local administration within the centralized system of governance.[101] This was in part because of Ottoman Egypt's lack of manpower and resources to exert direct control over the vast territorial extensions of the newly conquered lands.

As a result, administrative divisions according to tribal allegiances emerged. In this system the collective challenges to the centralized authority in the core areas were minimized by favoring central riverine communities over more remote populations. In particular, this excluded non-collaborative leaders and subjected resisting non-Arabized and non-Muslim groups in Kordofan and southern frontier to slave-raiding.[102] For instance, O'Brien has pointed out that

Shayks took on the added role of representative of an outside power – the central government authority in the 'tribe'. Their tribal authority and power therefore gained a limited degree of freedom from the consent of the governed. In other words, the structure and the nature of the groupings (tribes) were modified, distorted and transformed. Instead of an 'original' flexible organization of a core group that represented a 'power centre' to which followers were attracted, there started to emerge more stable power centres to which attachment became involuntary.[103]

These power centers, formed around Arabized Muslim elites, organized along religious and tribal lines. In this system, ethnic identity of Arabized Muslim "tribes" was portrayed as primordial, unchanging, and inherently incompatible with non-Arabized and non-Muslim "other" considered as having lower status.[104] Such an exclusive form of group definition, compatible with the prevailing social hierarchy, extended to the northern *Turkiyyah* as means of consolidating the local elites' political and economic position. These dynamics buttressed the idea of superiority particularly among sections of the north-central groups collaborating with the regime in the newly founded political order. Social and political prominence was contrasted against "the other", the most extreme manifestation of which were the black, non-Arabized, and non-Muslim peoples in the south who were subjected to slavery. This logic driving the social concentration of economic and political power later developed into portraying "the north" as a common Arabic and Islamic region, as opposed to "the south".

During the *Turkiyyah*, sectors of local subjects despised the official doctrine of religious orthodoxy. This is largely because it undermined local, more familiar, Sufi practices that had characterized the central Sudanese society during the Funj sultanate,[105] and weakened the position of traditional Sufi leaders. Consequently the *ulama*, the guardians of religious orthodoxy, encountered resistance and failed to gain similar popularity enjoyed by the Sufi *tariqa* and the holy men in the rural areas of northern *Turkiyyah*.[106] Still, the imposition of orthodox Islam was successful in consolidating the centralized administration over the traditional religious elite in north-central core areas, although opposition remained which in the 1880s facilitated the rapid spread of Mahdism in the midst of popular discontent.[107]

The regime chose to collaborate with the *Khatmiyyah* religious order based near Kassala. This was due to *Khatmiyyah* promoting Islam doctrinally compatible with government aspirations, and allowed extending the regime control towards Abyssinia. Having arrived to the area only recently before the *Turkiyyah*, and with lesser capacity to organize resistance than some of the more established orders, the *Khatmiyyah* leadership decided to benefit from collaborating with the administration. This converted it into the most prominent and politically influential religious group during the period. Although *Khatmiyyah*'s own religious centers were not tolerated, it enjoyed periodic privileges, such as subsidies and tax exemptions, which increased its economic prominence.[108] Many of the *Khatmiyyah* supporters were *Shaigiyyah*, who collaborated with the administration, resulting in social convergence of state and religion.[109] Moreover, this convergence enforced the logic of "tribalism", politicizing ethnic and religious affiliation, which was deliberately used to consolidate the regime by creating divisions and competition among religious and ethnic elites.

The collaboration of the abovementioned groups with the colonial masters generated resentment among other sections of the society. The administration's favoritism of sections of the *Khatmiyyah* and *Shaigiyyah* caused competition between dominant Sufi orders.[110] It excluded prominent sectors of another influential central riverine group, the *Jaaliyyin*. Some responses to the regime also culminated in violent tax revolts, such as the 1822-3 *Jaaliyyin* and the 1870s Darfur uprisings,[111] which were organized by local elites in a number of recently conquered territories against the imposition of a heavy tax regime.

Incorporation of Southern Frontier to *Turkiyyah*

Forces linking southern Sudan to the regional and the international in the 19th century were largely geopolitical, economic, and cultural. During the Turco-Egyptian period, the penetration and the subsequent exploitation of the territories in the southern margins of the *Turkiyyah* was mostly economically motivated. The exploration of the interior was propelled by depletion of slaves and ivory, amongst other commodities, in the more easily accessed areas of southern Darfur, southern Kordofan, and the Blue Nile. After opening up of the southern frontier in Bahr al-Ghazal, the Upper Nile and Equatoria, the extraction of local commodities increased due to local, regional, and international demand in the north-central *Turkiyyah*, Egypt, Libya, the Ottoman and Arabian markets, and Europe.

During this time, contacts with peoples beyond the White Nile grew significantly. The official slave raids soon gave way to equally violent private commercial ventures and increasingly permanent outposts. This was in part due to Ali's abandoning of the state monopoly, and the idea of creating a slave army because of diminishing supply of blacks and their considered lack of resistance to stress and disease, along with their local opposition and tendency to stage uprisings.[112] However, local resistance also hindered *Turkiyyah*'s expansion.[113] As long as the most powerful southern societies were able to uphold their traditional political structures and manpower to withstand northern encroachment, they appear to have retained the ability to repel the attempts of external domination.

By the 1850s, the presence of external actors in parts of the southern frontier became increasingly permanent because the administration established fortified trading posts up the Nile. According to Gray, "The Arab servants [of the Europeans] settled, obtained wives and slaves from the neighbouring tribes, and established themselves as a ruling caste . . . ".[114] As Ibrahim contends, ". . . their frequent resort to violence and reported contemptuous attitude towards the African population succeeded, with other important actors, in nurturing the distrust and fear that today dominates relations between the northern Sudan and those so-called marginalized regions, the South in particular".[115] Thus these Arab merchants, called *jallaba*, tended to extend their view of the Arab-Muslim dominated social hierarchy in the southern frontier through their attitude and behavior.

Interactions which formed the social relations between the *jallaba* and the local populations became potentially highly conflictive. The growing presence and violent entrepreneurship of many *jallaba* in the southern frontier made them the living representation of foreign oppression in the eyes of many Nilotics. Ibrahim argues that

> The *jallaba* played an important role, and perhaps pioneering too, in extending the frontiers of Arabic and Islam in the south, Darfur and the Nuba mountains. But their frequent resort to violence and reported contemptuous attitude towards the African population succeeded, with other important actors, in nurturing the distrust and fear that today dominates relations between the northern Sudan and those so-called marginalized regions, the South in particular.[116]

The narrative of violence, slavery, and oppression maintained through oral histories remained in the collective memory of the local communities, and became a story often referred to by prominent southerners.[117]

The *jallaba* benefited economically from the new political order, which further boosted their social status, converting them a privileged class in the southern frontier. For instance, the *jallaba* often served as middlemen between the administration and the population, providing currency for taxpayers to meet contributions to be paid in cash. At times, they joined military raids in the frontier lands and purchased captives from soldiers who were paid in slaves partly due to the lack of liquid currency, enabling the *jallaba* to influence the prices of slaves.[118] This tied many *jallaba* increasingly to the slave trade because the administration accepted slaves as a form of tax payment.[119] Thus, their increasingly prominent societal role laid a foundation for their political importance in Sudanese politics after decolonization.

Some *jallaba* were also militarily powerful. For instance, famous slave lord Rahman Mansour al-Zubair commanded a private army and became strong enough to control territory and fend off the state's incursions in the southern borderlands. As a result, the most powerful *jallaba* operated largely beyond the state's reach,[120] with their private forces made of slave soldiers, army renegades, and other *jallaba*, some of who had joined after escaping taxation in the central riverine Sudan. By the 1860s *jallaba* settler communities evolved increasingly around the state's *zeriba* (fortified military-trading posts) that had been used to facilitate the expansion of administration and commercial exploitation southwards along the Nile River. With state control of territory, rudimentary administration with limited influence was put in place. This resulted in the state's imposition on some local communities in southern Sudan, often resulting in devastation due to violence and slave-raiding, while a number of local communities fought against the violent foreign intrusion.[121] The impact of this order of limited state authority and violence was that local resistance was extensive. In fact, the southern frontier remained largely ungoverned by the weak administration, and the state constituted only one actor that faced powerful local groups and private entrepreneurs.

The inability of the outposts to impose government authority in the southern territories played a role in the *jallaba* domination of commercial interests in these areas. According to Gray, this was because European entrepreneurs "Confronted with reality[,] saw that private individuals, without an imperial intervention, had no hope of establishing a legitimate commerce in Equatoria".[122] Consequently, the European commercial interests faded due to the lack of state protection, and the private ventures of many less-affected *jallaba* able to ensure the security of their economic activities flourished.

The local Nilotic populations played an important role in the wider political situation in areas of the southern frontier. Some sections participated in slave trade, but others organized counter-expeditions to recover captives and commodities, which often created fear among the targeted Arabized frontier communities.[123] However, as the social order in a number of southern communities became increasingly disrupted in the latter 19th century due to the persisting violence, the counter raids gradually weakened and fighting between Nilotic groups intensified. This owed in part to external manipulation to divide local alliances,[124] which the Ottoman colonial state and private actors used to gain influence in the southern frontier. Conversely, while the southern resistance was localized, and involved mostly different subgroups lacking broader political alliances, some leaders, such as Subek-lo-Logunu,

Zemio, Bafuka, and Hamas Musa, who recognized that external actors made powerful allies, used alliances and strategies of extraversion to their advantage against local rivals.[125]

The inter-group violence in the southern frontier was characterized essentially by a three-way struggle. It unfolded mainly between the *Turkiyyah* soldier-administrators attempting to assert their authority, powerful slave lords often beyond official control, and the local groups.[126] By the turn of the 1880s, violence and destruction had become a prevalent feature of interaction between the different actors in the southern frontier. As Gray points out,

> The zeriba district had the 'aspect of a country destroyed by fire'; granaries were empty and harvests ruined; 'thousands and thousands' of natives' had fled for refuge to the Azande of the inaccessible swamps of the Dinka; many of the armed slave troops had scattered through the country establishing themselves as petty tyrants or . . . had fallen in the hands of the Arab frontier tribes . . . thus formidably increasing the strength of these virtually independent tribes; and, apart from this destruction and upheaval, about four thousand [northern] Arabs . . . hoped to continue their [commercial] activities as before.[127]

Here Gray refers to Arabized groups near the southern frontier and other northerners as "Arabs", which has historically resonated in southern Sudan where "Arab" does not necessarily refer to Arabs *per se* but has been often used to describe the mistrusted "other" from the north. This use of the "Arab" was further institutionalized in the political rhetoric during the long insurgencies, and has since been adopted in the media in the context of describing the war in Sudan.

Finally, during the *Turkiyyah*, the administration's attempt to expand its control to the southern frontier largely failed. Its inability to subdue resistance by local groups and impose government authority over non-state actors, such as slave lords and merchants, demonstrates that the centralized administration was never extended effectively to the southern areas and that the attempted external domination became manifested in prolonged violence and disorder. This contributed to a legacy of resistance, mistrust, and the fear of imposition of "Arab" domination by the centralized administration from the north.

The Demise of the *Turkiyyah*

The determinants for the decline and the eventual collapse of the *Turkiyyah* include an array of international and regional factors, and internal governance aspects. Suppression of slavery, economic stagnation, high taxation, official religious doctrine, and the so-called "civilizing" or "modernization" mission[128] were among these determinants. In addition, the eroding legitimacy of the administration in the eyes of the subjects in the northern rural areas due to corruption, and the "divide and rule" strategy which dispersed social elements and favored principally the *Khatmiyyah* leadership and sections of the *Shaigiyyah*, contributed to grievances leading to rebellion and collapse of the Ottoman rule.[129]

First, the local populations were subjected to state taxation during *Turkiyyah*. It was conducted either by employing the irregular soldiers (*bashi bozuq*), freed from taxation, who often used force, or the religious (principally *Khatmiyyah*) and communal leaders who were willing to collaborate with the regime in exchange for tax exemption. On lands under irrigation, taxes were collected on a fixed rate based on the number of water wheels, *saqiyyah*, which favored labor-intensive agricultural production. In other cultivated areas land tax was imposed based on the size of land rather than the level of production. This encouraged the use of slaves and migrant workers. When faced with the state's tax regime, a number of people, such as many of those who became *jallaba*, left their land, leaving other villagers to pay for their collective share of taxes which compounded the economic hardship of their home communities.[130] A practically insurmountable burden was added in 1877 when taxes were increased to fill the severely stretched coffers of the Egyptian Ottoman government due to a prolonged war against Abyssinia.[131] The heavy tax regime generated discontent and uprisings against the administration.

Second, by the end of the 1860s Ottoman Egypt had entered into financial difficulties. At this time, Ottoman Sultan faced increasing British pressure to push Khedive Ismail to suppress the slave trade in the *Turkiyyah*. The British, as major creditors, persuaded him to recognize Ismail's territorial acquisitions since 1866, and to grant him and his successors the dominion over the ports of Sawakin and Massawa on the east coast of *Turkiyyah*, but they also pushed for the end of slavery in Egypt and slave trade in the Red Sea by forcing the appointment of British officers as *Turkiyyah* administrators.[132] After negotiations in which Ismail attempted to seek Britain's support in the face of other European creditors, Egypt and Britain eventually signed a Convention for the Suppression of Slave Trade in 1877.[133] Yet, Ismail was forced to resign two years later before the treaty became fully effective, which resulted in the sharp decline of external funding for the *Turkiyyah* administration and left more room for slave trade and challenges against the state.[134]

There existed strong local interests in support of slavery and the slave trade in the *Turkiyyah*, which constituted part of regional and international supply-demand network. During this time, many *jallaba* grew in influence, attained education, and achieved administrative positions up to the level of provincial governors. However, they had built their livelihoods on profits from commerce, and often with an emphasis on the lucrative slave trade in which they played an important role. This contributed to the resistance against abolitionism by many of those who benefited from slave labor in northern part of the *Turkiyyah*. By the 1870s, particularly many *jallaba* who engaged in slave trade embraced anti-regime rhetoric.[135]

Third, economic factors that debilitated *Turkiyyah* were both external and internal. Externally, after the opening of the Suez Canal in 1869 Britain and France became eager to control it. Faced with increasing debt crisis and looming general bankruptcy, in 1873 Ismail was pressured to accept an Anglo-French debt commission to manage Egypt's fiscal affairs.[136] The commission interfered in Egypt's internal affairs, including the crown succession and policies in *Turkiyyah*. As a result, Ismail was persuaded to leave power to his son Tawfiq, who subsequently ruled Egypt until 1892 under British tutelage.[137] Yet, Tawfiq's appointment angered many Egyptians who deemed him a European puppet, which motivated a killing of 50 Europeans in June 1882 disturbances in Alexandria and triggered a British invasion and occupation of Egypt.[138] Consequently, by 1890 British imperial policy in the region centered on Egypt and securing its lifeline, the Nile.[139]

Finally, Khedive Ismail's "civilizing" mission to modernize Egypt was not well-received by all in the *Turkiyyah*. Largely an attempt to introduce Western inspired reforms, it aimed at creating politically centralized administration with a "European" type economy. However, there were no long term resources for this project, and effective control by the administration never reached much further than the north-central and eastern areas of the polity, which also hindered economic transformation. Elsewhere in northern and southern territories small military garrisons and fortified posts were in charge of vast territorial extensions and unable to impose sustained control. Moreover, the state's legitimacy eroded further due to a lack of supervision of the tax collectors, a number of who roamed the countryside and arbitrarily pocketed taxes, while unemployed soldiers engaged in illegal activities that spread criminality and corruption.[140] Thus, it was largely the growing local grievances and the declining state power and legitimacy which led to the emergence of violent challenge to the *Turkiyyah*.

These abovementioned factors gave impetus to Mahdism, which began as a regional movement in Kordofan. Muhammad Ahmad ibn as Sayyid Abd Allah, a holy man originating near Dongola, realized the malcontent among the illiterate population during his travels in northern areas of the *Turkiyyah*. He proclaimed himself as the expected prophet, *al-Mahdi al-Muntazar* (the awaited guide in the right path), in 1881, preaching against the Ottoman rule and advocating Islamic purity and simplicity. Muhammad Ahmad claimed to be the personification of the expected Mahdi, and called for the holy war, *jihad*, against the *Turkiyyah*, while also advocating Islamic nationalism for a pure corruption-free society. However, lacking capacity and considering Muhammad Ahmad's preaching against the regime initially harmless, the administration in Khartoum ignored the early incitation. It was not until Mahdi's growing number of followers stopped paying taxes that an order for his arrest was finally issued. Yet, Mahdi escaped capture by returning to Kordofan and continued mobilization. Abdallahi ibn Muhammad, a son of a Taaisha Baggara leader from southern Darfur, assisted him in gaining support among religious leaders.[141]

Owing largely to Abdallahi, Muhammad Ahmad attracted followers primarily among sections of the Arabized semi-nomadic Baggara,[142] but also among the *Jaaliyyin*. His followers were known as the *Ansar* and devoted to fulfilling his aim of restoring justice and righteousness in the world, preparing the second coming of the Prophet Isa, and replacing the *Turkiyyah* regime with a true Islamic community.[143] In the prevailing conditions, facilitated by the state's communications network, Mahdi used his politico-religious rhetoric to mobilize the *Ansar*, and organized an uprising that spread quickly from the Baggara inhabited areas of Kordofan to other regions, including the southern frontier, Darfur, and the east. Mahdi recruited among the growing number of disaffected highly-taxed peasants, pastoralists, and slave soldiers, and drew support from certain local groups in southern Sudan.[144] It was not only Mahdi's personal appeal that made many Baggara and *Jaaliyyin* join his cause, but many also resented the regime's favoritism of the *Khatmiyyah* and *Shaigiyyah* and hoped to establish a new political order in which they would gain a more prominent role. Eventually the Mahdist forces overwhelmed the *Turkiyyah* administration.

What arises as particularly relevant from this narrative is that the *Turkiyyah* established a centralized state in Sudan, and that its legacy lived on in the subsequent administration(s). In addition, it was during the *Turkiyyah* that the foundations for the exclusive and narrowly based state's political elite were forged. Education had been reserved mainly to the cadres of riverine regime collaborators, while Arab culture and Islam had consolidated as identifiers of the governing sociopolitical and socioeconomic actors. This way the *Turkiyyah* regime had "manipulated the minds"[145] of local peoples and built a centralized regime on the structures of pre-existing stratified and hierarchical social organization.

The Mahdist Period

Succeeding the *Turkiyyah*, the Mahdist period contributed to the emergence of "northern" Sudan. It further consolidated the political order of state marginalization of peripheries particularly in the southern frontier that was partially integrated as a territory for violent extraction of resources. The Mahdist period laid basis for prominent political actors in Sudan, and left a legacy of proneness to uprisings in northern Sudan and violent subjugation in southern Sudan, which affected the political dynamics of the succeeding Anglo-Egyptian colonial administration and beyond.

Mahdist Administration, Economy, and Legacy

The Mahdist *Ansar* confronted the *Turkiyyah*'s military by engaging its small and scattered armed forces. Suppressing the spreading revolt proved overwhelming, and the *Ansar* conquered most of the area previously controlled by the regime.

C. Outmost Limits of the Mahdiyyah

Source: *U.S Library of Congress*

90

After driving out the former masters, Mahdi sought to consolidate his rule. In the course of the rebellion the objective of the Mahdist protest movement had become to establish a militant Islamic theocratic state and revive an ideal community by transforming society through armed struggle.[146] However, in January 1885 Mahdi died of typhus and power fell to his successor, Abdallahi, one of his three Khalifas, who became the ruler and the commander of the Mahdist armies (*Amir Juyush al-Mahdiya*).[147] As a result, it became Abdallahi's task to complete Mahdi's dream for an Islamic state.[148]

Following the conquest, many of the officials who had been working for the previous regime were employed by the Mahdist state. The *Turkiyyah*'s centralized system of administration allowed the consolidation of power of the Mahdist ruling elite backed by the *Ansar*. The new regime sought to dismantle the Sufi orders, which not only posed as a powerful threat but also professed interpretations of Islam the Mahdists rejected. Particularly the former regime collaborator, the *Khatmiyyah*, was targeted, and its leadership took refuge in the British-held port of Sawakin.[149] However, the Mahdist regime was more lenient towards the *Shaigiyyah*, whose educated cadres were necessary for administering the *Mahdiyyah* due to the insufficient number of highly educated and qualified *Ansar*.

This resulted in certain continuities of state organization and governance, drawing on the earlier *Turkiyyah* experience. According to Holt,

> Faced with the prospect that the brief unity of the northern Sudanese would again dissolve, the Khalifa from the outset endeavoured to restore the administrative system. He could do this only by bringing back the men and methods of the old régime and thereby much of the corruption, dilatoriness, and oppression which the Mahdi had hoped to sweep away.[150]

Further efforts were undertaken to impose centralized rule through the imposition of laws aimed at debilitating and co-opting rural strongmen.[151] Therefore, there was a continuation of strategies of centralizing administration and co-opting potential opponents to unify the heterogeneous communities under consolidated rule. These strategies were adopted later by the Anglo-Egyptian Condominium and post-independence governments.

However, the jihadist nature of the Mahdist state meant that it was continuously at war. Armed conflicts with neighboring polities and internal dissent consumed most of the state's resources, while the warring affected the economy. Despite inheriting colonial infrastructure, the *Mahdiyyah* had little capacity to maintain it. The Mahdist state became relatively isolated from the world economy, while competing with its neighbors and imperial powers.[152] Policies such as invalidation and subsequent confusion about currency, as well as inadequate responses to a drought that plagued Sudan in the early 1880s, compounded the economic hardship as trade declined generally except in some urban centers.[153]

Two legacies of the Mahdist era are particularly relevant for later periods. Firstly, it witnessed the rise of the Mahdist *Ansar* as a new social constituency for a section of Arabized elites and the continued prominence of the riverine groups. The Mahdist order allowed rural northern and western areas dominated by the Baggara to become a new constituency for a section of the state elite, which continued to provide it a claim to political and economic power.[154] In addition, elements of riverine groups, mainly *Jaaliyyin*, *Shaigiyyah*, and *Danaqla*, continued to maintain prominent positions as administrators and merchants, a status further heightened by collaboration with the regime during the following Anglo-Egyptian period.

Secondly, the *Mahdiyyah* significantly influenced the construction of regional identity of "northern" Sudan. The Mahdist conquest was glorified among a number of tribal and religious elites in the northern Arabized Muslim territories (particularly among the *Ansar*). Lesch points out that "Thus, the Mahdiyya was reconstructed in the national imagination of the north as a period of liberation and assertion of cultural values . . . [, and it] . . . invigorated their [the Arabized Muslim elite's] national image and held positive symbolic significance as a golden age".[155] This has provided historical justification for the Arabized elites to portray "northern" Sudan as one, rather homogeneous, entity, in part because Mahdism brought together distinct groups in the northern territories to challenge the rule of foreign oppressors. In this way, the stories of Mahdist conquests served nation-building by advancing the idea of northern Sudan as a relatively uniform Arabized Muslim region. The importance of the Mahdist conquest can be observed in the manner in which it has been interpreted by northern intellectuals. For instance to Beshir the Mahdist movement is the only nationalist movement of the 19th century Africa that emerged successfully against imperialism, and confirmed the power of the Sudanese religious orders to mobilize the population and form a state along Islamic principles.[156] This view propagated by northern Sudanese scholars, which sees Mahdism essentially as "Sudanese", has buttressed the power of the Arabized Muslim religious and tribal elites in northern Sudan[157] and contributed to a perception of national unity based on Arab culture and Islam. It is in sharp contrast with the constructed perceptions in southern Sudan of what constitutes the Sudanese nation.[158]

Mahdist Wars in the Southern Frontier

In the mid-1880s the Mahdist conquest spread to the southern frontier and deeper into Darfur. For instance, Bahr al-Ghazal became increasingly plagued by violence between a loose alliance of the Dinka, Nuer, and Shil-luk, and the Rizaigat section of the Baggara, against the remaining *Turkiyyah* military.[159] After the defeat of the *Turkiyyah* in Bahr al-Ghazal, the area re-mained in turmoil. The Agar Dinka leadership mobilized its ranks against the *Ansar*, albeit unsuccessfully.[160] Others with ties to Darfur and Kordofan joined the Mahdist cause, and some further south participated in eradication of the remaining *Turkiyyah* outposts.[161] Moreover, many *Danaqla* and *Jaali-yyin*, mostly *jallaba* residing in the southern frontier, joined forces with the *Ansar* because government policies, mainly the suppression of slave trade, went against their established livelihoods.[162] Thus, Mahdists gained only limited support in the southern territories through alliances with rivals with the same strategic objective. However, this was not enough to gain effective control over the area.

The rebellion also challenged the state's presence in the southernmost Equatoria region. Although the Turco-Egyptian garrisons in Equatoria were well-manned, the fall of province after province weakened morale and result-ed in desertions of regime-supporting *Danaqla* to the side of the Mahdi.[163] Yet, the first Mahdist invasion of Equatoria was delayed until January 1885 due to a revolt of southern *jihadiyya*[164] slave soldiers, many tired of harsh treatment by the Mahdists.[165] After moving forward, the Mahdists, joined by the *Danaqla*, made steady progress in Equatoria despite fierce resistance, but then departed for Darfur, which was considered a higher priority, allowing the province to succumb into inter-communal feuds.[166] Thus, the Mahdist in-vasions not only debilitated local societies but also encouraged violent con-testation by altering power relations within and between them.

Absorbed by warfare against Abyssinia and Egypt, it took more than three years for the Mahdists to return to the southern territories. In 1888, alarmed by the news of European force under explorer Henry Morton Stan-ley, sent to help Mehmet Emin Pasha (Isaak Eduard Schnitzer), the *Turki-yyah* governor of Equatoria, Abdallahi ordered an invasion of the territory.[167] Although eradicating the *Turkiyyah* from the southern frontier was clearly set as the principal objective, Abdallahi's decision was also driven by mil-itary and commercial interest. He sought to reinforce the depleted Mahdist armies by new *jihadiyya*, while responding to the pressure exerted by the in-creasingly powerful central riverine *Danaqla* and *Jaaliyyin* who were eager to resume their trading activities disrupted by the war.[168] By this time, the riverine groups enjoyed considerable and increasing political and economic influence, which later allowed them to dominate the state elite.

Despite defeating the remaining Turco-Egyptian forces in Equatoria in the course of 1888-9, the Mahdists faced difficulties in bringing the province under their authority. For instance, Sconyers states that

> The main Mahdist garrison in Rejaf found itself in the midst of a congeries of private slave armies led by mutineers, deserters, renegade Turks and ex-Jihadiyya. All of them were heavily engaged in the ivory trade, extensive slave-raiding, and picking off small detachments of Mahdists caught unaware.[169]

All these groups were operating in a remote territory surrounded by local populations with shifting alliances. Some local communities used military collaboration with the Mahdists to pursue their own objectives, but also turned against them when it was in their interest.

Southern Nilotic troops initially played an integral part in the Mahdist army. However in the longer-term, the animosity harbored by some *jihadi-yya* resulted in violent revolts. According to Sconyers, this was largely because "Convinced that they [the Blacks] had been created by God as slaves with no redeeming qualities, the Mahdist forces began to act on those convictions".[170] Similarly, Collins claims that

> The sophisticated Arab with a culture and tradition centuries old felt . . . that he was superior to the simple African who was created by Allāh to be a slave . . . [while] . . . the general Arab treatment of Negroids in Equatoria appears to bear out this relationship, which still exists and is the most unfortunate legacy of the Mahdīya in the Southern Sudan.[171]

This attitude by many *jallaba* and Mahdists generated apprehension and hostility among southern groups. Consequently, while the last remnants of the *Turkiyyah* withered away, a number of local groups resisted Mahdist incursions and rejected Islam, which resulted in a situation in which the Mahdist state hardly controlled areas in the southern frontier beyond the outposts near the Nile, despite generating widespread fear.[172] In the southern territories, the Mahdist presence was considered as the continuation of the attempt of domination from the north. As a result, the Mahdist violence buttressed the collective memory that the "northerner" was the primary source of danger[173] and categorically "the other". Faced with fierce resistance, the Mahdist administration was never able to fully control the southern frontier, and the area remained largely out of the state authority's reach.[174]

Conclusion

It has been shown in this chapter that the 19th century historical experience is essential to the understanding of contemporary Sudan. As demonstrated by the above account, a number of historical factors and processes are important in the emergence of a marginalizing polity and its core's relationship with its periphery territories.

First, during the 19ᵗʰ century, for the first time, the core of what constitutes contemporary Sudan was administered as one political entity. The peripheral areas were at times incompletely integrated to the state through oppressive means, and some, such as the southern frontier, only to a very limited degree. The Ottoman *Turkiyyah* was largely a product of external forces (aspirations of regional and international actors), but it created local elites that sought to benefit from the new order. This was particularly the case in the privileged core Arabized Muslim areas, where some leaders were able to use the new situation for economic and political ascendance. While the central administration was consolidated in the central Nile valley, where it found some of its main local collaborators, the state's influence hardly penetrated certain peripheries, such as in the south, which were largely subjected to violent extraction of resources. State formation was thus largely based on a selective, exclusionary, and marginal incorporation of the periphery, manifested in regional terms through the use of religion, race, and language, to define group boundaries and inclusion/exclusion in the dominating sociocultural (political and economic) discourse of the Arabized elite. Over time, this deeply-rooted historical center-periphery division evolved into a structural condition of state and society because adherence to Arab culture and Islam determined access to power. To an extent, this marked continuity from the polities pre-dating the *Turkiyyah* and *Mahdiyyah*.

Second, during the 19ᵗʰ century, the Arab-Muslim dominated social hierarchy championed by the regime collaborators, namely the heads of sectarian groups and communal leaders, was consolidated. Islam was not only emphasized as part of identity, but portrayed as a unifying force and instrumentalized politically to claim prominent societal position. This enabled the eventual projection of an image of northern Sudan as a region in which Arab culture and Islam prevailed. However it hardly represented the whole reality, as demonstrated by the resistance of "Arab"-domination by some non-Arabized elements.

The *Mahdiyyah* witnessed the prelude of the *Ansar* as the constituency of the Mahdist movement. This not only challenged the external Ottoman rule, but also sought to assume societal prominence and counter the power of *Khatmiyyah* and *Shaigiyyah* favored by the Turco-Egyptian administration. It set the stage for the political competition over state power between the Mahdist and *Khatmiyyah* sectarian power elites. At the same time slave trade and violence in the southern frontier culminated, and their continuation, in part perpetrated by the *jallaba*, provided a context of protracted fear and mistrust carved in the memory of local communities. Maintaining this memory adhered to the interests of those sectors of the southern elites willing to antagonize the relations with northern intruders.

In sum, major legacies of the 19ᵗʰ century history that impact contemporary Sudan include the inheritance of centralized administration, the construction of the "Arab" as the dominating political identity category, and the memory of slavery, violence, and unequal (marginal) incorporation of the peripheries to the centralized polity. These are powerful forces that continued to dictate political, economic, and social realities of what became a particular kind of marginalizing state in Sudan. The next chapter shows how the Anglo-Egyptian Condominium period promoted the consolidation of the governing elite, and state marginalization as a socially institutionalized form of governance, and set the stage for insurgency formation in Sudan.

Endnotes

1   Iyob and Khadiagala (2006: 19).
2   On the long history of slavery in Sudan see for instance O'Fahey (1973), Collins (1992), Sikainga (1996), Fluehr-Lobban and Rhodes (2004), and Segal (2002).
3   For more discussion on this identity category see the following section.
4   Here a constructivist-instrumentalist position is adopted, deeming regional categories (center-periphery and north-south) as (re)constructed largely through extension of identity discourses of dominant elites and instrumentalized for political purposes.
5   Deng (1995a, 1995b) and Lesch (1998).
6   de Chand (2000: 25) and Jok (2001, 2007).
7   In north-central Sudan, the idea of *awlad al-balad* was adopted by the "fathers" (earlier generations) to claim socially prominent position. Adam, Bartlett, and Nour (2009: 7) assert that *Shaiqiyyah* and *Jaaliyyin* are often considered *awlad al-balad,* and further explain that

> The term awlad albalad was invented in early 1880s when the Mahdi chose Khalifa Abdullahi from Darfur to be his successor which outraged his cousins who came out with the term to explain that they had more right than the *gharrabi* (western Sudanese for male) for the position of his first deputy. The term has become as a signifier of exclusion ever since. It has been used [sic] northern Sudanese to exclude the non-northern Sudanese Muslims from other parts of the country including even the non-northern Sudanese Arabs. Of course Christians and adherents of traditional African believe [sic] systems are automatically pushed away through Islamic discourse.

8   See Jok (2001, 2007) and Iyob and Khadiagala (2006: 20-2).
9   The constructed concept of "northern" Sudan refers to Islamicized and to an extent Arabized areas of Sudan, encompassing the central riverine Nile region, Darfur, far northern territory (Nubia), and the Red Sea region in eastern Sudan, Kassala, and Kordofan. They are all predominantly Muslim, with parts of local

populations adopting influences from Arab culture. However, there are a number of borderland areas within "northern" Sudan, such as the Nuba Mountains, which are far less Arabized and less Islamicized than those lying in the central Nile Valley.

10   Iyob and Khadiagala (2006: 19-20).
11   Beswick (1994).
12   Holt (1961: 17), Henze (1991: 25), and Iyob and Khadiagala (2006: 22).
13   Mazrui (1973: 72-3) and Deng (1995b: 80).
14   'Abd al-Rahim (1970: 135-6), and Iyob and Khadiagala (2006: 22).
15   Hasan (2003: 14), and Iyob and Khadiagala (2006: 23).
16   'Abd al-Rahim (1970: 236-7).
17   Mazrui (1973: 73).
18   Holt (1961: 16-8).
19   Henze (1991: 25), and Iyob and Khadiagala (2006: 23).
20   Holt (1961: 20-3) and Collins (1962: 8).
21   Spaulding (1985: 75-7) and Sikainga (1996: 2).
22   Holt (1961: 20), and Iyob and Khadiagala (2006: 23).
23   This is why the region bears the name Dar Fur, "Land of the Fur". See e.g. Abdul-Jalil (2006: 22). See also Holt (1961: 25-6) and LOC (1991).
24   Holt (1961: 27-8).
25   Iyob and Khadiagala (2006: 25).
26   Lusk (2005).
27   Sufi refers to a particular type of Islam in which mysticism and diverse rituals emphasize the love for fellow men and a personal relationship with God, *Allah*. Sufism has been at times considered inappropriate, or even impure, by some advocates of orthodox Islam. Some claim that Sufism even predates Islam to some extent.
28   'Abd al-Rahim (1970: 239), and Iyob and Khadiagala (2006: 24-5).
29   Iyob and Khadiagala (2006: 24-5).
30   Bayart (1993: 24).
31   Johnson (2006: 95).
32   Deng (1995a: 369-400, 484-5).
33   "Almost racial" here refers to Deng's concept, not race *per se*. It should be noted that many Islamicized peoples in the periphery of contemporary state in Sudan, such as the Beja in the east, the Fur in the west, and the Nuba in the southern fringes of "northern" Sudan, remain less Arabized even though many are Muslims, and feel more empowered by preserving their traditions in their local contexts.
34   Woodward (1997: 98).
35   One such area is the Nuba Mountains in southern Kordofan which has been subjected to Arab and Islamic influences for centuries. "Arab" identity has not grown deep roots in the area for a number of reasons, violence and the legacy of slavery being among the most important ones, and Arabization has generat-

ed resistance. In Darfur the term "Arab" has often been considered an insult to the nomads. See e.g. Lusk (2005).

36 Although Arab and Islamic cultural influences also spread east and westwards, these processes are not highlighted here due to this monograph's emphasis on insurgency formation in southern Sudan.
37 Woodward (1997: 96).
38 Gray (1961: 34, 46, 140-1, 143-4) and Deng (1995b: 80).
39 See Spaulding (2006: 401-2).
40 Spaulding (2006: 401).
41 See also Rolandsen (2005: 23).
42 Beswick (1994).
43 Hasan (2003: 100).
44 Gray (1961: 15), Collins (1962: 7), Hasan (2003: 100-1), and Rolandsen (2005: 23).
45 Thomas (2012: 26).
46 Mazrui (1973: 72) and Hutchinson (1996). This tradition has made army, police, and other occupations related to security services as locally respected professions, encouraging many young men to join the state's security apparatus or rebel organizations during insurgencies. The extent of militarization of southern societies is related to the long periods of violence they have experienced.
47 Gray (1961: 11).
48 For instance, Nuer spiritual leaders had a historical network of relationships extending to Ethiopia. According to Johnson (1986), the Nuer have also historically formed the western "Nilotic frontier" of imperial Ethiopia.
49 Collins (1962: 4) and Hasan (2003: 104-5).
50 Collins (1962: 5), Hasan (2003: 102), and Rolandsen (2005: 23).
51 Beswick (1994: 172-85).
52 Gray (1961: 10).
53 Hasan (2003: 105-6).
54 Hasan (2003: 107).
55 Ahmad (1977: 31-9).
56 Walz (1978: 29ff).
57 Niblock (1987: 3).
58 O'Fahey and Spaulding (1974: 55-56).
59 Niblock (1987: 3).
60 Beswick (2004: 201).
61 Thomas (2010: 28).
62 This was particularly the case when slave-raiding intensified during the *Turkiyyah* with the use of Islamic law as justification for it. See e.g. Mire (1986: 115).
63 Hasan (2003: 107-8).
64 Hasan (2003: 198-9) and Beswick (2004: 220).
65 Hasan (2003: 109).
66 See more on this in the next section.

67 The growth of trade also had other effects. It facilitated the expansion of the *Turkiyyah* to Darfur since the commercial activities in Bahr al-Ghazal in the southern frontier deprived the Keira sultanate of its resource base, contributing to its demise in 1874. In addition, expansion of demand for confectionary items and paper in Europe provided an incentive for a rapid increase of gum arabic production, particularly in the El Obeid region in south-central area of Kordofan, linking local economy with the world market. Other economic developments included the spread of private ownership of land in riverine Sudan and wider circulation of liquid currency. These economic developments also advanced a capitalist mode of production in which southern captives provided the main labor. See e.g. Holt (1961: 72-4) and Niblock (1987: 7-8, 10).

68 Alier (1990: 12).

69 See Björkelo (1984: 90-1, 1989: 123-4, 142-3).

70 Alier (1990: 12).

71 See e.g. Hill (1959: 49), Holt (1961: 64), and Ibrahim (2000: 5).

72 Björkelo (1989: 114-6) and Tiyambe Zeleza (1993: 300).

73 The *jallaba* refers to the Arabic word *jallab*, which in this context means the one who "brings slaves". See Ibrahim (2000: 8) for more.

74 Warburg (2003: 7).

75 This argument surfaces continuously in the "north-south" relations in Sudan. "Northerners" continue to be criticized for their limited understanding of "southern" Sudan.

76 Muhammad Ali (1972: 3-21), Tignor (1987: 181), and Björkelo (1989: 118).

77 Niblock (1987: 9) and Ibrahim (2000: 6).

78 Gray (1961: 46).

79 In central and northern Sudan slaves were often cooks, blacksmiths, and construction workers, apart from their more traditional duties as servants, soldiers, and agricultural laborers. See e.g. Lesch (1998: 27), Hasan (2003: 58), and Sharkey (2003: 17, 19).

80 Warburg (2003: 13).

81 Björkelo (1984: 92-5).

82 Gray (1961: 36), Jok (2001: 95), and Sharkey (2003: 19). Sharkey (2003: 17-8) also points out that "In the northern regions . . . , where Islam and Arabic language prevailed, a centuries-old slave trade had bestowed servile connotations on the adjective 'Sudanese'", and "To the Northerners, who regarded themselves as Arabs, being "Sudanese" meant being "Black" . . . and being "Black", in turn, meant having low social status".

83 Despite recognizing the controversial debate over *Turkiyyah*'s nature, the author considers it having been essentially a colony if defined according to commonly accepted definition as: Country or area ruled by another political entity with political elite originating from the latter.

84 ESIS (2004).

85 Ibrahim (2000: 7).

86 First, during 1820-22 Ali extended Ottoman Egyptian rule over central northern Sudan, annexing Dongola and the weakened Funj Sultanate in the central Nile

Valley, while founding Khartoum as an administrative center in 1824. By 1822 the Mamluk resistance in Sudan had been dispersed, and the Funj Sultanate conquered, while subsequent expansion took place in 1840 when Ottoman rule extended to Kassala. In 1865 the conquest reached the Red Sea coast where the ports Sawakin and Massawa were taken. Subsequently, Ali's grandson Khedive Ismail completed the second phase of expansion in the course of the 1870s by annexing Bahr al-Ghazal in 1871 and Darfur in 1874. See e.g. Henze (1991: 26), Ibrahim (2000: 7), and Warburg (2003: 6).

87 The term *Turkiyyah,* or "Turco-Egyptian" used by Holt (1961), refers to Muhammad Ali's invasion and occupation of areas that account for large parts of contemporary Sudan in 1820-1885. Among the principal motivations behind Ali's decision to occupy the lands south of Egypt were controlling the origin of slaves, and building an army based on Nilotics capable of undertaking the expansionary campaigns through which he envisioned challenging the Ottoman Sultan's hegemony in the Near East; the search for the mythical riches of the Sudanese kingdoms that he was personally obsessed with; and ending the looming threat that the Mamluks posed to his rule. See e.g. Holt (1961: 36-7), Collins (1962: 5), and Ibrahim (2000). Holt (1961: 37) further emphasizes that one should see Muhammad Ali's expedition to Sudan as private endeavor. Therefore, the term "Turco-Egyptian" describes Egypt as dominated by Turkish speaking Ottoman elite, composed of senior officers and officials ruling over Arabic speaking Egyptian subjects. The administration of Sudan was equally largely non-Egyptian, as the officials were largely Greeks, Kurds, Albanians, and Europeans, leaving Egyptians junior posts in the army and administration. As a result, the Sudanese referred to the new rulers as *al-Turk,* "the Turks", despite their distinct nationalities. Thus, "Turco" here refers merely to the Turkish speaking elite and their Ottoman culture.

88 *Zeriba* were first introduced as fortified government military and trading posts during the invasion of Sudan, but in the southern frontier, where the administrative presence of the regime was largely absent, they later became bases for merchants and slave lords. The slave lords commanded large private armies and became powerful enough to avoid centralized tax regime. The most powerful of them, Rahman Mansour al-Zubair (Zubeir Pasha), incorporated Darfur to the *Turkiyyah.* See e.g. Cordell (1985: 18).

89 Gray (1961: 16-20), Sconyers (1978: 10-1), and Collins (1990: 66-8).

90 Holt (1961: 58).

91 The geopolitical importance of the Nile had increased due to three particularly significant developments: The "discovery" of the sources of the Nile in Lake Victoria in 1862, the completion of the Suez Canal in 1869, and the bankruptcy of Egypt in 1876. First, when John Hanning Speke "discovered" the sources of the Nile at Lake Victoria on 28 July 1862, attention of European powers turned towards the Equatorian lakes and controlling the Nile flow down to Egypt. Second, the opening of Suez Canal on 17 November 1869 attracted the attention of European maritime nations with interest in Asia because it reduced the travel

time to the Orient by half. Third, Egypt had experienced a financial boom in the 1860s when it took over as the cotton supplier for the British Isles from the United States due to the American Civil War. But by 1876 Egypt was bankrupt because of spending on massive modernization projects and luxury items, and Britain and France eager to exert influence over the Nile and Suez took control of its finances. See Collins (1990: 26-8).

92   Gray (1961: 20-1) and Ibrahim (2000: 8).

93   Warburg (2003: 12).

94   "Tribal" here refers simply to "Arab" social organization, not tribalism as manipulation of ethnic identity boundaries. See El Zain (1996).

95   The *Shaigiyyah* had first fought the Egyptian expansion, but after being defeated they began to collaborate with the state by participating in lower levels of the administration and signing up as *bashi bozuq*, irregular soldiers exempted from tax contributions, to perform violent tax collection raids. This suggests that sectors of the *Shaigiyyah* used strategies of extraversion to buttress their dominance in the local context, while the *Turkiyyah* administrators, on the other hand, found them culturally similar and relatively controllable due to their geographic proximity. See e.g. Warburg (2003: 7).

96   Ibrahim (2000: 7-8).

97   According to Holt (1961: 64), the new regime improved agriculture and exports to Egypt. Accordingly, new technology, through introduction of the waterwheel, *saqiyyah*, and Egyptian peasants teaching their counterparts, expanded area of cultivation and agricultural production. Moreover, Hill (1959: 7, 49-50) and Niblock (1987: 8-9) assert that the relatively successful experimentation with new crops, such as sugar cane and cotton, the establishment of warehouses, and the digging of watering holes for cattle to be exported, resulted in the expansion of the economy and trade over which Cairo initially maintained an exclusive monopoly.

98   A number of these existed, and their organization included socio-economic as well as religious societies. See e.g. chapters by Awad Al-Karsani and Abdullahi Mohamed Osman in *Al Majdhubiyya and Al Mikashfiyya: Two Sufi Tariqas in the Sudan* (1985). According to Woodward (2003: 96), "The politics of Islam from the eighteenth century onward was a reflection of the growth of the Sufi orders, or *turuq* (singular *tariqa*), who came into Sudan and steadily grew in size".

99   *Ulama* are highly educated Islamic scholars. They are perhaps most known for their juridical functions as arbiters of the Islamic law, *sharia*.

100 Warburg (2003: 6) and LOC (1991).

101 Hasan (1985: 11) and El Zain (1996: 524).

102 Al-Gaddal (1985: 9-10) and El Zain (1996: 525).

103 O'Brien (1979: 139).

104 See El Zain (1996: 523-9) for evidence on perceptions of "inherent" incompatibilities. Author's fieldwork has revealed further evidence of the paramount role of these elites in the process of formation of the Sudanese polity.

105 Ibrahim (2000: 8).
106 Warburg (2003: 8-9).
107 Holt (1958: 24).
108 LOC (1991).
109 MacEoin and Al-Shahi (1983: 63).
110 MacEoin and Al-Shahi (1983: 63).
111 Ibrahim (2000: 5) and Warburg (2003: 7).
112 Ibrahim (2000: 4).
113 For instance, referring to the Shilluk, Ibrahim (2000: 5, 6-7) has noted that
     Their [the Shilluk] determination to maintain . . . political institutions
     against the imperialists' plans . . . [to] . . . replace them was crucial factor
     for the deeply-rooted tradition of resistance to foreigners in the South . . .
     [becoming] a major stumbling block for the Turkish [Egyptians] and subse-
     quently European attempts to explore the upper reaches of the river [Nile]
     . . . [and] . . . Their daring resistance had in the end brought this imperialist
     advance in the South to a virtual and disastrous end.
114 Gray (1961: 46).
115 Ibrahim (2000: 8).
116 Ibrahim (2000: 8).
117 This affirmation is based on the author's interviews and field observations.
118 Warburg (2003: 16).
119 Fegley (2008: 36). Particularly the cattle herding Baggara nomads, who mostly
     live in the Sahelian transitional zone in southern Kordofan and Darfur, became
     dependent on the *jallaba*. This was because their possibilities to obtain cash
     diminished as a result of the end of cattle shipments to Egypt in the 1840s.
     As a result, a peculiar form of transactions emerged: The Baggara first sold
     their cattle to the *jallaba* for currency, and then the *jallaba* resold the cattle to
     the Baggara for slaves, which were considered more precious commodity. See
     Warburg (2003: 13). In Kordofan, the trade was more straightforward since the
     Baggara provided the *jallaba* with a direct supply of slaves largely obtained
     from the Nuba Mountains.
120 Gray (1961: 69) and Niblock (1987: 9-10).
121 Gray (1961: 69).
122 Gray (1961: 203).
123 An anonymous writer of the period asserted that "The Dinka, in great strength,
     also raid the Arabs as far as al-Rusayris and sometimes up to the neighbour-
     hood of Sennar, killing and destroying everything they meet, committing
     atrocities and carrying off the cows that they find and all human beings who
     have not been able to escape". See Ibrahim (2000: 6).
124 Ibrahim (2000: 6).
125 See e.g. Nyombe (2007: 108-11) on divisions among the Bari between those
     against slavery and those allying with the slave raiders.
126 See e.g. Gray (1961: 120-5), Sconyers (1978: 17), and Nyombe (2007: 89-90,
     108-11).

127 Gray (1961: 125).
128 Ali's grandson and a successor Khedive Ismail defined his attempt to emulate Europe, and introduce new reforms in Egypt and *Turkiyyah* as a "civilizing" or "modernization" mission.
129 See Holt (1958: 24-5) and LOC (1991).
130 Warburg (2003: 14).
131 Holt (1958: 29).
132 Holt (1958: 25-32) and Warburg (2003: 15).
133 Warburg (2003: 15) and Ibrahim (2000: 7). However, this provoked objection among the Arabized peoples since not only was slavery a permitted institution in their interpretation of Islam and common practice for centuries before *Turkiyyah*, but livelihoods of many depended on slave trade. Thus, they objected that Samuel Baker, a British non-Muslim, was appointed to suppress one of the most important economic activities. In 1873, Charles George Gordon, was appointed as the Governor in the Southern Equatoria province in an attempt to extend government authority, end the slave trade, and encourage legitimate commerce. See e.g. Holt (1958: 26-7) and Sconyers (1978: 16). However, as Gray (1961: 108-111), Sconyers (1978: 16-17), and Ibrahim (2000: 8-9) note, Gordon's efforts were eventually unsuccessful in bringing a degree of stability.
134 Warburg (2003: 15).
135 See e.g. Warburg (2003: 15-6).
136 The general bankruptcy in Egypt that peaked in the 1870s had an incapacitating effect on the administration. For instance, heavy taxation resulted in declining revenue from the *Turkiyyah* since it discouraged economic growth. In terms of government revenue, the inefficiency in tax collection and related corruption resulted in the loss of almost EG£1million in 1869-79, while in 1878 alone it was calculated that five out of eleven provinces were governed at a financial loss. See e.g. Warburg (2003: 14). This lack of finances meant that the envisaged economic reforms came to a standstill.
137 Henze (1991: 31) and LOC (1991).
138 Gray (1961: 152).
139 Collins (1990: 105).
140 LOC (1991).
141 Later, Abdallahi converted into Mahdi's successor. This paragraph draws mainly from LOC (1991), Henze (1991), and IAO (2004).
142 The Mahdist *Ansar* drew largely from the Baggara of Kordofan and Darfur. Similarly to a number of other Muslim groups in contemporary Sudan, the Baggara have manufactured genealogies for generations that trace their lineage back to Muslim ancestors, and, despite being genetically mixed, they embrace Arab culture due to its deemed high status. See e.g. Cunnison (1971: 186-96). However, their receptiveness to the Mahdist cause was not only because they were Muslims, but also because of Abdallahi's and other members of the Baggara elites' ability to mobilize them based on grievances towards the *Turkiyyah*. The first supporters of the Mahdist cause came among the Baggara,

providing part of the manpower for the Mahdist army. After the conquest the Baggara became increasingly connected to the central riverine area due to their involvement in the administration and the military. Many Baggara remain as the core constituents of the contemporary (neo-)Mahdist movement.

143 Henze (1991: 31) and Weiss (1999: 1).

144 Mahdism expanded rapidly in the rural areas in northern and western *Turki-yyah*. It fed on the resentment of rival Arabized and Muslim groups towards regime collaborators. Apart from the Baggara as its main constituency, the movement drew its followers from rural communities, among Beja people of eastern Sudan, the *jallaba*, and sectors of the *Jaaliyyin* and *Danaqla*, whose livelihoods were linked to slave trade that the *Turkiyyah* suppressed. See MacEoin and Al-Shahi (1983: 63), LOC (1991), and Henze (1991: 31).

145 Based on author's interview of a prominent *jallaba* in Juba on 29 September 2008.

146 Holt (1958: 100) and Weiss (1999: 12-14).

147 Holt (1958: 104).

148 Beshir (1974: 16).

149 'Abd al-Rahim (1970: 240).

150 Holt (1958: 246).

151 LOC (1991), Ibrahim (2000: 7-9), and Warburg (2003: 55). Mahdi also transformed the five pillars of Islam according to his vision of a perfect Islamic community. For instance, a true believer had to show loyalty to him as the representative of God's Prophet,while obligation to *jihad* replaced the pilgrimage to Mecca, and almsgiving (*Zakat*) became a system of state taxation. See e.g. LOC (1991) and Weiss (1999: 18-22). Some of these provisions, such as *Zakat*, have been used in later periods in Sudan in the context of state-promoted Islam.

152 See Tignor (1987: 181) and Warburg (2003: 51-2). According to Holt (1958: 255-7), trade with Egypt had seized after the Mahdist conquest, and the commercial activities that had previously connected *Turkiyyah* to the outside world diminished drastically. Part of the reason, the continuous wars aside, was the limited access to international markets since major transportation nods, such as the port of Sawakin and the railroad that linked Wadi Halfa with Egypt, remained under Egyptian and British control. However, Niblock (1987: 10) contends that a small amount of trade in camels in Egyptian markets, and informal exports of gum arabic and ostrich feathers, took place through Sawakin with British permission.

153 Niblock (1987: 10-1).

154 Its main manifestation has been the Umma Party. See Chapter IV for more.

155 Lesch (1998: 28-9).

156 Beshir (1974: 15).

157 Based on interviews in Khartoum, Nuba Mountains, and Juba (November-December 2005 and 2008).

158 Deng (1995).

159 Gray (1961: 155-59).
160 Collins (1962: 44-5).
161 Sconyers (1978: 18).
162 Holt (1958: 34) and Collins (1962: 22-3).
163 Gray (1961: 160) and Collins (1962: 46).
164 *Jihadiyya* is a common name for black southern slave soldiers (often riflemen) who were used during *Turkiyyah* and *Mahdiyyah*, forming an important part of the army. After the abolition of slavery, the tradition of the *jihadiyya* survived to the British colonial period during which these riflemen served in imperial campaigns and the two World Wars.
165 Collins (1962: 47) and Sconyers (1978: 19).
166 Collins (1962: 49-50, 54, 138).
167 Collins (1990: 74).
168 Collins (1962: 56-8).
169 Sconyers (1978: 21).
170 Sconyers (1978: 21).
171 Collins (1962: 72).
172 Collins (1962: 72, 73, 75).
173 Lesch (1998: 29).
174 Rolandsen (2005: 23).

CHAPTER IV

COLONIAL ADMINISTRATION:
The Anglo-Egyptian Condominium

C hapter III focused on the 19th century history of the region that became contemporary Sudan. Here, however, the emphasis is put on the Anglo-Egyptian Condominium period in an attempt to build on the previously underlined historical trajectories. These include the continuity of the colonial state, above all the centralized administration, governance, ruling methods, and favoritism of a selection of prominent elements of the Arabized Muslim elites. The sociopolitical organization of the Anglo-Egyptian Condominium period emerges from earlier realities and combines them with new administrative structures, policies, and changing regional and international context. It is argued here that the Anglo-Egyptian colonial state, which emerged from this combination of pre-existing and new factors, laid basis for the post-colonial systemic state marginalization.

Violent conquest and military campaigns marked the conquest and consolidation of the Anglo-Egyptian co-dominium, although colonial order was imposed under the pretext of "pacification". The colonial policies were aimed at maximizing extraction and minimizing political instability, centering on the economic growth pole strategy favoring the center and extending the pre-existing "divide and rule" principle of governance to the periphery. This paved the way for growing relative deprivation and poverty, and arguably provided a setting which facilitated insurgency formation in the long run. The colonial policies, which for decades differed between northern territories and the administratively separated southern periphery, maintained the previous social stratification, fostered ethnic politics and divisions, and enforced economic imbalances between and within groups and territories. The "differentiating" policies facilitated the strengthening of the sentiment of southern (and northern) regionalism, as perceptions of injustices and inequalities among southern Sudanese elite extended.

The colony's particular co-dominium status became a source of schism between Britain and Egypt, as both sought regional power and influence within Sudan. This served the narrow sections of the Arabized elite who concentrated economic and political power. The powerful Sufi movements became major actors in the local struggle of power, with sections of associated riverine groups, such as elements of *Jaaliyyin*, *Shaiqiyyah*, and *Danaqla*, also growing in power. Meanwhile Britain, as the administrator of the colony, separated its southern parts and isolated them from the rest of the colonial state, and its hegemony over Sudan set the stage for a rift with Egypt. This had serious implications in the process of decolonization that was propelled by the international post-World War II environment. As such, the dynamics and policies of the colonial state consolidated the 19th century foundation of a particular kind of marginalization in Sudan, maintaining a political reality which provided preconditions for insurgencies in southern Sudan.

Incorporation of the Region into the British Colonial Empire

The incorporation of the region covering contemporary Sudan into the British Empire was the prelude to the period of Anglo-Egyptian Condominium, a particular co-dominium arrangement between Britain and Egypt, during which the borders of the colony were forged and the marginalizing political system enduring to post-colonial period was cemented.

The Anglo-Egyptian Conquest

After overcoming the Napoleonic threat in the early 19th century, Britain established itself as a major world power. It exerted extensive economic control through its commercial fleet and the large navy, which heightened its overall influence. During the first half of the 19th century, British immigration to southern Africa had increased considerably, but its attention was diverted to northeast Africa after the inauguration of the Suez Canal that provided a new route from Europe to Asia. As a result, the British sought to control the Canal, which in geopolitical terms meant controlling Egypt. In 1875 the British government purchased Khedive Ismail's personal 44% share of the Suez Canal, and in 1882 the Egyptian nationalists staged an uprising against the growing European influence[1] which gave London a justification to occupy Egypt militarily. Although the French also had a claim on the Suez Canal, British strength persuaded them and other competing powers to settle for a Treaty within the 1888 Convention of Constantinople. Consequently, the Canal was declared neutral territory but *de facto* controlled by the British who maintained a military force stationed in Egypt until 1954.

Meanwhile, the "Scramble for Africa", initiated by the 1884-5 Berlin Conference, had forced Britain to review its imperial policy. London sought to protect Egypt and the Suez Canal, which made British officials consider the occupation of the Mahdist state to control the Nile waters that came to be perceived as Egypt's lifeline. For Nicoll, this argument at least partly justified the invasion of the *Mahdiyyah*, as did avenging the death of highly-esteemed British official Charles George Gordon which had created a public uproar in Britain.[2]

In the context of the scramble in the late 1880s, the *Mahdiyyah* became of interest to the British, French, Belgian, and Italian imperial powers. They all endeavored to extend their influence in the region. The first three powers sought control of the upper Nile area; Britain desiring to expand its African dominion as a continuous belt from Cairo to Cape Town,[3] the French aspiring to control territory from the Atlantic coast to the Red Sea, and Belgium's King Leopold II hoping to extend his dominion from the Congo to the source of the Nile and beyond.

Britain endeavored to thwart the threat presented by the Belgian and French claims to territories that were not colonized and assert its own power in Sudan. In 1889 the British launched an invasion of the *Mahdiyyah* from Egypt. Meanwhile in 1893-1902 in the southern margins of the *Mahdiyyah* Leopold embarked on a mission to extend the Congo Free State into the Equatorian Nile valley, which resulted in armed confrontations featuring local groups, the Mahdists, and the Belgian-Congolese troops.[4] The invasions from the north and the south further weakened the Mahdist regime, and contributed to its eventual defeat against the Anglo-Egyptian army on 2 September 1898 in the Battle of Omdurman. Soon after, the French occupied Fashoda in southern margins of Sudan, which led to British-French confrontation, the "Fashoda incident",[5] and almost triggered a war between Britain and France. However, seriously weakened by a domestic political scandal and unable to challenge the British naval superiority, the French decided to withdraw, and Britain asserted its dominion over the area. It subsequently came to an agreement with Belgium, leasing Lado Enclave[6] to Leopold in 1894 for his lifetime.

Once the main Mahdist opposition and the French threat had been neutralized,[7] the British sought to consolidate their claim over the conquered territories. On 19 January 1899, an agreement between Britain and Egypt was signed, which established joint colonial rule over the Anglo-Egyptian Condominium.[8] The hybrid nature of the agreement was a carefully thought outcome of the correspondence between officials in London and Evelyn Baring (later referred to as Lord Cromer), who was the British Consul General in Cairo. The attempt was to deal with Egyptian opposition to the conquest of the *Mahdiyyah* and ward off criticism of other European powers regarding British colonial expansion.[9] However, Egypt's function was also to cover the financial costs of governing the colony; a task the British parliament was unwilling to assume itself.[10] Hence, the agreement enabled Britain, which controlled Egypt, to become the *de facto* ruler of the conquered territories, without assuming the main financial responsibility.

The agreement designed by Britain stipulated the areas south of the 22nd parallel as the Anglo-Egyptian Condominium. It established the northern boundary with Egypt, while a pact with France dividing central Africa in the spheres of influence defined the border between the Anglo-Egyptian Condominium and the French dominion in the west. Later, the eastern border with Eritrea was agreed upon with the Italians, and a border agreement with Abyssinia and delineation of border with the colonial dominion of Uganda were concluded in 1913.[11] According to Kebbede, "Within the first two decades, most of the . . . border was defined and nearly all territory of today's Sudan came under the firm control of Britain".[12] Thus, similarly to other African colonies, the Anglo-Egyptian Condominium's borders were drawn largely by agreements between the colonial powers according to their geopolitical interests and irrespective of local ethnic and geographical boundaries.

Administrative Structures and Initial Policies

After the initial conquest, it took time for the new Anglo-Egyptian masters to establish their control of the territory of colonial Sudan. In the northern areas, there were a number of communal uprisings, such as those of the Funj in 1919, Garidi in 1925, and Eliri as late as 1929.[13] Darfur was granted an autonomous tributary position, but when Sultan Ali Dinar turned against the British in 1915 to side with the Ottomans in World War I, Anglo-Egyptian forces conquered the sultanate in 1917, killed Dinar, and annexed it. The attempt to bring the southern frontier under centralized administration was initiated in 1918.[14] However, the campaigns to consolidate colonial authority continued in the form of punitive patrols until the 1930s, and parts of it continued isolated from the centralized administration well beyond the colonial period.

During the Anglo-Egyptian Condominium, the frontier lands of southern Sudan and Darfur became formally part of the Sudanese polity. Focusing on monopolizing political power for the administration, the British introduced a paternalistic and bureaucratically authoritarian colonial government in charge of a provincial system under a Governor-General based in Khartoum.[15] The administration relied partly on the governance legacies of previous *Turkiyyah* and *Mahdiyyah*, including the "divide and rule" logic by encouraging politically competitive ethnicity through "tribalism", manipulating ethnic and sectarian divisions among the subjected groups while favoring carefully selected prominent sectors of society.[16] According to El Zain, British governance accentuated the effects of ruling methods initiated during the *Turkiyyah* to the extent that " . . . the tribe became 'tribalist', the sect became 'sectarianist', and culture became a source of domination and racism".[17] El Zain's assessment is informative, although, as often the case with northern Sudanese narratives, it also appears apologist as it appears to fail to recognize that the origins of social subjugation in Sudan have been largely dictated by slavery and slave trade which predated the Anglo-Egyptian Condominium.

When governing Sudan, the British were concerned about uprisings capable of challenging the colonial rule. As a result, in order to prevent unity between communities that could pose a threat similarly to the *Mahdiyyah*, or convergence into a national political identity, the British employed "divide and rule" ideology by encouraging "tribalization" and exclusive perceptions of ethno-political identities. However, these efforts were conditioned by the pre-existing ethnic, cultural, and religious realities drawing from the dynamics of domination, and the persisting logic of the highly exclusive *Turkiyyah* political system rife with favoritism, corruption, and mismanagement that marginalized most sectors of the society.[18] The Anglo-Egyptian administration reinforced the type of governance and ruling methods it inherited from earlier administrations, adapting them to its needs and passing them on to post-colonial Sudan.

The Anglo-Egyptian political organization was to a large extent a result of the experience of governing northern territories during the gradual conquest of Sudan. It owed much to the example of administration practiced in the Dongola area where a type of military administration had been established.[19] Drawing on the model applied in Dongola, the British instituted a provincial system dividing the Anglo-Egyptian Condominium initially into six provinces; Dongola, Barbar, Kassala, Fashoda, Kordofan, and Khartoum. However, after World War I, the number of provinces was increased to fourteen before it was finally cut back to nine, including Bahr al-Ghazal, Equatoria, and Upper Nile in the south.[20] In the early stages, a British military officer, assisted by British inspectors at district level, governed each province, while the Egyptian administrators (*mamurs*) were in charge of lower level governance and assisted at the local level by "tribal" community leaders.

111

However, the policy of indirect rule based on native administration, or rule by local leaders appointed by the government at the grassroots level, only became the governance system in the 1920s in response to a nationalist current extending from Egypt to northern Sudan, and until then the local leaders did not receive pay from the colonial administration.[21] In the southern provinces the British military officials dealt directly with the local leaders, and gave way to the northern administrators during the process of decolonization.

D. Provinces of the Anglo-Egyptian Condominium

Source: *Courtesy of the University of Texas Libraries,*
The University of Texas at Austin

The type of administration established was carefully designed. In Africa generally, the colonial state was "all-powerful and arbitrary".[22] Mazrui has called the type of political order it espoused as "ethnocratic", since it sought to gain and maintain control by monopolizing power to one group and excluding others.[23] The colonial state politicized the ethnic sense of affiliation and belonging by promoting exclusive, and at times antagonistic, view of identity. Colonial Sudan followed this general pattern, as the British, who sought not to repeat the mistakes of the *Turkiyyah*, wanted an efficient, all powerful, and inexpensive government. Therefore, colonial elite consisting of a small number of British and Egyptian administrators was established, representing state power and seeking to extend authority over the vast territory with minimum resources by carefully selecting local collaborators and deliberately marginalizing others. To achieve this, they exploited local alliances through a number of strategies, including favoritism and nepotism.

The British monopolized political power around the figure of Governor-General[24] and his political advisors who acted on behalf of the colonial government.[25] The Governor-General reported to the British Consul in Cairo, and the Anglo-Egyptian administration, as its counterpart in Egypt, was placed under the supervision of the British Foreign Office instead of the Colonial Office. This owed partly to the fact that Egypt, which was an equal partner in administering the colony, was still legally under Ottoman authority and not a British colony.[26] Free from the Colonial Office's supervision, the Condominium government had more room than most other British colonial administrations for dictating policy. Despite organizational differences, the colonial government's monopolization of political authority maintained the pattern of exclusive exercise of political power from the earlier periods. It therefore set the precedent for the political dynamics that prevailed in post-colonial Sudan, although institutions corresponding to democratic rule were created during decolonization.

At the highest level of administration, the military personnel gradually gave way to highly educated British civil servants. The latter formed the Sudan Political Service, initiated in 1905, and consisted of men mainly educated in Oxford and Cambridge. They became a fluently Arabic-speaking ruling elite of approximately 140 individuals, governing over 9 million colonial subjects.[27] The colonial administration's initial policies were aimed at consolidating its rule, which was a process in which it heavily relied on Egyptian personnel some of which had served the *Turkiyyah*. Partly with the idea of curbing the threat of religiously incited revolution, and to avoid collapse similar to the *Turkiyyah*, the British committed themselves to separating church and state. They sought to divert the attention of the leading

Sufi movements, the *Khatmiyyah* and neo-Mahdists,[28] away from politics and religion, granting them economic concessions.[29] In addition, the model imposed in India was used to secularize the criminal and penal codes, and the civil and religious laws were kept separate, while subjecting personal matters of the Muslim population to customary *sharia* law in separate courts.[30] The Governor-General exercised arbitrary power to appoint the judges of the civil and religious courts, as well as other officials, which resulted in the colonial state in Sudan being both authoritarian and highly exclusive.

Colonial Rule and the Emergence of Nationalism in Northern Sudan

The rise of the Arabized Muslim elites in what became known as the "northern" Sudan, and the emergence of nationalism during the Condominium period, is significant for analyzing armed conflict formation in southern Sudan. The attempt here is to show how opportunities were created primarily for the prominent sectors of the central riverine groups, some of which embraced the opportunity to collaborate with the regime to elevate their socioeconomic power and political importance.

The Consolidation of Arabized Muslim Elites

In the Condominium, both accumulation of economic wealth and reinvestment became important in defining socioeconomic power. Since the British were aware of the role the heavy taxation had played in the demise of the *Turkiyyah*, they oriented government tax regime from the population to the produce by taxing cotton. As a result, the Condominium subjects became lightly taxed relative to the subjects in a number of other colonies, and selected individuals were able to accumulate significant fortunes that enabled them to increase their socioeconomic status and political influence.

Cotton growing was concentrated in large schemes that gradually excluded small farmers, resulting in an uneven socioeconomic pattern. For instance, the Gezira scheme, which became the main venture for large-scale production of agricultural goods, hardly improved the livelihoods of the majority of subsistence-oriented farmers.[31] In contrast, the socioeconomic effects of Gezira, and other large schemes producing cotton for export (and other products), favored the economic prominence of chiefs and other heads of communities who controlled the land in the area where such ventures were located. According to Niblock, "Large landowners (mostly tribal leaders) were able to obtain a significantly larger share in the scheme than smaller landowners or those without land".[32] Since many village leaders were also able to register communal land as their private property, they became large landowners and accumulated wealth through the schemes. These leaders often benefited from government's economic favors oriented to buy their loyalties and minimize possible uprisings, which in turn increased their influence and capacity to use patron-client networks to control their constituencies. Consequently, a major socioeconomic implication of early Condominium policies was the concentration of wealth in the hands of the already prominent social actors, which further increased their societal importance.

Holding economic power often meant gaining political influence, particularly for those who were socially well-established. The pattern of economic power that emerged in the early Condominium period therefore led to two kinds of economic inequality that had deep political implications. The first was socioeconomic, allowing those who benefited from the Condominium rule to reinvest and strengthen their economic and political status. The second was "regional", referring to the deliberate concentration of economic development to the central riverine areas that left other areas largely underdeveloped. These two types of inequality were vital in shaping the dynamics of politics in contemporary Sudan.[33] They concentrated political power exclusively to the privileged groups at the center of the polity, and created grievances among those excluded in the marginalized periphery.

Moreover, the Condominium policies encouraged the strengthening of an economic elite which played an important role in the process of decolonization and the national politics. Among the most significant groupings within this elite were religious and ethnic leaders, merchants, and high-level civil servants and professionals. However, the Condominium policy also pushed the majority of subjects to become increasingly economically marginalized, and permitted the continuation of slave-like exploitation of labor.[34]

Religious leaders were among the best positioned to benefit economically from the Condominium rule. This was particularly the case with the leading neo-Mahdist and *Khatmiyyah* Sufi orders.[35] The British initially supported the *Khatmiyyah*, the rival of the neo-Mahdist movement, which had taken refuge in Sawakin during the *Mahdiyyah*, but after realizing its pro-Egyptian proclivities they shifted towards endorsing the neo-Mahdist[36] movement despite the initial fears of its capacity for staging uprisings. Egypt, in turn, sought to support the *Khatmiyyah*, which shows the existing rivalry in the co-dominium rule.[37] Referring to the resultant economic power of the leader of the neo-Mahdists, Sayyid Abd al-Rahman al-Mahdi, it has been noted that "On Aba Island alone he had a labour force of about 4500. He was in 1936, by any standards, economically prosperous and politically important".[38] This

115

economic and political prominence of heads of the leading Sufi orders, supported by their collaboration with the colonizer, positioned them above other social groups.

However, the competition over resources heightened the rivalry between the Sufi orders. The colonial rulers exploited this contest, which facilitated their mastery over Sudan particularly because each order required extensive economic resources to feed its patron-client networks and social bases.[39] The colonial masters sought to play the one against the other to minimize the risk of uprisings, while both movements used strategies of extraversion, shifting between collaboration and resistance in response to the different Condominium policies.

Although religious leaders were the protagonists of the struggle for economic and political power, secular leaders of local groups in the cotton producing areas also formed part of the new economic elite. Integral to the system of native administration that guaranteed the British policy of indirect rule in the remoter areas, they grew in importance.[40] Particularly after the nationalist uprising in the mid-1920s, the local leaders in administration became pronounced because the British sought to minimize Egyptian influence in Sudan. They expelled many Egyptian civil servants and deemed younger educated Arab-Muslims and "detribalized blacks"[41] as unreliable substitutes.[42] Therefore, in 1927 the Powers of Sheiks Ordinance was passed which gave the local leaders a growingly prominent role, as they were granted legal authority over tribal courts and local policing to enforce customary law.[43] This also entailed economic benefits since the government backed them in collecting taxes, and when the influence of these strongmen extended over semi-urban, mostly merchant-inhabited, areas in the northern provinces they were able to accumulate wealth through control over trade licenses and commercial activities.[44]

Historically, merchants had played a prominent social and economic role in the territories of today's Sudan. Many of them benefited from the Condominium rule, as the relative political stability, renewed economic growth, and expansion of cash economy allowed opportunities particularly in export trade. Although the Condominium period witnessed the arrival of Greek, Lebanese, and Syrian traders, similarly to the later *Turkiyyah* period,[45] local *jallaba*, headed by the al-Shaykh Mustafa al-Amin family, occupied a significant role in the export business.[46] Thus, in the southern provinces, as well as elsewhere in the periphery of the colonial state, trade remained among the most lucrative activities for accumulating wealth, but it remained largely in control of the *jallaba* and foreign companies and individuals.[47] This strengthened the position of those *jallaba* participating in the regional and

116

international trade networks, and benefiting from high gum arabic prices and the booming exports especially after railroad was extended to El Obeid.[48] Moreover, by the 1940s and 1950s the exportation of livestock, principally to Egypt and Saudi Arabia, together with the flourishing oilseed trade, became concentrated in the hands of gradually more prominent merchants, who, due to their increasing financial wealth, were in a position to reinvest.[49] Some *jallaba* also invested in education, which eventually led to some of them gaining a significant role in the northern political elite.

The fourth group of colonial subjects that gained prominence during the Condominium period was civil servants in high positions and highly-trained professionals.[50] However, it was only in the 1950s when individuals from this group began to acquire capital and land.[51] Thus, it took until the independence of Sudan when civil servants and professionals became well-positioned to exercise their newly acquired economic and political power.

Finally, southern Sudanese residing in the northern provinces also continued to work in the area where most of the economic development took place. Largely owing to the centuries of slave trade, southern blacks had become a relatively large section of the population in the northern Sudan, reaching 1/3 of the total by 1898.[52] Most southern Sudanese in the northern territories remained enslaved, or working in slave-like conditions, during the colonial period, despite the formal abolition of slavery in the British Empire in 1833. The government was generally unwilling to free slaves because the colony suffered from a labor shortage, and enforcing abolition would have angered prominent sectors of northern Sudanese[53] as had been the case during the period leading to the Mahdist uprising. The labor shortage was also alleviated by West African Muslim migrants, the *fellata*, who largely settled around the Blue Nile and worked primarily in agriculture with low pay,[54] as well as by many Darfurians who migrated to the productive agricultural areas of central Sudan. In other words, economic growth in the central regions during Anglo-Egyptian period, similarly to earlier times, was based on labor from the marginalized peripheries under the supervision of locals who viewed themselves as culturally superior to the laborers. This promoted the perception of being "northerners", an association defined in terms of celebration of Arab culture and Islam as opposed to the non-Arab "other" originating from the peripheries.

Colonial Policies, Racism, and the Social Construction of "Northern Sudan"

The Condominium policies reinforced the cultural rift between "northerners" and the rest. They emphasized differences between Arabized Muslims of the northern provinces and the non-Arabized peoples of the peripheries of the colonial state. Contrasting Arab culture and adherence to Islam the most, the blacks of the southern territories were considered the outmost manifestation of "the other". The Southern Policy, which was imposed to isolate the three southern provinces, Bahr al-Ghazal, Equatoria, and Upper Nile,[55] administratively from other parts of the colony, contributed to this polarization as it subjected "north" and "south" to distinct Condominium policies that prevented the formation of common political consciousness. In addition, according to Ruay, the enforced policy of "tribalism", or creating new boundaries of ethnic politics by reshaping group leadership, became " . . . largely responsible for the legacy of backwardness in the South and for magnifying the superiority/inferiority syndrome which characterized relations between South and North".[56] Thus, the divisions on cultural and racial basis encouraged views of superiority, and resulted in further consolidation of exclusive group identities, domination, and subjugation as integral to the political system and culture in Sudan.

The British colonial racism, influenced by 19th century Victorian intellectual currents emphasizing social and cultural progress, influenced the attitudes on cultural race in the Condominium. According to O'Fahey, "Virtually every Sudanese . . . [has experienced] discrimination in Egypt and elsewhere in the Arab world. The discrimination they [Arab Muslim northerners] impose on their Southern or Western co-citizens is imposed upon them as they go down the Nile".[57] Indeed, faced with such outside perceptions, the local elites needed to justify social differences in order to legitimize the exclusive concentration of power to them. Gradually, the differentiation involving internal and external perceptions influenced the Condominium administrators' views and categorization between the northern "Arabs" and "blacks", and "detribalized blacks" of southern origin living in northern part of the colony providing labor.[58] Despite the emergence of abolitionist ideas " . . . the second half of the 19th century saw increased ideological elaboration of white supremacist attitudes, supported by pseudoscientific arguments associated with social Darwinism and related ideologies".[59] In this way, northern Sudan became to be considered semi-civilized relative to what was seen as its more sophisticated neighbor, Egypt, while southern provinces were deemed largely savage. This partly justified the protective European over-rule that was deemed both instructive and civilizing especially in southern Sudan.

During the Condominium, "tribalism" became further institutionalized as a form of governance through which indirect rule, native administration, and later Southern Policy were articulated.[60] The colonial policy promoted exclusive view on identities, politicizing them based on perceived cultural and ethnic attributes functioning as basis for group association. Such exclusionary group organization became the main source of political identities, and, by focusing and manipulating cultural and ethnic identity differences, to an extent neutralized the homogenizing forces of state centralization. These ethnic politics becoming the order of the day had far-reaching consequences for post-colonial Sudan.

Coexisting with the "tribalist" organization of colonial society, the rigid social hierarchy based on the generations-old northern socio-cultural attitudes towards the southern peoples continued throughout the Anglo-Egyptian period. Once acquiring slaves became more accessible and prevalent in the northern provinces, the sphere of activities dedicated for slave labor increased, and even poorer northern riverine families could hold one or two slaves.[61] Despite the reduction of major slave-trading activity, Spaulding points out that the persistence of slavery itself constituted the principal context through which the constructed socio-cultural Arab-Muslim led domination and subjugation continued to be manifested.[62] The persisting domestic slavery, to which the British initially turned a blind eye, maintained the attitude of supremacy of the Arabized Muslim peoples over the southern blacks.[63]

In addition, slave raids in the borderlands of the colonial state continued. Slaves were smuggled through the largely uncontrolled western and eastern borders, for instance, to French Sudan and Ethiopia.[64] Despite the occasional crackdown of slave traders, the practice remained and slave labor was even encouraged by the Sudan colonial government when faced with rising labor costs in the main cotton schemes.[65] According to O'Fahey, " . . . small-scale slave-owning created a very peculiarly Sudanese form of racism",[66] and unable and unwilling to eradicate the widespread practice of domestic slave-holding in northern Sudan, the British dealt with it by calling slaves "servants" and owners "masters".[67] Thus, during the colonial period the racial categorization in which "African" is deemed subordinate to a superior "Arab" buttressed power of the Arabized elites which had elevated their position in the social hierarchy through their economic prowess and social and political influence. In this context, slavery continued as a structural condition that subjected black southerners to the lowest social status.

Throughout the Condominium period, the issue of slavery continued to be intimately related to the Sudanese "Arab" identity. It served the elite interest to justify its social prominence, as well as maintaining the prevailing social hierarchy. Thus, it was important for the Arabized populations to continue to emphasize their "Arab" identity. According to Jok, part of this identity is manifested in

119

> . . . a conception that Arabism has a superior rank to Africanism, based on the way they view the racial hierarchy. A problem, however, arises when it comes to those Northerners with physical features such as pigmentation, shape of the nose, and hair texture that are typically African. Most people in the North share these features with Southerners, and yet regard themselves as Arab.[68]

Hence, it was perceived necessary to use other means to justify the constructed "Arab" identity that was associated with social, economic, and political prominence. This resulted in embracing standard Arabic language, attained through education, an educated view of Islam, and creating ethno-history based on Arab and Muslim genealogies.[69] The discourse has glorified Arab history of conquest, and has maintained high respect for the Mahdi as the father of "Sudanese" nationalism.

The Condominium order provided a context which facilitated promotion of the perceived Arab superiority. This is in part because colonial policies favored Arabized Muslim elite collaborators by granting them almost exclusive and selective access to economic opportunities and higher education in Gordon College in Khartoum.[70] As a result, the northern Sudanese were considered to contrast the black, "acultural", southerners, which became integral part of constructing and asserting the "Arab"-Muslim identity that has dominated the social hierarchy. Perceiving the southerners as the contrary, this view justifies the exclusive political and economic power of the Arabized Muslim elites through the logic of cultural superiority. It became an important element in the construction of "northern" Sudan, which was increasingly portrayed as one Muslim region according to the interests of the Arabized elites in its core riverine areas.

Over time, part of this elite employed in the colonial administration became increasingly familiar with the exclusive dynamics and governance practices of the colonial state. A cultural and racial justification of superiority was important part of its policies, which marginalized the large majority of the population through economic exclusion, especially since the colonizers based their rule on deliberate creation of poverty as a control mechanism.[71] Learning from the Condominium administration, and equipped with knowledge of the dynamics of colonial governance, sectors of the Arabized Muslim elite that inherited power in Sudan applied the same methods. They imposed exclusive policies that continued to create poverty and marginalize the majority of population in post-colonial Sudan.

Finally, however, when the prominent sectors of the Arabized Muslim elites monopolized the nationalist political movement in the 1940s, and later the national politics, they imposed their own cultural identity and racial views. Such views became integral part of perceptions that guided institutions, and they influenced exclusionary policies perpetuating systemic marginalization within and by the Sudanese state. Therefore, political philosophy guiding governance was to an extent inherited from the colonial administration. It became linked with the perception of "northern Sudan" as a "regional" entity, which contrasted the southern Sudan as the categorical "other".

Nationalism and Political Consolidation of "Northern" Elites

In March 1919, a nationalist revolt in Egypt against British overrule[72] caused an abrupt change in the administration of Anglo-Egyptian Condominium. The colonial administration embarked on a reactionary policy because officials feared Egyptian incitation of the local nationalists. Their main fears included the movement for the "Unity of the Nile Valley", which sought to unite Sudan with Egypt[73] and in which social networks of educated cadres who had studied in Khartoum, Cairo, and Beirut played a major role. However, the measures adopted to curb the nationalist sentiment failed to prevent disturbances organized by members of the Arabized riverine elites in 1920-4[74] in the northern provinces. Although eventually put down, these revolts severed the Condominium government's relations with the educated cadres in northern Sudan along with its attempt for large-scale Sudanization of public administrations until well into the 1930s.[75]

A selection of nationalist individuals played a prominent role in organizing the uprisings. Ali Abd al-Latif and Obeid Haq al-Amin, who together founded the White Flag League (WFL),[76] were the most famous leaders of the movement. Al-Latif was a southern Dinka, and his prominent role in the early northern Sudanese nationalist movement provides evidence of the permeability and malleability of ethnic and "tribal" boundaries among the educated sectors of the society. This shows to an extent that the widely argued incompatibilities between the northerners and the southerners are not inherent or primordial, but socially constructed, manipulated, and situational.

Britain's attempt to minimize Egyptian influence emerged as the major development from the nationalist uprisings. While having first claimed that Egypt had legitimate rights over the Anglo-Egyptian Condominium, the British now attempted to disconnect the latter from the nationalist influences of the politically turbulent Egypt. The Condominium government sought to diminish reliance on Egyptian personnel through Sudanization of administration. In addition, in 1920, it made indirect rule through native administration the doctrine in order to minimize Egyptian influence and to curb the elites affected by the nationalist current. This policy reinforced power of traditional leaders along "tribal" logic, and created divisions between the nationalist clique connected with the major Sufi movements and the largely less educated rural "tribal" leadership in order to diminish challenges to the colonial overrule.[77] Thus, apart from their already existing tax collecting duty, "tribal" leaders became endorsed with judicial and administrative power and additional responsibilities.[78] They were granted the right to exercise customary law, whenever it did not substantially contradict British interests, and encouraged to expand their following through amalgamation and homogenization of communities[79] to constitute more governable "tribal" entities. The promotion of "tribalism", according to El Zain, already originated in the Ottoman-Egyptian period when the Egyptian administration converted the Sufi leaders and local shayks as the intermediaries of its policy of extraction. It was institutionalized in the governance structures " . . . within the power relations of the colonial system . . . " and " . . . governs power relations in Sudanese politics today", making "tribalism" and sectarianism " . . . the two pillars of the Sudanese political system".[80] This institutionalization of colonial governance practices, characterized by creation of "tribal" ethnic divisions that politicized geographical and psychological boundaries along regional, ethno-cultural, and religious lines, developed along strong political and economic networks, which have made the "tribal" logic resistant to attempts of creating non-ethnicized political and local administrative formations.[81]

However, in the 1930s, the northern nationalists found new room for maneuvering. This was largely due to regional and international events that affected the local reality. In 1935 Italians, who had colonized Eritrea since 1890, invaded Abyssinia and threatened both the British position in northeastern Africa and the recently independent Egypt's interests in the Nile. This prompted, on 26 August 1936, the coming together of the co-dominium allies in the Treaty of Alliance, which invited the Egyptian military and civilians back to Sudan, and consequently reinitiated the Anglo-Egyptian competition over the local and regional influence.[82] The reinvigorated rivalry offered the local nationalists in northern Sudan increasing opportunity to express their demands and exploit their position through political and economic extraversion. In 1938 the Gordon Memorial College graduates founded the Graduates' General Congress (GC), which consisted exclusively of well-educated Arabized Muslims and assumed the role of the main voice of "Sudanese" nationalism.[83] Thus, sections of the "northern" elite monopolized the nationalist movement and their political identity became to define its essence.

The restoration of the Condominium government's education policy in the course of the late 1930s allowed the establishment of the GC. The organization assumed the role of a leader of the nationalist political activity, and claimed to represent the interests of all Sudanese colonial subjects. In 1942, the GC submitted a twelve-point memorandum to the Condominium government. In the memorandum it demanded self-rule, more educational opportunities, increased participation in the administration, reversal of the Southern Policy through abolition of the Closed District Ordinance and the related restrictions on trade and movement, and the cancelling of subventions to missionary schools in charge of education in southern provinces while adhering their syllabi with those in the northern provinces.[84] As a collection of Arabized elite individuals advocating interests of northern Sudanese constituencies, the GC positioned itself against the Southern Policy and perceived the barriers it had established as " . . . typical machiavellian devices aimed at prolonging the British rule and to separate the South from the North".[85] Partly influenced by the commercial interests of the *jallaba*, the GC claimed the southern provinces as an integral part of the "northern Sudan" largely due to historical and economic reasons. As a result, the southern issue was paramount in consolidating alliances between sections within the central Arabized elite, which hoped to extend their political power over the southern provinces and resume unrestricted extraction of commodities and resources from the southern borderlands.

The colonial authorities responded initially with an attempt to split the nationalist movement. The administration claimed that the GC's demands were not justified because it represented only a fraction of the society, and it continued to deliberately provide uneven support to the major Sufi movements which served as the main social base for the nationalist sentiment. The movement developed along two lines, the neo-Mahdists advocating independence by raising the slogan "Sudan for Sudanese" and the *Khatmiyyah* promoting the "Unity of the Nile Valley" through association with Egypt.[86] Egypt's support to the latter forced Britain to favor the first as a counterforce to the attempts of extending Egypt's regional influence. Many sources indicate this factional rivalry having been the order of the day, but it mainly involved the privileged cadres of the Arabized Muslim elite and was heavily affected by each co-dominium masters' support.

Colonial Power in Southern Sudan

Colonial power articulated in the periphery of the colonial state in Sudan in terms of "regional" differences of political and economic integration. This resulted in drastic distinction specifically between the central (core) and peripheral territories of the colony, and contributed to the creation of a perception of incompatibility between northern and southern Sudan.

The Establishment of Condominium Rule in Southern Sudan

During the early Anglo-Egyptian period, resistance in the southern territories against the centralized administration took a pattern similar to the 19th century.[87] Military expeditions against the Nilotic Dinka were not completed until 1927, and even then sections of the Dinka posed a threat to the colonial administrators until 1932.[88] The British organized their last military campaign in colonial southern Sudan from 1928 to 1930, which resulted in the colonization of the Nuer.[89] The subjection of the main Dinka and Nuer groups, which paved way for colonial control of the main areas in the southern provinces, was made possible in part by conflicts among various groups of the majority Dinka themselves. The British sought to weaken southern groups by encouraging conflicts between them, while continued warfare and raiding involving sections of the Baggara, Dinka, Murle, and Nuer also weakened all of them and permitted further colonial consolidation.[90] Therefore, divide and rule strategies, including collaboration with a selection of local leaders, enabled the British to extend their influence in the territories of Sudan's southern frontier.

Yet after the conquest, many parts of southern territories remained without effective government presence. Ruay has argued that " . . . it was doubtful whether there was any real submission to the foreign rule".[91] Similarly to other parts of British Africa, the colonial administration's power was established and largely emanated from larger population centers. It was enforced through occasional military patrols and native administration (indirect rule), rather than permanent and effective state presence and supervision of the local administration in the periphery. In Condominium Sudan few resources were forwarded to administer or economically develop the periphery, as the motivation to extend Anglo-Egyptian administration southwards " . . . depended not on a desire to develop the resources or to meet the needs of the area itself, but on the decision to safeguard the Nile's waters as an inevitable extension of the British occupation of Egypt".[92] Consequently, periphery frontiers, such as those that became the southern provinces (Bahr al-Ghazal, Equatoria, and Upper Nile), were incorporated to the colonial system as marginal territories.

Effect of Colonial Political Economy on Southern Sudan

Policies during the Condominium period deepened the development divide between the core and periphery territories in Sudan. They contributed to the establishment of persistent and relative socioeconomic inequality between different groups of the population, largely along the lines of the prevailing social hierarchy. However, differences in the level of economic development, political awareness, social and cultural reality, and distinct status had already been established before the Condominium government engaged in such deliberate policy of differentiation.[93] Since the British had originally conquered the *Mahdiyyah* for external reasons, rather than due to the interest in the region itself, they had little interest in developing it[94] except for covering part of the administrative costs. However, the gum arabic and cotton exports along with improved communications, which made the colony an important producer even in terms of the world market, laid the foundation for a growth pole pattern of economic development. This became concentrated in the north-central core areas, the central Nile valley around and north of Khartoum, Gezira (between the Blue and White Nile immediately south of Khartoum), central Kordofan, and the southern part of Kassala province.[95] As Warburg affirms, "Thereby Greater Khartoum, with only 6 per cent of the population, contained 85 per cent of all commercial companies; 80 per cent of all banks; seventy three percent of all industrial establishments and 70 per cent of all industrial labour".[96] These areas central to the colonial political economy contained the administrative centers and the major agricultural schemes, with the privileged sectors of their population benefiting from higher education and development.

However, the focus on north-central Sudan deprived other parts of the colony of significant investment.[97] This pattern of economic concentration caused general underdevelopment of remote territories.[98] As a result, although the central areas experienced economic modernization and growth, the economy in more remote territories remained subsistence oriented and the communities became marginalized in terms of economic opportunities and development.[99] In addition, since the vast majority of peripheral populations were poorly educated they were also deprived of public positions, which favored the central riverine groups whose elites became to dominate public employment during the late colonial period.[100] Common accounts fail to mention that this partial incorporation, based on exploitation, generated grievances specifically among the rising "regional" elites in the peripheral areas that were excluded from benefits elites enjoyed at the core of the colonial politics and economy.

The regional economic differences had deep demographic and political effects. While the administrators used "divide and rule" strategies to minimize the possibility of development of common political and economic grievances that could serve as the rallying cry against the colonial state, the colonial policies encouraged urbanization and migration to more prosperous areas. At times they stimulated "regionalist" political sentiments among local elites in the peripheries since economic development and job opportunities in these marginalized areas were scarce.[101] Marginalization was particularly pronounced in the isolated southern provinces where the " . . . main contact with the state was through those organs which sought to tax, administer and control . . . " the local communities.[102] This led to the culmination of the perceptions of inequality, particularly during the last years of the colonial era when the emerging local political elites pointed to cultural differences, slavery, and prevailing social hierarchy as causes for their economic and political marginalization. Yet, marginalization appears to have been less severe in other parts of the periphery of the colonial state, which were partly Arabized and largely Muslim. In general, they were more connected to the politics and economics of the state's core areas through their leadership, cultural affinities, and voluntary labor migration.

In sum, the interplay between historical, social, and cultural dynamics, regional economic inequalities, and marginalization contributed to specific political trajectories in the peripheries of the colonial state. In southern Sudan, the presence of alien but extractive central administration, uneven development, and socio-economic deprivation relative to the core, all contributed to discontent and the emergence of sentiments of relative deprivation and injustice.[103] This took place especially from the 1940s onwards when mainly the younger sections of the elites, which had received a degree of modern education, began to regard themselves as different from the politicized cultural project of the Arabized Muslim central riverine power elite. The history of conflict and slavery, and the differential treatment by the Condominium government, facilitated (re)construction and reinforcement of the sense of difference from the core in southern Sudan.

The Southern Policy

Imposition of Southern Policy in Sudan was one of the British reactionary strategies to the Egyptian and Sudanese nationalist uprisings. While the colonial authorities set up a system of indirect rule along Lugardian principles,[104] they also isolated southern provinces from northern areas. Since the southern provinces were seen to play an important geo-strategic role to obstruct the spread of nationalism and " . . . block out Arabism and Islam from Black Africa",[105] by 1920 it was argued that they were to be separated from the rest of the colony.[106] However, dictated by the Closed District Ordinance Act of 1920, the Passport and Permit Ordinance Act of 1922, and Permits to Trade Ordinance Act of 1925, the Southern Policy of isolation was not fully implemented until 1930.[107] It was designed to facilitate the consolidation of local administration isolated from northern Sudan, curbing *jallaba* presence and northern cultural influences. Although adopted largely in response to nationalist currents destabilizing northern Sudan, the policy also aimed to suppress slave trade, curb the political influence of the two influential Sufi movements (neo-Mahdists and *Khatmiyyah*) that were becoming increasingly powerful, and minimize the remaining threat to colonial rule at the local level posed by two resistant southern leaders, Ngundeng and Ariadhdit.[108]

Thus, elimination of Arab and Islamic influence in the southern provinces became a major objective of the Condominium policy. Aiming to protect Sub-Saharan regions from the spread of Arabic culture and Islam, Christianity and mission education were favored as "civilizing" forces following Lugard's proposals. Consequently, the Condominium government promoted English, vernacular languages, and Christianity instead of Arabic and Islam, and sought to consolidate "tribalism" as a tool of governance similarly to the northern provinces.[109] Accordingly, colonial authorities encouraged "tribalism" through native administration, established security apparatus based on territorial command, and promoted Christian mission education despite rudimentary Arabic being spoken in parts of the southern territories. They considered eventually incorporating the southern provinces to British East Africa to protect them from northern influences and due to their perceived close cultural affinity.[110]

The idea of annexing southern Sudan with colonial territories south of it gained intensity as a result of Milner Commission report which outlined the reasons for the Southern Policy. The report suggested measures of decentralization, and its directive statement in 1930 was issued to prepare the southern provinces to be annexed to the British East Africa.[111] However, the commission's recommendations were never implemented, in part because this would have required redrawing colonial boundaries and also because it was rejected by the British East Africa administrators who were not interested in annexing the unproductive and "savage" southern Sudan to their dominion.[112] Yet another factor was Egypt's and northern Sudanese nationalists' resistance to any such policy because both wanted to secure their own economic and political interests, the former hoping to control the Nile waters by eventually annexing Sudan and the latter to resume economic activities and extend political influence over the region. Eventually, the effect of the Southern Policy " . . . was to deepen and enhance the differences between

the Southern and Northern parts of the Sudan".[113] The isolation and specula-
tion about links with East Africa reinforced the projected view that southern
Sudan was inherently different from northern parts of the colony, and part of
Sub-Saharan Africa.

Therefore, the British briefly considered the southern provinces as a
buffer obstructing the spread of Arabic and Islamic influence to Sub-Saharan East Africa. A perception prevailed initially that southern Sudan had to
be protected and developed along more "natural" lines through the cost-ef-
fective system of indirect rule by native administration, with missionaries
allowed to Christianize and educate small numbers of southerners[114] who
would become the local ruling elite. The missionary involvement was not
only seen as more desirable than the spread of Arabic culture and Islam,
but it was also perceived to complement the modest economic development
initiatives planned in the region. The missionary education promoted intermingling among a handful of elite individuals, socializing them according
to Western norms, which laid the foundation for the "regional" elite tran-
scending ethnic and tribal lines. This elite became heavily influenced by the
Western views on northern Sudan.

Moreover, although divided along numerous ethnic affinities, the Condominium's Southern Policy considered southern provinces as one loose and
diverse "regional" entity subjected to the general policy of differentiation
from what the authorities viewed as northern Sudan. Markakis notes that

> . . . colonial rule in . . . Southern Sudan promoted a degree of regional
> integration through the establishment of institutions and processes linking
> the various districts and ethnic groups within each region, and provided
> them with a common vested interest in the existence of these institutions
> and processes.[115]

This contributed to the emerging perception of southern territories as "the
South", perceived as "native", "black", and inherently "African" cultural
and regional space, as opposed to "the North" defined as more sophisticated
"Arab" and "Muslim" region.

The Southern Policy sought the formation of the new elites in southern
provinces along Western cultural characteristics. It also largely prevented
the presence of northerners in southern Sudan.[116] The British military administrators of the southern provinces, the "Bog Barons", who considered that
northern army troops spread Arabic and Muslim influence, decided to create a local military force under British officers. Consequently, the Southern
Equatoria Corps (SEC) was founded and the northern soldiers were moved
out of southern Sudan by 1917,[117] which paved way for two largely separate
security apparatuses in Sudan.[118] This development has been less document-

ed, but it influenced a sentiment of southern regionalism in response to fears of northern domination. The formation of SEC also favored army service as a desired occupation for many southerners.[119]

The Southern Policy aimed at division and control. It sought " . . . complete separation in educational, socio-economic and political development . . . ".[120] For instance, in Bahr al-Ghazal and Darfur border, this translated into military posts set up to protect the Dinka from Rizaiqat raids aimed to gain access to pastureland in the southern territories.[121] According to Markakis,

> The South remained outside the framework of the colonial economy, producing nothing new, exporting little more than it had during the pre-colonial period, but importing more, including food, to meet the requirements of the non-productive population that gathered around the colonial administrative centers . . .[122]

Consequently, the urban centers in southern Sudan generated few opportunities that would drive urbanization. As a result, in contrast to a number of flourishing towns in northern Sudan, Juba, southern Sudan's largest town, had a population of only 9,000 by the time of independence in 1956.[123] Thus, it appears that the creation of poverty in "the South", as was the case more generally in the peripheries of the colonial state, formed part of the authorities' attempt to assert and maintain control.

The Southern Policy was formally fully adopted in 1930, and articulated through an effort to implement indirect rule by using "traditional" institutions. According to the 1930 Memorandum on Southern Policy, which dictated policy guidelines for provincial governors, the government's aim was to: (1)familiarize all British administrators with the local beliefs, customs, and languages of the people they administered; (2)produce non-Arabic speaking administrative, clerical, and technical staff; (3)diminish the amount of traders from northern Sudan, favoring Greek and Syrian merchants instead; and (4)use English wherever communication with vernaculars was impossible.[124] According to the authorities, "The policy of the government in the southern Sudan is to build up a series of self-contained racial or tribal units with the structure and organization based on whatever extent the requirements of equity and good government permit upon the indigenous customs, traditional usage and beliefs".[125] Thus the Southern Policy, which considered "the South" distinct from "northern Sudan", sought to generate regional entity with a regional identity that mixed Western and "African" cultural values.

As of 1930, the Southern Policy facilitated reconstruction and reorganization of "tribal" formations. It allowed local "traditional" administration, as long as this did not interfere with British ambitions.[126] Although the policy could be viewed as contradictory to the overall "civilization mission", it had more pragmatic objective in maintaining colonial control while preventing the undesired cultural influences from the northern territories. Its impact, however, was the reconfiguration of ethnic communities, recreating their boundaries and traditions, and fomenting competition for political influence through a process in which the selection of convenient "tribalist" leadership became paramount to the interests of the Condominium administration.

The Condominium authorities also sought to eradicate slave trade, which had contributed to the fragmentation of social order of a number of southern communities. Yet, although the international dimension of slave trade was largely suppressed and slavery overall publicly denounced, the British tolerated forced labor in Sudan which kept alive the violent memory of slave trade.[127] This memory highlighted the differences between northerners and southerners, and heightened local animosity against Arab cultural and Islamic influences in southern Sudan. Local leadership became instrumental in fomenting the memory of slave trade as part of historical narratives of northern domination, which encouraged collective "southern" identity. Such narratives, largely based on 19th century experiences, deeply influence attitudes in many local communities in southern Sudan, and served the perception of "Arab" as "the other", aiming to dominate, subjugate, and marginalize the southerners. These narratives have later been reinforced by literature and media.[128]

Mission education emerged important in the process of shaping the attitudes of sections of the southern elite. The British encouraged Christian missionary activity and education to counter northern influence to which they found the southerners particularly prone.[129] The government itself did not provide education initially in southern areas, and it delegated the laborious social and educational work to the missionaries.[130] Encouraged by the policy, a number of Christian missionary societies were active in the southern provinces. Consequently, the southern territories were divided in spheres of missionary activity between different denominations, while Christian missionaries were prevented from proselytizing in the northern territories because the government barred them from converting Muslims in the fear of reactions among both local and foreign Muslim communities.[131]

Locally in "the South" access to education remained limited partly because the missionary orders had no capacity to cater for the larger population.[132] This contrasted the situation in north-central Sudan, where there was wider access to education, including the Gordon Memorial College in Khartoum. The southern educational system was based on "bush schools" for grade 1 and 2 education in vernacular languages, followed by central district schools for grades 3 and 4 in English, after which the pupils who excelled in an exam were sent to an intermediate school beyond district level where they spent time with pupils from other ethnic communities, developing a common consciousness as more complete "southerners". The educated youngsters were then employed as clerks, medical assistants, and other junior officials, and a selected few went on to attain university education in East Africa. This mission-led process resulted in the construction and extension of "regional" southern consciousness, as opposed to "the North", which the members of mission-educated elite tended to advocate further.

In 1928, Rejaf language conference laid guidelines for the language of education in southern Sudan. At the elementary level local vernacular languages were used, while higher education was conducted in English.[133] The administration excluded Arabic from the southern education because it was seen to advance Arabization and Islamicization.[134] This proved contradictory to the later change of policy to maintain Sudan as one political entity in which official language was Arabic.

The Southern Policy, which was largely articulated through missionary education, went through two major stages. Firstly, the initial two decades of Condominium rule were characterized by the missionary societies being solely responsible for implementation of education in the southern provinces.[135] The education policy was oriented towards maintaining order and reinforcing "tribalism". This was undertaken by reinvigorating local social formations, and manipulating them to create differences and competition between communities. The policy of fostering "tribal" culture was also aimed at maintaining stability and introducing little change (e.g. through higher education), particularly inhibiting the spread of northern Arab and Islamic cultural influences.[136] Secondly, during the 1920s, the Condominium government began to subsidize missionary education with a vision to train locals to eventually replace the more costly foreign administrators, while education became gradually seen as essential in preparation of southern societies to withstand the effects of "civilization".[137] This policy resulted in the small but ethnically diverse mission-educated southern elite.

The effort to revive and maintain "African" identity and introduce Christianity in "the South" culminated when the Southern Policy was imposed in its strictest form. During 1930-46, Sunday was made the day of rest in "the South", while Arabic dress, customs, and names were banned, the few remaining northern merchants and officials expelled, and intermarriage with northerners heavily discouraged.[138] This favoring of local and Christian cultural symbolism fomented "southern" identity further, and polarized it against the promoted image of "the North" as the "Arab-Islamic other". One key ingredient of this separation was the reversal of the Condominium language policy, which marginalized the educated southern elite during the Sudanization process of public offices in the preparation of Sudan for self-rule.

The Southern Policy was based on a perception of fragility of southern communities and their perceived receptiveness to northern cultural influences. However, the perceived lack of sophistication and modernity of southern communities also generated doubts about southern Sudan's sustainability as a coherent regional entity. This led the authorities eventually to decide that southern provinces could not stand by themselves politically or economically.[139] Unlike central regions of the colony, the British administrators described "the South" largely as "primitive", with no prospects for economic development,[140] which also justified the unwillingness to invest in the region. The higher-level officials repeatedly frustrated economic development initiatives in the southern provinces, deeming private enterprise as a threat to the authority of the colonial state. The administration promoted only a few selected economic development initiatives of which the most famous was the Zande Scheme (Nzara Agro-Industrial complex) initiated in mid-1940s in Nzara near Yambio.[141] Economically, "the South" was put under "care and maintenance", subjected to the enforcement of a policy of "peaceful living" and tax collection.[142] Pastoralism and subsistence farming remained as the main sources of livelihoods in the southern provinces, and southerners were encouraged to uphold traditional economic activities for cultural conservation.[143] This policy formed also part of a larger geo-political strategy aimed at securing control over the Nile, deeming local development and increasing use of Nile waters undesirable because it might undermine water resources available for Egypt. This was despite the sentiment among some officials that economic development and well-being of the people should have been promoted.[144]

The overall effects of the Southern Policy were manifold. It reinvigorated and remade southern communities after the 19th century violence, but the relative peace brought by the Condominium rule after 1930 caused restructuring of local chiefs' leadership. The policy guided the local social organization increasingly towards heterogeneous "tribalist" order, creating and encouraging ethnic divisions and competition between communities. Moreover, the Southern Policy encouraged the perception of the "North" and the "South" as separate but socio-politically somewhat homogeneous entities. However, although sectors of local elites used this view to establish prominence, local populations remained highly diverse and heterogeneous. Finally, the Southern Policy accentuated differences, laying ground for economic and political grievances that eventually culminated in calls for autonomy and self-determination among sectors of the emerging contemporary mission-educated southern elite. The perceptions of injustices and relative deprivation of southern Sudan eventually became a regionally homogenizing force among the contemporary local elites, which organized regional political movement around them. Southern regionalism partly based resistance on the perceived "Arab" domination to counter the northern nationalist movement's exclusive control of national politics. The promotion of Christianity and English also encouraged the emergence of regionalist and separatist tendencies. This is because they became two cultural elements embraced by the mission-educated elites in opposition to the imposition of northern cultural traditions, namely Islam and the Arabic language, after independence.

Co-dominium Political Effects

By the 1940s, the co-dominium order stimulated preparation for decolonization. In this process a combination of local, regional, and international factors intertwined, resulting in the independence of Sudan. The analysis here centers on highlighting the processes that led to the marginalization of the southern elite and propelled opportune conditions for insurgency formation.

Egyptian Influence and the Emergence of "National" Political Elite

From the beginning of the colonial period, the British were aware of the extensive influence Egypt had on the Condominium. This centered on the importance of the Nile River, some harboring the memory of the *Turkiyyah* as a "natural" extension of Egypt, which culminated in cultural and trade links, the presence of Egyptian administrators in Sudan, and many prominent individuals from northern Sudan either studying in Egypt or having Egyptian teachers.[145] In the co-dominium arrangement, however, Egypt had had to settle for becoming the junior partner and accepting the international border that separated it from Sudan.

In addition, Egypt had particularly strong influence on the Sudanese military officers who were largely from the Arabized central Nile riverine communities. Thus, as the nationalist demonstrations of the 1920s culminated following the assassination of the Anglo-Egyptian Condominium's Governor-General Oliver (Lee) Stack in November 1924 in Cairo, they inspired an uprising of northern Sudanese junior officers in Khartoum Military Academy.[146] This was suppressed, but resulted in government reprisals and a meticulous crackdown of the Sudanese nationalist movement. It provided a pretext for the British administrators to pursue policies to minimize Egyptian influence in Sudan.

By the mid-1940s the Sudanese nationalist movement had re-surfaced. However, gaining increasing space in the public sphere accelerated political competition between its factions. The Condominium government's concessions to the demands expressed in the GC's 1942 memorandum not only stimulated the drive for decolonization but also generated competition among nationalists seeking to replace the colonial government. In 1943, Advisory Council for Northern Sudan (ACNS) was established as the first step to allow formalization of the nationalist movement by allowing the registering of political parties.[147] As a result, prominent nationalist Ismail al-Azhari, and other intellectuals, immediately founded the *Ashiqqah* party associated with the pro-Egyptian *Khatmiyyah* faction. This later formed the National Unionist Party (NUP) with other three organizations that had similar interests and advocated union with Egypt. Meanwhile, the neo-Mahdist's founded the independentist Umma Party in 1945, which was strongly linked to the British interests of curbing Egyptian influence in Sudan.[148] Woodward concludes that "That rivalry of Islamic movements, which also incited the alienation of southern politicians, was to be at the heart of party politics during the periods of liberal democracy in post-independence Sudan".[149]

Faced with internal and external pressure towards decolonization, the British agreed to study the prospects of more important role of locals in the administration. This led to the Sudan Administrative Conference (SAC) in 1946, which laid the basis for the establishment of the national parliament. In 1948 Legislative Assembly[150] was founded, along social composition that mirrored the ACNS, with individuals from various sections of the northern economic and intellectual elite. These individuals, backed by the powerful Sufi movements, formed political parties and monopolized national politics. According to Niblock,

> This shows how economic prominence and social status served to gain political influence. In the first parliament . . . some 70-75 per cent of the members of the House of Representatives came from one of these four groupings, and between 75 per cent and 85 per cent of the members of the Senate.[151]

As a result, the social actors that came to dominate Sudanese political processes were overwhelmingly Arabized Muslims from the central riverine communities, with socio-economically prominent backgrounds. The unifying interest among these individuals was to extend the political hegemony of the northern political elite to the peripheries and particularly southern Sudan.[152]

134

Reversal of the Southern Policy

In the course of the 1940s, the Condominium administration revised and reversed the Southern Policy. Both external and internal factors contributed to the decision.[153] The external determinants were mainly linked to the post-World War II (WWII) international environment that affected regional dynamics, as the world order was in the process of succumbing into the Cold War. Both the United States (U.S) and the Soviet Union (U.S.S.R.) were critical of European imperialism and eager to impose their political and ideological hegemony, permitting many nationalist movements in Africa to gain strength.[154] In this context Britain found itself torn by tensions within its imperial discourse.[155] It negotiated with Egypt on post-WWII arrangements for the Condominium, while facing increasing financial burden due to the colonies and pressure to undertake policy changes due to growing anti-colonial momentum propelled by the Middle East bloc in the United Nations (U.N.).[156]

Thus, Britain became gradually inclined to decolonize Sudan. Meanwhile, after WWII, Egypt's growing influence had converted it into a major regional actor. Egypt sought increasing power by promoting the "Unity of the Nile Valley" and the re-incorporation of southern provinces to ensure sufficient Nile water for its own use.[157] This became troubling to the British who hoped to avoid losing Egypt's support. Finally, faced with Egypt's and the Sudanese nationalist's demands for the re-annexation of southern Sudan, the British justified the reunification by portraying the southern provinces as unviable for independence.[158]

At the same time, with the lead of Civil Secretary James Robertson, the Condominium administration sought to delay the process of decolonization. This was aimed at curbing Egypt's regional power by allowing the local elites to decide their future relationship with Egypt. An internationally supervised plebiscite was envisioned despite Egyptian and U.S. pressure; the U.S. being interested in securing northeastern Africa through extension of Egypt's sovereignty.[159] Meanwhile, the British felt obliged to create national political institutions to prepare Sudan for self-governance. Such concessions were aimed at appeasing external powers demanding decolonization, as well as the neo-Mahdists who had developed a wide following in parts of northern Sudan.

The SAC established a sub-committee on central government and on local administration. The central government sub-committee was monopolized by members of the riverine Arabized Muslim elite and had minority British participation. It made the status of southern Sudan a major political issue because the British sought to appeal to Egypt and the U.S. (maintaining Sudan as one), and due to the eagerness of the northern nationalists to reincorporate southern provinces to northern Sudan. A SAC delegation visited southern provinces to explore ways for closer association of locals with the central administration.[160] After the tour, the sub-committee recommended that the southern provinces should be annexed and ruled under one government of Sudan, reflecting the agenda of the Arabized political elite seeking to re-annex the southern provinces.[161] Consequently, it wrote a report that called for the founding of the Legislative Assembly and a conference to discuss the future status of the southern provinces. The sub-committee demanded abolition of the Permit to Trade Order that would enable the northerners to resume their economic activities in the area, and advocated the unification of the educational system between the regions and the adoption of Arabic teaching in all schools in southern provinces.[162] This reflected the earlier demands of the GC, and was based on the interests of the reduced but increasingly powerful sectors of the Arabized Muslim elite that sought to extend its political hegemony to the southern provinces by converting them into a territorially integral, but politically and economically marginalized, part of the post-colonial Sudanese polity. The SAC was the first formal forum to discuss the future of the southern provinces without southern participation.[163] This led to a pattern of marginalization of the southern elite in national politics and in the decisions concerning the southern provinces.

The Emergence and Marginalization of "Southern" Elite

Experiencing international and regional pressure, also channeled through the imperial policy, the Condominium government adhered to the collective demands of the Arabized nationalist elite. It began to justify the reversal of the Southern Policy. In May 1946, briefly after assuming the position of Civil Secretary, Robertson claimed that the southern provinces were unable to represent themselves in the SAC and needed time, or special arrangements, to prevent from becoming helpless prey to the educated Arabized elite in the new political institutions.[164] However, on 16 December 1946, the Condominium administration's position differed drastically in the Memorandum on Southern Policy which stated that

> The policy of the Sudan Government regarding the Southern Sudan is to act upon the facts that the peoples of the Southern Sudan are distinctively African and Negroid, but that geography and economics combine (so far as can be foreseen at the present time) to render them inextricably bound for future development to the middle-eastern and arabicized Northern Sudan: and therefore to ensure that they shall, by educational and economic development, be equipped to stand up for themselves in the future as socially

136

and economically the equals of their partners of the Northern Sudan in the Sudan of the future.[165]

This laid the basis for the abolition of the Southern Policy and determined the future of southern provinces as part of northern Sudan.[166] Although Robertson stated that rapid development of the southern provinces was one policy objective, the less than ten years of dedicated to it before Sudan's eventual independence in 1956 was simply inadequate.[167] It is questionable whether even Robertson himself believed in the possibility of southern provinces catching up, while Sudan's self-rule was nearer than the British initially expected.

The government also felt obliged to improve education in the southern provinces, and harmonize it according to the Arabized elite's demands. This is why it assumed the main responsibility of education from the missionary schools.[168] The new policy implemented from 1946 was to prepare the local youth for the unification of Sudan by establishing a secondary school, providing higher education at the Gordon Memorial College for talented students from the southern provinces, and introducing Arabic as a subject at the intermediate school level.[169] While this is often viewed as proof of British goodwill towards the southern provinces, it can be considered as rather superficial move since education remained confined to narrow sections of the population.[170] After prohibiting Arabic for years and suddenly introducing it in the few intermediate schools to serve millions of southerners was neither enough to significantly boost the collective Arabic skills nor to drastically improve the overall educational level in the southern provinces.

Hence, largely due to the short time period, the economic development and education policies seeking to make southern Sudan stand on its own largely failed. However, the Condominium policies did create an embryonic core of an educated class keen on defending southern regional interests. This local mission/government school educated intelligentsia identified itself not only through its diverse ethnic affiliations, but growingly as "southern" in contrast to what was perceived as the Arab and Muslim "North".[171] Thus, education had produced new elite capable of overlooking ethnic distinctions and seeking to promote southern regional identity. Yet this nucleus was weak, easily outmaneuvered by the northern elite, and divided in terms of political goals. Individual or "tribal" interests often prevented collective stance.

After the SAC decision initiated the process of re-annexation of southern provinces to northern Sudan, the British military administrators ("Bog Barons") in southern Sudan voiced their joint concern. They submitted a letter accepting the general conclusions of the SAC, but denounced the "selling-out" of the southern provinces to the northern "Arab" elite and com-

plained that the southerners had not been heard on the issue.[172] Largely due
to their joint complaint, Robertson decided to organize a conference in June
1947 in Juba to hear concerns of southern chiefs and civil servants on the
issue. However, although it was later suggested that the annexation should
take place under safeguards and a period of trusteeship, the decision to unify the two parts of the colony had already been taken. The conference in
Juba was convoked merely to justify that hand-picked representatives of the
southern elite agreed to the transition already in process.[173]

Meanwhile, a handful of mission-educated southerners had been employed in the colonial service as assistants and junior officials. Aware of receiving less pay than their "Arab" counterparts, on 25 March 1943 they had
staged a strike in the Malakal Hospital demanding equal wages. According
to Collins, this had been initiated by an

> ... inferiority complex, which their northern fellow workers took every
> opportunity to reinforce and which seemed confirmed by the government
> paying them less ... [due to which] ... the southerners felt a bitter sense
> of injustice ... But the tumergi strike was a visible symbol, of a practical
> and personal nature, of the differences between north and south upon which
> discontent of the educated southerners could focus on a regional, and there-
> fore a specifically southern issue.[174]

There was a growing sentiment among the southerners that their rights had
been denied, and because of being perceived as socially inferior not being
credited properly for their work. Thus, arguably the unequal treatment, in
which racist perceptions drawing from the legacy of slavery were inherent,
stimulated southern sentiments of difference and regionalism in a particular
way that differed from other areas of the colony's marginalized periphery.

The mobilization for equal pay led to the founding of the Southern Sudan Welfare Association (SSWA).[175] It was the first southern professional
organization, formed in November 1946, with headquarters in Juba and
branches established in the following years in Wau, Malakal, Kapoeta, Torit, Yei, Amadi, Maridi, and Yambio. Akol credits the SSWA for raising the
wage issue, and notes that despite not being primarily a political organization it provided experience to some prominent southern politicians such
as Stanislaus Paysama and Paul Logale.[176] These members of the emerging
southern political elite had been previously shaped by mission education,
which contributed to their overall view of the "Arab" and the "southerner"
that were later confirmed by the Condominium policies and their interaction
with the northern elite. Thus, these individuals projected a view of a "southern region" to which the memory of slavery and 19th century atrocities was
instrumental when in search for unified resistance to "Arab" oppression. Yet,

at the same time, general political awareness in "the South" hardly existed.

Subsequently, the British decided to hear southerners on the re-annexation issue. Consequently, a conference was convened in Juba, but in a situation in which the Condominium administration had already decided upon the future annexation of the southern provinces. Indeed, during the opening day of the conference the British insisted that the purpose of the conference was to explore the most adequate manner in which the southern region would be incorporated to the future Sudan.[177] Since there were no provincial councils to appoint representatives for the southern provinces, the British had hand-picked prominent southerners to assess their capacity to represent southern Sudan.[178]

By the time the Juba Conference took place, the embryonic southern intelligentsia had become aware of the prevailing economic imbalances and inequality between northern and southern Sudan. This served to advance the sentiments of injustice and relative deprivation between the two heterogeneous territories, increasingly viewed as "regional" entities. It is important to note, however, that neither the narrowly based Arabized Muslim elite, nor the emerging southern mission-educated leadership and local chiefs,[179] could claim to fully represent the diverse and numerous ethnic groups of their respective imagined "regions". While in "the North" the exclusive north-central riverine elite had gained strength and developed a relatively coherent approach towards the non-Arabized peripheral regions (which it found to contrast its hegemonic goals), in the "South" the contemporary elite emerged later and faced external forces which undermined its strength from the 1940s onwards. This situation emerged in part due to the northern nationalist elite's efforts to divide the ranks of the southern intelligentsia that was generally positioned against its exclusive hegemony. It also sought to undermine a common "southern cause" that it saw as a challenge to its dominant position founded upon the constructed view of "Arab" superiority and Islam.

The two-day Juba Conference took place on 12-13 June 1947. Attending it were British administrators, including civil secretary and assistant civil secretary, governors of the southern provinces, and director of establishment, together with six prominent members of the northern elite, and seven chiefs and ten junior officials representing "the South".[180] Judge Mohamed Shingiti led the northern delegation, while Clement Mboro, who later became a prominent politician, headed the less educated southern representation that had hardly any political experience.[181] Diverging positions between the two delegations characterized the first day of the conference proceedings. While the delegation of "the North" sought southerners' acceptance to participate in the future Legislative Assembly with minority representation, the southern representatives "expressed deep fears of the North", "rejected the idea of closer association", and insisted that "development should be accelerated" and that "the South should have its own Advisory Council like the North before joining the proposed Legislative Assembly".[182] For instance, Chief Lolik Lado expressed reservations towards northerners by stating that "The ancestors of the Northern Sudanese were not peace-loving and domesticated like cows. The younger generations claim that they mean no harm but time will show what they will in fact do".[183] Moreover, Chief Buth Diu, who later became a prominent politician, voiced the general suspicion among the representatives of the southern provinces by stating that "Northerners claim to have no desire to dominate the South, but this . . . [is] not enough and there . . . [has] to be safeguards".[184] The mistrust and fear of northern "Arab" intentions were apparent.[185]

However, the second day brought sudden reversal to the position of the southern representatives. They no longer expressed the views they had vigorously defended the day before, and accepted the position of the northern delegation that southern members would participate in the Legislative Assembly as part of the region's re-annexation in northern Sudan. Yet, this abrupt and radical change of position came unexpected even to the British who suspected foul play from the side of the northerners.[186] Although some consider that part of this sudden change of opinion could be attributed to the southern inexperience, some southern intellectuals and politicians have later alleged that their delegates were bribed, threatened, and blackmailed by the northern representatives the night between the sessions, and tricked into believing that the unity was not constitutional but merely administrative.[187] Indeed, there is evidence that Shingiti had talked to Mboro until late to try to reverse the southern position, which allegedly led to the latter to change his mind and state the next day that it was in the best interest of the southerners to join the Legislative Assembly.[188] James Tambura, one of the southern delegates, claimed that "Judge Shingeiti had said that if they did not participate, they would have no say in the future Government of the Sudan".[189] Yet despite these claims, it is possible that some southern delegates were inclined to adhere to the northern position.[190] Although the reasons for the southerners' change of heart are obscure, what is clear is that their position expressed during the first day of proceedings was eventually not respected.

The Juba Conference was used to accelerate the process of reunification. Despite the southern delegates' suspicions, the British administrators used the proceedings to justify the re-annexation of southern provinces by arguing that it was the wish of southerners articulated through their delegates. At least 13 representatives elected by provincial councils were to represent "the

South" in the future parliament, while education policy would be unified and trade and communications between the two "regions" would ensue.[191] However, it was also the opinion of the British administrators to grant safeguards until the southerners could consider themselves socially and economically equal to the northerners. This was enough to keep those British administrators and southerners who had been against the reunification at bay, although the authorities knew that it would be difficult to convince the northern nationalist elite about such measures.[192] Consequently, the barriers between northern and southern Sudan imposed by the Southern Policy were eradicated by the end of 1947.

Finally, the Juba Conference became one of the defining events in the construction of "southern" historical narrative. In this way, it left a legacy of bitterness among southern communities while reinforcing the northern elite's view of southern inferiority.[193] Although the unity of Sudan had been decided already before the conference, it was cemented in the southern historical narrative and criticized for persuasion and bribery. This view was often complemented by the legacy of slavery and the perceived northern attempt to extend social hierarchy perpetuated by the perception of "Arab" superiority and local inferiority in "the South". The British and the Egyptians further fostered perceptions of southern lack of sophistication in the northern provinces, affecting North-South inter-group relationships.

Such exclusionary views on ethnic, cultural, and "regional" identity prevailed because their promotion was in the interest of power elites seeking to construct "regional" identity entities. Projecting northern superiority and southern inferiority created animosity and grievances that were useful for political mobilization and asserting claims that either supported the maintenance of a hegemonic position (northern elite) or served demands for access to power and resources (southern elite) at the national level. The gross categorization between "the North" and "the South" also projected an image of large, contradicting, relatively unitary, regional political, economic, and social entities, which contrasted the reality of highly heterogeneous northern and southern populations and territories. Thus, the institutionalized and socially (historically) derived political and economic marginalization, coupled with the regional/local elites' instrumentalization of exclusionary identity politics drawn along the North-South or center-periphery divide, and expressed through race, culture, language, and religion, laid the structural and systemic base for the chronic political instability and insurgencies in post-colonial Sudan.

Conclusion

The Anglo-Egyptian Condominium continued the pattern of external dom-ination in Sudan. It cemented exclusive governance seeking to minimize costs and maximize economic extraction. Generally based on "divide and rule" logic through "tribalism", manipulating, reinventing, strengthening, and politicizing ethnic identities, the colonial rulers sought to play local groups against each other and to use heads of the most established social groupings in the north-central Sudan for political control. This helped to consolidate those elites collaborating with the regime, while poverty and dependency were created in the peripheries as a control mechanism. By in-tegrating southern provinces in the colonial polity, at the same time isolating them and encouraging distinct political, economic, and social trajectory as opposed to the northern provinces, the colonial state and its policies con-tributed in the establishment of a marginalizing political culture among the governing elites. A state system emerged which included the local elites' cre-ation of "imagined regions", "the North" and "the South", forging political, economic, social, and cultural cleavages that would later affect the process of decolonization.

Meanwhile, by the 1940s, political and economic marginalization of southern provinces and its elites had become increasingly apparent relative to the favoring of the more central northern riverine and cotton producing ar-eas. Such imbalances were permanent part of the governance structures and ruling methods of the colonial state, and remained so after the reunification of Sudan.

The Arabized power elites in the northern provinces forged an illusion of common "northern" identity based on Arab culture and Islam which project-ed the area as one politico-cultural entity. In contrast, the emerging mission-ary-educated sectors of southern elites (re)constructed differences against "the North" based on their own identities, interests, and visions for the "South". Such dynamics, containing the legacy of slavery and subjugation, led to the making of the idea of the "northern region" and its utmost contrary image, the "southern region", both portrayed as relatively homogeneous and contrasting their relative "other".[194] It was the northern Sudanese regime col-laborators who reached higher-level positions in the colonial administration, inherited the state leadership, and later sought to consolidate their power by maintaining colonial type governance based on marginalization that was justified by race and culture (language and religion).

Finally, the Condominium government reversed the Southern Policy by reincorporating southern provinces into northern Sudan as a subservient pe-riphery. As will be shown in the next chapter, this was undertaken while obstructing effective political representation of "the South" at the national level and maintaining poverty and dependence by hindering development in southern Sudan. This propelled sentiments of injustice and relative deprivation, further fed by feelings of mistrust and fear, which became significant in insurgency formation in southern Sudan in the process of decolonization.

Endnotes

1   A joint Anglo-French commission oversaw Egyptian finances during the country's bankruptcy. Many Egyptians perceived this as foreign overrule, which inspired nationalist sentiments. See e.g. Izzedin (1981: 2).
2   See Nicoll (2004).
3   Cecil Rhodes, who sought to build a "Cape to Cairo" railroad, was the main architect of this plan.
4   Collins (1962: 109-77).
5   Analyzing the Fashoda incident is beyond the scope of this book. However, there are many illuminating accounts and reports related to the conquest of the *Mahdiyyah* and the "Fashoda incident". See e.g. Abdel Rahim (1969), Bates (1984), Bueno de Mesquita and Lalman (1992), Daly (1986), Henze (1991), Holt (1958), New York Times (1899), Ruay (1994), Tignor (1987), Vandervort (1998), Warburg (2003), and Weiss (1999).
6   After Leodpold II's death, Lado Enclave, which extended from Kiro (today's Central Equatoria) to the shores of Lake Albert, was returned to Britain in 1910. Southern part of it was annexed to British Uganda in 1912.
7   In 1902, the remaining Mahdist military in the southern frontier gave way to Anglo-Egyptian domination. It retreated towards Darfur and its influence withered away. See e.g. Collins (1962: 172-3, 176-7).
8   Abdel Rahim (1969: 32).
9   Daly (1986: 11).
10 Abdel Rahim (1969: 30-1).
11 O'Ballance (1977: 25).
12 Kebbede (1999: 12).
13 Ruay (1994: 34).
14 Johnson (2003: 9-10).
15 Tignor (1987: 188).
16 Tignor (1987: 196-7) and Daly (1991: 396).
17 El Zain (1996: 525).
18 Daly (1991: 395-6, 398).
19 According to Daly (1986: 71), this had been based on a leadership of a commander, *mudir*, and divided into three areas and eleven districts, as it had been during the *Turkiyyah*. A British-trained Egyptian military *mamur* was in charge of each administrative unit.
20 Abdel Rahim (1969: 49) and Daly (1986: 72).
21 Abdel Rahim (1969: 49-51).

22   Ake (2000: 35).
23   Mazrui (1975).
24   Governor-General was a British officer and held the supreme authority in the territory that he administered. The Governor-General officially served Egypt, but was largely independent, and was appointed by the Egyptian court with British recommendation. He could neither be appointed nor dismissed without British approval. See e.g. Abdel Rahim (1969: 33).
25   Abdel Rahim (1969: 47) notes that in 1910 a practice of bringing together experts to make decisions on technical issues was institutionalized in the Governor-General's Council. The Council consisted of an inspector general, civil, financial, and legal secretaries, and 2-4 other British officials appointed by the Governor-General. The Council was a colonial government responsible for dictating ordinances, laws, regulations, and budget issues, and implementing policies to maximize benefits and minimize costs of the administration of the colony. The Governor-General had veto power over the Council, which took decisions on the majority basis.
26   Tignor (1987: 188).
27   Meredith (2005: 5) and Collins (2008: 35, 38).
28   The term "neo-Mahdist" refers to the Mahdist movement after the *Mahdiyyah* under leadership of Sayyid Abd al-Rahman al-Mahdi. It is used here henceforth to refer to the Mahdist movement since the Anglo-Egyptian conquest.
29   Sconyers (1978: 38) and Tignor (1987: 197).
30   Daly (1986: 38-9, 61).
31   Daly (1986: 428).
32   Niblock (1987: 15).
33   Niblock (1987: 49).
34   See e.g. Niblock (1987: 49-50) and Daly (1986: 234).
35   This owes to major Sufi orders having played an important role in pre-Condominium politics, having strong centralized organizations, and commanding large number of followers. The British were eager to divert their attention from any possible political and religious agitation against the regime by favoring them with privileged treatment and economic concessions.
36   Tignor (1987: 197).
37   For instance, the British initially endorsed the economic standing of the head of the *Khatmiyyah*, Sayyid Ali al-Mirghani, who received substantial allowances including land in the Red Sea area and elsewhere in the northern provinces to develop agriculture. The Condominium government also gave land to the leader of the Mahdist movement, Sayyid Abd al-Rahman al-Mahdi, and converted a substantial loan made to him in 1926 into a gift. See e.g. Beshir (1974: 141) and Niblock (1987: 52).
38   Beshir (1974: 141).
39   Tignor (1987: 197).
40   Niblock (1987: 53-4).
41   Sharkey (2003) calls those southerners who have to an extent been assimilated to "northern" social order as "detribalized Blacks".

42 Sharkey (2003: 78-80).
43 Johnson (1991) and Sharkey (2003: 81).
44 Niblock (1987: 53).
45 Such were, for instance, Condomichalos & Co., George Haggar Company, and M. D. Bittar family company.
46 Tignor (1987: 195-6). According to Niblock (1987: 55-7), while British and Greek companies dominated the import trade, the *jallaba* largely organized the exportation of gum arabic, livestock, and oilseeds.
47 Niblock (1987: 146).
48 Daly (1986: 217-8).
49 Niblock (1987: 56-9). (Niblock (1987: 58-9) and Tignor (1987: 195-6) further assert that many gained economic power by expanding their commercial networks, engaging in food processing, or petty manufacturing, such as flour milling, printing, or production of consumer goods such as soaps, soft drinks, and sweets.
50 This took place after a Condominium government committee, instituted in 1946, made a plan in 1948 to Sudanize slightly over 62% of the positions held by foreign administrators within 14 years. See e.g. Abdel Rahim (1969: 158). In the end, this was undertaken much faster, which became highly contentious particularly in the case of southern Sudan.
51 They acquired " . . . urban real estate, and a small number were investing in mechanised dry farming, pump schemes and contracting businesses" (Niblock, 1987: 60).
52 Spaulding (1982).
53 Daly (1986: 235-9).
54 Daly (1986: 238).
55 This policy was also applied to the Nuba peoples of the Nuba Mountains area in Southern Kordofan.
56 Ruay (1994: 42).
57 O'Fahey (2002: 56).
58 Sharkey (2003: 20-1).
59 van Dijk (1993: 55).
60 Eriksen (1993: 88) argues that "Contemporary ethnicity, or 'tribalism', is not . . . relic in the past but a product of modernization processes leading up to the present".
61 Sharkey (2003: 19).
62 Spaulding (1988).
63 Daly (1986: 232-239) and Jok (2001: 6).
64 Daly (1986: 444-5) and Jok (2001: 95).
65 Daly (1986: 442-5).
66 O'Fahey (2002: 56).
67 Daly (1986: 239) and Sharkey (2003: 18).
68 Jok (2001: 77).
69 Eriksen (1993: 94), Jok (2001: 77), and Johnson (2006: 95).

70 Sharkey (2003: 21, 23, 24).
71 See Munene (2001).
72 According to Abdel Rahim (1969: 58), " . . . resentment of the formal declaration of their country as a British protectorate, the apparent success of the Arab Revolt of 1916, and President Wilson's fourteen points and doctrine of self-determination greatly stimulated the already-growing sentiment of nationalism in Egypt".
73 Sidahmed and Sidahmed (2005: 24) and Collins (2008: 37).
74 These first nationalist protests in 1920-4 were led by politically active Arabized Muslims of the Sudanese Union Society, which consisted of junior government officials, army staff, merchants, workers, clerks, and judges.
75 Abdel Rahim (1969: 65) and Daly (1986: 292-6).
76 In May 1923, Ali Abd al-Latif (of Dinka origin) and Obeid Haq al-Amin founded the WFL upon al-Latif's release from prison. He had been jailed because of writing a controversial article calling for Sudanese self-determination. The WFL received wide support in the northern provinces and became the earliest manifestation of contemporary nationalism in Sudan. See e.g. Abu Hasabu (1985: 45-6), Deng (1995a: 104-5), and Sidahmed and Sidahmed (2005: 24).
77 Abdel Rahim (1969: 67), El Zain (1987: 17-23, 1996: 525), and Daly (1991: 413).
78 The new duties included tax assessment, and road, well, and other water storage facility maintenance.
79 Abdel Rahim (1969: 68-70), Ruay (1994: 40-1), and El Zain (1996: 526).
80 El Zain (1996: 525, 526).
81 At the local level, "tribalism" became paramount political system which has endured efforts of implementation of new forms of local government that have chronically lacked sufficient economic basis and incentives to co-opt prominent local actors. Instead, efforts to formalize local administration have often stimulated "tribal" opposition and further empowered "tribalist" competition. See e.g. El Zain (1996: 523, 526). This contestation was over public positions through which wealth could be acquired and resources channeled to constituencies.
82 Abdel Rahim (1969: 84-5, 120-1).
83 Sidahmed and Sidahmed (2005: 25).
84 Abu Hasabu (1985: 109) and Ruay (1994: 49).
85 Ruay (1994: 49).
86 Abu Hasabu (1985: 109), and Sidahmed and Sidahmed (2005: 26).
87 According to Alier (1990: 13-4) two types of leaders were significant in the resistance: "One of these was the religious man who gained his following through the administration of his spiritual powers to members of the community in need. He was either prophet or in possession of supernatural powers . . . " and "The second category of leaders of resistance gained community respect . . . through . . . acts of bravery and courage . . . settlement of disputes in the community and improvement in its welfare and yet others through inheritance from ancestors".

88 Mawut (1983: 21-39) and Meredith (2005: 4).

89 Hutchinson (1996: 115).

90 Mawut (1983: 46).

91 Ruay (1994: 34).

92 Gray (1961: 203).

93 Johnson (2003: 8).

94 Sidahmed and Sidahmed (2005: 23).

95 Niblock (1987: 143) and Kebbede (1999: 12).

96 Warburg (2003: 140).

97 The imbalance of the economic development was of such magnitude that by 1955-6 Khartoum, Northern, and Kassala provinces received 60%, the three southern provinces, Bahr al-Ghazal, Equatoria, and Upper Nile, 5%, and the west, Kordofan and Darfur, 12%, of the overall private, governmental, and public corporation investment. See e.g. Harvie and Kleve (1959: 88). According to Niblock (1987: 144), this was demographically disproportionate because at that the time the combined population of Khartoum, Northern, and Kassala provinces (2,319,000) was smaller than that of the southern provinces (2,783,000) and Kordofan and Darfur (3,091,000).

98 Dhal (2004: 15).

99 For instance incomes varied greatly between provinces. While the three northern provinces and the Blue Nile summed 33 and 42 Sudanese Pounds (S£) per capita by 1955-6, respectively, the three southern provinces produced only S£14 (Harvie and Kleve, 1959: 80).

100 Markakis (1998: 111) and Jok (2007: 81-2).

101 Niblock (1987: 143-7) and Markakis (1998: 108).

102 Niblock (1987: 147).

103 For instance, Niblock (1987: 146) asserts that regional movements surfaced during the late colonial period among those groups excluded from the economic benefits generated during the Condominium. These included e.g. the Fur in Darfur, the Nuba of southern Kordofan, the Beja around Kassala, and Equatorians in southern Sudan.

104 This was a product of Frederick Lugard's views of how to conduct colonization, outlined in his *The Dual Mandate in British Tropical Africa* (1922).

105 Ruay (1994: 38).

106 Abdel Rahim (1969: 75).

107 Abdel Rahim (1969: 75-6), Daly (1986: 413, 1993: 8), and Niblock (1987: 153-4).

108 Alier (1990: 17-8).

109 Abdel Rahim (1969: 73-5, 79). Kitchener's memorandum from 1892 describes the British fear for Arabization and Islamicization of Africa, claiming that "Unless the Christian powers held their own in Africa, the Mohammedan Arabs will I believe step in and in the center of the continent will form a base from which they will be able to drive back all civilizing influences to the coast, and

the country will then be given up to slavery and misrule as is the case in the Sudan at present" (quoted in Collins, 1971: 17).

110 Abdel Rahim (1969: 71, 75-83), Sconyers (1978: 58), Woodward (1995: 94), and Keen (2001: 223).

111 Sconyers (1978: 58) and Niblock (1987: 153).

112 Niblock (1987: 157).

113 Abdel Rahim (1969: 73).

114 Sharkey (2003: 81) and Rolandsen (2005: 24).

115 Markakis (1998: 107).

116 However this was not altogether coherent, as for instance in 1932 a dispute between the British and Egyptians over the construction of a mosque for the *jallaba* who remained in Juba resulted in the British allowing it to take place.

117 Niblock (1987: 153).

118 Beshir (1968: 38) and Sarkesian (1973: 6).

119 It became prestigious particularly to those who embraced warrior tradition, but also due to social respect related to having a uniform, a gun, and personal income.

120 de Chand (2000: 15).

121 Mawut (1983: 46).

122 Markakis (1998: 108).

123 Markakis (1998: 108).

124 Reproduced in Sconyers (1978: 268-72).

125 Quoted in Said (1965: 30).

126 Abdel Rahim (1969: 244-9) and Albino (1970: 19).

127 Daly (1986: 232-9) and Ruay (1994: 37), and Jok (2001: 90-5).

128 These often mention a rift between "Christian and Animist South" and "Arab and Islamic North".

129 Niblock (1987: 150-1).

130 Abdel Rahim (1969: 72).

131 Beshir (1968: 31), Abdel Rahim (1969: 72), and Ruay (1994: 43-4).

132 For instance, according to Abdel Rahim (1969: 83) and Niblock (1987: 152), by 1926 the entire southern region summed 31 elementary, two intermediate, and one trade school, and by 1930 one more elementary and intermediate school. The first government school opened in Atar in the late 1940s. Meanwhile, e.g. the Gordon Memorial College in Khartoum had been active since 1902.

133 Niblock (1987: 152).

134 Beshir (1968: 44).

135 Daly (1993: 8) and Ruay (1994: 44).

136 Niblock (1987: 152) and Warburg (2003: 138).

137 See Niblock (1987: 152), Daly (1993: 8), and Ruay (1994: 45).

138 Abdel Rahim (1969: 78, 73) and Niblock (1987: 153, 155).

139 Sarkesian (1973: 7).

140 Ruay (1994: 37).

141 Sanderson (1985: 106-9) and Daly (1991: 181-2).

142 Markakis (1998: 108).

143 As Heraclides (1987: 217) has put it, the British forced " . . . the Southerners to develop at their own pace, along their own lines, under the administration of the legendary British 'Bog Barons', who ruled the South in splendid isolation, with a twist of paternalism coupled with a certain admiration for the defiant tribesmen". This admiration of the southerners owed partly to the British administrators' glorification of the southern resistance to the 19th century Arabic and Islamic encroachment.

144 Sanderson (1985: 106-17).

145 Yohannes (1997: 262) and Warburg (2000: 75-6).

146 Burr and Collins (1999: 55).

147 The advisory council consisted of Governor-General, who acted as its president, the civil, financial, and legal secretary, along with 18 members from provincial councils in the northern provinces. Eight were appointed by the Governor-General and two by the chamber of commerce. See e.g. Niblock (1987: 159).

148 Sidahmed and Sidahmed (2005: 26). Describing the nationalist movement and its effect Woodward (1997: 97) notes that " . . . the postwar [WWII] movement was to be not united secular movement, but one in which the Western-educated nationalist politicians of northern Sudan were mainly members of the neo-Mahdist Ummah Party of the *Khatmiyyah*-backed Unionists, later to become the National Unionist Party (so-called because of their links with Egypt, i.e., against Britain *and* the Ummah Party)". Allegedly, the Umma was to an extent constructed, and largely backed, by the British to counter the *Khatmiyyah* associated with Egypt.

149 Woodward (1997: 97).

150 The terms Legislative Assembly, Constituent Assembly, and Parliament found in the literature all refer to the Sudanese national parliament.

151 Niblock (1987: 60-1).

152 Ruay (1994: 49).

153 A combination of international and regional (f)actors was paramount to the political concessions to nationalists, including international pressure for decolonization involving the anti-colonial block in the U.N., the American-Soviet Cold War competition, self-determination principle based on the 1941 Atlantic Charter, and doubts about the viability of colonies.

154 Campos Serrano (2000: 20, 28).

155 According to Cooper and Stoler (1997: IX), such tensions emerged "between the universalizing claims of European ideology and the particularistic nature of conquest and rule, the limitations posed on rulers by the reproduction of difference as much as by the heightened degree of exploitation and domination that colonization entailed".

156 Daly (1991: 234-7), Austen (1996), and Campos Serrano (2000: 28, 30).

157 Warburg (2000: 76-81).

158 Abdel Rahim (1969: 169), Alier (1990: 19), and Daly (1991: 236-8).

159 Alier (1990: 19), Daly (1991: 167, 235-6), and Hanes (1995: 134-6).

160 Daly (1991: 236) and Ruay (1994: 50).

161 Abdel Rahim (1969: 167).

162 Ruay (1994: 50), and Sidahmed and Sidahmed (2005: 26). In 1947 the Farouk School in Arabic was established in Juba, from which the brightest pupils went on to study in al-Azhar Islamic university in Cairo. This, and the abovementioned Juba mosque issue, indicates Egypt's influence in Sudan.

163 de Chand (2000: 16). Yet, including southerners would have been difficult because it required recognition of who could speak for "the South". This was more apparent in the case of "the North" where the educated Arabized central riverine nationalist elite was deemed as the legitimate representative of the general population.

164 Daly (1991: 236) and Ruay (1994: 50).

165 Reproduced in Sconyers (1978: 275).

166 Rogier (2005: 9).

167 Niblock (1987: 156) notes that this was undertaken by " . . . conditioning southerners to increased contacts with northerners, drawing the South into national political institutions, and making southern education compatible with the educational system established in the North". These policy measures coupled with the establishment of agricultural and industrial schemes paralleled the northern elite's agenda of assimilating the southern provinces. Cotton cultivation had already been introduced in the area between 1925 and 1930 for educational purposes to convert the "natives" into modern "economic men" who would desire imported consumer goods. In the late 1940s, however, the development efforts were stepped up. For instance, cotton production was stimulated in Maridi and Zande, while a ginnery, an oil mill processing cotton-seed, a soap factory manufacturing scheme, and sawmills were set up at Katire, Gilo, and Loka. See Ruay (1994: 48, 57) and Dhal (2004: 19). In the process, the Zande Scheme (Nzara Agro-Industrial complex) producing cotton and cloth, established in 1946 and managed through Equatoria Projects Board, became the most elaborate development project in the southern provinces. Later, in the early 1950s, other economic ventures such as Yirol sesame oil mill and an electric power unit using charcoal were built. See Dhal (2004: 19, 22). However, all this came few and late to boost southern development before independence.

168 Dhal (2004: 25-6) and Ruay (1994: 44).

169 Miner (2003).

170 According to Niblock (1987: 152-3), by 1948 there were only 45 boys' and 26 girls' elementary schools, and three intermediate schools, serving 6,600 and 549 pupils respectively, while in 1950 a secondary school was established in Rumbek.

171 This was largely because intermingling across "tribal" lines in district level schools had produced a common spirit that became gradually recognized as "southern".

172 Abdel Rahim (1969: 170) and Daly (1991: 237).

173 Alier (1990: 21), Daly (1991: 237-9), and Ruay (1994: 51).

174 Collins (1983: 41).

175 The SSWA leadership included Lino Tombe as President, Renato Ondzi Koma as Vice-President, Gordon Apec Ayom as Secretary-General, and Paul Logale as Treasurer.

176 Akol (2007: 41-2).

177 Ruay (1994: 51).

178 Abu Hasabu (1985: 146).

179 Although Simonse (1992: 138) has claimed that the network of chiefs in the southern provinces was the main legitimate interlocutor for the South, his single example of Chief Lomiluk from Tirangore falls short of representing the elites of vast and heterogeneous southern provinces.

180 Ruay (1994: 51).

181 Collins (1983: 289-90) and Baraja (2004).

182 Ruay (1994: 52).

183 RJC (1947: 12).

184 RJC (1947: 13).

185 Sarkesian (1973: 7).

186 Daly (1991: 240) and Ruay (1994: 52). The British had different interpretations of the sudden change of southern delegates' opinion. Some suspected the change of heart being "fear of losing improved terms of service", while others interpreted it as "pathetic defencelessness against plausible thugery [sic]" (quoted in Daly, 1991: 240).

187 Eprile (1974: 19) and Ruay (1994: 52-3).

188 Collins (1983: 290) and Daly (1991: 240).

189 Quoted in Collins (1983: 290).

190 Said (1965: 72) and Howell (1973: 164).

191 Abu Hasabu (1985: 146-7).

192 Daly (1991: 241-2).

193 Ruay (1994: 53) claims that it contributed to a view among the northern elite of southerners being easily corrupted and naive. This view draws from the attitude of Arab-Muslim superiority and the established view of social hierarchy.

194 However, both constructed "regions" are highly heterogeneous. As the time went on, various local elites began to struggle for prominence within each "region" in the context of national level elite competition.

CHAPTER V

DECOLONIZATION:
The Emergence of the First Insurgency in Sudan

Anyone who finds injustice in his country is sure to fight it.[1]

The process of decolonization provided the context for the first insurgency in southern Sudan. Although the situation in southern Sudan had become increasingly volatile, the authorities did little to diffuse tensions. This was particularly the case in Equatoria province, in which there were regionalist sentiments among the elite. Consequently, Equatoria became the hotbed of anti-northern sentiments fomented by some prominent individuals. As the political processes resulted in the marginalization of the emerging southern political forces, and subjected them to the "northern" governing elite's hegemony, the shattered hope of improved social, economic, and political position among the southern elite induced some to adopt radical measures. Marginalizing governance and institutional structures passing from the Anglo-Egyptian Condominium authorities to what was viewed by many in the southern leadership as "Arab" elite in control of the political scene, was perceived as subjecting the southern provinces and its peoples to perpetual domination, subjugation, inequality, and underdevelopment.

The international, regional, and local contexts had been conducive to the abandonment of the Southern Policy. However, the process of preparation of Sudan for self-rule was equally complex affair, involving local, regional, and international actors. The main players included the northern nationalists, Britain, Egypt, and indirectly the U.S. Yet, decolonization left the social hierarchy deriving from slavery, which determined political and economic power, largely intact, and paved way for its institutionalization in the political structures the post-colonial state inherited from the highly hierarchical colonial polity. In this situation, the fear of domination, as an anti-northern sentiment, became a powerful mobilizing force particularly in Equatoria.

Some local leaders, frustrated by the inability to capture individual and collective gains through the political process, capitalized upon it by staging and radicalizing demonstrations that led to disturbances and an army uprising. In the process, the government securitized the situation in the southern provinces, and answered violent incidents with repression. This led to growing local animosity that fueled armed opposition to the state.

Moreover, the continued exclusivity of the socio-culturally and racially[2] derived political and economic power became a key feature in developments after independence. Its concentration in one narrow group buttressed the dynamics of what had become a structurally and systemically marginalizing polity. This condition led to further institutionalization of exclusive governance practices, policies, and organization of administration, which propelled political instability between competing elites in and between the center and peripheries. Armed insurgencies in the peripheries, and coups and revolutions at the center, became the outmost manifestations of this intractable instability. In its origins, the periphery elites' perceptions and sentiments towards the exclusive rule of north-central riverine elites in the state's core have been crucial. For many southerners the exclusive power and oppression by the "Arab" regimes has been unacceptable, encouraging sentiments of political regionalism and secessionism, while the governing elites have sought to securitize the southern challenge to the state by representing it as a threat.

Decolonization of Sudan

Sudan's transition to self-rule formalized the political hegemony of the narrow northern intelligentsia over the marginalizing post-colonial state. In this both internal and external factors were important, but external actors were particularly prominent in influencing the internal politics of decolonization and contributing to the continuity of state marginalization that emanated from the colonial period. They promoted the dominance of the leading elite in "the North", which led to the exclusion of its counterpart in "the South" from an effective role in national politics.

Regional Political Developments and Decolonization

By the late 1940s, in the international context of emerging superpower competition between the U.S. and the U.S.S.R., Britain was under pressure to leave Sudan. As a result, Egypt had gained international leverage and increasingly challenged Britain's dominant position in the colony. Egypt sought to recover its position as a regional power and emphasized its historical links with Sudan, with Egyptian historians claiming Sudan as an integral part of

154

Egypt due to centuries' interaction, cultural affinity, and being connected by the Nile.[3] The waning of Britain's power in the Middle East and the rising pan-Arab nationalism, an ideology that the northern Sudanese nationalists readily adopted from Egypt, reinforced this sentiment.[4]

In addition, ensuring rights to the Nile waters became a crucial aspect of Egypt's foreign policy.[5] Egypt had sought to regain influence in the Anglo-Egyptian Condominium by reaffirming the 1899 co-dominium agreement through the 1936 Treaty of Alliance, which reversed the 1920s policy of de-Egyptianization of public service and military in Sudan.[6] However, in the longer term, this failed to satisfy Egyptian nationalists who sought to annex the Condominium and affirm control over the sources of the Nile, which led to intensifying competition with Britain that preferred pro-British Sudan not too closely associated with Egypt. This competition manifested itself through the support of the most powerful political-sectarian movements: Egypt intensified its backing of the nationalist movement by supporting the *Khatmiyyah* and the NUP for the "Unity of the Nile Valley", and the British endorsed the Umma that sought "Sudan for the Sudanese".[7]

Growing rift between the co-dominium allies ensued. On the one hand, any process aimed at self-governance and independence of Sudan went against Egypt's interests since it considered Anglo-Egyptian condominium as integral part of its territory and subject to its authority.[8] On the other hand, the British rejected such claims and argued that the local nationalists themselves should decide about their future. They threw their weight behind those nationalists who advocated independence, with the hope that the latter would establish a pro-British Sudan that would be a member of the Commonwealth and over which Britain could maintain political and economic influence.[9] Both co-dominium partners focused on the northern elite as the exclusive political and economic force in Sudan, and as the "natural" inheritor of power, while excluding the periphery elites from the process of decolonization.

By 1947, Britain had committed itself to the process of preparing the Condominium for self-rule. This attracted the attention of the U.S., which consequently became a major player forcing decolonization of Sudan. It pressured Britain to engage in an accelerated political process. However, this pressure pushed Britain to engage in a process of decolonization which did not allow southern Sudan time to develop a political elite that could match its counterpart in the northern provinces, or to reach an economic level that could alleviate the local mistrust, fears, and perceptions of injustice and relative deprivation. The U.S. was mainly concerned about maintaining regional stability, while it favored Egypt in order to fill the regional power vacuum left by the British decolonization, and to prevent Soviet Union from gaining ground in Middle East[10] and North Africa.[11]

In August 1947, after fruitless Anglo-Egyptian negotiations, Egypt presented its claim against Britain in the U.N. Although unsuccessful, Egypt remained adamant about its demands, while the British countered by accelerating the political process to strengthen the northern pro-independence nationalists position.[12] This situation, in which both powers supported their favoite factions of the Sudanese nationalist elite, continued until 23 July 1952 when the Egyptian monarchy came to an end in a coup of free officers loyal to the half-Sudanese General Muhammad Naguib.

The events in Egypt further accelerated the decolonization of Sudan.[13] Soon after taking power, the Egyptian military regime shifted its approach towards the British and Sudanese pro-independence nationalists' position. The new Egyptian leadership sought British exit, which would lessen its influence in the region and either allow Egypt to persuade Sudan for unity or secure Sudan's future membership in the Arab League in which Egypt was a major player.[14] Consequently, aware of the growing U.S. interest in the region to prevent Soviet incursion, the Egyptian regime separated the dispute over British troops in the Suez Canal from Sudan's future. Egypt moderated its position by indicating willingness to allow the Sudanese nationalists to decide between union with Egypt and independence, which contributed to the U.S. decision to support Cairo and decisively reversed the American endorsement of the British inclination to delay Sudan's self-rule because it diminished the prospect of armed sectarian conflict in the increasingly polarized northern Sudan.[15] The U.S. desired to extend its hegemony over the region, and sought alliance with Egypt to hinder leftist tendencies in Arab nationalism, considering both neo-Mahdists, influenced also by the nationalist currents in Libya and Eritrea, and the *Khatmiyyah*, as the local protagonists of decolonization in Sudan.[16] Concentrating on the two movements was enough for the U.S., which discarded the leading elites of Sudan's peripheries in its policy. This included the intelligentsia in southern Sudan, which had a strengthening regionalist sentiment.

Consequently, although the British had withstood Egypt's demands, the U.S. pressure for Sudan's self-determination turned the tables. In December 1950 the Sudanese Legislative Assembly passed a resolution requesting more extended powers, which the British were compelled to accept, leading to the founding of the Constitutional Amendment Commission (CAC) in March 1951 calling on the administration to prepare a Self-Government Statute that was promulgated in the following year.[17] Meanwhile the military coup in Egypt resulted in a shift in foreign policy orientation, with Cairo taking up an anti-imperialist, non-aligned, stand. The interests of Britain and the U.S. on Sudan's self-determination converged, and resulted in the acceleration of the decolonization process as well as the push towards Sudan's independence. Both sought to curb Egypt's regional influence.

At the same time, the Egyptian support became paramount to the Sudanese unionists. Its contribution facilitated the coming together of factions, and the formation of the NUP under the leadership of Ismail al-Azhari, as well as seeking to reverse the position of the independentist Umma Party.[18] This involvement reinforced the main northern religious movements' domination over national politics,[19] and it heightened competition between Egypt and Britain over Sudan's future.

On 10 January 1953 Egypt signed an agreement with representatives of northern Sudanese nationalists in Cairo. The treaty was manifold, but one of its stipulations demanded southern Sudan's unconditional annexation.[20] It called for the removal of southern safeguards from Sudan's self-government legislation, which reflected only the view of the northern nationalist elite because southern representatives were excluded from the Cairo negotiations on the grounds that they had no registered political organizations.[21] This decision, despite the existence of political formations representing the southern provinces, reinforced the precedent set in the 1947 Juba Conference of marginalizing the southern representation in national politics.

The U.S. supported the Cairo agreement. The same year, it put pressure on Britain to sign an agreement for political transition in Sudan within three years. However, the U.S. was also aware that by pushing Britain to leave Sudan, and attempting to keep it within Western sphere of influence through its own foreign policy, it would risk a rebellion in Sudan's southern provinces.[22] Yet, it appears that this was viewed as more acceptable in strategic calculations than the possibility of losing Egypt to the Soviet camp. At the same time, the British still hoped to hold on to southern Sudan for the time being, and two documents surfaced signed by prominent southerners which demanded either federal system for Sudan or the upholding of special powers of the Governor-General to protect the southern region from northern domination. The Americans considered these pleas initially as of British making, and only after the U.S. Liaison Officer in Sudan, Joseph Sweeney, submitted his report of a fact-finding mission in the southern provinces did the U.S. government realize that the threat of a secessionist uprising in southern Sudan was imminent.[23]

Still, the American assessment of the situation remained that accelerating the process towards Sudan's self-government would be the best option. This would keep the issue of southern Sudan away from regional politics and the Suez problem, and internalizing it would give the British no excuse to hold on to Sudan.[24] The U.S. policy therefore constituted yet another factor contributing to the marginalization of southern Sudan and its political movement. It subjected the southern provinces to the hegemony of the narrow governing elite in "the North", forcing southern representatives to participate, with minimal preparation and low numbers, in institutions of a state they largely felt was alien and whose policies they were unable to influence.[25]

Finally, on 12 February 1953, the co-dominium partners signed the Anglo-Egyptian agreement on self-government and self-determination of Sudan. According to the treaty, Sudan would become an independent state after a transitional period. By accepting the agreement, Britain achieved its strategic objective, but disregarded the southern safeguards that some Condominium officials had previously defended. According to Burr and Collins, the agreement " . . . opened the floodgates for unlimited and visible Egyptian influence in which the Sudanese army and particularly its intelligence services were the principal recipients".[26] It also contributed to the formalization of the northern Arabized Muslim elite's domination of politics in Sudan.

Formalization of the Arabized Muslim Elite Domination

The process of preparation of Sudan for self-government had been officially initiated in December 1948 through the formation of the parliament, the Legislative Assembly. The southern members of parliament[27] were the only non-Arabized Muslim elite representatives, but their small number and lack of support in north-central Sudan deprived them of influencing the national political trajectory dictated by the latter.[28] The southern safeguards, which the British had initially considered necessary, were the Legislative Assembly's first conflictive issue. While the northern majority was collectively against any concessions to the southern provinces, over which its members sought to extend Arab and Islamic influence, some colonial officials " . . . envisaged a short federal status for the South, which was to be expressed for the time being through the Governor-General's reserved powers . . . "[29] in the 1948 Legislative Assembly Ordinance. The attempt was to maintain political safeguards until southern leaders would become numerous and capable enough to be able to advance southern regional interests at the national level. Arguing that "Without protection the Southerners will not be able to develop along indigenous lines, will be overwhelmed and swamped by the North and deteriorate into a servile community hewing wood and drawing water", these British officials were faced by others who asserted that the southern territories should not enjoy any special status because that would " . . . only arouse old suspicion in the North and intensify a wound that is beginning to heal".[30] This mix of opinions undermined the British position, and under pressure from the U.S., which sought to secure the Suez Canal and Egypt as the gate to Middle East, the safeguards were left out of the Executive Council and the founding document for the Sudanese parliament, the Legislative Assembly Ordinance.[31] This decision was made also without the participation of southern representatives, who were considered to already have been sufficiently consulted in the 1947 Juba Conference.

However, the southern elite objected vigorously to the decision to drop the safeguards. Until then, it had been generally understood that the British administrators were committed to protect the southern provinces against extension of "Arab" domination. This assessment was valid to an extent that some administrators, particularly in the southern provinces, had argued for the safeguards. Further disappointment was brought by the news that southern demands for revision of the ordinance were rejected on the grounds that the population of the northern provinces opposed any special treatment of the southern territories.[32] Yet, although sections of the northern elite, the British administrators, and the U.S. were aware of the southern fears, none of them engaged in diffusing them by pushing for a special arrangement, significant inclusion of southern representation in the national political processes, or addressing the growing mistrust among southerners in other ways. This, in part, led to some within the southern elite to come to an understanding that the British bowed to the pressure from northern Sudan and Egypt, which reinforced apprehension and expectation of the resumption of "Arab" domination and subjugation. The fears and mistrust, in turn, heightened the preparedness for popular mobilization among sections of southern communities particularly in Equatoria which hosted many members of the mission-educated elite.

The early policies drafted by the Legislative Assembly came to reflect the collective objectives of the dominant part of the northern nationalist elite. One principal goal that united its intelligentsia beyond the immediate riverine core was the consolidation of its hegemony in northern Sudan, and extension of its domination to the southern provinces by encouraging commercial extraction and assimilation through Arab language, culture, and Islam. This included, according to Ruay, the deliberate continuation of the marginalization of the culturally and "racially" distinct southern political representatives in the Legislative Assembly by consistently voting down, and occasionally ridiculing, their initiatives.[33]

The Executive Council and the Legislative Assembly acquired full control of the national political process, while the power of Governor-General faded. However, the newly established political institutions faced difficulties regarding reunification of northern and southern provinces. Consequently, efforts at overcoming differences were undertaken by encouraging the movement and transfer of personnel between the regions, allowing the Governor-General to take specific decisions over the southern territories, and ensuring the minimal southern presence in the ministerial councils.[34] Arguably, however, the minority participation of southern representatives in the ministerial councils and Legislative Assembly set the precedent of the northern elite using such token participation in political institutions to seek an impression of effective incorporation of southerners in the national decision-making processes. Yet, the southern representatives had no power to affect policymaking.

In an attempt to extend its influence to the southern provinces, the governing elite decided to unify educational policy. The result was a complete reversal of the education system in the southern territories where English and Christianity had been encouraged, while the education system in northern areas remained unaltered. Already in 1948, the newly established education ministry had introduced Arabic as a subject in southern secondary schools since it had been argued that the government should " . . . take such immediate steps as it thinks necessary to ensure that Arabic is taught as a main subject in the schools of the Southern provinces as soon as possible".[35] This was a major step to impose Arabization and Islamicization in the southern Sudan,[36] as it sharply contrasted the colonial policy that had sought to fend off Arabic and Muslim cultural influences. The policy appears to have been implemented with little consideration of its possible consequences in southern Sudan.

Guidelines were put in place to secure the government objectives. These included mission administered schools having to contract proficient Arabic teachers by 1951, Arabic being encouraged as the spoken language in all schools, and school authorities themselves being instructed to learn Arabic.[37] Although the education minister attempted to explain that the purpose of the policy was to make the southern population proficient in Arabic so that it could work anywhere in the country, this did little to clear the existing fears of "Arab" domination in the southern provinces. The new education policy served to further politicize the already inflammable issues of language and culture, as sections of southern elite sought to actively resist what they perceived as the northern aspiration to assimilate and incorporate southerners as a subjugated servile community to buttress the northern "Arab" elite's hegemony.

160

1953 Parliamentary Election

The first parliamentary election in Condominium Sudan took place in November-December 1953. It was preceded by electoral campaign heavily influenced by Egypt,[38] which rallied to endorse the NUP, headed by Azhari. A product of unionist groupings established in 1952 with Egyptian support, and officially promoting the "Unity of the Nile Valley", the NUP gained advantage over its main rival, the Umma. This was in part due to Egypt's support, and because it was well-organized and drew from Arab nationalism and the rising anti-British sentiment. Meanwhile, the Umma had been weakened by the defection of some non-Mahdist communal leaders who formed Social Republican Party together with a small number of intellectuals.[39] This competition within the nationalist political movement, as well as the southern issue, served the British who still harbored hopes of slowing down Sudan's transition to independence.

During the electoral campaign, Egypt attempted to persuade southerners to vote for the NUP. According to Ruay, among their promises were, " . . . that Southerners would be able to occupy all the senior posts in the government that were occupied by the British in the South and that, in general, they would have a quarter of the jobs in the Sudan".[40] These pledges were backed up by a paper signed by Azhari, which outlined the party's election strategy and claimed that Sudanization of public administrations would give priority to southerners in the southern provinces, encouraging competent southerners to find employment at a high level in the central government, local government institutions, and development committees.[41] Overall, Cairo sought aggressively to sway local opinion towards favoring union with Egypt.

The 1953 election was largely decided upon between the neo-Mahdist Umma independentists supported by Britain, and the *Khatmiyyah*-influenced unionist NUP backed by Egypt. In the end, the NUP triumphed by obtaining 46 of the 92 seats available in the Legislative Assembly's House of Representatives.[42] The election outcome was largely a result of the *Khatmiyyah* leadership's control of the NUP, and mobilization of Azhari's following, converting the party into a dominant force in the first Sudanese government.[43] It has been indicated that the election outcome was also due to the aggressive campaigning by Egypt for NUP support in parts of the southern provinces where the election process was less understood among the population.[44] But the NUP's success in southern Sudan also owed to the strategies adopted by sections of the southern elite to join the NUP to advance their own interests in the national political scene. This strategy was a likely consequence of the elite realizing the difficulty to attract support for southern parties at the national level, and particularly in central and northern Sudan where southern political initiatives were largely dismissed.

In the southern provinces, the aftermath of the election was characterized by growing mistrust. The promises made during the election campaign had a significant effect on southern people's future hopes.[45] Particularly the assurances related to government jobs were important because public employment was perceived as a path to prosperity and higher social standing. However, the promises made in southern Sudan remained unfulfilled and local leaders became growingly dissatisfied, which was reflected in the sentiments of their followers.[46] This was particularly contentious in the context of decolonization, and the heightening discontent towards perceived northern domination.

Emergence of the "Southern Problem"

The rise of the Western-educated intelligentsia as the political elite in southern Sudan led to the northern governing elite to portray "the South" as a "problem". This is because the southern elite sought to extend its vision of "the South" as distinct from "the North", and based its project on self-determination (and separatism). In Khartoum such political movement was perceived as a threat to Sudan's unity and the aspirations of building a nation based on Arabic culture and Islam, which propelled the view of "the South" as a threat and the securitization of the southern issue. In the process, the southern resistance was converted into the "Southern Problem" which the government handled hard-handedly.

Regional Political Movement in Southern Provinces

Southern Policy had fostered distinct cultural attributes and led to the propagation of separate regional identity. It had isolated the southern provinces from the nationalist current monopolized by sections of the northern elite. While the British had felt obliged to provide northern nationalists economic resources to ensure their loyalty,[47] the emerging mission-educated southern political intelligentsia had greater dependence on the colonizer. It could not pressure the Condominium administration for resources, which contributed to its inability to build a vibrant political movement in the short period of decolonization.[48]

In this context, the sentiments of injustice and relative deprivation in southern provinces, together with the legacy of subjugation and resistance, served as grievances for propagating the regional political project of "the South". Perceived inequality based on uneven development and imposition

162

of "Arab" culture could also be harnessed to serve the regional political resistance. The feeling of being distinct from "the North" largely explains why sections of the elites in southern Sudan reinforced local apprehension towards the "Arab" government, and aspired to reach beyond ethnic affiliations to build a "regional" movement. This culminated in the agenda to preserve "southern" lifestyle by opposing the Arab and Islam-centric assimilationist view from northern Sudan. Still, despite the existence of common grievances and common subjection to the Southern Policy, local ethnic community identities remained strong in part due to the shortage of "regional" homogenizing forces. This contributed to distinct, and at times competing, political views, and different approaches to counter the perceived "Arab" domination. The existence of such distinct strategies is contrary to the claims of a number of scholars who tend to portray the early southern intelligentsia as lacking political vision.[49]

The emerging contemporary political elite in the southern provinces differed from the traditional local leadership and its counterpart in the northern provinces. It had received largely Western education, and had for the most part not been affected by Arab nationalism, culture, and Islamic teachings. Importantly, it had absorbed the constructed North-South identity cleavage, which allowed defining a collective "regional" identity beyond narrower ethnic affiliations. Unlike the Arabized elites, which received cultural and ideological influences largely from Egypt and other Arab regions, the southern intelligentsia emerged mostly independent from such outside currents and it did not initially identify with the nationalist thought that came from Arab states. Socialized according to Western norms, and heavily dependent on the missionaries and the British administrators,[50] the southern intelligentsia became more interested in safeguarding the position of the southerners and their imagined "region" as opposed to "the North". This suggests that the British and missionary influence on this emerging educated "regional" elite had been fundamental in shaping its worldview and attitudes towards "the Arab".[51] As noted above, it was clearly in the interest of the British and the missionaries to manufacture and reinforce southern elite's incompatibilities with the northern "Arab" Muslims during the Southern Policy, especially when it was briefly envisioned that southern provinces would be transferred to British East Africa.

This education was integral to the shaping of attitudes, morals, identity, and political orientation of the emerging southern elite. Local cultures, encouraged by the Southern Policy, combined with Westernization and became a cultural distinction that differentiated the educated southern elite from its northern counterpart. It produced a Christianized cadre that had better dominion of English than Arabic. As a result, Christianity was reinforced as a unifying force in the southern provinces, although many locals continued to practice traditional beliefs or became only superficially Christian.[52] What is also evident is that the missionaries not only educated but also supported at least some members of the southern elite either directly or through church organizations. Some were given the possibility to pursue higher education in East Africa or beyond, and after their expulsion from southern Sudan in the 1960s the church organizations provided moral and financial support to the southern opposition. The presence of the missionaries also facilitated securitization of the southern issue, with the northern elite seeking to portray them as creators of southern political opposition. Therefore, among the northern elite, the missionaries were to an extent seen as being behind the "Southern Problem", which was considered a menace to the unity of Sudan. This was despite southern regionalism's limited impact on the northern elite domination, at best somewhat hindering the extension of the national project based on Arabic culture and Islam in southern Sudan. Still, northern political elite's practice of portraying southern political movement as a secessionist threat, which largely began in the 1950s, not only served to securitize the issue and justify repressive measures in southern Sudan, but also had far-reaching consequences because it at times reinforced separatist sentiment among sections of the southern Sudanese elite.

Gradually, the emerging African nationalism also became a factor in the political orientation of part of the southern elite. While the decolonization model concentrating power in the hands of the Arabized elite was perceived as unacceptable by many in the southern intelligentsia,[53] the violent struggle that broke out in the 1950s against the central government fed the sentiment of "Africanism" in contrast to what was generally viewed as northern "Arabism".

However, the emerging mission-educated southern elite suffered from relative isolation in terms of spreading its regionalist message. In southern provinces, relative to northern Sudan, there was a shortage of communication technology and infrastructure. Movement over the vast territorial extensions and hardly penetrable terrain was difficult, which discouraged gatherings and establishment of political clubs and associations. This was one factor that encouraged grassroots ethnic politics between territorially close neighbors, while the few scattered intellectuals extended their influence primarily over their ethnically defined constituencies. The British policy of "tribalization", and indirect rule, further encouraged this form of political organization. In fact, the Juba Conference was the first occasion when representatives of the dispersed southern elites[54] officially came together.[55]

In the process of decolonization, southerners obtained minority representation in the Legislative Assembly. The three heterogeneous southern provinces were represented by 12 members of parliament who were largely marginalized and subject to manipulation by the more experienced northern representatives. They drew support almost solely from their local constituencies, and differed from the vast majority of population in southern provinces which had practically no Western educational attainment and modern political consciousness.[56] Their agendas focused on pressing for political recognition and economic development for the southern provinces.

Political organization had existed in the southern provinces at least since the Southern Officials' Welfare Committee rallied successfully for equal pay. However, it was not until 1951 that southern political cadres began pushing for political representation at the national level. Disgruntled of being repeatedly voted down by the northern political forces, Buth Diu, the only southern member in the CAC, decided in 1952 to establish a southern political party together with Stanislaus Paysama and Abdel Rahman Sule.[57] In 1953, in preparation for the first Sudanese parliamentary election, the three educated southerners, a Nuer, a Dinka, and a Bari, respectively, founded the Southern Party.[58] The initial demand of this political group was to delay the independence of Sudan so that the southern provinces could catch up to northern Sudan in terms of development, but later it changed its objectives to call for Sudanese independence and special treatment for the South within unified Sudan.[59] Northern nationalists' persuasion to have prominent southerners siding with full independence of Sudan contributed to this change in the agenda.

The Southern Party was registered before the upcoming election in 1953. In the election, it sought to promote southern interests and independence by opposing union with Egypt, which its members viewed partly responsible for the exclusion of southerners from the three-party negotiations between Britain, Egypt, and northern representatives on Sudan's self-determination.[60] Yet, the party remained weak during its early years since it was largely manipulated by the dominant sectarian parties eager to co-opt southern representatives.[61]

This dynamic set the precedent for the northern elite political forces to create strategic alliances with some individual southern representatives to gain minority constituencies from and in southern Sudan. By and large, these alliances have since then aimed at dividing the southern leadership, and generating support and wider legitimacy for the northern elite factions, while attempting to create an illusion of effective representation of southern interests at the national level. The northern elite has since co-opted southern leaders, and some southern leaders have collaborated with northerners for personal gain. This approach has been adopted by some individual southern politicians because it has benefited them personally, and possibly their immediate constituencies, or otherwise increased their political influence. Yet, such strategies undermined unity among the southern leadership. Due to these reasons, and others, the few southern representatives at the national level have had no power to alter key government policies. At times their own strategies, and the northern elite elements frequently collaborating with each other to capitalize upon divisions among the southern leaders, prevented common stand and unity among the southern political movement.

In 1954 the Southern Party sought to expand its constituency to counter the NUP. It changed its name to Liberal Party,[62] and convinced many southern independents and former NUP supporters to join, but was unsuccessful in attracting support in the northern provinces. As a result, its name was changed first to Southern Liberal Party and then back to Southern Party.[63] Meanwhile, NUP members in the southern provinces engaged in propaganda to undermine Umma's local support.[64] While southern parties were largely unable to gain support in the northern provinces, in part due to the prevailing attitudes, the northern elite parties bickering amongst themselves over slavery in southern Sudan likely undermined their support locally.

The Road to 1955 Southern Disturbances

The political developments in the aftermath of the 1953 election fostered fear and mistrust of "Arab" intentions among sectors of the southern population, particularly in Equatoria. These sentiments were further enforced by broken electoral promises and the end of the Sudanization process that deprived locals of most public positions in the southern provinces.

After the formal annexation of southern Sudan, the growing presence of northern civil servants and traders aggravated the situation. Although those *jallaba* who remained in the southern provinces generally maintained good relations with the locals, the arrival of new northerners after the annexation of "the South" changed the attitudes of many,[65] as intermingling with southerners was increasingly viewed as undesirable and despised.[66] In these circumstances, many *jallaba* began to show collective unwillingness to interact with locals on equal terms, and projected a superior attitude subjugating southerners. The northerners saw locals as wild, primitive, and godless, while themselves forming exclusive social groups limited to those embracing Arab culture, language, and customs.[67] In response to the influx of those considered "Arabs", mistrust among the locals grew and relationship between the two groups deteriorated.

166

Not surprisingly, the attitude of superiority invoked negative feelings among many southerners. Owing largely to the northern perception of a social hierarchy rooted in slavery (but also to the British attitude placing the northerners above locals), the ill-feelings were further exacerbated by the Umma Party's effort to gain support in southern provinces by accusing the *jallaba* of exploiting southerners.[68] The southerners were often referred to as *abeed* (slaves), following the historically forged social hierarchy.[69] Many of the new arrivals after the annexation of southern provinces were civil servants, army officers, and other influential "Arabs", and the racial attitudes they projected became reflected in local responses.

The accelerated process of Sudanization following the election hardened local attitudes in the southern provinces. According to the 1953 Anglo-Egyptian Agreement, a Sudanization Committee was instituted to distribute the remaining government jobs occupied by the exiting British. On 20 February 1954, the five-member committee, which was composed of a British, Egyptian, NUP, Umma, and Pakistani member, was established, and four months later it announced that some 800 senior positions remained to be filled.[70] However, to claim more positions for its constituents, the newly elected NUP government replaced the Umma Party member with another unionist, giving the NUP-Egyptian coalition more influence.[71]

The Sudanization process became highly exclusive. The Committee dictated that the criteria of recruiting and promoting personnel were composed of three main elements: seniority, experience, and qualifications.[72] The authorities adhered to the three categories to ensure the efficiency of the civil service, which according to their view formed an important part of maintaining good administration.[73] The process filtered out the large majority of southerners on the grounds of insufficient command of Arabic, which was the new official language of the government. Although some southerners had occupied a reduced number of junior government posts during the Condominium, which made the members of the southern elite to hope increasing representation, the hiring process excluded most of them.

Under the pretext of efficiency, southerners were systematically turned down and members of the north-central riverine elite and their constituents were favored. Those southerners who felt qualified for government jobs considered themselves victims of a process characterized by favoritism and patronage. In an attempt to conserve administrative posts for their supporters, factions of the northern political elite promoted a number of head clerks several levels up to deputy governors in the northern provinces, while southern administrators that occupied junior posts were largely left without promotions.[74] In the end, the southerners obtained 6 of the 800 posts in the final Sudanization process,[75] which resulted in an influx of northern administrators, teachers, and senior army and police officers in the southern provinces. Thus, rather than governed by the stated policy of promoting technical quality, the final Sudanization process of public employment was dictated by political patronage that ignored growing social tensions in the southern provinces.

In October 1954, the final senior civil servant appointments to conclude Sudanization were announced. Only 4 Assistant District Commissioner (ADC) positions were granted to southerners in the southern provinces, which triggered rapidly-spreading general restlessness. Sectors of the disappointed southern intelligentsia that had been marginalized in the process fomented mobilization. In addition, many southern independents and members of the NUP who lost the prospects of government posts, which had lured many of them to the party, defected to the Liberal Party.[76] The state had failed to accommodate the local elites in "the South".

Many southern leaders came to view the Sudanization process generally as Arabization, or "internal colonization", of southern Sudan. Sections of its members fed the fears of "Arab" domination, which spread the belief among some that another era of slavery by "the Arabs" was at hand.[77] These sentiments extended among communities in various parts of southern provinces. Characterizing the general feeling of "Arabs" taking over the administrative positions, one southern merchant stated that "The results of Sudanization have come with a very disappointing result . . . Well as it appears, it means our fellow northerners want to colonize us for another hundred years".[78] This way, the sight of arriving "Arab" administrators and *jallaba*, together with the shattering of hopes of expected political representation, jobs, prosperity, and development, encouraged the feeling of despair. The anxiety was so widespread that the situation became a threat to state's security,[79] as local animosity centered on an attitude to confront the "Arab" to correct perceived injustices, particularly in Equatoria. The subjection could be characterized as "internal colonization" in which cultural and "racial" subjugation played an important role.

A significant response to Sudanization among the southern political cadres was the call for self-determination within Sudan. This raised tensions between sectors of southern leadership and the government. Disappointed with the process, in October 1954 the Liberal Party decided to convene a meeting in Juba for June 1955, and in April 1955 convoked southern representatives over party lines to form a Southern Bloc to demand political concessions and demand federal status for southern Sudan.[80] Southern politicians also asked their constituents to get ready for sacrifices,[81] seeking to organize opposition to the perceived "Arab" domination.

In the context of rising tensions, the government securitized the southern issue. After the NUP victory, Azhari had become Prime Minister and had decided to visit southern Sudan. However, he received a cold welcome, with many locals either booing or ridiculing him.[82] The spreading anti-government sentiment alarmed Azhari to the extent that he implemented measures to raise salaries of local prison custodians, police officers, and clerks to the level of those in the northern provinces, but this failed to soften southern opposition because many leading southerners were not included in public employment.[83] In these circumstances the government became increasingly inclined to apply repressive measures in "the South". Khartoum informed that it was aware of the conspiracies weaved in the southern provinces and would use "force of iron" against any southerner who would "dare attempt to divide the nation".[84] This shows how despite its federalist agenda, the southern opposition became to be portrayed as separatist. Propagation of this image served the government interest to present southern political agitation as a threat to the state security. In "the North", it served to justify the application of repressive and violent measures to quell southern opposition.

In response to growing tensions in the southern provinces, the government ordered the administrators who almost all hailed from northern provinces to introduce stricter measures of control. It transmitted such instructions through the public Radio Omdurman, which resulted in them making their way to the ears of many southerners.[85] At this stage, sectors of the northern elite began to perceive views expressed within the southern political cadre as a challenge to their attempt to extend state authority in the southern provinces. They began to refer to the situation as the "Southern Problem". The threats of use of force escalated the situation. They fed sentiments for dissent which united many southern leaders around the call for federal solution as a "regional" political objective.[86]

Moreover, the Sudanization policy had resulted in northerners controlling the army. This had important implications in the South since both police force and the SEC -the latter being a contingent composed of southerners under a mix of British and northern officers- now became officered exclusively by northerners. For instance, 24 of the total of 32 officers in the SEC became northerners, while 8 officers were southerners, and the former were entirely in charge of detachments of the southern units in Bahr al-Ghazal and Upper Nile.[87] Among the troops in Equatoria, there were more southern junior officers relative to their northern superiors than in other regions, which to an extent facilitated organized action for dissent.

In the situation of increasing tension, many southerners felt that they were about to be subjected to northern rule as second-class citizens, which could only be resisted by advocating self-determination. Beshir notes that at this time "Political agitation and organization developed and began to take shape under the leadership of the educated Southerners . . . [as] . . . Southern Sudanese became convinced that their regional interests were of greater value than the larger association with the Sudan as a whole".[88] Although there were those who continued to collaborate with the central government, the majority in the southern political class was disappointed and perceived itself as marginalized. Many sought to mobilize constituents for opposition, and looked for political concessions from the government.

The 1955 Uprising

In the circumstances of growing animosity towards the "Arab" North in southern Sudan, the government grew increasingly preoccupied. As a result, Azhari sought to prevent a conference the southern political forces had convoked in Juba to coordinate their demands,[89] but the attempt compromised the administration's legitimacy further. Soon after, a local member of the Legislative Assembly[90] was arrested and the southern work force at the Zande Scheme in Nzara was downsized,[91] which generated riots in the context of growing mistrust. In response, the local authorities attempted to regain order by force, but this resulted in many deaths.[92] The Yambio and Nzara incidents were significant in strengthening the anti-government sentiment in Equatoria, resonating also elsewhere in the southern provinces.[93] This situation gave sectors of southern politicians, particularly in Equatoria, higher leverage for mobilization for dissidence and violent action against the government.

After the Nzara disturbances, the government became concerned that the growing anxiety and tension in the region would result in a general uprising. This elevated pressure to send northern army troops to the region, as it had become clear that the current security forces had almost no control over the southern territory, nor could the government count on the southern military and police which were increasingly consumed by the local sentiments of mistrust and fear. Indeed, the Nzara incident had affected the SEC. On 7 August a plot was revealed after politically active southern soldier, Saturlino Oboyo, tried to kill a northern assistant postmaster. In a search conducted in his premises, documents indicating a plan to kill northern officers in the southern provinces was unveiled.[94] The investigation also exposed a network of connections linking the Liberal Party and the SEC to the conspiracy,[95] which the government subsequently attempted to use to justify neutralization of the southern political leadership.

Local administrators sought to act upon the threat posed by the conspiracy. A decision was made to request Khartoum for more troops and law enforcement was asked to arrest the civilians involved in the plot, but this provoked further riots.[96] Despite the escalation and the call for troops to be sent to maintain order, in Khartoum the situation's severity was not fully understood and the initial pleas for troops were dismissed. However, on 10 August 1955 the government airlifted a detachment of 500 soldiers to Juba. Meanwhile, the anxiety and fear had reached such level that upon the arrival of the soldiers many locals left Juba because they thought that the soldiers were sent to kill them.[97] Yet, the government's intention was to maintain order and neutralize the threat posed by the SEC in Equatoria by transferring troops based in Torit to Khartoum.[98]

At this point, some southern leaders in Equatoria fomented the fears further. They circulated a false and controversial telegram,[99] and encouraged rumors that the southern troops that were to be transferred would be eliminated.[100] Northern officers evacuating their families from Torit on 14 August was taken as a sign that the northerners were preparing to attack the SEC.[101] In these circumstances the southern troops became consumed by fear and anxiety.[102]

Yet, despite the knowledge of a real chance of mutiny the orders for transfer to Khartoum were imposed. This disregarded the mounting political tension in a situation in which the northern officers of the SEC and administration had lost their legitimacy among their subordinates and the general public, and were increasingly viewed as oppressors. The eventual go-ahead order of the transfer provoked a mutiny among the SEC in Torit.[103]

The outrage among southerners first consumed Torit and then spread to other parts of Equatoria, before extending to Bahr al-Ghazal and Upper Nile. In other garrison towns of Equatoria, Juba, Yei, Yambio, and Maridi, a total of 190 southern soldiers revolted.[104] The disturbances affected practically all Equatoria province, as northerners were systematically rounded up, imprisoned, and then executed, variably sparing women and children.[105] Despite some southerners attempting to save northern lives, most of them were either tricked or forced to give way.[106] In other words, what seems to have been a planned scheme of successive mutinies provoked by propaganda was joined by thousands of tribesmen and hundreds of southern police officers and prison wardens, transforming it into a general uprising against perceived northern "Arab" subjugation.[107] On 20 and 21 August, the mutineers also made plans to fight the northern troops and invade Juba but, in the midst of general disorder and in the absence of support that they had hoped to receive from the British, many deserted and such offensive became impossible.[108] It appears that the expectations of British assistance had been due to fabricated beliefs that the British would support the southern cause, since some of the

British administrators had sought to protect the southern provinces during the process of decolonization.

The breakdown of order that ensued was characterized by brutality against anything "Arab". In fact, despite the seeming chaos, there was little damage and looting done to non-northern property. The disorder became of such magnitude that the northern army's No. 5 Company Camel Corps stationed at Juba was able to maintain order only around Juba airport, while the rest of the town remained out of its control.

However, the mutiny did not reach the same extent in Bahr al-Ghazal and Upper Nile. Some disturbances occurred, but only in Rumbek and Malakal did they result in deaths. This was partly due to the administrators and some non-Equatorian southern leaders loyal to the government being successful in calming the population and keeping the southern security forces at bay. For instance, in Bahr al-Ghazal northern administrators left Wau and temporarily suspended the administration, which calmed down the situation until the arrival of northern army units in the end of October.[109] The fact that the dissident politicians and leaders who were mainly Equatorian were unable to mobilize other areas than those hosting their social constituencies speaks of the ethnic diversity and the importance of social connection for political mobilization in this case.

When the news about the scale and extension of the disturbances reached Khartoum,[110] they caused confusion among the northern elite about appropriate state response. This is in part due to most northern politicians in Khartoum having been ignorant of the local realities and situation in "the South".[111] It was hard for many northerners to understand why the southerners had rebelled against their perceivably superior and more sophisticated northern Arab-Muslim administrators. However, when evidence about the brutality against northerners became apparent, a sentiment of revenge emerged.[112]

The view of a hostile, uncivilized, and problematic southern Sudan contributed to the government's decision to resort to violent measures. On 19 August, Khartoum declared a state of emergency in the southern provinces and sent army reinforcements.[113] Yet, the initial government measures to end the disturbances were unsuccessful. Prime Minister Azhari attempted to convince the mutineers to surrender, but his demands were answered by a counter demand for the immediate withdrawal of northern soldiers from southern provinces and either a British intervention or a U.N. investigation. The mutineers felt that the northern "Arabs" were not to be trusted,[114] and that the northern army would attack and retaliate.[115]

Those involved in the mutiny's leadership were aware of the political situation, and to an extent the international context. Telegrams were sent to the

British Prime Minister and the headquarters of the British troops in Sudan in hope of support, while the northern opposition politicians, Egypt, the former British administrators of the southern provinces, and the southern Liberal Party demanded British or joint British-Egyptian military intervention to resolve the situation.[116] However, the British government did not interfere on the side of the mutineers because it feared that this could give Egypt a pretext to extend its regional influence by undermining independent Sudan as a counter force.[117]

In contrast, the British decided to aid Khartoum to suppress the revolt. After news of the disturbances reached Governor-General Alexander Knox Helm, who had already departed for Britain, he returned to Sudan, brought transport planes airlifting 8,000 northern troops to the southern provinces, and negotiated with the mutineers about the terms of their surrender.[118] On 25-26 August, Helm dispatched two messages backing Prime Minister Azhari in which he demanded the mutineers to disarm and guaranteed that they would be treated as military prisoners with the respective rights. He also promised a full investigation into southern grievances, and to send his advisor, a British official, to oversee the surrender in Torit. Faced with these conditions, on 27 August the mutineers accepted, but the mistrust and fear again became significant factors since the rebels, except their leader, junior officer Renaldo Loleya, and a handful of others, abandoned Torit convinced that they would be killed by the northern units upon surrender.[119] Although in his correspondence with the mutineers Helm had exploited the trust the southerners had towards the British, his influence could not prevent part of the mutineers from escaping without turning in their weapons and establishing themselves in the border territories of the neighboring countries.[120] This was the beginning of armed opposition in southern Sudan, based in the borderlands between Sudan and its southern neighbors. Yet, only later did it develop into a full-fledged insurgency.

The southern disturbances required official British and Egyptian response. Internationally, the British government belittled the situation to prevent Egyptian involvement, and in turn sought speedy finalization of decolonization, preferring to leave the problem to the Sudanese government.[121] In contrast, the Egyptians insisted on British-Egyptian military cooperation to maintain order.[122] However, fearing that Egyptian troops could strengthen the prospects for "Unity of the Nile Valley", Britain rejected the Egyptian plan.

By the end of October 1955 order had been restored, and the army recovered control of the major towns where disturbances had taken place. The surrendered mutineers were put on trial, and despite the initial promises many of them were executed.[123] The British also attempted to negotiate the return of mutineers who had escaped to Uganda, but they were unable to pursue this because the U.S. pressured Britain to withdraw from Sudan in order to calm Egypt. As the British left Sudan, they decided that it would now be the Sudanese who would have to resolve the "Southern Problem" they predicted would continue.[124] Although at this point the British might still have attempted to divide Sudan along Condominium lines, as had been proposed earlier, faced with pressure from the outside powers and the Sudanese northern elite they decided to withdraw leaving Sudan intact. This indicates that in the process of decolonization, international geo-political considerations weighed more than Sudan's internal politics. The British withdrawal left the northern elite controlled Sudanese government to resolve the political rift that had developed between the northern and southern leadership.

The disturbances provoked violent government repression through which Khartoum sought to regain authority. Apart from the trials of the mutineers, the government closed schools, took political prisoners, committed tortures, and killed many southern officials and police and prison warders, while it transported approximately 2,000 southerners to northern labor prisons.[125] Many southerners believed that the reprisals that extended for months far outweighed the southern brutality during the initial events.[126] This generated bitterness particularly among younger cadres of the population, some sabotaging government infrastructure and joining the rebels.[127] In the consequent cycle of violence, which included the putting down of a demonstration over pay in February 1956,[128] hatred grew among many southerners particularly in Equatoria. Political consciousness centered increasingly on a perception of the "Arabs" as enemies.

The southern elite sought to capture the increasing anti-"Arab" sentiment as it continued to build the regional political project. It was further encouraged by northern ignorance of "the South",[129] an attitude of superiority, and the playing down of the southern political elite. This collided head on with the northern elite's assimilationist project that would uphold the exclusive social hierarchy and render the southerners second-class, or socially lower, in the Sudanese nation defined in terms of adherence to Arab culture and Islam.[130] The competition of these political projects was significant in the escalation of the situation towards growing support of violent dissent in southern Sudan.

Finally, several policy measures were introduced that added to the discord. For instance, army troops composed of northerners were made responsible for maintaining order in the southern provinces, while the SEC was abolished, which heightened the feeling of "Arab" subjugation and colonization, and resulted in many former southern soldiers escaping in the bush.[131] Moreover, southern soldiers and students[132] were prohibited to enlist in the armed forces until 1956, and the two secondary schools in Juba and Rumbek were moved to the North.[133] This led to an exodus of students to Kenya, Uganda, and Belgian Congo, which spread awareness of the unfolding situation in southern Sudan.

On 1 January 1956 Sudan acquired independence. A constitutional debate followed in which the most extreme demands were those for instituting an Islamic state on one side and a federal system on the other side. However, neither proposal prevailed because sectarian wrangling between the northern parties characterized the early post-colonial political scene. In July 1956 Prime Minister Azhari faced a non-confidence vote in which the rivals, Umma and NUP parties, came together to establish a new government. The non-confidence vote had been made possible in part by the earlier defection of a number of members of Azhari's government and their founding of the People's Democratic Party (PDP). It was in part triggered by the "Southern Problem" and the difficult economic situation Sudan faced after independence. Soon Sudan entered in economic recession triggered by its uncompetitive cotton exports that faced decreasing world commodity prices, and by 1958 Sudan's currency reserves had reached a Sudanese Pounds (S£) 8 million low.[134]

The same year general elections were held. Umma Party won[135] and formed a coalition government with PDP,[136] which was headed by the Umma secretary Abdullah al-Khalil. The NUP moved into the opposition. However, the leading forces entered into political wrangling mainly about foreign policy orientation, with Umma preferring the West and PDP and NUP favoring Egypt and Arab countries. This was coupled with heated debates on American aid and the accumulated unsold cotton. Moreover, the Western orientation of Prime Minister Khalil made it difficult for Sudan to renew the deal on Nile waters with Egypt, which was viewed to be of outmost importance. This debilitated the governing Umma Party's position.

Abboud Regime and Forced Arabization and Islamicization

The establishment of the new government did little to end the bickering among northern parties. This played in the hands of political forces from the peripheries, strengthening the challenge to the exclusive rule of the Arabized elite as many rallied behind the southern cause.[137] In these circumstances, and in the regional environment in which military coups had recently occurred in the Middle East and Egypt, Prime Minister Khalil, who was a former army general, engineered an army intervention.[138] His aim was to disrupt the weakening democratic order and set up an authoritarian regime that could deal with Sudan's economic problems and protect the northern elite's exclusive hold on power against challenge from southern Sudan. By military intervention Khalil hoped to promote Umma's hegemony, and prevent Sudan from drifting to the Soviet sphere and under increasing Egyptian influence. He approached the U.S., and after initial hesitation Washington accepted the plan while convinced that Egypt was about to take over Sudan. Consequently, a bloodless military coup was staged in the morning of 17 November 1958 which brought a regime headed by General Ibrahim Abboud to power.[139] Although Beshir has argued that the coup was not a northern conspiracy,[140] the objective was, at least in part, to preserve Umma's power and the political hegemony of the northern elite, as well as ensuring Sudan's Western orientation.

Commander-in-chief of the Sudanese army, Ibrahim Abboud, became the president and the figurehead of the new regime.[141] By concentrating more power on the presidency, he embarked on a plan for further centralization of the state and administration.[142] Meanwhile, under pressure from the U.S., the regime, formed along personal ties among the Umma Party,[143] attacked the political left.[144]

However, following the military coup the level of general anxiety in the southern provinces heightened further. This is because the army coup was viewed as an attempt to avoid political concessions,[145] and it was feared that it would result in protracted repression. These fears had foundation, as the regime almost immediately turned its attention to the "Southern Problem". It radicalized the cultural assimilation policies adopted by the Azhari and Khalil governments,[146] following the widespread opinion among the northern elite that the southern dissent could be quelled by hard-handed eradication of language, culture, and religious differences through Arabization and Islamicization, which would also strengthen government authority and centralized administration.[147] Yet, the repressive policy of Arabization and Islamicization adopted by the regime, together with violent counterinsurgency measures, resulted in further local hostility towards "the North" in the southern provinces.[148]

The government also embarked on another wave of northernization of personnel in all the principal administrative posts in southern Sudan. Although some southerners had acquired civil servant positions in the southern provinces during the democratic period, now, apart from banning southern political representation overall, all southern governors and district commissioners were replaced with northern inspectors. In addition, while southern junior officials were transferred to the northern provinces, army and police rank and file in southern Sudan became overwhelmingly northern, and provincial and executive councils were put under northern officials' direct supervision and control. Moreover, the imposition of cultural Arabization and Islamicization as forces of forced assimilation, relying on coercive power of the security forces, was to consolidate the state in southern Sudan by giving it long-term legitimacy.[149] However this policy backfired because the repressive measures led to the escalation of the armed conflict.

The government also viewed Christian missionaries increasingly as instigators who contributed to the "Southern Problem".[150] They were deemed to be a remain of colonialism and represent imperialist external interests, as well as supporting mutineers and inciting southern dissent, which was seen to undermine the government agenda of Arabization and Islamicization.[151] This led to progressive restrictions on Christian missionary and religious activity,[152] but at the same time it increased the number of converts because many southerners faced with insecurity found comfort in Christian religion as a counterforce to the imposed Arabization and Islamicization.

In the latter 1950s scattered armed attacks on government personnel and installations occurred in Equatoria. These were largely undertaken by the mutineers who had escaped in 1955, and those who had joined them. They caused concern for the regime, and it launched counterinsurgency measures which resulted in killings, torture, bombardment, and the burning of villages accused of sheltering the so-called "outlaws".[153] At this point the rebels posed only a localized threat to the regime authority in the peripheral parts of southern Sudan,[154] but the oppressive counterinsurgency campaign generated an upsurge of southern opposition, strengthened by many of those subjected to regime violence and escaping to more remote areas. In this context of escalating violent incidents a growing number of southerners were caught between threats and violence by the army troops and the "outlaws".[155]

By 1960 the conflict began to disrupt local living conditions on a wider scale. This affected the lives of the local people in two major ways. First, by 1960, the fear of both government retaliatory raids[156] and those of the foraging rebels forced displacement.[157] Second, in 1960 and 1962, demonstrations took place in southern schools in the midst of other disturbances and rumors about the formation of a new guerilla force,[158] which led to organized boycotts in protest of state repression that provoked yet further government reprisals.[159]

Growing insecurity and disrupted livelihoods encouraged displacement because those who stayed were likely to suffer from violence by the security forces or the rebels.[160] Thus, many discontinued their traditional sedentary crop cultivation and/or cattle herding. This created more dependency on alternative forms of subsistence, such as fishing, hunting, and gathering, which were often not enough to sustain families. Chief Thon Wai described that

> Whenever the boys came in the middle of the night, they would find food, they would find cattle, they would find a goat, they would eat but then leave . . . That is how we lived, avoiding one another, crossing our paths, each man coming and another going.[161]

However because of the growth of such activities, available local resources became easily exhausted. Consequently, displacement and labor migration emerged increasingly as alternatives.

Although labor migration had formed part of the economy in Sudan already during and prior to the colonial period, the growing number of displaced due to the situation in the southern provinces increased the pool of cheap labor in northern Sudan. This complemented the expansion of capitalist agriculture, while the displaced southerners allegedly worked in slave-like conditions as agricultural laborers or in other low-level employment.[162] Although the migration northwards during the 1950s and 1960s was not as extensive as during the later southern insurgency, more than a million southerners came to live in the northern provinces. Fomenting further violence in southern Sudan became synonymous with increasing cheap labor for agriculture in northern Sudan.[163] In the northern provinces, this situation further reinforced the social hierarchy emanating from the 19th century and beyond.

In the early 1960s, the regime began explicitly targeting the southern political elite as a counterinsurgency strategy. Already in December 1960 the regime plan to imprison southern elites to disrupt the southern political movement was unveiled,[164] and a decision was made to transfer the few remaining southerners serving as officials to the northern provinces, which initiated an exodus of prominent southerners to the bush and the neighboring countries.[165] A few administrators and teachers with secondary or higher education moved first, and a less educated group led by secondary school students and junior government employees (such as prison warders and policemen) followed them to hiding in the southern forests, borderlands, and capitals of the neighboring states. The example set by the elite escalated the wave of emigration in southern Sudan,[166] and by the mid-1960s there were about 70,000 Sudanese refugees in the neighboring countries.[167] By the end of the conflict in the early 1970s, the number had reached over half a million.[168]

The Founding and Consolidation of the Anya Nya

Despite often being considered to have started as two separate forces, the armed and political opposition in southern Sudan were closely connected. Their union galvanized in the main rebel organization, Anya Nya, an umbrella of armed groupings that consolidated when the rebellion grew regional.

Emergence and Consolidation of Armed Opposition

In the course of the late 1950s, the "outlaws" staged occasional attacks, ambushes, and shootings which caused minor damage to the government.[169] They sustained themselves by engaging in banditry, organizing a force of approximately 500 lightly armed fighters into small bands according to ethnic and regional lines, all exercising military discipline to maintain organizational coherence in the face of government pressure.[170] The movement, which centered on the figure of chief Lomiluk during 1955-1959,[171] was composed of largely independent commands under provincial commanders-in-chief who operated locally and imposed their authority on individual villages.[172] Largely because the government was unable to destroy the insurgents, and impede recruitment and access to arms, the guerrilla warfare survived.[173] In fact, harsh but non-comprehensive government measures stimulated recruitment further, which sustained the movement despite the scarcity of armament.

In 1960 the rebel forces continued largely dispersed. The early guerilla survival period was characterized by the foraging of food, while the stated motivations for armed violence centered on perceived and experienced social injustices rather than any borrowed political ideology. Moreover, in the early 1960s the rebels were mainly armed with arrows, spears, and machetes, and only possessed approximately 200 old firearms.[174] Johnson points out that, "The guerillas . . . had no external military support, arming themselves mainly by theft from police outposts, the occasional ambush of army patrols, or through the defection of Southern police or soldiers".[175] However, in the early 1960 this changed. Fleeing government repression, growing numbers in Equatoria, including many of the 800 southerners jailed after the 1955 mutiny and released in 1961, joined the rebellion. This led to the formation of a more coherent and politically oriented force in 1963 under a single umbrella organization called the Land Freedom Army (LFA).[176]

The LFA engaged in guerrilla warfare against the government. The force was organized in territorial units according to British military model, and run by regional commanders under the authority of supreme commander, Major General Emedio Tafeng. Soon after its founding, the LFA adopted the name Anya Nya[177] and established base camps and training facilities[178] in the hard to access terrain of the neighboring countries bordering southern Sudan.[179] But until the end of 1963 the rebel operations consisted largely of scattered assaults on isolated government posts, the most significant attack taking place in Pochalla, Upper Nile.[180] This convinced some civilians in Upper Nile of Anya Nya's capacity, attracted new recruits, and helped to spread the movement's Nuer branch in the province.[181] Gradually, the Anya Nya commenced a concerted campaign to destroy bridges, block roads, ambush northern troops, and coerce southerners who were either unhelpful or collaborated with the regime, while government troops raided communities thought to support the rebels.[182] This escalation generated further displacement to the forests, neighboring countries, and northern Sudan.

The first major Anya Nya operation was its unsuccessful attempt to take Wau, the main town in Bahr al-Ghazal.[183] The failure in Wau paralyzed the Anya Nya's attack capacity and forced it to go back to recruiting, training, and reorganization, while it seized arms sent by Egypt and Algeria to the Congolese Simba rebels through Khartoum and obtained arms from the Simba from August 1964 to 1965.[184] Following the Simbas' defeat, the conflict in DRC, in which independent Uganda was also involved, produced 9,000 refugees to Equatoria, including some former Simba.[185] This allowed Anya Nya to acquire further armament.

By the mid-1960s Anya Nya had become a threatening force,[186] although it continued to suffer from a number of weaknesses.[187] Meanwhile, by 1964 the political opposition, which had been initially separated from the armed insurgency,[188] was developing links with the movement's Bahr al-Ghazal command.[189] Although both had their roots in regime repression, sections of the political and armed opposition differed considerably; the armed struggle being led by defected junior officers and lower level security personnel who were not necessarily familiar with, or fond of, the political elite. However, the links between the two became obvious in September 1964 when part of the southern political opposition shifted from the initial commitment to non-violence to an attempt to gain control of the Anya Nya.[190]

The Rise of the Political Opposition

Although a handful of southern politicians were connected to the conspiracy before the Torit mutiny, the southern political opposition developed somewhat separately from the early insurgency. Initially, the deliberate targeting of southern intelligentsia weakened the political organization behind a common southern cause. In 1961 the Sudan Christian Association had been founded to counter Arabization and Islamicization, but due to Captain Joseph Lagu's initiative in February 1962, who then was a sectional leader in the Anya Nya,[191] the prominent southern political leaders[192] transformed it into the largely separatist Sudan African Closed Districts National Union

180

(SACDNU) which engaged in diplomacy and propagation of the southern cause and demanded independence. Equatorian politicians were the early protagonists of pushing "the southern" agenda,[193] and the SACDNU leaders[194] assumed a prominent role in the southern political opposition. Advocating secession of southern Sudan was therefore largely an initiative among some Equatorian leaders, and to an extent a result of hardening positions in the midst of the escalating violence in southern Sudan.

In an April 1962 meeting in Leopoldville (Kinshasa), SACDNU's name was changed to the Sudan African National Union (SANU). From 1964 it was headquartered in Kampala where a vibrant southern diaspora community already existed, but also continued to have a factional base under William Deng in Leopoldville.[195] By this time, the SANU leadership was affected by the emerging African nationalism, which in the case of Sudan could be interpreted as the southern liberation struggle from the perceived northern "Arab" domination and "internal colonialism". By 1964 factionalism had deepened[196] and resulted in Deng, an ethnic Dinka, to advocate a federal solution in opposition to the secessionist Equatorian majority of SANU-in exile.[197] He moved to Khartoum to establish SANU-inside, to enter in Sudanese domestic politics, and to compete against the Khartoum-based, and to an extent Dinka influenced, southern political opposition, the Southern Front (SF).[198] Thus, distinct political objectives, personal competition, factionalism, and "tribalism", weakened the southern political movement from its early stages.

The exile southern political opposition emerged largely in response to regime repression. The imposition of Arabic culture and Islam, and restriction of Christianity, created conditions in which the southern political opposition was able to increasingly mobilize sections of local communities.[199] The SANU focused initially on efforts to gain political recognition and alliances by resorting to propaganda of oppression of black "Christian Africans" by repressive and racist "Arab-Muslim" regime.[200] It informed the press and sent appeals to the U.N. and the Organization of African Unity (OAU).[201] Moreover, the SANU contacted church organizations and missionaries, which brought it moral support and additional resources, leading to international protests against the regime and contributing to further targeting of Christians by the regime.[202] In this way, race and religion became increasingly politically instrumentalized, as the regime imposed Arabization and Islamicization, while the SANU sought to promote Africanism and Christianity as counter forces to them. These dynamics set the precedent for the use of religion, race, and cultural attributes to attract external support in the context of the Sudanese conflicts.

Regionalization of the "Southern Problem"

Initially the Abboud regime sought international recognition for legitimizing its power and to extravert material resources from external actors for consolidation. The bipolar Cold War environment proved receptive to these aspirations. In this effort, the regime recognized China, negotiated two trade agreements with the Soviet Union in 1961 and 1963, obtained aid, loans, and credits from Britain, West Germany, and the U.S., and as a member of the World Bank since 1957 acquired a loan from the International Development Association in 1958 to develop rail and water transportation systems.[203]

The regime also sought to improve the relationship with Arab countries and particularly its neighbor, Egypt. Abboud's military rule in Sudan facilitated negotiating the Nile Waters Agreement and other bilateral treaties, while, having previously served in the Egyptian army, he expressed reliance on Egypt as a protective force for Sudan. The regime also established good relations with other Arab states, including Algeria, Libya, Syria, Iraq, North Yemen, Jordan, and Saudi Arabia, and showed solidarity towards Palestine. Moreover, it supported Iraq's and Syria's pan-Arabist aspirations by channeling arms to the largely Muslim Eritrean rebels. However, in 1963 Khartoum stopped supporting Eritreans and negotiated a defense treaty with Ethiopia to curb possible Ethiopian support to the Anya Nya, while seeking to maintain good relations with Arab states siding with the Soviet Union and growing increasingly confrontational with the U.S. backed Israel and Ethiopia.[204]

By mid-1960s the "Southern Problem" had become regionalized. One major element in this was SANU publicizing the southern cause internationally, including searching for southern Sudan's recognition through a self-determination plebiscite and claiming that southerners were being exterminated.[205] Also, Deng sought to gain U.N. attention by encouraging a series of armed raids on police posts in southern Sudan from the neighboring states in 1963, and by traveling to Geneva to spread the word on the SANU cause which resulted in a GB£175,000 grant for Uganda to alleviate the conditions of southern refugees.[206] Although this shows that Deng exerted influence over sections of the Anya Nya, the SANU's diplomatic effort failed to attract significant support at the level of regional and international organizations.

African countries remained reluctant to officially support the southern rebellion. This was largely due to the OAU charter. Yet, from 1963 onwards, southern politicians connected with the Anya Nya were in contact with Israeli embassies in Uganda, Ethiopia, DRC, and Chad to make arrangements to channel Israeli aid to the rebels through those countries.[207] In addition, despite a 1963 defense treaty with Khartoum, Ethiopia, which by now hosted large southern refugee camps in its territory, gave covert support to the Anya

Nya. In the late 1960s Ugandan army under Idi Amin also aided the rebels by briefly facilitating Israeli support through northern Uganda, while DRC and Kenya lent vague and largely moral support.[208] This shows that links between the political and armed opposition already existed in the early 1960s, and that the "Southern Problem" had become a regional issue.

Meanwhile, the regime sought foreign support to contain the insurgency and accused certain organizations and neighboring countries of supporting the rebels. Supplied militarily and financially by Arab states, Sudan itself drifted closer to the Soviet Union.[209] The northern Sudanese political elites began to perceive the strengthening rebellion in the southern provinces increasingly as a Christian crusade in which the "outlaws" served the designs of Ethiopia, Israel, and the World Council of Churches,[210] and the regime continued to resort in various repressive measures. First, it increased the army contingent in southern Sudan to 8,000, which was 40% of the army's total strength, but engaging the rebels was mostly unsuccessful and in frustration the army often destroyed entire towns suspected of aiding them.[211] Khartoum also imprisoned many junior southern officials, police, and prison staff, although many managed to defect and join the Anya Nya.[212] These measures were counterproductive because they provoked increasing hatred towards the regime.

Second, Khartoum sought to isolate southern Sudan from undesired external influences. It removed all the remaining Christian missionaries and put restrictions on foreign merchants active in southern Sudan. After the army claimed that missionaries had been behind the attack on Wau in February 1964, the regime argued that there was evidence beyond doubt that they were inciting the southern rebellion and replaced the approximately 300 foreign missionaries with Sudanese clergy.[213] This drove Christian organizations to support southerners in exile in light of what was viewed as persecution.[214] There was external support from religious organizations, which was largely channeled through an Equatorian priest, Father Saturnino Lohure,[215] who became an important figure in the southern political struggle.[216] Gray has further asserted that " . . . the fact that a Catholic priest [Lohure] played so prominent role in the emerging conflict undoubtedly strengthened Khartoum's conviction that the influence of foreign missionaries was a major obstacle to achievement of national unity".[217] At the same time, foreign traders, mostly Greek and Syrian, were only allowed to reside in the southern provincial capitals because they were similarly suspected of helping rebels.[218]

Third, the regime also accused neighboring states of fomenting the "Southern Problem". It blamed DRC for harboring rebels, and Israel for providing training in a military facility in Uganda.[219] This led to army incursions across borders, such as an attack on an Anya Nya camp on 8 May 1964 over the border in DRC from where Khartoum claimed the assault on Wau had been organized.[220] Yet, the regime was more reluctant to enter Uganda, which remained a British protectorate until 1967 and whose position towards the Anya Nya remained obscure since it accepted refugees but persecuted some pro-rebellion southern politicians.[221]

Finally, the relationship between Sudan and Ethiopia was also affected by the situation. This was because large numbers of refugees began to arrive in Ethiopia, which contributed to its Anya Nya support as well as its collaboration with the U.S. and Israel. On 3 May 1964 Sudan signed an extradition treaty with Ethiopia to cut Anya Nya from support but this was never implemented, and Ethiopians relieved their refugee burden by spreading rumors locally about an alleged Sudan-Ethiopia crackdown that initially caused mass exodus of refugees from Ethiopia to Uganda and Kenya.[222] Overall, already by 1964, Ethiopia and Uganda hosted tens of thousands of southern Sudanese refugees, and eventually Uganda became the main receptor of southerners until the end of the first episode of armed conflict in 1972.[223]

Conclusion

In the process of decolonization, both co-dominium powers sought to use the southern issue to their advantage in their competition to cast influence over the Sudanese political elite. At the same time, the U.S. pressed for decolonization, knowing that it would likely lead to a rebellion in southern Sudan. On the other hand, the north-central riverine nationalist elite used the competition between the colonial masters to consolidate an exclusive relationship with them. This facilitated " . . . the transfer of the colonial structures intact from Britain to the northern Sudanese nationalists",[224] and fomented further marginalization of the southern elites. Thus the collective strategy of the leadership of the northern nationalists targeting Egypt to impose itself as the main recognized voice in Sudan was largely successful, as Egypt embraced the northern elite as means of increasing its own strength in the co-dominium end game. As a result, Egypt's strengthened negotiation position due to local support in the northern provinces, and the U.S. pressure that the northern elites also sought to stimulate, compelled even those British initially defending Southern Policy to accept the northern nationalists as the leading group to which political power should concentrate. This led to complete exclusion of peripheral elites from political power at the national level, and allowed the political and economic hegemony of the northern nationalists to prevail in the exclusive governance and institutions inherited from the Condominium.

184

These dynamics led to southern Sudan's subjection to the rule of the northern political elite controlled central government. As a result, the southern political elite was largely deprived of political positions even at the local level, and it was provided few incentives and resources to act as an integrating force in the process of re-annexation of the southern provinces to the state. Instead, this situation led to the southern elite's resistance to the political and economic imposition of the northern elite by mobilizing opposition to nation-building based on Arab culture and Islam. Both of these identity elements were found alien and undesirable among the elites in southern Sudan in part because they deemed non-"Arab" and non-Muslim southerners as second-class, hindered their possibilities of social ascension, and transformed the regional social order led by the Christian, mission-educated, elite. Decolonization, which led to annexation of southern provinces to northern Sudan as subordinate territories, marginalized southerners politically and generated grievances among many in the southern elite and its constituencies against the northern "Arabs", particularly after northerners took over local administration of the region. Together with the history of violent incursions to the southern frontier, slavery and the Southern Policy, latter of which had isolated southern provinces from northern influences, the perceived injustices and relative deprivation served to generate political and armed opposition in southern Sudan. Additionally, the influx of northerners placed in locally high positions appeared for many southerners as "internal colonization" and resuscitated memories of the 19th century subjugation.

The general historiography on rebellions in southern Sudan has largely failed to emphasize the importance of external processes and dynamics in the insurgency formation during the era of decolonization. These were of utmost importance in influencing local actors and dictating political and economic trajectories. In the case of Sudan, it was not only Britain's inability to finance colonial administration, but also the geopolitical power competition between Britain and Egypt in the Cold War context in which the U.S. and the U.S.S.R. competed for regional influence, which determined its decolonization. Although they knew that the unification of southern provinces with northern Sudan without safeguards would likely cause political violence, the British went on and transferred administration from the hands of the colonial government to the sections of the narrowly based northern nationalist elite. The latter, with intent to consolidate its position and extend its influence in the southern provinces, propagated its political project based on its self-proclaimed Arab culture and Islam irrespective of local cultures in the state peripheries. Portraying and extending Arab-Muslim identity thus converted into a political rational behind state policies.

However, this policy was contested particularly in the southern provinces by those sections of the local mission-educated elite that felt marginalized in the new political landscape. Many prominent southerners sought to defend their political visions, interests, and views of southern Sudan, and promote them as the foundation of regional identity. At the same time, many southerners viewed the "Arab"-Muslim state as alien, and a source of fear, since its assimilationist aspirations were deemed to threaten southern way of life. The southern "regional" elite, as a contrasting force to the extension of "Arab" hegemony, therefore propagated resistance to the exclusive vision of the northern elite. The early southern demands articulated in calls for a federal system of governance that could ensure the region's political rights.

In this situation, the violent manifestation of the "Southern Problem" triggered in Torit. Initially it mostly involved the Equatoria province, the home of the most prominent and numerous southern leaders conspiring against the government. From the beginning, the armed opposition was connected to political leaders despite often been considered as initially separate. The violence led to the northern governing elite's securitization of the southern calls for self-determination by referring to them as "Southern Problem". This justified coercive reprisals to the mutiny, and violent counterinsurgency measures to the unfolding insurgency.

Finally, the policies of the Abboud military regime were an important factor contributing to the radicalization of the opposition and the growth of the armed movement. They led to a growing polarization between northern and southern Sudan due to forced Arabization and Islamicization that assaulted southern identities, and also played a role in increasing rebel recruitment. In these circumstances, the Anya Nya rebel opposition acquired increasing quantities of arms, while attracting other resources and moral support. Facilitated by the consolidation of the rebellion, this led to the escalation of the "Southern Problem" into full-fledged armed opposition. Neighboring states and external powers were involved in regionalizing the insurgency, and it was only at the end of the 1960s when clouds of peace began to gather.

Endnotes

1   President Jaafar Nimeiri of Sudan in an interview on the war in Chad. Sudanow (Jan. 1982: 10).

2   This refers to the social hierarchy, and Deng's concept of "social race". See Deng (1978, 1995a, 1995b).

3   Warburg (2000: 75-6).

4   Yohannes (1997: 262).

5   Egypt's concern of securing enough water for irrigation and other uses emerged

already in the 1920s when Lord Edmund Allenby threatened, in response to Sudan Governor-General Stack's assassination in Cairo, that the British would permit Sudan to use as much of the Nile water as required without a need to take into account the interests of Egypt. This led the Egyptian politicians to focus on ensuring sufficient quantity of Nile water in the future, which became an important factor behind their insistence on the "Unity of the Nile Valley" instead of self-determination for Sudan. See e.g. Warburg (2000: 76-7). Nile waters continue to play a crucial role in Egyptian foreign policy today.

6   Abu Hasabu (1985: 47) and Holt (1961: 141).

7   Abdel Rahim (1969: 120-2) and Daly (1991: 50-61, 82).

8   Ruay (1994: 60).

9   Yohannes (1997: 261, 263).

10   According to Lyons (1978: 8), the following year Soviet Union recognized Israel and later supplied it with Czech military material.

11   Yohannes (1997: 261).

12   In October 1951 Egypt pressured Britain by abrogating the 1899 and 1936 co-dominium agreements, opposing a proposed Constitutional Amendment Commission (CAC), rallying for support within Sudan, and issuing decrees proclaiming its King Farouk I as the King of Sudan with the right to draft its new constitution. See e.g. Ruay (1994: 61-2).

13   Daly (1991: 280) and Woodward (2006: 29) assert that the coup was partly inspired by increased anti-British sentiment over a military base at the Suez and Egypt's impotence regarding the Condominium in Sudan.

14   Ruay (1994: 64-5), Yohannes (1997: 264), and Warburg (2000: 77).

15   Niblock (1987: 203), Yohannes (1997: 264, 266), and Sidahmed and Sidahmed (2005: 27).

16   Yohannes (1997: 265).

17   Daly (1991: 280-2), Ruay (1994: 61, 63), and Sidahmed and Sidahmed (2005: 26).

18   Sidahmed and Sidahmed (2005: 27).

19   Niblock (1987: 203), and Sidahmed and Sidahmed (2005: 26).

20   The treaty recognized the Sudanese right for self-determination, called for an international commission to supervise first elections, sought Governor-General's support in policy issues, stipulated that a commission would be set up to supervise the final steps of the Sudanization of public employment, demanded a schedule of the removal of British and Egyptian troops, and insisted on the removal of the southern safeguards from the draft of the Self-Government Statute.

21   Oduho and Deng (1963: 21), Ruay (1994: 66), and de Chand (2000: 23).

22   Yohannes (1997: 267).

23   The report was based on approximately 200 interviews of southern politicians.

24   Yohannes (1997: 267-9).

25   Deng (1995b: 77-8).

26   Burr and Collins (1999: 56).

27 The representation of the southern provinces was 13 members, which constituted a minority against the 52 representatives of the northern Arabized elite.
See e.g. Niblock (1987: 159).

28 Niblock (1987: 61-81).

29 Ruay (1994: 54).

30 Duncan (1957: 197-8).

31 Alier (1990: 21), Daly (1991: 242, 265-6), Hanes (1995: 134-5), and Louis
(2006: 657).

32 Ruay (1994: 55-6).

33 Ruay (1994: 56-7).

34 Alier (1990: 22).

35 Legislative Assembly Proceedings quoted in Ruay (1994: 57-8).

36 Miner (2003).

37 Ruay (1994: 58).

38 The electoral campaign was characterized by competition among the political
parties of the dominant "northern" forces. Accoring to Ruay (1994: 69), "It
was a situation of political wrangling, coaxing, excitement and all forms of
flattery, bribery not excluded", in which Britain, Egypt, and the local administration were heavily involved. Egypt played an important role in supporting
the NUP, although it had previously agreed as part of the Egyptian-Sudanese
Agreement to ensure a neutral electoral climate. See Daly (1991: 356-7). For
instance, Cairo appointed a Special Minister for the Sudanese Affairs, used
radio propaganda, granted money gifts, and sponsored local nationalists to visit
Egypt. It also sent representatives to Sudan, and provided grants to local private schools to encourage vote for the NUP. See RCIDSS (1956), O'Ballance
(1977: 37), and Ruay (1994: 68-9).

39 Niblock (1987: 202).

40 Ruay (1994: 69).

41 See the NUP election manifesto reproduced in Howell (1978b: 123). Among
the most significant efforts to convince southerners for the unity with Egypt
was a tour by Egyptian officer, Major Saleh Salem, to the southern provinces.
In convoked gatherings, Salem promised repeatedly that the 40 senior government posts occupied by the British in the southern provinces would go to
the locals. See O'Ballance (1977: 37). In addition, according to Ruay (1994:
69), he sought to convince the southern public that southerners would acquire
technical positions, disregarding the fact that these required expertise and spe-
cialization that the great majority of local people did not have. Collins (1983:
448) adds that at one time, in an attempt to convince some locals for the unity
with Egypt, Salem joined a Dinka dance with his upper body exposed.

42 Umma gained 23, Southern Party 9, and other parties 11 seats of the overall
total. See e.g. Bechtold (1976: 181). The NUP claimed 5, Southern Party 9, and
other southern political formations 8 seats, respectively, of the 22 allocated for
the southern provinces. See SEC (1954: 27).

43 Niblock (1987: 207) and Warburg (2003: 134-5).

44 O'Ballance (1977: 37).
45 According to Ruay (1994: 69), "The impact of all these [electoral] promises on the Southerners was nothing short of extreme feeling of satisfaction, happiness and the desire to kick out the British from the country as quickly as possible".
46 Although many had voted NUP, the growing grievances threatened the party's position in the southern provinces after the elections. This was largely because increasingly influential mission-educated sectors of local leadership positioned themselves against union with Egypt, a sentiment which was further exacerbated by a visit of Umma politicians and southern representatives in Khartoum to the southern territories in mid-1954 during which they criticized the NUP government. See Sarkesian (1973: 9). Al-Azhari granted three ministerial positions to southern politicians, but the move, which benefited mostly those politicians and had little impact on the southern opinion, did little to alleviate the growing discontent. It appears that Al-Azhari overestimated the local influence of southern politicians in Khartoum at the time, and assumed wrongly that they and their constituencies favored the government they joined.
47 Keen (2001: 222).
48 Woodward (1995: 95).
49 See e.g. Niblock (1987) and Daly (1991).
50 For instance, Howell (1978b: 55) has noted that southern educated elite depended " . . . upon the tutelary temperament of the local administrator or missionary".
51 For instance one rather controversial northern scholar, Mohamed Ahmed Hassan Makki (1989: 76), has alleged that "In mission schools the boys were taught that their brothers from the North were the source of all their hardship. In the teaching of religion and history every opportunity was taken to keep the memory of slavery alive".
52 Beswick (2004: 205).
53 Deng Ajuok (2008: 136).
54 The emerging Western-educated southern elite was weaker, less politically experienced, narrowly based, scattered, and culturally distinct from the northern intelligentsia. See Niblock (1987: 156-7).
55 RJC (1947: 26).
56 Howell (1973: 164-5). Author's interviews in Juba and Kampala indicate this as it appears that general awareness remained very scattered.
57 Badal (1994: 105) and Ruay (1994: 66-7).
58 Howell (1973: 165) and O'Ballance (1977: 36).
59 Ruay (1994: 67) and Markakis (1998: 111).
60 Sarkesian (1973: 8), Eprile (1974: 20), and Ruay (1994: 64-7).
61 Howell (1973: 165). Southern representatives often swayed away from a collective southern stand to force concessions. This was due to divisions and floor-crossing caused by bribery, co-option, and other persuasion by northern political forces. For instance according to Paysama, "The money was there, a great amount of money, from the Government and the Umma Party, and every

time elections [voting] came, they [the Southerners] are destroyed like this" (quoted in Badal, 1994: 105).

62 Howell (1973: 166).

63 O'Ballance (1977: 36-7).

64 Sarkesian (1973: 9).

65 Based on an interview with a prominent member of the University of Juba (22 September 2008). As noted in the previous chapter, some *jallaba* had been present in places like Juba, even during the Southern Policy, to engage in trade and to provide commercial services which the British perceived as essential.

66 Ruay (1994: 75).

67 Deng (1995a: 136).

68 RCIDSS (1956: 20).

69 According to Ruay (1994: 74-5), this attitude of many *jallaba* could be observed in daily business in situations such as insisting to sit in the front seat, skipping queues in the local administrator's office or hospital, and keeping locals waiting in line in government offices while casually chatting with officials.

70 Howell (1973: 166), Daly (1991: 370), and Markakis (1998: 111).

71 Daly (1991: 370).

72 Niblock (1987: 216).

73 Ruay (1994: 71).

74 Albino (1970: 33) and Ruay (1994: 71).

75 Taisier and Matthews (1999: 203).

76 Howell (1973: 166) and O'Ballance (1977: 38).

77 Ruay (1994: 72), Markakis (1998: 111), Rogier (2005: 10), and Jok (2007: 79-82). Individuals such as Chief Lomiluk, a politically influential "rainmaker" who was fired from the government service in May 1955 by the northern District Commissioner for opposing the annexation of the South, were important in this process. See Simonse (1992: 118-119).

78 Quoted in Collins (1975: 65).

79 Ruay (1994: 72).

80 Oduho and Deng (1963: 22-24), Sarkesian (1973: 9), Alier (1990: 23), Ruay (1994: 76), and Markakis (1998: 111). The Liberal Party's Juba Conference took place on 18-21 October 1954 and included chiefs from the three southern provinces (Bahr al-Ghazal, Equatoria, and Upper Nile), southern Sudanese representatives in Khartoum, NUP members from the South, and a number of individuals of northern origin who considered themselves southerners, along with Liberal Party members. Chaired by Benjamin Lwoki, President of the Liberal Party, the conference decided unanimously to support Sudanese independence, and to push for federal form of government, with 7 NUP members abstaining from the vote. See MLPCJ (1954).

81 Said (1965: 173).

82 RCIDSS (1956: 21).

83 RCIDSS (1956: 21) and Ruay (1994: 74).

84 Quoted in Ruay (1994: 73).

85   Ruay (1994: 74).
86   Markakis (1998: 111-2).
87   RCIDSS (1956: 24-5).
88   Beshir (1968: 73).
89   RCIDSS (1956: 86). Khartoum portrayed an image that most southern leaders were against the conference by commissioning the northern District Commissioner and his assistant in Yambio to tour their district in Equatoria province and to pressure local chiefs to sign in support of preventing the meeting. The Assistant District Commissioner convinced 13 local Azande chiefs from Tembura sub-section to sign a telegram declaring that they sided with the government and objected to the Juba conference, and after obtaining the signatures he sent a telegram to Khartoum claiming that the southerners were generally against the conference. Radio Omdurman was subsequently used to spread propaganda against the conference. See RCIDSS (1956: 21, 87-8), Eprile (1974: 40), and Ruay (1994: 76).
90   Khartoum's strategy had initially the desired effect as it provoked a confrontation between the chiefs who had signed the telegram and and Elia Kuze, Legislative Assembly representative of Yambio, who supported the conference. On 7 July 1955 in a public meeting in Yambio it was decided that the chiefs who had signed the telegram should be dismissed and Kuze's position as the peoples' representative at the national level affirmed. But instead of accepting the decision, which would have stripped them from leadership, the chiefs resorted to Assistant District Commissioner who was behind the plot, and demanded Kuze's arrest and trial. Consequently, on 25 July Kuze was arrested and sentenced initially to 20 years in prison for criminal intimidation. However, the trial was a dubious and violated the legal immunity of a parliament member, and the sentence was ten times the maximum described in the penal code for criminal intimidation. In addition, the chiefs were both the plaintiffs and the judges in the process. Upon the announcement of the sentence, which was finally adjusted to 2 years adhering to the penal code, a crowd of 700 following the trial called for Kuze's release. Small groups gathered in the Yambio market, raided a *jallaba* shop, and assaulted individuals they considered "Arabs". See Eprile (1974: 40), O'Ballance (1977: 40), and Ruay (1994: 76-7).
91   July 26, 1955, a demonstration began when a petition of 60 employees for higher wages was under consideration, and 250 workers of the Weaving and Spinning Mill left the factory and grouped outside the General Manager's office. Carrying sticks and tools, which they used to break windows of the offices, the crowd shouted "go back to your own country", and was joined by others equipped with bows, arrows, and spears, which increased the size of the crowd to between 700 and 1,000 individuals. Starting with the salary issue, the demonstration was also possibly related to the Kuze trial and the dismissal of 300 Equatorian workers in June and early July from the Zande Scheme, the only major economic development project in the southern provinces. Despite the dismissal of the local workers having been at least in part an economic de-

cision, with little consideration of its consequences, some southerners became convinced that it had taken place due to "Arab" colonialism to deprive the locals of their livelihoods. The fact that the decision had been made after more northern staff had been hired strengthened such beliefs. See RCIDSS (1956: 22, 102), Eprile (1974: 41), Daly (1991: 385), Ruay (1994: 78), and O'Ballance (2000: 7).

92 Upon receiving news about the demonstration, District Commissioner dispatched a unit to the scene. It consisted of 11 soldiers and 5 policemen under the authority of Assistant District Commissioner, but by the time the unit arrived the situation had become increasingly threatening and two *jallaba* shops had been looted. Consequently, the authorities attempted to disperse the crowd, first by warnings and tear gas, but after this appeared impossible, and faced with overwhelming odds, the unit fired at the crowd. The shooting, which was joined by two *jallaba* merchants with their own guns, dispersed the mob, but left six Azande demonstrators dead and several injured, while two others drowned when escaping in panic. See RCIDSS (1956: 22, 80, 102), Eprile (1974: 41), O'Ballance (1977: 40), Daly (1991: 385), and Ruay (1994: 78-9).

93 According to the RCIDSS (1956: 102), " . . . the [Nzara] incident itself had a bad effect on the minds of the Southerners and was regarded by them as the beginning of a war; and if there was some confidence left in the administration, it had then disappeared completely". The events in Yambio also fed this perception. In fact, what took place in Nzara received no investigation from Khartoum, but rather resulted in an ultimatum that was broadcasted and circulated. For instance, the later Commission of Inquiry in the Disturbances in the Southern Sudan came to a conclusion that the situation in Nzara was mishandled, and defined the government's dealing with the events of 1955 as a series of blunders. See RCIDSS (1956: 21-2, 102), Eprile (1974: 41), and Ruay (1994: 78-9).

94 RCIDSS (1956: 25-7), O'Ballance (1977: 41), Daly (1991: 385-6), and Ruay (1994: 79).

95 During the investigation it was also discovered that Oboyo's intent had been to kill the northern acting officer in charge of the SEC; that he was a member of the Liberal Party and in contact with politically oriented clerks in Juba; that he knew about government plans to send northern troops to southern Sudan and believed they would come to kill southerners; that he had spread propaganda among southern troops and planned a systematic killing of northern officers in the three southern provinces in early August 1955; that he had counted with a total of 24 conspirators within the SEC placed in Torit, Malakal, Kapoeta, Trek, Juba, and Leave; and finally that he had intended to persuade southern junior officers to fire on arriving the northern troops and capture strategic locations in Juba. However, after the junior officers declined to participate, he had pleaded resignation from his position as the president of southern corps and the military leader of the conspiracy from the Liberal Party Committee in Juba. See RCIDSS (1956: 25-7).

96   Due to the government's limited capacity and decreasing legitimacy in southern Sudan, which complicated making arrests in the SEC, it settled for investigating the extent of the conspiracy among the troops, while detaining two civilian clerks, Marco Rome and Daniel Jume, on 8 August in Juba. This again provoked demonstrations. The situation grew tense the following day as a crowd demanded release of the two accused, and although the District Commissioner was inclined to compromise and send the accused to Torit for investigation, the crowd assaulted him. However the District Commissioner escaped and tear gas bombs were used to disperse the crowd. See RCIDSS (1956: 30) and Eprile (1974: 41).

97   RCIDSS (1956: 30-1), Eprile (1974: 41), Ruay (1994: 79), and O'Ballance (2000: 7).

98   On 16 August 1955, the government ordered the No.2 Company of the SEC in Torit to prepare for transfer to Khartoum. The unit was to participate in a parade to celebrate the withdrawal of colonial troops from Sudan. However, the No.2 Company along with other sections of the SEC was increasingly fearful due to the rumors circulated by some southern politicians and because of the recent events. See RCIDSS (1956: 32, 84-102, 105) and Ruay (1994: 79).

99   This highly publicized document had been circulating in the southern provinces since July 1955. Allegedly signed by Prime Minister al-Azhari, but which originated from an unidentified politically active southern clerk in Juba, it stated ". . . Do not listen to the childish complaints of the Southerners. Persecute them, oppress them, ill-treat them according to my orders. Any administrator who fails to comply with my orders will be liable to prosecution . . .". See RCIDSS (1956: 82), Ruay (1994: 79), and O'Ballance, 2000: 7).

100 To add to other rumors, including that the southern troops would be disarmed, Second Lieutenant Taffeng Ladongi, one of the nine junior officers in the SEC, spread the word among his men that the order was a trap to let northern troops to do what they wanted with the women and children of southern soldiers, while they would be executed in Khartoum. See RCIDSS (1956: 106), Markakis (1998: 112), and Ruay (1994: 80).

101 RCIDSS (1956: 105).

102 RCIDSS (1956: 106) reports that their links to civilians and some southern politicians was apparent. It became widely known that when the No.2 Company was to be transported to Khartoum it would disobey the order.

103 Shortly after Captain Yuzbashi Salah Abdel Magid addressed the soldiers in a threatening manner, stating that if they mutinied they would be killed, the No.2 Company soldiers broke into the armory and fired upon two northern officers, killing one of them. Although the mutineers began to hunt down other northern officers, some of them escaped. Many southern civilians joined the revolt and began looting *jallaba* shops, provoking a situation which led to the drowning of an estimated 55 southerners while crossing river Kinyeti when trying to escape the violence. The next morning, the violence and looting continued. Enraged by exaggerated reports spread by southern junior officers Renaldo

Loleya and Mandiri Onzaki that northern troops had massacred many southern soldiers and civilians in Juba (the exact number being four), the mutineers looted more *jallaba* shops and northerners' houses. On 20 August, the havoc continued although Loleya had been thought to be in charge, and the mutineers killed several northern *jallaba* merchants, their families, and northern officials and officers. For instance, they killed some *jallaba* and their families who had taken refuge in prison cells by firing at them through ventilation windows and doors after the prison warden had denied them the keys. Later, 11 of the northern survivors in Torit were taken to hospital, while some escaped and others were forced to clean the blood from the cells, while yet others had to load and unload dead bodies on a truck after which they were rounded up and the majority shot dead. Other atrocities committed included further arbitrary killings and executions of northerners. For instance, the 11 northerners who were in a hospital run by missionaries were joined by two northern officers, but following demands of southern officers they were taken to army cells, and on 25 August the two officers were executed by Ladongi's brother who mistakenly thought his brother had been killed in Juba. Two northern merchants released to bury them were also shot dead before a missionary housed and protected the remaining northern prisoners. See RCIDSS (1956: 34-6, 38, 53), Albino (1970: 38), and Eprile (1974: 42-3).

104 O'Ballance (1977: 41, 2000: 7) and Markakis (1998: 112).

105 RCIDSS (1956: 47-66).

106 Eprile (1974: 43).

107 Ruay (1994: 81) and O'Ballance (2000: 7-8).

108 RCIDSS (1956: 42-5) and Collins (1975: 67).

109 RCIDSS (1956: 37, 53, 66-77, 80) and Daly (1991: 386).

110 The overall number of known casualties in the southern disturbances was 336 of which 261 were northerners and 75 southerners. According to official sources, the deaths by location were the following: Torit, 78 northerners and 55 southerners who drowned; Zande District (Yambio and Nzara), 45 northerners; Eastern District (Kapoeta), 35 northerners; Yei, 32 northerners and 1 southerner; Moru District (Maridi), 27 northerners; Loka, 17 northeners; Kateri, 9 northeners and 6 southerners; Malakal, 1 northener and 9 southerners; Terekeka 7 northerners; Tali, 6 northeners; Juba, 4 southerners; Lainya, 3 northerners; Rumbek, 1 northerner. See RCIDS (1956: 80).

111 Claiming northern ignorance of the local realities in the South, Collins (1975: 66) asserts that "No one lounging in the cool of the evening on the veranda of the Grand Hotel [informal meeting point still favored by the northern elite] or sipping tea in the sūq of Omdurman would ever have predicted that the tempest would rage for seventeen years".

112 Ruay (1994: 82).

113 O'Ballance (1977: 41) and Daly (1991: 386).

114 At the time, such sentiment, promoted by elements of the southern elite, had already developed among the southerners due to perceived northern disrespect

194

of agreements and commitments with the southerners since the 1940s. Abel Alier's *Southern Sudan: Too Many Agreements Dishonoured* (1990) makes this case.

115 RCIDSS (1956: 37-40), O'Ballance (1977: 42), and Ruay (1994: 82).

116 O'Ballance (1977: 42) and Daly (1991: 386-7).

117 Daly (1991: 386-7).

118 RCIDSS (1956: 40), O'Ballance (1977: 41), and Ruay (1994: 82).

119 RCIDSS (1956: 40-2).

120 O'Ballance (1977: 42), Ruay (1994: 83), and ICG (2002: 9). On 3 November it was announced that 959 mutineers had surrendered, while an estimated 360 remained at large. Over 3,000 southerners, including 140 mutineers, had fled to Uganda fearing government reprisals. See Daly (1991: 387) and O'Ballance (2000: 8).

121 Daly (1991: 387), Johnson (2003: 29), and Rogier (2005: 10).

122 O'Ballance (1977: 42).

123 Although al-Azhari attempted to hold back pressure to seek revenge for the atrocities committed during the disturbances, the trials of the surrendered mutineers were conducted in an atmosphere of retaliation, in part because a number of northern survivors, including the District Commissioner and Assistant District Commissioner of Yambio, sat in the tribunal. Consequently, the civil courts issued 147 death sentences by mid-December 1955, out of which Helm, who departed from Sudan permanently on 15 December, authorized 121. Northern Sudanese judges ordered further death sentences in 1956, also executing Loleya to who Helm had personally promised safe conduct and fair trials. See Albino (1970: 38), Eprile (1974: 47), O'Ballance (1977: 42-3, 2000: 8), Daly (1991: 387), and Ruay (1994: 83).

124 See Daly (1991: 387-8), Yohannes (1997: 269), and Woodward (2006: 29).

125 Oduho and Deng (1963: 33). According to Albino (1970: 38), "Life became very cheap, and people passed away daily in firing squads, from random shooting, torture in prisons, or in secret night arrests".

126 Eprile (1974: 48, 54-55).

127 Simonse (1992: 177). For instance, many pupils returning to school found that their role models (e.g. familiar police officers or officials) had been killed and that northerners had taken over the schools and administration. The northerners appeared also more present in the streets, and enjoying the company of southern women. These developments generated bitterness particularly among sections of the youth.

128 From 18 to 21 February 1956 demonstrations of some 700 tenant farmers from Guda cotton project (Guda Agricultural Scheme) in Kosti took place. The farmers demanded equitable pay for their labor in form of increase in the share of profits, more efficient auditing, and a role in formulating management and sales policy. Clashing with the demonstrators, the police force suffered casualties but killed 18 and imprisoned either 334 or 281 depending on the source. 190 or 192 detainees died in custody due to suffocation and heat stroke. As a

result, the press demanded the Azhari government's resignation, but it outlived the crisis after having been questioned on the incident. See Yohannes (1997: 293) and O'Ballance (2000: 6).

129 The Southern Policy had contributed to this ignorance and prevented a phasing out of attitudes based on slavery, which affected northern behavior and government policies leading up to the 1955 disturbances.

130 Jok (2007: 3, 4-5).

131 O'Ballance (1977: 42) and Jok (2007: 79, 81-2).

132 A plan had existed among some students to enlist in the army to learn military skills and then rebel.

133 O'Ballance (1977: 43).

134 See Collins (2008: 69-70).

135 According to Niblock (1987: 212) and Sidahmed and Sidahmed (2005: 30), the Umma-People's Democratic Party (PDP) coalition received 62 and 26 seats, respectively, leaving the NUP with 42 seats in the Parliament. O'Ballance (1977: 46) gives slightly different numbers: the Umma 63, the NUP 45, the PDP 27, the Southern Bloc (Federal Party) 37, and the Anti-Imperialist Front 1. Niblock (1987: 215) also quotes numbers from Bechtold (1976: 190) and presents the following results: the Umma 63 and 14, the NUP 44 and 5, the PDP 26 and 4, the Southern Liberals 40 and 7, of the total seats of the House of Representatives (173) and the Senate (30), respectively. Finally, Hasan (2003: 172) states the following numbers: Umma 63, NUP 45, Southern Liberals 38, and PDP 27.

136 Beginning in October 1955, al-Mirghani pressured for non-sectarian and secular Azhari government's replacement. He masterminded a breakaway of 3 ministers and 18 parliamentarians leading to an internal division in the NUP that culminated in the formation of the PDP on 30 June 1956. The PDP composed of anti-Azhari ex-NUP elements, which, unlike Azhari who broke with Egypt in support of Sudanese independence, maintained relations with Nasser's Egypt and its patron, the Soviet Union. The PDP reached over sectarian lines to act in concert with Umma to depose Azhari. See Niblock (1987: 208-10), Yohannes (1997: 285), and Hasan (2003: 172).

137 The Southern Sudan Federal Party founded by Saturnino Lohure and Ezboni Mundiri had gained a number of seats. After Mundiri spoke about a federal solution for the South in the Legislative Assembly, he was imprisoned and the party banned. Lohure replaced it with the Southern Block. See Veenhoven and Ewing (1977: 243).

138 Hasan (2003: 174) and Collins (2005: 205).

139 First (1970: 225, 228-30), Niblock (1987: 217-8), Woodward (1995: 95-6), Yohannes (1997: 290, 291), O'Ballance (2000: 12), and Hasan (2003: 173).

140 Beshir (1968: 80).

141 He assumed the title of Commander-in-Chief, presiding over the twelve-member Supreme Council of the Armed Forces (SCAF) that became the political authority exercising all constitutional powers. A cabinet of ministers was formed

to assist the SCAF, seven of whose members, including Abboud, belonged to the SCAF, while another six were civilians, including Santino Deng as the only southerner. See First (1970: 232), O'Ballance (2000: 12), and Hassan (2003: 175).

142 First (1970: 231).

143 For example, Yohannes (1997: 291) and O'Ballance (2000: 13) assert that early on these personal ties were based on a family relationship between the former Prime Minister al-Khalil and his son-in-law, General Ahmad Abd al-Wahab, who initially became Deputy Commander in Chief, Minister of the Interior and Local Government, and a member of the SCAF.

144 O'Ballance (1977: 49) and Yohannes (1997: 292-4). However, political wrangling and two Arab-nationalist and anti-Western coup attempts resulted in the incorporation of anti-western elements, and the regime sought consolidation orienting increasingly towards Egypt with which it concluded the Nile Waters Agreement in October 1959. See Albino (1970: 44) and Collins (2005: 205). According to Niblock (1987: 221) and Warburg (2000: 78), this raised the Sudanese water allocation from the 1/22 stipulated in the previous treaty to 1/3, or 18.5 billion m^3 respective to Egypt's 55.5 billion m^3.

145 Oduho and Deng (1963: 35) and Albino (1970: 44).

146 According to Collins (1990: 304), "After the dissolution of parliament, the military government sought to quell southern dissent by the bonds of Sudanese nationalism, expressed in Arabic language, Arab culture, and the Arab past fused with the traditions of Sudanese history and the deep emotions of Sudanese Islam. These are strong and dynamic themes in the northern Sudan. They have less relevance among the southern Sudanese, who had frustrated the ambitions of the Mahdi and the efforts of the Khalifa 'Abd Allahi at the end of the nineteenth century to advance Islam up the Nile and in the twentieth century, supported by British imperial policy, formed an African bastion against Islam".

147 For instance, the regime initiated a school building program, backed by the United States Agency for International Development (USAID) that funneled money to the Sudanese economy. During that time the Americans considered the anti-Communist Abboud regime heading to the Western camp. The resources provided by the U.S. were largely used to establish schools to learn *Qur'an*, along with one secondary and a number of intermediate schools, as well as Islamic institutes. Conversion to Islam was encouraged among students, and Arabic replaced English as the medium of instruction at the intermediate level in the southern provinces. The government also built mosques, replaced Sunday with Friday as the official day of rest, and subsidized Muslim propaganda in southern Sudan through the Department of Religious Affairs. See e.g. Beshir (1968: 81), Niblock (1987: 224), Yohannes (1997: 294-5), Jendia (2002: 65), Johnson (2003: 30), and Collins (2005: 209).

148 O'Ballance (1977: 51-2), Niblock (1987: 223-4), Daly (1993: 149, and Jendia (2002: 64-5).

149 Collins (2005: 207-8).

150 While many prominent members of the northern elite, such as Siddig al-Mahdi and Islamists, are known to have advocated the spread of Islam to deal with the "Southern Problem", the missionaries continued to see themselves as a bastion of Christianity to curb the Islamic encroachment in the South. See O'Ballance (2000: 15).

151 O'Ballance (1977: 51), Niblock (1987: 224), and Jendia (2002: 56).

152 According to Collins (2005: 209), in 1961 religious gatherings outside the churches and catechetical teaching became forbidden, and missionary activities became increasingly curbed. In the following year, on 15 May 1962, the regime decreed a Missionary Societies Act, which limited the activities to basic religious functions. Johnson (2003: 31) has noted that "Ironically, conversions to Christianity increased dramatically once the churches were subjected to this government assault".

153 Eprile (1974: 55-6) and Chan and Zuor (2006: 13). These measures aimed at coercive dominance, appeasement, and assimilation by force. Arrests, tortures, and other retaliatory actions were taken, but this facilitated development of southern opposition. See e.g. Eprile (1974: 55-6), O'Ballance (1977: 52), Daly (1993: 13-4), Johnson (2003: 31), and Iyob and Khadiagala (2006: 81). According to O'Ballance (1977: 51), for instance in 1957 the government troops destroyed 700 huts in Yei district as punishment for collaborating with the rebels.

154 Howell (1978a: 425). For instance, O'Ballance (1977: 51, 59) asserts that ". . . the 'rebels', or 'outlaws' as the Khartoum Government officially designated them, were few in number and they lacked cohesion, organization and central direction; their scarce firearms were the old British rifles, sten-guns they had taken with them when they had deserted" and " . . . their hatred of northerners manifested itself in the occasional ambush, shooting incident or minor attack".

155 O'Ballance (1977: 51).

156 According to Niblock (1987: 224), "The violence employed by the police and armed forces in suppressing dissent caused growing numbers of southern civilians to escape from government control, either by fleeing into exile or by absconding into the bush".

157 O'Ballance (1977: 52-3, 57) and Niblock (1987: 225).

158 For instance awareness in schools led to coordinated, repeated, and annual strikes to which the authorities responded heavy handedly, including dismissing the brightest students. In contrast, pupils often considered those colleagues interacting with northern teachers unnecessarily as traitors.

159 O'Ballance (1977: 52) stresses that pupils began boycotting schools either in the fear of becoming targets of the government or the rebels. See also Niblock (1987: 225).

160 Replying to the question of what war meant, Chief Thon Wai said, "Our brothers [the Northerners], in their anger with us, harassed all those people who remained at home, including their chiefs. Even if the people of the forest [the

rebels] had only passed near a camp, they would come and say, 'They are here inside the camp.' They would proceed to destroy the camp. Children would die and women would die. The chief would only stand holding his head. If you tried force, you fell a victim. Whatever you tried, you fell a victim. Nothing made it better. You just sat mourning with your hands folded like a woman" (quoted in Deng, 1978: 167).

161 Quoted in Deng (1978: 168-9).
162 Duffield (1992: 52). Duffield (2001) also discusses this in the context of the second southern insurgency.
163 Woodward (2002: 9-10) and Johnson (2002: 2).
164 Eprile (1974: 21, 92) and O'Ballance (1977: 53).
165 According to Eprile (1974: 92) and O'Ballance (1977: 53), Dominic Muerwel, a former southern member of the Legislative Assembly, had attempted to leave the country already in 1959 to establish an exile political movement. However, William Deng, a Dinka from Tonj, Bahr al-Ghazal, and the Assistant District Commissioner of Kapoeta, was prominent among those seeking exile after the plot, claiming having been victim of obstruction and nepotism.
166 Many southerners began to flee to Uganda, Kenya, Ethiopia, the CAR, and DRC, and some found refuge and assistance among ethnic kin across the border.
167 Bariagaber (2006: 70).
168 Beshir (1968: 84).
169 According to Simonse (1992: 313) between " . . . 1955 and 1959 a series of attacks was carried out against government targets and against chiefs who were regarded as collaborating with the government . . .". These were individual incidents in which single soldiers were killed, but larger battles against army troops were avoided.
170 O'Ballance (1977: 57, 59).
171 Simonse (1992: 119).
172 Howell (1978a: 425, 426), Wakoson (1984), and Chan and Zuor (2006: 15-6).
173 Howell (1978a: 426).
174 O'Ballance (2000: 18).
175 Johnson (2003: 31).
176 See O'Ballance (1977: 59, 2000: 19), Woodward (1995: 97), and Chan and Zuor (2006: 13).
177 "Anya Nya" means "snake poison" or "venom of the Gabon viper" in Madi and other Equatorian languages.
178 According to Chan and Zuor (2006: 13), "In late 1963, the first training centers outside the country were opened in Zaire at the villages of Bangadi and Nyangera with Captain Marko Bangusa as the person in charge of training. The camps started out with such weapons as spears, swords, pangas, sticks, and etc.".
179 O'Ballance (2000: 19-20).
180 In Pochalla, the rebels, recruited to organize in Nuer refugee camps in Ethio-

pia, killed all northern *jallaba* except one female, and occupied a police post for a week. See Eprile (1974: 96), O'Ballance (2000: 20), and Chan and Zuor (2006: 14-5).

181 Chan and Zuor (2006: 15).

182 O'Ballance (2000: 20).

183 On 11 January 1964 a force from a Dinka branch of the movement under Captain Bernandino, armed with British rifles, sten guns, and Molotov cocktails, unsuccessfully attacked the government defenses. Bernandino and sixty men were captured. Subsequently, he and two of his men were hanged, while the rest were imprisoned. See Eprile (1974: 96) and O'Ballance (2000: 20).

184 Eprile (1974: 96-7), O'Ballance (1977: 60-1), and Chan and Zuor (2006: 14).

185 Musa (1988: 457).

186 By early 1964 most of Sudan's army of 18,000 was operating in southern provinces, but by September there were thousands of Anya Nya recruits to be trained. By the end of the year the Anya Nya military force already reached 2,000, which forced decreasing the recruitment due to the shortage of firearms. See Eprile (1974: 96), O'Ballance (1977: 61-2), and Iyob and Khadiagala (2006: 81).

187 According to Eprile (1974: 97), who has compiled a list of observer accounts, the rebels experienced " . . . smallness of the educated elite; lack of discipline; personal misuse of money; poor sense of organization; poor time sense; little combat experience; poverty; inferior military equipment; shortage of external sources of supply; lack of support of neighbouring African countries; no developed resources to sell in return for foreign backing; an extremely high death rate from disease; poor to non-existent communications and transport; lack of knowledge of techniques used by other guerilla movements". All this added to ethnic differences that were difficult to overcome. See Eprile (1974: 98) and Chan and Zuor (2006: 15-6).

188 According to O'Ballance (1977: 53-4), the SANU President Joseph Oduho, a Lotuko from Lobira in Equatoria, initially condemned the rebellion, which seemed to disconnect the political movement from the insurgency in 1960.

189 Bernandino appears to have carried out the Wau attack according to Deng's orders. See O'Ballance (1977: 60-1).

190 O'Ballance (1977: 61).

191 Albino (1970: 44), O'Ballance (1977: 53), Markakis (1998: 117), and Chan and Zuor (2006: 16).

192 According to Collins (2008: 79-80), these were Saturnino Lohure, Joseph Oduho, and William Deng.

193 These Equatorian leaders included Lohure, a Lotuka, Agrey Jaden, a Pojulu, Oduho, a Lotuka, Rume, a Kuku, Ezboni Mundiri, a Moru, Albino Tombe, a Lokoya, Tafen Lodongi and Lazaru Mutek, both Lotukas, Benjamin Loki, a Pojulu, Elia Lupe, a Kakwa, Elia Kuze, an Azande, and Timon Boro, a Moru.

194 Lohure was linked to the Catholic Church and channeled support to the SACDNU, while Joseph Oduho became its first President, Marko Rume the Vice-President, Deng the Secretary General, and Jaden the Deputy Secretary

General. See Eprile (1974: 92), O'Ballance (2000: 17), and Chan and Zuor (2006: 16).

195 Albino (1970: 44), O'Ballance (1977: 54), Markakis (1998: 117), and Chan and Zuor (2006: 16, 17). The SANU continued diplomacy and earlier propaganda through publications, but its leadership consisted of prominent individuals of different ethnicities and regions many of who had played part in the emerging southern political movement. Consequently, SANU remained divided between demands for federalism and independence, and personal ambitions and competition. See Eprile (1974: 92-3), O'Ballance (2000: 17-8), and Chan and Zuor (2006: 16-7).

196 First major disagreement had occurred between Oduho and Deng over the movement's name. When the leadership was voted upon during the first SANU convention in 7-16 November 1964, Deng was absent in Europe on a diplomatic mission, resulting in him being deliberately sidelined. In 1964, the Abboud regime collapsed in the October Revolution following pressure from the sidelined Arabized elite's opposition and the Sudan Communist Party (SCP) which had mobilized their civilian constituencies in northern Sudan against repression, nepotism, corruption, deteriorating economic conditions, and the deepening "Southern Problem". It was replaced by al-Khalifa's caretaker government, which sought to negotiate with the southern opposition. According to Chan and Zuor (2006: 17), this led to an offshoot when sidelined Deng responded positively to al-Khalifa government's request for peace negotiations against the will of the rest of the movement. See also Hasan (2003) for an excellent account on this.

197 Many exiled southern politicians advocated independence as a solution to northern domination.

198 Chan and Zuor (2006: 17) assert that the SF was a southern political organization with constituency among the displaced southerners in the northern provinces. Mboro, a Ndogo from near Wau in Bahr al-Ghazal, and Abel Alier, a Bor Dinka, were among its leading members. The existence of the SF may have influenced Deng's decision to go to Khartoum.

199 Markakis (1998: 117).

200 According to Markakis (1998: 117), an attempt was made to " . . . solicit support abroad, particularly among Africans, portraying the conflict as racial, and relying heavily on the theme of Arab oppression of black Africans".

201 The OAU had been founded on 25 May 1963 as culmination of pan-Africanism, but was at the same time based on a charter prohibiting involvement in the internal affairs of member states. On SANU appeals to the OAU and the latter's charter, see O'Ballance (1977: 53-4), Alier (1990: 73), Markakis (1998: 117), Jendia (2002: 114), and Murithi (2005: 2, 3, 23).

202 Markakis (1998: 117) and ICG (2002: 93-8).

203 O'Ballance (1977: 50), Heldman (1981: 65), and World Bank (2003).

204 Zartman (1985: 83), Jendia (2002: 114, 121), and Woodward (2003: 120).

205 O'Ballance (1977: 60, 63).

206 O'Ballance (1977: 60-1, 63, 64).

207 Beshir (1975: 91).

208 Jendia (2002: 114, 117-9) and Akol (2007: 107-8).

209 Heldman (1981: 65) and Jendia (2002: 114).

210 Sikainga (1993: 81).

211 O'Ballance (2000: 21) and Markakis (1998: 117).

212 O'Ballance (1977: 62).

213 The total number of the deported missionaries varies by source between 300 (272 Roman Catholic and 28 Protestant) and 335. See Eprile (1974: 85-6), O'Ballance (1977: 62), and Niblock (1987: 224).

214 Alier (1990: 75).

215 See Paterno (2007) on the story of Father Saturnino, a Lotuka Catholic priest, and his prominent role in the southern struggle.

216 O'Ballance (1977; 2000), Heraclides (1987: 226-7), and Gray (2002: 120).

217 Gray (2002: 120).

218 O'Ballance (2000: 21).

219 O'Ballance (1977: 62-3).

220 O'Ballance (2000: 21).

221 O'Ballance (2000: 21). In fact, Uganda did not provide military aid initially to the Anya Nya in part because it hoped to gain U.N. financing by hosting southern refugees. Meanwhile, Uganda tracked down southern politicians, such as Joseph Oduho, who was arrested in February 1964 in Kampala, soon after assuming the leadership of the SANU from Deng, on charges of recruiting Anya Nya fighters from the refugee camps. See O'Ballance (1977: 63).

222 O'Ballance (2000: 22) and Jendia (2002: 114). Allegedly this exodus was also partly due to SANU's engagement in a propaganda campaign, in which it claimed that 14 refugee camps in Ethiopia had been attacked by the government soldiers and that Ethiopia was to extradite thousands of refugees. See O'Ballance (1977: 63).

223 Bariagaber (2006: 70).

224 Johnson (2003: 22).

CHAPTER VI

FROM WAR TO PEACE:
The Return to Authoritarian Rule

In the latter part of the 1960s, the insurgency in southern Sudan intensified. Political developments during this period demonstrate how peace initiatives were unable to address the situation for years, and how their failure led to deepening violence. This changed only when a combination of interlinked local, regional, and international dynamics related to another regime change became conducive to a peace settlement in the early 1970s. External forces and actors were important particularly in the latter stages of the first insurgency in southern Sudan, and they combined with opportune the internal political dynamics to bring about the peace settlement.

In the late 1960s the southern elite continued to be largely marginalized and excluded from power at the state level. Some of its members were granted symbolic state positions in an attempt to end the rebellion, but these did not amount to effective political power. From the narrative of the latter part of the war, it becomes also clear that despite political violence there existed no primordial or inherent incompatibility between the constructed "northern" and "southern" identity, which would impede a single state solution to the war. Rather, as has been argued in the previous chapters, the conflicting identity differences are (re)constructed, manipulated, and instrumentalized in the political competition for power and resources. As shown, they become salient especially in circumstances of political repression and violence.

Transitional Government and Failed Peace Efforts

Abboud's downfall in 1964 facilitated efforts to deal with the "Southern Problem" politically. However, the government which succeeded the regime was unable to find compromises that would satisfy the demands of the fragmented southern opposition.

The Transitional Government

In the course of the early 1960s, the support of the Abboud regime had declined in the northern provinces. This was largely due to its authoritarian policies, deepening economic malaise, and the war in the South, which inspired popular opposition. By 1964, northern opposition political parties had joined with professional, labor, and student organizations to organize the opposition. The same year they staged a wave of popular demonstrations that swept northern Sudan, culminating in a general strike and the much celebrated October Revolution that eventually toppled the military regime.[1]

On 30 October 1964, a caretaker government of al-Khatim al-Khalifa took office.[2] After some initial difficulties with reluctant elements of the exiting military regime, and after having fought back the Sudan Communist Party attempt to take power following the civilian overthrow of the military regime, the new government was able to consolidate itself and push for democratic order.[3] Composed primarily of a wide spectrum of northern elite opposition groups, which had used the disaffection of regime repression, economic deterioration, nepotism and corruption, and the worsening "Southern Problem" to gain power, the new government had to confront the legacy of the northern elite's inability to govern together. Now, as the new state leadership ruling over political system featured by the established culture and practice of marginalization, the collection of northern elite factions in power confronted the same problems related to political and economic organization that had been faced by the earlier governments. When the leadership took measures to establish political stability,[4] it gradually succumbed into the dominance of the most prominent parties that sought to wrestle power from the radical forces. The initial cabinet was reshuffled, which resulted in the Umma and NUP re-consolidating their position, while the Islamic Charter Front (ICF) arose as a new constituency based on radical religious values.[5] In this situation, the better-established sections of the northern elite recovered state leadership from the radical coalition that had initially commanded wide popular support.

Meanwhile, the fall of Abboud regime had been generally well-received in the southern provinces. It appeared that the end of dictatorship might undo the worst repression and propel reconciliation efforts. Many southern elite members were also pleased about having representation in the cabinet and the transitional parliament, and that Khalifa, who was also well respected in southern Sudan, assumed power. However, most exile leaders expressed concerns about the real intentions of the new government. This was despite it having shown goodwill by releasing 32 southern political prisoners and re-establishing Sunday and Christmas Day as official holidays in southern

Sudan. At the same time, the SANU was embroiled in a leadership struggle between Deng in Europe, Lohure in Nairobi, and Joseph Oduho and Agrey Jaden in Kampala.[6]

Moreover, motivated in part by its attempt to deal with the "Southern Problem", a coalition of northern elite parties attempted to reinforce relations with Arab states. By making arrangements with Algeria and Egypt, Sudan allowed Russian arms to be transported through its territory to the Simba in the Congo and the Eritrean Liberation Front (ELF), which had emerged in 1961 and 1964 respectively.[7] However, these arrangements backfired in the war against the Anya Nya because the rebels captured some of the arms shipments.[8] In January 1965, Khartoum finally suspended the arms deliveries amidst allegations that five planeloads had been delivered to the Simba. But it resumed the support to the ELF, which was later permitted to open offices in Sudan when a new government elected in 1965 shifted its focus from assisting the Simba to also arming Chadian insurgents.[9] This dynamic established Sudan as a supply route and sanctuary for the Congolese, Eritrean, and Chadian rebels with support of a number of Arab states. It promoted a pattern of culturally oriented foreign relations through political alignment with Arab countries, to which southern opposition responded by seeking "anti-Arab" and "African" ties. As a result, the diverging foreign relations pursued by northern and southern elites, respectively, in the midst of the armed conflict, polarized the country further. Thus, engaging in relations with the Anya Nya became attractive for Israel and some Western actors (including covertly the U.S.), as well as Uganda, Ethiopia, and DRC, and to a lesser extent CAR and Kenya, some of which suffered from instability caused by "Arab" support to rebel groups operating in their territories. This facilitated development of regional networks beyond those dictated by ethnic affinities,[10] and promoted the perception of the insurgency in southern Sudan as an "African" struggle against an "Arab" hegemon. As such, the complex landscape of foreign relations polarized the perceptions of northern and southern "regional" identities further, and hindered prospects for a negotiated settlement to the insurgency.

Failed Peace Efforts

As the conflict dragged on and the Anya Nya strengthened,[11] Khartoum faced increasing pressure to find a peaceful solution to the "Southern Problem". Consequently, an attempt was made to reconcile with the main southern political forces, the SANU and the SF, latter of which was composed of a small number of highly educated southern civil servants, led by Mboro, and engaged in non-violent opposition in Khartoum. While Mboro, who was appointed as the Minister of Interior in Khalifa government, was pushed to negotiate a cease-fire and appeal for peace in southern Sudan, other SF member Ezboni Mundiri was sent to Uganda to sign an agreement to repatriate Sudanese refugees and begin negotiations with the SANU.[12] This made the SF integral to the transitional government's policy towards southern Sudan, which also included the "southernization" of local government positions in southern Sudan.[13]

Meanwhile Deng had unilaterally addressed Khalifa with a letter that proposed a constitutional conference to deal with the "Southern Problem". Deng sought SANU's return as a political force in Sudan, while promoting federalist system and return of refugees, exile politicians, and missionaries.[14] However, his views did not represent the position of those majority in the SANU leadership that by now demanded secession and full independence of southern Sudan. Still, envisaging the possibility of bringing southern politicians back within the limits of state control, the government acted in response to Deng's demands. In December, after returning from a two-day trip to the Southern provinces with Mboro, Khalifa declared an unconditional amnesty for all southerners who had left Sudan since 1955, called for freedom and equality, and to leave behind all racial, religious, and political differences, while offering southern leaders federal autonomy.[15] Yet, the statement gained limited support among southern leadership since the majority of SANU leaders rejected the offer.

However, despite the reconciliation initiatives, the political situation remained tense. It resulted in a riot by southerners in Khartoum in December 1964,[16] which came to be called "Black Sunday" because it was the first time the violence related to the "Southern Problem" was felt in the capital. The "Black Sunday" caused immediate migration of many southerners back to southern Sudan in the fear of reprisals. Although this event reinforced the sense of urgency for a political resolution, some intellectuals within the northern elite continued to consider the difference in political views between the two regions as insurmountable.[17] Because of continuation of polarizing opinions, further sharpened by the war, the government faced growing difficulties in reconciling with the southern exile leadership. After Khartoum presented an offer for federal autonomy, the SANU spokesman stated on 5 January 1965 that "SANU must use all means to eject the Arabs from the South Sudan. Negotiations have failed; the next step is force".[18] However, the movement itself remained deeply divided.[19]

With an attempt to weaken the SANU by capitalizing on its internal divisions, and deeming Deng as the main interlocutor, the government began to favor him exclusively. On 25 December 1964, after consulting Deng, Khartoum announced that the SANU had agreed to participate in general elections in March 1965. Yet, Deng worked rather independently, while promoting the impression that his views on the "Southern Problem" represented the majority position among southern leaders.[20] The government readily adopted Deng's position, and further propagated his proposal to set up a Round Table Conference to discuss southern grievances. But SANU-in-exile demanded that any such conference should be held in a neutral territory outside Sudan, observed by the international community, and that the return of southern delegates would be conditional to any agreement in such meeting.[21] The conference was to take place in February 1965 in Juba, but this was subjected to government guarantee of the safety of the SANU delegation, and its commitment to a cease-fire and the lifting of the state of emergency in southern provinces.[22]

SANU's preparatory meeting in Kampala was inconclusive because it remained divided between the two positions. Although there was no solution in sight, Deng parted for Khartoum and announced that SANU was ready for the conference, dragging the divided organization into the negotiating table largely unprepared.[23] It is difficult to assess to what extent Deng was influenced by the government that sought to weaken the southern position,[24] but his individual ventures in the context of internal power struggle within SANU were detrimental to achieving a common stand.

The Round Table Conference was delayed.[25] This gave time for new "southern" parties to emerge in early 1965. While remaining small, many were driven by disagreements among southern leaders. Principal among these were Santino Deng's Southern Unity Party, calling for federalism, the resurrected Liberal Party of Stanislaus Paysama and Buth Diu, and the Southern Peace Party.[26] However, it is also likely that Khartoum, and sectors of the northern elite, endorsed some of these new southern factions to further divide the southern position articulated by SANU and SF. One possible indication of this is that the leaders of most of these other parties were from the older generation of southern politicians, many of who had a background of collaborating with the northern elite governments.

Furthermore, the northern political parties were divided between different views on the political arrangement for southern Sudan. The left wing organizations, such as the SCP, the Anti-Imperialist Front, and pro-Egyptian elements, were prepared to allow a higher degree of autonomy to appease and stabilize the nation, while the traditional parties advocated a more centralized political arrangement and less concessions to southern Sudan.[27] However, the northern political forces managed to organize a relatively unified delegation prepared to allow some limited constitutional compromises towards regional government strictly within the context of unified Sudan, but recognizing that these concessions would not be sufficient to satisfy many southern leaders.[28]

The Round Table Conference was finally held during March 1965. It consisted of 45 participants of who 18 represented northern political forces and 27 various southern political factions. The conference included observers from Uganda, Kenya, Tanzania, Ghana, Nigeria, Algeria, and Egypt. Southern representation remained divided over Deng's position,[29] and the competition between the SANU-in exile and SF secessionists.[30] During the conference, southerners demonstrated their mistrust, having witnessed the brutality of the Abboud regime, and remained divided,[31] while the northern elite delegation was largely influenced by its traditional attitudes against concessions to southern provinces.[32]

As a result, divergent positions emerged. Many of the southern delegates, including some more unity-minded, advocated that Sudan as one centralized entity had failed, while the northerners insisted on unified Sudan in which southern Sudan could possibly have regional government.[33] Meanwhile, the northern delegation pointed to external imperialist aspirations having created the problem and undermining the unity of Sudan.[34] They also disputed the common position of southern politicians that southern provinces should be treated as one region, fearing its power and possible secession, and preferred to treat the region as several administrative districts.[35] This intentionally undermined the unity of the southern delegation and weakened its "regional" position.

Ultimately, the diversity of positions and difficulties to reach compromises hindered the prospects of reaching a settlement. Nevertheless, the dominant SANU-in-exile and SF were able to make clear their demands for a referendum for unity, federalism, or separation to be held in southern Sudan under the supervision of external observers of the conference.[36] This was the first occasion in which southern leaders collectively called for a referendum of self-determination.

In contrast, adamant to preserve southern provinces as part of Sudan, the northern delegation rejected the demand for plebiscite. It demonstrated willingness to accept only a limited autonomy based on a regional government system.[37] Eventually, however, a reform plan to normalize relations between the two regions was agreed upon, which included some government concessions to address local grievances.[38] In addition, it was agreed that although there continued to be an impasse in the constitutional status of the southern provinces, the debate over the southern issue should continue in another conference in three months' time.[39]

Finally, while the northern political forces did not pronounce the conference as a failure, the southern participants generally considered it unsuccessful. Khartoum sought to project the perception amongst conference observers that negotiations were to continue, attempted to minimize the chance of intensification of Anya Nya activity, and looked for SANU and SF support before the coming elections.[40] On the other hand, the southern participants generally believed that the measures promised by the northern delegation would not be implemented, and many deemed that the governing elite had only tested the capability of the southern negotiators and sought Anya Nya surrender.[41] Many southern politicians saw no credible prospects that political and economic marginalization of southern Sudan would be remedied.

Parliamentary election followed the Round Table Conference in April-May 1965.[42] Having deemed the conference as a failure, southern politicians declared a collective election boycott to which Khartoum answered by announcing that the election would go ahead but not be conducted in the southern provinces due to security reasons.[43] The government then used the southern boycott to hand representative positions in southern provinces to government loyalists. A later Supreme Court decision allowed 21 southern representatives to claim their seats by default, which enabled 14 *jallaba* supported by the government to enter the Legislative Assembly.[44] Johnson has argued that in this political process, "The Southern parties were . . . effectively denied voice in the parliament".[45] The prevailing political culture and dynamics of the northern elite dominated state had again prevented southerners from gaining effective representation at the center of the political system. Arguably, the 1965 election also set the precedent for the future governments to instrumentalize the armed conflict in southern Sudan for maintaining the *status quo*.

Soon after the election, in which Umma prevailed ahead of the NUP, the two dominant parties came together and made an amendment to the transitional constitution. This granted Azhari permanent presidency of the Supreme Council,[46] and allowed the main parties of the northern elite to reclaim their paramount role in the political scene. The move had significant repercussions for the following years because it gave Azhari power over the government and direct command of policy decisions. Hence, the election results and the constitutional amendment ensured the continuation of the *status quo* of power relations by marginalizing the "radical" forces that had been prominent in the transitional government.[47] In this situation, the failure of the Round Table Conference and the political exclusion of the main southern political forces contributed to the intensification of the insurgency in southern Sudan.

Nimeiri Assumes Power

After failed peace negotiations, the successive governments resumed the search for military solution to the "Southern Problem". However, in 1969 they were brought down by another military coup in the context of changing international and regional alliances, which initially intensified the conflict but finally led to a peace agreement.

The Coup and its Aftermath

In July 1965 the new Umma-Democratic Unionist Party (former NUP) coalition government under Muhammad Ahmad Mahgoub took office, and leftist elements that had been prominent in the transitional government were pushed into opposition. However, during the following three years the political situation remained volatile as result of sectarian bickering between the neo-Mahdists and the *Khatmiyyah*, an internal power struggle within Umma leadership which split the party into two, the polarization of the political scene between government and opposition, and the continuing conflict in southern Sudan.[48]

During Mahgoub government, conditions in the South worsened because the state sought to curb rebel support through repressive measures, backed by foreign policy overtures towards the Eastern Bloc.[49] The repression resulted in continued atrocities, including assassinations of Deng and Lohure, and the targeting of retired southern leaders.[50] Yet, this strengthened rather than weakened the insurgency, although both southern political and armed opposition remained divided. Power struggles within the southern political opposition became manifested increasingly through ethnic and "tribalist" terms, as politicians sought to form political-military constituencies through control of the ethnically and regionally divided Anya Nya armed groups. As a result, political-military organizations emerged, main ones being the Azania Liberation Front (ALF), the Southern Sudan Provisional Government, SSPG (the later Nile Provisional Government, NPG, that suffered an offshoot the Anyidi Revolutionary Government, ARG), and Sue River Revolutionary Government (SRRG). Some of these were able to control territory in southern Sudan, and function as rudimentary administrations raising taxes and providing services.[51]

The escalating violence in the southern provinces, along with economic deterioration in the northern provinces, contributed to yet another army coup. Inspired by its Egyptian counterpart, in the morning of 25 May 1969 socialist Free Officers' Movement (FOM)[52] seized the government and brought to power a military regime headed by Colonel Jaafar Nimeiri.[53] In the morning of the coup the new leadership addressed the nation, declaring the founding of the Democratic Republic of the Sudan, and stated having claimed power in the name of the 1964 October Revolution to change the course of the country whose history had been a series of catastrophes, and to end the rule of self-interested political parties.[54] Although the northern elite leadership denounced the coup, in part because it was removed from power and because the SCP was allowed back to national politics after being purged, the general public received it well.[55] This was largely because of the frequently changing and ineffective governments had not been able to deal with major issues concerning the nation.

The FOM took immediate measures to consolidate its leadership. The provisional constitution was suspended along with the government and the parliament, and the public service commission and electoral commission were dissolved, while public gatherings were banned and newspapers temporarily closed. Moreover, seeking to end the Umma-DUP sectarian dominance, leaders of the main political parties, including Azhari and Mahgoub, were imprisoned, the parties outlawed, their property confiscated, and army officers posing a possible threat to the new regime retired.[56] These measures concentrated power in the FOM-led sectors of the military, and a selection of northern elite forces collaborating with it.

Initially aligned with the Soviet Bloc, the regime pursued a socialist model of economic development. It reformed the main political institutions accordingly, but maintained them in control of the northern elite sectors, particularly the high-level army officers, the SCP, and Arab socialist and nationalist politicians. The Revolutionary Command Council (RCC) and the cabinet were made the main institutions exercising political power.[57] Babikir Awadallah, an influential leftist with pro-Egyptian and Eastern Bloc tendencies who had earlier been involved in the overthrow of Abboud, became the head of the cabinet, which outlined the Nimeiri regime's initial foreign policy. This helped the modeling a new socialist domestic economic policy according to Egyptian example of centralized planning, with heavy public sector involvement. Two southerners, Joseph Garang (SCP) and Abel Alier (SF), served as ministers of supplies and housing, respectively, which was in line with the already established practice of symbolic southern token representation in the government.[58]

In addition, the new regime instituted Sudan Socialist Union (SSU) as the sole political party. This aimed to consolidate the new government by centralizing political and economic power and transferring it away from the northern sectarian movements. The SSU, a mass organization of radical elements, came to constitute the center of the political system, with elected committees exercising power at the local level. It replaced the indirect rule based on native administration of the *nazir* and *shayk* in the northern provinces, which sought to undo the constituencies of the sectarian organizations at the local level.[59] The new system led to elaborate bureaucratic structures concentrating power on the presidency,[60] while the state's relation with its marginalized peripheries remained largely unchanged.

However, soon after Nimeiri assumed power differences emerged within the governing military-civilian alliance, leading to political squabbles within the regime.[61] The government used repressive measures against those not aligned with its policy as part of an attempt to eliminate challenges from the northern political forces and help Nimeiri to consolidate his personal position.[62] The SCP was blamed for the soon apparent failures of socialist economic order and was subsequently sidelined.[63]

The marginalization of the SCP indicated Sudan's drift from the Soviet Bloc towards the Western camp. This came in part as a response to an allegedly U.S.-financed,[64] March 1970 neo-Mahdist, abortive coup attempt. *Imam* al-Mahdi had staged an uprising in Omdurman and armed *Ansar* to force Nimeiri to step down, which triggered a massive regime response with 40,000 troops and air support against the Mahdist stronghold in Aba Island on the Nile where 30,000 *Ansar* had assembled. The attack ended in a massacre in which *Imam* and 3,000 *Ansar* lost their lives.[65] The events of Aba Island showed the strength of the new regime and removed the immediate sectarian threat by pushing their leaderships into exile.

By early 1971 the regime's effort to curb the Communist influence had escalated into an attempt to dismantle the SCP. Consequently, the SSU was allowed as the only legal political organization. The SCP and its mass constituencies were banned, part of the SCP leadership was co-opted to the SSU and the government, and the remaining leaders were tracked down and arrested. Only Joseph Garang, a southerner and now the Minister of Southern Affairs from the non-conformist SCP faction, survived the regime onslaught[66] because he was viewed useful in seeking rapprochement with the southern opposition.

The confrontation with the SCP resulted in another coup attempt on 19 July 1971. This time it was organized by the Sudanese Communists aided by Mahgoub, who had returned from exile and used his influence on loyal army officers to execute the plan that led to a three-day change of power during which Nimeiri was imprisoned.[67] However, the coup eventually failed due to Egyptian-Libyan intervention, and because large part of the army remained loyal to Nimeiri.[68] Khartoum alleged that the coup had been supported by the Soviet Union, which led to the deterioration of Sudan's relationship with the U.S.S.R. and a gradual turn towards the West.[69] By phrasing allegations and purging the SCP elements, Khartoum clearly indicated its interest in changing alliances and to enter in patronage of the Western powers. Since the socialist forces were seen as a threat, Nimeiri used foreign policy shift to tighten the regime's grip on power.

Consequently, the regime reduced its reliance on the Soviet Bloc and the Arab socialist states allied with it. Sudan lowered the number of Soviet and eastern European diplomats, and accused Eritreans, who received support from the Soviet allied Arab states, of having taken part in the 1971 coup attempt. This justified ending support to the ELF and opened the possibility to deal with the "Southern Problem" because it allowed negotiations with Ethiopia, a U.S. ally, regarding ending its and Israel's assistance to the Anya Nya.[70] At this point the government faced increasing pressure to engage in a diplomatic effort to end the costly rebellion in southern Sudan due to the lack of external support to finance counterinsurgency and to quell domestic opposition to the war.[71] This converged with U.S. geo-political interests, as it sought to count on Sudan as part of a Western alliance in the Horn of Africa, and allegedly withdrew previous CIA support from the Anya Nya in an attempt to force it to negotiate with Khartoum.[72] This shows how Nimeiri sought to benefit from the superpower competition and extravert support to boost the regime's domestic position, but also how the U.S. was able to influence Sudan's domestic politics by contributing to the pressure for negotiated solution to the "Southern Problem".

After dismantling the SCP, the regime was obliged to seek new domestic constituency in the context of a foreign policy shift towards the West. This resulted in an unprecedented change in the domestic political landscape because the northern elite parties posed a threat to the regime and were exiled. In the need of domestic alliance, Nimeiri decided to bring in the southern political forces. This benefited the regime in two ways. First, by allocating southern elite political positions at the national level, and conceding to some southern demands for self-governance, the regime could appease the southern opposition and possibly find a negotiated end to the insurgency. Second, having southern Sudanese constituency would strengthen the state as it would fill the gap left by northern political forces and silence separatist voices in southern Sudan. The changing foreign policy orientation and the absence of any considerable opposition by the northern elite forces to negotiate with the deemed "outlaws" freed Nimeiri to look for a negotiated solution to the war.

Moreover, Nimeiri sought popular support to strengthen his grip on power. Still under threat by the exiled northern political parties, a referendum was put forward on his presidency. It returned 98.6% favorable vote, demonstrating the coercive power of the regime and fomenting a more personalized system of power concentrated on the army, the RCC, and the SSU.[73] The maintenance of this political organization, and elaborate bureaucracy, became conditioned to a degree by resources extraverted from the exterior through the regime's foreign policy.

Consequently, foreign policy became an important element expressing the regime's ideology and approach to economic organization and development. The state's initial reforms aimed at building a socialist centrally planned economy proved largely counterproductive.[74] Although the wide range of nationalizations and confiscations,[75] influenced by Nasserist centralized economic model, concentrated the Sudanese economy under the regime control, they, and the alliance with socialist and Arab countries, brought few positive results in terms of economic development. Instead, since the establishment of the new economic order coincided with the change of Sudan's foreign policy, the socialist economic experimentation was bound to fail and Khartoum reinstated the capitalist economic system.[76]

Although Sudan's relationship with the Eastern Bloc deteriorated after Nimeiri's change of heart,[77] relations with Arab states remained stronger. Closer regional collaboration tied Sudan increasingly to Egypt and Libya,[78] as Khartoum continued to follow Egypt's "Arab" foreign policy orientation by supporting the Palestinian cause against Israel.[79] Until it began to prepare to seek negotiations with the Anya Nya, the regime also allowed the ELF to operate in Sudan and actively encouraged Arab and other states to support Eritrea. Thus, relations with other Arab states, except Saudi Arabia that hosted major Sudanese exile opposition,[80] were strong and allowed Khartoum to draw military and technical support against the Anya Nya.

Sudan's Eastern Bloc orientation in the late 1960s had prompted U.S. to implement a policy of containment. Fearing the weakening of its geo-political position in the Horn, the U.S. orchestrated a campaign through Israel[81] and Ethiopia to provide arms, training, and sanctuary to the Anya Nya. This strengthening of the armed opposition was aimed at countering the regime's Soviet, Egyptian, and Libyan support. As a result, southern opposition drew covert support from Ethiopia and Israel, but also until early 1970s through northern Uganda controlled by the head of the Ugandan army, Idi Amin.[82]

Meanwhile, Sudan had participated in the Egyptian and Libyan initiative of joining the three states in an "Arab" alliance.[83] Statements concerning this political process outraged southerners because it defined Sudan as "Arab".[84] Yet the initiative was short-lived, and Khartoum's new Western foreign policy orientation after SCP coup attempt led it to withdraw from the process and search for a new domestic constituency and external allies.[85] This led to Nimeiri, " . . . lacking the active collaboration of any major political, sectarian or regional grouping, . . . to turn away from the politics of the past".[86] The regime's independence from the northern elite constituencies opened the possibility, in an unprecedented manner, for it to ally with southern political forces. However, Nimeiri also knew that becoming part of the proposed Arab Federation would have undermined any plan for negotiated agreement with the southerners, and led to the exiled northern elite's future coup attempts in part because their prominent sectors were opposed to state union with other countries. Thus Nimeiri's new foreign policy orientation, and the seeking of an alliance with the southern political leadership, formed part of strategic calculations for regime survival.[87]

Remedying the "Southern Problem"

Nimeiri designed wide-ranging strategies to tackle the "Southern Problem". These included a combination of foreign policy efforts oriented towards regional and international actors, and direct coercive and development measures in the search for a negotiated end to the conflict.

Nimeiri's Initial Approach to the "Southern Problem"

Nimeiri's approach to the "Southern Problem" differed from those of preceding governments. It combined coercive measures with incentives for cooperation, lessening marginalization and exclusion, to convert southern leaders and population into new domestic regime allies. The policy mixed hard-handed military measures, development efforts, and political concessions, but continued to view secession as an unacceptable solution to the "Southern Problem", describing it as a "crime".[88] The regime responded to the Anya Nya operations, which grew more organized and sophisticated by 1970-1, through a combination of intense military action and foreign policy to cut off Anya Nya' external support. On 9 June 1969, a policy statement was broadcasted[89] for which southern politicians in Khartoum had provided groundwork. In it Nimeiri invited the southerners to accept peace through a special arrangement within united Sudan.[90] Although the statement was not followed immediately by any concrete action except for the creation of the Minister for Southern Affairs position held initially by Joseph Garang, the proposal for wide economic concessions demonstrates the regime's larger space for political maneuvering than in the case of earlier governments dependent on the sectarian political dynamics.[91]

The southern reaction to Nimeiri's June declaration was mixed. Some southerners celebrated the statement in Khartoum on 12 June 1969 because it marked the first time a minister working directly for southern Sudan had been appointed.[92] Meanwhile, political-military groups, such as the NPG and the ARG, demanded southern secession to be recognized, but other more moderate factions in exile headed by the ALF expressed their interest in the proposal.[93] Some southern factions perceived the June declaration as an opening to introduce themselves as political forces within the center of the political system. The NPG representatives stated they would change their stance if Nimeiri would agree to total independence, while other factions pronounced that they would not recognize any agreement between other southern factional governments and Khartoum, and the Anya Nya military movement remained silent.[94] This indicates continued southern divisions regarding the terms for peace.

In April 1968 the major military campaign in southern Sudan seized and the Anya Nya had suspended large operations. During this period, Colonel Joseph Lagu, a Madi from Equatoria who had defected from the Sudanese army in 1963[95] and had been regional commander of the Anya Nya Armed Forces (ANAF) in eastern Equatoria, established an independent command that was initially separated from the political opposition.[96] Subsequently, Lagu used his control of arms supplies from Uganda to expand influence over the southern military and political leadership. He challenged the ARG leadership through an alliance with Colonel Samuel Abujohn, the Anya Nya commander of the SRRG in western Equatoria (Zandeland) in February 1970, and allied later with James Loro, commander of central region from Yei to Juba.[97]

The calmer period encouraged some southern refugees to return to southern Sudan. It was agreed that the World Food Program would provide US$435,000 in 1969 and US$11,427,000 in 1970 in food aid for the refugees, which the regime used as an incentive for repatriation as it sought to cut southern opposition off from its support base outside the country. In total, 49,500 refugees and 80,000 internally displaced returned in June 1969-December 1971 period but the refugee situation remained complex.[98] Although incentives for peace followed with US$4 million dedicated to a development program, southern intellectuals in Khartoum criticized the slowness of the implementation of the policy.[99]

In late 1969, the Anya Nya resumed its major operations. These were in part a response to Joseph Garang's failed efforts to force negotiations because of distrust on his insistence that the "Southern Problem" could be resolved by erasing economic inequalities,[100] as was claimed by the regime.

216

At the same time, Lagu's leadership capacity and control of arms supplies from East Africa through eastern Equatoria had enabled him to take over rival factions and improve troop discipline across the local commands.[101] In November, with heightened capacity, the Anya Nya launched a campaign in Equatoria and Upper Nile consisting of attacks on bridges, convoys, and remote army posts.[102]

In response to the re-activation of the Anya Nya campaigns, Khartoum reinforced the armed forces in southern Sudan.[103] This consisted principally of acquiring military hardware and strengthening the officer corps with Soviet and Egyptian support and operational assistance.[104] Consequently the newly equipped army of which 1/3 was deployed in southern Sudan by 1970 strengthened from 26,500 men in 1969 to 36,000 by 1972, and faced an estimated 5,000-10,000 generally poorly equipped Anya Nya.[105]

By the end of 1969 Khartoum launched a large-scale retaliation offensive. During the campaign, civilians and their material possessions were deliberately targeted as a counterinsurgency strategy in order to eliminate support base for the rebels.[106] The intense fighting that continued until mid-1971 was complemented with a propaganda campaign, accusing Western powers and Israel of Anya Nya support. The army also embarked on a campaign of arbitrary kidnappings and assassinations targeting southern leaders, and these attacks were subsequently blamed on the rebels.[107] Moreover, the government staged the most intensive aerial campaign of the war in 1970-1, which involved aircraft, helicopters, Egyptian commandoes, and Russian air transported troops.[108] In this situation, faced by the strengthened army, the Anya Nya increasingly appealed for external support[109] which it obtained mainly from NGOs and private individuals.[110] Thus, the intensification of war reflected the regime strategy to push for peace by weakening the southern military opposition.

However, after the July 1971 SCP coup attempt, Khartoum scaled down its military operations and began a search for negotiated settlement. Not only did it seek secret contacts with the insurgents, but it made strategic appointments to promote southern regime collaborators; Abel Alier becoming Vice President of Sudan and Hilari Logale the Commissioner of Equatoria. Mboro was released from prison and southerners were again allowed positions in the army, police, and civil service. In addition, funds were forwarded for economic development of southern Sudan and the plans for an Arab Federation definitely given up.[111] Furthermore, the government imposed a stricter code of behavior for its troops in southern Sudan, improved the security in the camps for the internally displaced (also called "peace villages" in which southerners had been concentrated to live in precarious conditions), reopened medical facilities, started agricultural projects, and initiated a program to build and repair roads and bridges. While these attempts were only gradually initiated because of small amount of allocated funding and southern apprehension, by April 1970 the regime had opened 40 resettlement areas to restart agricultural activities and established medical facilities in population centers under its control in Gogreal, Wau, Malakal, Nasir, Dodo, and Kodok.[112] Meanwhile, the Anya Nya-held countryside experienced little improvement in this respect. As a whole, the new regime policy sought to gain grassroots support for peace by turning local communities against the war.

In addition, as part of the effort to end the war, in the latter 1971 Nimeiri intensified the diplomatic effort with Ethiopia and Uganda to neutralize external assistance to Anya Nya. This aimed to curb the rebel supply channels and constituencies among refugees that allowed them to organize, recruit, and plan operations, but was problematized by Sudan's assistance to Eritreans and Milton Obote's supporters after Idi Amin took power in Uganda. However, after Nimeiri pledged to end Sudan's support for Eritreans during mutual state visits with Haile Selassie in November 1971 and January 1972, an agreement was signed between Sudan and Ethiopia to end aid to each other's respective rebels. This decreased Anya Nya's external support in Upper Nile, where the guerrillas lost their main cross-border source of ammunition and supplies from Ethiopia by 1972.[113]

Moreover, Uganda's Anya Nya support ended although this had little to do with Nimeiri's efforts. After Amin had taken power in January 1971, remnants of Obote's Acholi and Langi forces had sought refuge in southern Sudan where they were given sanctuary and reorganized with Khartoum's support to overthrow Amin. Amin sought policy convergence with Sudan, and adhered to Nimeiri's petition to end Anya Nya support in exchange for Sudan pledging to stop assisting Obote, after realizing that he could not neutralize Obote through arms. A bilateral agreement was signed in 1971 in which each regime refrained from supporting the other's opposition.[114]

Amin's increasingly pro-Arab and anti-Western orientation, including improved relationship with Libya, likely influenced his decision to go along with Nimeiri. While Sudan was still obscure about its move towards the West, improved relations with Uganda contributed to the curbing of Israeli support to the Anya Nya. The cutting off of a major supply route to Lagu's main force, and diminishing facilities for the southern refugees, pressured the largest southern armed opposition faction to negotiate with the regime.[115] On 24 March 1972 Amin expelled Israelis from Uganda, and Sudan forced out the few thousand strong Ugandan opposition forces from Equatoria to Tanzania from where Obote staged an assault on Amin's regime in September 1972.[116] This unprecedented pressure on Lagu's Anya Nya force, which largely depended on the Israeli aid channeled through Uganda, contributed heavily to the rebel decision to agree to negotiate with the Sudanese regime.

Unification of the Anya Nya Leadership

By the end of 1960s the Anya Nya leadership had gradually unified and centered on Lagu's leadership. In October 1969, the Anya Nya High Command Council was instituted with the purpose of adding coherence to the movement, control and coordinate its operations, obtain and distribute military equipment, and engage in administration in areas under rebel control.[117]

At this point, many southern exile politicians who still remained separated from the armed movement envisaged to gain control over it. However, their personal ambitions, competition over obtaining of external aid, and low capacity and influence beyond immediate ethnic loyalties all contributed to factionalism, weakening the movement until Lagu's force finally absorbed the remaining competing political-military groups in April 1970.[118] The escalation of warfare in 1970-1 facilitated Lagu's influence further when it accentuated the role of the Anya Nya military capacity and control of external supply, pushing the southern politicians to the margins of the opposition.[119] Ability to control Israeli aid from Uganda allowed Lagu to assert control over other armed constituencies because he could withhold supplies, which motivated many to join Lagu who in turn was able to push for organizational coherence and discipline to counter disobedience, insubordination, and banditry.[120] In April 1970 Lagu's forces absorbed the ARG, pensioning off its leader Tafeng who had left the main Anya Nya in July 1969, and after winning over Abujohn, Lagu brought the NPG under his control in July 1970. As a result, Lagu's Anya Nya command could claim to be the legitimate authority in southern Sudan. By 1971 the military organization had also co-opted most of the southern exile political movement, which Lagu sought to rebuild by consolidating his position through concentration of power. He then convoked southern military and political leaders in January 1971 to officially launch the Southern Sudan Liberation Front (SSLF), which had already been in formation since October 1969.[121] Lagu assumed both the political and military leadership of the SSLF, promoted himself to Major-General, and named the movement's political wing as Southern Sudan Liberation Movement (SSLM), while commanding a broad-based constituency including a diverse mix of military and political leaders.

This control allowed a more concerted effort to define the ideological basis and objectives for the southern struggle. The SSLM declared its objective being the ridding of southern Sudan of northern colonialism, since many southerners considered that the struggle was a continuation of the 1955 mutiny to defend the southern identity and African values.[122] Accordingly, the SSLM issued a document called "What We Fight For in South Sudan", stating that

> The goal of our struggle is . . . the right of self-determination for our people. We want our people to be able of its own free will and under no threat or fear, to determine its destiny, either to remain in a unitary Sudan as a truly autonomous region, or to have nothing whatsoever to do with the North and tie our future with that of our African brothers in their states on our Southern borders . . . Our specifically African—as distinct from Arab—identity and the common aspirations which unite all our tribes in a common struggle fully qualify us for nationhood and the right of self-determination . . . by rejecting the attempted arabization of Southern Sudan and by adhering to our African identity and heritage we exercise a basic human right which is bound to be recognized by everybody sooner or later . . . by waging our own war of Liberation we also block Arab and Russian imperialist expansionism southwards and protect our brothers in East and Central Africa.[123]

This suggests that despite the generally low educational attainment of a large part of the southern leadership, the ideas and objectives behind the insurgency appear to have been more refined than claimed by much of the posterior historiography and current opinions.

In early 1971, Lagu moderated his rhetoric in response to the first covert negotiation contacts with the regime representatives. By not excluding the possibility of a settlement in the framework of "one Sudan", as advocated by the regime, he asserted that the Anya Nya had been founded in 1963-4 to fight for southern rights and political power without which it would be hopeless for the southerners to control their economic and cultural development.[124] Rather than defining a clear ideology by Western standards, the attempt was to explain why the insurgents were fighting and emphasize international significance of the resistance to boost the declining external support. Although in the literature it has been argued that the southern opposition continued to lack objectives in terms of any defined political ideology, it is apparent that the "ideological" cornerstones of the struggle were tailored in the particular context of the struggle to adhere with the rebel objectives of ensuring southern rights, especially self-determination, and securing "southern" identity and cultures.

Lagu used the SSLM political structure to allocate positions as a reward to those politicians who were willing to collaborate.[125] Despite the war, by 1971 a rudimentary civil administration using the British legal system had been established by founding courts for communal and civil cases. A number of medical centers and dispensaries, including training facilities, as well as cotton, soap, salt, and cooking oil production, and hundreds of basic elementary schools, were set up mostly around Juba and Yei area.[126] The rebel administration and most services centered on Equatoria where the leadership of the rebel movement originated from and where Lagu's influence was strongest. As a result, the Anya Nya established local state-like structures, extracting taxes and offering protection and services along the principle of "social contract", in the areas under its administration.

Finally, despite the diminishing external support, the SSLM sought to maintain pressure on the army throughout 1971. More ambitious operations facilitated by the unity and new equipment extended out of Equatoria, but leadership fissures appeared. For instance, senior leader Abujohn was dismissed after being accused of non-cooperation, lack of seriousness, disobedience, and plotting against Lagu, while some hard-line separatist officers remained reluctant to accept negotiations within the regime-proposed framework of "one Sudan".[127]

Arrival to the Addis Ababa Peace Accord

The developments that led to the signing of the Addis Ababa Agreement, ending major hostilities in southern Sudan, are linked to the opportune and intertwined local, regional, and international factors. The changing political environment was instrumental for the success of the negotiations that resulted in the treaty.

Towards Negotiated Settlement

In 1971, Nimeiri's strategy to convince southern leadership to provide him a new constituency had become synonymous with the pressure to decentralize Sudan. The devolution of political power had been demanded by other emerging regional movements in the peripheries of northern Sudan, including those representing the Beja in the east and the Nuba in southern Kordofan. The call was motivated by the attempt to engage provinces increasingly in decision-making, and facilitating economic development, while diminishing the northern elite's exclusive concentration of political and economic power which mainly benefited the north-central riverine Sudan.[128] The regime recognized that administrative decentralization would allow it to continue controlling national resources, while granting more organizational autonomy at the local level would help to appease dissenting regionalist voices in the peripheries. This logic also applied to the later negotiations in which the government sought to neutralize the "Southern Problem".

The regime's search for a negotiated settlement in southern Sudan began with a diplomatic effort. Nimeiri visited CAR, Chad, Ethiopia, Uganda, and Zaire, and in August 1970 Sudan reached an agreement for economic cooperation with Uganda. This was followed by the signing of a more extensive deal with Ethiopia in March 1971 to adhere to the OAU conventions, curb support to each other's rebel movements, and set up a joint commission to inspect refugee camps for rebel activity in each other's territory.[129]

However Amin, who was initially pro-Anya Nya, took power in Uganda. As a result, external support continued briefly before Uganda's foreign policy reoriented towards Arab states, gradually impeding the Israeli support for the SSLM. Israel's assistance to Anya Nya had flourished in the late 1960s in the context of polarization of Arab-Israeli relations, as Israel had sought to support proxy forces against "Arab" regimes. Yet, in the course of 1971 Nimeiri and Amin concluded bilateral agreement to cease support of each other's rebels, similar to the one that Sudan reached with Ethiopia, and by the end of the year Amin had severed relations with the West, concluded a deal for aid from Libya and Saudi Arabia, and ended Israeli support to the SSLM. Amin's change of policy had a direct impact on the southern opposition, as it undermined the SSLM's capacity and pressured it to negotiate.[130]

In response to the agreement with Ethiopia, Sudan curbed support to the ELF temporarily. Nimeiri ceased briefly the shipping of Arab military material to the Eritreans through Sudan, and transferred pro-Eritrean officials out of Kassala province in response to his visit to Ethiopia in November and Haile Selassie's reciprocal visit to Sudan in January 1972.[131] Although Ethiopia remained as a sanctuary for the southern refugees (particularly Nuer whose ethnic kin extends to the Gambella region), allowing the eastern sections of Anya Nya to organize, it became interested in facilitating peace negotiations between Khartoum and the rebels. This was in part because its Western patrons promised aid for the process, and Addis Ababa hoped that Khartoum's pledge to curb its support to the Eritrean rebels was genuine.[132] In turn, Sudan's demonstration of goodwill was aimed to weaken the Anya Nya and to secure opportune conditions in the peace talks envisioned in Ethiopia.

By the second half of 1971 the search for peace had gained momentum. Nimeiri needed a domestic constituency that would minimize the threat of internal opposition and complement Khartoum's new foreign policy orientation, while he was interested in heightening the regime's popular support by ending the costly and destabilizing southern insurgency.[133] For its part, the SSLM confronted the reinforced army and was faced with diminishing external support. In this situation, Nimeiri was aware that the regime's Western orientation would reduce the SSLM support further.[134] To an extent, Nimeiri's approach to seek external support to undo domestic threat against close domestic rivals followed the central dynamic of the politics of northern Sudanese political elite since decolonization. It was not much different from the southern elite's established practice to either seek support from sections of the northern elite, or from external actors, against local rivals, which the SSLM also sought. Both approaches of internal (within the polity) and external extraversion had important continuities from earlier colonial and pre-colonial periods.

The unification of southern factions under Lagu's leadership was an important factor facilitating the peace process. It forced southern politicians and officers fearing to be left out of the negotiation process to speak with one voice, although many were wary about initiating negotiations based on the unity of Sudan, and some, among them John Garang, the future figurehead of the second insurgency, preferred to continue war.[135] This was particularly the case with separatist hardliners who objected to negotiations in the framework of "one Sudan".

Aiming to strengthen the regime, and prepared to reduce marginalization and exclusion of southern Sudan through limited political concessions, Nimeiri sought to initiate secret contacts with the SSLM in the course of 1971. Alier, the Minister for Southern Affairs, who was more trusted in the southern provinces than his predecessor Joseph Garang, was put in charge of the process. With support of the World Council of Churches (WCC) and All African Council of Churches (AACC), Alier was put in contact with the exile leaders. Meanwhile, the United Nations High Commissioner for Refugees (UNHCR) and Western NGOs involved with the approximately half a million registered Sudanese refugees in the neighboring Ethiopia, Uganda, Zaire, and Central Africa, also endorsed the peace efforts.[136] In this context, the domestic, regional, and international political environment encouraged negotiations.

The role of mediation was critical for putting the two parties together and setting the climate for negotiations. On the government side Alier had a prominent role in the preparation and initiation of the process, working closely with Nimeiri, assessing opinions within the northern political cadres, visiting the interested European governments and NGOs, encouraging contacts with the WCC and the AACC, and sending southern delegations from Khartoum to meet southern opposition groups within and outside Sudan.[137] Following Alier's trip to Europe, the WCC and AACC visited Sudan in spring 1971 and met government officials and southerners in various parts of the country.[138] After the visit, church organizations began contacting southern leaders and targeting those who accepted government demands for negotiating on the basis of "one Sudan",[139] with a limited autonomy for the southern provinces as one region. Draft proposals were circulated among them, and their demands were forwarded to the regime in January 1971.[140] Interested in the continuation of the process the regime met some of the demands,[141] which led to the first secret meeting between its representatives and those of the SSLM in November 1971 in Addis Ababa[142] in the context of Nimeiri's state visit to Ethiopia.[143] In Ethiopia, the regime recognized the SSLM as the representative of southern Sudan, adhered to the SSLM demands for negotiations to take place in a third country, made preparations to halt its military offensive and tone down anti-Anya Nya propaganda, and yielded to a cease-fire.[144]

The formal negotiations took place in February 1972 in Addis Ababa. The regime sent an experienced eight-member delegation[145] that faced the SSLM negotiating team,[146] with southern politicians from Khartoum observing the proceedings. However, apart from two leading southern politicians, Oliver Albino and Ezboni Mundiri, other exile politicians did not participate in the negotiations. Allegedly this was because a number of them opposed Lagu's leadership, which to an extent undermined the legitimacy of the SSLM to represent the southern Sudan as a whole.

Indeed, although some hardliners opposed the single state solution the SSLM leadership was committed to it. The SSLM also remained adamant about including African observers and arbitrators. It was keen to ensure the integrity of the process, but may also have wanted to demonstrate its "African" and "Christian" leaning. The SSLM preferred Haile Selassie's personal participation, but it was agreed that his representative Nabiyelul Kifle would become an observer along with Leopoldo Niilus and Kodwo Ankrah from the WCC, Burgess Carr from the AACC, who also acted as the moderator, and Samuel Athi Bwogo from the Sudan Council of Churches.[147]

When the negotiations got underway, a number of controversial issues emerged. These included the federal political arrangement, the role of Arabic language, three major territories that could be removed from southern provincial jurisdiction, financial and economic stipulations important for enforcing the southern autonomy, regional political institutions and administration, and the issue of security forces.[148] However, initially negotiations over federal arrangement, the most important matter for many southerners, were abandoned because the regime delegation claimed it had no mandate to agree on a federal solution since this would affect the structure of the whole state. In contrast, the southerners stated that they perceived Arabic language as an instrument of cultural and political domination. This may have led some in the southern delegation to become preoccupied with leadership and administrative positions,[149] but the main objective of the SSLM negotiating team continued to be the ensuring of southern rights, especially self-determination.

In the proceedings, particularly the issue of North-South boundaries and the future security arrangements through which the Anya Nya was to be integrated became contested. First, the North-South boundary was controversial because Abyei, southern Blue Nile, and Kafia Kingi (*Hufrat al-Nahas*) resource-rich border areas had previously been juggled between the two regions.[150] Second, the security arrangements became heavily debated. Contesting the integration of rebels into the national army, Captain John Garang, a newly-commissioned Anya Nya officer with only six months' experience, proposed an alternative arrangement of two separate regional armies for Sudan and a national force drawn equally from northern and southern Sudan for national defense.[151] However the government delegation rejected this, and an arrangement was reached in which the Anya Nya contingents would eventually be integrated in the Sudanese security forces. Yet, some in the SSLM leadership, including Lagu, opposed the initial approval of the security conditions by the SSLM negotiating team, along with some other parts of the agreement, but not having been personally present in the negotiations they felt obliged to accept the treaty as initially agreed.[152] This was likely due to a consideration that the rebellion had become increasingly unsustainable, local demands for peace within southern Sudan, and the diminishing SSLF fighting capacity due to the reduced external support. In the end, Khartoum had been able to force through an agreement that was favorable to it, and the implementation of which it could control.

The Addis Ababa Agreement was eventually signed on 27 February 1972.[153] In it, the southern region composed of Bahr al-Ghazal, Equatoria, and Upper Nile provinces achieved a limited autonomous status. This inspired demands for self-determination from elites in other marginalized areas, such as Nuba Mountains, Darfur, and the east, which had been calling for federal system for the whole country. Economically, southern Sudan remained subordinate and dependent on transfer payments, grants, and economic planning from Khartoum, but the regional government owned the land and was able to stop Arabization and Islamicization policies which contributed to ensuring the continuity of local cultures and languages. English became the regional administrative language, as opposed to Arabic at the national level, and the regional administration operated the school system.[154] Once the agreement had been signed, Nimeiri and Alier toured southern Sudan for ten days to project an image of the regime's goodwill.[155] Overall, the treaty was a victory for the government because it ensured presidential powers over the region and transformed it into a regime constituency, while the Arabic version of the agreement was left deliberately vague and subject to future manipulation.

Finally, the Addis Ababa treaty would have hardly been possible without the domestic, regional, and international actors and forces that provided incentives for peace.[156] The period during its signing marked the initial stages of the most intense competition for client states between the U.S. and the U.S.S.R. in the Horn of Africa. While the U.S. was heavily engaged in Vietnam, Khartoum's and Moscow's relations had been severed after 1971. The U.S. hoped to stabilize Nimeiri after his turn to the West by pressuring the SSLM for peace. As has been mentioned, the regional support for the rebels also waned and Nimeiri sought domestic consolidation. These factors had facilitated the WCC and the AACC mediation for the final agreement. In this way, Nimeiri had been able to provide a credible illusion of a reduction of the marginalizing effect of the state in the southern provinces through a political arrangement that maintained Sudan as one state. This created a political environment that temporarily encouraged the weakening and convergence of the socially constructed "Arab-African" identity rift that had previously been reinforced by the war.

Responses to the Agreement

Despite the outright rejection of the Addis Ababa Agreement by a number of exiled political factions, which viewed it as an unacceptable sellout to the southerners, it was regionally and internationally overwhelmingly welcomed. European, American, African, and Arab press reports praised the achieved peace, along with the role of a number of African leaders and politicians, the OAU and the U.N., in the process, and Nimeiri was nominated for the 1973 Nobel peace prize.[157] As Nimeiri had calculated, the agreement extended his local popularity particularly in southern Sudan, and further consolidated his national leadership.[158]

After the signing of the agreement, Nimeiri sought aggrandizement through its publicity value. In contrast, the southern leadership encountered deepening rift among its leadership and constituencies. On 3 March, in a political rally in Wad Nubawi, Nimeiri presented the treaty as a major success, declaring the day National Unity Day, announcing a cease-fire, and signing the Southern Provinces Self-Government Act which converted the agreement into a law.[159] Lagu issued orders for the cease-fire the same day, but upon the SSLM delegation's return from Ethiopia it faced fierce opposition from separatist southern officers and politicians who were reluctant to accept anything less than a full secession and a separate southern army.[160] As a result, mixed reactions took place among the Anya Nya. Whereas Lagu was generally viewed as a hero, being the figurehead of the southern armed struggle, for instance the Anya Nya command in Bahr al-Ghazal rejected the treaty as a wholesale surrender to the "Arabs".[161] Still, Lagu's influence had been sufficient to convince his nearest Anya Nya commanders to abide by the cease-fire,[162] which convinced most of the remaining contingents to end hostilities.

However, a number of Anya Nya officers, less influenced by Lagu, planned to disobey the agreement. Meeting secretly in Loboke to assess their collective opinion, Emmanuel Abuur Nhial, Alfred Deng Aluk, Alison Manani Magaya, Habbakkuk Soro, Stephen Madut Baak, Disan Ojwe Olweny, Kamilo Odongi, Paul Awel, Albino Akol Akol, and John Garang drafted a document rejecting the treaty, and circulated it in the Anya Nya camps. The pamphlet was an attempt to resist implementation of the agreement and rally for Lagu's replacement. Yet, allegedly Saturnino Arika, Commander of Eastern Equatoria, handed the document over to Lagu, which led to Odongi's and Ojwe's arrest and the abandoning of the discovered plot.[163] In a later interview, John Garang also indicated that the officers wanted to give peace a chance because people desired it, although being aware that the root causes of the conflict had not been addressed and that the integration of the Anya Nya was an attempt at neutralizing the southern fighting capacity.[164] In the end, the plotters returned to their home areas to wait for the absorption of their troops into the national army.

Conclusion

The intertwined local, regional, and international factors led to the intensification and the eventual negotiated settlement of the first insurgency in southern Sudan. Although ending the Abboud dictatorship, second parliamentary period (1964-9) had been characterized by a return of factional feuds and bickering within the northern elite establishment over political power. While another opportunity had been given to establish a democratic system, the prevailing political culture and dynamics founded upon marginalization and exclusionary identity politics, which contributed to the intensification of the war in southern Sudan, prevented transformation of the political system. The democratic experiment failed largely because the exclusive northern elite political parties remained largely detached from the marginalized part of the society (particularly the people of state peripheries). Concerned mainly with their own interests, they channeled benefits to their narrow social constituencies in north-central Sudan. In these circumstances, party leaderships squabbled over personalized politics and engaged in sectional and sectarian competition involving widespread nepotism and corruption, while the economy deteriorated and the war in southern Sudan intensified and reinforced the socially constructed polarization along the "Arab" versus "African" rift.

In this context, the state remained in the hands of sectors of the northern elite, whose foreign policy orientation in the 1960s towards the Eastern Bloc and leftist-oriented Arab states perpetuated the conflict. This inspired external support for the Anya Nya by actors aligned with the West, which made the war increasingly part of regional political dynamics. As it intensified, the conflict became ensconced as a struggle between "Arab-Muslims" and "African Christians and non-Muslims", which in turn had implications for identity (re)construction and reinforcement. While the military coup that installed Nimeiri in power replaced the northern sectarian parties with military leadership, it transferred the power firmly to other northern elite section. Subsequently, to consolidate the new configuration of political and economic power, the regime embraced southern Sudan to compensate for the loss of the northern sectarian constituency. As has been shown, this move was purely strategic and bound southern Sudan to the state through a political arrangement that emphasized its subservient position and reinforced its economic dependence on Khartoum.

However, the Addis Ababa Agreement shows that the political differences between "northern Arabs" and "southern Africans" could be overcome initially in one state settlement. Both categories have been socially constructed, reinforced, and used by local elites to portray their fight as "regional" when they seek to influence their constituents in the "North" and the "South", respectively. Yet, although to an extent assuming these categorizations because they form part of their own identities, these "regional" and "national" elites are capable of looking beyond the differences when settling conflicts of interest, as was the case in Addis Ababa. This points to an existence of continuing transformation and adjustment in terms of identity (re)construction, reinforcement, and emphasis over time. In this way, the gradually fluctuating softer and harder stands on political identities contribute significantly to peace and war.

Moreover, the Addis Ababa Agreement also shows that transformation of the exclusive political and economic governance by the leading state elites is necessary for achieving peace. This took place in Sudan in opportune local, regional, and international conditions in the early 1970s, allocating concessions to the southern opposition that ensured a degree of self-determination. It did, however, require carefully coordinated domestic and foreign policy in a favorable regional environment for reaching peace in the context of the Cold War. Yet, the regime's inclusion of southern Sudanese constituency was merely strategic, and neither elaborate nor lasting, which facilitated the later resurgence of war.

Furthermore, the limited autonomy prepared southern Sudan for a new period in which its local political elites led the southern provinces as one political entity for the first time. It provided them with political opportunities, possibilities for self-enrichment, and extending influence, and challenged them to politically unify the highly heterogeneous "region" organized politically through "tribalist" group identities. This became an opportunity to strengthen "the South" in terms of political and social coherence, but was simultaneously seen as a threat among sections of the northern elite that regained influence in the course of the 1970s.

Finally, the narrative in this chapter suggests that genuine and appropriate political arrangements, demonstrating goodwill through the dismantling of structures and policies of marginalization and subjugation, may effectively end an insurgency. Although in the case of Sudan this would have likely translated into improved security and well-being in southern Sudan in the long term, the internal and external political realities related to governance and the logic of the Sudanese state prevented such development. Thus, during Nimeiri's leadership, the political trajectory dictated by the exclusive and marginalizing governance and political culture continued, leading to internal political developments that in conjunction with external (regional and international) political realities led to the resumption of rebellion in southern Sudan.

Endnotes

1   For a detailed account on the downfall of the Abboud regime, see e.g. Hasan (2003).

2   Al-Khatim al-Khalifa, head of the Khartoum Technical Institute, was a former assistant under secretary of education in southern Sudan, and respected politically independent individual. He formed a transitional government composed of 14 cabinet members, out of which five were from the northern parties (Umma, NUP, PDP, SCP, and Muslim Brothers), two were southern representatives (Clement Mboro and Alfred Wol, soon replaced by Ezboni Mundiri) from the SF formed in the same month, and the remaining being representatives of the Professionals' Front, the SCP, professional organizations, public servants, and universities who all had played a vital role in the October Revolution. See Holt and Daly (2000: 156) and Collins (2008: 81). According to O'Ballance (1977: 67) and Alier (1990: 26), the process culminated in the formation of

a five-man Council of the Sovereignty (former SCAF), which included one southerner, Luigi Adwok.

3   O'Ballance (1977: 66-7).

4   The transitional government restored the old provisional constitution suspended by the military regime, dismantled its council system, abolished censorship, legalized political parties, re-established the autonomy of the university, and took anti-corruption measures. See O'Ballance (1977: 68, 2000: 27) and Holt and Daly (2000: 156).

5   According to Holt and Daly (2000: 156-7) and Warburg (2003: 147), the Professionals' Front was composed of radical elements and established political parties willing to maintain the prevailing socioeconomic and sociopolitical order. These collided as the established political parties were eager to push for elections to restore their exclusive control of national politics, while the Professionals' Front argued that as long as there was state of emergency in the South elections should not take place. Some radical proposals produced offshoots in the Professionals' Front, while the confrontation was brought to an end by an *Ansar* demonstration in Khartoum that triggered the resignation of the cabinet on 18 February 1965. Subsequently, al-Khalifa was asked to form a new cabinet, which he did five days later, but the new cabinet was dominated by the Umma, the NUP, and the ICF, leaving the SCP and the PDP associated with the professional elements in minority.

6   Beshir (1968: 89), O'Ballance (1977: 68), Alier (1990: 26-7), and Holt and Daly (2000: 156).

7   See Grundy (1971: 123), Eprile (1974: 96), O'Ballance (2000: 34), Sherman (1980: 73-4), and Collins (2005: 221). In April 1965, two ministers, one from the ICF and another from the NUP, were accused of smuggling weapons to the ELF, and later 18 tons of Czechoslovakian arms originating from Syria destined to the ELF were seized at the Khartoum airport. Four military officers were made scapegoats although Khartoum itself was implicated. See e.g. Beshir (1975: 29) and O'Ballance (1977: 77, 2000: 34). According to Yohannes (1997: 301), this resulted in a low point in Sudan's relationship with Western states, particularly with the U.S., which perceived its aid to the ELF as an effort to undermine its military presence in Eritrea.

8   The rebels obtained arms by ambushing the deliveries going through the South and relieving the defeated and fleeing Simba of their arms in early 1965. They obtained an estimated 6,000 guns this way and began to receive arms from the DRC government seeking to avenge the Sudanese support for the Simba. See e.g. Eprile (1974: 96-7), Johnson (2003: 31), and Collins (2005: 221-2).

9   See more on Sudan's support for the ELF and the Simba in Burr and Collins (1999: 56), O'Ballance (2000: 30), and Deng and Zartman (2002: 26).

10   These are found, for instance, among the Nuer in Upper Nile and western Ethiopia, the Acholi in Equatoria and northern Uganda, the Azande in Equatoria and northeastern DRC and eastern CAR, and among other major groups in Equatorian southern Sudan, such as the Madi, the Kakwa, the Lugbara, the

Mortu (all extending to DRC and Uganda), the Karamojong (Uganda), and the Toposa (in Uganda, Kenya, and Ethiopia).

11 Collins (2005: 222) and O'Ballance (1977: 98) note that due to its growing size and continuing internal divisions, the Anya Nya experienced individualism, frequent indiscipline, and desertion, which led to local armed struggles and infighting along ethnic lines, murders, arson, and theft of cattle, goods, produce, and women.

12 The SF visited Nairobi and Kampala to meet with the SANU leaders to hear their views, and on 12 November 1964 Mboro persuaded the Anya Nya to agree to a one-month cease fire while he toured the South on a fact-finding mission. See e.g. O'Ballance (2000: 27) and Alier (1990: 26-7).

13 Beshir (1968: 89), Johnson (2003: 32), and Collins (2005: 219-20).

14 See Beshir (1968: 88-9) and Alier (1990: 28).

15 Beshir (1968: 89) and O'Ballance (1977: 69, 2000: 27-8).

16 On 6 December, when a plane that was to bring Mboro back from his tour in the South was late, the southerners who had come to receive him became increasingly restless. This was largely due to rumors, which included a claim that the northerners had murdered him. As a result, an angry crowd amongst the up to a million southern laborers now living in the northern provinces initiated a riot, damaging property and targeting northerners. Northerners countered by attacking them with sticks and stones, and after the police had been able to disperse the crowd the following day, seemingly nine southerners, four northerners, and one Greek had been killed, and over four hundred people injured. Yet, the absolute number of casualties is difficult to establish as estimated deaths range everywhere from seven to hundreds. See O'Ballance (2000: 28), Alier (1990: 27), Holt and Daly (2000: 157), and Collins (2008: 82).

17 Holt and Daly (2000: 157) and Collins (2008: 83).

18 Quoted in O'Ballance (1977: 69).

19 While in the first SANU convention in November 1964 in Kampala the posts of the President and the Secretary General were abolished and cabinet was formed, two prominent leaders, Deng and Oduho, pursued their individualistic aspirations. Deng, an advocate of the federalist approach in a unified Sudan, continued to speak for the SANU and claiming to be its Secretary General. In a party election during the convention Oduho lost the presidency to Jaden and moved to Kenya. See O'Ballance (2000: 29).

20 O'Ballance (2000: 29) notes that he wrote a series of proposals of a federal constitution which were addressed to the government, clearly against the SANU's policy of seeking secession. Deng suggested that Sudan should withdraw from the Arab League of which it had been a member since 1956, remain a member of the recently formed OAU, and restore the SEC. He also demanded that southerners should again be appointed to the government service and the police, and advocated that southern politicians should have freedom to campaign in "normal circumstances" in the next elections.

21 Albino (1970: 50-1).

22 Alier (1990: 28), LOC (1991), O'Ballance (2000: 30), Holt and Daly (2000: 157), and Collins (2005: 220).

23 O'Ballance (1977: 70) and Alier (1990: 28). Collins (2005: 220) states, "Deng's precipitate action divided the southerners and destroyed their solidarity. Indeed, the failure of southern leadership to remain united and the propensity of southern politicians to follow the dictates of their own egos and interests remained a principal factor in prolonging the problem of the South and may well be decisive in its future".

24 Encouraging southern disunity, the government initially invited only SANU to the conference. This deliberately challenged the SF, claiming to be the only legitimate political organization for the South. See e.g. O'Ballance (1977: 70). Collins (2005: 220) mentions that it also invited southerners who differed from SANU and SF positions. Ostensibly, this was aimed at confusing the southern position and prevent a common stand.

25 However, this was because of the problems within SANU and due to the government itself being weak and divided. Meanwhile, the security situation around Juba deteriorated. Khartoum was suggested as an alternative venue, but SANU-in-exile declined, which led SF to propose a third country only to be rejected by the government. Finally, Deng's presence in Khartoum forced the other southern factions to bow to Khartoum as the venue. See Beshir (1968: 91-2), O'Ballance (2000: 30-1), Holt and Daly (2000: 157-8), and Collins (2005: 220).

26 Albino (1970: 57) and O'Ballance (2000: 31).

27 O'Ballance (2000: 30).

28 Beshir (1968: 93) and Daly (1993: 15).

29 Deng continued to be a controversial figure. The SANU delegation reluctantly accepted him as a member, while Deng himself insisted that he was the leading representative of the SANU. The government deliberately avoided declaring his exact status. See e.g. Albino (1970: 52) and O'Ballance (2000: 31).

30 Beshir (1968: 92, 95), Albino (1970: 50-2, 54), O'Ballance (1977: 73, 2000: 30), and Alier (1990: 29).

31 Markakis (1998: 117) and Rogier (2005: 11). Such political factionalism exists in the South today, and it continues to debilitate regional political coherence. See e.g. Badal (1994: 105-24).

32 Alier (1990: 29), Daly (1993: 15), and Warburg (2003: 147).

33 Deng (1995b: 87) and Chan and Zuor (2006: 66).

34 Albino (1970: 52).

35 Collins (2008: 84).

36 Beshir (1968: 94-5), Albino (1970: 54), and Daly (1993: 15).

37 Beshir (1968: 93), O'Ballance (1977: 74), and Rogier (2005: 11).

38 These included resettling southern returnees, the "southernization" of administration, police, and prison officers, equalizing salaries, establishing a university and girls' secondary school, religious freedom, allowing the free movement of Christian priests, establishing a commission for socioeconomic planning,

and dedicating increased funds for development in southern Sudan. See Beshir (1968: 95), Albino (1970: 55), Alier (1990: 32), and Daly (1993: 15).

39   An appointed twelve-man committee, composed of six northerners and six southerners, was first to report the resolutions of the conference and then supervise their implementation. See e.g. Albino (1970: 56), O'Ballance, (2000: 32), Alier (1990: 31-2), and Holt and Daly (2000: 158).

40   Alier (1990: 31). It is likely that it also sought to divert international attention from the "Southern Problem".

41   Albino (1970: 56) and Alier (1990: 32).

42   According to Daly (1993: 15) and O'Ballance (2000: 32), participation in the 1965 parliamentary election in the North was low and some incidents of violence occurred. However, they were conducted successfully and resulted in the victory of Umma, which reportedly gained 76 seats of the total of 173 ahead of NUP 54, SCP 11, Beja Tribal Association (later Beja Congress) 10, ICF 5, PDP 3, and Independents 15. Again, some discrepancy over exact results exists as Holt and Daly (2000: 159) provide a slightly different allocation of seats: Umma 76, NUP 54, Beja representatives 10, SCP 8, Nuba Mountain Federation of Independents 7, Independents 7, ICF 5, and PDP 3.

43   O'Ballance (1977: 75), Johnson (2003: 34), and Sidahmed and Sidahmed (2005: 31).

44   Albino (1970: 58), Beshir (1968: 99), and O'Ballance (2000: 32).

45   Johnson (2003: 34).

46   Alier (1990: 41) and Holt and Daly (2000: 159).

47   Daly (1993: 15).

48   O'Ballance (2000: 22), and Sidahmed and Sidahmed (2005: 31).

49   The policy came in response to the worsening security situation. Its objective was to eliminate the opposition in the South, both the armed factions and unarmed intelligentsia, collaborate with southerners interested in unity, and continued policy of Arabization and Islamicization of the region. See e.g. Beshir (1968: 99, 1975: 26-7), Collins (2005: 221), and Alier (1990: 33).

50   See Beshir (1968, 1975), Eprile (1974), O'Ballance (2000), Collins (2005), and Johnson (2003).

51   See Eprile (1974), Beshir (1975), Collins (1975), O'Ballance (1977), Markakis (1998), and Johnson (2003).

52   Collins (2005: 227) and Niblock (1987: 235) note that the FOM had been first founded in the 1950s as a Sudanese version of the group of officers behind the 1952 Nasser coup. But rather than introducing social and economic change, its initial policy was to improve the efficiency of a government dominated by sectarian interests, which in its view was responsible for the deteriorating economy, absence of constitution, and lack of ability to deal with the "Southern Problem".

53   There have been accusations surrounding Prime Minister Mahgoub's private connections to military leaders of the Hashimab clan, which might have facilitated the coup. See e.g. Alier (1990: 42). There was also failed attempt by

regionalist political organizations from the periphery to take power, which according to Eprile (1974: 133-5) may have inspired Mahgoub's decision to hand power over to the military to maintain the northern elite's exclusive position.

54 O'Ballance (1977: 103), Alier (1990: 43), and Holt and Daly (2000: 166).

55 Alier (1990: 43).

56 LOC (1991), and Holt and Daly (2000: 166).

57 The RCC was first composed of the six officers behind the coup, and Awadallah, but three more young officers, Lieutenant-Colonel Babikir al-Nur, Major Abu al-Qasim Hashim, and Hashim al-Ata, were also included. The inclusion of the latter was intended to reinforce the regime since al-Nur and al-Ata were associated with Communists and al-Qasim Hashim had links with the Arab nationalist, Nasserist, clique closely related to Egypt. The Cabinet was the regime's executive branch, deliberately composed of politically radical elements, including a total of 23 members from the SCP, the Arab socialists with links to the Iraqi Baath Party, the Arab nationalists of whom some had links to the DUP, some PDP members, and independent radicals such as those linked either to the Professionals' Front or having served in the Transitional Government of 1965. See e.g. Niblock (1987: 241-2), Alier (1990: 45), and Holt and Daly (2000: 166-7).

58 Alier (1990: 44-5) and Johnson (2003: 36).

59 Niblock (1989: 259, 264), Alier (1990: 46), and Holt and Daly (2000: 173).

60 Above the local structure, branch (village or rural), district, sub-provincial, and provincial party committees and party conferences (councils) were installed, copying Egypt, Tanzania, and Yugoslavia. The SSU was to serve as the socialist vanguard and have 50% representation of farmers and workers in its committees or conferences. In this highly hierarchical system of centralized administration, geographical delineation replaced ethnic boundaries at the local level, and the regime appointed chairmen to the provincial councils, asserting its control. The institutions below provincial level were allotted no resources to undertake administrative change, leading them to become redundant. At the national level, there were the People's Assembly (or National Congress, former Constituent Assembly), the party presidency, the secretariat-general, the central committee, and the political bureau, which were all subjected to Nimeiri's personal decision-making in varying degrees, particularly after he began to concentrate power increasingly on the presidency and purging the opposition. The system was deemed highly bureaucratized and inefficient. See Niblock (1987: 259, 264), and Holt and Daly (2000: 173).

61 Niblock (1987: 253) and Alier (1990: 61-2) note that this was initially because the SCP leadership split due to its leader's Abdel Khaliq Mahgoub's cautious approach towards the new regime. The "conditionalists", including al-Ata, al-Nur and Farouk Osman Hamadallah, a leading Arab Baath socialist, and Muawiyah Ibrahim's and Ahmed Suleiman's "unconditional" supporters of the regime prepared to dissolve the SCP and join the SSU. Also, the RCC was affected by Egypt and composed of a number of pro-Arab Federation offi-

cers, which led to an intensified attempt to expel Mahgoub's "conditionalists" to avoid the same difficulties faced by Egypt in the early stages of Nasser's revolution. See Alier (1990: 62).

62   According to Niblock (1987: 254-5), already in October 1969, a government reshuffle resulted in Awadallah's and four SCP-related ministers' destitution, followed by the SCP leader Mahgoub's arrest in April 1970 and three-month deportation to Egypt. Further destitutions took place in November 1970 involving members associated, or sympathizing, with the SCP, such as al-Nur, al-Ata, and Hamadallah, latter of which was one of the six free officers behind the 1969 coup. In addition, Communists were dismissed from the army, government, and administration. Nimeiri also assumed the Prime Minister's position to complement that of the President.

63   Yohannes (1997: 303), and Holt and Daly (2000: 167).

64   Such unconfirmed allegations of US$18 million Central Intelligence Agency (CIA) plot involving Israel, Uganda, Roman Catholic organizations, British intelligence and mercenaries, are based on the testimony of German mercenary Rolf Steiner during his trial in August 1971 in Khartoum. Steiner was first sentenced to death for his subversive activities against the state, but the sentence was then reduced to 20 years in prison. Steiner later became ill and was transferred to Germany. See e.g. Beshir (1975: 94-5) and Howell (1978a: 428-9).

65   LOC (1991) and Holt and Daly (2000: 167), and O'Ballance (2000: 59).

66   Niblock (1987: 255), O'Ballance (2000: 60-1), and Johnson (2003: 36).

67   Niblock (1987: 256), O'Ballance (2000: 61), and Sidahmed and Sidahmed (2005: 32).

68   Alier (1990: 61, 62), Deeb (1991: 76), and Holt and Daly (2000: 168-9). Although the coup was never approved by the majority of the SCP's decision-makers, it gave Nimeiri an excuse to execute the party's leadership after regaining power on 22 July 1971. This included Mahgoub, Garang, and Shafi Ahmad al-Shaikh (secretary general of the Sudan Workers' Trade Union), together with the officers, al-Ata, al-Nur, and Hamadallah, all allegedly behind the coup attempt. See Niblock (1987: 256), Alier (1990: 61, 63), Korn (1993: 85-8), and Johnson, 2003: 36). Subsequently, Nimeiri appointed Alier as the Minister for Southern Affairs.

69   Yohannes (1997: 304). For instance, Sudan's main export article, cotton, had been used as credit to acquire Soviet financing, collaboration, and arms. The heavy reliance on the U.S.S.R. had severed the ties with the West, which could not be quickly recovered despite the purging of local Communists. See also Eprile (1974: 32).

70   Deeb (1991: 77) and Yohannes (1997: 303).

71   Eprile (1974: 32), Alier (1990: 63), and Rogier (2005: 13).

72   Howell (1978a: 434).

73   Alier (1990: 63), and Holt and Daly (2000: 169).

74   During the first two years of Nimeiri rule the foreign investment declined approximately S£300,000 and S£400,000, respectively, while cotton remained

the main export consisting of anywhere between 58.6% and 61.3% of the total export value in 1969-1972 despite an attempt to encourage other sectors. Similarly, although initially stable, the foreign trade balance turned drastically negative in 1974 when it dropped to negative S£125.5 million from positive S£400,000 of the previous year. See Mohamed Ali (1989: 52, 56, 61). Finally, Henze (1991: 102, 107) indicates that while military outlays consumed approximately 20% of the government budget in 1971-2, the Sudanese GNP per capita declined from US$442 to US$420.

75 Niblock (1987: 243-4). According to Warburg (2003: 159), nationalizations were also aimed to minimize threat to the new regime by neutralizing the economic power of the traditional northern establishment through confiscation of the property of the *Ansar* and the *Khatmiyyah*, the latter being treated less harshly (largely due to its ties with Egypt). By the end of 1970 over 80% of Sudan's foreign trade was controlled by the state. See Yohannes (1997: 302).

76 Niblock (1987: 284-6). According to Yohannes (1997: 303), among the first signs of this was Sudan's borrowing with commercial rates from the West that elevated inflation to an unprecedented level, with the counterinsurgency campaign in the South simultaneously requiring 60% more military spending.

77 Ties had been forged with the Soviet Bloc countries by recognizing East Germany and exchanging delegations in June and July 1969. Nimeiri toured China, Eastern Europe, and North Korea in the following year, which led to trade agreements and military, technical, and financial assistance. See Reich (1980: 354-5), Niblock (1987: 244-6), Mohamed Ali (1989: 55), Alier (1990: 44, 67), and Holt and Daly (2000: 169).

78 Particularly, there was increasing interest in Arab affairs propelled by the Arab socialism embraced by Gamal Abdel Nasser and Muammar Qadhafi. In this context, the relations with Egypt, and initially also with Libya, became among the most prominent in Nimeiri's foreign policy, and already in July 1969 Egypt and Sudan announced the formation of joint economic committee leading to the Economic Integration Agreement in September. Also, Qadhafi's coup in September 1969 induced Sudan to deepen relations with Libya. In December 1969 Egypt, Libya, and Sudan signed a Tripoli Charter to cooperate in defense, foreign policy, and economy, with a view to establishing a federation, which Nimeiri supported publicly despite domestic elite opposition. This led to a Tripartite Economic Agreement in April 1970 and the constitution of a council for economic integration in Cairo, while in November further commitments were made towards integration. See Niblock (1987: 246-7), Yohannes (1997: 303), and Holt and Daly (2000: 169). Nimeiri's calculations in maintaining good relations with Egypt and Libya paid off when both intervened during the SCP coup attempt, contributing to upholding the regime.

79 Alier (1990: 44).

80 Sudan's turn eastwards had also enraged Saudi Arabia, which began collaboration with the exiled northern elite political opposition parties. While it provided sanctuary to the main northern political groups, the Saudi cooperation pro-

moting Islamic resurgence in the Arab world through financing strengthened principally the Muslim Brothers.

81   O'Ballance (2000: 74) notes that Israeli training camps were established in Ethiopia, DRC, and Uganda.

82   Alier (1990: 67-8) and O'Ballance (2000: 75). While Ethiopia and Israel had increased their support to the Anya Nya in the latter 1960s, Amin had become involved in the Israeli operations in Uganda in 1968 to help the southerners who had allegedly visited him with Israeli officers. Amin came originally from the Sudan-Uganda border area and recruited 500 southerners to overthrow Obote in January 1971. He employed 1,300 southern Sudanese in his army overall, which, together with facilitating Israeli support, encouraged him to side initially with the Anya Nya. See O'Ballance (2000: 74-5) and Johnson (2003: 36-7).

83   Egypt and Libya promoted immediate measures to form common political structure and foreign policy, but Nimeiri proposed a more gradual approach starting with economic integration.

84   Beshir (1975: 87-88) asserts that this was particularly the case after Nimeiri had stated in November 1970 in Cairo that the tripartite could defend the Arab civilization in Africa. Nimeiri's statement led southern students and youth groups to submit him a joint memorandum denouncing the statement that defined Sudan as Arab, and undermined southern cultures and relations with the African states.

85   According to Niblock (1987: 247-8), when in April 1971 Egypt, Libya, and Syria announced their intention to form federal institutions Nimeiri abandoned the process. The subsequent SCP coup attempt in July left the regime vulnerable in the domestic context, and contributed to its new foreign policy orientation and alliance with southerners.

86   Holt and Daly (2000: 170).

87   The latter was pushed by Western oriented technocrats, who had replaced the Communists in the aftermath of the July 1971 coup attempt as an influential grouping within the state apparatus. They sought to prevent the formation of an Arab Federation and repair the deteriorated diplomatic relations with the West due to the 1967 Arab-Israeli War, the U.S. support for Israel, Israel's aid to the Anya Nya, and Sudan's nationalization of foreign banks and enterprises. See e.g. Niblock (1987: 266), Alier (1990: 67-8), and Holt and Daly (2000: 169).

88   O'Ballance (2000: 68).

89   It pledged recognition of the historical and cultural differences between the North and the South, and blamed British colonial legacy and traditional northern elite for inequality, promising that, "The Southern people have the right to develop their respective cultures and traditions within a united Sudan". It outlined a rudimentary Regional Autonomy Program for the South, including extension of the amnesty to those who would abandon rebellion, promoting economic, social, and cultural development, training, and the setting up of a special budget and economic planning board for the South. All this was condi-

tional upon the South's full participation in "a broad socialist-oriented demo-cratic movement", the SSU. See Beshir (1975: 72-3, 75).

90 Alier (1990: 48-9), and Holt and Daly (2000: 169-70).

91 Wai (1973: 219-220) and Collins (2005: 227-8).

92 Beshir (1975: 75) and Alier (1990: 43, 49).

93 O'Ballance (2000: 68).

94 O'Ballance (1977: 115), Johnson (2003: 33), and Collins (2005: 228).

95 Lagu had attended Army College in Khartoum, but reportedly during a visit to see family he allegedly saw atrocities committed by the army that convinced him to join the Anya Nya. He fled to the Congo where he became one of the exiles planning military operations against the regime, and became the com-mander of the Anya Nya in central Equatoria until 1965. Subsequently, Lagu established his own command in eastern Equatoria. See Collins (2005: 228). Largely due to his training, Lagu became a prominent member of the Anya Nya military leadership.

96 O'Ballance (1977: 96).

97 Howell (1973: 177), Wai (1973: 164), O'Ballance (1977: 88, 116), Holt and Daly (2000: 170), and Collins (2005: 228). However, the Anya Nya never con-verted into a conventional force with sufficient power to challenge the army elsewhere than the South. Its leadership, along with southern politicians, un-derstood that the movement lacked capacity to destroy any large army garrison or control a sizeable town in the long-term. The ANAF continued as locally based, with a low level of armament and training, and even Lagu's High Com-mand, under which other armed factions were increasingly co-opted, remained prone to factionalism. The relatively weak position compared to the army was also manifested in the Anya Nya's external dependence on a few suppliers of ammunition, medical supplies, and mostly antiquated military hardware, such as rifles and mines, while it continuously sought recognition among African states and by the Cold War powers. It used propaganda to dichotomize the struggle between "Arabs" and "Africans" and to give the rebellion deliber-ately racial and anti-Communist tone. See Howell (1978a: 426, 427-30). This reflects the later media reports of rebellions in southern Sudan, and defies the reality that the "Arab" and "African" are constructed and fluid categories rath-er than primordial manifestations of inherent incompatibilities, and that the problem in Sudan is rather the institutionalized system of narrow distribution of political and economic power.

98 The war led to the complex refugee situation in which Sudanese, mostly Acholi and Azande, refugees with ethnic links to the neighboring countries, supported the Anya Nya. Also some of the Ugandan and Congolese refugees in Sudan would confront their respective regimes. A similar situation unfolded between Sudan and Ethiopia where particularly the Eritrean refugees, but also those from other regions, played a role.

99 Beshir (1975: 75-7, 79-80, 87, 106).

100 Deng (1995b: 91) and Johnson (2003: 36).

101 Eprile (1974: 98-9).
102 O'Ballance (1977: 116) and Collins (2005: 228).
103 The Mahgoub government had previously failed to acquire helicopters and air-
     craft from the U.S. government, but it had concluded a cotton-for-arms barter
     agreement with the Soviet Union in August 1968. Nimeiri benefited directly
     from the deal and in February 1970-August 1971 the U.S.S.R. supplied the
     regime with modern military hardware, including 16 MIG-21 fighter jets, five
     Antonov-24 transport planes, anti-aircraft guns, 150 tanks (including T-55's
     and T-59's), and other armored vehicles of an overall value of US$150 million.
     See Eprile (1974: 104), O'Ballance (1977: 118, 2000: 70), LOC (1991), and
     Yohannes (1997: 303).
104 O'Ballance (1977: 117) and Collins (2005: 228). As a result, Soviet financ-
     ing increased, and the number of advisors, instructors, technicians, and pilots
     along with eastern European personnel grew to anywhere between 200 and
     3,000, until the July 1971 coup attempt after which Soviet presence began
     to diminish. Some of these personnel were located in the South. Amin, who
     initially aligned himself with the Anya Nya channeling Israeli support, alleged
     that Obote had collaborated with Soviet instructors in northern Uganda to sup-
     port Khartoum's war effort. While waiting for military equipment from the
     U.S.S.R., the regime had sought military aid also from Egypt. Egypt assisted
     the air force to the extent that allegedly Egyptian and Soviet pilots flew mis-
     sions in the South. See Eprile (1974: 103-6, 108, 112), O'Ballance (2000: 70-
     1), Alier (1990: 68), ICG (2002: 10), and Collins (2005: 229).
105 Eprile (1974: 100, 108, 134), O'Ballance (2000: 71), and LOC (1991).
106 The main objectives were Anya Nya bases, against two of which the govern-
     ment attacked in December. In January 1970, international attention focused
     on unusually intense fighting in the South during which it was claimed that
     the government forces had committed numerous massacres. For instance, ac-
     cording to *The Christian Monitor*, 700 people had been machine-gunned in
     one incident, while 2,000 had been killed and their cattle captured on another
     occasion. See O'Ballance (2000: 72). Eprile (1974: 49-52) notes that while the
     Anya Nya had also treated civilians harshly, this had been on a different scale
     as reports of further army massacres in the South in the course of 1970 indicate.
     Reportedly an estimated 3,200 civilians were massacred and 100,000 cattle
     killed or confiscated between April and August 1970 in Bahr al-Ghazal alone.
     See Eprile (1974: 50-2) and Alier (1990: 57). Eprile (1974: 52), O'Ballance
     (1977: 125), and Collins (2005: 229) further assert that in September-Novem-
     ber 1970 the government staged a large-scale offensive against the Anya Nya
     base in Mortu (prior headquarters of the ARG), near the Sudan-Uganda border,
     during which the rebels engaged the army in conventional warfare, repulsing
     the government offensive on three occasions, but when the army eventually
     overran the base about 800 villagers perished and many women were raped.
     Khartoum later used Mortu as a base for Uganda's former president Milton
     Obote's guerrillas against Idi Amin's regime. See O'Ballance (1977: 137) and

Alier (1990: 70).

107 Eprile (1974: 53) and O'Ballance (1977: 138).

108 Eprile (1974: 105-6). For instance, in November 1970 a major air strike allegedly claimed lives of 800 people, followed by a number of attacks in January 1971 in which people, cattle, and infrastructure were destroyed, leading to allegedly the most devastating air raid in February 1971 that reportedly killed 1,000 people. See Eprile (1974: 105) and O'Ballance (1977: 122-3, 137). Finally, O'Ballance (1977: 122-3) reports that the aerial offensive, which did not prove efficient against the rebels in the densely vegetated South but was devastating to the civilians, was suspended in summer 1971 after it had caused the number of southern refugees registered by the UN High Commissioner for Refugees (UNHCR) to rise to a total of 176,000 (of which 59,000 remained in DRC, 20,000 in Ethiopia, 72,000 in Uganda, and 25,000 in CAR).

109 In November 1970, it sent letters to the U.N. Secretary-General and the General Assembly, denouncing the "Arab" domination of the South, exclusion of the Africans from the government, religious persecution, social domination and discrimination, spread of famine and disease, absence of education and health facilities, and accusing the government of genocide. It also accused Algeria, Egypt, Libya, Kuwait, the U.S.S.R., and East Germany of supplying the regime against the South, which in a letter in December 1970 it claimed the U.N. should end. This triggered a U.N. resolution for a formal investigation of the southern claims, and a recommendation for a peacekeeping force. The resolution appealed to an international committee to investigate the situation, and to the International Red Cross for food and medicine. See Beshir (1975: 89).

110 This included rallying exile networks in Europe and Africa. In London, the Southern Sudan Association began publishing the *Grass Curtain* (1970-2), and influential political associations were set up in Italy and Norway that affected the public opinion and civil society organizations particularly in the latter. These groups were successful in publicizing the situation in the South and attracting some financial and material aid to the refugees through civil society and humanitarian aid organizations, such as Caritas, Church Relief Work, Action Committee for Africa, and Verona Fathers, while a number of wealthy and influential private Western individuals provided support in terms of arms, publicity, finance, and medicines. Allegedly, a company known as Southern Air-Motive in Kampala, owned by British individuals, facilitated Israeli arms transfers to the rebels through their representatives in Europe, Addis Ababa, Kampala, Nairobi, and DRC. See Beshir (1975: 90-1).

111 Collins (2005: 229-30).

112 O'Ballance (2000: 77-8).

113 Howell (1978a: 433).

114 Howell (1978a: 433) and Rogier (2005: 13).

115 Rogier (2005: 12-3).

116 Howell (1978a: 434).

117 O'Ballance (2000: 79). O'Ballance (1977: 133-4) further notes that although

the body was to meet annually, it was not until June 1971 when it was able to convene, and even at that time logistical difficulties prevented all commanders from being present at the same time.

118 Wai (1973: 163-5) and Beshir (1975: 65).

119 Collins (2005: 229).

120 However, the SSLM continued to suffer from the indiscipline that had characterized its predecessors, and the rebel practice of killing the captured government soldiers persisted (O'Ballance, 1977: 137).

121 Wai (1973: 164), O'Ballance (1977: 135, 2000: 79-80), Johnson (2003: 37), and Collins (2005: 228-30).

122 Deng (1995a: 141).

123 Quoted in Beshir (1975: 66-7).

124 Eprile (1974: 100).

125 By 1972 the High Command consisting of Lagu, Brigadier Joseph Akwon, Colonel Frederick Maggot, and Colonel Emmanuel Abur, was joined by the High Civil Authority under Elia Lupe, which included the Commissioner of Equatoria, Elisapana Mulla, the Commissioner of Upper Nile, Antipas Ayiei, and the Police Commissioner, Dishan Ojwe. In an effort for increasing international propaganda, Lagu appointed Emissaries Mading de Garang in London, Lawrence Wol Wol in Paris, Dominic Mohamed in Washington, D.C., Angelo Voga in Kampala, and Job Adier in Addis Ababa. See Eprile (1974: 99) and O'Ballance (2000: 82-3).

126 Eprile (1974: 101, 102) and O'Ballance (1977: 136, 2000: 81, 82-3). They further note that Lagu sought to regularize the civil administration and appointed Mulla, a former principal, to organize it according to the British model, and to establish a civil administration training center in Langayu near the Ugandan border where tax collection and legal administration were taught. By January 1972, the SSLM had founded 500 bush schools, each with 200 pupils, organized through a system of community education in which teaching staff was supplemented by literate adults. See Eprile (1974: 101).

127 O'Ballance (1977: 139) and Johnson (2003: 37).

128 Warburg (2003: 165).

129 Beshir (1975: 83-4) and Rogier (2005: 13).

130 O'Ballance (1977: 127-8), Howell (1978a: 432), ICG (2002: 11), and Rogier (2005: 13).

131 Alier (1990: 91-2) and Erlich (1983: 65-6).

132 Woodward (2003: 121).

133 Johnson (2003: 37) and Rogier (2005: 12). According to Daly (1993: 19), " . . . Nimayri moved to settle the war in the South, in order to placate the army, enhance his prestige at home and abroad, and win for himself the Southern support that all Khartoum regimes had lacked since independence".

134 Western NGOs supported southern refugees while being aware that rebels organized among them. See Alier (1990: 58, 68-9).

135 Johnson (2003: 37) and Rogier (2005: 12). John Garang stated later that "Late Brigadier Emmanuel Abur, Lewa (Major General) Joseph Kuol Amum – now with us, myself and many young officers, sat down, analysed the situation and decided to oppose the Agreement" because " . . . its basic terms and the basis of Agreement were first to absorb the Anya Nya into the National Army, second to integrate it after absorption and third to destroy it" (Heritage, 1987a: 4). This was despite general sentiment for peace in southern Sudan.

136 Beshir (1975: 99), Alier (1990: 56-9), Daly (1993: 19), O'Ballance (2000: 86), Johnson (2003: 36), and Rogier (2005: 12-3).

137 Beshir (1975: 83, 99), Howell (1978a: 432), and Alier (1990: 54-84).

138 Beshir (1975: 81, 99-100) and Alier (1990: 76). Beshir (1975: 81-2) notes that during the visit the church representatives became convinced that the conflict was not purely religious, as they had understood it, but combined also race, social, political, and economic factors which in their view had to be resolved through a political process.

139 Madut Arop (2006: 21) argues that the role of the WCC and the AACC was controversial. Celebrating the regime's willingness to negotiate, they pressured southerners to negotiate largely on the basis of terms dictated by the regime, which eventually led to an agreement that fell short of southern interests. Once the negotiations got underway, the southerners had neither time to be consulted on the ground nor educated about what was to be negotiated upon. In fact, the final peace agreement was to an extent imposed on the southerners, with Lagu being forced to accept the negotiations without having participated in much of the process he presumably assumed to be a result of genuine goodwill in Khartoum.

140 These included the full cessation of hostilities, the supervision of the cease fire by African or OAU team with unrestricted access, the release of Mboro and other political prisoners pleaded by the WCC/AACC delegation, and the recognition of the SSLM as the regime's only negotiation partner. The talks were to be chaired by an African country or the OAU, and the negotiations to take place outside Sudan. See Beshir (1975: 104) and Alier (1990: 76).

141 It also made a symbolic gesture by returning a sacred spear of the Bor Dinka from Khartoum in August 1971. See Alier (1990: 84).

142 In this meeting Alier and General Mohamed al-Baghir Ahmed, Minister of the Interior, met the SSLM representatives Wol, de Garang, Mulla, Job Adier, Anania Wolo, Paul Puok, and their legal advisor Dingle Foot. See Beshir (1975: 105-6) and Alier (1990: 76, 79-84).

143 Beshir (1975: 83, 99), Howell (1978a: 432), and Alier (1990: 54-84).

144 Alier (1990: 77-84, 90) and Johnson (2003: 37). In December, handing over the passengers of a crashed Sudan Airways plane unharmed improved Anya Nya's image among many northerners. See Alier (1990: 87-8).

145 The delegation consisted of Alier and al-Baghir, together with Mansour Khalid, the Minister of Foreign Affairs, Gaafar Mohamed Ali Bakheit, the Minister of Local Government, Abdel Rahman Abdalla, the Minister of Public Service

and Administrative Reform, Brigadier Mirghani Suleiman Khalil, a nephew of former premier al-Khalil, Colonel Kamal Abashar Yassin, and ambassadors Ahmed Salah Bakhari from Addis Ababa and al-Amin Mohamed al-Amin from Nairobi, all of them familiar with the South and many in contact with southerners. See Beshir (1975: 107) and Alier (1990: 91, 92-5).

146 This included Mundiri, Wol, de Garang, Maggot, Albino, Puot, Adier, and Lagu's personal assistant Angelo Voga. See Beshir (1975: 107) and Alier (1990: 96).

147 Beshir (1975: 107) and Alier (1990: 97, 98).

148 Alier (1990: 98-105).

149 John Garang later claimed that at this point the southern leadership's paramount interest became political posts, military positions, and other jobs. See Heritage (1987a: 4). However, these accusations from an individual who did not form part of the negotiations have neither been substantiated nor corroborated.

150 For instance, Abyei, mainly inhabited by the Ngok Dinka, had been part of Southern Kordofan from 1905 and then Bahr al-Ghazal until 1951, but removed due to the personal position of a local chief. The southern part of Blue Nile, home of the Burun people, had belonged to Upper Nile until 1951 when it was removed due to difficult access. Kafia Kingi (*Hufrat al-Nahas*) was originally part of Bahr al-Ghazal, but had been joined in southern Darfur in 1961 when the Abboud regime decided to affirm control over its copper and uranium deposits. See Alier (1990: 99, 101). According to Thomas (2010: 12), the area is thought to have also gold and petroleum.

151 Interestingly this became reality about 30 years later as one of the main security stipulations of the Comprehensive Peace Agreement of 2005 negotiated by the leadership of the main southern organization of the second rebellion.

152 Eprile (1972: 15) and Howell (1978a: 434).

153 The North-South boundary was demarcated along the provincial borders as they stood at the time of independence in 1956, and a right to referendum was agreed on for those border populations that wished to join the autonomous Southern Sudan. In addition, the southern demand for a separate regional army was abandoned, and an agreement was concluded to form an army Southern Command of 12,000 troops with half being recruited from the South. Moreover, the specific sources of revenues for the southern region were stipulated, despite allegations that the regime delegates had an interest in advancing southern poverty and its consequent economic dependency on the regime. Finally, the southern regional political institutions, the High Executive Council (HEC) and the Regional Assembly, the executive and legislative organs respectively, were accorded. It was also agreed that considering the disrespect of past agreements by the Arabized elite political forces, the final treaty was to be enacted into a law, Southern Provinces Self-Government Act, that could only be amended through 3/4 majority vote in the national parliament and with confirmation of 2/3 majority vote in a referendum conducted in the southern

region. See e.g. Beshir (1975: 107) and Alier (1990: 101-5).

154 Beshir (1975: 111) and Alier (1990: 100-2).

155 O'Ballance (2000: 87).

156 Ethiopia played a major role in the peace process partly because its Western supporters offered the regime aid in exchange for facilitating peace efforts. In addition, after the shift in Uganda's foreign policy orientation by the end of 1971, Ethiopia became one of the most important forces supporting the SSLM and could use this position to its advantage in terms of the negotiations. Finally, it was in the context of the relationship between the local protagonists, the regional setting, and the international Cold War politics in which the peace treaty became possible.

157 Beshir (1975: 108-9), Graham (1990: 132), and Madut-Arop (2006: 18).

158 Awur (1988: 61-2) and Madut-Arop (2006: 18).

159 Beshir (1975: 107-8, 120), Awur (1988: 61, 62), Akol (2007: 132), and Collins (2008: 111).

160 Howell (1978a: 434) and Akol (2007: 132).

161 For instance when the commander of Bahr al-Ghazal, Emmanuel Abuur Nhial, arrived to Kampala to inquire about the details of the negotiations from exiled Bahr al-Ghazal politicians, Lagu had already ratified the agreement in Khartoum and prepared his return to Juba. Although Bahr al-Ghazal politicians had rejected it, in Lobone, the Anya Nya headquarters, Abuur understood that orders had been given for the Anya Nya troops to demobilize, relocate, and wait for absorption into the national army. See Madut-Arop (2006: 19). The flow of information among distinct territorial commands, therefore, was too deficient to allow an overall assessment of the "southern" view of the negotiations before they were finished.

162 O'Ballance (2000: 87).

163 Madut-Arop (2006: 19-20).

164 According to Garang, "We calculated that the clique in Khartoum would erode the government in Juba because its basis for the Agreement was first to absorb the Anya Nya into the National Army, second to integrate it after absorption and third to destroy it. So you have the process of achieving a cheap victory over the Anya Nya forces . . . We also accepted to be absorbed because we knew that the North would dishonour the Agreement, and the south would be ready for war. Then we would be ready to launch a genuine movement, the people's revolution" (quoted in Madut-Arop, 2006: 20).

CHAPTER VII

AUTONOMOUS SOUTHERN SUDAN:
An Era of Uncertainty

The 1972 Addis Ababa Agreement was a result of the regime's and southern opposition's willingness to make peace in favorable local, regional, and international conditions. Pushed also by external actors, the agreement became the framework for peace in Sudan. Southern Sudan, encompassing Bahr al-Ghazal, Upper Nile, and Equatoria, gained self-government and limited political autonomy as one region.

However, despite allowing the establishment of southern political institutions, the agreement lacked financial guarantees for the region. Southern Sudan remained economically under regime control. This was less than an ideal starting point for southern self-government, as was the southern political elite's lack of experience representing the highly heterogeneous southern region as one entity. These factors contributed to the competing elites within "the South" engaging in a struggle over local political power and resources.

In the course of the 1970s, Islamic resurgence provided a context in which southern autonomy became increasingly contested. Natural resources, and particularly petroleum, discovered in the South during the second half of the decade, played an important role in the infringement on southern self-government. In this context, sections of the southern leadership again resorted to ethnic politics and "tribalism", while the regime sought to exploit such fissures among the southerners, and weaken the unity of the region and its capacity to challenge the hegemony of northern elite at the national level.

In the circumstances of deepening local political discord, and the struggle over southern regional rights, differentiation and polarization of identities again emerged. While individual southern politicians continued to hold office in the regime and the parliament, their influence remained marginal and insufficient to affect regime policies towards southern Sudan. As the 1970s progressed, the regime's infringement in southern politics deepened and finally resulted in the president's unconstitutional abrogation of the self-government in southern Sudan.

The institution and implementation of southern self-government gener-ated a number of difficulties, and resulted in the deterioration of the political scene. Early southern regional politics were characterized by the members of the political elite assuming positions in order to defend interests of con-stituencies formed according to politicized ethnic and religious identity af-filiations (tribalism), which largely followed the pattern established already during the colonial era. The logic behind their exclusive political strategies mirrored that of the representatives of the national regime, although it was not based on the attitudes of inherent cultural and racial superiority. In the leading circles of the regime, and among the northern elite opposition seek-ing to undermine Nimeiri, the southern region was perceived as potentially too strong relative to the center, which was used to justify measures leading to its weakening relative to the central government. In this situation, the sen-timents of disappointment of the autonomy largely due to the difficulties re-lated to the self-governance and the former Anya Nya integration, continued northern domination and violation of southern autonomy, lack of economic development, insecurity, and inequality and relative deprivation, contributed to the resurgence of discord between southern leadership and the regime.

Thus, the period of southern self-rule was characterized by the regime's engagement in violating the commitments made in Addis Ababa, and sectors of the disgruntled southern military elite gaining power that in the end sur-passed that of the local politicians. In this context, the internal, regional, and international political realities reinforced the projected "Arab" vs. "African" identity rift, re-strengthening the marginalizing dynamic of the political sys-tem towards southern region. This was instrumental to the process of organi-zation of the second insurgency in southern Sudan.

Post-War National Political and Economic Context

The national political and economic landscape of which southern Sudanese region formed part, was marked initially by Nimeiri's strategy to reduce marginalization and exclusion through more extensive incorporation of "the South". However, the prevailing political realities of northern elite's com-petition over state leadership, together with the limits of the autonomy as a restricted political and economic arrangement in which the southern region remained subject to a high level of regime influence, ultimately resulted in reinforced polarization of the regional "North-South" rift.

246

From Exclusively "Arab" to "Arab-African"

The 1972 agreement in Addis Ababa had brought the first war in southern Sudan to an end. It has been estimated that between 500,000 and 1.5 million had perished, with one million having become refugees or internally displaced.[1] During the war, the activities and operations of the warring parties had targeted largely civilians,[2] which shows that attacking and using civilians as a cover, constituency, and a source of "asset transfer",[3] is not a new post-Cold War phenomenon.[4] Although this occurred at a large scale also in the second insurgency in southern Sudan (1983-2005), the onset of the second conflict, which due to its leadership can be largely considered as continuation of the first, predated the post-Cold War political environment in which rebellions in Africa appeared initially to increase.[5]

The Addis Ababa peace agreement stipulated that the three highly diverse provinces of Bahr al-Ghazal, Equatoria, and Upper Nile, unified by the armed opposition to the national government, would constitute the southern region. Accordingly, the southern region was to preserve its boundaries with northern provinces, largely (but not fully) demarcated in 1956, with its capital based in Juba. In addition, the agreement specified the authority of the central government over critical aspects of political sovereignty and economic affairs, leaving the southern regional government to manage local affairs but with significant limitations. For instance, the central government was to remain in charge of national defense, external affairs, currency and coinage, air and inter-regional river transport, communications and telecommunications, customs and foreign trade, immigration, emigration, and naturalization, planning of education and economic and social development, and performing public audit.[6] Meanwhile, the southern regional parliament was allocated powers to legislate to safeguard public order and internal security, efficient administration, and regional cultural, economic, and social development, detailed in 20 specific clauses and appendixes of the agreement.[7] This shows that while the regime's attempt was to form a limited alliance with the southern region by recognizing its interests, the autonomy arrangement was deliberately maintained too limited to break the dynamics and the logic of state marginalization that resulted from the central government's control of funding and national administration. The region continued economically and politically dependent on the central government as the core of the Sudanese political system.

According to the agreement, two main political institutions were created in the southern region to manage its affairs. These were the High Executive Council (HEC), a regional government exercising executive power, and the People's Regional Assembly, endowed with the legislative power. The

HEC was formed by a president of the region, appointed by the national president, but with the recommendation of the Regional Assembly, which in practice meant that the national president was largely in control of the selection process of the regional leadership.[8] The President of the HEC, in turn, appointed the ministers of his cabinet with the decision being subject to the approval of the Regional Assembly. The ministers were responsible for the annual budgets of the ministries that were to be approved first by the Regional Assembly, prior to their presentation to the National Assembly (Sudanese parliament). Finally, the Regional Assembly consisted initially of partly appointed (up to 25%) and partly elected members, all of which in the later legislatures were to be elected directly by a secret vote.[9] These institutions formed the core of the political system in southern Sudan. In principle, similar to the national level, the democratic institutional structure contradicted the regime's authoritarian political management. At the same time, the incorporation of the southern region remained limited because only a small number of southern politicians represented the region at the national level. They continued to have little say in the national politics, including in the case of the government's policies towards the southern region. In this institutional context, prominent sectors of the southern political class resorted back to the "tribalist" political culture, which generally reduced the appeal of individual politicians to their ethnic constituencies that often manifested in loyalty of subordinates in exchange for resources provided by the "big man".

The main security provisions of the agreement included integration of the Anya Nya units to the state's security institutions. This was an important issue for the SSLM, because it was seen to reward southern troops for their efforts. Although the security arrangements after the initial cease-fire had been the main impasse during the peace negotiations, the SSLM, alarmed by the integration of its forces to the national security apparatus, pushed "the South" to have its own army. However, the government delegation vehemently opposed this because it would have increased power of the southern region relative to the regime, although, on the other hand, it would have served as a minimum security guarantee for the southern region. In the end, Haile Selassie's proposal for a 12,000-strong Southern Command composed of 6,000 southerners matched with an equal number of northerners had prevailed in the final agreement.[10] The integration was to be supervised by a Joint Military Commission composed of an equal number of senior northern officers and their southern counterparts, and was to include international observers.[11] This served as a minimal guarantee for the southern leadership, and many southern leaders and soldiers decided to collaborate with the regime in the hope that the autonomous political arrangement would remedy southern Sudan's marginalization.

Moreover, the agreement included general amnesty for war-related crimes. All criminal acts committed during the conflict were forgiven and prisoners released within 15 days of the ratification of the agreement, which led to the freeing of over 2,000 people imprisoned in southern Sudan.[12] On 3 March 1972, a general amnesty provision was signed into a law as the Indemnity Act.[13] This was another sign of Nimeiri's initial strategy to appease southerners and reduce the dynamics of marginalization of southern Sudan.

However, the Addis Ababa peace agreement was plagued by a number of weaknesses. First, it was an internal treaty with no mechanism for external monitoring or supervision. Second, it had no external arbitration mechanism in case of violations of its provisions.[14] Third, it failed to provide financial and physical guarantees for southern Sudan, doing little to remedy the region's chronic dependency on the regime financing and to deal with the proliferation of modern weapons and the persisting killing of civilians, kidnapping of women and children, and cattle rustling, all which had been intense during the war and still continued afterwards.[15]

Furthermore, in 1970 Nimeiri had declared the restructuring of Sudan's political institutions. Although many of the reforms to be implemented were not completed before the finalization of the Addis Ababa Agreement, he used the opportunity of cessation of hostilities to introduce a permanent constitution promulgated on 8 May 1973 to replace the largely modified temporary constitution of 1956.[16] The new constitution became manifestation of the regime's initially secular approach,[17] as Nimeiri favored the technocrats and southern politicians over sectors of Arab nationalists, conservatives, and religious radicals, and purged them from national politics.[18] Incorporating the Addis Ababa Agreement, the new constitution initially tackled national identity and religion by defining Sudan as "Arab" and "African",[19] attempting to resolve the contentious matters relating to the national identity of the country. However, this failed to transfer into a social reality since the social hierarchy dominated by Arab culture and Islam continued to determine social status and opportunities in Sudan. The institutionalized state marginalization of the peripheries encouraged further the constructed "regional" identities, which in the North-South context continued to reinforce the instrumentalization of "Arab" vs. "African" and "Muslim" vs. "non-Muslim".

The 1973 constitution also concentrated extensive powers on the presidency. In particular, it allowed Nimeiri to declare a state of emergency, suspend the constitution, and have the judiciary directly responsible to him. Converting Sudan into one-party state with the SSU under his chairmanship, Nimeiri's personal influence extended widely through elaborate patronage politics.[20] Although the National People's Assembly, the parliament, was portrayed as a largely independent institution that checked presidential powers, Nimeiri used presidential position to neutralize it by filling it mainly with regime supporters loyal to him.[21] As such, the permanent constitution centered political power on Nimeiri's presidency and purged the northern elite parties opposing the dictatorial regime by proclaiming them illegal. Faced with these measures, the main northern opposition parties took refuge in the neighboring Arab states and operated in exile against Nimeiri's government.

Throughout the early 1970s, Nimeiri survived a number of coup attempts organized by anti-regime elements, some with foreign support.[22] This owed in part to the narrow base of the regime, which relied extensively on sectors in the military loyal to Nimeiri and to an extent on the southern support. In 1975, another aborted coup[23] convinced Nimeiri to pass constitutional amendments to center further power on the president, and to give the State Security Organ (SSO) freedom to perform preventive arrests in weeding out dissent.[24] This led to ever growing authoritarianism, but also convinced Nimeiri to seek alliances with sectors of the exiled northern elite to strengthen his power and diminish the threat of a successful coup.

Political Arrangements for Southern Autonomy

The southern negotiators' swift signing of the peace agreement created confusion in southern Sudan. The SSLM delegation's negotiation result was disappointing to many southern leaders, which led to delaying the agreement's ratification and an initiative to renegotiate it.[25] However, this came too late, as Uganda and Zaire, both of which supported the Anya Nya and hosted large numbers of southern refugees, announced their support of the treaty and pressured the SSLM to comply.[26] The indecision was related to the composition of the SSLM leadership that consisted of a number of secondary power centers under Lagu's leadership. Some of these sectors in southern political leadership and military command, especially among hard line secessionists such as those that became part of the underground officers' movement and of the Anya Nya II, rejected the agreement, which brought about enduring internal instability in "the South". The agreement had important consequences in part because it initiated a process through which considerable part of political and economic power held by the rebel military officers during the insurgency shifted to the civilian politicians who assumed the political leadership in the self-governed region. Thus, after the war, grievances heightened among the southern military due to the loss of power, integration to the Sudanese army, and impotence to defend southern Sudan in the face of infractions on its self-government.

The ratification of the Addis Ababa Agreement on 27 March 1972 by Nimeiri and Lagu marked the formalization of the accord and paved way for its implementation. However, against expectations, Nimeiri interfered in the process. He deprived Lagu of the appointment as the President of the Interim HEC, removed him from political leadership, absorbed him into SSU structures, and emphasized that he was a military man.[27] Instead, Nimeiri rewarded Alier with the Interim HEC presidency.[28] Although Alier himself has claimed that his appointment as the President of the Interim HEC was coherent with the SSLM view,[29] Collins has argued that it was unexpected and finalized without consultation.[30] In fact, according to Lagu, he had been previously falsely promised the presidency.[31] Regime collaborator Alier's appointment as the head of the southern region generated renewed suspicion within sectors of southern leadership.[32] It was also the prelude to bitter political competition between him and Lagu, which polarized the main southern political forces behind the two protagonists.

External Challenges to the Regime's Reliance on Southern Support

Although Nimeiri felt the weakness of his regime due to the several coup attempts, external, regional, and international factors played an important role in inducing Khartoum's shift from the southern constituency to again embrace the northern elite forces.

External Factors in Political Reversion

Nimeiri regime, relying largely on southern support, continued to face challenges. This was to a large extent because the favorable external conditions for the alliance with the South, which had been useful for obtaining the much needed domestic constituency and end the insurgency, were changing. Although sectors of the northern elite opposition remained in exile, socialist officers overthrew Haile Selassie in Ethiopia in 1974 and Addis Ababa shifted to the Soviet camp to join Libya that sought to destabilize the U.S.-allied Sudan. In 1976, the National Front (NF), a coalition of exiled northern elite political parties founded in 1974,[33] attempted to seize power. Qadhafi, who had not forgiven Nimeiri for refusing to implement the Tripoli Charter that would have allowed Libya extend its influence, backed the unsuccessful attempt.[34] The aborted coup, again involving northern opposition elements, pushed Nimeiri to seek alliances with the exiled sectors of the northern elite. This came in the expense of the regime's alliance with the South, which was considered inadequate to secure Nimeiri's power against the exiled northern opposition's challenge. The short-lived incorporation of the South to the state's political system was coming to an end.

In the aftermath of the coup attempt, Nimeiri accused Libya, Ethiopia, and the Soviet Union. These accusations were carefully expressed to cement American support and to portray the affair as a design of international Communism. This was not completely unfounded, as Ethiopia, Libya, and the U.S.S.R. supported the dissidents, with Ethiopia seeking to install a pro-Ethiopian regime in Sudan to purge ELF's supply networks which persisted.[35] Whereas the U.S.S.R. was interested in reversing Sudan's pro-Western foreign policy orientation towards Egypt, Saudi Arabia, and the U.S., a successful coup in Sudan would have extended Qadhafi's influence in the Sahel towards Darfur and Chad where Libya supported a rebel faction led by Goukouni Oueddi against the regime of Felix Malloum who himself had come to power in a coup in 1975. The most immediate repercussions of the aborted coup attempts were that Nimeiri sought to extravert more support from the U.S., and, concluding that southern constituency was insufficient to stabilize the regime, revert back to seeking alliance with sections of the exiled northern elite.

Nimeiri's rhetoric portraying Sudan as surrounded by the Communist threat paid off. The U.S. elevated its support for Khartoum and converted Sudan into the focal point of its geopolitical machinations in the Horn of Africa, which in the following decade became its main zone of interest in the continent along with Southern Africa.[36] By this approach the U.S. aimed to neutralize the growing Libyan influence in Sub-Saharan Africa,[37] and began rebuilding the Sudanese army,[38] sending arms to Sudan,[39] and formed a regional alliance of states and sub-state groups centering on Sudan while seeking internal stability by investing on Sudan's economy.[40]

Increasingly alarmed by the threat of the formerly dominant exiled political organizations, Nimeiri sought to re-legitimize the regime. He embarked on a policy of "national" reconciliation with the northern political forces. However this reconciliation required the sidelining of the South because, unlike Nimeiri, most northern elite representatives refused concessions to southern Sudan which they considered subservient region that should be unconditionally subjected to the northern elite dominated state. As a result, dictated by Nimeiri's negotiation with the NF, and affecting Sudan's periphery regions only in terms of general amnesty and the release of 1,000 political prisoners, the reconciliation was hardly "national".[41] In this situation, also affected by the regional context of Islamic resurgence and the growing power of political Islam, Nimeiri reversed the earlier policy of persecution of the northern sectarian parties and Islamists.[42] He announced elections to be held in 1977, luring the exiled northern factions back to Sudan where he could exert control over them by facilitating token representation in political institutions. The return of the NF would also diffuse pressure from Saudi Arabia, which pushed for reconciliation of northern elite political factions and whose financial investment on Sudan Nimeiri partly depended upon.[43]

In contrast, the NF had been severely debilitated by the failed coup attempt. It could not afford another challenge against the regime, which was backed by the reinforced army, the U.S., and Egypt.[44] In these circumstances, the northern opposition factions accepted Nimeiri's invitation and regained limited access to the political institutions.[45] The return of the main northern political forces neutralized their direct threat to the regime, particularly since they were now more controlled in the domestic political scene. However, Nimeiri's change of power base from the earlier support groups, the secular technocrats, Communists, and southern politicians, towards the northern elite, was also marked by an attempt to divide the northern elite opposition. Considering the regionally rising Islamism from which the Sudanese regime could benefit, he favored Hassan al-Turabi's Islamist section[46] of the northern opposition elite, and deliberately sidelined the sectarian power centers, the neo-Mahdists and the *Khatmiyyah*, which were considered as the most potent threat to the regime. Although this division of the northern elite brought a certain level of stability in the short term, it resulted both in the alienation of the South (because the NF resented any concessions to the region) and in the growing strength of the Islamist constituency within the regime that eventually threatened Nimeiri's personal position.

In 1977 Nimeiri's term as the president had come to an end, and after a plebiscite convoked for re-election he continued in power. In February 1978 the parties returning from exile were allowed to take part in the election of the People's Assembly, but they failed to challenge the regime which prevailed by taking 164 of 304 available seats.[47] However, the lower than expected share of seats for the regime demonstrated its persisting weakness.

As a result, Nimeiri embarked on a mission to weaken the opposition. By associating himself with the Islamist section of the northern elite he emphasized the role of Islam, while gradually resorting to support the Islamic law, *shari'a*. This move was mainly strategic, but it encouraged the growth of the Muslim Brothers, counting on Saudi Arabian support, from a small urban organization to a mass political movement.[48] Playing the Islamic card was convenient in the regional political context because, apart from helping to cement the economic relationship with Saudi Arabia, the leftist radical ideologies had subsided to the Islamic resurgence in Egypt and militant Islam had emerged in Iran and Algeria.[49] In Egypt, Sadat had endorsed the Muslim Brothers and Islamic student organizations to undermine the opposition to Nasserist-dominated professional and student organizations, and amended the constitution so that *shari'a* became the main source of all legislation.[50] This had far-reaching consequences in Sudan in the following years because Nimeiri, and northern Sudan, continued to look towards Egypt for inspiration.

Whereas the sectarian parties had hesitated to collaborate with the regime, the Muslim Brothers ceased this opportunity. According to Collins, Turabi " . . . openly committed himself to the regime in order to rebuild the Muslim Brothers under his patronage", and used a network of contacts with individuals and organizations in the Arabian Peninsula to gain support for the movement, counting largely on diaspora financing to build up its resource base.[51] Nimeiri cleared the way for the Muslim Brothers, who decided to work within the state apparatus by supporting the regime and purging the opposition parties competing for influence, while declining to push forward the reforms towards political opening demanded by other NF elements. The Muslim Brothers were rewarded with a number of positions in the government and state machinery, which culminated in Turabi's appointment as the Attorney-General in 1979 and allowed the movement to gain further influence, while also granting generous Islamic banking concessions that allowed the Muslim Brotherhood to gain economic power by managing financial flows largely originating from the Gulf States.[52] From 1979 onwards Nimeiri's actions became increasingly compromised by his failing health, and, upon return to Khartoum after surviving a second cardio-vascular surgery in 1982, he became obsessed with completing his Islamic vision for Sudan.[53] By this time Turabi was exercising wide powers, and many considered him to have become *de facto* president.

Initially, Western powers considered Islamicization compatible with Sudan's foreign policy orientation. This view was facilitated by the regime's relationship above all with Western supported Egypt and Saudi Arabia, which, like Sudan, used strategies of extraversion to obtain external resources to maintain power. Such regional context allowed a more advantageous climate for domestic Islamic resurgence which the U.S. supported in the Middle East as a counterforce to Communism. In these circumstances Nimeiri became convinced that the survival of his regime depended on Western and Arab patrons, largely because Sudan was on the brink of a bankruptcy due to its deteriorating domestic economic conditions that had worsened further in the international context of the 1973 petroleum crisis. The situation had led to the exhaustion of foreign exchange reserves to a negative S£53 million by

July 1977, together with mass unemployment, inflation, and inadequate supplies of basic commodities and food stuffs.[54] This also explains Nimeiri's opportunist rhetoric to extravert Western assistance by emphasizing Soviet, Libyan, and Ethiopian threat.

The U.S. administration sought to keep Sudan in the Western camp. In this situation, motivated in part by Libya's threat to Western interests, and the perceived unreliability of Ethiopia in the long term, it overlooked the murder of two American diplomats in 1977[55] and encouraged Nimeiri to negotiate for the release of Americans who had been captured by Eritreans. The U.S. also pushed for American investments and oil prospecting in Sudan, which had intensified with Chevron forwarding a payment of US$1 billion to secure a contract over a large area in 1974. Moreover, Washington encouraged the plan to convert Sudan into a "breadbasket" of the Arab world by promising U.S. companies an important commercial role. All this resulted from the focus on Sudan as the center of the U.S. policy in the Horn of Africa after the Ethiopian socialist revolution in 1974.[56]

In the regional context, Sudan's relations with Egypt remained intimate. While Egypt's military presence in Sudan helped to save Nimeiri from several coup attempts, increasingly open economic arrangements followed. They were formalized through a program of political and economic cooperation signed in February 1974, and a defense treaty concluded in 1977. In 1979-80, Sudan boycotted Egypt's decision to offer Nile water to Israel for irrigating the Negev desert, but had to consolidate its alliance with Egypt to continue a joint effort to curb Libyan encroachment in Chad and Darfur. The close association with Egypt continued until the October 1982 Integration Charter, which committed Egypt and Sudan to establish a number of joint political institutions, including the Higher Council and the Nile Valley Parliament.[57] This mirrored the earlier calls for the "Unity of the Nile Valley" during decolonization.

Similarly, Sudan's relationship with Saudi Arabia improved after its departure from the Communist path. The Western-oriented Saudi Arabia perceived Sudan as strategically important to counter Soviet influence emanating through Ethiopia, but feared the weakening of the regime and encouraged Nimeiri to reconcile with the exiled political parties that it supported. The Saudi assistance to the northern Sudanese parties was in part due to cultural affinity and the warm relationship between them. For instance, *Khatmiyyah* originated in Saudi Arabia, and the Mahdist movement was considered in some circles as a guardian of Arab culture and Islamic values in Sudan. Moreover, more radical pro-Islamist Saudis funneled financing for the Muslim Brothers, particularly after they assumed control of the Islamic banking sector in Sudan. Finally, by the mid-1970s, both Egypt's military assistance and American and Saudi Arabian economic support were indispensable to the Sudanese government which was ruling in deteriorating economic conditions.

However, Sudan's relations with a number of its other regional neighbors deteriorated after the signing of the Addis Ababa treaty and reorientation of foreign policy. Both Libya and Ethiopia, the staunchest collaborators of the Soviet Union in the region during the 1970s, positioned themselves against Nimeiri. In the case of Libya, Qadhafi was personally disappointed with Nimeiri's move to negotiate peace with Sudan's southern rebels and distance Sudan from the Tripoli Charter. This provided him yet another incentive to support Sudanese dissidents and undermine Nimeiri by fomenting instability in Darfur in relation to the war Libya was fighting in Chad.[58] In addition, threatened by deepening collaboration between Western supported Egypt and Sudan, Qadhafi formed a Tripartite Alliance with the Soviet-backed Ethiopia and South Yemen in August 1981. This Soviet influenced alliance formed part of a larger strategy through which the U.S.S.R. sought to extend its geo-political control south of the Suez Canal and over the Red Sea shipping passage to the Indian Ocean.[59]

Furthermore, in the course of the 1970s, the war in Chad became more complex. It included Soviet-backed Libya, U.S.-supported Egypt, and Sudan, as well as the old colonial master France. In 1975 Chadian President François Tombalbaye was killed in a coup executed by General Felix Malloum, and by the mid-1970s the principal warring parties had disintegrated into a number of factional armies. Although the National Liberation Front of Chad (FROLINAT) continued as the main rebel force, even it had not been able escape factionalism. This resulted in Egypt and Sudan supporting Hissene Habre, and Libya backing Goukouni Oueddi. In 1979, Oueddi deposed Malloum and established a Government of National Unity until the resurgence of war in 1981, which led to Habre conquering N'Djamena in July 1982 and assuming power. The war dragged on and its repercussions were felt on the Sudanese soil, particularly in Darfur, in the form of a Libyan incursion that posed a threat to Nimeiri.

The Addis Ababa Agreement had been a high point of Sudan's relationship with Ethiopia in the early 1970s. This relationship had culminated in the demarcation of the frontier between the two states and Kenya. However, Khartoum's continuing support to the Eritrean rebels soured relations particularly after the Marxist regime of Mengistu Haile Mariam assumed power in Ethiopia.[60] While the increasingly Islamic agenda and the facilitation of the assistance of Arab League states to Eritrea continued to play a role in the latter 1970s, the ethnic and cultural ties of eastern Sudanese communities with Eritreans were also a factor.[61] In response, by 1976 Ethiopia had begun supporting residual Anya Nya II groupings active in southern Sudan and based in its western borderlands. These had not accepted the Addis Ababa treaty, demanded secession, and caused instability in the region by continuing armed violence.[62] This became an important element in the insurgency formation process in southern Sudan in the early 1980s because Ethiopia already provided support and a sanctuary for southern armed dissident groups.

Sudan-Uganda relations during the decade of the 1970s were also relatively turbulent. In 1971, Amin had seized power from Obote with the support of approximately 500 Anya Nya and other soldiers, many summoned from ethnic groups extending from northern Uganda to Sudan's southernmost Equatoria province. Amin's shift from an alliance with Israel towards Libya helped to conclude the Addis Ababa Agreement and the establishment of a relationship of mutual tolerance between Khartoum and Kampala during the 1970s.[63]

However, Amin's downfall in 1979 generated unprecedented flow of refugees from Uganda into southern Sudan. They totaled 39,000 in 1979 and 80,000 in August 1981, elevating to an estimated 200,000 by the second half of 1983 when the war in southern Sudan had resumed and again reversed the flow.[64] The incoming Ugandans affected most heavily the conditions in Equatoria where the influx of refugees strained local agricultural and social resources as well as the ecosystem.[65] Seeking to benefit from the situation, the respective regimes used refugees to extravert resources through humanitarian aid. Finally, the refugee crisis also illustrated the strength of the cross-border ethnic connections between southern Sudan and neighboring states.[66] This exchange of refugees featured strongly in Sudan's relations with Uganda, Ethiopia, Kenya, and Zaire, while groups living near the border with northern Sudan often sought refuge there.

Sudan's turn to the West manifested itself in its partnership with the U.S. After receiving news about deteriorating Soviet relations, the Americans quickly announced that Sudan was eligible for buying U.S. military equipment, which paved the way for Washington to resume diplomatic ties with Khartoum in July 1972. This resulted in a significant flow of American aid and in the reversal of the nationalization policy in 1974, in the context of Ethiopia drifting to the Soviet sphere, which in turn encouraged U.S. investment in the development of financial and commercial infrastructure, communications, and mining sector. In 1977 further economic and military support followed, and in 1981 Nimeiri allowed Americans to use Sudanese military bases and negotiated an arms contract with the U.S. after the news about Libyan Tripartite Alliance with Ethiopia and South Yemen.[67] Holt and Daly have noted that "The perceived threat of Soviet-backed regimes in Ethiopia and Libya, increasing dependence on Western and especially American Aid, and Nimeiri's apparent belief in the domestic value of close American support, produced strong bilateral relations that lasted until the end of the regime".[68] By the early 1980s Sudan had become the second recipient of U.S. economic and military assistance in Africa after Egypt.[69]

In this situation, Sudan began collaborating with Western commercial and financial agencies, governments, private companies, and international organizations.[70] In addition, Khartoum sought to promote agricultural production for which Sudan had high potential. This attracted those Arab states seeking to secure future foreign food supply to invest in agriculture in Sudan, promoted as the "breadbasket" of the Middle East.[71] In 1972, promises for significant Arab financial assistance and investment began to arrive. The United Arab Emirates donated US$1 million as rehabilitation funds for southern Sudan, and the following year the Kuwaiti Fund for Arab Economic Development (KFAED) announced significant financing for irrigation projects, while the Arab Fund for Economic and Social Development agreed on an investment of US$6 billion to cover the first ten years of Sudan's projected 25-year program.[72] After Nimeiri's "national" reconciliation and alliance with the Muslim Brothers, relations with a number of Arab states improved further.

By the mid-1970s the business of development had converted into the main economic undertaking in the country. It included massive investment and expenditure.[73] Plans were made for agricultural, industrial, infrastructure, transportation, and communications development, counting largely on investment from Arab states. Efforts were concentrated on north-central Sudan[74] where ventures owned by sectors of the northern elite benefited most from the investment.

Still, despite having attracted generous external financing by the end of the decade Sudan was facing an economic crisis.[75] This was largely because Nimeiri's neo-patrimonial state was absorbing ever-growing amount of resources, while from the mid-1970s the investment flows to Sudan had begun to decline. At this time, the soaring oil prices, due to Organization of Petroleum Exporting Countries maneuvering to punish Western powers that had supported Israel in the 1973 Arab-Israeli War, resulted in a global economic slump that diminished external investment.[76] The domestic effect of the financial crisis was a recession, which in turn had a direct effect of aggravating social grievances and strengthening opposition to the regime that culminated in the mid-1980s. This was in part because of the inability of the increasingly bankrupt regime to maintain its extensive neo-patrimonial clientelist networks that upheld Nimeiri's power.

The rapid economic decline forced the government to turn to the international financial agencies for economic adjustment. Although the World Bank had previously refused to help Sudan financially due to its economic problems, in 1978 it agreed to provide support, which the IMF followed up in May 1979 by alleviating Sudan's immediate financial burden in exchange for austerity measures. The imposed remedies for export-led recovery included repeated devaluations, cutting subsidies of consumer goods, and further privatization to establish free market environment, while rehabilitating the previously neglected Gezira area to recover cotton production. The World Bank approved projects included livestock marketing, improvement of port facilities, mechanized farming, and agricultural research.[77]

Yet, the austerity measures could not remedy the deteriorating economy. They rather worsened the situation by weakening the state's political control through strict downsizing of the bureaucracy, subsidies, and services. In this way, the intervention of the international financial organizations resulted in the state losing control of its neo-patrimonial support structures, and contributed to Nimeiri's eventual downfall by opening space for the Islamist infiltration into the state structures.[78]

Institution of Southern Self-Government

Khartoum played the main role in the implementation of the Addis Ababa Agreement, while the southern administration with inadequate funding faced insurmountable burden of successfully promoting the political rights and economic development of the region.

Addis Ababa Agreement Implementation

After Alier's appointment as the President of the HEC, the implementation of the Addis Ababa Agreement began. In the process, three southerners were appointed to the central government,[79] but, as had been the case previously, they were granted marginal ministerial positions with limited influence. The posts were carefully designated to politicians who had no capacity to challenge the *status quo* of state power.

On 4 April 1972, Nimeiri issued a presidential order for appointing the chairman and the Interim HEC, and on 22 April the HEC cabinet took the oath of office in Khartoum. Two days later Alier flew to Juba with his 11 regional ministers of who seven were returnees from exile and four from within Sudan.[80] The attempt was to include southern politicians, both from

259

domestic and exile opposition, with a just ethnic and regional representation (two ministers from Bahr al-Ghazal, six from Equatoria, and four from Upper Nile, including the HEC president). However, at the same time, largely due to ethnic and personal rivalries, the autonomous government failed to neither integrate traditional authorities nor many of the educated returnees into its institutions, which generated protest. Smaller groups, and those who were discontented, alleged that the Dinka (Alier) and the Equatorians (Lagu) had disproportionally high representation in the southern political institutions, and that the former SF and SSLM politicians and rebels were favored over other groups.[81]

Subsequently, the southern leadership appointed the officials of lower echelons of the region's administration.[82] The organization of the local government was adopted from the persisting structure during the colonial period. According to Johnson,

> This administrative structure, despite many re-namings of units and offices, remained essentially the same after independence and during the brief period of the southern Regional government (1972-83), with chiefs being supervised at the district level by local government officials, who reported to a civil administrator within the province or a region, who was in turn subordinate to the provincial commissioner/regional governor, a political appointee.[83]

By June 1972 the administration of the region had for the first time become "southern".[84] However, the administrative continuity and the groups in power in the South, products of the prevailing political context in Sudan, and relevant external political and economic dynamics affecting the country, generated continuity of exclusionary view on political identities and "tribalistic" ruling methods. In the long run, the divisive ethnic politics proved more powerful and resilient to the institutional changes in the context of continuing divide and rule practices than any wider extension of a cohesive "southern" regional political identity that was largely restricted to the elites.

Initially, after the peace agreement, most of the southern region continued in a state of uncertainty. Many southerners had to be disarmed, or integrated in the state security apparatus or civilian sector, while more than 500,000 refugees were to be repatriated and another half a million of internally displaced resettled, with many fearing for their personal security.[85]

On 21-23 February 1972, an international conference was held in Khartoum to extravert aid for the returning southern refugees and the internally displaced. Attended by representatives of the OAU, U.N., NGOs, and observers from African and Arab countries, the conference supported the government efforts, and various institutions and states pledged emergency relief and resettlement and rehabilitation assistance.[86] As part of its effort to consolidate Sudan as an ally, the U.S. made US$22.45 million available for resettling and rehabilitation of a total of 680,000 refugees registered mainly in Ethiopia.[87]

Subsequently, a Resettlement Commission[88] was established to oversee repatriation and rehabilitation. A Repatriation and Relief Commission was constituted to transport refugees back to Sudan, while it also assisted the internally displaced. The commission was given powers to work internationally together with the UNHCR, and it was assisted by a number of NGOs.[89] In 1974, rehabilitation and resettlement had become a priority in the South, and was focused on reviving basic services, such as education, health, and water, and providing agricultural inputs and support to the returnees.[90] However, the effort suffered from the lack of expertise and resources reaching the South, leading to discontent towards the central government and the southern authorities.

The overall achievements of repatriation and rehabilitation were slim. Reportedly, more than 300,000 refugees went without benefit from the process and many, remembering the horrors of war, preferred to stay with their ethnic kin in the neighboring states.[91] The internally displaced were inclined to return to the "peace villages" or other parts of the country,[92] while the regime preferred to alleviate population pressure in Khartoum and other population centers which it considered a possible security threat. Soon the number of returnees overwhelmed the repatriation effort that was sustained principally by external cooperation,[93] while the regime continued to concentrate on economic development in benefit of the north-central Sudan and deprived the South of additional resources.[94] Thus, the dynamics of exclusive governance continued during the 1970s, which reveals that Nimeiri's partnership with the southern leadership was only strategic, aimed at strengthening the regime also in relation to southern Sudan which it sought to maintain economically dependent. This dynamic continued to produce conditions in the South that maintained its subordination and marginal incorporation to the national politics and economy.

Moreover, the Addis Ababa Agreement's Cease-Fire Protocol was a key condition stipulating the conditions for the cessation of hostilities and monitoring mission. Use of violence and provocative troop movements were forbidden and a Joint Cease-Fire Commission composed of equal representation, along with a mission of foreign observers, was established. It was mandated to oversee the cease-fire, repatriation and registration of returnees, and to inspect cease-fire violations and recommend actions to handle them.[95]

Although a number of incidents occurred in 1972-4, they were contained.[96]

Another crucial condition for peace had been the assurance that Anya Nya rebels were provided viable livelihoods after the war. The protocol, Temporary Arrangements for the Composition of the Units of the People's Armed Forces in the Southern Region, called for recruitment of male southerners to the Army's Southern Command. A Joint Military Commission, constituted in April 1972 by a presidential decree, supervised the process of absorption of former Anya Nya units into the Southern Command made of 6,000 southerners and 6,000 northerners, while 4,500 Anya Nya were to be recruited as police, prison wardens, and game scouts, and the remaining rebels placed in non-military occupations ranging from road construction to veterinary and agricultural work.[97] The Joint Military Commission stipulated the selection criteria for absorption, which included being member of the Anya Nya, academically sufficiently qualified, healthy, and willing to continue as a soldier.[98] The process included training for the Anya Nya forces to match their northern counterparts. The Joint Military Commission recommended a two-stage process; the absorption of the former Anya Nya in the army structures as their own units, followed by integration through which the Anya Nya would be placed under army commands.[99]

The Anya Nya absorption and integration were gradual processes confronted with the difficulty of uniting former enemies. The former warring parties continued generally suspicious of each other at an individual and collective level, and the Anya Nya remained wary of situations that would expose them to the northern forces. According to the HEC, the process, consisting to several stages[100], was to be completed by 3 March 1977, within five years' time from the signing of the Addis Ababa Accord.[101] Its final part, the integration process, proved as the most problematic due to the complexity of related issues[102] and accompanying suspicion and rumors,[103] while some were obliged to retire, accept lower than expected rank, or settle for non-military occupations perceived as less prestigious.[104] Negative aspects of absorption and integration contributed to the resentment, and many Anya Nya members and civilians came to perceive the process as a deliberate government policy to neutralize southern security forces.[105]

The incorporation of the former rebels to the army became contentious. Since the army's rank and file was mostly composed of western Sudanese (Darfurians) under orders of north-central riverine, principally *Shaiqiyyah*, officers, it was hardly an unbiased representation of the national ethnic plurality.[106] Fearing that their privileged position would be undermined by the incorporation of the Anya Nya, northern officers had difficulty accepting the process and some resigned in protest.[107] Others interpreted the arrangement only as temporary, and considered that after five years the influence of the Anya Nya would fade due to troop transfers, dismissals, and retirement.[108] In fact, the regime did design a covert policy to demote, retire, and lay off senior ex-rebel officers to neutralize the movement's leadership, which caused resentment and contributed to underground anti-regime mobilization by southern officers in the course of the 1970s.[109]

On the other hand, there were varying interpretations and opinions concerning the integration process. Some ex-rebels and southern politicians returning from exile considered the five-year period as time dedicated for training in separate units before the integration, while others perceived the arrangement as consisting of two separate parallel armed forces. Both views originated from a sentiment that full integration would be dangerous for southern regional integrity and should be resisted. This was despite Alier reiterating that the HEC policy stipulated full integration within five years.[110]

Furthermore, a number of issues related to disarmament, demobilization, and reintegration also became problematic. These included the question of personal armament, the army's rules over promotions, the material rewards of absorption, and sentiments of suspicion and superiority among northern officers.[111] Occasionally, explosive outbursts followed which were tantamount to the sentiments that contributed to instability among the military in the South.

Yet, even more importantly, some officers deliberately slowed down the process.[112] These actions by some, mainly secessionist, ex-Anya Nya officers reflected their rejection of the peace treaty. They were also linked to these officers' resistance to their declining role in regional politics after the war, and the resurgence of the southern political class as a major force dictating political power in the region after the peace treaty. To an extent, such actions also drew from the general feeling among the absorbed ex-Anya Nya and many civilians in the South. They were suspicious, mistrustful, and feared a possible coup that would change the regime into more conservative one since it appeared that Nimeiri had brought the war to an end against general northern opinion.[113] It was feared that such more conservative government would likely revert to policies of Arabization and Islamicization of the South.

The following integration phase proved even more problematic. The government aimed to incorporate the ex-Anya Nya first by uniting the provincial ex-rebel commands. The plan was to mix individual or smaller detachments of former rebels, and then incorporate them into the army structures. As part of integration, the regime established a covert program to send senior ex-rebel officers for training abroad or other branches of the armed forces, detaching them from their loyal subordinates, after which they were

placed elsewhere.[114] After this, their units would be transferred[115] or dismantled, but by the end of 1973 this attempt to neutralize the Anya Nya units had
raised unprecedented controversy and tension. As a result, Lagu and Alier
toured garrisons and clarified the integration plan. They recognized that
non-confidence was not limited to ex-rebels, but that it was a generalized
sentiment that resembled the overall political uncertainty in the South. Lagu
sought to diffuse the tension by ordering that northern officers in the South
should be made to feel more comfortable, but at the same time banned from
socializing exclusively with the *jallaba*, while corrupting rumors causing
instability should be isolated. By identifying these and other factors, he was
aware of the events that had led to the southern disturbances and mutinies in
the 1950s, and emphasized the northern officers' need for cultural sensitivity
and the potential dangers of *jallaba* influence.[116] The first phase of the integration was completed[117] in the context of widespread suspicion in the South.

However, by 1973 the process had caused growing fear and anxiety,[118]
and opposition to integration strengthened. At around this time, Garang appeared in Bussere, the cradle of the early disobedience led by some ex-Anya
Nya officers,[119] and allegedly secretly assumed the leadership of an underground movement of officers in opposition to the Addis Ababa Agreement.[120]
After his role in stirring opposition to the integration had become obvious,
a delegation was sent from Khartoum to arrest Garang as an alleged leader
of the underground resistance movement. Yet, it had to return empty-handed
when the officers associated with Garang threatened to revolt if he was detained. These officers portrayed themselves as the protectors of southern interests, seeking to remain prepared to resume the war in case of a successful
coup against Nimeiri would undermine the peace agreement.[121] The development of southern underground dissidence together with other incidents, such
as the grenade attack in Wau that appeared to target northern officers, led
to measures by the regime to accelerate its attempt to neutralize the former
Anya Nya by re-organizing the ex-rebels at platoon, company, and battalion
levels.[122]

Initially, the southern political institutions sought to allocate civil service positions according to the ethnic composition of the region. However,
in practice, the process was plagued by favoritism, personalized politics for
self-gain, and corruption. From the beginning, it generated inter-ethnic and
inter-regional competition and tensions which characterized the southern regional government overall, and which were exploited by the national regime.
In addition, the regional government had limited resources, which fell short
of providing employment for the majority of the remaining ex-Anya Nya
due to financial dependency on the regime.[123] Indeed, Khartoum's special

fund for southern rehabilitation was limited and ran out already in 1974. As a result, many ex-rebels became unemployed, and approximately 3,500 were directed to farming, which many of them resented because state employment, particularly in the army, was generally preferred over farming and trade.[124] Consequently, the regime preferred to employ southerners as low-cost manual labor in agro-industrial sugar schemes in the northern provinces, which the Interim HEC declined. Instead, the HEC suggested implementation of two sugar schemes in the Kenaf in the South, which the regime rejected because it concentrated economic and technical resources on agricultural projects in the north-central Sudan, and sought to maintain the South dependent and as a source of cheap labor. This incomplete process generated a pool of southerners with military knowhow and experience in living in the bush, which could be exploited for mobilization for armed violence.

Southern Regional Politics

The first and second regional assemblies provided the setting for southern politics. Already by the mid-1970s, the southern political scene had grown divisive in the context in which personalized and exclusive agendas became dominant in local politics.

First People's Regional Assembly, Dec. 1973-Dec. 1977

The Interim HEC laid the foundation for the first People's Regional Assembly, the southern regional parliament. Major part of its mission was to prepare and conduct elections in which new representatives would be chosen at the end of the 18-month period it had been in power. The HEC first established an Election Commission in September 1973, and then convoked the election in October-November 1973. Out of the 60 available seats 30 were designated for elected southern representatives of the SSU, and the remaining 30 distributed between provinces; 11 for Bahr al-Ghazal, 10 for Equatoria, and 9 for Upper Nile. Alier's constituency of the former SF and Lagu's SSLM leaders gained majority.[125]

The first seating of the southern parliament, which dealt with the issue of selecting the new HEC president, was tense. In December 1973 Nimeiri appointed Alier as the sole SSU candidate for the HEC presidency, thus violating the Addis Ababa Agreement that was now part of Sudan's 1973 constitution. The agreement stated that the People's Regional Assembly would recommend a candidate for the HEC presidency to the national president who would then appoint him.[126] While Nimeiri's move practically renewed Alier's term in office,[127] it contradicted the constitution and set a precedent for further interventions on the southern affairs. This undermined integrity of the regional administration. Therefore, from early on, it became clear that the type of regional autonomy stipulated in the Addis Ababa treaty failed to free southern Sudan from the dependence on the regime and its leadership. It was therefore insufficient to transform the dynamics and logic of state marginalization and the subordinate position of southern region in the Sudanese political system.

The first Regional Assembly, which assumed power in December 1973, was the only one to serve a full four-year term. It was the regional legislative organ that was to keep the HEC in check amidst of frequent accusations of corruption and the use of security apparatus to curb the opposition.[128] Among the principal issues faced by the first regional assembly was the military integration process.

By 1974 the government had accelerated and expanded the process of integration with the view to complete the integration program within the agreed five-year period. Many southerners considered this deadline unrealistic,[129] but the southern political leadership in Juba accepted the policy of speedy integration pushed by the regime, and was aware of it involving troop transfers.[130] The accelerated process faced growing resistance that led to violent confrontations, such as in Juba in December 1974[131] and February 1977, Akobo in March 1975, Kapoeta-Rumbek in January 1976, and Wau in February 1976, which were often triggered by soldiers' fears of being transferred to the North or rumors of being attacked by northern troops.[132] However, these uprisings were generally individual expressions of frustrations that lacked organization to produce sustained armed opposition.

From 1975 onwards, however, a number of more destabilizing incidents took place. For instance on 2 March 1975, prior to Unity Day celebrations in Akobo, a number of former Anya Nya soldiers and officers of the garrison staged a mutiny.[133] According to Madut-Arop,

> The Akobo troops were reportedly acting on the rumour that a contingent of Northern Sudanese troops was on its way to disarm them before they would subsequently be transferred to Northern Sudan . . . [and] . . . the mutineers were hoping that their move would have sparked a mutiny all over the south to mark the return of the war for total independence of the South Sudan . . .[134]

Many of them eventually surrendered after being subjected to intense persuasion by both regional and national authorities, and were subsequently arrested and executed.[135] However, some escaped to western Ethiopia and became part of the armed groups of Anya Nya II operating in eastern southern Sudan,[136] which Ethiopia actively supported to pressure Nimeiri to end his assistance to the Eritreans.[137] Whereas the main Anya Nya II military organization consisted principally of the Nuer, other armed groups calling themselves Anya Nya II also emerged in the late 1970s and early 1980s in Bentiu, Fangak, Akoka, and northern Bahr al-Ghazal.[138] In essence, this was the beginning of intensification of insecurity caused by organized armed groups, which culminated in the second insurgency in southern Sudan.

In this context, a pattern of armed force developed in which the northern regime officials and the army in the South (including former Anya Nya officers and troops) sought to crush the dissidents. This imposition of hard measures against the mostly former Anya Nya dissidents, instead of seeking a negotiated approach, endangered the implementation of the agreement because it provoked violence and discontent that inspired further mutinies, although initially personal interventions by Alier and Lagu helped to avoid escalation.[139] Yet incidents and organized attacks, involving sentiments of suspicion and fear of northern aspirations as one mobilizing factor, continued to occur in 1976[140] and 1977.[141] While disgruntled junior-level ex-Anya Nya officers organized most such events, in some cases, similarly to the political agitation that led to the first insurgency, southern hardline politicians were implicated.[142] Indeed, the events in January and February in Wau, Rumbek, and Kapoeta point to a plan in which the southern politicians involved seem to have fed the ex-Anya Nya junior army officials' and soldiers propaganda, seeking to instill resentment, suspicion, and fear over integration and slow promotions. This aimed at promoting the already increasing grievances in the South manifested in the context of political uncertainty and insecurity, which would allow mobilization along re-polarizing "Arab"-"African" political identity rift.

The seriousness of the situation prompted Alier to attempt to diffuse tension. He suggested that the integration process should focus on internal ex-Anya Nya integration first, and to be followed by integration and transfer within the South before any measures would be taken to move southern units to the North.[143] However the regime, conditioned by its new alliance with radical religious elements of the northern elite, insisted on the policy which would to neutralize the Anya Nya sooner. The government proceeded by transferring southern units to the North, and retired former Anya Nya officers, applying similar measures to police, prisons, and wildlife departments, but it was forced to leave the most resistant ex-Anya Nya battalions in the South intact.[144]

The integration coincided with other political developments that did not involve the military but affected the ex-Anya Nya and the civilians. Issues that added to the increasingly generalized discontent included the 1977 military and integration agreement with Egypt that was seen to reaffirm Sudan's "Arab" ties, and the growing competition among southern politicians that undermined regional political unity.[145]

The question of lack of southern development[146] was important. In particular, controversy arose over the externally influenced Jonglei Canal project and oil prospecting,[147] since it appeared that the regime aimed to keep the South poor and dependent by confiscating its resources for the benefit of the government and its external allies.[148] First, in February 1974 Nimeiri signed an agreement for political and economic integration with Egypt, which contributed to the Jonglei Canal project to build a 175-mile channel to cut the rate of evaporation in the *Sudd* by 50%, adding irrigated cultivable area in northern provinces by 3.7 million acres.[149] It was presented to the local authorities as a project in benefit of the South, and portrayed as a measure of the regional government's commitment to southern development. Yet, the project was linked to the regime's financial blackmailing of the southern administration, and after minimum guarantees for its benefits for the South the regional government was forced to accept it. This generated sentiments among southerners that the central government was stealing southern water resources for developing northern Sudan and Egypt, both of which depend heavily on the Nile for irrigation.

Second, in 1974, after foreign petroleum companies suggested conducting oil exploration in the southern region, many members of the northern elite became alarmed. It was feared that finding petroleum, a high-value resource, in the South would strengthen secessionist sentiment in the region that already enjoyed limited autonomy.[150] However, the interest to attract foreign investment prevailed, and oil prospecting was supported by adopting a new legislation which enabled companies such as British Ball and Collins, American Pacific International, Oceanic Exploration (U.S.), and Chevron (U.S.) to secure exploration contracts. Chevron was provided an exploration deal in southern Sudan, but Nimeiri allegedly pocketed the proceeds of the contract despite the southern regional government having been the rightful authority to receive the funding according to the Southern Provinces Self-Government Act that formed part of the Sudanese constitution.[151]

The controversy over southern resources contributed significantly to the re-securitization of the North-South relationship. However, some in the northern elite feared that in the case oil was found, part of the southern intelligentsia would be empowered to claim that conditions justifying Sudan's unity (southern dependence on northern Sudan) had ceased to exist and would advocate secession. These fears fed the position among some northern politicians in Khartoum to be against oil exploration in the southern region in the first place. Consequently, after petroleum was discovered in the North-South border area in 1978,[152] intensification of securitization of the relationship between the regime and the South followed. Some elements in the northern elite again portrayed southern Sudan as a separatist "problem" menacing the state's unity. This position, which had previously weakened during the early years of Nimeiri rule, gained strength again after the regime's alliance with the more radical Islamist elements of the northern elite. Still, facing deepening economic difficulties, the state sought petroleum also in the South in order to establish a new source of financing. This was attractive to Nimeiri because it would provide resources to maintain the *status quo*, including the state's neo-patrimonial and clientelist structures, while maintaining Islamists as a minor partner and strengthening the regime's economic position against opposition. It would also diminish the reliance on external sources for state funding.

The first People's Regional Assembly came to an end on 19 December 1977 in a situation in which politicians from various parts of the southern region were increasingly divided. There was an element of envy and bitterness attached to the views of some politicians who were left without a position in the administration, viewing the HEC as a privileged club of individuals with high salaries, housing, cars, telephones, and a generous resignation payments. This led to some of the excluded politicians to use ethnic hostility, accusations, and propaganda to bring down ministers and attempt to enter the ministerial cadre.[153] Although such conduct had not prevented the democratic regional political institutions from functioning, it had reinforced further the use of "tribalist" strategies as a major tool of competition for political positions.[154]

While many divisions among southern politicians were of their own making, Nimeiri's machinations deliberately exacerbated ethnic tensions in the South. The regime sought to play southern leaders, mainly Alier and Lagu who Nimeiri knew personally, deliberately against each other by favoring the one after the other in an attempt to undermine southern regional unity. This became more apparent after the regime's "national" reconciliation with the exiled northern elite factions because these sought to rebuild their influence in Khartoum by undermining the southern self-government. As a result, they portrayed the Addis Ababa Agreement as an unacceptable concession to the southern provinces, an expression of southern separatism, and an obstacle to a constitutional reform embracing Islam. Behind their anti-South political agenda was the objective of retaining access to southern resources,[155] resuming direct state control of southern Sudan as a subordinate territory, and extending northern elite's influence in the southern provinces by imposing social transformation through assimilation to Arab culture and Islam. This was the case particularly following Turabi's Muslim Brotherhood's association with the regime because it replaced southern Sudan as the major regime constituency. Thus, arguably, the regime's approach to southern Sudan was to a large extent dictated by the marginalizing dynamics and political culture of the Sudanese state which continued to generate grievances in the South. In this context, the return of sections of the traditional northern elite forces to the government reinforced the re-polarization of regional identities between the North and the South, and led to the re-securitizing of the South as a separatist problem.

Second Southern Regional Assembly, Feb. 1978-Feb. 1980

By the mid-1970s, divisions among southern politicians had grown to hinder political processes in the region. These were exacerbated by the exclusion of influential politicians from the first HEC and the People's Regional Assembly, and transfers of officials to unwanted posts, while four ministers were dismissed and a number of southern politicians arrested by the state's security organs.[156] Most of those leaders excluded from political positions threw their weight behind Lagu, who resented Nimeiri favoring Alier and was considered by many as the best guarantee against northern infringement to southern politics.[157] The rifts in the political elite became the seeds of personalized power struggles, of which the most significant centered on Alier and Lagu.[158] This undermined further the South's position relative to the regime because Nimeiri was able to cast considerable influence over the two leaders.

The first regional assembly ended its term in December 1977, after which elections were conducted. These resulted in the victory of a loose coalition of leaders demanding change.[159] This owed in part to Nimeiri's efforts, to a degree influenced by army officers and civilian officials aspiring to remove Lagu from the army. Sections in the northern elite, particularly traditional and conservative factions returning from exile, also felt threatened by the possibility of Lagu becoming one of the highest-level army officials. They generally resented some of the Anya Nya officers' influential positions in the Southern Command, while the northern politicians had received assurances from Nimeiri for the revision of the 1972 Southern Provinces Self-Government Act during the "national" reconciliation.[160] Their pressure, and principally the influence of the growing power of the Islamist section of the northern elite within the regime, became instrumental in the push to undermine the Addis Ababa Agreement.

270

As one of the initial steps to demonstrate the regime's authority over the semi-autonomous South, Nimeiri adhered to the demands to remove Lagu from the army. He shifted Lagu from the military to the political sphere by appointing him as the president of the HEC, which was likely a move to diminish the political capacity of the southern executive because Lagu was principally a soldier, not a politician. The NF endorsed the plan, Sadiq al-Mahdi supporting Lagu's candidature both morally and financially,[161] and southern politicians who had been excluded during the first regional assembly welcomed it in part because they were led to believe that Lagu could propel economic progress.[162] In 1978, Alier received notice from Abu al-Gasim Muhammad Ibrahim, a member of the SSU political bureau and Nimeiri's cabinet, that it was the president's personal view that he should give up the race for the HEC presidency which Alier duly accepted.[163] Although it was clear that the move aimed to promote regime authority over the South by creating further division among the local politicians,[164] opposing the decision would have been detrimental to Alier's personal relationship with Nimeiri and his future political aspirations. This way, the personal ties between northern and southern leadership reflected the projection of the regime authority and northern manipulation of southern politics. The presence of such personal ties, which had developed for the most part since the 1950s, and their persistence through periods of rebellion and southern self-governance until today, show that there are no inherent incompatibilities between northern and southern elites that produce violent conflict. Rather, these differences are a result of (re)construction and manipulation of political identities related to the respective elites' interests.

In the first meeting of the second People's Regional Assembly on 27 February 1978, Lagu was accepted unanimously as the President of the HEC.[165] This represented change in the southern leadership, Lagu benefiting from the support of a wide range of southern ethnic constituencies,[166] principally in Equatoria. However when sworn in, Nimeiri told Lagu not to appear again in military uniform.[167] In this symbolic manner Nimeiri effectively removed Lagu from the army, which also figuratively marked the end of the SSLF military organization's potential to challenge the regime. Although the SSLM military had been largely dismantled, sections of the northern elite paradoxically continued to portray southern Sudan as a separatist threat.

By the end of the decade, the situation in southern Sudan had turned increasingly turbulent. Ethnically defined squabbling became the order of the day, as differences emerged between Lagu, his cabinet, and the Speaker of the Regional Assembly.[168] Personal wrangling alienated Lagu from the wider inter-ethnic constituency that had brought him to power. His uncomfortable

271

personal relationship with Nimeiri, and contacts with other influential northern factions, were another impediment in relations with the regime. By 1979 Lagu had put pressure to create a number of new administrative posts, mostly under directorates in the ministries of finance, public service, and agriculture, and to upgrade other already existing positions. Ostensibly, he sought to appoint his Equatorian constituents to higher echelons of administration and to curb what he claimed as Dinka domination, while strengthening his own position through the increasing Equatorian influence in the political institutions.[169] While Lagu's argument was not completely unfounded in that the Dinka and Nuer administrators tended also to favor their ethnic kin in the allocation of positions and provision of services, the Equatorians had been well represented[170] in part because of having larger numbers of educated individuals than the two Nilotic groups. Given the much larger size of the Dinka and Nuer population, Equatorians often had less positions in southern political institutions. In any event, the focus on ethnic allegiances promoted "tribalism", resulting in increasingly divisive ethnic politics between Lagu and the Equatorians and Alier and the Dinka. This reversed the momentum for inter-ethnic political consensus, and the seeking of common and widely recognized "southern" identity.

In 1979, a secret report of the army headquarters for the northern officers of the Southern Command came to light. It was discovered by Colonel Andrew Makur Thaou, transferred from Wau to Juba to fill in for Colonel Umar who was on a pilgrimage to Mecca. Umar had forgotten a copy of the report describing how to handle the absorbed forces, the police, prison warders, and wildlife officers in case of a rebellion. Makur took it to Lagu, the President of the HEC, who pointed out that he was no longer a military officer with authority over the ex-Anya Nya, but rather a civilian official. However, he recommended Makur to draft an immediate counter-plan.[171] This incident became known among the ex-Anya Nya officers, and contributed to the strengthening of the underground movement because its leaders, including Garang, became convinced that regime sought to neutralize the southern military. Consequently, efforts to remove ex-Anya Nya senior commanders faced more resistance, and by 1980 it had become clear that the former Anya Nya maintained an organized underground network. This prompted the government to plan ways in which to remove the absorbed forces from the South without provoking resumption of war.[172] The tensions within the security apparatus in the South continued to escalate, while sentiments of mistrust and fear heightened.

Meanwhile Alier, and some other politicians who opposed Lagu's presidency, struck back. They accused Lagu of embezzling US$2.5 million, reportedly donated by Abu Dhabi in 1978, and demanded his resignation.[173] The accusations came at the time when " . . . there was little doubt in Juba that corruption had become conspicuous in direct proportion of his dispensation of patronage, particularly to the Dinka Samuel Aru Bol, vice-president of the HEC and speaker of the Assembly, a post Lagu had created".[174] The opposition, headed by Mboro, Malwal, Alier, and an overwhelmingly Dinka constituency supporting them, accused Bol of mishandling S£30,000 for the resettlement of refugees, which fueled further demands for Lagu's resignation.[175]

The dispute over ousting the speaker had significant repercussions. Immediately, 24 members of the Regional Assembly claimed that the dismissal of Mboro was unconstitutional, and that the president was acting beyond his powers, forwarding the matter to Nimeiri in 1979 and asking for Lagu's destitution.[176] This gave an excuse to Nimeiri, also under pressure of the radical elements of the northern elite, to dissolve the Regional Assembly in February 1980 in an unconstitutional move. Bol was then arrested and charged with corruption, while Nimeiri also dissolved the People's National Assembly where he faced growing opposition.[177] The disbanding of the Regional Assembly was in part justified by the escalation of inter-ethnic disputes, which was not completely unfounded due to the militarization of many Dinka and Nuer groups in the course of the 1970s.[178]

Prior to the dissolution of the southern parliament and dismissing Lagu, Nimeiri had promulgated the 1980 High Executive Council and Regional Assembly Act. It gave him powers to dissolve the People's Regional Assembly. The law stood in direct confrontation with the 1973 national constitution, but this was largely left unchallenged in the South because Alier's faction celebrated the move to destitute Lagu.[179] By decreeing a law that contradicted the constitution and using it to justify infringement on southern autonomy, Nimeiri had removed the final safeguards of the limited southern autonomy.

Conclusion

The implementation of southern autonomy created a political climate in which, despite the incorporation of the southern leadership as new regime constituency, the continued dependence of the southern region on the regime became apparent. Even though the Addis Ababa Agreement had a constitutional status as the Southern Provinces Self-Government Act, the political dynamics perpetuated the position of southern Sudan as a marginal and subordinate territorial entity within the authoritarian state. Although Nimeiri's strategic efforts initially appeared to remedy the constructed "Arab"-"African" political identity rift, the regime deliberately deprived southern region of resources for self-administration against the spirit of the Addis Ababa Agreement. In the end, the agreement was too weak to protect southern self-governance from the central government influence and was subject to regime manipulation.

As a result, when the regional and international political environment turned inopportune for the regime to continue to rely on southern Sudan as a major constituency, the self-government agreement became increasingly contested. After Nimeiri survived a number of coup attempts and faced strengthening northern opposition in exile, he embarked on the "national" reconciliation to negotiate its return to Sudan. In the regional context of Islamic resurgence, the regime looked towards northern Sudanese Islamists, backed by regional and international powers, as the new regime constituency. The Islamists' and other northern elite factions' perceptions of the South undermined the regime's partnership with the southern region, and converted Addis Ababa Agreement from a political asset to a burden.

In this situation the view of southern Sudan categorically as "the other" was again reinforced within the northern political circles, and the Addis Ababa Agreement was increasingly seen as the initial step to southern secession. Particularly after the discovery of petroleum in the southern territory, influential sections in the northern elite became preoccupied by its potential economic capacity to survive as a separate political entity from Sudan. This was largely because their idea of Sudan as one, and its national identity deriving from Arab culture and Islam, was constructed on the subjugation of the South as the economically unviable and dependent "other". Keeping the South poor was therefore seen to minimize its possibility to secede and to maintain it as a source for extraction of natural resources and cheap labor for northern Sudan.

In the mid-1970s, in context of growing political uncertainty, the regime's relationship with the South was reconstructed through securitization of southern region as a threat. Southern political cadres seemed unable to agree on common goals, and some military elements continued the rebellion in the region while others refused to integrate to the state's security apparatus. The refocus of portraying the South as the explicit "other", and as a threat to the state, also explains largely why the second insurgency emerged in southern Sudan instead of other parts of the marginalized periphery of the Sudanese state.

When the breach between sectors of southern soldiers and politicians, which had originally surfaced during the first rebellion, became re-emphasized, the southern military grew increasingly reluctant to accept integration. This is largely due to the shifting power from the Anya Nya officers to the politicians, while some in the ex-Anya Nya officer core felt that they posed as the guarantee of the Addis Ababa Agreement and should remain able to secure the southern self-government. In the fear of becoming redundant as part of the integration process, sections in the southern military sought to conspire against the regime which aimed at neutralizing the ex-Anya Nya.

At the same time, many southern soldiers continued to be affected by the sentiments of sections of the local population. Civilians had grown mistrustful and fearful during the ailing of the limited autonomy that appeared incapable of ensuring security, stability, and economic development. Perceptions of many southern politicians becoming corrupt, motivated by a struggle for positions, and manipulated by Khartoum to the extent that they only stood for "tribal", not southern, interests, facilitated increasing militarization and insecurity. In these circumstances of growing uncertainty, and the activities of armed groups causing local insecurity, which drove people to their ethnic kin for protection, the reinforcement and instrumentalization of ethnic, religious, sectional, and regional distinctions became paramount. When the lack of progress of the implementation of the Addis Ababa Agreement, and the intentions to undermine it, became apparent, general disappointment spread in the South. This elevated the perceptions of insecurity and injustice, and related grievances, among many southern civilians and soldiers. Finally, the political climate of uncertainty and lawlessness propelled primarily military opposition willing to capitalize on the situation.

Endnotes

1   Alier (1990: 261) and O'Ballance (1977: 13).
2   However, according to Alier (1990: 261) the losses of the fighting forces were drastically smaller: an estimated 500-2,000 Anya Nya and equal number of government troops died fighting. This reflects the extent in which oppressing and targeting civilians had been an aspect of counter-insurgency measures and rebel tactics.
3   See Duffield (2001).
4   Kaldor's (1999, 2009) "new wars" thesis argues this.
5   One factor leading to this perception was that some already ongoing armed conflicts became more visible.
6   Addis Ababa Agreement, Chapter IV, Article 7. Available in Alier (1990) and Akol (2007) as an annex.
7   Addis Ababa Agreement, Chapter IV, Article 11 and appendix B.
8   Akol (2001: 2) has claimed that this set the precedent for regime involvement in the regional politics, and for the highly contested nature of the southern

presidency among southern elite factions.

9   Addis Ababa Agreement (1972), Chapter IV, articles 8-10.

10 Kulusika (1998: 101), and Collins (2008: 111).

11 Addis Ababa Agreement, Agreement on the Cease-Fire in the Southern Region, articles 6 and 8.

12 Alier (1990: 141).

13 Alier (1990: 141) and Akol (2007: 138).

14 Kulusika (1998: 103). Jendia (2002: 94) points out that the agreement was based on the 1965 Round Table Conference that had been unable to provide a solution to the "Southern Problem" in part because the government delegation had only offered limited autonomy to the southern provinces and given the national government the ultimate authority in key areas. This was a deliberate effort to keep the South in check by maintaining its dependency on the center.

15 Although addressing insecurity was one of the main tasks of the regional political institutions, this was only partly possible due to the continued availability of arms to fuel local conflicts, and a growing dissatisfaction among civilians and within the southern security apparatus. See Johnson and Prunier (1993: 120-4), and Prunier (1986) for more details.

16 Holt and Daly (2000: 173), Warburg (2003: 149), and Collins (2008: 116).

17 Warburg (2003: 150, 166) asserts that "The significance of this constitution was that it attempted, for the first time since independence, to accommodate all religions on the basis of equality and openly to promote secularism . . . Yet, if we take into account both the realities prevailing in Sudan and the radicalization of Islam in surrounding countries, including Egypt, the 1973 Constitution could be viewed as a step towards liberalization and coexistence in a multi-ethnic society". While the regime established a secular constitution, northern Islamist hardliners demanded Islam as the state religion, the head of state to be a Muslim, and all legislation to conform to Islamic jurisprudence. See Alier (1990: 145). Still, as Warburg (2003: 150) points out, they were purged by the regime and had to settle for the provided framework. In the context of the regional Islamic resurgence, and Nimeiri's reconciliation with the Arabized elite political forces in exile from mid-1970s onwards, the constitution was heavily amended and undermined after the traditional, conservative, and radical northern political forces re-entered in the Sudanese political scene.

18 Niblock (1987: 266).

19 The multifaceted document, relying on approximately 225 articles, described Sudan as secular and free in terms of religion, but with the society guided by Islam. The state provided the possibility to express the values of Islam and Christianity, and on paper Sudan embraced both Arab and African identity. This was allegedly exemplified by the incorporation of Addis Ababa Agreement as a Southern Provinces Self-Government Act in the permanent constitution. See Holt and Daly (2000: 173) and Collins (2008: 117).

20 Holt and Daly (2000: 173-4).

21 Niblock (1987: 261-2), Holt and Daly (2000: 174), and Collins (2008: 117).

22   A coup in January 1973 was aborted, as was a subsequent Libyan backed attempt to murder Nimeiri in April 1974. The riots which followed were put down, dissidents arrested, and by the end of the year Nimeiri had declared a state of emergency and replaced cabinet members with more loyal personnel. See Collins (2008: 128).

23   In September 1975, Nimeiri suffered yet another coup attempt that made him strengthen presidential powers towards absolute autocracy. Paratroopers of western Sudanese origin under Lieutenant Colonel Hassan Hussein, motivated by Khartoum's disregard of Darfur and Kordofan, took control of Radio Omdurman and announced that Nimeiri was under house arrest. However officers loyal to Nimeiri put an end to the attempt, him actually never having been captured by the plotters. Southern soldiers of the Sudanese army in Khartoum played an indispensable role in undoing the coup, and also participated in bringing down an attempt in 1976 by the northern political opposition in exile, which exemplifies the degree of success of Nimeiri's policy to consolidate southern support. See Rogier (2005: 14), Akol (2007: 140), and Collins (2008: 127). Interestingly, similar claims to those in 1975 were made by the Darfur armed opposition movements during the exclusive two-party peace process that ended the second insurgency in southern Sudan in 2005.

24   Akol (2007: 140-1) and Collins (2008: 127-8).

25   Howell (1978a: 434-5) and Akol (2007: 132).

26   Akol (2007: 133). Meanwhile, Lagu headed a new delegation to Addis Ababa. Together with Oduho, he discussed privately with Alier the possible modifications to the agreement. While Alier reminded the southern leaders of the difficulty to revise the treaty, and told them that many southerners already celebrated the end of hostilities, he announced that the regime had yielded to Lagu's and Oduho's demand for ensuring that the 6,000 southerners in the Southern Command would be exclusively Anya Nya troops. See Akol (2007: 133) and Collins (2008: 111). According to Howell (1978a: 435), their other demands never materialized because Lagu was both unable and unwilling to demand further concessions that could have unraveled the negotiated pact.

27   After the ceremony, Lagu and a number of southern leaders cautiously proceeded to Khartoum where Lagu held a press conference and on 1 April was appointed as Major-General of the Sudanese army and Commander of the army's Southern Command. This adhered to the SSLM demand that Lagu should be in condition to supervise the Anya Nya, while he was awarded SSU membership. See Alier (1990: 127), Akol (2007: 134), and Collins (2008: 112).

28   Akol (2007: 136) and Collins (2008: 112).

29   Alier (1990: 127).

30   Collins (2008: 112).

31   Madut-Arop (2006: 22).

32   According to Alier (1990: 127), while some in Khartoum viewed the process as a defeat against the 'outlaws', many in the South considered that Lagu had been bought by the northern "Arabs", and he was condemned by politicians

277

such as Jaden and Gordon Muortat Mayen. Despite Alier's disappointment, Lagu remained committed to the peace process and married a daughter of a *jallaba* merchant killed during the Torit disturbances as a gesture of his goodwill. See Madut-Arop (2006: 22).

33   These included the Umma Party of the neo-Mahdist *Ansar*, the DUP of the *Khatmiyyah*, and the ICF of the Muslim Brothers.

34   Yohannes (1997: 312) and Collins (2008: 128). The coup was to take place in the morning of 2 July 1976 upon Nimeiri's arrival from France and the U.S. But due to his earlier than expected landing Nimeiri was able to escape. Troops loyal to him, among which there were many southerners, arrived in the capital and suppressed the *Ansar* dominated uprising, killing more than 700 and arresting a number of religious leaders and dissidents. The plan was masterminded from Britain by Sadig al-Mahdi, leader of the Umma, but also involved Sharif Husayn al-Hindi, a former NUP minister of finance, and other exiled leaders of the NUP, the DUP, and the ICF, all part of the NF. It had been executed by training 2,000 mostly *Ansar* dissidents with Soviet help in two of the 20 training camps established for Qadhafi's Islamic Legion in the southern Libyan desert. They were sent to the capital as seasonal workers, burying their guns in the sand in Omdurman and waiting for Nimeiri's arrival. See LOC (1991), Holt and Daly (2000: 174), Rogier (2005: 14) and Collins (2008: 128-9). According to John Garang, many of the forces of the aborted coup were foreign mercenaries, which motivated the Sudanese army to counter the "invasion" (quoted in Heritage, 1987b: 4). In any event, Yohannes (1997: 312) notes that Nimeiri had been saved by the American intelligence that knew about the coup and advised him to change his schedule.

35   Yohannes (1997: 313).

36   Yohannes (1997: 313).

37   The U.S. was particularly preoccupied by Qadhafi's designs of converting Libya into a regional power, establishing an Islamic bloc by extending the boundaries of its influence to Sub-Saharan Africa, which culminated in its triple alliance with Ethiopia and South Yemen in 1981. One of Libya's main strengths was its financial capability, as it offered US$855.1 million to its two allies, while the triple alliance agreement included propping up military strength by raising 60,000 troops to aid rebels in Somalia and aiding the existing residual Anya Nya bands supported by Ethiopia in southern Sudan to undermine Nimeiri. See Woodward (1987: 182-3) and Yohannes (1997: 314).

38   The focus on armed forces was justified by the relatively small and poorly equipped army of 50,000, depending on antiquated Soviet military hardware in 1977, relative to Ethiopia with 150,000-300,000 soldiers with new Soviet equipment. Libya used US$5 billion in 1974-8 and US$12 billion in 1981 for arms from the U.S.S.R. to distribute them both to its relatively small 22,000-strong army and for subversive activities to extend its regional influence. See Yohannes (1997: 314). Woodward (1987: 182) alleges that Libya had spent US$1.4 billion solely for subversive activity in 1975-80.

39 Legum and Lee (1979: 18, 124) note that in 1977 Sudan imported US$500 million worth of Western armament, with the U.S. pledging to supply Nimeiri with 12 F-5 jets and six C-130 transport planes as part of a US$70 million military aid package, and US$80 million promised for the following year. France pledged to supply 15 Mirage jets, 10 helicopters, and armored vehicles worth US$85 million, paid for covertly by Abu Dhabi. Britain offered its military expertise and opened its arms market to Sudan.

40 Yohannes (1997: 314).

41 According to Alier (1990: 235-6, 237) and Yohannes (1997: 320-1), the NF factions sought to propel Sudan's Arab identity and the state's adherence to Islam. They resented the 1973 constitution and the 1972 Southern Provinces Self-Government Act. Particularly Muslim Brothers, but also other NF factions gave Nimeiri the impression that he would gain full support of the conservative northern political forces by revising the Southern Provinces Self-Government Act, and would be remembered as a great Sudanese leader by implementing an Islamic constitution. Nimeiri promised to democratize the SSU, re-evaluate part of the 1973 constitution, particularly Article 16 that gave Christianity and traditional religions equal standing with Islam, and review the Addis Ababa Agreement that the conservative parties viewed as a surrender to the South.

42 While initially Nimeiri forced the judicial authorities to condemn Sadiq and al-Hindi to death in absence, he secretly met Sadiq, the leader of the NF, in Port Sudan. This led to an accord announced in July 1977 on the return of the Umma and the *Ansar* militants in Sudan. It was agreed on a condition that both recognized the SSU one-party state and presidential system. Nimeiri declared amnesty, including for the Muslim Brothers, and promised political reforms. Despite initially demanding further concessions, al-Hindi's DUP, which could not afford to be left in exile when its rival had been reincorporated into the authoritarian politics in Sudan, disputed the elections of the National Assembly in 1978. While Sadiq and Nimeiri had reportedly discussed Nimeiri's fear of Soviet aspirations, and the need for the political stability and unity of the northern political factions, they also talked about their common apprehension of the South. See Holt and Daly (2000: 174), Sidahmed and Sidahmed (2005: 33), Collins (2008: 129-30). According to Khalid (1985: 171), Sadiq praised Nimeiri's fermenting Islamist tendency, and expressed his willingness to work within the one-party framework if it was opened further and made more effective and representative. The "national" reconciliation included a general amnesty of formerly banned opposition, which was also made to apply to southern political prisoners. See Akol (2007: 141).

43 Warburg (2003: 153).

44 Yohannes (1997: 313), Holt and Daly (2000: 174), and Collins (2008: 130).

45 This is how in the regional context of Islamic resurgence, Sudanese Muslim Brothers, backed by a network of individuals and organizations from the Arabian Peninsula, seized the opportunity to infiltrate into the state apparatus. See e.g. Prunier and Gisselquist (2003: 116-8), and Rogier (2005: 15).

46 Yohannes (1997: 321) and Warburg (2003: 159-60) note that during his 1971 visit to Saudi Arabia after the aborted SCP coup, Nimeiri had first met leaders of Muslim Brothers who had escaped from Sudan in 1969. At that time, Nimeiri also discussed with King Faysal his future plans for Sudan's Islamic path, initially securing Saudi financing which was soon withdrawn when Sudan passed the 1973 secular constitution.

47 The candidates of the Umma, the DUP, and the Muslim Brothers together obtained 80, and independents 60 seats (Holt and Daly, 2000: 174).

48 Melvill (2002: 7).

49 Warburg (2003: 152-3).

50 Zeidan (1999), Zubaida (2000: 70), and Warburg (2003: 153).

51 Collins (2008: 130). Later the movement was able to control financial flows and dominate the Islamic financial system implemented in Sudan, extending its influence by providing employment, creating Islamist middle and higher class, appealing to the poor through charitable and civil society organizations, and elaborating patronage system that allowed infiltration into the state machinery. This could be seen as unprecedented pragmatism since Turabi was the first Islamist leader in the Arab world to cooperate with officially socialist government. See e.g. Sidahmed and Sidahmed (2005: 33), and Musso (2009).

52 Melvill (2002: 7) and Warburg (2003: 159).

53 Collins (2008: 146).

54 Legum and Lee (1979: 127), and Yohannes (1997: 311).

55 In 1977 a Belgian diplomat, the American Ambassador, and his deputy were abducted and assassinated in Sudan by Black September branch of the Palestinian Liberation Organization during the first anniversary celebration of the Addis Ababa Agreement. The murders were understood as an expression of unenthusiastic Arab opinion about the peace agreement, and an attempt to undermine the Sudan-U.S. relations. Black September executed the hostages after the U.S. government refused to negotiate the release of Palestinians in captivity. Nimeiri promised to deal with the perpetrators after their arrest, but commuted their initial life sentences to seven years in prison after which he handed them to PLO to be punished. This severed U.S.-Sudan relations momentarily and the American aid to Sudan was suspended for a brief period. See Alier (1990: 145, 154), Yohannes (1997: 304-5), and Akol (2007: 139).

56 See Yohannes (1997: 305-6, 311).

57 Khalid (1990: 326), Holt and Daly (2000: 175-6), and Jendia (2002: 122-3).

58 Jendia (2002: 124-5).

59 Eprile (1974: 115-7) and Jendia (2002: 117).

60 Turner (1998: 204) and Jendia (2002: 115).

61 Turner (1998: 204), and Chan and Zuor (2006: 59).

62 Rolandsen (2005: 26), and Chan and Zuor (2006: 59).

63 Adefuye (1985: 64) and Jendia (2002: 119).

64 Crisp and Ayling (1985: 3), Musa (1988: 457), and Jendia (2002: 119).

65 Musa (1988: 466).

66 This is said to have been important factor in rebel support not only in the Anya Nya war but also during the later SPLM/A insurgency during which the rebel movement received logistical and material support in different degrees from the territories of Ethiopia, Uganda, Zaire, Kenya, and the CAR. See Rapoport (1996: 267).

67 Jendia (2002: 129, 130-2).

68 Holt and Daly (2000: 175).

69 Malwal (1985: 25).

70 To demonstrate its goodwill towards a capitalist mode of production and to satisfy International Monetary Fund's (IMF) stabilization requirements, including reducing the public sector, liberalizing trade, eliminating subsidies, implementing policy against inflation, and devaluation, Sudan agreed to implement the required policies in exchange for an initial loan of US$24 million in 1972. The government returned a number of companies to their owners and passed legislation to protect private ownership, initially promulgating the 1972 Development and Promotion of Industrial Investment Act and 1974 Development and Encouragement of Industrial Investment Act. The transition from socialist economic order towards capitalism was embodied by the transformation of the previous development plans. The Five Year Industrial Development Plan undertaken in 1970 was transformed into two interim programs (1973-4 and 1976-7), and the S£2.7 billion Six Year Plan (1977-83) along IMF policy guidelines. However, the ambitious plan, which was to draw S£1.8 billion from foreign sources, required seizing Arab financing and implementation of Western technology, necessitating continuity in its new foreign policy orientation. See Legum and Lee (1979: 127), Elhassan (1985: 153-7), Niblock (1987: 279, 282), Yohannes (1997: 312), and Collins (2008: 118-9).

71 This was to be achieved by applying Western technology and Arab financing. At an Arab summit held in 1976, commitments were made with a pledged US$700 million in agricultural aid during a 10 year period. Kuwait agreed to invest US$ 61 million, Saudi Arabia US$28 million, and the World Bank US$42 million, to bring new land under cultivation, Qatar, Kuwait, and Saudi Arabia donating US$10 million, and Kuwaiti Fund for Arab Economic Development (KFAED) lending another US$50 million, while joint American and Saudi investment financed a US$40 million cement factory to support development of infrastructure. According to the strategy, Sudan was to supply the Arab world 42% of its vegetable oil, 58% of its basic food commodities, and 20% of its sugar by 1985. See Yohannes (1997: 318) and Jendia (2002: 140).

72 Niblock (1987: 279), Holt and Daly (2000: 177), Jendia (2002: 139-40), and Collins (2008: 117-9).

73 The 1976 Development of Agricultural Investment Act aimed to attract foreign investment, along with a diplomatic visit to the U.S. to encourage private investment in long-term agriculture and other projects for up to US$1.1 billion. Consequently, there was an increase in expenditure from S£278 million in 1972-3 to more than S£1 billion in 1976-7. See Legum and Lee (1979: 128),

Niblock (1987: 280-2), Yohannes (1997: 312), and Collins (2008: 118-9).

74 Jendia (2002: 141, 142) and Collins (2008: 119-20).

75 According to Niblock (1987: 283), this was in part because only a few of the major projects had finished on time, those completed could often not meet the planned levels of production, and neglect of the already existing agricultural and industrial projects led to decline of their production levels, resulting in decreasing output. In addition, by 1978 relentless borrowing had resulted in massive and increasing external debt, which alimented inflation, hindered the ability to acquire foreign inputs, and led to severe decline in Sudan's exports. The problems were compounded by low world prices of Sudan's mostly agricultural exports, mismanagement, black market, and record levels of corruption that implicated Nimeiri's closest financial advisors, such as Saudi businessman Adnan Khashoggi. See Holt and Daly (2000: 177) and Collins (2008: 126, 153).

76 Niblock (1987: 279) and Collins (2008: 118).

77 Holt and Daly (2000: 177), Collins (2008: 153), and World Bank (2008).

78 In 1980 the regime decreed the Encouragement of Investment Act, but failure of the overall strategy could be attributed to the extent of deficient planning of the overall development program, and external factors such as oil crisis and emigration of labor to the Gulf States. See Niblock (1987: 279, 283, 285-6). According to Holt and Daly (2000: 177, 179) and Collins (2008: 153-4), the series of devaluations that raised the prices of imported goods, and the drastic lowering of subsidies of basic commodities, proved costly for the regime because it gradually lost control of the masses, facing continuous riots and demonstrations as of 1979. They constituted an important ingredient in the process that led to the demise of the regime. Warburg (2003: 159) adds that by April 1985 when Nimeiry was overthrown, Sudan's foreign debt was approximately US$13 billion, with debt arrears to the IMF alone amounting to US$130-50 million.

79 Wol became the Minister of Planning, Bona Malwal the Minister of State of Information and Culture, and Samuel Lupai the Minister of State of Local Government, which raised arguments about insufficient southern representation and counterarguments for the southerners getting more than they deserved. See Beshir (1975: 112).

80 The returning exiles (and their ministries) in the Interim HEC included Elia Lupe (Public Service and Labour), Mading de Garang (Information, Culture and Tourism), Gama Hassan (Agriculture and Animal Production), Michael Towili (Natural Resources and Rural Development), Joseph Oduho (Housing and Public Utilities), Ezboni Mundiri (Transport, Roads and Communications), and Michael Wal (HEC Affairs). Those appointed from within Sudan included Abel Alier (President) and Hilari Logale (Finance and Economic Planning), who had been prominent politicians in the banned SF, Samuel Aru Bol (Regional Administration), a skeptic of the peace agreement who yielded to serve after been pressured by his constituents, Dr. Toby Maduot (Public Health), who

had formed part of the banned SANU-inside, and Luigi Adwok (Education), who was independent. See Beshir (1975; 112, 113), Alier (1990: 128, 131), and Madut-Arop (2006: 22).

81   Beshir (1975: 112), Alier (1990: 128-9), Holt and Daly (2000: 171), and Collins (2008: 112).

82   According to Alier (1990: 129) and Akol (2007: 314), these included senior administrative positions, such as two secretaries-general, nine ministerial positions, three provincial governorships, and five posts in security services (including Lagu's appointment as Major-General, and regional police and prison commissioners and their assistants). Moses Chuol Juak (Upper Nile), Henry Bagho (Equatoria), and Ezekiel Kodi (Bahr al-Ghazal) were appointed as commissioners of the three southern provinces, with added responsibilities related to relief, resettlement and rehabilitation of social services, maintenance of security, and confidence-building in their respective provinces.

83   Johnson (1998: 67).

84   Beshir (1975: 133) and Alier (1990: 129-30).

85   Alier (1990: 124-6). Alier also claims to have taken steps to ensure the security of the *jallaba*, believing that they played a role in the South as merchants, receiving returnees, and in confidence-building, but some left for the North. See Alier (1990: 132).

86   Beshir (1975: 106-7). The UNHCR pledged US$17.7, out of which only S£3 million were received from the OAU, the central government, a number of northern provinces, private sources, exile communities, NGOs, and states such as Qatar, Dubai, Saudi Arabia, Morocco, Gabon, Somalia, Cameroon, Ethiopia, Tanzania, Cyprus, Italy, the U.S., Britain, Egypt and Yugoslavia. See Beshir (1975: 116).

87   Yohannes (1997: 304).

88   Chaired by Mboro, it received donations and supervised the administration of financial and technical assistance. It was supported by the regime's Special Fund, chaired by Mahmoud Beheiry and assisted by Peter Gatkwoth, and assisted principally by the Food and Agriculture Organization (FAO), United Nations Development Program, UNCHR, the World Bank, World Health Organization, and foreign governments. See Beshir (1975: 115), Alier (1990: 128-9, 134), and Akol (2007: 137). This allowed for extraversion of material support to the South, which overall remained limited in part due to Khartoum's unwillingness to channel extensive resources to the region.

89   According to Beshir (1975: 115-6), Alier (1990: 133-4), and Collins (2008: 112-3), these included the African Committee for the Relief of the Southern Sudanese, both German and Norwegian Church Aid, Oxfam, Lutheran World Service, the Catholic Relief Organization, Caritas, the World Council of Churches, Save the Children, and the Red Cross.

90   Alier (1990: 133) and Akol (2007: 137).

91   Alier (1990: 133).

92   Collins (2008: 113).

93   UN agencies and engineers from Britain, West Germany, and the Netherlands, revived health infrastructure and services, building 16 bridges, and rehabilitating schools in which 113,230 children were enrolled in 1972-4. See Alier (1990: 134-5). This was facilitated by Sudan's Western orientation.

94   This has been pointed out by many in the South.

95   Beshir (1975: 117) and Alier (1990: 135). Alier (1990: 135) also notes that Brigadier Abdel Latif Dahab and Colonel Frederick Maggot, the main regime and the SSLM representative, respectively, had been enrolled in the Sudan Military College and worked together securing the cease-fire so that the parties agreed to discard almost all foreign observers.

96   For instance, in September 1972 in Wau a northern police officer opened fire on a crowd. The civilian authorities responded by detaining all northern political officers, including the police commissioner, suspected of plotting against the peace agreement. Moreover, in the context of growing tension among the absorbed Anya Nya over the military integration process, on 24 January 1974 in Wau, Chinese made grenades were thrown into a cinema, a bachelor mess, and a non-commissioned officers' club mostly occupied by northerners, killing one and injuring others. The incident was allegedly attributed to the Anya Nya underground movement at Bussere camp, a hub of officers scheming against the peace treaty. See Alier (1990: 136) and Madut-Arop (2006: 26, 29).

97   Beshir (1975: 117), Awur (1988: 65), and Madut-Arop (2006: 23-4).

98   The recruitment process was intended to function in equal terms, allocating 2,000 troop and more than 200 officer positions together with 1,500 police and prison forces posts for each of the three southern provinces. According to Beshir (1975: 118), 1 Major-General (Lagu), 4 Colonels, 7 Lieutenant Colonels, 18 Majors, 57 Captains, 48 Lieutenants, and 66 Second Lieutenants of the former Anya Nya were absorbed. In the end, out of 15,832 aspirants, 6,079 entered the army, 1,860 in the police and prison services, and 5,489 to work in civil administration, while 2,414 medically unfit were recommended for work in the public administration. See Beshir (1975: 117) and Alier (1990: 138).

99   Beshir (1975: 117-9).

100   The plan included several phases of which the first (May 1973 - June 1974) consisted of increasing the administrative and technical capability of the absorbed Anya Nya through specialized training to match their northern counterparts. The next stages (June 1974 -November 1975) concentrated on internal integration of the absorbed Anya Nya, and consecutively to form mixed troops with northern units. Finally, the fourth stage aimed to complete the Southern Command as a fully integrated and functioning force in the structure of the army, allowing a possibility for Nimeiri as the Supreme Commander of the People's Armed Forces to transfer the absorbed Anya Nya anywhere in the country with the recommendation of the President of the HEC. See Awur (1988: 68), Alier (1990: 151-29, Collins (2008: 114), and Madut-Arop (2006: 25-6).

101   See Awur (1988: 69, 79) and Alier (1990: 148). The Regional Assembly had

the right to recommend an extension to this.

102 For instance, negative views of some northerners about the incorporation, corresponding perceptions among the Anya Nya, the lack of Anya Nya cohesion and training, lack of logistical and housing capacity for large-scale troop movements, adjustment of rank, seniority, replacement of personal armament, and rules of promotions affecting the absorbed Anya Nya officers, were all potentially contentious issues.

103 This is an important element resulting from suspicion and mistrust. It is a powerful tool for mobilization if adopted and extended through rumors and other strategies in an organized manner. While rumors were an integral part of this kind of mobilization for the southern disturbances in 1955, there are other situations in Sudan in which rumors have generated indiscipline but not led to organized armed opposition because they have not been part of a systematically orchestrated mobilization effort.

104 See Alier (1990: 148-50), Madut-Arop (2006: 24), and Collins (2008: 113).

105 Kulusika (1998: 103).

106 Collins (2008: 113).

107 There were a number of arguments against the Anya Nya integration, including lower efficiency and non-recognition of the special treatment of the South, which hindered the integration further.

108 Alier (1990: 148) and Collins (2008: 113).

109 Chan and Zuor (2006: 35).

110 Awur (1988: 69, 79) and Alier (1990: 149).

111 First, during the process the personal weapons of the ex-Anya Nya had to be replaced, but many refused to exchange their arms for what were considered inferior Chinese-produced weapons, while the ex-rebels expected compensation for their weapons they considered personal property. Many also insisted on keeping their personal arms, which were consequently licensed, while the ex-rebels left outside state's security apparatus were disarmed through a financial compensation scheme for which a special budget was provided. Second, a dispute over the rules of promotions of non-commissioned officers became a contentious issue. They were not allowed to rise to higher ranks, which resulted in some ex-Anya Nya officers threatening to head back to the bush in 1976, and simultaneously the southerners' admission to the Military College was deliberately scaled down to 5% from the promised 1/3 in 1974-82. Third, some were dissatisfied due to the lack of material rewards after being absorbed, while suspicion of being eliminated, and an inferiority complex due to lower education, training, and experience relative to the army troops, translated into occasional defensive and violent outbursts. See Alier (1990: 150-2, 242) and Collins (2008: 139).

112 For instance, at Malek camp near Bor in Upper Nile the Technical Committee of Absorption headed by Brigadier Mirghani Suleiman faced Captain John Garang, who had been against the peace treaty and adamantly stated over his commanding officer that the troops in the province were not ready for absorp-

tion. However, the troops had to yield to the absorption in August 1972. See Johnson and Prunier (1993: 121-2) and Madut-Arop (2006: 23). For instance in Bahr al-Ghazal and Upper Nile, Major Magaya, a member of the commission, reported a number of difficulties in selecting forces for the Support Arms and Services department because of inability to convince the commanding officers to allow integration. In Malek near Bor, the commission representatives faced Major William who would not allow the process without orders from the provincial command in Malakal despite the Technical Commission's mandate from Juba. At Malou garrison near Rumbek the reception of the members of commission by some of the officers was hostile and aggressive, which thwarted the effort to initiate the process. The next garrison where the initiation of integration was attempted was in Bussere south of Wau, but it was problematized again by the commanding officer, Joseph Kuol, who responded that no one person, even Lagu, had the right to decide the faith of the South alone, that he unilaterally rejected the plan because it was against the Addis Ababa Agreement, and that the proposed integration at battalion instead of brigade level was unacceptable because it would assimilate the Anya Nya into the army structures, that the troops should remain separate for the five year period, and that Lagu should come in person to explain the integration instead of sending lower rank officers to do the job. See Awur (1988: 71-2).

113 Awur (1988: 73).

114 This separation targeted particularly the officers resisting integration, such as John Garang, the future leader of the SPLM/A, who was first transferred to Bor and Khartoum and then sent to study in the U.S., while others were sent to Great Britain, Egypt, Pakistan, Cyprus or India. See Alier (1990: 151), Madut-Arop (2006: 26-7), and Collins (2008: 114).

115 According to Awur (1988: 70), any mention of transfer to the North raised tensions among the absorbed ex-rebels because many were told about the 1955 events when the mutineers had been persuaded to return, disarmed, and reportedly later killed. Yet, very few individual Anya Nya soldiers dared to question the process, fearing a transfer to the North, while the ex-rebels in Bahr al-Ghazal tended to be afraid of moving alone and continued to sing Anya Nya war songs against "Arabs". See Madut-Arop (2006: 25, 26).

116 As Awur (1988: 76) notes,

> These jallaba have contributed considerably to the problem of the southern Sudan. They do not behave as the citizens in a part of their country, but as "settlers", and therefore think that the Northern government – represented in the army – is there to "protect" them. They are the first to invite newly transferred Northern Officers (or any other government officials) to their homes and tell them imaginary things and advise them how they should behave towards the local people. I have observed a good number of Northern Officers and officials who for the first two weeks in a town of the South and before coming into contact with these jallaba have behaved and considered themselves as Sudanese and just as the locals, but after meeting with jalla-

ba, changed their behavior completely and adopted colonial attitudes.

117 On this paragraph see Awur (1988: 57, 69-70, 74-7) and Madut-Arop (2006: 24-6).

118 For instance, on one occasion, consumed by suspicion and mistrust, an absorbed battalion in western Juba refused to move to a new location between the Juba General Army Headquarters and the Nile River, because its southern officers feared that in the case of resumption of hostilities it would be isolated and not able to take refuge in the bush. See Madut-Arop (2006: 28).

119 Madut-Arop (2006: 26) asserts that, for instance, at the Bussere camp Lagu was ill-received and mocked as a traitor, which made him respond that the troops were nothing but a Dinka tribal army. This shows the "tribalistic" nature of politics that penetrated also the civilian-military relations.

120 This included Lietenant Colonel Alfred Deng, Lieutenant Colonel Joseph Kuol Amuom, Major Stephen Madut Baak, Major Albino Akol Akol, Major Thomas Dhol, Major Santino Ajing Dau, and various junior level officers. See Madut-Arop (2006: 25). According to John Garang, " . . . we were in frequent contact . . . [and] . . . active. We were even engaged in sabotage activities in places like Wau, Malakal and other places. We were active during the ten years between 1972-1982 planning to launch the Peoples Revolution" (quoted in Heritage, 1987a).

121 Madut-Arop (2006: 25-8).

122 This led to the formation of battalions Aweil 110, Rumbek 111, Wau 103, Malakal 104, Bor 105, Juba 116, and Torit and Kapoeta 117, and the abolition of the defiant Bussere camp by integrating its forces into battalions 103, 110, 111, and 113, the latter also in Wau. Garang was transferred to Bor, then to Khartoum, and sent to pursue training and doctoral studies in the U.S. Other officers, such as Lieutenant Colonel Stephen Madut Baak, were sent to the North or spread among other battalions. In the process, lack of confidence and suspicion continued to generate resistance towards internal integration. Individual battalions were transferred between regions, which was resisted because it was considered by some soldiers as part of a plan to move southern units to the North. But this was only occasionally achieved, as between Kapoeta and Rumbek where troops were interchanged. See Awur (1988: 77-8) and Madut-Arop (2006: 26-7, 29).

123 Short-term labor intensive projects and occupation in the forestry department, construction, rehabilitation, wildlife department as game scouts, local administration, agriculture, fisheries, roads, resettlement, and traditional farming was offered. Bilateral projects funded by the Overseas Development Agency, the World Bank, governments of West Germany and the Netherlands, the European Economic Community, and USAID also employed ex-Anya Nya personnel. Employment elsewhere than in the military was generally less desired within former Anya Nya cadres largely due to the local warrior traditions and the militarization of society caused by the prolonged conflict. See Alier (1990: 139, 143, 152), Akol (2007: 138) and Collins (2008: 114).

124 Alier (1990: 143-4) and Collins (2008: 114).

125 Beshir (1975: 113-5), Akol (2007: 138-9), and Collins (2008: 114).

126 Akol (2007: 139, 148) and Collins (2008: 115).

127 Alier was confirmed as the president of the HEC through a vote, but in fact this was just a formality since the relevant members of the assembly had already met previously as the SSU representatives, giving full support to Alier who was the only candidate (Akol, 2007: 140).

128 Akol (2007: 140). According to Collins (2008: 114-5),

>   During its four-year term the Assembly was characterized by lively debates, feeble understanding of parliamentary procedure, and motions of censure frequently proposed for no other reason than personal vindictiveness. Nevertheless, the Assembly passed mundane legislation without which the Regional Government could not function, and resolved serious and potentially explosive issues over the safety of southerners sent north for training, and charges of corruption over a large purchase of educational materials which precipitated heated charges and counter-charges that nearly dissolved the Regional Assembly before the matter was peacefully defused. The contentious question of the language of instruction in schools was satisfactorily settled by instruction in the vernacular languages, English, and Arabic in an ascending level of the educational ladder.

129 Awur (1988: 78).

130 Akol (2007: 148).

131 The first politically threatening incident took place in Juba in December 1974 when an absorbed ex-Anya Nya Battalion 116 was ordered to move according to the integration policy. The soldiers disobeyed, fearing that the transfer would lead them into a trap and expose them to possible northern aggression. They detained and beat their commanding (also ex-rebel) officer Peter Cirillo because he had accepted integration. Defying their threat to execute the officer if someone came to his rescue, Alier, the President of the HEC, entered the barracks and liberated him. See Awur (1988: 78), Kulusika (1998: 103), and Madut-Arop (2006: 28).

132 See Alier (1990: 152), Chan and Zuor (2006: 35), Akol (2007: 142), and Collins (2008: 114).

133 They killed Colonel Abel Chol, who had been given orders to implement integration by joining the absorbed Anya Nya with army forces, along with seven recently integrated northern soldiers, and injured permanently Captain Philip Dok and others when they went to reason with the mutineers who had sealed off the town and held the barracks for five days. See Nile Mirror (1975), Alier (1990: 154) and Madut-Arop (2006: 29).

134 Madut-Arop (2006: 29).

135 Alier (1990: 154-5) and Madut-Arop (2006: 29).

136 For instance, Lieutenants Vincent Kuany Latjor and Benson Kur, and Corporal James Bol Kur Alangjok, managed to escape to Ethiopia with a reduced number of men and were sentenced to death *in absentia*. These mutineers joined

forces with other discontented former Anya Nya elements, some in Ethiopia, which had either never accepted the peace treaty or were disenchanted with it, forming Any Nya II and conducting scattered guerrilla activity in southern Sudan with Ethiopian and Libyan support. They also counted principally on Nuer refugees, other previously disarmed Anya Nya in Ethiopia, students, and politicians, such as Yong Kier, who had spread propaganda among the discontented ex-rebels with the intent for them to desert and start another war for the complete liberation of the South. See Alier (1990: 155), Chan and Zuor (2006: 21-2), Madut-Arop (2006: 29), and Akol (2007: 142, 169).

137 These insurgents were heavily dependent on Ethiopia, which was eager to establish a rebel movement in southern Sudan. This is why the deserters were immediately consulted in 1975 about their willingness to establish a guerrilla movement, and with their approval five politicians in exile, among who were Muortat and Elia Aduang, were invited to Addis Ababa to form the rebel organization. Yet, Ethiopia was not interested in supporting a full-scale war that would lead to the disintegration of Sudan because of its own regional secessionist problems, but wanted to provide means for the southerners to wage "residual guerrilla warfare" with a limited scope that hardly destabilized the South until 1983 when a succession of larger scale mutinies took place. In order to hide their support, and assert control over the rebel organization, the Ethiopians ordered the formation of the movement to be announced elsewhere, monopolized support so that it could be withdrawn at any moment if there was a shift in policy, and insisted on operating the military camp in Bilpam where the rebels were based. Consequently, the birth of the movement, whose short-lived political wing became known as the Anya Nya Patriotic Front, was announced in Nairobi where a BBC journalist labeled it as Anya Nya II. Muortat became President, assisted by Moses Malek Chol, while Aduang became the General Secretary and Bol Kiir Diew his deputy. See Johnson (2003: 59-61), Chan and Zuor (2006: 22-3), and Akol (2007: 169).

138 Most of these groups had no connection to the main Anya Nya II, some of them being essentially Dinka militias fighting against Baggara raiders. See Madut-Arop (2006: 64-5) and Akol (2007: 169).

139 Awur (1988: 79) and Alier (1990: 153-4, 155-7).

140 In January 1976, the two companies of Kapoeta and Rumbek Anya Nya garrison were given orders to exchange forces. However, both were reluctant to obey commands, which again required Alier and Lagu to address the troops. Due to rumors of conspiracy to send the Kapoeta troops to Khartoum to be disbanded and neutralized, the soldiers and their officers were in a mutinous mood roaming the streets, but the southern political and military leadership convinced them to accept the orders. Similar diplomacy was required when troop transfers took place from Aweil to Rumbek. A month later, an incident occurred that required further action from the regional authorities. By that time many absorbed troops had become frustrated about the integration, and were often aggressively instigating minor problems. In connection with the earlier

mutinous mood in Kapoeta and Rumbek, the desertion of troops that took place in February 1976 among the Battalion 103 in and around Wau was part of a larger conspiracy to retake arms. It was also due to the personal preoccupation and disappointment of an absorbed officer Alfred Agwet Awan regarding his integration from Battalion 111 in Bor, and not obtaining promotion like many colleagues of the same rank. Having been transferred to Wau from Rumbek to be integrated into the northern army units, the troops camped in the center of the city and had to be convinced by the Commissioner, Isaiah Kulang Mabor, to move to the barracks. Agwet had proceeded with the plan prematurely. On 16 February he deserted with his troops, escaping to the bush outside Wau, believing that the former Anya Nya in the army, police, prisons and wildlife departments in the South would defect and join him. His troops allegedly repelled a reconnaissance force sent after him. Again the army suggested pursuing and destroying the deserters, but the southern authorities, Kulang and Provincial Security Committee, agreed only to send a few volunteering officers to convince them to return. Yet, on 19 February Agwet had the negotiators, the police inspector Captain Bullen Kuca, the first cousin of Agwet, Brigadier Emmanuel Abbur, and Gabriel Abdalla Mabok, shot. Agwet killed Abbur after having explained his bitterness about having been excluded from higher officer cadre. While Captain Lawrence Aleu, along with some non-commissioned officers, returned to Wau, and deserters revealed the whereabouts of the majority of Agwet's hidden arms, some men followed him to CAR where Agwet was arrested months later, returned to Sudan, convicted, and executed along with five of his non-commissioned officers, while most of his troops were reintegrated. Agwet's execution generated tension among the absorbed forces in Aweil and Rumbek, which the regional authorities sought to diffuse. See Awur (1988: 80), Alier (1990: 149, 157-62), Madut-Arop (2006: 29-30), and Akol (2007: 142).

141 In another development in February 1977, sections of the absorbed forces attacked unsuccessfully the Juba airport. The attack was repelled, but, if successful, the plan would have included further maneuvers. During the confrontation four northern soldiers were killed. The incident was considered a military attempt to take power in the South, and led to an arrest of Oduho and Peter A. Sule until December 1977 when they were pardoned as part of Nimeiri's "national reconciliation" policy. This incident was not only a manifestation of dissatisfaction regarding the integration, but also allegedly linked through Philip Abbas Gaboush, a Nuba politician regarded in the South as northerner, to the northern NF factions that had attempted to depose Nimeiri the year before. Reportedly, Habbakuk Soro, and the members of Battalion 116 under his command, had responded to a letter circulated by two students from the University of Khartoum, Walter Kunijwok Ayoker and Lual Acuek, intended for all ex-Anya Nya officers, and prisons, police, and wildlife personnel. It informed that a coup was to take place against Nimeiri and ex-rebels should be ready to act, but Soro and his men were persuaded back to barracks after reassurances that

such conspiracy did not exist. See Awur (1988: 80-1), Alier (1990: 162, 174), Madut-Arop (2006: 28-9), and Akol (2007: 142, 149).

142 In 1976, a letter from the Deputy Speaker of the Regional Assembly, Benjamin Bol, in Wau, to the Minister of HEC, Joseph Oduho, in Juba, and Malath Joseph Luet, came to light, detailing a plan for a general desertion among the ex-Anya Nya, consisting of hiding their arms in the bush and proceeding to take refuge and engage in training in the neighboring countries, while preparing another full-scale rebellion. It became clear that Bol had specifically asked Oduho to prevent the transfer of Anya Nya troops from Kapoeta to Rumbek, while he went to seek further support for the plan from retired Major Kawac Makwei, a member of the Regional Assembly, whose help would have been essential because he enjoyed wide influence over ex-Anya Nya. Consequently, both Bol and Oduho were detained briefly. See Alier (1990: 159, 160, 174) and Madut-Arop (2006: 30).

143 Madut-Arop (2006: 30-1).

144 These were battalions 103, 104, 105, 111, 116, and 117 (Madut-Arop, 2006: 31).

145 Awur (1988: 81-2).

146 After the 1972 Addis Ababa Peace Agreement, it would have taken an unprecedented effort to lift the southern economy. Yet, such effort was not undertaken and the regime starved the southern regional government of financing for reconstruction, rehabilitation, and development. Although plans were made to rehabilitate the southern economy and concentrate on rebuilding basic social and economic infrastructure in the context of a national five-year development plan, these were not respected. The expenditure matched 20.1% of the projected budget allocation in 1972-7, falling short of the original budget by 60% in 1972-3, 90% in 1973-4, 83.8% in 1974-5, 77.3% in 1975-6, and 76.4% in 1976-7. See RMFEP (1977: 226) and Yongo-Bure (1988a: 382, 1993: 56). Large scale economic development in the region therefore did not take place. See Jendia (2002: 144-5).

147 Chan and Zuor (2006: 33) argue that the Jonglei Canal project and oil prospecting became politically explosive and destabilizing issues in this context of widening North-South socio-economic drift, economic discrimination, and inadequate development financing for the South. They are particularly representative of the regime's approach towards the southern region, and significant in the southern alienation and resurging grievances. Jonglei Canal project's presentation led to student riots in many major towns of the South in October 1974, which were forcefully put down and two pupils were killed as the police fired upon the demonstrators. See Awur (1988: 82), Alier (1990: 197-8, 200-1), Jendia (2002: 149), and Collins (2008: 120-1).

148 This is shown by the regime's decision to create Unity State that encompassed Bentiu, Upper Nile, where oil had been first discovered in 1978. This way the resource-rich region could be claimed to fall under its direct administration.

149 See Collins (1990: 310, 312, 313) and Yohannes (1997: 323).

150 Alier (1990: 215).

151 Widatalla (1988: 420-1, 425, 427), and Chan and Zuor (2006: 33)

152 ICG (2002: 100) and HRW (2003: 92).

153 Alier (1990: 173), Holt and Daly (2000: 173), and Collins (2008: 115).

154 According to Chan And Zuor (2006: 28),

> This tribal sentiment was responsible for reshuffling of the ministerial posts according to how people knew each other as opposed to how good they can do the job. Nepotism became the policy of survival as people tried to pact ministerial positions with their kin-men . . . as tribal sentiments and personal rivalries overwhelmed many of them to the point of giving up the Southern national interests. The situation was like a dream come true to those who were enjoying its fruits i.e., access to the national resources through ministerial portfolios and assignments.

Madut-Arop (2006: 36) adds that

> . . . it was common for some officials to favour some of their tribesmen when filling some positions that would have genuinely been offered for public competition through merit in accordance to the existing public service regulations. Some of these examples were reported, especially in the recruitment of police, local government, and wildlife departments; the recruitment process was controlled by Dinka and Nuer officers.

155 Rogier (2005: 15).

156 For instance, Mboro's brief detention ordered by the SSO in Khartoum for the suspected involvement in the 1975 coup attempt, and Bol's and Oduho's short arrests in 1976 due to inciting rebellion, were particularly controversial. See Alier (1990: 174) and Collins (2008: 133).

157 Alier (1990: 174), Akol (2007: 144), and Collins (2008: 133).

158 There were those supporting the continuity of Alier's leadership, facing those grouped behind Lagu looking for change. The latter came from the group of politicians in search of high positions that they could not obtain under Alier, along with those detained in mid-1970s, those losing positions in the 1973-7 legislature, and those pointing to the failure of economic policies. See Alier (1990: 176).

159 Akol (2007: 144).

160 Alier (1990: 175).

161 Collins (2008: 133).

162 Alier (1990: 175).

163 Alier (1990: 177) and Wakoson (1993: 41).

164 Collins (2008: 133).

165 Samuel Aru Bol was appointed as Lagu's deputy, and Clement Mboro as the Speaker.

166 Alier (1990: 177) and Akol (2007: 144). Lagu stated in his Regional Policy Statement (RPS, 1978: 6-7) before the Regional Assembly that

> My dear countrymen, before the advent of the May revolution, the very fabric of the Sudan as a nation was almost torn apart by the divisive forces

of religious sectarianism, racialism, and party factionalism. But now, national unity has been achieved and the divisive forces curbed. The policy of the Regional Government, therefore, is to consolidate national unity and combat forces hostile to our peace, security, and prosperity. I wish to call upon every member of this House, and upon every Southerner to maintain Regional unity. We will not allow tribalism to divide us. My election as President of the High Executive Council proves that the South is politically mature and nationalistic enough to rise above ethnic and geographical differences when choosing leaders. At last, the basis to build and develop a Southern personality within the united, diverse Sudan now exists.

167 Alier (1990: 177).
168 See Alier (1990: 178) and Akol (2007: 144-5).
169 Alier (1990: 179) and Collins (2008: 134).
170 Chan and Zuor (2006: 37).
171 See Madut-Arop (2006: 31-2).
172 Madut-Arop (2006: 32) and Akol (2007: 150).
173 Alier (1990: 178) and Akol (2007: 145).
174 Collins (2008: 134).
175 Collins (2008: 134).
176 Alier (1990: 178), Akol (2007: 145), and Collins (2008: 134).
177 See Alier (1990: 178-9), Holt and Daly (2000: 171), Akol (2007: 145, 150), Collins (2008: 134). Chan and Zuor (2006: 37) state that Nimeiri had intervened in the process of selecting the President of the HEC in 1973, 1978, and 1980, and would do so in 1982, and dissolved the southern political institutions in 1980 while using the fear of many Equatorians of possible Dinka domination by encouraging Lagu's propaganda and demands for the re-division of the southern region.
178 Jok and Hutchinson (1999: 125-45).
179 Akol (2007: 145).

CHAPTER VIII

POLITICIZATION OF ISLAMICIZATION:
The Resurgence of War

Deteriorating political and economic conditions in the South gave rise to circumstances conducive to insurgency formation and the resumption of large scale political violence. The combination of internal, regional, and international dynamics led to the re-intensification of marginalization of the southern leadership, and the culmination of the regime's undermining of southern autonomy to reinstate the region's subordinate status. In order to reach this objective, Khartoum deliberately deprived the South of resources and development, and sought to neutralize southern resistance by feeding political divisions and integrating the southern military, the units composed of ex-Anya Nya rebels, into the national security apparatus. As indicated, this process was influenced by Sudan's major allies' support for Islamism, and the regional dynamics of the Islamic resurgence in the neighboring Arab states which convinced Nimeiri to resort to the Muslim Brothers as a regime constituency. As a result, given the political project of the northern elite, and particularly that of the Muslim Brothers, oriented against the South as "the other", Nimeiri's partnership with the South became problematic. This favored Islamicization of Sudanese domestic political and economic scene, and, coupled with an unstable and insecure regional political situation, gave further impetus to the existing southern grievances in the context of the northern leadership's reinforcing of the constructed "Arab"-"African" political identity divide.

The process of insurgency formation highlighted here shows how the local and external political and economic contexts of the final years of the Nimeiri regime were crucial in the deterioration of the situation in the South, leading to the re-emergence of armed opposition. Although considered a feasible short-term strategy, the efforts to neutralize the former Anya Nya in the conditions of increasing insecurity, the abrogation of the Addis Ababa Agreement, and resorting to radical Islamism and neglecting the heterogeneous nature of the highly diverse state, were counterproductive in the long run. The dynamics and logic of deepening state marginalization re-polarized the political scene, empowering those sectors of the military in the South willing to re-initiate armed struggle.

The Context of Islamicization

The rise of Islamist politics in the region, which penetrated Sudan through the change of the main constituency of the regime, contributed to the circumstances conducive to renewed insurgency in southern Sudan.

Nimeiri's Islamic Path

By the mid-1970s political and militant Islam had gained momentum in Algeria, Iran, and the neighboring Egypt, resulting in the decline of Nasserist Arab nationalism in the region, and contributing to Nimeiri's growingly religious inclination.[1] At this time, Anwar al-Sadat, who followed Nasser as President of Egypt, promoted Islamic student groups and the Muslim Brotherhood to consolidate his power, while Nimeiri, influenced by Cairo and in need of a new regime constituency, saw an opportunity in the resurgence of Islamic groupings with economic connections to Saudi Arabia to save the deteriorating economy in Sudan.[2] Thus, the Islamic political approach served to strengthen political leadership in Sudan through extraversion of funding and support from Saudi Arabia, other Gulf States, Egypt,[3] and Western allies who perceived Islamism as a desired counterforce to Communism. Although Nimeiri knew that an Islamic approach advocated by the main sections of the northern elite since independence would alienate the South, he sought to replace southern support for the regime with sectors of the northern elite which could strengthen the government against exile northern elite factions that had staged a number of coup attempts. This reinforced political Islam and Arab identity (considered as a source of social prominence and power) in the state's discourse, which had been in decline in the early 1970s due to its partnership with the southern elites. It led to the re-strengthening of regional identity-based political projects; the northern assimilationism and expansionism, and southern resistance.

The aborted coup in 1976 had been a turning point for the regime policy. Although Nimeiri had considered endorsing some northern factions as a regime constituency as early as 1971, the 1976 events showed him that counting on southern support continued being widely rejected by the traditional northern elite forces in exile, and relying on small Sufi orders[4] for the state's legitimacy in northern Sudan was not enough to stabilize the regime.

296

As a result, pressured by Arab states in 1977, Nimeiri reconciled with the exiled NF political factions, which led to the Muslim Brothers seeking actively to collaborate with the regime.[5] In order to honor the new alliance, in April 1977 Nimeiri founded a Committee for the Revision of Sudanese Laws on Islamic Principles to study the possibility to adjust laws to be coherent with the Islamic law, *shari'a*. He appointed Turabi, the leader of the Islamic Charter Front (ICF), the major political wing of the Muslim Brothers, as its chairman. Nimeiri also chose other Muslim Brothers as members of the committee, demonstrating the regime's preference to cooperate with the ICF instead of other NF factions.[6] This strategy deliberately avoided working with the neo-Mahdists and the *Khatmiyyah*, which Nimeiri considered as the regime's main threat following a number of coup attempts and due to their attempt to regain political influence in northern Sudan.[7] Choosing the path towards Islamicization of the state was the initial step for the preparation of legal framework for the declaration of September Laws in 1983,[8] and was detrimental to the South's prominent position as a regime partner due to the Islamist discourse that rejected its political self-determination and sought to transform its socio-cultural landscape through assimilation to Arab culture and Islam.

However, as Nimeiri had anticipated, the maneuvers towards Islamicization of the state initially strengthened the regime. They elevated its support domestically in northern Sudan, boosted its international legitimacy, and widened its resource base, but also initiated a process in which Nimeiri sought to outplay the Muslim Brothers in terms of political influence by appealing to the northern Sudanese Muslim population through Islamic reforms.[9] Yet, since he lacked any strong constituency apart from the Islamist section of the northern elite, Nimeiri became increasingly conditioned by the policy of the Muslim Brothers.

Gradually, the Muslim Brothers converted into the main constituency of the regime. Turabi's growing influence and knowledge of Islamic jurisprudence, law, and economics helped him to manipulate the politico-religious context, and enhanced the movement's political and economic influence particularly through the establishment of a network of banks in Saudi Arabia supporting Islamic financial institutions in Sudan[10] and the management of finances of many of the approximately 350,000 Sudanese migrant workers in the Gulf States.[11] This enabled the Muslim Brothers to operate from an expanding financial platform. Similarly to their counterparts in Egypt, the Muslim Brothers provided employment for their constituents and services for the poor through Islamic civil society organizations, while contributing to the emergence of an Islamist "middle" and "top" class based on a broad social base of patronage.[12] The Muslim Brothers attacked the regime from within, and their strategy culminated in the infiltration of members in the state institutions, including the military,[13] public administration, and the public education system, with the long term objective of assuming state power.[14] In addition, Turabi's appointment as Sudan's Attorney-General in August 1977, along with the directorship as the chairman of the law revision committee, put him in a powerful position to influence policy.[15] In the process, political Islam gradually penetrated the state.

The response by international actors to these domestic developments in Sudan followed the lead of the U.S. Washington perceived growing Islamism as a desired counterforce to the Soviet geo-political aspirations, and supported it covertly in Afghanistan and elsewhere. This bound Sudan inextricably to the American Middle East strategy, which led to active support by the U.S. through the CIA to train, arm, and transport Sudanese Islamists to Afghanistan, as well as supporting their military careers.[16] Consequently, Islamists became a major force in the Sudanese military, particularly among the younger officers, which increased their political power.

In this political context, following the foreign policy inclinations of Egypt, Sudan continued to count on the American support. The U.S., on the other hand, continued to view Sudan as the cornerstone of its regional policy, which contributed to the propping up of its military against threats from the neighboring states.[17] Nimeiri took an active part in the U.S. regional strategy, and resumed support of armed opposition in Ethiopia.[18] This complemented the U.S. policy view of the importance of Eritrea to undermine Soviet-backed Ethiopia and minimize its intervention in Sudan.[19] However, in return, Ethiopia supported armed opposition elements in Sudan to destabilize Nimeiri.

The U.S. also viewed Libyan encroachment in Chad as an important security threat to Sudan. Knowing this, Nimeiri used Libya to extravert resources and political legitimacy[20] by claiming that it sought regime change in Sudan.[21] Indeed Libya used Darfur for its military aspirations, but this was mainly to support its expansionist campaign in Chad. However, Libya faced Sudan-U.S. support for Chadian anti-Libyan forces under Hissene Habre that used villages in the Sudanese side of the Chad-Darfur border as sanctuaries. In any event, Tripoli was a potential enemy of Khartoum, and Nimeiri's claims adhered to the CIA's agenda to weaken Libya.[22] This justified the U.S. financial, military, and diplomatic support to secure Nimeiri's regime,[23] which largely ensured its prolongation until the mid-1980s despite its deep internal political and economic problems.

By the late 1970s Nimeiri's government was nearing bankruptcy. As part of revitalizing the economy, deemed essential for his survival, the U.S. recommended measures to change the course of what was considered structurally statist economic conditions. While funneling funds for development, an attempt was made to reschedule debt, encourage investment, promote rural development through international agencies and NGOs, devaluate the currency, and pursue market oriented approach especially in agricultural pricing.[24] These efforts included a number of experimental NGO projects in southern Sudan, which in some cases replaced the local government provision of services and justified the regime's lack of transfers to fund local administration in the South.[25] The measures pushed externalization of economic and political power away from the regional authorities and institutions.

Moreover, the political power dynamics and the exigencies of the northern governing elite continued to concentrate development projects even in unviable areas of north-central Sudan.[26] This contributed to the economic crisis composed of a number of factors, including incapacity and rampant corruption.[27] Thus, systematic state marginalization encouraged the sustenance of a pattern of uneven development, deliberately concentrating economic benefits of development in central riverine areas and excluding the periphery to maintain its dependence on the center. At the same time, the governing elite sought to expand the privatized area of resource exploitation towards the southern periphery through land expropriation, and promotion of mechanized farming schemes owned mainly by its leading cadres.[28] This continued to be part of a larger strategy of the dominant sections of the northern elite to maintain exclusive power position, creating inequality, poverty, and dependence in the periphery.[29]

Although realizing that there was little desired impact from the increased financing, the U.S. continued channeling funds to Sudan.[30] Yet, the American economic aid, motivated to bring about a *laissez faire* capitalist system, was conditional, which had weakening effect on the regime by undermining its control of the economy.[31] Other actors, principally the Islamists who extracted a growing amount of external funding, took advantage of this opening of economic space which led to a re-polarization of dichotomous North-South political identities since more resources were used to "Islamize" the state and society contrary to the desire of many southerners.

By 1978 Sudan could no longer service its external debt,[32] which invited increasing international intervention. The agricultural sector that dominated the economy had reached a standstill,[33] with the declining production levels having translated into lower export earnings, while import expenditures continued to grow.[34] The overall economic deterioration, which the increasingly unfavorable imports-exports ratio illustrated, became a threat to the political stability of the regime. This had led to the introduction of the IMF's three-year economic recovery program,[35] with the overall strategy to increase production of agricultural exports and donor investment guided through primarily macroeconomic adjustments that heightened regional economic disparities in terms of salaries and well-being.[36] They also turned a blind eye to the neo-patrimonial networks, which required resources to maintain state strength and political stability. The imposed austerity became politically explosive and generated riots already in 1979,[37] but although the IMF understood that the policies had a disturbingly destabilizing effects it proceeded with them.[38] The IMF and the World Bank estimated that the completion of Sudan's recovery program required 10 years of sacrifices,[39] while the International Labor Organization recommended economic reforms which the regime failed to implement.[40] The intervention of some of the international organizations weakened the regime further, although Sudan's patron, the U.S., provided direct relief aid.[41]

Furthermore, in the process of extension of Nimeiri's personal influence over the decision-making processes, public agencies had become politicized, bloated, and more and more redundant.[42] This tendency, which reflected the expanding neo-patrimonial and clientelist networks as the Nimeiri regime's form of governance, impeded economic recovery. The political system was also characterized by nepotism in which positions were filled and created according to patronage, and family links and connections, which in turn fostered corruption from the level of highest officials to the local government employees.[43] Lacking resources, the state became vulnerable to the Islamist takeover of its institutions and economy. Gradually the Islamist financial networks, involving foreign private investors, organizations, Islamic banks, and the Sudanese expatriates in the Gulf States, infiltrated in the state and replaced the regime's patronage structures.

In this context, the soaring prices of consumer goods became politically destabilizing.[44] The imposed structural adjustments eradicated price controls and affected not only the poorest, but also wealthier sectors of urban population. The growing regional wealth disparities continued to provide an incentive for the rural poor, particularly from the South and Darfur, to migrate to the main urban centers of north-central Sudan, which in turn led to rapid growth of urban population and created a vast number of unemployed and homeless in the urban areas.[45] To combat the exponential growth of the population centers, in 1980 the government initiated a program to transport migrants back to the countryside.[46] This program, much resented in the South and elsewhere in the periphery, set a precedent for the periodic expulsions of internally displaced southerners carried out during the course of the war in the 1990s and early 2000s.

By the late 1970s, Nimeiri needed urgent relief for the financial troubles faced by the regime. In this context, and with the stated objective to decentralize political authority to channel increasing power to provincial councils, the regime passed the 1980 Regional Government Act that divided northern provinces into five regional governments (Darfur, Eastern, Khartoum, Kordofan, and Northern) placed under the authority of the Central region.[47] This policy was portrayed as a measure to bring local governments closer to the regime, advance local autonomy, and appease periphery elites by creating new administrative positions, but it was used as a cost-cutting measure to reduce the financial responsibilities of the central government at the local level.[48] The policy enabled the regime initially to diffuse the pressure related to the demands of elites in the state peripheries, but it also elevated anxiety in the South since it constituted an experiment that could be replicated in an attempt to divide the southern region.

In fact, many southern politicians considered the law as an assault to regional integrity. Some perceived it as opening the door for the resumption of "divide and rule" and exploitation of southern natural resources, particularly since expropriation of land in benefit of the regime-associated factions of the northern elite had taken place in the late 1970s and Chevron had discovered oil in Upper Nile.[49] This reaction was a direct response to the voices emanating from Khartoum about the eagerness of powerful sections of the northern elite to restore the central government's direct control of the southern region.[50] Indeed Turabi, who sought to establish a system based on *shari'a* law, had orchestrated the decentralization campaign with an ultimate objective to abolish the Addis Ababa Agreement, which the northern political elite in exile had opposed from the beginning.[51] This economic and political context became conducive to the re-emergence of insurgency in the South where many associated decentralization with "Arab-Muslim" central state domination.

By 1983-4 the Sudanese economy had reached its unprecedented low point.[52] The ever-worsening situation that had begun in the late 1970s had severe effects on most sectors of the population, which led to strikes and demonstrations. The increasing instability, in turn, pushed Nimeiri to proceed with Islamicization of the state, implementation of *shari'a* law, and the decreeing of martial law on 30 February 1984.[53] At the same time, the Islamicization of state and society was left exclusively to Turabi's Islamist faction that collaborated with the regime. While favoring the ICF the state simultaneously persecuted other Islamist groups, particularly the Republican Brothers, which led to Egypt distance itself from Sudan.[54] This was a significant blow to Nimeiri, who had relied in part on Egypt's long-term support.

301

Nimeiri's other external patrons also grew resentful of the increasingly Islamist domestic policy based largely on the views of Turabi's Muslim Brothers. Particularly the U.S. found the intensifying Islamism problematic because by the early 1980s it seemed that the type of political Islam on the rise opposed Western liberalism and American values, which undermined the U.S. in Sudan and the Horn of Africa. In addition, Americans feared that Islamicization might provoke new large-scale rebellion in southern Sudan, which could allow Ethiopia and Libya to undermine Nimeiri and result in re-orientation of Sudan's foreign policy and extension of Soviet influence.[55] After all, Nimeiri was already facing lack of legitimacy.

Political Context of the End of Self-Government in Southern Sudan

In the early 1980s, political and economic dynamics in southern Sudan in the context of state marginalization intensified political confrontation at the national level and within the South. In this, the regime's infringement of the autonomy for direct control of southern Sudan and its resources resulted in intensifying political conflict.

Third Southern Regional Assembly, June 1980-Oct. 1981

Weakness of the limited southern political autonomy became more apparent during the period of the third regional assembly. It commenced after Nimeiri's direct intervention to dissolve the southern parliament and dismiss Lagu as the HEC president. Some claim the reason for the dismissal having been Lagu's lack of action to quell southern demonstrations triggered by the news of Khartoum's plan to allow American company Chevron to exploit the newly found oil deposits in Bentiu.[56] However, Lagu himself believed that it had been motivated by Abel Alier's and his Dinka political constituency's pressure on Nimeiri as the largest group in the South seeking to dominate the regional administration.[57] In retrospect, both assessments hold justifiable elements as Nimeiri sought to fragment the southern region politically by encouraging his preferred faction, Alier's largely Dinka constituency, to regain power, while at the same time seeking to exploit Lagu's and other Equatorians' Dinka animosity. This appears to have been part of a strategy to extract southern oil and relieve the regime's financial burden. Yet, it constituted a violation of the 1972 Southern Provinces Self-Government Act and the 1973 national constitution in which it had been integrated.

In 1980 elections were due in the South. They demonstrated the deep polarization in the southern leadership which had developed in the course of the 1970s. On the one hand, Lagu had become the figurehead of the Equatorian Central Committee of Individuals (ECCI) that sought decentralization of the South, which the regime increasingly supported. The logic was that Equatoria would have its own region and escape what some Equatorians perceived as the majority "Dinka domination" of regional affairs. This faction was mostly composed of Equatorian politicians, intellectuals, and returnees, including elites, soldiers, and businessmen, many having held high positions in Amin's regime in Uganda and now mainly blamed the Dinka for their economic malaise. Many in the ECCI leadership were interested in the lucrative administrative positions and also hoped that re-division would generate economic development in Equatoria.[58]

On the other extreme there was the group led by Alier. His constituency stood for unity of the southern region. It endorsed the *status quo* that had prevailed in southern politics in 1973-7, and was mostly composed of Nilotics, principally the Dinka, with strongholds in Bahr al-Ghazal and Upper Nile. This was the majority position in the South partly because it sought to keep southern regional self-government intact to filter the central government's direct influence on southern Sudan. Alier's faction also had some support among Equatorians, which undermined Lagu's minority divisionists.

The 1980 electoral campaign was characterized by the confrontation between Alier's and Lagu's factions. While Lagu's divisionists were encouraged by the regime to undermine the southern autonomy through demands that focused on intra-regional tensions, Alier's unity-minded followers considered their adversaries as unpatriotic and punishable. The diverging views led to violent incidents between the militants. At the same time, aware that regime support was crucial for winning the HEC presidency, both Alier's and Lagu's constituencies courted Nimeiri for support.[59] Khartoum seemingly sided with Alier, but maintained its covert plan for dividing the South and continued to encourage Lagu.

In the midst of growing tension in the South, Nimeiri announced publicly that he would not endorse any decentralization of the region. He referred to the 1972 Southern Provinces Self-Government Act as part of the national constitution, and recognized that the majority of southerners opposed such policy. This outraged Lagu, who insisted that people did want decentralization, and intensified his faction's "Equatoria region now" and "equal division" (*kokora* in Bari language) campaign.[60] By this time Lagu had become heavily influenced by Nimeiri's secret plan for decentralization, which the regime sought to execute later. Nimeiri's decision to portray himself as the defender of the unity of the South at this stage may have been largely due to the rising insecurity, and the persisting problem of integration among the former Anya Nya units.

Finally, Alier became the new HEC president with Nimeiri's backing.[61] He selected a cabinet with a meticulous Dinka-Equatorian balance that would maximize support in the southern parliament, the People's Regional Assembly, but at the same time relied on a number of politicians who had participated in the HEC during his earlier terms in office.[62] Alier was also aware of the realities that had led to Lagu's rule in 1978, namely the short-comings of economic development, the controversial oil and water issues distancing the HEC from the regime, and the need to maintain the fragile peace in the southern region.[63]

Under Alier, the HEC continued the push for more concessions for the South.[64] However, Nimeiri sought to extend the decentralization policy and was aware of Alier's and the HEC's insistence on maintaining the South as one region. In mid-1980, against the backdrop of the 1980 Regional Government Act, and also seeking to control the resource-rich southern border territories (especially oil areas), the parliamentary representatives of the northern elite initiated a debate on the North-South boundary.[65] At this time, southern representatives in the People's National Assembly noticed a map attached to a proposed boundary law, which violated the territorial integrity of the southern region stipulated in the 1972 Southern Provinces Self-Government Act, annexing the oil-rich Bentiu area[66] and fertile farming territories of northern Bahr al-Ghazal and Upper Nile to the northern provinces.[67] This map was part of a move that attempted to secure more grazing land for the local Baggara Arabs, gain land for the northern elite large-scale agriculture schemes around Kosti, and, most importantly, provide access to oil wealth on the southern side of the boundary.[68]

The discovery of the altered boundary map provoked outrage among southern leaders. An extraordinary meeting of the HEC condemned the regime's deliberate effort to annex the Bentiu oil zone, Renk agricultural land, and the mineral-rich Kafia Kingi to the northern provinces, and demonstrations were staged in major towns in the South.[69] Alier denounced the move and passed a joint petition by the HEC and the regional assembly to Nimeiri, who appointed an investigation committee headed by Chief of Justice Khalafallah Rasheed which against expectations resolved the dispute in favor of the South.[70] Nimeiri accepted the conclusions of the committee and issued a presidential decree accordingly,[71] which suggests that he was reluctant to put further pressure on the South at this point despite the regime's main ally, the Muslim Brothers, having orchestrated the attempt to alter the boundary. In any event, the rivalry over resources had a re-polarizing impact on regional

"Arab"-"African" political identities by heightening southern grievances towards the regime.

Moreover, in the context of the state's financial crisis, other incidents took place that indicated the regime's financial desperation and push to exploit southern resources. In November 1980, Nimeiri addressed the People's National Assembly and stated that an oil refinery would be built in Kosti.[72] This decision had been taken secretly as an alternative plan to exclude the southern leadership from decision-making, and enable Khartoum to take the proceeds of oil extracted in the southern region. The decision raised an uproar among the southern politicians because it overrode previous assumptions that a refinery would be placed in Bentiu, according to a common practice to build refineries near the oil fields. In the dispute that emerged arguments and counterarguments were exchanged between the regime and HEC,[73] but Khartoum rejected any amendments. Nimeiri contended that the decision had been based on economic and technical arguments and not political reasoning. However, in his declarations for the refinery being built in Kosti, Nimeiri had again used publicly the discourse of the South as a separatist threat to the state, while asserting that Equatorian divisionists in the South preferred that the revenue generated by the refinery would be placed in the central government treasury so that all regions in Sudan could benefit from it equally.[74] In the end, the proposed oil refinery was replaced by a plan to build an oil pipeline through northern Sudan to the Red Sea.[75] Yet, the dispute had again encroached on southern autonomy, infuriated southern leaders, and exposed the growing southern grievances as a reflection of the increasingly polarizing North-South relations.

The dispute also revealed the weakness of the HEC, which became inclined to accept the plans for oil exploitation. However, pressure from the People's Regional Assembly[76] and the southern public resulted in its outright rejection in the South. The growing disenchantment of the weakness and corruption of the HEC since the 1970s had resulted in declining legitimacy of the regional government, which was considered increasingly similar to the despised central government and some of its foreign collaborators.[77] These sentiments encouraged radical elements particularly among the ex-Anya Nya.[78]

Faced with the economic crisis, and opposition from the South to develop the oilfields that could provide financial windfall to the bankrupt regime, Nimeiri prepared political measures to end southern resistance. Under pressure from the Muslim Brothers and other collaborators of the northern elite, Nimeiri proceeded with a plan to decentralize the southern region into three regions corresponding to its three original provinces.[79] In March 1981, the issue was brought to the People's Regional Assembly, where it was rejected as a violation of the Southern Provinces Self-Government Act.[80] However-er, although Nimeiri had miscalculated the extent of Lagu's support in the regional parliament, he continued with the plan by pointing to Lagu's dis-course of "Dinka domination" and excessive "centralization"[81] and sought to divert the regional opposition to the regime by encouraging Lagu's pro-di-visionists' anti-Dinka sentiment and propaganda.[82] Nimeiri promoted de-centralization among sections of prominent Equatorians with promises of high-level administrative posts and development money.[83] This contributed to further polarization of sentiments between unity and decentralization, and re-strengthening of the "tribalist" logic promoting Equatorian-Dinka (Nilot-ic) ethnic divisions.

Yet, although the southern factions differed radically in their approach towards the regime, they both sought to ensure the rights of southerners in general and their respective narrower constituencies. On the one hand, Lagu believed that a number of smaller regions would ensure the rights and in-terests of smaller ethnic groups, emphasizing their self-determination with respect to larger groups and the state as a whole. To achieve this, a strategic partnership with the central government was necessary to bypass regional political institutions in which his constituency was in a minority position.[84] In this perception, southern regional political institutions were deemed as instruments of regional domination by majority ethnic groups and should be abolished.

On the other hand, however, Alier's unity-minded regionalist constitu-ency viewed regional autonomy and institutions as the only way to ensure the rights of southerners collectively. One southern region was seen to have more power relative to the state, and consequently more influence and bar-gaining power to secure southern rights and favorable policies and economic arrangements. Therefore, Alier and his allies focused on consolidating the South as one region, standing as the only guarantee of serious consider-ation of southern interests in the state center dominated by the northern elite which was seen to manage the systematic marginalization of the South.[85] To promote the opinion for southern unity, Alier's Council for the Unity of the Southern Sudan (CUSS)[86] commissioned a propaganda book[87] which appeared in 1981. Attempting to undermine the regime's encroachment on the South, and to justify the maintaining of the southern region as one polit-ical unit, it expressed widely-held southern views. Yet, in response, Nimeiri intensified his efforts to neutralize the resistance to the planned re-division. The situation put the regime aspirations and southern unity in direct con-frontation, while the southern political scene polarized further, resulting in increasing propensity for radical action.[88]

In September 1981, Nimeiri launched his campaign to divide the southern region. Prompted by his growing discontent towards the southern political institutions, and pressure by the Islamist constituency to revoke the Southern Provinces Self-Government Act, Nimeiri raised the issue in the SSU Political Bureau. Arguing for the termination of southern self-government, he again relied on the 1980 High Executive Council and Regional Assembly Act which had allegedly been drafted with Alier's collaboration to dissolve Lagu's earlier HEC. On 5 October 1981 Nimeiri dissolved the HEC and appointed Transitional Regional Government (TRG) under General Gismallah Abdullah Rasas, a Fertit[89] southerner and Lagu's friend.[90] He also dissolved People's National Assembly to prepare for the vote that by law required 3/4 majority at the national level to approve the re-division[91] of the South. According to the law, it would additionally need a 2/3 majority support in the People's Regional Assembly to become effective.[92]

The new Nimeiri-appointed southern administration took office immediately. Although it was set to function only six months, mainly to oversee preparation for a referendum on the division in southern Sudan, Rasas refused to convoke a referendum before the elections for a new People's Regional Assembly would take place in part because this was resisted by a number of his TRG cabinet members who were former high-level Anya Nya officers.[93] Some of these officers belonged to an underground organization planning armed resistance, and attempted to stall the disintegration of the South, while Nimeiri had sought to neutralize their military influence by moving them from the army to political positions. However, the ex-Anya Nya had joined the TRG with the belief of being reinstated in the army after its dissolution.[94] Several of them were disenchanted by their waning political influence and economic prominence as military officers after the war, and sought to reinstate their prominence as military leaders.[95]

The news of the disruption of regional politics resulted in disorder in the South.[96] Demonstrations ensued against the dissolution of the southern political institutions, also targeting Rasas who was perceived as a symbol of intensifying northern domination.[97] Suspecting the CUSS of an attempt to undermine the TRG, Nimeiri ordered Rasas to distance himself from Alier's constituency but Rasas proved less enthusiastic about dividing the South.[98] In December 1981, during growing political tension, Nimeiri visited the major towns in the South but faced demonstrations.[99] In response, Nimeiri, who claimed to have been personally insulted, demanded recommendations from southern political forces concerning a suitable manner to proceed with the decentralization of the southern region.[100]

Measures were also taken against Alier's anti-divisionist leadership. On 22 December, the CUSS sent a communiqué to Nimeiri in which it demanded recognition of the southern majority anti-divisionist stand,[101] calling for neutral and equal treatment of the two main southern political factions and the legalizing of the CUSS as a political formation, while also requesting support outside Sudan.[102] The letter prompted the regime to arrest the CUSS executive committee, the southern members of the national parliament against re-division, and a number of their student followers,[103] accusing the CUSS politicians of harboring connections with Libya and plotting to undermine the constitutional foundation of the one-party state.[104] However, the arrests of southern politicians triggered riots in which northerners in the South were targeted, and the regime felt obliged to calm the situation by releasing the detained politicians in January-February 1982 to allow them to participate in elections in the southern region that were scheduled for April.[105]

When Nimeiri proceeded to end the southern autonomy, the growing political tension became increasingly conducive to the resumption of major armed opposition. Driven by self-initiative, rising pressure from his allies,[106] and external factors, the concentration on de-centralization and re-division of the South helped Nimeiri to divert attention from the state's economic crisis. The support against southern autonomy enabled Khartoum to adopt hard position towards southern Sudan, although the regime was aware of the increasing possibility of resumption of rebellion in the South[107] that could undermine the regime in northern Sudan.

Fourth Southern Regional Assembly, May 1982-June 1983

Although poised to divide the southern region, Nimeiri was wary of the impact of abolition of southern self-government in a situation that by now had generated riots in various parts of the country. Consequently, the regime shifted its approach towards the South briefly in February 1982[108] as a strategic move to diffuse pressure at the national level.[109] By portraying a change of position towards the South, Nimeiri sought to minimize reactionary vote to oppose re-division in the upcoming southern elections. However, although calling for the next elected representatives to restore democracy in the South, Nimeiri did not forget to mention that proper application of the 1981 People's Local Government Act, together with other de-centralizing measures, was necessary for the whole country, and that the southern factions should reach a compromise on the issue.[110] In this way, de-centralization of the state as a whole was used as a pretext to justify the future re-division of the South.

Meanwhile "tribalism", in terms of personalized, and ethnically and sectionally fractional politics, became increasingly apparent in the South. Under pressure from both Lagu's constituency and the central government, personal rivalries over the presidency of the HEC resulted in divisions in the CUSS which undermined a concerted campaign to defend southern autonomy and territorial integrity.[111] By March 1982, the issue of re-division of the South had monopolized the electoral campaign and pitted Lagu's ECCI against Alier's CUSS.[112] At this stage, the ECCI's propaganda for de-centralization was adopted in the major towns in Equatoria and in parts of the rural areas where many local farmers had experienced armed confrontations with Dinka migrants looking for pastures for their cattle in the aftermath of extraordinary flooding of the Nile around Bor and Yirol.[113] The ECCI's propaganda and the violent events had polarizing impact on the (re)construction of inter-ethnic grievances in the South, which in turn had far-reaching consequences on the re-emphasis of the "otherness" of the Dinka among Equatorians (and vice versa).[114]

The electoral process polarized the re-division debate further and again produced violent confrontations. In April 1982 the voting took place and Lagu's divisionists won most seats in Eastern and Western Equatoria, while Alier's faction prevailed in most other districts of southern Sudan (Bahr al-Ghazal, Jonglei, Lakes, and Upper Nile).[115] The newly formed People's Regional Assembly then elected Joseph James Tembura, an Equatorian divisionist covertly backed by the regime,[116] as the President of the HEC over the unity representative Clement Mboro.[117] Tembura had obtained financial resources from members of the Islamic Brotherhood, Abdel Hamid Saleh and Yassin Omer, while some members of Alier's increasingly disunited constituency succumbed to bribery and voted for his presidency. Meanwhile, the southern unity position had been undermined by propaganda, promises for cabinet positions, and false assertions of Nimeiri's reluctance to re-divide the South.

After Tembura's election, Nimeiri again hardened his approach towards southern Sudan. Immediately after the elections he replaced Alier with Lagu as the Second Vice President at the national level,[118] with an attempt to neutralize the leadership of the political opposition to re-division. In addition, when the TRG handed power to the new HEC in June 1982, the former Anya Nya officers were dropped from the new executive and directly retired. This was part of Nimeiri's strategy by to minimize the risk of a renewed rebellion, but it led to restlessness in the South because of being seen as part of an overall attempt to neutralize the leading cadres of the former rebels.[119] In tandem with the campaign to undermine the Addis Ababa Agreement, another element to Nimeiri's strategy was the transferring and integration of the remaining elements[120] of battalions 103, 104, 105, 110, 111, 116, and 117, composed of the former Anya Nya. These measures to remove the security guarantees of the limited southern autonomy raised further tension, particularly among many of the ex-Anya Nya who feared becoming redundant.

The accumulated effect of the regime's policy was a growing sentiment of insecurity in the South. This was because especially in the environment of growing uncertainty, many viewed the former Anya Nya in the military, police, prisons, and wildlife department as the protectors of the South and the guardians of the Addis Ababa Agreement.[121] These circumstances of increasing political divergence and removal of former rebel officers encouraged conspiracies and mutinies among ex-Anya Nya troops loyal to them.[122]

In June 1982, the new People's Regional Assembly initiated its work in the midst of growing tension. Nimeiri applied pressure to the HEC to implement the division of the South, but the project continued to face resistance in the southern political institutions, which led the regime to manipulate the SSU regional congress voting results on the issue.[123] However, although Tembura neither adhered to nor rejected Khartoum's pressure,[124] the regime's machinations were gaining momentum.

In early 1983 Nimeiri moved forward to complete the re-division. In March, the regime engaged in coercive measures in response to political resistance to re-division and calls for referendum for self-determination in Abyei,[125] and Nimeiri subsequently instructed Tembura to comply with the re-division plan.[126] On 5 June 1983, claiming that de-centralization of the South had been recommended by the HEC, Nimeiri announced the Republican Order No. 1 (the dissolution of the southern region) in a televised press session with Lagu at his side, and declared the division of the region into its three constituent provinces (Bahr al-Ghazal, Equatoria, and Upper Nile) for an initial period of 18 months, while denying that this was at odds with the Southern Provinces Self-Government Act.[127] The declaration stripped the southern region of self-government under largely self-elected leadership, turning it into three provinces with regime appointed leadership answerable to the national government and without right to formally question national legislation concerning it.[128] The abolition of the southern region in this unconstitutional move resumed the northern elite-dominated state's direct subjugation of southern Sudan. It re-intensified political and economic marginalization by terminating the limited southern self-determination, and ended the South's ability to decide on, or contest, any policies concerning it.

In addition, consumed by the Islamic influences of the Muslim Brotherhood, the regime resumed Arabization of the South. Terminating the regional administration, public service, and internal southern security bodies neutralized regional resistance and permitted direct control of the three southern

territories. This allowed the regime to reinstate Arabic as the official language, and declare the use of other languages (vernacular and English) being
subject to special permission.[129] Nimeiri implemented these measures with
the hope to strengthen his position, while faced with the northern elite opposition demands to neutralize any collective southern influence at the national
level. The end of regional authority in the South, and the new language policy, caused political instability in the southern territories, and cleared the path
for the sections of the southern military to feed on the rising fear, grievances,
and radicalization of parts of local communities in the face of what appeared
as an onslaught on southern Sudan.

The re-division of southern Sudan also represented the high-point of the
regime's collaboration with Muslim Brothers. Nimeiri defended the re-division by asserting that the Addis Ababa Agreement had been a personal deal
between Lagu and himself, and that both wanted it changed, while the referendum to effect any change to the Southern Provinces Self-Government Act
required by the constitution was unnecessary since he was mandated by the
people of Sudan to do what he saw as essential.[130] However, Nimeiri's final
decision to go through with the division largely owed to the Islamists' influence and their radical stand against the southern autonomy, which prevented the establishment of an Islamic constitution.[131] In addition, through the
abolition of the southern autonomy, the Muslim Brotherhood also achieved
the definite removal of southerners as a competing regime constituency that
Nimeiri could resort to. This made him almost exclusively dependent on
Muslim Brothers for providing domestic constituency and legitimacy for the
weakening regime. It removed the main obstacle for Turabi and his associates to consolidate themselves as the main political force in Sudan.

Following the division, new governments in the southern territories were
set up. The instituting of three separate administrations and territorial entities (Bahr al-Ghazal, Equatoria, and Upper Nile) caused massive migration
since many individuals who had settled elsewhere in the South during the
autonomy were evicted from their residences and now returned to their areas
of origin.[132] This also applied to the political cadres and those civil servants
who had been made redundant, many of who now returned to participate in
the administration of their respective newly created "region".[133] Subsequently, Nimeiri appointed new governors, cancelled elections, abolished the local
institutions to extract revenue from regional trade and resources, and made
the security apparatus in the South formally responsible to Khartoum instead
of Juba.[134] The division also marked re-intensification of ethnic politics and
"tribalism" that affected particularly many Nilotics (Dinka and Nuer) who
had resided in Equatoria during the Addis Ababa period. The politics of in-

tolerance caused mass exodus, and many uprooted people headed towards the Ethiopian border while some joined the active rebel organizations.[135] This elevated insecurity in southern Sudan considerably as the number and strength of local armed groups increased.[136]

Local Ethnic Struggles and Militias

Although the Addis Ababa Agreement had provided a setting for the pacification of southern Sudan after the war, the process had been gradual and could not be completed before insecurity and violence again gained momentum. Particularly many rural areas in southern Sudan experienced outbreaks of violence and persistent insecurity throughout the period of southern regional self-governance, and many of the absorbed Anya Nya units placed in the remote rural army outposts were affected by this. While the lack of security in rural areas was mainly related to local ethnic feuds and raiding, it became also linked to the activities of the disparate Anya Nya II that persisted throughout the period of southern autonomy.[137]

The Anya Nya II groups and armed bands organized along ethnic lines. They tended to use guns distributed by the government during the 1960s as part of its strategy to debilitate the Anya Nya, as well as small arms traded along the Ethiopian borderlands. As part of its counter-insurgency approach, Khartoum had summoned, armed, supplied, and sometimes paid southern militias to fight other groups,[138] with an attempt to encourage "tribalization" of local ethnic conflicts. More guns were readily available in the Ethiopian border areas, where arms trade had existed already long time before the emergence of the "Southern Problem", and the proliferation of guns had contributed to the intensification of internal Nuer conflicts in Ethiopia which had spread to the Nuer communities on the Sudanese side of the border.[139]

Similarly, historical inter-ethnic feuds in the North-South border zone, manifested in the context of inter-group relations between conflict and co-operation, had intensified in conjunction with the first southern insurgency. Although these conflicts[140] had already surfaced during the colonial period, particularly in the controversial Darfur-Bahr al-Ghazal boundary demarcated 14 kilometers south of the Bahr al-Arab (or Kiir in Dinka) river in 1924, they had manifested themselves in the al-Muglad massacre in 1965 in which sections of the Humr Misiria had killed over two hundred Ngok Dinka.[141] The relationship between these sections of Baggara and Dinka remained volatile throughout the 1970s despite traditional conflict resolution efforts.

The combination of more destructive military technology and deterioration of the traditional inter-ethnic conflict resolution councils undermined the settlement of local conflicts. The introduction of advanced armament, such as semi-automatic weapons, compounded the debilitating effect of Ni-meiri's abolition of Native Administration in 1971, which had led to the de-crease of state presence in areas where local ethnic conflict was prevalent.[142] Although the southern regional government had sought to restore Native Ad-ministration in the South, particularly focusing on the chiefs' courts, similar structures ceased to exist in the borderlands of northern Sudan facing Bahr al-Ghazal, which undermined inter-ethnic conflict resolution.[143]

During the late 1970's the relationship between sections of the Baggara and the Dinka in the North-South boundary deteriorated further.[144] This took place in the context of persisting droughts until the early 1980s, and the subsequent contest over pastureland and water,[145] which reinforced "tribal-ism" as people sought security through adhering to their exclusive ethnic identities and considering neighboring groups as different and sometimes as the enemy. This politicized ethnicity further, and after more intense conflicts emerged between parts of the Rizaigat (Baggara) and Malwal (Dinka) by the end of the 1970s,[146] instability spread to the Humr Misiria (Baggara)-Ngok (Dinka) relations in 1983-4 and led to organized militia activity by the Humr by 1985.[147] The *murahalin* militia, consisting of sectors of the Baggara, had originally been used to patrol the North-South border during the Condomini-um period, but at this point it began to target primarily Dinka civilians.[148] Despite this situation, Khartoum made no effort towards inter-ethnic conflict resolution, and began to use militias systematically against southern armed groups and civilians.[149]

The regional political situation contributed to deteriorating security sit-uation in rural southern Sudan. One contributing factor was the fall of the Selassie regime in Ethiopia in 1974 that led to the decline of Sudan-Ethiopia relations, and the wider availability of small arms through Ethiopia's sup-port for southern Sudanese guerrilla bands in response to the intensification of Sudan's assistance to its rebels. Similarly, the fall of Idi Amin in 1979 in Uganda added to the growing insecurity in the South due to the flow of weapons from northern Uganda to Bahr al-Ghazal and Jonglei by the late 1980, and because most of the southern military personnel and mercenaries who had served under Amin found themselves now unemployed in Sudan.[150] By 1980, there were various ethnically diverse armed groups and militias in the South referred to as Anya Nya II, of which some drew on ideological motivations and others on grievances related to the implementation of the Addis Ababa Agreement.[151]

Consolidation of Armed Factions and Underground Movements

Origins of southern military conspiracy, which culminated in the formation of the large-scale armed opposition in southern Sudan in the early 1980s, go back to the years immediately after the Addis Ababa Agreement. Although in the context of growing dissatisfaction of the political situation among southerners a number of secret political organizations[152] emerged, it was the military groupings, namely the underground movement of ex-Anya Nya officers and the diverse Anya Nya II formations, which became the most powerful.[153] In fact, many of these groups, ranging from bandits and cattle rustlers to militias and rebel organizations, engaged in politically motivated violence at a varying degree.

However, the Anya Nya II cluster that became significant in the emergence of the second insurgency in southern Sudan was active in the Ethiopian border area.[154] Collectively known among the southerners as the main secessionist Anya Nya II, or Anya Nya Patriotic Front (APF),[155] it operated from Bilpam in western Ethiopia, and received support from both Ethiopia and Libya[156] for the stated objective of liberating southern Sudan.[157] Yet, its external backers, which also briefly included Sadiq al-Mahdi after the 1976 aborted coup attempt, restricted the material support carefully so that the APF was only able to inflict limited damage and political instability.[158] Although at this stage groups that did not receive external backing provoked most of the armed incidents in the southern territories,[159] Bilpam became a symbol for armed struggle against the regime since the mere existence of dissidents there encouraged ex-Anya Nya troops to threaten with revolts if they were to be transferred away from southern Sudan.[160]

In the early 1980s the Anya Nya II groups began disrupting security and economic activity in the South on a larger scale.[161] This led to a military response involving harassment and shooting of civilians,[162] and the stepping up of the attempt to detach the resistant former Anya Nya units from their leadership.[163] As a result, the Anya Nya II activities declined by the end of 1981, but the repressive measures were not comprehensive enough and provoked re-escalation of violence. By 1982 the Ethiopian-backed Anya Nya II faction, which had previously received only rudimentary support, began to assert its dominance over diverse dissident bands in Jonglei, Upper Nile, and Lakes provinces, and forwarded recruits, who had in part been generated by the army repression, for training in Ethiopia.[164] In this context, a network connecting leaders of various armed groups emerged,[165] and some Anya Nya II units began attacking targets associated with northern "Arab" repression.[166]

In 1982, the political environment in the South had become conducive to supporting a rebellion.[167] In this situation, the underground movement composed of southern officers and dignitaries seized the initiative in attracting covert external support and extending its network among southern soldiers, politicians, professionals, and students.[168] For instance, John Garang, a military officer and one of the underground leaders, appealed to individual commanders of the absorbed forces, and maintained contacts with Anya Nya II,[169] while deepening his personal connection with leaders William Chuol, Gai Tut, and Chagai Atem who smuggled weapons to their respective armed constituencies.[170] The underground movement's links with Anya Nya II, which allegedly began in 1982,[171] were used to organize a series of mutinies in 1983 and the defection of the Anya Nya units absorbed in the army, while also encouraging wider desertions among southerners in the security forces.[172]

Yet, differing political views and personal rivalries between the ex-Anya Nya leaders and many of their former comrades (now Anya Nya II) hindered collaboration. It was only when Nimeiri's reputation in southern Sudan reached its unprecedented slump, when the local grievances that had motivated many Anya Nya II were to a large extent overtaken by regional and national issues.[173] In these circumstances, despite the growing northern army presence, local violence, and suspicion of Khartoum, the core units of the ex-Anya Nya troops involved in the underground movement remained in the army until the mutinies in 1983.

Conclusion

By the early 1980s, Sudan's external alliances, regional realities, and domestic developments reinforced the dynamics and the logic of state marginalization. The interconnection between domestic, regional, and international spheres led to the prominence of those forces in the national political and economic context that resulted in the exclusion of the South and its elites from national processes. The domestic scene was receptive to the intervening regional and international actors and forces, mainly the penetrating effects of the regional Islamic resurgence and the Cold War political dynamics. Nimeiri's alliance with the Islamist section of the northern elite in the context of revival of political Islam undermined southern autonomy, and it was further affected by the state's economic problems and close collaboration with the U.S. in which American interest on southern Sudanese oil played an important role.

The marginalization and exclusion of southerners as central government's major political constituency coincided with the regime's embracing of the Islamist section of the northern elite. This, in turn, reinforced the securitization of the South as a threat to the state's Islamicization aspirations. Among the most influential cadres of the northern elite, its regional self-government became increasingly considered as a source of strength for a possible secession. Faced with economic difficulties, Khartoum became increasingly inclined to encroach on southern autonomy to extract its high-value resources, while fomenting divisions among its leadership and depriving it of economic development.

Moreover, the state aimed at maintaining the political and economic *status quo*. Any successful implementation of the Addis Ababa Agreement in the long term would have altered the established patterns of political and economic power in Sudan, which the northern elite collectively opposed. It would have undermined the northern governing elite's privileged position as the most prominent section of the society, and the historically established hierarchical social order dominated by a particular view of superiority of Arab culture (language and customs) and Islam.

Another dynamic that undermined regional cohesion of the South was the political competition among and within its local elite factions. The most visible example of this, the competition over political power between Alier and Lagu, and their constituencies, generated growing politicized identity divide as the leaders promoted distinct political arrangements to secure the rights of southern Sudanese. At the same time, the factionalism weakened the collective stand against the central government. This undermined further the survival of the South as an autonomous region.

Finally, the regime's shifting alliances, which led to the tampering with the Addis Ababa Agreement, resulted in increasing discontent, insecurity, and violence in the South. Khartoum's strategies encouraged political "tribalization" within the region and re-intensified identity polarization along the divide between the northern "Arab" ruling sections and the major part of the southern political and military leadership. These circumstances led to deterioration of conditions in the South since the political and economic context encouraged sections of former Anya Nya military leaders to challenge the leadership of the local politicians whose legitimacy waned through their inability to stand against the central government manipulation of southern politics and preference to concentrate on local rivalries and self-enrichment. The southern regional administration increasingly under threat, militarization and growing insecurity became the order of the day, with political power in the southern territories concentrating increasingly to the leadership of the armed factions. After armed groups resurged, factions of military officers conspired against the regime, and the situation culminated in the renewed armed rebellion.

Endnotes

1   This was in part due to his poor health and belief that divine forces had saved his regime. Nimeiri began consistently attending Friday prayers, with a distinct location announced every Thursday by the President's office, and associated himself increasingly with *Sufi* orders, inviting their leaders for annual Ramadan reception, providing them with palace grants, organizing an annual *Qur'an* contest, and instituting the Ministry of Endowments and Ministry of Religious Affairs to gain support of smaller *Sufi* orders. In 1980 the first of Nimeiri's two books explaining his Islamic inclinations was published. In it he explained how a return to conviction and commitment to Islam was necessary for Sudan, which had been condemned to backwardness by the Western colonialism that continued to affect the Sudanese society. See Warburg (2003: 152-3) and Collins (2008: 145-6).

2   In 1974 Nimeiri began to invite members of Sufi *tariqa* for pilgrimage to Mecca, financed by the government, while the President's report to the SSU National Congress expressed the view that faith was not only a private issue but also a major building block for the social and political institutions of the society. See Warburg (2003: 153) and Collins (2008: 145).

3   Egypt's official stand in the early 1980's was for moderate state-led Islam, but al-Azhar praised some of Nimeiri's more radical reforms.

4   Nimeiri had appointed leaders of smaller Sufi orders into the SSU apparatus, government posts, and minor ministries, and allowed them new opportunities in secondary schools and universities. Consequently, through political influence these drew financing from Arab states, which increased their power relative to the traditional Arabized elite factions in exile until 1977. However, some of their members escaped dependence on Nimeiri, who was not perceived as ideal religious leader, and joined more radical non-*Sufi* organizations, mainly the Muslim Brothers. See Karsani (1993: 144-7), Warburg (2003: 154), and Collins (2008: 145).

5   Despite Nimeiri having planned partnership with the Muslim Brothers already in 1971, it was not until 1977, after Turabi had calculated that they would benefit most by infiltrating in the state institutions, when the movement opted out of the NF and began active cooperation with the regime. This was only months before the "national" reconciliation. See Warburg (2003: 160, 184) and Collins (2008: 149).

6   See Legum and Lee (1979: 113-4), Daly (1993: 20), Warburg (2003: 155), and Collins (2008: 145).

7   For instance, since the "national" reconciliation, the leader of the Umma, Sadiq al-Mahdi, who since the Aba Island incident had also become the *Imam* of the *Ansar*, sought to fix the movement's relationship with the army and strengthen its organization in Sudan. He was also highly critical of the Muslim Brothers,

perceived as elitist opportunists willing to work within Nimeiri's framework and support rigid policy based on a traditional pattern, such as the literal interpretation of the *Qur'an* and *shari'a* not suitable for a contemporary Muslim society. In addition, Sadiq and the *Ansar*, along with their rivals the *Khatmiyya* and smaller *Sufi* orders, became preoccupied with the infiltration of the Muslim Brothers into the SSU, secondary schools, universities, and Islamic banks. Moreover, Sadiq criticized Nimeiri's Islamist policy as a desperately calculated attempt to falsify Islam and use it to purge his opponents in the North and the South to save his collapsing regime. This led to Sadiq's periodic detentions along with other *Ansar* leaders, and the exclusion of the Umma from Nimeiri's Islamic project. See Warburg (2003: 173-6) and Collins (2008: 150).

8   Awur (1988: 98).

9   Daly (1993: 20-1) and Yohannes (1997: 321).

10   In the early stages the financial needs for the expansion of the movement were met by donations from Arab states and wealthy Sudanese businessmen who hoped to serve *Allah*. However, as the movement's influence grew, Turabi was able to propel the Islamicization of the economy, and from 1978 to at least partially control Islamic banking and other financial institutions, which allowed for a profitable manipulation of economic processes and secured financing to extend political influence. The Muslim Brothers benefited from the banks' dominance of the import/export sector and foreign currency market, which permitted them to hijack the state's control of the economy. Allegedly, in 1978-1987, approximately US$11 billion of Sudan's external aid was transferred abroad through the Islamic banking system. Turabi, himself, was closely linked to the board of directors of both the Faisal and Tadamon Islamic banks, which facilitated the funnelling of donations to build a large mosque near the University of Khartoum and an Islamic university in Omdurman. Moreover, in the 1970s and 1980s the Muslim Brothers were heavily engaged with the northern Sudanese emigrants in the oil producing Arab states, who sent not only official remittances back to Sudan in benefit of the national economy but also informal funds to the Muslim Brothers. According to a study in 1984-5, an estimated US$3 billion was smuggled back to Sudan annually, part of which trickled to the Muslim Brothers. After all, the movement encouraged the emigration of Sudanese male workers, particularly those with Islamist tendencies, cared for the social needs of emigrants in the receiving states, and encouraged women's education and the role of the wives of the emigrants in public life. See Duffield (1993: 333, 346), Yohannes (1997: 321), Warburg (2003: 190-1), and Collins (2008: 149).

11   Yohannes (1997: 321) and Musso (2009).

12   Yohannes (1997: 321) and Musso (2009). Originally an organization of urban educated individuals, the Muslim Brothers broadened its social constituency by creating a patron-client network through which it distributed a portion of its wealth to merchants, artisans, students, taxi-drivers, and others, converting

them into a social constituency. Turabi preferred this strategy over religious agitation. See Yohannes (1997: 321).

13 After 1977 the Muslim Brothers gained more influence in the military. According to Warburg (2003: 189), "Their better-educated membership, experience, superior organization and relative financial affluence, gained as a result of the new Islamic banking system introduced by Numayri with their active assistance, enabled the Brothers to achieve greater success in the army too". Not only were they appointed to organize courses of Islamic ideology for senior officer corps, which facilitated their influence, but graduated Muslim Brothers were encouraged to become officers upon completing their studies and soldiers were persuaded to join the movement. Two major strategies of the Muslim Brothers included the use of the army as a vehicle to impose an Islamic state, and the formation of an Islamic army to replace the elements that guarded the secular *status quo*, as in the case of a number of states in the Muslim world. See Warburg (2003: 189-90) and Collins (2008: 149).

14 Turabi sought increasing political and economic power by enlisting students of secondary schools and universities who would later be professionals. This included school teachers, professors, lawyers, doctors, engineers, civil servants, and cadets. Other channels were infiltration in the army and manipulation of the Islamic economy, such as launching a bill converting *zakat* into a compulsory tax, followed by the Islamicization of financial institutions and the monetary system. See Yohannes (1997: 321), Jendia (2002: 144, 155), Warburg (2003: 155, 185), and Collins (2008: 149).

15 See Yohannes (1997: 321) and Warburg (2003: 184-5). Turabi's political and pragmatic majority overtook Abdallah Abd al-Majid's and Jaafar Shaykh Idris's ideological minority that was more closely connected with Egyptian Muslim Brothers. See Warburg (2003: 185-6) and Collins (2008: 149).

16 de Waal (1994: 48-61).

17 Nimeiri drew US$101.5 million in U.S. security assistance in 1982, followed by similar amounts until 1985, for the modernization of the Sudanese army. From the US$520.6 million budget requested for the Indian Ocean and African countries for 1984, US$498.9 million was divided between Sudan, Somalia, and Kenya in a regional containment strategy. This included US$500,000 in covert support, and hardware provided by Saudi Arabia, allocated annually to the Eritrean and Tigrayan rebels through Sudan, despite their leftist agendas. See Woodward (1987: 373, 384) and Yohannes (1997: 315).

18 It allowed Ethiopian rebels to beam anti-Mengistu propaganda, and challenged the Eritrean question's status as a domestic crisis at the OAU by stating that it was in fact internationalized conflict due to the refugee problem affecting Sudan. This automatically justified the implication of the latter, and the claim that Ethiopia had unilaterally abolished the U.N.-dictated federal system and provoked the war. See Legum and Lee (1979: 124).

19 Yohannes (1997: 316).

20 Nimeiri's rhetoric about regional threats deviated international attention from

319

Sudan's internal problems. Militarization in the name of external threats ensured the persistence of authoritarianism. The arms shipments to Sudan were normally treated as commercial transactions financed by Saudi Arabia, which in 1977-9 used US$320 million for this purpose. The financing schemes for foreign military sales included grant aid paid by American tax payers, and cash or credit, with any shortfall financed by a third party, mostly Saudi Arabia. See Lefevbre (1991: 210) and Yohannes (1997: 317-8).

21 For instance, he produced 10,000 undocumented refugees and pointed to Libyan spies as evidence of Tripoli's aspirations to attack Sudan, while claiming that Libya had established military facilities on the Chad-Sudan border. See Yohannes (1997: 316).

22 For instance, in September 1981, CIA produced evidence that Libyan air force had attacked Sudanese villages near the Chadian border (Yohannes, 1997: 316). Such events were used to legitimize external support to Nimeiri.

23 In 1981-2 the U.S. helped to finance the failed OAU intervention force in Chad, funneling US$30 and US$100 million as security assistance and sending radar aircrafts to Sudan, while supporting Habre's rebels in Chad with US$25 million. See Yohannes (1997: 317).

24 Yohannes (1997: 319) and Rolandsen (2005: 25-6).

25 See Rolandsen (2005: 26). This contradicts Chandler's (2006) thesis that externally dictated state capacity-building and reinforcing is a strategy developed by Western powers and international organizations in the context of their unprecedented power after the Cold War. Instead, in the 1970s and 1980s this phenomenon was already part of the U.S. approach to Sudan and used by the Nimeiri regime.

26 For instance, plants making tomato paste and dehydrated milk were established in date-producing and cow-free areas. See Whitaker (1988: 74).

27 First, harsh climactic conditions in the Sudanese desert areas impeded more delicate projects, such as sugar refining. See Whitaker (1988: 74). Second, technical incompetence and corruption played an important role in obstructing modernization of productive infrastructure. For instance, the Kenana sugarcane complex that was to become one of the major projects was halted by financial incoherence. Although the scheme was originally evaluated at a cost of US$150 million, between October 1973 and September 1976 the calculations had been revised several times to US$475 million. The government announced it was still lacking US$260 million, while the companies building the projects charged high management and execution fees. See Legum and Lee (1979: 130). Corruption in the administration, as referred to above, was also rampant, with the use of public property for personal benefit, transfers of government assets to the officials (such as valuable farmland sold for cheap prices), and even on one occasion the national bank lending US$200 million to a businessman with a fictitious company. See LOC (1991). Finally, experimenting with Islamic reforms in the economy encouraged the spread of Islamic banks, exempt from taxation in Sudan, and provided a channel for the transfer of ille-

gitimately obtained funds abroad without controls, spreading state corruption and eroding the legitimacy of the regime. See Yohannes, (1997: 320).

28   This was permitted by the replacement of the colonial system, based on tribal leaders, with northern Sudanese administrators, and new legislation strengthening the powers of the state over the rural populations. Expropriation under the 1970 Unregistered Land Act had become commonplace, allowing the elites associated with the government to obtain land from rural peoples, and the 1974 Law of Criminal Trespass further obstructed the access of pastoral people and small farmers to the expropriated land. See Johnson (2002: 2) and Pantuliano (2007: 3). Expropriation of land was particularly apparent in the North-South border region, such as southern Kordofan's Habila area where many uneducated and illiterate local farmers and pastoralists experienced their land either being registered to someone else or being annexed into mechanized farming schemes. See Simpson (1981: 201) and Pantuliano (2007: 3).

29   This could be seen in the governing elite's concern of economic development in the South, which in their view would feed a secessionist sentiment. The continuity of such an attitude had been expressed when the Abboud regime had removed resource rich areas, such as *Hufrat al-Nahas*, from the southern provinces in the 1960s, again during the Addis Ababa negotiations, and finally in the early 1980s when the Nimeiri regime attempted to remove resource rich areas from the South.

30   In 1976-85 the American transfers amounted to US$1.358 billion, or 9.5% of the total allocated for Africa. After putting down US$100 million, the Americans convinced other Western countries and institutions to contribute another US$800 million. In 1983, the World Bank and the IMF also became involved, the former sponsoring a Paris Club meeting raising US$780 million for Sudan and the latter supervising structural adjustment and debt rescheduling measures promoted by the U.S. See Yohannes (1997: 319).

31   The requirements attached to U.S. support, which included advancing free market reforms, prices, privatization, removal of subsidies on consumer articles, devaluation, and adherence to the World Bank and IMF programs, reduced Nimeiri's hold on the Sudanese economy, and weakened the regime that used repression and refused to democratize, creating political instability during economic deterioration. See Yohannes (1997: 319-20).

32   It had amounted to US$2.25 billion, and Sudan began to default debt service payments which increased the public debt further by US$130.9 million. See Elhassan (1985: 202) and Collins (2008: 153).

33   The plunge in agriculture was largely due to the large landowners' propensity to prefer quick profit, and unwillingness to work in less profitable conditions. This led to unsustainable use of land by ignoring regulations of land management, the lack of use of fertilizers and soil conservation methods, shifting cultivation to virgin areas without rehabilitating the exhausted soil, and abandoning business due to higher input prices or lower terms of trade in the international market. Still, by 1977 over 8 million acres had been intensively cultivated by

large landowners, which enriched a number of them enormously despite dwindling production. See Simpson (1981: 203-7) and Collins (2008: 150-1).

34 As gross domestic output fell 4.3% in 1978-9 and 1% in 1979-80, import expenditure grew steadily, generating trade deficit of S£564.2 million in 1980. External borrowing led to foreign debt soaring from US$3 billion in 1978 to US$5.2 billion by 1982. See Elhassan (1985: 199) and Niblock (1987: 23, 356).

35 The objective was 4% annual growth and reduction of inflation to 10% through fiscal measures such as reduction of external debt, domestic borrowing, money supply, and announcing pre-seasonal faming prices, while investing in essential productive ventures, including agricultural projects, and rejuvenating infrastructure and communications. See Jendia (2002: 152-3) and Collins (2008: 153).

36 See Jendia (2002: 152-3).

37 Brown (1986: 498).

38 The regime was increasingly incapable of managing its economy, and "Weak world prices of Sudan's dwindling exports, shortages that led to inflation, black-marketeering, the crippling of production, and mismanagement and corruption on unprecedented levels all required drastic action" (Holt and Daly, 2000: 177).

39 Holt and Daly (2000: 177).

40 Khartoum sought to expand large-scale agricultural and industrial schemes, and neglected small-scale industries and commercial ventures in an effort to satisfy Arab investors and large landowners. See Jendia (2002: 152).

41 In 1981 and 1982, 41% and 62% of the total U.S. budget for Africa was divided between Sudan, Liberia, Kenya, Somalia, Zaire, and Zambia, with Sudan being the largest recipient throughout the early 1980s. To justify this, Sudan was portrayed as a capitalist democracy with a moderating influence in the Horn of Africa, supporting the Camp David Accord and mediating in the Eritrean issue. See Yohannes (1997: 313).

42 The public administrations were more reluctant to make decisions, passing them to ministerial offices, while macroeconomic efficiency was hindered by bloated bureaucracies, summing 250,000 civil servants in 1976 to service 15 million Sudanese, and another 100,000 working for public enterprises. See Collins (2008: 152). When it became apparent that Sudan lacked the will and capacity to implement fully the recovery program, in part because of inefficiency of the civil service and Nimeiri's obsession with controlling decision-making personally, the IMF introduced more stringent austerity measures in 1981. See Jendia (2002: 153) and Collins (2008: 152).

43 Over 800 cases of fraud exceeding S£1,000 reported in 1975-1982 provide some indication of the level of corruption in public bureaucracies and corporations. See Yohannes (1997: 320), Holt and Daly (2000: 177), and Collins (2008: 152-3) on this.

44   Prompted by the cutting of subsidies on basic commodities due to the IMF recovery measures, stagnating wages, and increasing prices of sugar, cooking oil, and gasoline, the gap between the rich and the poor expanded and the growing poverty generated discontent and urban unrest. See Jendia (2002: 154) and Collins (2008: 151). This was affected by devaluations, which made imports more expensive for consumers and hit particularly the urban bourgeoisie that had developed a taste for imported luxury goods.

45   Khartoum alone grew by a rate of 6.6% annually, reaching 1,343,000 inhabitants by 1983. See Collins (2008: 151). This program set a precedent for expulsions carried out during the 1990s and early 2000s.

46   Collins (2008: 151).

47   Each had their own governor and a minister. See Khalid (1985: 205-10).

48   See Niblock (1987: 287), Arou (1988: 168), Holt and Daly (2000: 173), and Warburg (2003: 166).

49   See e.g. Alier (1990: 215-24), Warburg (2003: 166-7), and Rogier (2005: 16).

50   Malwal (1985: 30-7).

51   Officially the Muslim Brothers blamed the colonial powers, Egypt and principally Britain, for the "Southern Problem", and the Mahdists for neglecting it. According to them, this allowed the South to be penetrated by the imperialists from Zaire. They recognized no Arabized elite responsibility of the origin of the "Southern Problem". The sectarian parties were also reluctant to accept such responsibility. See Warburg (2003: 167-8) and Rogier (2005: 16).

52   At this time the cotton harvest was 550,000 bales, less than 1/3 from ten years before, and foreign debt had amounted to over US$7 billion. See Collins (2008: 153). Debt arrears to the World Bank had reached US$786 million in 1981, while Sudan's debt to the IMF reached US$1.1 billion a few years later. Also, Nimeiri's strategy of drawing US$6 billion investment from the Arab states had backfired because the already injected US$2.3 billion had been misallocated in part due to rampant corruption. LOC (1991) and Yohannes (1997: 323-4).

53   In June 1981, 8,000 Sudan Railway Workers' Union members went on a strike but were forced back to work by the army; 45,000 were dropped from the public salary list, and labor law was amended to make strikes acts of treason. Sensing the mounting discontent, Nimeiri attempted to appease the population, but in December 1981 nationwide demonstrations organized by students took place which turned into violent riots. Despite being forcibly suppressed by the security apparatus, similar events occurred in January 1982 in which the police killed five students in Wad Medani. Nimeiri felt threatened by these events and called a meeting of national leadership, including members of his political bureau, representatives of the SSU, generals, under-secretaries of ministries, and youth and workers' union representatives. The meeting was designed to be inclusive, and sought to minimize direct criticism of regime policies, but many participants pointed to corruption and demanded political and economic reforms along with the return of more executive power to ministries and public

administrations. Nimeiri responded to corruption accusations in public administrations by suggesting that many of the conferees were implicated in corruption themselves, and announced that if the Sudanese were not satisfied with his
work he would quit. However, his threat to resign was a strategy he had used
previously in 1969 to eliminate civilian leadership from the regime's highest echelons, again in 1975 to introduce sugar tax, and in 1980 to assess the
support of the regime. Yet, Nimeiri continued in power and purged 23 critical
senior army officers in an attempt to reassert his position. See Brown (1986:
502), Alier (1990: 187-9), Jendia (2002: 154), and Collins (2008: 151-2).

54   For instance, Muhammad Najib al-Muti, a recently exiled Egyptian Muslim
preacher involved in agitation against the Copts, was allowed to express his
radical Islamic perceptions on Sudanese television, which resulted in the arrest
of Republican Brothers due to accusations of heresy. This led to a conflict between the regime and the Republican Brothers, which culminated in the public
hanging of an influential leader of the Republican Brothers, Mahmud Muhammad Taha, in January 1985. However, although rejoiced by some Islamists,
the hanging was condemned by Egypt's president Mubarak who withdrew his
support from Nimeiri. See Warburg (2003: 160-5) and Collins (2008: 147-9).

55   Yohannes (1997: 322).

56   Alier (1990: 179) and Collins (2008: 134).

57   Awur (1988: 89).

58   See Madut-Arop (2006: 36, 37) and Collins (2008: 136).

59   Madut-Arop (2006: 37).

60   For instance, this was showcased by printing t-shirts and hats. Lagu's *kokora*
campaign was to an extent financed by Khartoum.

61   Since Nimeiri was interested principally to maintain control of the South at a
personal level, and weaken the region by playing the southern political factions against each other, he ensured that Alier renewed his HEC Presidency.
Alier won against Aru, other unity-minded candidate, by 68 to 37 in a regional
assembly vote, and Angelo Beda from Alier's constituency was elected as the
Speaker. See Alier (1990: 180), Jendia (2002: 152), Madut-Arop (2006: 38),
Akol (2007: 146), and Collins (2008: 134).

62   The following individuals were granted ministerial positions: Gatkwoth
(Vice-President and Finance), Logale (Regional Administration), Malwal (Industry and Mining), Oduho (Public Service and Labour), Gama Hassan (Agriculture and Natural Resources), Justin Yac (Rural Development), Joseph Ukel
(Information), Andrew Wieu (Education), Samuel Abu John (Wildlife Conservation and Tourism), Toby Maduot (Health). See Alier (1990: 180) and Collins
(2008: 134).

63   Madut-Arop (2006: 38).

64   For instance, Gatkwoth and Malwal were sent to Khartoum a number of times
to persuade Nimeiri not to meddle with southern regional politics and its natural resources. See Madut-Arop (2006: 39). Particular focus was aimed at encouraging projects in agro-industrial and transportation sectors, since the main

agricultural ventures in the South, including the sugar schemes, had stagnated. On the other hand, prospecting for oil and minerals had continued uninterruptedly, and in 1980 the French Total Oil had been granted a concession in Bor, Pibor, and Kapoeta region, within Bahr al-Ghazal, Equatoria, and Upper Nile, with the possibility to explore the Ilemi Triangle, which had been under Kenyan administration since the colonial period. See Widatalla (1988: 427) and Alier (1990: 182, 216). In August 1981 Nimeiri sent a delegation under the Minister of Finance, Bedr al-Din Suleiman, including senior officials of the Bank of Sudan and agricultural, industrial, and commercial banks, to visit the South and inquire about its lack of development. This led to bank branches being established in Juba, while US$9 million from the KFAED was pledged for rehabilitation of the Nzara agro-industrial venture. See Alier (1990: 182) and Collins (2008: 134-5).

65 Before Sudan's independence the British had annexed Abyei to Kordofan, and in 1960 Abboud had transferred the mineral-rich Kafia Kingi enclave (*Hufrat al-Nahas*) to Darfur from the southern territory. However, the Addis Ababa Agreement explicitly stated the commitment to return to the 1956 border between northern and southern Sudan. See AAA (1972: Article 3.iii). Yet, this went against Nimeiri's interests and in the absence of the stipulated referendum the people of the Abyei border region had become increasingly discontent. See Awur (1988: 83-4) and Alier (1990: 101). Referendums dictated by the Addis Ababa Agreement to establish the status of the areas with ethnic ties to the South, such as Abyei and *Chali al-Fil* in the Blue Nile, were never conducted. See Chan and Zuor (2006: 34).

66 These oil wells were located within the boundaries of the Bentiu Area Council, despite the central government's claim that they were part of Southern Kordofan. Symbolically, the central government also named the first oil well in the area as *heglig*, an Arabic term of a tree known in the Bentiu area as *thou* in Dinka language. Similar name changes were commonplace in the disputed Renk agricultural region to give an impression that areas with Arabic names belonged to the northern provinces. Alier (1990: 219) and Warburg (1993: 350). These were designs to prepare the areas to be annexed to the northern provinces.

67 See Awur (1988: 84), Alier (1990: 182, 218), and Akol (2007: 147). This attempt had been preceded by Nimeiri's failed effort to annex Kafia Kingi (*Hufrat al-Nahas*) permanently to Darfur in 1978, which the southerners had prevented through a collectively rejection. See Chan and Zuor (2006: 34).

68 Awur (1988: 84).

69 Awur (1988: 84) and Dallalah (1988: 441)

70 See Awur (1988: 84), Dallalah (1988: 441-2), and Alier (1990: 218). The investigation on the issue revealed secret contracts between the government and Chevron, favoring the latter over other oil companies. It was also discovered that Kafia Kingi, located in a presumably petroleum rich area in western Bahr al-Ghazal, had been secretly leased to Chevron in 1979. While Kafia Kingi

had been part of the southern region since the Addis Ababa Agreement, it had been a previously controversial region in 1961 when Abboud had temporarily annexed it to Darfur because uranium deposits had been detected in the area. When the issue resurfaced in 1980-1 as part of the boundary dispute, it reinforced the perception of the regime's deceitfulness. See Alier (1990: 218-9).

71 Dallalah (1988: 442) and Alier (1990: 218).

72 See Dallalah (1988: 443), Alier (1990: 219), and Akol (2007: 147). The U.S. oil company Chevron suggested a technical committee made up of both southerners and northerners to study the feasibility of locating the refinery in Bentiu, but the regime representatives fabricated evidence that the southern leadership was secession-minded. Nimeiri used this to justify the decision in favor of Kosti, while Chevron offered a nominal incentive package including Kosti-Renk-Malakal road improvement, enhancement of sanitation, health, and education, and establishment of a development council with S£1 million base money in the Bentiu area, reviving also a plan for a topping plant and transportation of refined products to the South. However, the central government advised both companies not to collaborate with the HEC and Chevron declined to take up the development work it had initially promised. It recruited mainly northerners. In contrast, Total did cooperate with the southern regional administration against Khartoum's advice. See Alier (1990: 220-21) and Jendia (2002: 150).

73 Alier wrote a letter to Nimeiri explaining that despite Chevron's reluctance, Khartoum should insist on building the refinery in Bentiu to advance development in the area and permit the southern government to collect taxes from its undertakings, diminishing the regime's responsibility to fund the South. Nimeiri disagreed and invited Alier and Malwal, the HEC President and the Minister of Industry, to debate the issue in Khartoum. Chevron officials and al-Tuhami explained that building refinery in Bentiu would not be economically viable since it would be operative in only three to five years, while a refinery in Kosti could be finished in two. Moreover, Kosti was closer to industries needing oil and better connected through essential transportation links. This did not convince the southern delegates who pointed out that the local population could benefit from jobs, economic development, byproducts (such as tar to build roads), fair sharing of oil revenues, and services, such as dispensaries, hospitals, and schools. See Awur (1988: 85-6), Dallalah (1988: 443-4), Alier (1990: 219-20), Chan and Zuor (2006: 33-4), Madut-Arop (2006: 39), and Akol (2007: 147).

74 Awur (1988: 85-6), Alier (1990: 220), Chan and Zuor (2006: 33-4), and Madut-Arop (2006: 39).

75 This was because Chevron preferred more immediate profit from unrefined Sudanese oil in international markets, and the palace clique sought access to export commissions despite Sudan's need of oil for domestic consumption, leading to plans to build a 1,455km pipeline from Bentiu to Port Sudan for US$437 million. See Dallalah (1988: 446), Alier (1990: 221-2), and Khalid

(1990: 332). At the same time, the regime deemed a southern initiative of building a pipeline to Mombasa politically and economically unfeasible, despite the fact that it had promised to lease land to American, Greek, and Saudi businesses to pipe oil from the Gulf States through Africa to Gabon where it could be shipped onwards by avoiding areas of Soviet influence. Although Western geo-political security policy aimed to avoid the Red Sea, the Mediterranean, the Gulf of Aden, and the Indian Ocean for oil exports, the regime insisted on piping oil out through Port Sudan. See Alier (1990: 222). Not only was the regime disingenuous towards the South to administer oil exclusively, but its internal policy for petroleum overrode the larger geo-political considerations of the Cold War situation.

76   In 31 March 1981, the Regional Assembly had adopted a resolution to "Disapprove of the attitude of the Chevron Oil Company in blatantly and deliberately taking part or side in a politically motivated decision which clearly adversely effects the interest of the people of the Southern Region" (RPRA, 1981).

77   See Dallalah (1988: 445), Alier (1990: 221), and Akol (2007: 147). The southern attitude for instance towards Chevron had a later repercussion after the armed hostilities against the regime began because the rebels targeted personnel and installations of the company very early on.

78   Such ex-Anya Nya members claimed that they had fought the government previously without knowing about the oil, blamed the HEC for not fighting for the refinery even physically if necessary, and asserted that they would take up arms if Nimeiri deceived them. See Alier (1990: 221) and Jendia (2002: 151).

79   Bringing up the issue in the SSU Central Committee meeting in February 1981, he claimed that "Now that devolution of powers has become reality in the North . . . we consider the possibility of devolving administration in the South itself" (Arou 1988: 168 and Akol, 2007: 151), arguing that division would bring administration closer to people, facilitate people's participation in the political process, and limit domination of one single ethnic group over others. Nimeiri's proposal was based on an earlier ECCI suggestion to divide the South. At this point, the regime's central committee took no action because the motion had only minority support from Lagu's constituency. See Arou (1988: 168-9), Akol (2007: 151), and Collins (2008: 135).

80   Chan and Zuor (2006: 37).

81   Malwal (1985: 30) and Dak (1988: 191).

82   In March 1981, 12 southern politicians submitted a written petition for Nimeiri to dissolve the southern government and divide the region. See Arou (1988: 174). This was followed by the publication of Lagu's booklet, *Decentralization: A Necessity for the Southern Provinces of the Sudan* in April 1981, echoing his thesis of Dinka domination and arguing that the Dinka had disproportionate representation in the higher echelons of the southern administration. Lagu (1981: 1) argued against the Dinka political elite by asserting that "Political leadership, with a strong tribal orientation having satisfied themselves that the only way to remain in power is to fan up tribal loyalties from their tribe,

which they believe must dominate because of sheer numbers are now turning around to point a finger at those who want to correct the situation as 'power hungry' politicians". The regime financed Lagu's booklet published by the Samar Printing Press in Khartoum, which was widely circulated free of charge by Lagu's associates. See Awur (1988: 89), Akol (2007: 151), and Collins (2008: 135).

83 Nimeiri allegedly told prominent Equatorians who had been defeated in the regional elections in 1980 that decentralization would create 2/3 more high level administrative positions in the southern provinces, and that all three regions in the South Bahr al-Ghazal, Equatoria, and Upper Nile, would be granted initially S£15 million for economic development. See Alier (1990: 234). Still, according to Awur (1988: 90) and Dak (1988: 191, 192), Equatorians became increasingly drawn in only when the propaganda was given a more development-oriented tone, and some senior politicians, such as Mundiri, reversed their initial posture after realizing that the regime was a significant force behind it.

84 On the other hand, the divisionists pointed to the conduct of affairs in regional politics since 1972 and argued that instead of endorsing unity the southern governments had propelled division through discrimination. This generated space for a wide array of grievances that were channeled for a call to equal division, *kokora*, of the southern region, to free Equatorians and others from "Dinka domination". For many, "Dinka domination" had become a legitimate fear, at least in the manner it was portrayed as referring to nepotism, and there was also a genuine attempt to achieve economic development. In general, the message of the divisionists, which was transmitted through a campaign of political mobilization, was able to capture vast support in Equatoria. Indeed Lagu's assertion at a political rally in Khartoum in March 1981 that the South did not have to be strong and unified anymore was applauded, while some southern politicians felt embarrassed by a Member of Regional Assembly's and the Chairman of the SSU Assembly Body's, Ambrose Ring Thiik's, response to Lagu in which he claimed that South's struggle against the northern Arabs was not over. Thiik was later arrested for his support of unity of the southern region. See Madut-Arop (2006: 37) and Akol (2007: 155-8).

85 The unity faction argued that decentralization was simply Nimeiri's strategy to undermine southern autonomy and resume direct control for the region by Khartoum. History lent support to this discourse because many southerners believed that successive northern governments had been keen to divide and rule the region. They further argued that the southern region's unity was the only guarantee of its strength, and that intra-regional differences should not weaken a common stand against any northern plot to undermine autonomy, the only valid manner altering the provisions of the Addis Ababa Agreement being the referendum. During the campaign the unity faction defended its prior term in office that had been tainted by a number of letdowns, such as the failure to hear public opinion during the 1981 refinery dispute, and continued using legalistic

arguments, largely by Alier, a lawyer by training, in defense of unity, which was perceived by some as an attempt to defend their jobs and other personal interests. Moreover, while defending unity they continued to function within the SSU Political Bureau and declined to take responsibility for the CUSS activities. See Akol (2007: 155-7). Some of this was perceived negatively in the South, where people were turning increasingly hostile to Nimeiri and the regime and were also disenchanted by their own politicians.

86   The CUSS was chaired by Mboro, who was assisted by Aru, and Oduho served as its Secretary General. The CUSS also included 24 prominent southern politicians in its executive committee. See Akol (2007: 160-1).

87   The book, *The Redivision of the Southern Region: Why it Must Be Rejected*, also known as *The Solidarity Book*, described southern officers' heroism to save Nimeiri from coup attempts, warned him not to tamper with southern resources and development, and treated "Arabs" scruffily in the context of Arab-Israeli relations. See e.g. Alier (1990: 183), Madut-Arop (2006: 40), and Collins (2008: 135). On the situation of the South, its authors wrote that

Tribalism is still a very strong force in African politics ... [;] ... it is in our determination that tribalism, however little, is condemned and uprooted . . . [and] ... tribal loyalties and activities are simple agitations and moves not based on relevant justifications ... But obviously, redivision is not the accurate prescription for this disease (quoted in Awur, 1988: 91, 92).

The book was rejected in Khartoum, declared illegal and banned (Awur, 1988: 92), and Alier was summoned to explain. Although he argued that the book had been written by members of the People's National Assembly and some students of the University of Khartoum as an answer to Lagu's propaganda, it having been printed by the Nile Printing Press in Juba was enough to infuriate Nimeiri and other northern elite individuals and facilitate a consensus among northern political forces that the South positioned itself against their perception of "national" interest. See e.g. Awur (1988: 90), Alier (1990: 184-5), Madut-Arop (2006: 39-40), Akol (2007: 152), and Collins (2008: 135).

88   The divisionists warned about a revolt, and the unity-minded about the resumption of war in the South. See Madut-Arop (2006: 40). Both parties included ex-Anya Nya elements.

89   Historically, Fertit were people who engaged in subsistence life in the margins of pre-colonial sultanates in Darfur and evaded state control.

90   Arou (1982: 185, 1988: 174), Rogier (2005: 16), and Akol (2007: 153).

91   Nimeiri's move was meant to undermine the unity-minded southern leadership and lower the southern representation at the national level below the stipulated 25% to facilitate the South's division, adhering to the 1981 People's Local Government Act that had been applied to previously decentralize the North. See Dak (1988: 176), Alier (1990: 186), and Madut-Arop (2006: 32).

92   Awur (1988: 94-5).

93   Arou (1988: 174), Chan and Zuor (2006: 37), Madut-Arop (2006: 32), and Akol (2007: 153). Apart from the Vice-President, and Minister of Commerce

and Industry, Makur, who had found the army orders to act against a rebellion in the South in 1979, some of the former Anya Nya officers in the TRG were: Brigadier Joseph Kuol Amuom, the Minister of Administration and Local Government, Colonel Habbakuk Soro, Minister of Wildlife Conservation, Colonel Alison Manana Magaya, Commissioner of Western Equatoria, Colonel Saturnino Arika, Commissioner of Eastern Equatoria, Colonel John Kaong Nyuon, Commissioner of Jonglei Province, Colonel Peter Mabil, Commissioner of Upper Nile, Colonel Alfred Deng Aluk, Commissioner of Bahr al-Ghazal, and Major General Samuel Mabur Malek, Commissioner of Lakes Province. Particularly Makur had become suspected of forming part of an Anya Nya conspiracy and was kept out of the South on political duties. If this were not the case, it was feared that former Anya Nya units would desert and reinitiate hostilities against the Nimeiri regime. See Madut-Arop (2006: 32, 33, 40).

94   Madut-Arop (2006: 32).

95   During the insurgency their political influence and the chances for self-enrichment had been greater than after the war when they had been absorbed and integrated into the state's security apparatus.

96   While the unity-minded in Alier's faction, including leaders from Bahr al-Ghazal, Upper Nile, and some Equatorians, were disappointed and rejected Nimeiri's order because it was aimed to dismantle the Addis Ababa Agreement and weaken the South, Lagu's divisionists celebrated the move because it opened the window for re-division, to escape the alleged Dinka domination, and was believed to bring material benefits for Equatoria in the form of administrative jobs and development financing. See Arou (1988: 175) and Madut-Arop (2006: 32, 33).

97   Alier (1990: 186) and Collins (2008: 135-6). On 6 October 1981, Alier appeared on the radio to diffuse tension in Juba, and, having promised Nimeiri a peaceful transition, provided Rasas with the necessary government information.

98   He even made public remarks about the importance of unity of the region. See Alier (1990: 187) and Akol (2007: 154).

99   For instance in Wau and Rumbek he was received with demonstrations. Bussere Secondary School students and other school children, as well as pupils of the Secondary School in Rumbek, ridiculed him and threw stones. After this humiliation Nimeiri became increasingly uncompromising. See Khalid (1985: 237), Alier (1990: 190), Madut-Arop (2006: 41) and Collins (2008: 136).

100 See Alier (1990: 190-1), Madut-Arop (2006: 41-2), Akol (2007: 163-4), and Collins (2008: 136). Nimeiri preferred the term de-centralization instead of division to minimize protests.

101 This view was prevalent in the People's Regional Assembly, and among southern members in the People's National Assembly and the SSU.

102 Khalid (1985: 236-7). It attempted to capture the attention of the neighboring countries, such as Ethiopia that was supporting residual armed factions in the South, which might be most inclined to help the cause of the anti-divisionists

through the OAU. A letter was written in which the measures taken by the regime to undermine the southern autonomy were detailed. See Arou (1982: 341-2).

103 Arou (1988: 175), ESPAC (2002: 33), Madut-Arop (2006: 42), and Akol (2007: 161).

104 Arou (1988: 175, 176). There was reason to believe in the Libyan connection because the letter stating the formation of the CUSS gave some indication to that direction, and Alier, who was aware of Qadhafi's designs to undermine Nimeiri, had met him personally in 1975 in Wau. See Arou (1982: 346-9) and Alier (1990: 170-2).

105 These resulted in numerous deaths, including three school children in Wau. The southern riots took place in the context of overall economic deterioration and tension in the country, resulting in large-scale demonstrations in December 1981. The detained southern politicians were released after some of them were charged with establishing a political organization, which violated the one-party national constitution. See Arou (1988: 176-7) and Akol (2007: 161).

106 According to Alier (1990: 230), "For a President who wanted to manage things alone, the autonomy of the South was an undesirable limitation to his powers. And for those who wanted to revive the call for a theocratic system of government based on Islamic fundamentalism, the autonomy was a constitutional barrier to their cherished goals".

107 In October 1981, Nimeiri warned Alier and Beda that he would use force against any armed uprising in the South, and out of suspicion delayed Alier's return to Juba and sent Rasas with him to neutralize risk of a rebellion. See Alier (1990: 185, 186).

108 In the opening of the Fifth People's National Assembly he told the southern leadership that he perceived de-centralization as excessively divisive and against national interest, and announced that elections were to be held in the southern region in April. See e.g. Awur (1988: 95), Alier (1990: 189), and Akol (2007: 154).

109 The December riots all over the country, following the dissolution of the national and regional assemblies in October 1981, had shaken the regime. A sign of decreasing legitimacy, this had not only led Nimeiri to organize a meeting with the national leadership, but also convinced him to reassert his position in the army, the SSU, the parliament, and the cabinet. Nimeiri needed time for this reassertion of personal authority, and the issue of the South became temporarily a lesser concern. Second, after assessing that it was practically impossible that the southerners would vote for de-centralization in a free and fair referendum because only a minority, mostly Equatorians, supported Lagu's divisionists, he decided to postpone the plan to divide the southern region. See Alier (1990: 189) and Akol (2007: 153). Nimeiri wanted temporarily to minimize any destabilizing effect from the South, which could debilitate his position further.

110 See Arou (1988: 186), Akol (2007: 154-5), and Collins (2008: 188).

111 See Akol (2007: 161, 162). Whereas Alier and his associates sought the presidency, undermining Mboro's candidature only to endorse him later after having damaged his credibility, Toby Maduot and Othwonh Dak reached an agreement with Equatorians on forming a government, and Brigadier Andrew Makur Thaou announced his competing candidature for the HEC presidency of a Government for Regional Reconciliation. This initiative is widely believed to have been sponsored by Nimeiri to undermine the unity faction. See Akol (2007: 162-3).

112 According to Alier (1990: 189),

> There were many reasons for this which had to do with interaction between groups and their neighbours, a tradition of resistance to foreigners of all types, the unequal distribution of education in the region, the uneven impact of the civil war—which affected Equatoria most of all—and the recent upheavals in Uganda. A large number of soldiers, workers, elites and businessmen, all Southern Sudanese, who worked in Uganda during the administration of Idi Amin had rushed to Equatoria between October 1979 and January 1980 after his overthrow. Most of them were without jobs and all were from Equatoria. The unemployment and comparative poverty they found at home contrasted sharply with the prosperous lives they had lived in Uganda. Their frustrations led them to actions that were sometimes beyond the norm and the 'liberation' of Equatoria from the Dinka was one of them.

113 Alier (1990: 189) and Collins (2008: 136). Other factors contributing to the Dinka migration had been the war and the following Addis Ababa period that encouraged the movement of people.

114 This was relevant regarding the alliances during the second southern insurgency and beyond.

115 Arou (1988: 178) and ESPAC (2002: 33).

116 Tembura's election was rife with accusations of regime manipulation. Tembura, who was able to secure votes from an ethnically larger variety of regional assembly representatives, including 20% of his vote coming from the Dinka, received assistance from Siddiq al-Banna, Nimeiri's close relative in charge of the army's southern command, together with a delegation from Khartoum headed by Ezzil al-Din al-Sayed, the Speaker of the national parliament. Allegedly, unity faction politicians were told that Nimeiri would not proceed with the division, which resulted in almost 30 members breaking away to the divisionist camp and enabled the election of Tembura. See e.g. Arou (1988: 178, 180-1), Alier (1990: 190), Nyaba (2000: 29), and Madut-Arop (2006: 34).

117 Tembura won with 62 votes to 49. Arou (1988: 180-1) and Alier (1990: 192). Matthew Obur was elected as the Speaker.

118 See Awur (1988: 95, 96).

119 For instance, 103 of the 203 original ex-Anya Nya officers had been relieved from the army by 1982. At the same time, the number of the still active former Anya Nya soldiers had declined to 2,000 from the original 6,000, and the ex-

Anya Nya in police, prison, and wildlife forces had diminished. Non-promotion, retirement, disability, and death were the main reasons for the decline, while officers and soldiers were deliberately not replaced by other southerners. See Kulusika (1998: 103) and Madut-Arop (2006: 34).

120   Since 1980 the policy of transferring former Anya Nya had been intensified, according to the demands of the army headquarters in Khartoum and despite the HEC leadership's warnings. Those officers who had avoided transfer by threatening to revolt, particularly in Ayod, Bor, Kapoeta, Rumbek, and Torit, were placed under regime vigilance. See Madut-Arop (2006: 36, 369).

121   See Madut-Arop (2006: 34).

122   According to Madut-Arop (2006: 34, 36), " . . . [This] undoubtedly opened doors for the former Anya Nya underground movement to agitate and ring bells of the resumption of insurrection in the South. Indeed, the government's policies and reactionary propensities of the Southerners naturally synchronized the rhythm towards war that was gaining momentum day by day".

123   According to Akol (2007: 155), in the first meeting the HEC insisted on the implementation of the reforms dictated by the Nimeiri regime. However, after the regional congress of the SSU, which Nimeiri convoked to raise the issue of division in January 1983, voted overwhelmingly in defense of the Southern Provinces Self-Government Act, he applied pressure on Tembura and Zein al-Abdin M. A. Abdel Gader, who were in charge of publishing the voting results, to change the resolution from rejection to acceptance. Soon after the vote Tembura met Nimeiri and suggested a reshuffle of the HEC, but Nimeiri insisted that by February 1983 three separate governments should be formed in the South and the People's Regional Assembly dissolved. The plan for the division consisted of three stages, including appointment of one minister each for Bahr al-Ghazal, Equatoria, and Upper Nile responsible to the HEC for 1-2 year interim period, followed by the appointment of vice-presidents administering each region and reporting to the HEC, and finally the formation of governments for each region following the end of Tembura's four-year term after which the HEC and the People's Regional Assembly would gradually cease to function. See Alier (1990: 191-2, 234), Chan and Zuor (2006: 37), Madut-Arop (2006: 42), and Collins (2008: 136-7).

124   According to Alier (1990: 192) and Akol (2007: 164), both non-Equatorians, Tembura proceeded privately, writing a letter to Nimeiri calling for the division of the southern region, and submitted his plan to initiate the formation of three separate governments in the South in February 1983. However, Chan and Zuor (2006: 37) assert that "Tambura, the descendant of a prominent Azande family, recognized that most people in Upper Nile and Bahr al-Ghazal opposed re-division, and did not act on that request".

125   The regime arrested the members of the Abyei central committee, who had just returned from Juba to call for the Abyei referendum as stipulated in the Self-Government Act, because they were allegedly encouraging Anya Nya II activities in northern Bahr al-Ghazal where 12 northern merchants had been

killed in Ariath, north of Aweil, in January 1983. See Niblock (1987: 288) and Madut-Arop (2006: 42-3, 65). The SSO also arrested Obur, the Speaker of the Regional Assembly, and Dhol Acuil Aleu, the Vice-President of the HEC, who had previously supported Tembura, after having held a rally in the University of Khartoum. They had told students about the forgery of the Regional Assembly voting results on the re-division issue, accusing Tembura and ministers of the central government of manipulating the outcome, asserting that Nimeiri would not divide the South due to his religious conviction as a Muslim, and that they would oppose any possible violation of the Southern Provinces Self-Government Act. See Alier (1990: 192, 234) and Madut-Arop (2006: 42). According to Akol (2007: 164), both were imprisoned in Kobar until mid-1984 and upon release joined the newly emerged rebels in Addis Ababa.

126 In May 1983, Nimeiri had received a delegation of northerners and southerners demanding the division of the southern region. Headed by Lagu, it included Philip Obang, Luigi Adwok Bong, Othwon Dak, Oliver Albino, Ahmed-Hameed Saleh, and the Speaker of the National Assembly, Izz al-din al-Saeed. They were discontented with Tembura, claiming that being Azande determined his positioning against the division. Subsequently, Tembura was called to Khartoum, and in a meeting with Nimeiri on 5 June 1983 he was told that the president would announce the division the same evening and that he would become the Governor of Equatoria Region, Daniel Kuot Matthews the Governor of Upper Nile Region, and Wol the Governor of Bahr al-Ghazal Region (Madut-Arop, 2006: 54-5).

127 See Alier (1990: 235), Akol (2007: 164), and Collins (2008: 137-8). Nimeiri also decreed the transfer of the personnel from the regional institutions. See Malwal (1985: 34) and Madut-Arop (2006: 55).

128 Rogier (2005: 16), Akol (2007: 166, 167, 168), and Collins (2008: 138).

129 Alier (1990: 227-9, 232), Akol (2007: 166-8), and Collins (2008: 138).

130 Khalid (1985: 239).

131 Alier (1990: 164) and Collins (2008: 138).

132 Alier (1990: 235), Madut-Arop (2006: 55-6), and Akol (2007: 165).

133 For instance, Tembura returned to Juba in his capacity as Governor of Equatoria where he was received with joy by Lagu's constituency. However, after he left out some of the staunchest supporters of division of the South (including Albino, Eliaba James Surur, Luka Monoja, Samson Kwaje, and Jino Gama), political strife took place in Equatoria along ethnic and sectional lines. Demands were encouraged for further de-centralization, manifested in the fractionalization of Equatorian politics before political life was disrupted by the intensifying armed conflict. The pledged improvement of conditions after the division did not materialize, and, as grievances spread and Nimeiri's machinations became more apparent, some members of the Equatorian intelligentsia later joined southern rebels despite them being principally Dinka (Madut-Arop, 2006: 56-7).

134 Chan and Zuor (2006: 37).

135   Awur (1988: 87) and Madut-Arop (2006: 56).

136   The situation encouraged the underground political opposition in the South. This network had been active since the 1970s and included a number of organizations, such as the National Action Movement (NAM), the Juwama African People's Organization, the SSLM, and the Movement of Total Liberation of Southern Sudan. None of these groups survived the early 1980s, but some of their prominent members, such as Samuel Gai Tut and Akwot Atem (NAM), and Pagan Amum and Nyachugak Nyachiluk (SSLM), became prominent in armed organizations after the war broke out. See Akol (2001: 2-3).

137   For instance, continuously during the 1970s, the Murle, a people with a deep-rooted warrior culture, carried out cattle raids on their neighboring Bor, Twic, Nyareweng, and Ghol Dinka and Lou Nuer groups. See de Waal (1993: 154), and Johnson and Prunier (1993: 120). This invited retaliatory raids, while the availability of firearms made the confrontations more devastating. This inter-ethnic relationship can be considered normal in places such as Jonglei where such raiding produces deaths and destruction even today.

138   See e.g. Johnson and Prunier (1993: 119, 120).

139   Johnson and Prunier (1993: 120).

140   These conflicts took place between sectors of the nomadic Rizaigat and Misiria, both perceived culturally as Arab Baggara, and sections of Malwal, Twic, Ngok, and Ruweng Dinka, sectors of the Nuer, and parts of the Nuba.

141   de Waal (1993: 144). According to Alier (1990: 255-6), these feuds continued throughout the Anya Nya insurgency, and halted only when some Baggara negotiated agreements with local Anya Nya leaders to continue their grazing activity by paying taxes in form of money and bulls.

142   The replacement of Native Administration through which the colonial state had encouraged local mechanisms for conflict settlement, with the system of local People's Councils, resulted in resistance of the new structures by some chiefs opposing the regime, while some locals ignored all local administrators. See de Waal (1993: 145).

143   For instance, in the 1971-6 period there were no regular traditional meetings to resolve Rizaigat-Malwal Dinka feuds, and it was only in 1979 after army intervention by southern troops from Aweil that a system of three consecutive annual meetings was imposed, the Malwal complaining that they were not treated fairly by the Rizaigat court and the Rizaigat expressing discontent over the intervention by southern forces. It should also be mentioned that in the southern Kordofan/Abyei area, which the regime defined strictly as an "Arab" dominated region belonging to the North, similar instability existed throughout the 1970s. In this case, both Ngok Dinka and Humr Misiria were under the same Area Council, which potentially facilitated local conflict settlement, but also subjected the Ngok to domination of the local Baggara groups. See de Waal (1993: 145). Sectors of the Baggara form an important constituency of a section of the Arabized governing elite. These received limited backing from the regime authorities, attempting to assert control and buttress Baggara superiority locally.

144 de Waal (1993: 144-6) and Madut-Arop (2006: 63-5) point out that the conflicts involving Dinka and Baggara ethnic militias had intensified from 1965 onwards, and had acquired ethnic and racial dimension in the context of the first insurgency that had encouraged sections of Dinka youth to join the Anya Nya. They had led to the inclusion of the referendum clause in the Addis Ababa Agreement through which the Ngok Dinka inhabited Abyei could be joined to the South, but at the same time the Khartoum-backed Baggara militia *Quaat al-Marheel* had protected the Misiria who had continued to use traditional Dinka land in Abyei for grazing. The presence of Misiria cattle, in turn, encouraged cattle-raiding in the deteriorating economic conditions that were compounded by drought and famine in the early 1980s. This cycle of violence heightened the polarization of the constructed politico-cultural identity between the "Arab" and "African".

145 Johnson and Prunier (1993: 121).

146 For instance, in 1978 a militia group under Michael Miokol Deng Majok surfaced as an inter-clan militia of the Ngok Dinka of Abyei and Malwal Dinka of Aweil against sections of the Baggara (Misiria and Rizeigat) in response to an escalation of traditional conflicts over water and grazing land. This militia was formed in the context of escalating local violence related to cattle-raiding that also involved the neighboring Twic and Rek Dinka.

147 de Waal (1993: 146).

148 Johnson and Prunier (1993: 121).

149 This was despite its engagement in resolving local conflicts in Darfur in the early 1980s. See de Waal (1993: 146, 147).

150 Johnson and Prunier (1993: 119-22).

151 Kulusika (1998: 103).

152 These included the National Action Movement, led by Oduho, Akwot Atem, Benjamin Bol Akok, and Samuel Gai Tut, the Movement for the Total Liberation of Southern Sudan, an Equatorian led student movement with connection to the southern Sudan student association in Egypt, and Juwama African People's Organization.

153 However, the secret opposition organizations were scattered throughout the 1970s, and it was only after the organized mutinies in 1983 when an effort was made to unite the armed struggle between the underground movement and the Anya Nya II. See e.g. Johnson and Prunier (1993: 121-6), Johnson (1998: 57-61, 2003: 59-66), Nyaba (2002: 28-41), Madut-Arop (2006: 59), and Akol (2007: 149-50).

154 In 1975-6, remnants of the absorbed ex-Anya Nya who had deserted in Akobo and Wau had found safety in Ethiopia. There camps for those Anya Nya fighters who had not accepted the Addis Ababa Agreement, and other refugees, already existed. Many of these former guerrilla were Nuer who drew support also from local Nuer communities in western Ethiopia. In the late 1970s, particularly discontented, and mostly poorly educated, Nuer youth were encouraged to join armed groups, but often an embryonic political leadership succumbed

into ideological difficulties and the groups engaged in banditry, many without political objectives. See Johnson and Prunier (1993: 121), Johnson (1998: 57-8, 2003: 59), and Madut-Arop (2006: 62). Non-Nuer groups among these included the Revolutionary Committee of James Bol Kur (Shilluk), Bernard Bakam (Anuak), Thaan Nyibil (Shilluk), and Joseph Mubarak (Nuba) founded in response to Nuer animosity towards non-Nuer recruits. See Madut-Arop (2006: 62).

155 Madut-Arop (2006: 60-1) asserts that in 1975 a group of Anya Nya II had constituted the APF led by Muortat, consisting of some of those condemning the Addis Ababa Agreement and former members of the NPG with a secessionist agenda to liberate southern Sudan. However, the separatist agenda and non-Communist orientation was not appealing to Soviet-aligned Ethiopia, and failing to maintain unity the political leadership of the APF gradually waned out.

156 For instance, the mutineers from Akobo led by Kuany and Bol reached an agreement with Ethiopia for limited political and material backing after Sudan continued its support for the ELF despite Ethiopia's official warning in 1976. In this situation, Ethiopia became interested in destabilizing Nimeiri and to curb Sudan's support of the ELF, Tigray People's Liberation Front, Oromo Liberation Front, and Gambella People Liberation Force. See e.g. Nyaba (2000: 35-6), Johnson (1998: 57, 2003: 59), Chan and Zuor (2006: 24), and Madut-Arop (2006: 60).

157 Most mutineers were based in Bilpam and became active among the armed bands around Akobo, which forms part of an ethnically Nuer and Anuak region extending from Gambella (Ethiopia) to Upper Nile. See Johnson (2003: 59) and Madut-Arop (2006: 60). According to John Garang, "When I was at the General Headquarters in Khartoum, we used to be briefed about Bil Pam. The reports we had is that Gordon Koang had 7,000 strong, that Yagoub Ismail was with several thousand men and Abdalla Zakaria had many thousands..." (Heritage, 1987b: 4).

158 This was in part because the Anya Nya II was incapable of confronting the army, Ethiopia not wanting to involve its own military, and because Ethiopia would not support secessionist insurgency in Sudan while fighting separatist insurgents at home. For instance, an Anya Nya II section called the Sudan People's Revolutionary Party became the main force among the armed bands due to initial Ethiopian and Libyan support in terms of military material. However, the namely 150 rifles forwarded to the group by Sadiq, along with training and some financing, only gave it enough capacity to conduct limited recruitment in the Nuba Mountains and Khartoum but not to found a mass rebel movement. See e.g. Johnson (1998: 58, 2003: 60), Turner (1998: 205), Chan and Zuor (2006: 23), and Madut-Arop (2006: 62). The scope of activities of these groups included occasional attacks on civilians and government posts, but mostly cattle-raiding near the Ethiopian border, and providing cover for Sadiq to beam radio propaganda to Sudan after the 1976 aborted coup. See Johnson and Pru-

nier (1993: 122), Johnson (2003: 59), and Chan and Zuor (2006: 24).

159 Johnson and Prunier (1993: 122).

160 Madut-Arop (2006: 60-1) asserts that Bilpam was referred to as the place of hope where a transformation of the situation in the South could originate. Many southerners warned the authorities about moving to Bilpam when feeling that they were pressed by the regime's policies.

161 Although most of the armed bands had engaged in looting and raiding civilians, by 1980 attacks on police posts and merchandise trucks (that required more organizational coherence) began to take place in a number of locations, including Jonglei, Upper Nile, Bahr al-Ghazal, and Lakes. See Johnson and Prunier (1993: 122-3), Johnson (1998: 57, 58), and Chan and Zuor (2006: 23).

162 In the midst of rumors and the growing tension particularly after more northern army troops arrived to the South, incidents including harassment and killing of civilians became more commonplace in Aweil, Bentiu, Nasir, and Malakal.

163 Johnson and Prunier (1993: 121) assert that the attempt was to minimize the threat of renewed insurgency since the ex-Anya Nya officers' underground movement in Bussere was viewed to be associated with Anya Nya II activity, but it created a new grievance among the southern troops directly linked to the mutinies of 1983. The suspected leaders of the former Anya Nya opposition were removed. For instance, Abuur was promoted to Brigadier and moved to Wau, Madut Baak was transferred to Jebeit in Port Sudan, and others, such as Andrew Makur Thaou, Joseph Kuol Amoum, Albino Akol Akol, Alison Manani Magaya, and Habbakuk Soro, were kept under surveillance and given posts in the government. John Garang, a Twic Dinka from Wangulei north of Bor, had been sent to the U.S. for training, where, among other studies, he completed a doctorate degree in agricultural economics. However, after his return in 1981, in part because of the deteriorating situation, Garang retook underground activities in Khartoum where he was appointed as an assistant researcher for the army and a visiting lecturer. In addition, absorbed junior officers, such as Ngor Makiech, Salva Kiir Mayardit, William Chuol Deng, and Chagai Atem, became increasingly active in the movement. See Madut-Arop (2006: 43).

164 See Johnson and Prunier (1993: 121-3), Johnson (1998: 58, 2003: 60), Chan and Zuor (2006: 23), Madut-Arop (2006: 43), and Collins (2008: 140). In these circumstances, southern soldiers in Upper Nile and Jonglei tended to complain about the conduct of the army, and people began to talk better about the Anya Nya II groups, which in turn sought recruits. See Johnson and Prunier (1993: 121, 123) and Johnson (2003: 61). According to Chan and Zuor (2006: 24), by the early 1980s Addis Ababa had become inclined to support wider rebellion in Sudan because its limited aid to the Sudanese dissidents was insufficient to pressure Khartoum.

165 Adwot Atem, a Twic Dinka from Kongor and a leader of one of the Anya Nya II groupings active in Jonglei area, became the link between the underground movement commanders, including Garang, Major William Chuol Deng, and

Lieutenant General Samuel Gai Tut, latter of which was heavily engaged in sending Nuer youth secretly to Bilpam. See Johnson and Prunier (1993: 123) and Madut-Arop (2006: 43). Gai Tut was a Nuer from Akobo and former Israeli trained Anya Nya, who had been expelled from the army in 1974 after having threatened Lagu with a pistol. Previously he had served as a regional minister under Lagu and Rasas. Chuol, who had resigned from the army upon dismissal of Gai Tut, was originally a Dinka but became a Lak Nuer through naturalization and residence. See Alier (1990: 251, 252) and Collins (2008: 140).

166 According to Johnson and Prunier (1993: 121, 123) and Johnson (2003: 60), there was a gradual change of targets among Anya Nya II active in the Nasir area, which began assaulting more and more objects associated with the "northern Arab" and persuading absorbed police and military to their side. The decrease of attacks on civilians resulted in growing support for the main Anya Nya II groups.

167 Madut-Arop (2006: 43) asserts that in these circumstances, the underground movement of the absorbed Anya Nya officers strengthened its network and gained impetus through unpopular regime measures and mass arrests of leaders seeking southern unity.

168 He resided briefly at Hajj Yousif in the eastern fringes of Khartoum, a location he chose for conducting his underground activities due to its relative remoteness. Garang also moved discreetly and associated himself publicly with northern top army officers, such as generals Yousif Ahmed Yousif and Sowar al-Dhahab, General Abu Kodok, the Chief of Staff of the Sudanese army, and professional cadres in Khartoum. According to Garang, "My calculation was that if there were intelligence reports about my activities . . . These generals would dismiss the reports . . . " (quoted in Madut-Arop, 2006: 47). Moreover, to avoid being suspected, Garang worked with Major Arok Thon Arok who was a popular security officer and a tutor at Wad Saidna Military College in Omdurman until April 1982 when he became a member of the southern Regional Assembly. See Madut-Arop (2006: 43-7).

169 For instance Garang was in constant contact with commanders such as Kiir in Malakal, and Chuol was assigned to attempt to coordinate with the Anya Nya II in Bilpam, while Chagai Atem passed messages between Bor, Juba, Malakal, and Khartoum. See Madut-Arop (2006: 44).

170 In early 1982 Gai Tut was discovered, dismissed from the HEC of which he formed part, and detained when caught on Juba Bridge in an attempt to smuggle weapons to Anya Nya II based in Ethiopia. See Johnson and Prunier (1993: 123), and Johnson (2003: 61).

171 For instance, Major Kerubino Kwanyin Bol, a Dinka from Paywayi, Bahr al-Ghazal, and Major William Nyuon Bany, originally Dinka but Nuer by naturalization, who both formed part of the underground movement, were ordered by the army to fight the Anya Nya II in Jonglei province, but eventually developed contacts with the latter in 1982 and reportedly visited Anya Nya II camps prior to the Bor mutiny the following year. See e.g. Alier (1990: 251), Johnson and

Prunier (1993: 123), Nyaba (2000: 29) and Johnson (2003: 61).

172   During this time, Anya Nya II in Bentiu, Fangak, and Nasir areas initiated contacts with the absorbed Anya Nya in police and military, explaining that their grievances were with the regime (Johnson, 2003: 58, 61).

173   According to Johnson (2003: 60-1), one example of this was a dissident contingent linked to the underground movement moving to Bentiu to protect the southern oil fields from northern intrusion.

Chapter IX

Fighting for Southern Sudan:
The Making of the Second Insurgency

By the early 1980s the political order of the Nimeiri regime had become increasingly contested. The Islamists, who now formed Khartoum's main constituency, were exerting their influence in the state apparatus and projected it onto the society. In these circumstances the threat of resumption of insurgency in southern Sudan had become increasingly real, as fear of reinforced "Arab" domination and repressive Islamism grew. However, in 1982 the scattered armed groups active in southern Sudan still lacked external support to obtain social and material means to launch any viable large-scale rebellion.

By the early 1980s, a section of Anya Nya officers who had been absorbed into the state's security apparatus had formed an underground movement. In 1983 they conspired and initiated the second rebellion in southern Sudan. The SPLM/A then asserted prominence over other armed groups and launched a military campaign that, coupled with initial external support principally from Ethiopia, led to its consolidation. Yet, complex motivations laid behind the rebellion, related to the dynamics of exclusionary state governance that dictated the narrow distribution of political and economic power and marginalized the southern military and political elites. As the deteriorating political and economic circumstances in Sudan, and particularly in the southern territories, led to insecurity, armed groups strengthened and the rebellion launched by a section of southern officers gained momentum.

The Conspiracy and Rebellion

The Conspiracy

Prompted by the deteriorating political situation, the underground officer movement devised a plan to launch an insurgency. They decided, in February 1983 in Khartoum, to initiate rebellion in southern Sudan in August 1983 by taking control of its major towns.[1] With this in mind, the underground movement sought to strengthen its contacts with Anya Nya II groups. John Garang, one of the members of the underground movement, at the time an army intelligence officer in Khartoum, assumed the leading role in the planning.[2] The intensifying contacts with the Anya Nya II in Bilpam linked the underground movement with a growing number of former Anya Nya commanders willing to join the dissidents, which Ethiopia recognized by elevating its support to the rebels.[3] After Nimeiri issued orders in early 1983 to transfer battalions 105, 110, and 111 to the north and west in order to remove the remaining influence of the former Anya Nya officers in southern Sudan,[4] the underground movement leadership considered initiating the rebellion earlier.

Meanwhile, in November-December 1982, a dispute had emerged over salaries of some of the former Anya Nya units absorbed in the army.[5] This culminated in March 1983 when an investigation due to irregularities in payroll sheets was launched.[6] An investigation was taken on the matter in part because army officers had become suspicious,[7] and this resulted in further polemic when commander of Battalion 105, Captain Bullen Alier, refused to revise the distorted salary lists that Major Kerubino Kwanyin Bol had used to demand overpay for his troops.[8] Through the salary scandal Kerubino drew unwanted attention to his violent activities of confiscating goods for self-enrichment while fighting the Anya Nya II, and it gave the regime yet another reason to accelerate transfers of southern troops to the northern provinces.[9] This situation put pressure on Kerubino to stage a mutiny in mid-May instead of August 1983, which had been the time initially agreed to among the leaders of the underground movement.[10]

In April 1983, Siddig al-Banna, the leading officer of the army's southern command, invited political representatives of Jonglei Province and military authorities to an emergency meeting in Juba.[11] In order to diffuse tension in Bor, a military committee of investigation, which included a number of underground officers,[12] was set up to determine if the salary disagreement was politically devised or a mere accounting problem.[13] Although the crisis worsened, al-Banna remained adamant. Following orders from Khartoum on hard stand against the Battalion 105 leadership, and having not received corrected payrolls from Bor, he froze salaries.[14] Al-Banna also detained a non-military delegation[15] sent from Bor with an allegation that it sided with the disobedient soldiers, and disregarded its message that the required S£107,000 for the salaries should be raised even as a loan if necessary to prevent a rebellion.[16] The military intelligence was aware of the military-civilian connection in the conspiracy, suspecting that local politicians were deliberately creating instability through the absorbed former rebel forces. As a result, the army officers decided to take control of Bor.[17]

In this situation, the leadership of the underground movement reconsidered its plan. Garang, who by now had ascended as one of the key figures in the leadership of the underground movement, took his annual leave and went to Juba on 9 May 1983 to meet the officers part of the conspiracy and some CUSS politicians and civil servants who supported the plan.[18] Fearing to be discovered by the regime in the midst of rising tensions due to the Bor incident, he pushed forward the plan for simultaneous mutinies.[19]

However, meanwhile Kerubino's troops had already rebelled and assumed control of Bor.[20] On 13 May 1983 Garang also left for Bor, and upon his arrival took leadership from Kerubino. There he received a message from other underground officer, Salva Kiir, from Malakal, about an imminent army attack from Juba, and an airlift of army units to Akobo with orders to attack Pibor and Pochalla.[21] Garang organized the defense of Bor accordingly,[22] and Kerubino received the army attack in the dawn of 16 May 1983.[23] Yet, due to the strength of the attack he was forced to withdraw towards Ethiopia by the following morning.[24] After emptying storages in Pibor and Pochalla, some southern army units followed the example in their respective towns,[25] and other garrisons followed the suit, some supported by Anya Nya II sections.[26] Overall in the course of May to July 1983, driven mainly by the Bor mutiny and the re-division of the South, soldiers and police revolted and deserted in Malakal, Nasir, Bentiu, Aweil, Wau, Rumbek, as well as in Nzara, western Equatoria, although many Equatorians were initially less enthusiastic about joining the rebellion considered as a Dinka initiative[27] to maintain the South as one region. Approximately 1,000 troops deserted in the initial stages,[28] but further defections and mutinies meant that by July there was a large concentration of rebels in the Ethiopian border region, with approximately 2,500 southern soldiers making their way to Bilpam and another 500 remaining scattered in Bahr al-Ghazal.[29]

Garang, who had assumed the leadership of the first rebelling units, also left for Ethiopia. As a central figure in the conspiracy and in the initial mutiny, he was received by the Ethiopian area commander who escorted him to Adura which Ethiopian authorities had designated as his command post.[30] Although there is mixed information about Garang's prior contacts with Ethiopians, it appears that plans for the mutinies had been made with Anya Nya II and with the awareness of the Ethiopian military, which was interested in organizing the Sudanese rebels under solid leadership to assert control over them.

Despite these developments on the ground in the South, Nimeiri remained poised to implement his designs. The growing insecurity facilitated further re-securitization of the southern issue and legitimized more regime repression, which served to justify the South's re-division and opened ground for the imposition of *shari'a.*[31] In the process of portraying southern Sudan as a threat that should be overcome through imposition of Arabization and Islamicization, which had been the policy of a number of previous governments, Nimeiri was heavily influenced by Turabi and pressured by the regime's main political constituency, the Muslim Brothers. In this situation, the violence in the South was presented as a result of failed southern regional politics and "tribal" feuds of primitive southern society, which justified stronger state intervention by repressive means, including enforcing the decentralization policy and extending Islamic influence and legal order.

Constituting the SPLM/A

During the 1970s, northern authorities had sought to use force in the cases of disobedience among the former Anya Nya units. However by the early 1980s in the context of political instability and increasing armed violence, the state's capacity to use punitive measures against ex-Anya Nya had declined. This, along with the weakness, lack of authority, and eroding legitimacy of the southern political elite,[32] led to circumstances that facilitated mass support for violent dissidence under the southern military leadership, and generated conditions conducive to war. To this extent the insurgency was a response to state policies that increased support for organizing and initiating a rebellion by reinforcing the "North-South", and "Arab-African", political identity divide, and the deepening of the collective sentiment of "Arab" subjugation among many southerners. Thus, to a large degree, non-material resources and factors, such as attitudes, rumors, sentiments, and feelings permitted initial mobilization and recruitment for the insurrection, while it appears that the role of material resources that facilitated its viability became pronounced later.

The succession of mutinies and desertions in the South undermined the regime's efforts to reaffirm its control over the region. In a number of provinces, such as Jonglei, the fighting initiated displacement and migration from towns to remote rural areas, which was compounded by the division of southern Sudan that obliged large numbers of people to relocate to their areas of origin. This happened in the context of fear of renewed regime domination and a deteriorating security situation. The divisive and exclusive politics by the regime and southern politicians, which heightened ethnic animosity, had not only encouraged attitudes adverse to regional unity, but emphasized divisions along ethnic lines and generated ethnic animosity in the circumstances of growing insecurity.

In the aftermath of the Bor mutiny, Ethiopian borderlands became an important sanctuary for the southern rebels. In these areas, a number of insurgent groups came together under the most prominent leaders; including Garang's and Kong's Ethiopian-supported Anya Nya II in Bilpam (Ethiopia), and Gai Tut's, Chuol's,[33] and Akwot Atem's organization in Bukteng (Sudan).[34] The rivalry between these groups was exemplified by their choice of different headquarters, as Garang set up his base in Adura in May and drew support from other members of the underground movement, dignitaries from Abyei, politicians such as Oduho and Majier Gai, and dissidents from Boma. This prevented Gai Tut, who assumed leadership in Bukteng, to extend his influence to Adura.[35] In the meantime, a growing number of mostly Nuer recruits continued to arrive to the camps.[36] After Garang's arrival, most of the thousands of people reaching Ethiopia were forced to choose if to join Garang in Adura, Kong in Bilpam, or Gai Tut and Atem in Bukteng. Adura attracted many southern dignitaries, which further reinforced Garang's position.

By the time the insurgents organized in their respective bases, Ethiopian government had recognized Garang's prominence.[37] News of his preferential treatment and private meeting with General Tesfy Mesfin, Chairman of General Joint-Chiefs of Staff of Ethiopian army, generated resentment in the other dissident camps, and Akwot and Gai Tut demanded that Ethiopian authorities would choose a clear leader among the Sudanese rebels. Consequently a delegation of Sudanese dissidents led by Akwot Atem, which included Gai Tut, Garang, Oduho, and Kiir, met with Mesfin.[38]

Ethiopia aimed at merging the armed groups and exerting control over them. In order to encourage unity among the insurgents, Ethiopian regime conditioned its assistance to them along this logic. Mesfin demanded a written statement of the Sudanese dissidents' policy objectives, which Akwot, advocating secession, drafted. However Mesfin rejected it as inadequate, most importantly because Ethiopia felt it could not support secessionism.[39] Ethiopia's official stand adhered to the OAU Charter condemning external intervention in sovereign member states, but it also feared that supporting secessionist elements in Sudan would strengthen the ongoing separatist conflicts in its own peripheries.

Subsequently, the rebel leadership was instructed to draft another policy document. Upon the return from Gambella, where they had presented the first memorandum, Oduho persuaded Garang to select a group to write a new version to secure Ethiopian support for his faction.[40] This document submitted to the Ethiopian authorities was finally made public on 31 July 1983, becoming the founding manifesto for the Sudan People's Liberation Movement/Army (SPLM/A).[41] It confirmed Ethiopian support for Garang, giving him upper hand over the leaders of the other southern Sudanese insurgent factions.[42]

The key SPLM/A objective was revolution, and the construction of a socialist, secular, and unified "New Sudan" that would eradicate social injustice and inequality.[43] With this agenda, the SPLM/A sought to differ from the exclusively "southern" view of the former Anya Nya. The SPLM/A manifesto described the political problem in Sudan on center-periphery basis, with the state being dominated by a minority group over marginalized majority in the periphery. It was made explicit that the southern issue was an example of the systemic problem of the entire country and that a socialist revolution to form the "New Sudan" instead of secession was the only viable solution.[44]

The acceptance of the manifesto by Ethiopian authorities[45] made the SPLM/A the sole Sudanese anti-government organization recognized officially by a neighboring state. A rebel delegation meeting with the Ethiopian Prime Minister, Mengistu Haile Mariam, in Nazareth near Addis Ababa, was a sign of its official approval.[46] Thus, Garang adopting a socialist agenda had been successful in securing Ethiopian support,[47] and enabled him to claim the leadership of the rebel movement in the making. Essentially, the SPLM/A's objective became liberation of the marginalized areas (in the state periphery) by removing power from the narrow northern elite clique, and the establishment of an effective democratic state with inclusive political participation producing regionally and socially equitable distribution of resources and economic development.[48]

Yet, the SPLM/A manifesto generated controversy regarding the true objective of the struggle within the movement. While the leadership that followed Garang was publicly committed to the unity of Sudan, some senior members and many followers perceived unity only as a tactical recourse, believing that given the history of the political and armed struggle in the South a successful reconciliation with Khartoum in the context of one state was hardly possible.[49] Consequently, in the minds of many, secession remained the main goal or at least an option. At a minimum, this view boosted the SPLM/A's leverage in any negotiation with the government.

Formation of the SPLM/A and Factional Conflict

The founding of the SPLM/A had taken place before some elements of the rebel leadership had arrived to Ethiopia.[50] This led to the SPLM/A leadership being not clearly defined, and the secessionist leaders who competed for its leadership against Garang being suspicious of his attempt to claim supreme position by dealing with Ethiopians. This led Akwot, who was hoping to assume overall leadership of the rebels, to demand formation of a SPLM government in which leaders of each faction would play a role already prior to the rebel delegation's meeting with Ethiopian Prime Minister.[51] Pressured also by the other leaders, and still unsure of Ethiopian support, Garang initially yielded to the demand. Consequently, by convoking his supporters, Akwot secured initially the position of Chairman of the SPLM/A, while Gai Tut was made the Minister of Defense, Oduho the Minister of Foreign Affairs, Majier the Minister of Legal Affairs, and Garang the Commander-in-Chief.[52]

The wrangling for leadership heightened tensions between the main factions. In this situation Oduho, a senior politician aligned with Garang, advised that the leadership dispute should be resolved only after some concrete support from Ethiopia would be secured.[53] The other leaders took his advice, and the SPLM/A delegation met Mengistu who promised Ethiopian material and moral support to the movement because it was committed to unified Sudan and socialist objectives of social justice and political and economic equality. However, Mengistu also advised that Ethiopia would no longer tolerate separatist elements operating from its territory.[54] In addition, Mesfin pointed out that Garang would be his sole contact with the SPLM/A, especially regarding military support and logistics.[55] Next, Ethiopia transferred the rebel operations to Itang where Kerubino and Colonel William Nyuon had arrived to join Garang.[56] This strengthened Garang's constituency in terms of leadership and manpower. Ethiopia's support for Garang, and its warning against separatist elements in its territory, posed a direct threat to Akwot and Gai Tut who based the legitimacy of their leadership on the claim of secession and sought to prevent the strengthening of Garang's constituency.

After securing Ethiopian assistance, Garang was in charge of the most powerful group within the SPLM/A. However, he was also heavily influenced by Ethiopia,[57] which added fuel to the factional rift. The Ethiopians insisted that both the political and the armed wing of the movement should be united under a single leader, Garang, because it would allow better control, but this pitted the latter against Akwot and Gai Tut who claimed SPLM/A leadership based on seniority in the former Anya Nya.[58] In the growing contention an effort was made to negotiate on the leadership issue, but the situation escalated[59] into violent clashes in which the Ethiopian army intervened in support of Garang and forced the group formed by Akwot, Gai Tut, and

Chuol back to Sudan despite the existence of rumors that Akwot had accepted Garang's leadership.[60] The ensuing bloodshed also involved Nyuon's SPLM/A-Garang contingent ousting Gordon Kong's Anya Nya II group, the prior recipient of Ethiopian arms, from its base in Bilpam,[61] causing most of the remnants of Kong's faction to coalesce with Akwot and Gai Tut. Yet, there were also those Anya Nya II forces and refugees that disagreed with Akwot and joined Garang.[62]

It has been argued that the factional violence related to the leadership struggle was shaped by differences of ideology and objectives, rather than ethnic imperatives.[63] The evidence presented for this has it that there were members of both larger southern ethnic affiliations (Dinka and Nuer) in each main rebel faction's leadership,[64] although the leaders of Akwot-Gai Tut-Chuol group were primarily Nuer and in Garang's group mainly Dinka. However, importantly, the Anya Nya II's rank and file was predominantly Nuer, while Garang's faction was composed principally of the Dinka also from early on. Although this categorization might have relatively little significance at the level of leadership, it is important to note that the factional struggle within SPLM/A evolved to have a Dinka-Nuer ethnic element at the grassroots level,[65] which persisted and culminated into a bloody Dinka-Nuer conflict in the context of the insurgency in the 1990s.[66] Given the ethnic identity factor, Nuer and Dinka recruits were in many cases inclined to join a group to which they had ethnic ties despite the ideological objectives of their leadership. The Dinka-Nuer cleavage culminated into an attempt to weed out Nuer Anya Nya II sympathizers from the SPLM/A, and had repercussions on the civilian population of both groups which frequently became target of violence by "the other".[67] Overall, the evidence points to the relative fluidity of ethnic identity categories at the level of rebel leadership, including the capacity to forge meaningful inter-ethnic alliances, while the (re)construction and application of ethnic identities affecting the constituencies appears to have produced a more rigid and exclusive view on ethno-political identity with respect to "the other".

In July 1983 the SPLM/A leadership structure was formally completed and the organization of the rebel forces became a priority. Garang was the figurehead of the movement, the Chairman of the SPLM and Commander-in-Chief of the SPLA, and surrounded by his most loyal supporters from the earlier underground movement.[68] While by July 1983 the ranks of recruits for the guerrilla forces in Itang had reached thousands, including 2,500 defected soldiers of the absorbed forces and the approximately 500 remaining in Bahr al-Ghazal, making it difficult to wield together an effective force,[69] it was mainly the soldiers of battalions 104 and 105 together with some Anya

Nya II fighters that formed the foundation of the movement.[70] Some rudimentary political structures headed by Oduho and Majier Gai were also put in place, with political headquarters in London,[71] but these were soon suppressed by the military organization which led to the arrest and sidelining of the two prominent politicians.[72]

The southern population was affected by the deteriorating security situation. Members of various sectors of local groups joined the rebels or opted for other survival strategies in the increasingly insecure local context. The resumption of violence and deterioration of physical security forced most southerners to decide if to participate in the rebellion, armed activities, or opt for non-violent survival strategies, including internal displacement or becoming refugees. Many of those who first joined the rebellion did so due to insecurity and widespread grievances. They came among pastoralists, students, laborers, youth, women, peasants, and intelligentsia, while school pupils, teachers, students and office workers joined after Nimeiri's imposition of *shari'a* in September 1983.[73] Ostensibly, many rallied behind the SPLM/A not because of its socialist ideology, which was little known in most parts of the South, but because of animosity against the "Arab" government, and as a reaction to the marginalizing and excluding state policies that produced local insecurity and fear.[74] Strong motivational factors for some recruits to join were the ideas and views of "the South" as one region, access to a gun for defense against the regime supported militias, gaining respect and higher social standing, or economic advancement, and engaging in criminal activity.[75] While some youth saw themselves as defenders of the ancestral land, or joined in defense of their families, others used recruitment to maneuver within the space between the dominant actors, the state and the SPLA, in order to gain resources to invest in their own future, in essence to continue to reproduce the local culture by relying on family as the most durable institution during the conflict.[76] The "Arab" vs. "African" dichotomy used by the SPLM/A to legitimize the rebellion, conviction for liberation of the South, and forced conscription, also played a role in the recruitment,[77] but in some areas the SPLM/A's call to arms had little response.[78]

The SPLA recruitment was encouraged through propaganda. A major tool for this was radio SPLA, "The Voice of the Revolutionary Armed Struggle", established in Naru, near Addis Ababa, in 1983. It countered the regime's media propaganda about the armed struggle and promoted recruitment by targeting people of the marginalized peripheral regions of Sudan, encouraging the poor, dispossessed, and oppressed to join the movement.[79] Radio SPLA also served to transmit ideological propaganda of the movement.[80] While this elevated the scale of recruitment much higher than in the case of the Anya Nya, it also facilitated the defection of some members of the northern elite from the government side.[81]

The recruits were trained according to SPLM/A principles. Ethiopians helped to organize training for the movement, with able-bodied men being sorted out and sent to the Bonga Training Center near Gambella used previously to train Anya Nya II, while women, children, and the elderly were sent to refugee camps in Itang, Panyudo, Dima, and Gambella.[82] SPLM/A training camps, characterized by strict discipline and training conditions in which many suffered and large numbers died, were set up in various locations,[83] while the recruits were taught socialist principles, following the example of Ethiopia, and forced through a process of indoctrination.[84] With an intent to build an effective military machinery, the training aimed to overcome ethnic, sectional, geographic, and professional differences, and canalize the anger of the recruits towards the "Arab" as the categorical "other", while installing a belief in superiority on the battlefield.[85] The process of indoctrination probably resulted in higher awareness among the troops about the political objectives of the movement than had been the case previously during the Anya Nya insurgency, but it often had physically and psychologically damaging effect. It also deliberately reinforced the "African" vs. "Arab" identity cleavage.

Furthermore, the SPLA military force was organized in divisions under area commands as a mass guerrilla movement.[86] This was strategically different from favoring relatively small rebel units that had been the case during Anya Nya insurgency. Critics claim that this resulted in premature conventionalization of the war and massive casualties because the SPLA fought in several fronts (against the Anya Nya II remnants, militias, and the army), and because of low quality of training of the SPLM/A relative to the army. The organization also suffered from desertions, low administrative capacity in the liberated areas, indiscipline, attacks on civilians, looting of property, and forced conscription that at times pushed migration away from the SPLM/A areas and encouraged local collaboration with the Sudanese government.[87]

Finally, the early SPLM/A leadership suffered from deep personal animosities[88] which resulted in fear of attempts to change the leadership. As a result, in order to minimize the possibility of being overthrown, Garang surrounded himself with loyal individuals, and systematically excluded some Nuer from the highest positions, while engaging in persecution of a selection of politicians and intellectuals.[89] The potential threat of plots was countered by orienting animosities towards the perceived enemies and teaching basic Marxist ideas, which to an extent elevated the SPLA's coherence but tied it further to its Ethiopian patron.[90]

Escalation of the Conflict

In September 1983 Nimeiri had announced that Islamic law, *shari'a*, would guide all legislation and judicial practices. Having been under pressure by the Muslim Brothers[91] threatening to stage a pro-*shari'a* demonstration, Nimeiri had swiftly decreed the Islamic law.[92] Openly supported and heavily influenced by Turabi, who was pushing for immediate implementation of the *shari'a*, Nimeiri feared that agreeing to Islamic law would strengthen him further, and thus replaced Turabi with Awad al-Jid Muhammad Ahmad as the Attorney General prior to announcing the decree.[93] Although this move was aimed at curbing Turabi's power, it did not undermine his political prominence that already rivaled that of Nimeiri.[94]

Reaction to the declaration of Islamic law was mixed.[95] To regain political legitimacy by attempting to elevate status as a religious leader in the regional context of rising Islamism, Nimeiri began to deliver speeches, and claimed to punish anyone who would stage a strike despite the economic malaise because it would obstruct the cause of God (*Allah*) for Sudan.[96] While Nimeiri engaged in these efforts to maintain power, the weakening of the state and the emergence of Muslim Brothers increasingly undermined his position.

The implementation of the Islamic law, in planning of which Turabi's role had been essential,[97] raised uproar in southern Sudan. While it affected directly southerners residing in northern Sudan, who also suffered from forced evictions (*kasha*),[98] in southern Sudan it was interpreted as an all-out attack on southern cultures, traditions, and lifestyle.[99] Another major reason for the southern leadership to condemn the Islamicization of national legislation was that many in the southern elite felt antagonism towards Turabi, perceiving him as the main instigator of the troubles during the early 1980s, which resulted in further support for the rebellion even among some Equatorian leaders who had been initially against it.[100] In this way, the imposition of Islamic law became a unifying force in the South since it generated another incentive for growing numbers of southerners to take refuge together, or join rebel training camps in Ethiopia. In these circumstances Christian organizations increased their activity as a uniting counterforce against Islamicization.[101]

Political developments of early 1980s led to a general sentiment in southern Sudan that the "Arab" threat from the North had returned. For instance, the declaration of Islamic laws generated ill-feeling particularly in Juba.[102] Giving many southerners perceivably genuine reasons to join the armed struggle against the "Arab domination",[103] opposition was formed in Equatoria leading to an increasing number of rebel recruits.[104] The Islamic law and forced expulsion from the North were deemed to exclude southerners from full citizenship on cultural (e.g. language, religion, and customs) grounds.

As a result, southern politicians sought to prevent the imposition of Islamic law. In June 1984 Alier and Lagu drafted a joint petition personally addressed to Nimeiri in which they asserted that "The South wanted a recognition and acceptance to simple objective and vital facts, namely the existence of diversity of cultures, historical differences and economic social backwardness of the South".[105] However in its response to the southern demands, Khartoum capitalized on the newly imposed territorial political order by pointing out that the three newly formed southern regional administrations had no authority to question its decisions.[106] The regime also announced repeatedly that *shari'a* would not affect Christians or southern Sudan.[107] Although this may have been an effort to neutralize grievances based on politicization of religion, it was incoherent with the state policies and failed to convince the majority of southerners experiencing the end of regional autonomy and expecting full imposition of *shari'a*.

The Islamicization was also extended to national economy. In an attempt to avoid responsibility for the economic malaise, Nimeiri announced implementation of *zakat* as a tax system[108] and described the core of Sudanese economy as successful because it helped the poor and attracted investment. However, in reality, the Islamic economic reforms deepened the economic malaise.[109] Consequently, in December 1984 the banking system was fully Islamicized contrary to recommendations of Nimeiri's financial advisors, which benefited the Muslim Brothers who gained control over it. Thus, the strategy of politicization and instrumentalization of religion facilitated the Muslim Brothers' ascent to economic and political power.

The deteriorating economic conditions[110] led to bailout attempts and adjustment measures.[111] Financial aid was channeled to Sudan, export-led strategies applied, and the currency devalued, which heightened discontent among urban dwellers accustomed to purchase imported goods that were now more expensive. However, the economic measures were unsuccessful in part because corruption[112] was the norm, with heavy implication of the high level officials. After the mushrooming of government departments coincided with the lack of resources, the system of political patronage reached a critical point and public administrations stopped functioning.[113] Sudan was on the brink of a bankruptcy, the rising cost of living, devaluations, and overall inflation infuriating common people who staged demonstrations and riots. They blamed the regime and international financial institutions; the World Bank having pushed the austerity measures and the IMF having canceled its standby credit to Sudan.[114] External support that Nimeiri's regime had largely relied on was coming to an end.

Meanwhile, the factional fighting within the SPLM/A had shifted from Ethiopia to southern Sudanese territory. Some of the opponents of Garang worked against the movement by targeting its recruits.[115] In response, the SPLA began attacking their constituencies, killing many Nuer civilians, razing towns, destroying grain harvests, and looting livestock.[116] This soon evolved into SPLM/A's campaign to neutralize the remaining Anya Nya II groups in the South by co-opting some and confronting others with Ethiopian support.[117]

In response to the insurgency, the regime sought to exploit ethnic animosities in the South to build a counterinsurgency campaign.[118] In addition, Nimeiri used religion[119] as a tool to rally for war in northern territories, and particularly among the Baggara groups in the North-South borderlands. Specifically, a proclamation of *jihad* (against the southerners) was linked to the hidden agenda of the Islamists, and circulated among members of the "friendly forces" (Muslim militias) and northern soldiers to defend the political *status quo* against the revolutionary rebels designated as "the other".[120] The regime created government militias in the South and the transitional zone, which led to sections of some groups neighboring the Dinka to take arms against them.[121] Part of this strategy was to neutralize and displace civilians particularly in the transitional area, to free resource-rich land for exploitation, and in this way hinder SPLM/A support and recruitment,[122] but it was also applied in areas such as Equatoria.[123] For instance, after the Bor mutiny, the Governor of Equatoria, Peter Cirillo, admitted openly that he facilitated arms deliveries from the regime to the Mundari militias for self-defense and to protect Juba from the SPLA.[124] This turned Equatoria into a terrain for activities of various armed groups and escalating violence. Thus, fomenting ethnic and religious differences, and seeking to mobilize groups for violent action along those distinctions, featured prominently in the regime's counterinsurgency strategy, as it attempted to keep the war from spreading from the southern periphery to the north-central heartland.

The militia activity and propaganda campaign provoked violent responses among the Dinka. Along with the Anya Nya II activity, they boosted SPLM/A's recruitment[125] and operations against communities of the groups aligned with the regime.[126] In addition, the destructiveness of traditional conflicts was heightened by the introduction of automatic weapons, as well as external manipulation and assistance. The fall of Amin in Uganda, the SPLM/A rebellion, and regime interventions all contributed to the proliferation of small arms and the rapid deterioration of conditions in southern Sudan.

In this situation, Gai Tut's faction converted into a regime militia.[127] Yet, the Akwot-Gai Tut-Chuol group continued torn between confrontation and seeking rapprochement with Garang. In early 1984, Gai Tut had made contacts with Garang ostensibly to reconcile, but was killed between March and May near Ethiopian border by Kerubino's *Jamus* SPLA battalion.[128] This frustrated the reconciliation attempt because Chuol, who claimed the leadership of Gai Tut's forces, became involved with the regime.[129]

By 1984, apart from the attempt to destabilize the SPLM/A, Nimeiri had become interested in supporting Chuol's forces. This would allow the regime to answer Sudan's creditors' and Chevron's demands to develop the oilfields in Bentiu by protecting the commencing oil extraction activities. Consequently, Nimeiri initiated negotiations with Chuol with the result that the latter, to adhere to the regime's request to become a government militia in exchange for assistance, separated his command from the SPLM/A and changed the name of his forces back to Anya Nya II. Chuol claimed spiritual powers and dressed in a traditional manner to legitimize leadership over his constituency, and began operations in Waat-Nasir area and around Zeraf River with Khartoum's military and financial support channeled through regime-appointed Governor of Upper Nile, Daniel Kuot Matthews.[130] Gai Tut's death alienated the Anya Nya II aligned Nuer further from Garang's SPLM/A.[131] Although Atem appointed Chuol as Gai Tut's successor, and he had also been appointed as Minister of Defense and Commander-in-Chief of the group, the two disagreed. Frustrated by Atem's overall leadership and his unwillingness to collaborate with Nimeiri to obtain badly needed supplies, Chuol murdered Atem in August 1984 and assumed the leadership.[132] He then converted the force into a government supported militia.

Subsequently, Chuol's strengthened group engaged in anti-SPLA operations,[133] and the government portrayed him as the main voice speaking for the rebels in southern Sudan.[134] Nimeiri used this to convince Chevron and other interested parties by exposing the agreement with Chuol, whose forces he called "a faction of the SPLA", while ordering Koat Chatim, Commissioner of Unity Province (the main oil extraction area), to negotiate with the local Anya Nya II to reach an agreement to secure petroleum operations.[135] In this way, by using militias in the South because of its own inability to secure the oil territory, the ailing regime sought to channel resources from the state periphery to the center to rejuvenate its finances and maintain its hold on power.

Thus, Nimeiri continued the policy to generate and capitalize on ethnopolitical divisions in southern Sudan. By appointing a handful of southern individuals along ethnic lines to redundant posts in the government, he sought to obscure northern elite's political domination and the structural social and regional inequality,[136] while supporting the ethnic militias in the South. Nimeiri intended to (re)construct and reinforce a perception of Dinka-Nuer ethnic conflict by allowing exclusively Nuer recruitment to the Anya Nya II, although by now the Nuer formed part of both main rebel groups.[137] It can be therefore asserted that the armed struggle was never inherently ethnic, but took place in the context of political situation in which the regime portrayed the SPLM/A as a separatist Dinka movement despite its inter-ethnic nature.[138] This was not completely unfounded, however, because the highest positions in Garang's SPLM/A tended to be occupied by individuals from the different sub-sections of the Dinka.

Finally, although the regime's policy of enlisting militias to counter the SPLM/A was somewhat successful in parts of Equatoria, it did not work in the majority of Bahr al-Ghazal. Despite James Tembura, in his new capacity as Governor of Equatoria, being able to summon sections of Toposa and Mundari as government militias in Equatoria, Governor Lawrence Wol Wol experienced recruitment difficulties in Bahr al-Ghazal where the majority Dinka expressed anti-government sentiments. As a result, Wol worked to overcome Fertit opposition intellectuals, including Clement Mboro, and mobilized narrow sectors of Fertit as a militia to raid Dinka in 1986-7 in Wau.[139]

Consolidation of the SPLM/A

After having eliminated the most immediate Anya Nya II threat during the first half of 1984, the SPLA prepared more extensive military campaign.[140] By this time, Ethiopian and Libyan logistical and material support, and recruits starting to graduate from the training camps,[141] enabled it to launch major guerrilla operations.[142] The material and manpower prerequisites in place, the SPLM/A launched an offensive in southern Sudan by first attacking police and army posts, mirroring the Anya Nya strategy of the early 1960s.[143] In November 1984 it initiated major operations that targeted Chevron's oil[144] and CCI's Jonglei Canal[145] operations, in order to undermine the regime's extraction of southern oil and water resources, as well as river transport used for army supply.[146] The attacks were also aimed at depriving the regime of oil income, while Nimeiri was engaged in negotiations with Sudan's creditors for financial resources to save the regime. The targets had been carefully selected due to their propaganda value since the SPLM/A leadership was aware of Nimeiri's close collaboration with the U.S. when it singled out the American Chevron as a symbol of exploitation of southern Sudan.[147] By the end of 1984 the SPLA had captured Boma and Yirol, which disrupted the regime's commercial activity in Bahr al-Ghazal and Upper Nile,[148] and the following year it conquered most of rural southern Sudan.[149]

The SPLA conquest led to the collapse of the already weak, and in many parts hardly present, central government's local administrations in southern Sudan. The major government-held towns aside, the civil administration was replaced by the dominance of insurgent groups and militias. In SPLM/A controlled areas, rebel military administration and related economic order was imposed. This did not necessarily improve environmental or human conditions because many SPLA commanders extracted natural resources for self-enrichment similarly to the armed groups during the 1970s.[150] Gradually the escalation of war and deteriorating security situation also pushed people from their homes, and displacement emerged as a strategy by the warring parties to assert territorial control, capture humanitarian aid, and relocate the focal points of the conflict.[151] Incidents of slave capturing and trade also emerged in the context of the conflict,[152] which became particularly controversial given the history of slavery in Sudan. The general northern attitudes of superiority towards the southerners persisted, rendering the use of cheap labor of the displaced for physically demanding and other non-desirable jobs in the northern provinces.

The escalating violence therefore reshaped southern social structure. The persisting insecurity and proliferation of small arms resulted in militarization of society, affecting social values and institutions such as the extended family, belief systems, and cultural practices, while also resulting in the loss of languages and sentiments undermining self-esteem and self-confidence.[153] The violence also undermined the functioning of the traditional social networks, which forced people to search for social relationships outside their traditional group boundaries. In many cases prolonged uncertainty, fear, and violence bound identities tighter around ethnicity and religion, favoring the tendency for "tribalist" group mobilization and enforcing religion, largely Christianity or Islam, as an important part of individual identities.

Initially the SPLA sought to govern newly acquired territory through military administration, while it tended to treat local civilian populations in such areas as conquered peoples.[154] Although the SPLA tried to present itself as the liberator and the protector of southern Sudan, there was first little emphasis on political administration and provision of social services in its militarized organization that remained largely dependent on external resources.[155] In 1984, the SPLM/A built the first administrative structures in the conquered areas in Bahr al-Ghazal. It also encouraged the defeated local militias to join its ranks, and adopted a dominant role in settling local conflicts and disputes.[156] The new military/civil structures of provisional administration were imposed,[157] and enforced by military battalions that formed part of their internal structures. Meanwhile the civil penal code was replaced by army disciplinary law, and local legal system developed by merging the general penal and procedural codes with customary law.[158]

In the course of 1984 Garang's SPLM/A constituency had established itself as the main armed group in the South. It initiated an offensive that led to heavy clashes in Jekau and Malwal Gahoth in eastern Upper Nile, resulting in the siege of Nasir, one of the largest towns in the South. Although this caused many SPLA casualties, its power had grown to the extent that Chuol's Anya Nya II could no longer hold back the movement. The SPLM/A had thus reached its early military objectives of forming a cohesive organization, capturing territory, and consolidating control over the conquered areas.[159]

On 2 March 1984, in response to growing opposition to his regime in the northern provinces and the escalating rebellion in the South, Nimeiri made an attempt for reconciliation.[160] In a speech on the 12th anniversary of the Addis Ababa Agreement, Nimeiri pledged that all Sudanese would benefit from development projects without discrimination and pleaded "general amnesty" to "all those who carry weapons in southern Sudan . . . [if they] . . . return to their units and villages".[161] Garang responded to Nimeiri the following day. He defined the SPLM/A objectives and outlined its grievances and goals.[162] Among other issues, Garang emphasized Islam and its politicization and instrumentalization which had consumed the regime and featured strongly in its counterinsurgency campaign. This appealed to many southerners since religious differences had not been a significant source of dispute within the South even between its local armed groups.[163] Therefore, the use of religion could be seen principally as a method of social control by the northern governing elites through which exclusionary identity construction leading to socially, ethnically, and regionally defined marginalization could be canalized.

Although Khartoum's external credibility and support was decreasing, the regime drew some assistance from its North African Arab neighbors. For instance, despite Libya's initial siding with the SPLM/A, pan-Arabists in Tripoli and elsewhere perceived it as a threat. This was because the SPLM/A taking power in Khartoum would have undermined the machinations of leaders, such as Qadhafi, actively supporting the consolidation Arab culture and Islam in Sub-Saharan Africa. As a result, the strengthening of the Arabized elite controlled state in Sudan was deemed important, despite Libya's support to the SPLM/A to destabilize Nimeiri whose alliance with the U.S. Tripoli detested. Egypt, for instance, with an intimate historical and cultural connection with sections of the northern Sudanese elites, found supporting Sudan's government vital to its own interests, which included safeguarding the flow of the Nile water. Yet, the persisting Arab support to the government became increasingly perceived in the South as oriented against the "Africans", as it had been during the earlier Anya Nya insurgency.[164]

In response to the escalating violence, the regime succumbed into deeper reliance on the U.S. assistance. Khartoum condemned the SPLM/A as a Communist organization due to its socialist agenda and its links to Ethiopia, which Washington found easy to accept. In fact, this rhetoric matched the Reagan Administration's strategic confrontation with the Soviet Union in the geo-political competition in the Horn of Africa and Middle East, and Nimeiri used it deliberately to extravert American moral and material support.

However, the reliance primarily on the U.S. and Egypt for support was not enough to strengthen the regime. Internal challenges of eroding legitimacy in northern Sudan, and the war and loss of territorial control in the South, had weakened it significantly. In these circumstances, Nimeiri grew increasingly desperate and resorted to a two-pronged strategy to maintain power. First, from late 1984 onwards, he called for negotiations with the SPLM/A several times. This was in part due to American pressure because Washington had become wary of the Islamist radicalization, and had realized the conflict's detrimental effect on its geo-political interests and aspirations to extract Sudanese oil. Attempting to establish confidence and to diffuse Western pressure, Nimeiri lifted the state of emergency on 29 September 1984, repealed the 1983 order that had divided the South, and halted the Islamic *ad hoc* courts that had been set up after the implementation of *shari'a* in September 1983.[165] On 19 November 1984 in Malakal, he extended an offer to "all brothers" in the South to engage in dialogue, which he later repeated several times, but the SPLM/A rejected these pleas.[166] In the following month Nimeiri visited Nairobi and convinced Clement Mboro to help in an initiative for peace, but this failed due to Lagu's intransigence and led to a failed attempt by Nimeiri to bribe Garang with financial and political rewards.[167] Aware of Khartoum's weakness, the SPLM/A responded to Nimeiri's pleas in January 1985 by stating that it would stop the war only "when Numayri's system [had] all been dismantled and thrown into history's dustbin".[168]

Second, Nimeiri sought to counter the deteriorating economic conditions and political instability through repression. In this situation, Nimeiri turned against his allies, the Muslim Brothers, by imprisoning their leadership in March 1985 and charging them of planning to overthrow the regime.[169] In the South, however, the regime continued to support militias and other anti-Garang groups that were unable to stop the SPLA advance. This resulted in mass killings, destruction of villages, looting, and kidnappings, and in the case of Baggara militias also in cases of enslaving Nilotics, which all contributed to a famine that broke out in the area in 1986-7.[170] The regime and its petroleum-interested allies[171] also encouraged militias to cause displacement away from the oil-rich areas.

Finally, however, Nimeiri's repressive strategy was neither sufficient to quell popular demonstrations nor to stop the SPLA advance. The demonstrations in northern Sudan continued and generated increasing instability. In the South, by mid-1984, the SPLM/A controlled the area east of the White Nile, and in December 1984 it launched a new military campaign that paved way for the conquest of most rural southern Sudan and several towns in the following year.[172] Faced with this situation, Nimeiri visited Washington in early April 1985. He sought to obtain more U.S. support by renouncing Islamism and submitting to an IMF economic austerity program.[173] Yet, during his absence, army officers with links to the northern opposition parties, particularly the Umma, staged a coup, and finally brought down the regime on 6 April 1985.[174] Nimeiri's narrowly based rule that had functioned through extraversion, clientelist patronage, and corruption, had finally come to an end.

Conclusion

The collapse of Nimeiri regime was due to the combination of a number of factors. According to Holt and Daly, it was caused by " . . . an unprecedented combination of foreign pressure, economic disaster, famine, civil war, popular disgust, and the overweening self-confidence of a ruler who had come to despise his own people".[175] Indeed, the factors leading to the regime's downfall included the overall economic deterioration (the external debt having risen from US$300 million to US$9 billion during Nimeiri's tenure), political Islamism that had undermined both the economic and political stability of the regime, and the intensifying southern insurgency which required resources and prevented oil extraction and the finishing of the Jonglei Canal for increasing irrigation for agricultural production.[176]

After the overthrow of the regime, a provisional military government was establishment to oversee the transition back to civilian rule. The Transitional Military Council received external assistance from Arab states, and particularly Libya, which shifted its support from the SPLM/A to the traditional northern political forces, principally the Umma and the new regime.[177] The external resources consolidated the new government despite the war in southern Sudan, and ensured the continuity of the northern "Arab-Muslim" elite controlled state. The state continued to serve the interests of the governing northern elite faction and north-central Sudan, while continuing to marginalize peripheries above all in the war-torn southern Sudan.

Endnotes

1   According to Madut-Arop (2006: 44), in a secret meeting a number of mutinies were planned with a prior full alert of all absorbed battalions, but particularly involving battalions 104 in Ayod-Waat-Akobo, 105 in Bor-Pibor-Pochalla, 110 in Aweil, 111 in Rumbek, 116 in Juba, and 117 in Torit-Kapoeta. A plan was also made to take Juba, Malakal, and Wau by surprise.

2   In early 1983 a telegram was sent to Garang to plan the groundwork for the rebellion with the excuse that his non-existent brother was ill in Malakal. When in Malakal, Garang received updated information about the security situation. He was briefed on Anya Nya II activities, and Chagai Atem and Chuol were assigned to meet Gordon Kong, a commander of the most powerful Anya Nya II group based in Bilpam, to convince him to support the rebels upon the outbreak of mutinies. See Madut-Arop (2006: 45). According to Alier (1990: 254), after having been rejected from army employment in the aftermath of the Anya Nya rebellion due to deficient eyesight, and after his job as laborer for the Department of Education had been suspended due to the end of post-war resettlement funds, Kong had moved to Ethiopia to his extended family and joined the Anya Nya II.

3   Chan and Zuor (2006: 24).

4   Collins (2008: 139). The move was possibly a response to the killing of 12 Arab merchants in Ariath in December 1982. It almost triggered a mutiny by Bol Madut, an officer in Battalion 110, who defected and began recruiting for an Anya Nya II faction in Tonj area. In December 1982, the general army head-quarters had already arranged the transfer of Battalion 110 in Aweil to El-Fash-er in Darfur despite complaints and resistance, but this was allegedly facilitated by collusion of one of its former commanders, Albino Akol Akol, who had been a leader of a cell in the underground movement. See Madut-Arop (2006: 45, 65-6) and Collins (2008: 139).

5   Allegedly, the quarrel over Battalion 105 soldiers' pay surfaced in the context of Kerubino's and Nyuon's relationship with the commanding officer of the first infantry division in the southern region, General Siddig al-Banna. The latter used the two officers to amass personal wealth for himself through their activities against the Anya Nya II, during which their troops looted money, gold, cattle, and wildlife goods. See Nyaba (2000: 29) and Chan and Zuor (2006: 40). Alier (1990: 243) and Madut-Arop (2006: 45) have argued that the situation emerged because Kerubino and Nyuon had been granted liberties, among other things to use funds of their units as they preferred, including Ker-ubino's misappropriation of financing, requests of increased funds, and manip-ulation of other administrative issues. See also Nyaba (2000: 29, 31). Nyaba (2000: 31) has also pointed out that in the process of insurgency formation "The uprisings were triggered off by a volatile political situation, emanating from the general crisis of the regime. Furthermore, those who ignited the fire in Bor were those very close to the army leadership in Southern Region – Major General Saddiq el Bana, a very close relative of General Nimeiri".

6   See Alier (1990: 243) and Madut-Arop (2006: 45). Kulusika (1998: 104) and Johnson (2003: 61-2) note that Kerubino, the commander of garrison in Po-challa, had become suspected of misallocation and embezzlement of funds, which made him wary of the possibility that the regime would discover the underground plan.

7   Kerubino formed part of the underground movement and had turned down orders in January 1983 for the Battalion 105 to be disarmed and transferred to North amidst of prevailing discontent, suspicion, and indiscipline among the troops. See Awur (1988: 87), Johnson and Prunier (1993: 124), Nyaba (2000: 29), and Johnson (2003: 61). These sentiments were generated largely by the deteriorating political climate in the South. The troops refused the orders for a number of reasons. These included the consideration that according to the Addis Ababa Agreement they were to serve in the South only, fear of being disarmed or sent to Iraq to join an existing Sudanese contingent fighting Iran, and that they would have to leave the cattle and cultivations they had in Bor. See Johnson and Prunier (1993: 124) and Johnson (2003: 61). Turner (1998: 205) adds that it was customary for the absorbed Anya Nya to supplement their low army salary, between US$10 and US$45 monthly, through farming and cattle-raising, and that many had developed local family and community ties, all of which made relocating them elsewhere problematic.

8   According to Alier (1990: 243) and Madut-Arop (2006: 45-6), he claimed that salaries and allowances were correct, while the soldiers were growing restless and circulating rumors about imminence of war.

9   See Johnson (2003: 62) and Madut-Arop (2006: 46, 47). This policy resulted in a garrison mutiny in Wangkay 160km west of Bentiu, which resulted in the killing of the commanding officer and a troop defection to the local Anya Nya II group. The army unit sent after the soldiers was ambushed, while around the same time Anya Nya II assaulted police posts in Warrap near Tonj and Ganylid near Rumbek. Also another southern garrison in Raja, Bahr al-Ghazal, declined to move to el-Fasher, rebelled, and fled to the bush. See Turner (1998: 205).

10   Assertion based on an interview with a mid-ranking SPLM/A official. As part of the preparations for the mutiny, Kerubino had visited Anya Nya II camps in 1982 prior to moving to Bor and used his personal relationship with al-Banna to justify the shuttling between Juba and Bor for weeks without interference to secure food, logistics, and other supplies for his troops for the rainy season. See Collins (1982: 140) and Madut-Arop (2006: 46, 47).

11   He expressed concerns about security in Bor and threatened Jonglei politicians that they would be held responsible if the soldiers continued to disobey orders, but the southern politicians responded that responsibility for the armed forces corresponded to Nimeiri. See Madut-Arop (2006: 48-9).

12   According to Madut-Arop (2006: 49), it consisted of the Vice-President of the HEC, Dhol Acuil Aleu, as the Chair, and the Minister of Education, Philip Obang, General James Loro, Brigadier Musaad Nueri, Major Arok Thon Arok,

and members of parliament, Abdel Latif Chaul Lom, Elijah Malok, Michael Wal Duany, Samuel Gai Tut, and Akwot Atem.

13   The committee met the disgruntled soldiers in Bor and sought to appease them by announcing that their transfer to the north was revoked, that their salaries of April would be paid immediately, and that their dismissed fellow soldiers would be rehired. However, al-Banna refused to pay the salaries despite the committee's suggestion that the army headquarters should pay the demanded sum.

14   See Alier (1990: 243) and Madut-Arop (2006: 48).

15   This delegation included, among others, two former commissioners of Jonglei Province, Jonathan Malwal Leek and Nathaniel Anaai Kur, the SSU Province Secretary Bul Bior, representative of the Bor Chamber of Commerce, and Abdullahi Elias, a northerner living in Bor. See Alier (1990: 243, 245), Madut-Arop (2006: 46, 48, 49), and Collins (2008: 139).

16   See Alier (1990: 245).

17   Nyaba (2000: 29).

18   These included Elijah Malok, Martin Majer Gai, and Thon Arok, latter of which had formed part of the committee of investigation on the salary dispute.

19   He visited al-Banna to assess the army's view of the situation. Garang, who had ostensibly been sent by Nimeiri to resolve the situation, planned to travel to Bor to take over the leadership of the mutineers from Kerubino, but wanted to make sure that al-Banna did not suspect his intentions. After hearing about Garang's intention to go to Bor where he had an agricultural project, al-Banna warned him about the mutinous Battalion 105 in Bor, Pibor, and Pochalla, but agreed on Garang's petition to fetch his family which the latter had deliberately sent to Wangulei. See Heritage (1987a: 4), Johnson (2003: 61), Madut-Arop (2006: 47, 49-50), and Collins (2008: 141-2).

20   During the first week of May, Kerubino had arrived from Pochalla to Bor and assumed the leadership of the discontent troops from Bullen Alier, confiscating 250 bags of sorghum (*dura*) from the market for the soldiers and taking over and fortifying the town. He had also forbidden a northern army company traveling by a steamer to dock at Bor on 8 May, and lynched an alleged government soldier sent from Juba to gather information prior to a planned army assault to retake the town. See Alier (1990: 243), Madut-Arop (2006: 46-51), and Collins (2008: 139).

21   See Heritage (1987a: 4) and Madut-Arop (2006: 51).

22   The threats were the main attacking force from Juba and an army company in Langbar. The Battalion 105 commanded by Kerubino and Bullen Alier received the attack from Juba, and Garang went to immobilize the troops in Langbar by presenting himself in his power as a senior to the leading officer there. He convinced the commander of Langbar not to attack Bor by arguing for the necessity of protecting Alier, who stayed in the area seeking to shield the workers of French CCI who were building the Jonglei Canal, and Dutch engineers of the DeGroot Company building a Malakal-Juba road. See Heritage

362

(1987a: 4), Alier (1990: 245), and Madut-Arop (2006: 52-3).

23   The forces led by Lietenant Colonel Dominic Kassiano launched an offensive on Bor and Pibor, during which the deputy commander of the army force was killed and Kerubino wounded, which led Bullen Alier to assume the leadership of the mutineers. See Alier (1990: 245), Madut-Arop (2006: 52), and Akol (2007: 169).

24   See Alier (1990: 245), Madut-Arop (2006: 53), and Collins (2008: 139). Depending on the source consulted, the exact date of withdrawal was either 17 May (Alier, 1990: 245; Collins, 2008: 139) or 18 May (Madut-Arop, 2006: 53). Reportedly, both sides suffered five casualties apart from the killed army officer. See Alier (1990: 245).

25   See Alier (1990: 245), Johnson and Prunier (1993: 124), Madut-Arop (2006: 53), and Collins (2008: 139).

26   For instance in Ayod, the local garrison under Major William Nyuon Bany of Battalion 104 intercepted an army convoy from Malakal, offering it accommodation but killing its officers when asleep and executing its northern soldiers. See Alier (1990: 245), Prunier and Johnson (1993: 125), Kulusika (1998: 104), and Madut-Arop (2006: 53). In succession, Nyuon and his force emptied the Ayod armory and headed towards the Ethiopian border where a concentration point for the rebels had been fixed. When the army attacked Ayod on 6 June 1983, battalions 105 and 104 had already withdrawn to Ethiopia in collaboration with the local Anya Nya II. See Johnson (1998: 58), Chan and Zuor (2006: 40), and Madut-Arop (2006: 53-4). Moreover, in Waat a company revolted, attacked the town garrison with local Anya Nya II, and left for the bush.

27   See Johnson and Prunier (1993: 124-5), Johnson (2003: 62), and Collins (2008: 142, 143).

28   Niblock (1987: 288).

29   Johnson and Prunier (1993: 125), Madut-Arop (2006: 54), and Collins (2008: 139-40).

30   Madut-Arop (2006: 54).

31   See Alier (1990: 245-7) and Nyaba (2000: 29, 31).

32   According to Nyaba (2000: 31-4), the reasons for this included greed for power, aspirations for material wealth, and personalized authority imposed through the military (e.g. to prevent Abyei and Kurmuk referendums), as well as ambiguity and obscurity of political stand weighing towards Islamicization and promotion of Arab culture.

33   Gai Tut, a Lou Nuer, and Akwot, a Twic Dinka, were both associated with the NAM, prominent in the Anya Nya II group led by Akwot, friends, and former ministers under Lagu in 1978-80. Similarly to Chuol, a Lake Nuer, they all formed the leadership of the residual Anya Nya II groups and were secessionists following the Anya Nya tradition. See Alier (1990: 251), Johnson and Prunier (1993: 125), Madut-Arop (2006: 67), and Collins (2008: 143). This is partly why they kept their own units separated from Garang who in the end committed to fight for just, but united Sudan. Another reason for this was that

their separatist followers ensured their prominent position and secured their strategic and military importance.

34 Gai Tut proceeded to contact other Anya Nya II groups. Faced with lack of external material and financial support, he turned to Kong's group in Bilpam with the hope to assert himself as the leader of the Anya Nya II before the leadership of the underground officers' movement would arrive. He suggested to Kong that he, Akwot, and Chuol would form the political leadership of united Anya Nya II groups, while Kong would remain in charge of the military operations under its political wing. However, despite an ethnic link (Nuer), Kong had been the sole leader of the Anya Nya II at Bilpam for years, had amassed wealth through his activities in Sudan in terms of money, cattle, and wives, and refused the offer knowing that the leadership of the underground movement was about to arrive and that Ethiopians would not permit the change of leadership of the Anya Nya II in Bilpam lightly. His rejection points to his personal interests and possible earlier contacts with Garang and the underground movement. See Alier (1990: 251) and Madut-Arop (2006: 67-8).

35 Lieutenant Colonel Francis Ngor and Salva Kiir had sought to invade Malakal before withdrawing to Ethiopia to join Garang. Madut-Arop (2006: 68) notes that soon after a group of Abyei Liberation Front members, led by their deputy and general secretary Chol Deng Alak and Deng Alor Kuol, respectively, who had been jailed in January-May 1983, also arrived in Adura. Yet another group that added to the support for Garang was the Southern Sudan Liberation Front of Pagan Amum Okiech, Nyachigag Nyachiluk, Lado Lokurnyang, and Oyai Deng Ajak, a movement of leftist southern university students established in Boma Plateau and seeking to conduct guerrilla. It had engaged in kidnapping foreign personnel for ransom, and received Ethiopian training and Libyan financing, but the group dissolved itself to join Garang. This was allegedly due to rumors about an envisaged socialist orientation of the SPLM/A in the making which adhered to its own ideology. See Turner (1998: 205), Nyaba (2000: 27-8), and Madut-Arop (2006: 68-9).

36 Initially they arrived to Bukteng and Bilpam to join the prior Nuer elements from Bentiu and Nasir, the Dinka of Jonglei and Lakes, and the students from Rumbek Senior Secondary School who had made the bulk of the rebel organizations hosted in Ethiopia prior to the Bor mutiny. See Johnson and Prunier (1993: 131), and Chan and Zuor (2006: 53).

37 Ethiopian army arranged Garang to be transported to Gambella for a meeting to discuss the Sudanese rebel organization in the making. See Madut-Arop (2006: 69). It is likely that this meeting was crucial in sealing strong Ethiopian support for Garang, as Mesfin and consequently Mengistu were convinced to assist a non-secessionist rebel movement.

38 See Madut-Arop (2006: 69).

39 Akwot wrote a statement that the Sudanese dissidents as a whole would adhere to a socialist ideology and to liberate the South, making it an independent political entity. For this, it was stated, external financial and logistical support

would be required. The draft document sought to prevent a rift between secessionists and those favoring unity of Sudan. See Madut-Arop (2006: 69-70).

40   Garang put forward three conditions: 1) the rebellion was to be for new united
Sudan that would bring equality and justice to the marginalized regions; 2)
the rebels were to advance a socialist ruling system; 3) and that the different
armed groups in the South, including the Anya Nya II, would be regrouped and
trained prior to launching a war. See Madut-Arop (2006: 70). He is said to have
used an earlier manifesto of the underground movement to define the three
main rebel objectives. It was clear that any attempt of overthrowing Nimeiri required Ethiopian patronage, conditioned by a commitment to maintain a united
Sudan. See Johnson (2003: 63), Madut-Arop (2006: 70), and Collins (2008:
142). As such, this not only provides evidence of existence of a conspiracy,
but also hints to prior contacts of the underground movement with Ethiopia,
which exerted influence over it as soon as its leadership crossed to Ethiopia and
sought to organize a rebel movement.

41   Consisting of 11 chapters, the manifesto defined the "problem of southern Sudan" as part of a more general relationship between the center and the back-
ward and underdeveloped peripheral regions of the country, neglected in terms
of economic development by the colonial and post-colonial ruling cliques. It
pointed out that the current rulers come from the most developed central region
of the country, and seek to establish their identity, defined according to their
Arab culture, language, and Islam, as the national identity. See SPLM/A Manifesto (1983: 1-2). The stated aims of the movement, with Marxist overtones
adopted from Ethiopia, included a radical restructuring of political power by
ending the exclusive rule of northern elite groups, an end to uneven development between the center and the periphery, the fight against racism embodied
in regime policies such as the *kasha*, elimination of tribalism, sectionalism, and
provincialism, and socioeconomic transformation of Sudan into an industrial
and agro-industrial society. In Chapter 3 the manifesto described the causes
of the Anya Nya insurgency, highlighting educational differences and job distribution as the main reasons for the rebellion, and stating that the SPLM/A
would fight for other objectives. The specific grievances stated in Chapters 4-6
of the manifesto were: 1) Khartoum's interference in the selection of southern
leaders; 2) Jonglei Canal; 3) the act of dissolving southern political institutions
unconstitutionally; 4) intention to tamper with southern boundaries; 5) the issue of oil refinery and consequent plans of exporting the petroleum unrefined;
6) deliberate exclusion of the South from socioeconomic development; 7) the
integration treaty and defense agreement with Egypt; 8) the re-division; 9) lack
of adequate livelihood provided for the former Anya Nya; 10) the incomplete
integration of the Anya Nya; and 11) the policy of transferring southern troops
to the North. The last three chapters defined the movement's enemies, such as
northern political parties, fundamentalists, southern Sudanese elites, and Anya
Nya members (secessionists), together with any external force interested in Sudanese resources. It stated that SPLM/A's friends were the workers, peasants,

students, intellectuals, and progressive elements in the army. See SPLM/A Manifesto (1983) and Chan and Zuor (2006: 57-8).

42   In fact, the Ethiopian desire to locate Garang, meet with him prior to any other leader, subsequent inclination to accept his statement of objectives drafted according to its policy, and later support for Garang in the fight between the factions of the dissident groups confirm this assumption.

43   This was to be modeled according to the U.S. federal form governance system of which Garang was familiar. In it regional governments would have autonomous status and be overseen by a central government committed to fight against racism and ethnic divisions. See Garang (1987: 19-21, 26-7) and Collins (2008: 141, 143). Sudan was to become socialist and secular, free of family rule and ethnic, religious, and regional discrimination, with a democratic redistribution of political power and national resources. See Heritage (1987b: 4), Kok (1992: 104), and Rogier (2005: 18).

44   This created a rift between the SPLM/A leadership and some followers who fought for the cause thinking that the movement was secessionist. There was hope that some northern political factions might embrace the manifesto, but it failed to convince northerners, including the SCP, to join any southern led political formation as had been the case since independence. See Chan and Zuor (2006: 58-9, 60).

45   It should be noted that despite the overwhelming influence of Ethiopia in the making of the SPLM/A, or claims about absence of ideology, the movement had socialist aims. The concept of New Sudan, focusing on eradicating uneven development, inequality, and injustice between the center and the marginalized periphery, could be considered a justice-seeking ideology in itself, despite its resemblance to Marxism. As a result, justice-seeking in the sense spelled out in the SPLM Manifesto, or the posterior refinement of the concept of New Sudan, focuses on the restructuring of political and economic power adapted to the case of Sudan and can be considered as the ideological foundation for the rebel movement.

46   Madut-Arop (2006: 71, 72).

47   Yohannes (1997: 323). However, it is unclear to what extent Ethiopia pushed the SPLM/A to draft a socialist revolutionary manifesto. It is likely that Addis Ababa conditioned its support for the armed opposition according to specific policy goals which the latter accepted.

48   However, Garang admitted in 1987 that he would encourage a mixed, not exclusively socialist, economy in liberated areas. See Heritage (1987c: 4).

49   Rogier (2005: 19). One of these leaders was Salva Kiir, who as a staunch supporter of Garang and also known for his secessionist inclinations.

50   For instance, Kerubino was still hospitalized and Nyuon was ostensibly extracting wealth, principally cattle and money, in the midst of the deteriorating conditions in the South. The latter appears to have been motivated by self-enrichment, without clear interest in forming part of the constituting of the SPLM/A despite being a senior officer. See Madut-Arop (2006: 71).

51 According to Madut-Arop (2006: 71), Akwot had been one of the leading members of the Anya Nya.

52 See Johnson (1993: 125) and Madut-Arop (2006: 71).

53 Madut-Arop (2006: 72).

54 Madut-Arop (2006: 72).

55 Ethiopians had decided to support the younger and well-educated Garang because out of the senior officers he appeared ideologically the most committed to the unity of Sudan, commanded large and effective force, held diverse experience, and drew support from some prominent exiled southern politicians opposed to the separatist agenda of Akwot, Gai Tut, and Chuol. See Alier (1990: 252), Johnson and Prunier (1993: 125, 126), Johnson (2003: 65), and Madut-Arop (2006: 72).

56 Kerubino and Nyuon had rejected Akwot's proclamation of leadership of the movement in part because they had previously fought his Anya Nya II group in Sudan as counterinsurgency forces during the Addis Ababa period. This elevated tension between the two increasingly polarized main factions, one led by Garang and other by Akwot and Gai Tut. See Johnson and Prunier (1993: 126), Johnson (2003: 65), and Madut-Arop (2006: 73).

57 Akol (2001: 25).

58 Johnson and Prunier (1993: 125, 126) and Johnson (2003: 65).

59 A committee of leaders including Oduho, Majer Gai, Chol Deng Alak, Kiir, Francis Ngor Makiech, Garjiek, Ganyjuj, Chuol, Kerubino, Nyuon, and Elijah Jon had been formed, but during its proceedings Kerubino shot Marial Alek, a young refugee and recruit, whom he alleged of insubordination of a senior officer. Akwot and Gai Tut accused Garang's faction of conspiracy, Gai Tut stating that Garang had been manipulated by Ethiopian Marxist ideology, and Akwot alleging that Garang had been sent by Khartoum and was supported by Ethiopia to take over their struggle. See Alier (1990: 252) and Madut-Arop (2006: 73). Chan and Zuor (2006: 42, 43) assert that while the Akwot-Gai Tut-Chuol faction remained adamant about Akwot's claim to rebel leadership, Garang's group initially preferred Gai Tut over Akwot due to Kerubino's and Nyuon's animosity towards the latter.

60 See Johnson and Prunier (1993: 126), Nyaba (2000: 38), and Chan and Zuor (2006: 43).

61 Nyaba (2000: 37-8), Johnson and Prunier (1993: 126), Johnson (2003: 65-6), and Madut-Arop (2006: 74).

62 Johnson and Prunier (1993: 126) and Madut-Arop (2006: 74).

63 It has been alleged that the fighting that ensued was principally motivated by the leadership struggle and ideological orientation of the movement. This is true at least at the highest level to the extent that despite the multiple candidates for the leadership, the two groups differed ideologically, the Akwot-Gai Tut-Chuol group representing secession according to the separatist tradition, and Garang's group emphasizing a socialist political agenda in the southern armed struggle while appealing for unity. See Johnson and Prunier (1993: 126),

Johnson (2003: 65), and Chan and Zuor (2006: 43-4). It should be remembered though that this agenda, attributed to Garang's ability to maneuver for securing Ethiopian support, was influenced, if not altogether dictated, by Ethiopia that aspired to destabilize Nimeiri.

64 For this argument, see Alier (1990: 251) and Chan and Zuor (2006: 42-3). For instance, Garang and Akwot were both Twic Dinka from the Bor district in Kongor, Gai Tut a Nuer, Kerubino a Dinka, and Chuol and Nyuon originally Dinka but had become ethnically Nuer through naturalization.

65 See Nyaba (2000: 49, 67).

66 Jok and Hutchinson (1999: 125-45) and Johnson (2003: 111-26).

67 See Nyaba (2000: 49, 50-1).

68 Chan and Zuor (2006: 73) and Madut-Arop (2006: 74) note that Kerubino became Garang's deputy in both functions, Nyuon was appointed as Chief of Staff of security operations, Kiir became his deputy, and Nyachigag Nyachiluk became an alternative member of the SPLM/A political-military High Command. Whereas some, such as Stephen Madut Baak, joined the SPLM/A ranks from exile, many prominent military members of the underground movement, among them Andrew Makur Thaou, Albino Akol Akol, Alison Manani Magaya, Peter Cirillo, Robert Mayuk Deng, and Scopas Juma, remained in Sudan during this period. See Madut-Arop (2006: 75). According to Garang, other early members of the High Command included Daniel Awet, Bona Baang, Riek Machar, Lam Akol, James Wani Igga, Kuol Manyang, and John Kulang. See Heritage (1987b: 4). Major Arok Thon also became part of the High Command, but was disenchanted upon his late arrival in July in Itang because his former junior officer, Captain Kiir, had been promoted over him despite Arok having been the only one in the SPLA trained in an officer school in Sudan. See Nyaba (2000: 30, 44-5), and Chan and Zuor (2006: 73). There was also friction between Arok and Garang because Arok challenged Garang's social prominence in their native Bor County and had extensive combat experience relative to Garang's almost none. In fact, Garang relied on more experienced field commanders Kerubino, Nyuon, and Kiir for military operations. See Johnson (2003: 66), and Chan and Zuor (2006: 73). Ostensibly, this is why Garang favored them in the SPLM/A organization.

69 According to Chan and Zuor (2006: 41), "With the arrival of large number of South Sudanese in Itang, and the two battalions brought by Major William Nyuon from Ayod and Major Kiruno from Bor, the question became what to do next with all these different armies and groups of people?"

70 See Nyaba (2000: 38), Johnson (2003: 62), and Collins (2008: 139-40).

71 Turner (1998: 206).

72 Chan and Zuor (2006: 67, 72-4) state that it became an authoritarian and highly hierarchical military organization, with no plurality in the decision-making, allegedly resulting in unilateral views of policy and human rights violations by individual leaders. These "big men" exercised extensive powers over their soldiers, operations, and jurisdictions. See also Nyaba (2000: 45).

73 Nyaba (2000: 27) and Chan and Zuor (2006: 53). In November 1983 the Sudanese parliament ratified the bills proposed by the three-man committee, imposing measures for Islamicization in two brief sessions without any debate. Along
with the Sources of Judicial Decisions Act, which allowed the implementation
of the Islamic law, a completely new Penal Code, a Code of Criminal Proce-
dure, the Civil Procedures Act, and the Civil Transactions Act were promulgated, enabling the Islamicization of penalties of criminal conduct. See Warburg
(2003: 156). Among other measures alcoholic beverages were destroyed and
became prohibited, and a spree of corporal punishments was carried out, including televised and radio-transmitted lashings, executions, and amputations.
When forced to follow his first public amputation along with other government
officials, Turabi, the mastermind of the Islamic laws, fainted. The day Nimeiri
announced the Islamic laws he also released 13,000 detainees from the Kobar
prison, and claimed that he forgave them as Muhammad had done to the people
of Mecca after they persecuted him (Collins, 2006: 146).

74 Nyaba (2000: 26-7).

75 de Waal (1993: 154), Nyaba (2000: 26, 42, 43, 72), and Chan and Zuor (2006:
45, 46).

76 See Leonardi (2007: 391-412).

77 The role of conviction to "fight for your rights", imposition of *shari'a*, and
acquisition of arms for criminal activity were also motivating factors.

78 According to Johnson and Prunier (1993: 127), for instance in Aweil, a pro-di-
visionist Dinka area, in Nuer areas of Upper Nile, and in most of Equatoria, the
response was less enthusiastic. Many among Equatorian youth were hesitant
to join the SPLM/A because it was viewed mainly as a Dinka movement rather than expression of legitimate fight against "Arab" domination. Also, later
SPLA atrocities against some Equatorians undermined recruitment. See Kulusika (1998: 110), Madut-Arop (2006: 37), and Collins (2008: 143).

79 The programming included grandiose news about battles fought against the
army, portraying even the ones lost as victories, as well as political commentary, war songs, and poems, beamed in Arabic, English, and local languages.
See Nyaba (2000: 27, 53) and Madut-Arop (2006: 92, 103).

80 Khartoum portrayed the movement as Marxist in part to convince the U.S. and
ensure the delivery of military support. On the other hand, Garang articulated
the movement's socialist agenda on the SPLA radio, and concentrated on hardship experienced by the people, including the collapsing economy, shortage of
basic food items, rising unemployment, deterioration of social services, repression by the SSO, inflation, and devaluation of currency. See Johnson (2003:
64) and Collins (2008: 143). This increasing use of radio as an anti-regime
propaganda tool by armed southern opposition followed Sadiq al-Mahdi's an-
ti-Nimeiri radio campaign during the 1970s from Ethiopia.

81 These included Khalil Osman, a textile entrepreneur, and Mansour Khalid, the
former Minister of Foreign Affairs. See Nyaba (2000: 27) and Madut-Arop
(2006: 92).

82   See Chan and Zuor (2006: 44-5) and Madut-Arop (2006: 77).
83   These were established in Bonga, Bilpam, Buma, Dima, and Itang, along with some mobile training units.
84   It has been further alleged that SPLA Combat Intelligence, a security unit modeled according to Nimeiri's SSO, was established to suppress any other political opinion. An immediate obedience in concentration camp-like conditions during the 3-4 months of training was also imposed, as the recruits were indoctrinated to worship the rebel leaders as parent-like figures and forced to vow personal allegiance to Garang. In the process, many were brutalized and dehumanized, generating an environment of distrust, fear, indifference, demoralization, and apathy, which translated into SPLA atrocities against civilians in the field. See Nyaba (2000: 38, 52-3), Chan and Zuor (2006: 44-7), and Collins (2008: 143).
85   Allegedly, this treatment of recruits was motivated by the claim that they had to be prepared for any situation, and the belief that the movement would never run out of human resources. Garang, Kerubino, Nyuon, Kiir, and Arok, were portrayed as mystic, almost god-like, leaders to who the soldiers dedicated moral songs and poems, and who became the figureheads of the "cause" to the extent that many rebels felt they were fighting personally for these leaders. See Nyaba (2000: 38, 44-5), and Chan and Zuor (2006: 46-8, 73).
86   The SPLA ostracized its soldiers by seeking to deploy them to areas different from their origin. While some Nuer recruits refused to leave their home areas for training in Ethiopia, most Dinka recruits were deployed away from their home areas. See Johnson (2003: 69-70).The *Jamus* (Buffalo) Battalion led by Kerubino became the first larger unit to finish training in 1983, followed by the *Jarad* or *Kaoryom* (Locust) Division in 1984 and Timsah and Tiger battalions led by Thon Arok and Kiir. See Chan and Zuor (2006: 45) and Madut-Arop (2006: 77, 111). While Nyaba (2000: 38) claims that the latter division was mainly composed of recruited university students and office workers, Madut-Arop (2006: 77) asserts that it was an amalgamation of defected soldiers from various areas of southern Sudan. The *Kaoryom* Division consisted of five branches: The Central Command under Garang included four battalions (Bilpam, Elephant, Hippo, and Lion); the Southern Axis under Thon Arok in southern Upper Nile consisted of three battalions (*Zindia*, Cobra, and Lightning); the Northern Axis under Ngor Makiech operated in the Southern Blue Nile; the Eastern Axis under Nyachiluk operated in Boma Plateau and east of Bor and consisted of the Scorpion Battalion; and the Western Axis under Makur Aleiou and Amum operated in Bahr al-Ghazal and consisted of the Rhino Battalion that early on overran Aluakluak and Tonj, took Yirol, and surrounded Wau and Rumbek. See Nyaba (2000: 54) and Madut-Arop (2006: 111-2).
87   See Nyaba (2000: 58-60) and Madut-Arop (2006: 114-5) on these allegations.
88   For instance, inspired by competition for positions under Garang's leadership, Kerubino developed a dislike of Ngor Makiech who he was able to keep out of the High Command Council despite the latter's long involvement in the under-

ground movement and seniority in military rank to Kerubino. Moreover, while some secretly sympathized with the movement, many others, such as General Akol Akol, declined to join. See Madut-Arop (2006: 84-6).

89   Allegedly, such persecution initially alienated politicians from the militarized movement particularly after the death of Benjamin Bol Akok, a respected individual, by the Ethiopian security in August 1984. His death possibly also involved SPLM/A leaders. See Madut-Arop (2006: 81-3).

90   See Nyaba (2000: 50-5).

91   In November 1982, Islamic militants had held a conference organized by the Society of Islamic Thought and Civilization in Khartoum. In the conference Turabi asserted that the priority for the Muslim Brothers was the Islamicization of Sudan, transforming Sudanese law to comply with *shari'a*, which was reflected in the conference resolutions calling for social reforms preceding gradual implementation of the Islamic law. This led to the SSU national congress, now widely influenced by the Muslim Brothers, to favor the "Islamic path" in June 1983, opening a path for legislation according to Islamic principles that began in the two following months when Nimeiri appointed a three-lawyer committee to Islamize Sudan's legal system. This committee proceeded to draft bills mostly according to Turabi's suggestions, which were to be promulgated as part of Provisional Republican Orders. See Warburg (2003: 155-6, 186-7).

92   This was despite Sadig al-Mahdi telling Nimeiri that proclaiming *shari'a* would not remedy societal ills rising from poverty. Nimeiri also declared himself *Imam* to assert power over the Muslim Brothers by further politicizing religion, simultaneously establishing a symbolic relationship with his senior officials that mirrored the leadership of the *Mahdiyya*. See Johnson (2003: 56) and Collins (2008: 146).

93   See Warburg (2003: 155, 187).

94   Some have even suggested that Turabi had become the "real" president behind Nimeiri.

95   According to Collins (2008: 147), it was characterized by disappointment in urban areas where people enjoyed activities prohibited by the *shari'a*, apprehension about following inquisition, utter disappointment and fear in the South where Nimeiri lost last of his support, and joy in some rural areas in which it was seen to purify religion and wash the urban areas from their heresy.

96   Collins (2008: 147). For instance in a speech on 22 September 1984 in International Islamic Conference in Khartoum, he defended the policy by stating that Islamic state guided by *shari'a* was necessary for creating a crimeless and just society prescribed by Islam. This was echoed by Turabi who claimed it being part of educational process, while other leaders, including Sadiq and the leadership of Republican Brothers, denounced it in various parts of the country. See Alier (1990: 230) and Warburg (2003: 156, 163). According to Nimeiri, since the adoption of the Islamic law crime had declined 40%, although this was hardly the case since due to economic and social deterioration, and the

previous liberation of criminals as a gesture of goodwill, armed robbery had reached unprecedented levels. See Sidahmed (1997: 139), and Warburg (2003: 158).

97   Turabi had advised Nimeiri to divide the South to prevent southern opposition to the implementation of *shari'a*. Johnson (2003: 57) and Warburg (2003: 167).

98   Homes of many southerners in Khartoum were bulldozed to motivate them to leave the capital, and many were transported to the South forcibly.

99   Awur (1988: 100).

100 Malwal (1985: 35), Alier (1990: 230), and Warburg (2003: 167). In fact, according to Awur (1988: 98),

> Within short time there was a spirit of reconciliation, confession and repentence [sic] among Southerners. Opposition to Sharia became united, and rallies, public prayers, demonstrations, and such like, were conducted in the big towns like Juba. Many pamphlets were circulated denouncing Sharia and calling all Southerners to put aside their differences and unite.

101 Their statements encouraged people consumed with fear to resort to Christianity to confront the perceived threat of Islamic law. Thus, strengthening of Christian beliefs in the South was reactionary, and directly linked to politicization of Islam by the regime and its manipulation of religion as a political tool. Such response as part of reactionary pattern of southern politics overall is partly related to the Christian legacy and colonial isolation of southern Sudan. See Nyaba (2000: 32). For instance, Catholic Bishops of the Sudan reminded that "Conflicts begin where there are injustices, discrimination and oppression; when people are asking for their rights and they are denied to them", while adding that " . . . where the Sharia Law conflicts with Christian tradition and customs, and violates the freedom of conscience, you must stand for Christ" (CBS, 1984: 4, 7). They also stated that " . . . you are Africans and Christians, and therefore have the right to live in this country according to your culture, customs and religion. These are your rights, not only as citizens but human beings" (CBS, 1984: 13).

102 A week after the declaration, a demonstration against Islamic laws was staged in Juba, and students, particularly in Equatoria, agitated people to join the armed liberation struggle. See Madut-Arop (2006: 57). This feeling was expressed and propelled by a number of local publications. One of them, *Memorandum*, written by Equatorian students and spread widely in Juba in July 1984 explained that

> Inspired by the struggle of our great fore-fathers and by the aspirations of the Southern Sudanese people for total freedom from enslavement, exploitation and subjugation of all kinds, we the students of Equatoria in the Universities and higher institutions shall proceed to pronounce in words and deeds our view-point and judgement [sic] on the prevailing strained political situation . . . (quoted in Awur, 1988: 100).

103 Nyaba (2000: 72) and Madut-Arop (2006: 57).

104   A pamphlet dated on 8 July 1984 was circulated in Juba, which described the goals of the South Sudan People's Liberation Movement (SSPLM), indicating that armed struggle was necessary for the total liberation of the people of southern Sudan (Awur, 1988: 101). Although SSPLM lost its momentum, in part because it was secessionist, and in part because it was an Equatorian initiative imitating the Anya Nya, it encouraged some Equatorians to take up arms against the regime. An added factor to this was the disappointment of Tembura's leadership, favoring the Azande along ethnic lines, that led to a gradual stream of Lotuko recruits to the SPLM/A, while some Acholi, Lokoya, and Moru also joined the movement from eastern Equatoria. See Johnson and Prunier (1993: 133).

105   Awur (1988: 103).

106   Alier (1990: 230-1).

107   See Awur (1988: 104-5). Initially, it had almost no effect on the local life in the South, where for instance local bars continued to function normally.

108   According to Warburg (2003: 156, 158-9), this had decreed income tax at 2.5%, with a similar tax also applicable to non-Muslims, and corporate tax at 10%. Both The Civil Transactions Act and Zakat and Taxation Act undermined the economy because the former ended limited liability and interest charges in intra-Sudanese transactions and the latter undermined the previous tax base.

109   Warburg (2003: 156) and Collins (2008: 149).

110   According to Niblock (1987: 288-9), these coincided with a drought in 1984-5 in the Sahelian Sudan, affecting principally the populations of Darfur, Kordofan, and eastern Sudan. However, it also had an impact in the conflict in the South as it pushed Baggara southwards to look for pasture for their cattle in Dinka territories.

111   For instance, the U.S. diverted US$18 million from the USAID to pay Sudan's debt arrears and pressured the IMF to accept a standby loan for Sudan in May 1984, but after a scandal of misappropriation of the funds the U.S. Congress ordered the donor countries not to pay off Sudan's debt. As a result, the U.S. and Saudi Arabia cancelled an initiative to pay US$25 million worth of Sudan's IMF fees. See Jendia (2002: 156). In June, the U.S. finally bowed to pay Sudan's arrears to the IMF, which led the IMF to release the first US$20 million of the standby loan. Despite this, Sudan's overall unsatisfactory financial performance and sluggishness to pay its debt arrears made the IMF consider expelling Sudan in January 1985. See Brown (1986: 487-11, 506).

112   According to Holt and Daly (2000: 178), apart from the state apparatus, the corruption had also adverse effect on the education system, medical care, and trade unions and professional associations.

113   Holt and Daly (2000: 178).

114   See Holt and Daly (2000: 178), Warburg (2003: 159), and Collins (2008: 153-4). While the Sudanese oriented their discontent towards the IMF and the World Bank, the government continued its collaboration with the international financial institutions until its Islamic economic system hindered foreign aid

and investments. In 1984, when the Islamic economy gained impetus, the regime announced that it would not need a regular budget, but that it would be issued on the basis of three-month periods until September, after which the fiscal year would respect the Islamic calendar. See Brown (1986: 498-501, 504) and Jendia (2002: 155). As a result, and because Islamic banking hindered the ability to control the money flow due to the abolition of interests and transaction costs, the IMF, which was about to approve standby financing for the government, experienced increasing difficulties to supervise the recovery program. See Khalid (1990: 327-8).

115 According to Johnson and Prunier (1993: 126), and Madut-Arop (2006: 77-8), after returning to Bukteng in Sudan, Gai Tut and Akwot engaged in recruitment and setting up roadblocks, harassing and killing principally Dinka recruits crossing through Upper Nile to Ethiopia to join Garang who they now perceived as their main threat. In this context, Akwot sought to persuade the recruits by claiming that he commanded the real SPLM/A which was secessionist. However, many of those captured escaped and arrived later to Ethiopia. One such concentration of recruits was a group from Aweil, consisting of over 10,000 individuals under the leadership of Lual Diing Wol, a former unity-minded member of the abolished People's Regional Assembly, who was later appointed as alternate commander in the SPLM/A High Command. During 1983-4, principally those recruits coming from Tonj, Aweil, Gogrial, and Abyei, and civilians on their way to Ethiopia, or moving with their cattle looking for pastures, were harassed or killed, while those going through Rumbek, Yirol, and Bor, avoiding main areas of Upper Nile, often made it to Ethiopia more safely. See Johnson and Prunier (1993: 127) and Madut-Arop (2006: 78-80).

116 Nyaba (2000: 49).

117 According to Johnson and Prunier (1993: 126), Garang pressured the Bukteng group and Gai Tut felt obliged to negotiate, which led him into a trap in Itang surrounded by Garang and the Ethiopians hoping to disarm him. However, Gai Tut and some of his troops were able to escape, capture weapons in Adura, and return to Sudan. In January 1984, the main SPLM/A with Ethiopian army support launched military operations against Gai Tut-Atem-Chuol-Kong forces and captured Bukteng, but suffered heavy losses attributed to the claim that some Nuer elements in the main SPLM/A allegedly sympathized with the Anya Nya II Nuer and turned against Garang's force. Meanwhile, Johnson (1998: 58) notes that a number of smaller Anya Nya II groups were absorbed into the rebel movement or became influenced by it, but unlike during the Anya Nya insurgency they were not allowed to operate independently.

118 For instance, according to Alier (1990: 252) and Johnson (2003: 69), the Gaajak, Jikany, and Lou Nuer suffered from the SPLM/A reprisals and began to kill individual SPLM/A soldiers and take their guns. In 1984, Nimeiri began to seek ways to encourage the Nuer against the Dinka by providing arms and financing, justifying this support by claiming that the SPLM/A was Dinka-dom-

inated and Communist organization. Encouraging ethnic conflict in the South by supplying militias enabled Nimeiri to portray the war as a local tribal conflict, which provided justification for strengthening the SSO, enforcing Islamism, and declaring a state of emergency in the South on 29 April 1984, while he accused the SPLM/A of being a Marxist and Leninist tool of Ethiopia and the Soviet Union. See Johnson and Prunier (1993: 128), Turner (1998: 206), Holt and Daly (2000: 179) and Madut-Arop (2006: 97, 100).

119 Khartoum exploited ethnic animosity in the propaganda emitted through Juba and Omdurman radio stations; seeking support from Western countries and Arab states, and embarking on a hate campaign that was also part of the Friday prayers in Three Towns. Nimeiri characterized the Dinka and the SPLM/A as poised to spread atheism and Communism in the Horn of Africa, and in his capacity as self-proclaimed *Imam* declared *jihad* against the rebel movement, while describing the military as army of God and promising paradise for soldiers killed in action. See e.g. Alier (1990: 252) and Madut-Arop (2006: 97, 98-9, 101).

120 Khalid (1990: 12), Kulusika (1998: 116), and Chan and Zuor (2006: 68).

121 During this period, according to de Waal (1993: 147), encouraging Baggara raids became part of regime's strategy. Among southern groups, apart from the Nuer (sections of which engaged in "tribalized" ethnic conflict against sectors of the Dinka), militias of the Murle, the Mundari, Equatorians, and Fertit were summoned to conduct raids against the Dinka. For instance, the Murle have a long history in cattle-raiding, targeting the Bor Dinka and Nuer communities in Ayod, while having been armed during the first insurgency by the government. The raiding activities of sections of the Murle in Akobo, Bor, and Waat continued throughout the 1970s almost every rainy season. See de Waal (1993: 154) and Johnson (2003: 68). They still take place today. After the Bor mutiny they became among the first regime supported militias, with arms provided to Ismail Konye, a Murle Chief and a former army officer active in Pibor, who alone organized eight raids in 1983. While the raids were aimed at civilian population (for settling old feuds and private gain), they devastated rural dwellers likely to support the SPLM/A, tying down SPLA units in the area, but also caused collateral damage to the Anya Nya II constituencies. See de Waal (1993: 154) and Johnson (2003: 68). Allegedly, according to Madut-Arop (2006: 105), in 1983 Nimeiri had convoked the governors of Bahr al-Ghazal, Equatoria, and Upper Nile, Lawrence Wol Wol, James Tembura, and Daniel Kuot Matthews, to summon counterinsurgency forces in their respective regions with generous government funding.

122 Rolandsen (2005: 45).

123 According to Johnson (2003: 67-8) and Madut-Arop (2006: 106), the regime sought to manipulate sectors of Equatorian groups against the Dinka. Some Equatorian politicians, including Lagu and Tembura, were consumed by the propaganda adhering to anti-Dinka sentiments to the extent that they supported an army assault on Bor, allowed the harassment of the remaining Dinka and Nuer in Juba, and permitted the backing by the Equatorian regional govern-

ment of the Toposa-organized long range raids to loot the Bor Dinka. While many prominent Equatorians denounced the regime's propaganda after experiencing its effects, some politicians, such as Francis Wajo, the Deputy Governor of Equatoria, exploited the rhetoric and convinced Gajuk Wurnyang Lupai, the Commissioner of Eastern Equatoria and Mundari leader, to agitate against the Dinka. See Madut-Arop (2006: 102).

124   According to de Waal (1993: 153-4) and Johnson (2003: 68), Kabora subgroup of the Mundari around Terekeka harbored animosity towards the Bor Dinka due to a long history of local conflict over grazing land that had escalated during floods in the 1960s and 1970s. Mundari militia gained strength particularly after December 1984 when a small Bor Dinka SPLA contingent looted, raped, and murdered Mundari after been received lavishly by the latter, causing many to flee to Juba and young men to enlist in an anti-SPLA militia for self-protection. See Kulusika (1998: 110), Nyaba (2000: 39-40) and Madut-Arop (2006: 106). However, while the Mundari militia oriented its activities largely against Dinka civilians, allegedly killing thousands and looting cattle, only some sections of Mundari communities were involved in these activities, and many of those married with Dinka remained less enthusiastic about taking arms against the latter. See Johnson (2003: 68) and Madut-Arop, (2006: 106).

125   According to Nyaba (2000: 26; 92) and Madut-Arop (2006: 102-3), many Dinka sought arms to protect their communities principally against the raiding parties, and the more educated cadres strengthened the SPLA officer corps by submitting themselves to training in Bonga, Gambella, where SPLM/A politico-military college was founded.

126   For instance, Johnson and Prunier (1993: 130) claim that the SPLM/A retaliated by burning Pibor, inhabited mainly by the Murle, in 1984, and turned its attention to the Mundari at Terekeka and Gemmeiza the following year.

127   The initiator of this relationship was Matthews, a Gaajak Nuer and Governor of Upper Nile. See Heritage (1987b: 4). The regime sustained propaganda campaign against the Dinka through Matthews, instrumentalizing the legacy of 19th century Dinka-Nuer hostility and portraying the Dinka as belligerent relative to the Nuer, while declaring that the SPLM/A was exclusively Dinka despite the movement also having a considerable Nuer element. See Johnson and Prunier (1993: 127), and Madut-Arop (2006: 107, 109). Matthews was a central figure in the creation of the regime's militia strategy of "friendly forces" in Upper Nile, and led the main components of the government-backed southern militias against the SPLM/A, arming and providing uniforms for the Nuer fighters that collaborated closely with the army. See Alier (1990: 254), Johnson and Prunier (1993: 128), and Nyaba (2000: 23). After finding out about the breach between Gai Tut and Garang, Matthews wrote a letter to Nimeiri appealing for resources to prevent the SPLA advance to Upper Nile. With these resources Matthews was able to influence the Anya Nya II leadership to the extent that by the beginning of 1984 the latter had allegedly abandoned its separatist agenda

in exchange for arms and financial resources. See Alier (1990: 252), Johnson (2003: 66) and Madut-Arop (2006: 107).

128 Nyaba (2000: 38), Madut-Arop (2006: 80), and Collins (2008: 143).

129 Alier (1990: 252-3) and Nyaba (2000: 38, 49). Apart from the attempt to destabilize the SPLM/A, by 1984 Nimeiri was interested in supporting Chuol's forces to protect the commencing oil extraction activities in Bentiu which were demanded by Chevron and Sudan's creditors. But, despite a number of protective military operations, the area remained insecure. As a result, Nimeiri initiated negotiations with Chuol, who, to differentiate himself from the SPLM/A and to adhere to the regime's demand to become a government militia in exchange for assistance, changed the name of his forces back to Anya Nya II. He claimed spiritual powers and dressed in a traditional manner to convince followers, and began operations in Waat-Nasir area and around Zeraf River with Khartoum's military and financial support that was channeled through Matthews. See Alier (1990: 252-3), de Waal (1993: 151-2), Madut-Arop (2006: 107), and Collins (2008. 143). According to Nyaba (2000: 49), Gai Tut's death, and possible Kerubino's denial of his proper burial, alienated the Anya Nya II-aligned Nuer further. Although Akwot in his authority appointed Chuol as Gai Tut's successor, the two disagreed. Frustrated by Atem's leadership, his unwillingness to collaborate with Nimeiri to obtain badly needed supplies, and despite having been appointed the Minister of Defense and Commander in Chief, Chuol murdered Akwot in August 1984 and assumed leadership. See Johnson and Prunier (1993: 127), Madut-Arop (2006: 81), and Collins (2008: 143). According to Madut-Arop (2006: 81), ethnic sentiment was strong in the murder of Atem as he " . . . was just executed as a Dinka, believed to have been sent by Garang in order to wreck the Nuer's movement from within". However, this could also have been an excuse for Chuol to justify his plan.

130 Alier (1990: 252-3), de Waal (1993: 151-2), Madut-Arop (2006: 107), and Collins (2008: 143).

131 Nyaba (2000: 49).

132 Johnson and Prunier (1993: 127), Madut-Arop (2006: 81), and Collins (2008: 143).

133 Regrouping the approximately 300 Anya Nya II troops loyal to him, Chuol set up his headquarters in Zeraf valley and cooperated with the Bul Nuer under Paulino Matiep's leadership. He sought to cut the SPLA supply lines, and harassed the recruits streaming from Bahr al-Ghazal, frustrating SPLA movements and causing considerable damage. See Johnson and Prunier (1993: 129, 131), Madut-Arop (2006: 108), and Collins (2008: 143).

134 According to Alier (1990: 253) and Madut-Arop (2006: 108-9, 117), in November, Chuol sought a political settlement with representatives of the regime, allegedly also meeting Nimeiri and proposing a solution to the southern problem through a confederation with two separate armies according to the SSLM suggestion in 1972. He also advocated replacement of Matthews, who was against a federal solution, with Peter Gatkwoth. However, rejecting the resur-

rection of an Addis Ababa type arrangement, such proposals were met with an outright rejection by the regime representatives who characterized the federal plan as worse than separation. Yet, since cooperation with Chuol was desirable the assistance was continued.

135 de Waal (1993: 152) and Madut-Arop (2006: 117).

136 Johnson and Prunier (1993: 128-9), and Kulusika (1998: 115).

137 Distinct sections of the Nuer were represented, including the Gaajak of Mai-wut, Mor Lou of Akobo, Lak and Thiang of Zeraf valley, and Bul from the west, along with the Jikany Nuer of which some were inclined to join Anya Nya II due to family ties and grievances against the SPLA. In contrast, sections of the Gun Nuer oriented towards the SPLA. See Johnson and Prunier (1993: 128-9) and Johnson (1998: 61).

138 While in the early days Garang faction's leadership was largely Dinka, the majority of low-ranking soldiers became Dinka only later after the movement had already become consolidated.

139 de Waal (1993: 153) and Madut-Arop (2006: 110).

140 According to Johnson (2003: 69), initially the rebel operations had consisted of small skirmishes conducted against the army near the Ethiopian border to cause damage, capture military hardware, and retreat.

141 See Yohannes (1997: 323), Chan and Zuor (2006: 50), and Madut-Arop (2006: 95, 97).

142 In 1984, SPLA armament came principally from Libya, but the SPLM/A also sought contacts and support from other Arab countries, such as South Yemen, Egypt, and Jordan. See Heritage (1987b: 4, 1987c: 4). Yohannes (1997: 323) and Madut-Arop (2006: 120) assert that the Libyan assistance terminated in the unsuccessful meeting for the unification of northern and southern dissident groups on 31 December 1984 in Tripoli.

143 See Johnson and Prunier (1993: 127-8, 131). Simultaneously military/recruitment expeditions, largely by the SPLA Rhino Battalion, were conducted to more far reaching areas in Aweil, Bor, Gogrial, Tonj, the Lakes districts, Bahr al-Ghazal, and Kajo-Keji, Equatoria, in June 1984. The objective was to obtain recruits from areas devastated by militia raids, and guide them to avoid Nuer areas in Upper Nile on their way to Ethiopia. Skirmishes against the army also took place, interrupting the railway connecting Aweil to northern Sudan. See Johnson and Prunier (1993: 133), Johnson (2003: 69), and Madut-Arop (2006: 87).

144 On 3 February 1984, an Anya Nya II remnant group assaulted a new Chevron base camp at Roba Kona, next to Bentiu, allegedly in collaboration with the SPLA, which had already made contacts with guerrilla groups in Aweil, Bentiu, and Southern Kordofan in early 1984 as part of its military/recruitment operations. In this surprise night attack, which took place despite repeated assertions by the Minister of Energy, Tuhami, that the army was able to protect the oil wells and Chevron personnel, three foreign employees were killed and

several wounded when the rebels shot into the barges used for housing. This triggered a confrontation between Chevron and Tuhami, Chevron eventually leaving Sudan having lost its US$1 billion investment, which led to the suspension of oil extraction and construction of the pipeline to Port Sudan. See Yohannes (1997: 323), Verney (1999: 14), ESPAC (2002: 34), Johnson (2003: 69), and Collins (2008: 144).

145 Garang staged military operations to suspend the excavation of the Jonglei Canal. His decision to target the canal was largely due to a controversy that arose in the Bor conference of the Jonglei Executive Organ, which included members of the Permanent Joint Technical Committee, representatives of international aid organizations, the Mefit-Baptie research team, and local Dinka leaders together with some SPLM/A officers. In the conference, which had taken place on 10 November 1983, local grievances had been expressed, along with SPLM/A warnings that the CCI should immediately stop the digging of the canal. Despite the warnings, the CCI had continued its operations and the SPLA had kidnapped seven French and two Pakistani workers. The CCI halted its activities until SPLM/A released the hostages, but resumed its operations in January 1984 which prompted Kerubino's SPLA *Jamus* Battalion to assault its camp in Sobat on 10 February 1984. The attack dispersed the army guards, and Kerubino took six hostages, telling the French director of the camp that the rebels would return after dark. Yet, a CCI steamer evacuated the workers to Malakal before nightfall, leaving the Sobat camp abandoned and the excavation of the Jonglei Canal suspended at mile 166. See Collins (2008: 144-5).

146 In February 1984 the SPLM/A admitted having attacked a Nile steamer, reportedly killing 150 passengers and successively blocking the river route from Malakal by sinking two barges. See Alier (1990: 261) and ESPAC (2002: 34).

147 For instance, there were no training schemes for southerners to work in the oil sector, while northerners were recruited, no jobs were created or financial contributions or development schemes were granted, and southern political leadership was excluded from petroleum management. See e.g. Alier (1990: 222), Kok (1992: 107), and Yohannes (1997: 322-3).

148 Majak (1997: 144) and Jendia (2002: 162-3, 165) note that soon after most economic ventures in the South closed down, barter trade between the Baggara and the Dinka in Bahr al-Ghazal was disrupted due to growing mutual animosity, and commercial freight between southern Sudan and Zaire, Uganda, and Kenya came to a halt.

149 Alier (1990: 262-3) and Nyaba (2000: 54).

150 During the autonomous period, various armed groups, some related to the national army, had engaged in spoliation of the southern natural environment. As a result, lucrative hunting of wild animals had involved government officials, soldiers, and others, intensifying in the 1980s when some northerners went to the South driven by the economic opportunity of the breakdown of centralized authority, while rebel leaders engaged in the same activity. For instance, private individuals who enriched themselves through such activities smuggled ivory to

East Africa from where it found its way to Asian markets despite the attempt of some southern authorities to prevent hunting. In addition, they amassed wealth from other resources in the insecure environment, such as tropical wood, gold, and cattle. See Majak (1997: 136, 140), Nyaba (2000: 29), Jendia (2002; 161-2), Chan and Zuor (2006: 40), and Madut-Arop (2006: 29, 71).

151 See e.g. Keen (1998, 2001) and Duffield (2001).

152 In the circumstances of insecurity and violence, the persisting perception by sectors of Arabized peoples of southerners as slaves allegedly manifested it-self in incidents of slave-capturing and trade. The Baggara militias engaged in capturing of individuals during their raids on Dinka villages in Bahr al-Ghazal. Ostensibly, there were incidents of southerners being sold in El Obeid and else-where in the northern markets, with some people allegedly being purchased to be taken to Libya and the Middle East. See Jendia (2002: 165). Still, these incidents were isolated and cannot be equated with the scale of the 19th century slave enterprise.

153 Buckley (1997: A22) and Jendia (2002: 164).

154 According to Chan and Zuor (2006: 48, 53-4), empowered by their guns, the SPLA soldiers tended to subjugate local people, at times rape women at gun-point, subject people to physical labor, force elders to obey them, conduct harsh punishments, and torture (at times leading to death), without respect of local cultures. While some of this behavior was due to indiscipline, punish-ments of the SPLA soldiers were scarce, although, for instance, according to the SPLM/A penal code of 1983 rape and looting were punishable by death. In fact, most cases against soldiers were resolved according to customary law, resulting in fines and other forms of compensation. This treatment provoked local opposition to the SPLA among some Nuer, Didinga, and Murle, although occasionally the penal code was applied to try SPLM/A personnel. See Kuol (1997: 12), Johnson (1998: 68-9), and Chan and Zuor (2006: 54).

155 Chan and Zuor (2006: 48).

156 Heritage (1987c: 4) and Kuol (1997: 33-42).

157 In this system, area commanders were in charge of district political-military high commands that held wide policy and executive powers. The district high commands included the district administrator, political officer, intelligence of-ficer, and the members of district councils. The district councils that provided education, judiciary, agriculture, medical, and veterinary services were under the district high commands. Below these were provincial, district, town, and village committees. Heritage (1987c: 4).

158 Chief's courts were maintained as the main institutions of local administration of justice, but the SPLM/A used its influence to interfere in the appointment of chiefs. SPLM/A zonal commanders carried the responsibility of overall admin-istration, aided by military/civil administrators supervising tax collection, but the chiefs maintained similar duties as during the British native administration system, their tasks including recruitment of labor and militias, collection of taxes, relief distribution, and dispute resolution according to customary law.

See Kuol (1997: 10) and Johnson (1998: 58, 66-7).

159 Turner (1998: 206-7) and Nyaba (2000: 58).

160 According to Turner (1998: 206), this followed Vice-President General Omer Muhammad al-Tayeb's public statement on 9 December 1983 that Ethiopia and Libya supported the SPLM/A, which had resulted in Egypt sending air and ground support units to Sudan.

161 ESPAC (2002: 34).

162 He pointed out how the northern riverine ruling elite, *awlad al-balad*, had divided and ruled other peoples of Sudan along ethnic, religious, and cultural lines, using "tribalism" and racist ideology. See Garang (1987: 19). Garang defined the objective of the SPLM/A to wage revolutionary armed struggle with political mass support to liberate Sudan "in which a few people had amassed great wealth at the expense of the majority", and to establish "a united Sudan under a socialist system that affords democratic and human rights to all nationalities and guarantees freedom to all religions, beliefs and outlooks". He continued by arguing that "This injustice has resulted in profound crises and distortions in our economy, politics, ethics and even religion which Nimeiri has perverted into an article of trade" (Garang, 1987: 19, 23). Garang also listed what he perceived as Sudan's major problems, including the fall in production, hyperinflation, deterioration of social services, institutionalization of corruption and bribery, constant fear of the SSO and *kasha*. He gave six main reasons for the war, including the dissolution of southern political institutions, integration treaty with Egypt, attempt to change boundaries, the oil and refinery issue, division of southern Sudan, and the intent to neutralize the absorbed ex-Anya Nya forces. Garang ended his speech by describing the first two SPLA military offensives of which the first one culminated in seven-day occupation of eastern Nasir in mid-December 1983, and the second consisted of an attack and destruction of Ayod, the CCI Camp, and a Nile steamer in Wathkei, while ending in the bombardment of Malakal on 22 February 1984. See Garang (1987: 19-22, 23-4) and Turner (1998: 206).

163 In fact, the SPLM/A has many Muslim constituents.

164 Kulusika (1998: 113).

165 Madut-Arop (2006: 118).

166 ESPAC (2002: 35).

167 He sent businessmen Adnan Khashoggi and Tiny Rowland to shuttle between Khartoum, Ethiopia, and Kenya, and offer Garang another Addis Ababa type arrangement, financial wealth, and the vice presidency. Later, Rowland turned against Khartoum and lent financial and logistical support to the SPLM/A. See Nyaba (2000: 65), Madut-Arop (2006: 118-9), and Akol (2007: 170).

168 ESPAC (2002: 35).

169 Allegedly, Nimeiri sought to reinvigorate Khartoum's relations with Washington, which had become increasingly undermined by the regime's Islamic orientation. See Holt and Daly (2000: 179).

170 Kulusika (1998: 105-6).

171 According to Abbink (2004: 7), at this time Chevron financed a Missiriya militia in southern Kordofan.

172 The early SPLA success owed in part to the superior combat experience of some of its troops, support of sections of southern civilians, terrain, and the army being demoralized and poorly equipped. See ESPAC (2002: 35), Niblock (1987: 288), Turner (1998: 207), and Madut-Arop (2006: 119).

173 According to Yohannes (1997: 324) and Jendia (2002: 155), this program would have removed subsidies for bread, gasoline, and sugar, and would have facilitated access to an IMF standby loan.

174 Yohannes (1997: 324).

175 Holt and Daly (2000: 178).

176 Heritage (1987c: 4), Henze (1991: 158), and Yohannes (1997: 323).

177 Johnson (1998: 60), Kulusika (1998: 112), and Turner (1998: 207).

Chapter X

Epilogue:
Understanding Insurgency Formation in Southern Sudan

Generally, insurgency formation is a complex process which combines historical continuities, social, political, and economic factors, and local, regional and international actors and forces. A multifaceted blend of these determinants, insurgency formation can only be comprehensively analyzed by conducting broad, inclusive, and interdisciplinary studies with an attempt to objectively evaluate its distinct dimensions.

This study has analyzed dynamics of the process of insurgency formation in the case of southern Sudan. It has taken up state marginalization as an overarching and holistic theoretical concept to highlight the role of elites and governance in Sudanese politics and in the formation of armed opposition. The analysis has sought to reach beyond the broad categorizations characterized by the historical literature, including "the North" and "the northerners" and "the South" and "the southerners", and the grossly simplified media images of the "Arab" and "African". These broad categories obscure the colonial responsibility, and how state- making and identities link with the processes of insurgency formation. They also fail to show the importance of elite agency and ability to mobilize followers for armed struggle.

In addition, this study of the two insurgencies in southern Sudan, the Anya Nya and SPLM/A rebellion, has demonstrated the significance of considering how governance and policies of state marginalization generate armed opposition. Moreover, the analysis has shown that insurgency formation in southern Sudan in the two occasions was not an isolated local or domestic process, but involved intersecting regional and international actors and forces which deeply influenced it. Thus, the study has shown that broad-based, refined, and in-depth analyses are necessary for more comprehensive understanding of the processes of insurgency formation in Sudan and Africa.

The analysis conducted in this study has highlighted the importance of state formation and construction manifested in political competition, strife, and conflict. It has shown that attitudes towards the state are shaped by the local context, including personal and community experiences and historical legacies. For instance, understanding the 19th century historical processes is essential for more comprehensive view of contemporary state and politics in Sudan. Indeed, taking into account historical factors and processes from the period of initial state formation is essential for explaining the emergence of a marginalizing political culture among the elites in Sudan. In this, the agency of particular elites which aspired to extend their legitimacy and authority through "imagined regionalism" is crucial, as is the historical relationship and experiences in southern Sudan with respect to the expansion of a particular type of state domination, incomplete incorporation, and marginalization.

Furthermore, this study has shed light on the processes of consolidation of socially and regionally based political and economic marginalization during the Anglo-Egyptian colonial period. It has sought to highlight the effects of the policy of isolation of southern Sudan, which ultimately resulted in the emergence of a "regional" elite whose political identity was to an extent shaped by the historical domination (e.g. slavery, social hierarchy, and violent extraction of resources) of southern Sudan. Similarly to its counterpart, the Arabized political elite in northern Sudan, this elite sought prominence in the southern provinces, and aspired to extend socially constructed southern "regional" identity in response to the history of northern domination and subjugation. This "regional" identity mixed local cultural attributes with those of the British colonizers, and promoted a contrasting political identity to that celebrated in northern Sudan.

From the analyses in chapters III and IV in this study it becomes apparent that the view of the state and nation promoted by the Arabized political elite in northern Sudan was based on a perception of superiority over southern Sudan as "the other". The latter was portrayed as socially, culturally, economically, and politically inferior. In contrast, a particular view of northern Sudan aspiring to extend its domination was instrumental in constructing a political vision and identity for "the South". In this way, the center of the state and its margins interacted and contributed to the nature of political organization and identities, which are constantly (re)constructed and (re)negotiated.

Chapter V of this study has pointed out the impact of the marginalizing state policies in the process of decolonization, which served as inspiration to the first insurgency in southern Sudan. It was shown how attitudes towards the state and its narrow governing elite, and local interpretations of specific events, rumors, and emotional factors, led to widespread fear of northern

"Arab" domination at the dawn of independence. This was particularly the case when the majority of the southern elite was excluded from higher level employment, political representation, and participation in decision-making processes at the national level.

The first insurgency in southern Sudan has been dealt with in Chapter VI, which highlights the factors that led to the end of the war. It has shown how the short term inclusion to the state of a number of southern representatives was incomplete. This is followed by Chapter VII focusing on the issues related to the implementation of the 1972 Addis Ababa Peace Accord in southern Sudan. While it has shown that state reforms accommodated interests of part of the southern elite for a brief period of time, the peace treaty failed to address southern grievances related to perceived injustices and relative deprivation in the long term due to the realignment of state constituencies and continuation of state marginalization. As the study has demonstrated, this reinforced the dynamics and logic of marginalization and led again to increasingly exclusive governance by the ruling factions of the northern political elite, and policies that undermined the southern autonomous position and role in the Sudanese political system.

Furthermore, in Chapter VIII the study has analyzed president Nimeiri's shifting alliances and the development of intimate ties with the Islamist section of the northern political elite. This shift of political constituencies led to the reorientation of state policies, and reinforced the marginalizing logic that had a deteriorating effect on political stability in southern Sudan. The increasingly controversial state policies, along with problems of integration of the former southern rebels to the armed forces, gave impetus to the plans of the military elite to reinitiate the insurgency. The continuation of this process has been highlighted in Chapter IX, which also discusses the early armed conflict during which the Islamist faction of the northern elite strengthened and later took its still enduring hold of the Sudanese state.

The Findings

First, based on the evidence shown in this study, it can be concluded that in the case of both insurgencies in southern Sudan the processes of state formation and construction were intimately related to the conflict formation. The fluctuating (non-static) character of the degree of marginalization and continuing (re)construction and (re)negotiation of the state and its center-periphery relations should be emphasized. This is because as it was shown, various sectors and factions within the northern Arabized political elite competed over the state power, resulting in changes of the state's marginalizing policies towards southern Sudan over time. This competition translated into periods of authoritarian and multi-party rule, with varying degrees of authority, legitimacy, and application of repressive policies towards southern Sudan. However, the northern political elite as a whole considered southern Sudan a threat to the continuity of its exclusive political and economic power. Uninterested in sharing power, the northern political elite sought to portray southern Sudan as a menace and securitized the southern issue from early on.

As the analysis indicates, insurgency formation and consolidation in southern Sudan took place during particularly repressive periods in its contemporary history. This confirms the assumption that the theoretical proposition based on the concept of state marginalization provides a holistic foundation for explaining insurgency formation in southern Sudan.

Second, the mixed constructivist-instrumentalist position of group identities that has been adopted in this study has pointed out the role political identities played in the formation of insurgencies in southern Sudan. The study has shown how the historically formed, socially, economically, and politically (re)constructed, "Arab Muslim" and "African" identities portray differences between "the North" and "the South" in Sudan. Chapter III has demonstrated how in the process of state formation in Sudan, the Arabized Muslim dominated social hierarchy became a major force within which group-based political and economic power was configured. The subsequent Chapter IV concentrated on the Anglo-Egyptian colonial period and showed how the colonial policies channeled power into the hands of particular sections of the Arabized Muslim elite. This extended into a socially constructed political project to foment the perception of imagined homogeneous "Arab-Muslim North" and its geographical extension as a "region", despite the highly heterogeneous nature of northern Sudan. It also highlighted how the colonial "Southern Policy" led to the formation of political elite in southern Sudan that, in response to "the North", projected similarly an imagined and socially constructed view of a southern "region", or "the South". Attempting to homogenize the possibly even more heterogeneous territorial entity, the elite project promoted "the South" as a culturally unified "African" region opposed to an "Arab North", building upon a narrative of history of "Arab" domination and slavery emanating from the 19th century and beyond.

The remaining chapters of the study have indicated the periodic changes in the collective identities. They point to the shifting positions among and between northern and southern political elites over time between polarizing and merging agendas. This has either propelled insurgencies, or in contrast promoted more peaceful interaction. The analysis here clearly shows how the political competition and strife led to the securitization of the "Southern

Problem" in the process of decolonization, and fostered a growing identity rift between the state, dominated by sections of the Arabized elite, and the powerful sectors of the southern political elite. During the latter part of the first southern insurgency this "North-South" and "Arab-African" identity rift was partially remedied, facilitating a negotiated settlement to the war.

The analysis also points out how the implementation of the new political structures meant to ensure political autonomy for "the South" ultimately failed, which contributed to the formation of the second insurgency. This was orchestrated principally by discontented elements in the southern military leadership, and to a lesser extent by a number of politicians. During this period, the identity rift prone to armed confrontation widened again largely due to actions by the elites. It is demonstrated that while the most powerful Islamist section of the northern elite pushed for more repressive state policies, sectors of the southern elite responded by increasing militantism which again led to a widening gap of collective identities between "the North" and "the South". At the end, the study has pointed out how the resumption of the insurgency polarized the political identity rift further.

Overall, the analysis conducted here has demonstrated that the (re)constructed and reinforced identity categories vary and change over time. They are closely connected to the changing views of the state and the nation. It is therefore proposed that the political identities adjust, responding to periods of distinct degrees of political instability, strife, and conflict, and are (re) shaped and at times instrumentalized in pursuit of the interests of the dominant elites. This facilitated periodic settlements to remedy violence and war within the structure of the Sudanese state and governments.

The study therefore confirms the constructivist assumption of (re)construction and gradual changes in political identities, rejecting them being primordial. As suggested here, it appears that identities are shaped in relation to the political (dis)order and (in)stability, and in particular the state. This makes the state not only a formal institutional body, but an entity shaping social reality that in turn motivates social action. The notion of the "state" and "marginalization" are therefore involved in the continuous identity (re) construction; the construction of narratives that highlight differential social status and distinct collective experiences portrayed as "regional". This is why identities are not merely instrumental, but rather (re)constructed, used, and manipulated.

In the end, it is shown here that strict political identity categorizations shaping popular views on war in Sudan as an inevitable primordial battle between culturally distinct "Arab vs. African", "Muslim vs. Christian and Animist", or "North vs. South", is largely not the case. Although identities are real and orient the behavior of individuals, political identity categories are constructed, constantly (re)negotiated, and gradually changing. It therefore becomes obvious from the analysis that a view promoting primordial nature of identities and inevitability of the conflict falls into the "ancient hatreds" argumentation, and obscures the agency of the elites. It also fails to outline the role and responsibility of external actors, such as the colonizing powers Britain and Egypt and other powerful states, whose policies have contributed to insurgency formation. Indeed, much of the historiography on Sudan has not discussed the obvious colonial influences in the construction of "regional" political identities in northern and southern Sudan, and the external determinants in insurgency formation.

Third, this study has shown the crucial importance of the external (regional and international) actors and forces in the processes of insurgency formation. This has been largely neglected in the literature on the political history of southern insurgencies in Sudan. The initial process of formation of centralized state was primarily conducted by external actors and led to the construction of a marginalizing polity in which social origins of political and economic power were exclusively linked to Arab identity and Islam. The progression of exclusive power and marginalizing cultural and ethnic identity was extended further by the Anglo-Egyptian domination, crystallizing in the marginalizing colonial state. Chapter V has demonstrated how in the contentious process of decolonization the state became dominated exclusively by sectors of the narrowly defined Arabized elite. Decolonization of Sudan was prompted principally by regional and international actors and interests contesting over regional hegemony and geo-political influence. Not only did regional and international actors and forces dominate the state formation in Sudan, but they were also integral to the insurgency formation in southern Sudan by forcing rapid decolonization without adequate preparation.

Moreover, external actors were present in the latter stages of the first insurgency in southern Sudan by directly supporting the protagonists. Some had an integral role in the mediation that facilitated the negotiated settlement to the war. Similarly other external actors affected the re-emergence of increasingly repressive policies of state marginalization, and external actors appear to have been significantly involved in the political and economic situation in which the second insurgency in southern Sudan materialized.

Thus, direct and indirect external involvement by regional and international actors and forces has been an important element in creating conditions conducive to both war and peace in southern Sudan. This refutes the thesis of some prominent authors about the local nature of the causes of insurgencies, and confirms the assumption that the mainstream literature on insurgency formation in southern Sudan tends to lack regional and international analysis. It clearly underemphasizes these important dimensions in the origins of insurgencies, as it has been demonstrated here that external actors and forces influenced directly and indirectly the processes of insurgency formation.

Fourth, this study has pointed out some reasons why large-scale insurgencies materialized in two occasions in southern Sudan, and, in relation to this, why major insurgencies did not take place in other parts of Sudanese periphery until much later. It is emphasized here that the specific historical trajectories of state formation and (re)construction, along with elite agency and domination, are integral to the understanding of the particularity of the case of insurgency formation in southern Sudan.

In this regard, the analysis points to the legacies of the 19th century and earlier history. It has sought to explain how the role of slavery and social hierarchy have affected inter-group relations in Sudan until today and established an enduring and particular logic of institutionalized and regionally manifested social domination. In addition, colonial history has been important in shaping societal and political structures and reinforcing highly hierarchical type of inclusion and exclusion that have shaped inter-group attitudes and identities in relation to state marginalization.

These processes have promoted cleavages between the elites in the northern and southern part of the country since they were socialized and equipped with distinct narratives about the state and nation. This contributed to the deterioration of the political climate during decolonization, which was characterized by exclusive views of social privileges and marginal reincorporation of southern provinces to the state. As Chapter IV indicates, colonial policies favored the emergence of regionalist elites in southern Sudan as the first area in the Sudanese periphery, owing in part to the promotion of a narrative derived from the historical experience and legacy of slavery and subjugation. This became increasingly important in the process of decolonization, and contributed to the emergence of the insurgencies in part due to the (re)construction of identities referring to "the North" and "the South" as opposing categories. The particularities of the relative identity (re)construction process were different between the northern governing elite and the southern regional leadership, and the governing elite and the leaderships in Sudan's other peripheries.

Fifth, the study has sought to examine armed conflict formation in order to determine if the two rebellions in southern Sudan were connected. Chapter V has shown how the first insurgency in southern Sudan was long and destructive, and, although it was ended through a negotiated settlement, residual organized armed violence lingered. Chapter VI points out the difficulties of peace implementation and continued grievances in southern Sudan. To this extent, as this study has shown, the second insurgency that triggered in the early 1980s can largely be considered as a continuation of the first. It was led by a number of rebel leaders of the earlier movement, and capitalized on unaddressed generalized local grievances, among other diverse motivations, which had largely emerged from perceptions of inequality, injustices, relative deprivation, and the lack of self-determination with respect to north-central Sudan. This analysis therefore refutes the assumption that the two insurgencies were inherently different. Rather, the evidence considered has shown that the formation of the second insurgency relied on political, social, and economic realities largely produced already prior to the first rebellion and by its insufficient resolution.

Sixth, the analysis conducted here has also indicated that insurgencies result from complex interacting processes and multiple motivations. This starkly contrasts simplistic views based primarily on economic indicators, such as greed or opportunity. Although rational choice logic is important to consider in the cases of political and military elites organizing an insurgency, it cannot be reduced to material greed alone. Other factors, such as domestic, regional, and international political developments, actors, and forces, control over constituencies, social and emotional resources for mobilization, and other material realities facilitating insurgency formation, are important. External actors and political developments may heavily influence the making of rebel movements, and dictate significant aspects of insurgency formation, such as ideological foundations, objectives, and necessary material resources.

Similarly, the factors affecting individuals' decision to join a rebellion cannot be reduced only to material greed. Attitudes, values, sentimental factors, fear, sense of belonging, and social networks often play crucial roles in the decision. In addition, one-sided interpretations based on *Homo Economicus*, economic opportunity and rational choice to rebel, merely explain part of the material reasons for organizing and joining an insurgency, leaving out other crucial material and non-material motivations. Such a view therefore reduces the reality according to academic disciplinary bias (economicism), which undermines its inherent explanatory value. In the end, motivations to organize a rebellion or to join an insurgent movement are many, and their extensive understanding requires a comprehensive interdisciplinary analysis.

In sum, evidence analyzed in this work demonstrates that particular historical (political, economic, and social) trajectories led to southern Sudan becoming a subordinate part of the Sudanese polity. This denied its political elite effective participation and influence in the centralized state, which since decolonization has remained in the hands of the northern political elite factions. The relationship between the state center, defined according to exclusive view on Arab culture and Islam, depriving others from effective political participation and economic opportunities, and the periphery, which has largely been portrayed categorically as "the other", is largely responsible for the persisting marginalization and insurgencies in southern Sudan. The history of state's marginalization of its peripheries also largely explains the particularity of the other regional insurgencies in Sudan, and why they materialized.

Finally, it can be concluded from the analysis conducted here that both rebellions in southern Sudan were potentially avoidable. As pointed out, this goes against a number of scholars arguing that they were inevitable. Indeed, it seems that the insurgencies in southern Sudan were conditioned during their formational periods by a combination of external actors and forces, and those related to the dynamics and logic of state marginalization in Sudan. In this, the particular political system and political culture, products of specific historical processes in Sudan, were paramount. They created a political context in which exclusive and narrowly distributed political and economic power to the most powerful sectors of the northern political elite became highly conflictive in the post-colonial state.

As has been shown here, both insurgencies were organized and deliberately instigated against perceived injustices and relative deprivation, which together with emotional and sentimental factors served large-scale mobilization. These dynamics could have been diminished through more sensitive state policies towards southern Sudan, particularly by avoiding generating widespread mistrust and fear towards the state and the "Arab" northerner which became important elements of insurgency formation. For instance, better preparation of the process of decolonization and transformation of the state towards more inclusive governance, accommodating sectors of the southern elite, could have changed the trajectory that led to the first insurgency. Avoiding renewed subjugation of southern Sudan due to the introduction of repressive policies, as well as ending its limited autonomy, could have halted the formational processes of the second insurgency and prevented it from becoming a reality.

Similarly, the regional and international aspects of insurgency formation could have been tackled by concerted policies by external actors. Such measures could have been aimed at diffusing tension through mediation and putting pressure on the Sudanese government to accommodate southern demands. The external actors could also have taken deliberate measures to deprive the opposition of material resources needed for organizing and maintaining an insurgency. Yet, such concerted measures were not taken in the Cold War environment.

Thus, the analysis conducted here suggests that the situation in southern Sudan could possibly have been remedied by more equal sharing of political and economic power. However, this was generally rejected by the northern political elite, seeking to maintain its exclusive control of the state and the economy. Yet, allowing political opening, effective political representation of periphery elites at the national level, and promoting economic opportunities and material well-being in the peripheries, could have gone a long way towards preventing the insurgencies from materializing in southern Sudan. Promoting inclusive political system and culture could gradually have broken the historically formed exclusionary dynamics of state marginalization, which continue to contribute to political instability and armed opposition formation in Sudan today.

BIBLIOGRAPHY

AAA. (1972) "The Addis Ababa Agreement on the Problem of southern Sudan". Available online: http://madingaweil.com/addis-ababa-peace-agreement-1972.htm [accessed 5 June 2012]

Abbink, Jon G. (2004) "Reconstructing Southern Sudan in the Post-War Era: Challenges and Prospects of 'Quick Impact Programmes'". Working Paper 55, African Studies Centre, Leiden.

Abdel Rahim, Muddathir. (1969) *Imperialism and Nationalism in the Sudan: A Study in Constitutional and Political Development*. Oxford: Clarendon Press.

'Abd al-Rahim, Muddathir. (1970) "Arabism, Africanism, and Self-Identification in the Sudan". *Journal of Modern African Studies*, **8**(2), pp. 233-49.

Abdul-Jalil, Musa Adam. (2006) "Land Tenure, Land Use and Inter-Ethnic Conflicts in Darfur" *In*: Ahmed, Abdel Ghaffar M. and Manger, Leif. *Understanding the Crisis in Darfur: Listening to Sudanese Voices*. Bergen: University of Bergen, 20-32.

Abrahamsen, Rita. (2001) *Disciplining Democracy: Development Discourse and Good Governance in Africa*. London: Zed Books.

Abu Hasabu, Afaf Abdel Majid. (1985) *Factional Conflict in the Sudanese Nationalist Movement, 1918-1948*. Khartoum: University of Khartoum.

Adam, Gamal A., Bartlett, Anne A., and Baballa H. Nour (2009). "Slavery in Sudan: From Stereotyping to Practice". Paper presented at the International Sudan Studies Conference, 8th University of South Africa, 25-28 November.

Adams, William Y. (1991). "North and South in Sudanese History". Paper presented at the 2nd International Sudan Studies Conference, University of Durham, 8-11 April.

Adefuye, Ade. (1985) "Kakwa of Uganda and the Sudan: The Ethnic Factor in National and International Factors" *In*: Asiwaju, A. I. *Partitioned*

Africans: Ethnic Relations across Africa's International Boundaries, 1884-1984. London: C. Hurst & Co., 51-69.

Aguirre, Mariano. (2006) "África: El debate sobre el crisis del Estado" *In*: Aguirre, Mariano y Sogge, David. *Crisis del Estado y dominios civiles en África.* Working Paper 30, FRIDE, pp. 1-11.

Ahmad, Hassan Aziz. (1977) "Some Economic Factors Hampering the Development of Sudanese Trade during the Nineteenth Century". *Sudan Journal of Economic and Social Studies*, **2**(1), pp. 31-9.

Ake, Claude. (2000) *The Feasibility of Democracy in Africa.* Dakar: Codesria.

Akok, Garang and Ulrike Schultz. (2009) "'Life Would Be Easy If I would Be Dinka': The Construction of Ethnic Identities in Southern Sudanese Communities after the CPA". Paper presented at the 8th International Sudan Studies Conference, University of South Africa, 25-28 November.

Akol, Lam. (2007) *Southern Sudan: Colonialism, Resistance, and Autonomy.* Asmara: The Red Sea Press.

Akol, Lam. (2001) *SPLM/SPLA: Inside African Revolution.* Khartoum: Khartoum University Press.

Al-Gaddal, Mohammed S. (1985) *Al-Imaam Al-Mahdi: A Profile of a Sudanese Revolutionary.* Khartoum: Khartoum University Press.

Albino, Oliver. (1970) *The Sudan: A Southern Viewpoint.* London: Oxford University Press.

Alexander, Lindsay and Dan Smith. (2004) "Evidence & Analysis: Tackling the Structural Causes of Conflict in Africa & Strengthening Preventive Responses". International Alert. Paper prepared for Commission of Africa. Available online:

http://www.commissionforafrica.org/english/report/background/alexander_and_smith_background.pdf [accessed 23 April 2008]

Alier, Abel. (1990) *Southern Sudan: Too Many Agreements Dishonoured.* London: Ithaca.

Anderson, Benedict (1983) *Imagined Communities: Reflections on the Origin and Spread of Nationalism.* London: Verso.

Anyanwu, John. (2004) "Economic and Political Causes of Civil Wars in Africa: Some Econometric Results". *Peace, Conflict and Development*, 4. Available online: http://www.peacestudiesjournal.org.uk/docs/CivilWarAfrica.PDF [accessed 23 April 2008]

Bibliography

Appandurai, Arjun. (1996) "The Production of Locality" *In*: Appandurai, Arjun. *Modernity at Large: Cultural Dimensions of Globalization*. Minneapolis: University of Minnesota Press, 178-204.

Arfi, Badredine. (1998) "Ethnic Fear: The Social Construction of Insecurity". *Security Studies* **8**(1), pp. 151-203.

Arou, K. N. Mom. (1988) "Devolution: Decentralization and the Division of the Southern Region into Three Regions in 1983" *In*: Arou, Mom, K. N. and Yongo-Bure, Benaiah. *North-South Relations in the Sudan since the Addis Ababa Agreement*. Khartoum: University of Khartoum Press, 166-88.

Arou, K. N. Mom. (1982) "Regional Devolution in the Southern Sudan 1972-1981". Unpublished PhD Thesis, University of Edinburgh.

Asiwaju, Anthony I. (ed.) (1985) *Partitioned Africans: Ethnic Relations along Africa's International Boundaries, 1884-1984*. London: C. Hurst & Co.

Austen, Ralph. (1996) *African Economic History: International Development and External Dependency*. New York: Monthly Review Press.

Awur, Deng Wenyin. (1988) "The Integration of the Anya-Nya into the National Army" *In*: Arou, Mom, K. N. and Yongo-Bure, Benaiah. *North-South Relations in the Sudan since the Addis Ababa Agreement*. Khartoum: University of Khartoum Press, 57-119.

Ayittey, George B. N. (1998) *Africa in Chaos*. New York: St. Martin's Press.

Ayoob, Muhammed. (2001) "State Making, State Breaking, and State Failure" *In*: Crocker, Chester A., Hampson, Fen Osler and Pamela Aall. *Turbulent Peace: The Challenges of Managing International Conflict*. Washington: United States Institute of Peace Press, 127-42.

Azam, Jean Paul. (2001) "The Redistributive State and Conflicts in Africa". *Journal of Peace Research*, **38**(4), pp. 429-44.

Badal, Raphael K. (1994) "Political Cleavages within the Southern Sudan" *In*: Tvedt, Terje and Harir, Sharif. *Short-Cut to Decay: The Case of Sudan*. Uppsala: Nordic Africa Institute, 105-25.

Badal, Raphael K. (1976) "Rise and Fall of Separatism in Southern Sudan". *African Affairs*, **75**(301), pp. 463-74.

Ballentine, Karen. (2003) "Beyond Greed and Grievance: Reconsidering the Economic Dynamics of Armed Conflict" *In*: Ballentine, Karen and Sherman, Jake. *The Political Economy of Armed Conflict: Beyond Greed and Grievance*. Boulder: Lynne Rienner, 259-83.

Ballentine, Karen and Heiko Nitzsche. (2003) "Beyond Greed and Grievance: Policy Lessons from Studies in the Political Economy of Armed Conflict". International Peace Academy Policy Report. Available online: http://www.worldpolicy.org/projects/arms/study/bak05_1.pdf [accessed 23 April 2008]

Baraja, L. Gwaki Wori. (2004) "Synopses of Past Events as Compared to Developing Events". *Sudan Vision Daily*, 28 August. Available online: http://sudanvisiondaily.com/modules.php?name=News&file=article&sid=2879 [accessed on 23 April 2008]

Bariagaber, Assefaw. (2006) *Conflict and the Refugee Experience: Flight, Exile, and Repatriation in the Horn of Africa*. Aldershot: Ashgate.

Barth, Frederik. (1969) *Ethnic Groups and Boundaries*. Boston: Little Brown.

Bates, Darrell. (1984) *The Fashoda Incident of 1898: Encounter on the Nile*. London: Oxford University Press.

Bates, Robert H. (2008) *When Things Fell Apart: State Failure in Late-Century Africa*. Cambridge: Cambridge University Press.

Bates, Robert H. (1983) "Modernization, Ethnic Competition and the Rationality of Politics in Contemporary Africa". *In*: Rothchild, Donald and Olorunsola, Victor A. *State versus Ethnic Claims: African Policy Dilemmas*. Boulder (CO): Westview, 152-71.

Bayart, Jean-François. (2005) *The Illusion of Cultural Identity*. London: Hurst & Company.

Bayart, Jean-François. (2000) "Africa in the World: A History of Extraversion". *African Affairs*, **99**(395), pp. 217-67.

Bayart, Jean-François. (1993) *The State in Africa: The Politics of the Belly*. New York: Longman Publishing.

Bayart, Jean-François. (1991) "L'Etat". *In*: Coulon, C. and Martin, Denis-Constant. *Les Afriques Politiques*. Paris: Editions La Découverte, 213-30.

Bayart, Jean-François, Ellis, Stephen, and Beatrice Hibou. (1999) *The Criminalization of State in Africa*. Bloomington: Indiana University Press.

Bechtold, Peter. (1976) *Politics in the Sudan*. New York: Praeger.

Bekoe, Dorina A. (ed.) (2005) *East Africa and the Horn: Confronting the Challenges to Good Governance*. Boulder (CO): Lynne Rienner.

Berdal, Mats. (2003) "How 'New' Are 'New Wars'? Global Economic Change and Study of Civil War". *Global Governance*, 9(4), pp. 477-502.

Berman, Bruce and John Lonsdale. (1992) *Unhappy Valley. Vol. 2: Violence and Ethnicity*. Oxford: James Currey.

Beshir, Mohamed Omer. (1975) *The Southern Sudan: From Conflict to Peace*. Khartoum: Khartoum Bookshop.

Beshir, Mohamed Omer. (1974) *Revolution and Nationalism in the Sudan*. London: Rex Collins.

Beshir, Mohamed Omer. (1968) *The Southern Sudan: Background to Conflict*. London: Hurst.

Beswick, Stephanie. (2004) *Sudan's Blood Memory: The Legacy of War, Ethnicity, and Slavery in Early South Sudan*. Rochester (NY): University of Rochester Press.

Beswick, Stephanie. (1994) "Islam and the Dinka of the Southern Sudan from the Pre-Colonial Period to Independence (1956)". *Journal of Asian and African Studies*, 29(3-4), pp. 172-85.

Betléhemy, Jean-Claude, Kauffman Céline, Renard, Laurence and Lucia Wegner. "Political Instability, Political Regime and Economic Performance in African Countries". OECD Development Center. Available online:

http://www.csae.ox.ac.uk/conferences/2002-UPaGiSSA/papers/Kauffmann-csae2002.pdf [accessed 23 April 2008]

Björkelo, Anders. (1989) *Prelude to Mahdiyya: Peasants and Traders in the Shendi Region, 1821-1885*. Cambridge: Cambridge University Press.

Björkelo, Anders. (1984) "Turco-Jallaba Relations, 1821-1885". *In*: Manger, Leif O. *Trade and Traders in the Sudan*, Bergen: University of Bergen, 81-107.

Bodley, John. (1999) *Victims of Progress*. Palo Alto (CA): Mayfield.

Bodley, John. (1988) "Introduction: Tribal Peoples and Development". *In:* Bodley, John H. *Tribal Peoples and Development Issues*, Mountain View (CA): Mayfield, 1-7.

Bowles, Samuel, Franzini, Maurizio and Ugo Pagano. (eds.) (1999) *The Politics and Economics of Power*. London: Routledge.

Branch, Adam and Zachariah C. Mampilly. (2005) "Winning the War, but Losing the Peace? The Dilemma of SPLM/A Civil Administration and the Tasks Ahead". *Journal of Modern African Studies*, **43**(1), pp. 1-20.

Brass, Paul R. (1991) *Ethnicity and Nationalism: Theory and Comparison*. New Delhi: Sage.

Bratton, Michael. (2004) "State Building and Democratization in Sub-Saharan Africa: Forwards, Backwards, or Together?", Afrobarometer Working Paper No. 43, Institute for Democracy in South Africa, Pretoria.

Bratton, Michael and Nicholas van de Walle. (1997) *Democratic Experiments in Africa: Regime Transitions in Comparative Perspective*. Cambridge: Cambridge University Press.

Brown, Michael E. (1996) "Introduction". *In*: Brown, Michael E. *The International Dimensions of Internal Conflict*. Cambridge (MA): MIT Press, 1-31.

Brown, Richard. (1986) "International Responses to Sudan's Economic Crisis: 1978 to the April 1985 Coup d'Etat". *Development and Change*, **17**(3), pp. 487-511.

Buckley, Stephen. (1997) "African Lives: Chaos of War Strips Sudanese of Dignity, Traditions, and Identity", *The Washington Post*, 24 August, p. A22.

Bueno de Mesquita, Bruce and Lalman, David. (1992) *War and Reason: Domestic and International Imperatives*. London: Yale University Press.

Buhaug, Halvard and Scott Gates. (2002) "The Geography of Civil War". *Journal of Peace Research*, **39**(4), pp. 417-33.

Burr, J. Millard and Robert O. Collins. (1999) *Africa's Thirty Years War: Libya, Chad, and the Sudan*. Oxford: Westview Press.

Buzan, Barry, Wæver, Ole, and Jaap de Wilde. (1998) *Security: A Framework for Analysis*. Boulder: Lynne Rienner.

Callaghy, Thomas M., Kassimir, Ronald, and Robert Latham. (eds.) (2001) *Intervention and Transnationalism in Africa: Global-Local Networks of Power*. Cambridge: Cambridge University Press.

Campos Serrano, Alicia. (2000) "La aparición de los estados africanos en el sistema internacional: la descolonización de África". *In*: Peñas, Francisco Javier. *África en el sistema internacional*. Madrid: Catarata, 15-50.

Carreira da Silva, Filipe. (2011) *G. H. Mead. A Reader.* Abingdon: Routledge.

Castells, Manuel. (1998) *End of Millenium*. Oxford: Blackwell.

Castells, Manuel. (1997) *The Power of Identity. Vol. II, The Information Age: Economy, Society and Culture*. Oxford: Blackwell.

Castells, Manuel. (1996) *The Rise of the Network Society. Vol. 1, The Information Age: Economy, Society and Culture*. Oxford: Blackwell.

Cater, Charles. (2003) "The Political Economy of Conflict and UN Intervention: Rethinking the Critical Cases of Africa". *In*: Ballentine, Karen and Sherman, Jake. *The Political Economy of Armed Conflict: Beyond Greed and Grievance*. Boulder: Lynne Rienner, 19-45.

CBS. (1984) *Lord Come to Our Aid: Message of the Catholic Bishops of Sudan on Christian Behaviour and Attitudes in the Face of the Current Situation in the Country*. Juba: Catholic Press Institute.

Chabal, Patrick. (2009) *Africa: The Politics of Suffering and Smiling*. London: Zed Books.

Chabal, Patrick. (2007) *State and Governance: The Limits of Decentralisation*. The Hague: SNV Netherlands Development Organisation.

Chabal, Patrick and Daloz, Jean-Pascal. (2005) *Culture Troubles: Politics and the Interpretation of Meaning*. London: Hurts & Co.

Chabal, Patrick and Daloz, Jean-Pascal. (1999) *Africa Works: Disorder as Political Instrument*. Bloomington: Indiana University Press.

Chaigneau, Pascal. (2002) "The Geopolitics of African Conflicts". *African Geopolitics*, **7-8**(Summer-Fall), pp. 85-91.

Chan, Hoth G. and Riang Y. Zuor. (2006) *South Sudan: A Legitimate Struggle*. Baltimore: PublishAmerica.

Chandler, David. (2006) *Empire in Denial: The Politics of State-building*. London: Pluto Press.

Clapham, Christopher. (ed.) (1998) *African Guerrillas*. Oxford: James Currey.

Clapham, Christopher. (1996) *Africa and the International System: The Politics of State Survival*. Cambridge: Cambridge University Press.

Clapham, Christopher, Herbst, Jeffrey and Greg Mills. (eds.) (2006) *Big African States: Angola, Sudan, DRC, Ethiopia, Nigeria, South Africa*. Johannesburg: Wits University Press.

Clare, Michael T. (2002) *Resource Wars: The New Landscape of Global Conflict*. New York: Henry Holt.

Clayton, Anthony. (2003) "Violence in Africa since 1950: Frontiersmen". *In*: Pumphrey, Carolyn and Schwarz-Barcott, Rye. *Armed Conflict in Africa*. Lanham (US): Scarecrow, 43-67.

Cobham, Alex. (2005) "Causes of Conflict in Sudan: Testing *The Black Book*". *The European Journal of Development Research*, **17**(3), pp. 462-80.

Coleman, James S. (1990) *Foundation of Social Theory*. Cambridge (MA): Belknap.

Collier, Paul. (2003a) *Natural Resources and Violent Conflict: Options and Actions*. Washington, DC: The World Bank.

Collier, Paul. (2003b) "The Market for Civil War". *Foreign Policy*, **136**(May-June), pp. 38-46.

Collier, Paul. (2000a) "Rebellion as Quasi-Criminal Activity". *Journal of Conflict Resolution*, **44**(6), pp. 839-53.

Collier, Paul. (2000b) "Economic Causes of Civil Conflict and Their Implications for Policy". Working Paper, The World Bank. Available online: http://www.worldbank.org/research/conflict/papers/civilconflict.pdf [accessed 10 February 2007]

Collier, Paul and Anke Hoeffler. (2004). "Greed and Grievance in Civil War". *Oxford Economic Papers*, **56**(4), pp. 563-95.

Collier, Paul and Anke Hoeffler. (2002a) "On the Incidence of Civil War in Africa". *Journal of Conflict Resolution*, **46**(1), pp. 13-28.

Collier, Paul and Anke Hoeffler. (2002b) "Understanding Civil War: A New Agenda". *Journal of Conflict Resolution*, **46**(1), pp. 3-12.

Collier, Paul and Anke Hoeffler. (1998) "On Economic Causes of Civil War". *Oxford Economic Papers*, **50**(4), pp. 563-73.

Collier, Paul and Nicholas Sambanis. (eds.) (2005a) *Understanding Civil War: Evidence and Analysis. Volume I: Africa*. Herndon (VA): The World Bank.

Collier, Paul and Nicholas Sambanis. (eds.) (2005b) *Understanding Civil War: Evidence and Analysis. Volume II: Europe, Central Asia and Other Regions*. Herndon (VA): The World Bank.

Collins, Robert O. (2008) *A History of Modern Sudan*. Cambridge: Cambridge University Press.

Collins, Robert O. (2005) *Civil Wars and Revolution in the Sudan: Essays on the Sudan, Southern Sudan, and Darfur, 1962-2004*. Hollywood (CA): Tsehai Publishing.

Collins, Robert O. (1992) "The Nilotic Slave Trade: Past and Present". *In*: Savage, Elizabeth. *Human Commodity: Perspective of the trans-Saharan Slave Trade*. London: Frank Cass, 140-61.

Collins, Robert O. (1990) *The Waters of the Nile*. Oxford: Clarendon Press.

Collins, Robert O. (1985) "The Big Ditch: The Jonglei Canal Scheme". *In*: Daly, Martin W. *Modernization in the Sudan*. New York: Lilian Barber Press, 135-46.

Collins, Robert O. (1983) *Shadows in the Grass: Britain in the Southern Sudan, 1918-1956*. London: Yale University Press.

Collins, Robert O. (1975) *The Southern Sudan in Historical Perspective*. Tel Aviv: Israel Press.

Collins, Robert O. (1971) *The Land Beyond the Rivers: The Southern Sudan, 1898-1918*. New Haven: Yale University Press.

Collins, Robert O. (1962) *The Southern Sudan, 1883-1898: A Struggle for Control*. New Haven: Yale University Press.

Cooper, Frederick and Ann Laura Stoler. (eds.) (1997) *Tensions of Empire: Colonial Cultures in a Bourgeois World*. Berkeley: University of California Press.

Cordell, Dennis D. (1985) *Dar al-Kuti and the Last Years of the Trans-Saharan Slave Trade*. Madison: University of Wisconson Press.

CPA. (2005) "The Comprehensive Peace Agreement". Available online: http://www.aec-sudan.org/docs/cpa/cpa-en.pdf [accessed 23 August 2010]

Cramer, Cristopher. (2006) *Civil War is Not a Stupid Thing: Accounting for Violence in Developing Countries*. London: C. Hurst & Co.

Cramer, Cristopher. (2003) "Does Inequality Cause Conflict?". *Journal of International Development*, **15**(4), pp. 397-412.

Cramer, Christopher. (2002) "*Homo Economicus* Goes to War: Methodological Individualism, Rational Choice and the Political Economy of War". *World Development*, **30**(11), pp. 1845-64.

Crisp, Jeff and Rachel Ayling. (1985) "Ugandan Refugees in Sudan and Zaire". Report, British Refugee Council, London.

Cunnison, Ian. (1971) "Classification by Genealogy: A Problem of the Baqqara Belt" *In*: Hasan, Yusuf Fadl. *Sudan in Africa*. Khartoum: Khartoum University Press, 186-96.

Currea-Lugo, Victor. (2008) "Los Estados Imposibles". Available online: http://www.semana.com/wf_InfoArticulo.aspx?idArt=109740 [accessed 1 January 2008] Dak, Othwonh. (1988) "Southern Regions: Decentralization or Recentralization". *In*: Arou, Mom, K. N. and Yongo-Bure, Benaiah. *North-South Relations in the Sudan since the Addis Ababa Agreement*. Khartoum: University of Khartoum Press, 188-201.

Dallalah, Salwa Kamil. (1988) "Oil and Politics in Southern Sudan". *In*: Arou, Mom, K. N. and Yongo-Bure, Benaiah. *North-South Relations in the Sudan since the Addis Ababa Agreement*. Khartoum: University of Khartoum Press, 430-55.

Daly, Martin W. (1993) "Broken Bridge and Empty Basket: The Political and Economic Background of the Sudanese Civil War". *In*: Daly, John and Sikainga, Ahmad Alawad. *Civil War in the Sudan*. London: British Academic Press, 1-26.

Daly, Martin W. (1991) *Imperial Sudan: The Anglo-Egyptian Condominium, 1934-1956*. London: Cambridge University Press.

Daly, Martin W. (1986) *The Empire on the Nile: The Anglo-Egyptian Sudan, 1898-1934*. London: Cambridge University Press.

Daly, Martin W. (ed.) (1985) *Al Majdhubiyya and al Mikashfiyya: Two Sufi Tariqas in the Sudan*. Khartoum: University of Khartoum.

de Chand, David. (2000). "The Sources of Conflict between the North and the South in Sudan". Paper presented at the 5th International Sudan Studies Conference, University of Durham, 30 August-1 September. Available online: http://www.dur.ac.uk/justin.willis/chand.htm [accessed 23 April 2008]

de Waal, Alex. (2007a) "Sudan: What Kind of State? What Kind of Crisis?". Occasional Paper 2, Crisis States Research Centre, London School of Economics, April.

de Waal, Alex. (2007b) "Sudan: International Dimensions to the State and its Crisis". Occasional Paper 3, Crisis States Research Centre, London School of Economics, April.

de Waal, Alex. (1994) "Turabi's Muslim Brothers: Theocracy in Sudan". *Covert Action Quarterly*, **12**, pp. 48-61.

de Waal, Alex. (1993) "Some Comments on Militias in the Contemporary Sudan". *In*: Daly, John and Sikainga, Ahmad Alawad. *Civil War in the Sudan*. London: British Academic Press, 142-56.

Deeb, Mary Jane. (1991) *Libya's Foreign Policy in North Africa*. Boulder: Westview Press.

DeNardo, James. (1985) *Power in Numbers: The Political Strategy of Protest and Rebellion*. Princeton: Princeton University Press.

Deng, Francis Mading. (1995a) *War of Visions*: *Conflict Identities in the Sudan*. Washington (DC): The Brookings Institution.

Deng, Francis Mading. (1995b) "Negotiating a Hidden Agenda: Sudan's Conflict of Identities". *In*: Zartman, I. William. *Elusive Peace: Negotiating an End to Civil Wars*. Washington (DC): The Brookings Institution, 77-102.

Deng, Francis Mading. (1978) *Africans of Two Worlds: The Dinka in Afro-Arab Sudan*. New Haven: Yale University Press.

Deng, Francis Mading and I. William Zartman. (2002) *A Strategic Vision for Africa: The Kampala Movement*. Washington (DC): The Brookings Institution.

Deng Ajuok, Albino. (2008) "Response of Southern Sudanese Intellectuals to African Nationalism". *The Journal of Pan African Studies*, **2**(5), pp. 130-41.

Deutsch, Karl W. (1953) *Nationalism and Social Communication. An Inquiry into the Foundations of Nationality*. Cambridge (MA): Cambridge University Press.

Dhal, Abraham Matoc. (2004) *The Colonial Economy and the Underdevelopment of the Southern Sudan, 1899-1989*. Khartoum: Communication Services.

Doornbos, Martin. (1994) "State Formation and Collapse: Reflections on Identity and Power" *In*: van Bakel, M., Hagesteijn, R. and van de Welde, P. *Pivot Politics: Changing Cultural Identities in Early State Formation Processes*. Amsterdam: Het Spinhuis, 281-93.

Dreyfus, Hubert L. and Paul Rabinow. (1982) *Michel Foucault: Beyond Structuralism and Hermeneutics*. Chicago: University of Chicago Press.

Duffield, Mark. (2001) *Global Governance and New Wars: The Merging of Development and Security*. London: Zed Books.

403

Duffield, Mark. (1993) "NGO's, Disaster Relief and Asset Transfer in the Horn: Political Survival in a Permanent Emergency". *Development and Change*, **14**(1), pp. 131-57.

Duffield, Mark. (1992) "Famine, Conflict and the Internationalization of Public Welfare". *In*: Doornbos, Martin, Cliffe, Lionel, Ahmed, Abdel Ghaffal M., and Markakis, John. *Beyond Conflict in the Horn: Prospects for Peace*. The Hague: Institute of Social Studies, 49-62.

Duncan, John Spencer R. (1957) *The Sudan's Path to Independence*. Edinburgh: William Blackwood and Sons.

El Zain, Mahmud (1996) "Tribe and Religion in Sudan". *Review of African Political Economy*, **70**(23), pp. 523-9.

El Zain, Mahmud (1987) "Politics of Native Administration in the Sudan". Unpublished B.Sc. Thesis, University of Khartoum.

Elbadawi, Ibrahim and Nicholas Sambanis. (2000) "Why Are There So Many Civil Wars in Africa?". *Journal of African Economics,* **9**(3), pp. 244-69.

Elhassan, Abdalla Mohamed. (1985) "The State and the Development of Capitalism in Agriculture in Sudan: The Case of the Savannah Rainland". Unpublished PhD Thesis, University of East Anglia.

Eltahir, Yashir Awad Abdalla. (2009) "Sudan Politics in Ethnicization: Mismanaging Diversity, Dismantling the State". Paper presented at the 8th International Sudan Studies Conference, UNISA, 25-28 November.

Englebert, Pierre. (2000) *State Legitimacy and Development in Africa.* Boulder: Lynne Rienner.

Eprile, Cecil. (1974) *War and Peace in the Sudan 1955-1972*. London: David & Charles.

Epstein, Arnold L. (1958) *Politics in an Urban African Community*. Manchester: Manchester University Press.

Erdmann, Gero and Ulf Engel. (2007) "Neopatrimonialism Reconsidered: Critical Review and Elaboration of an Elusive Concept", *Commonwealth & Comparative Politics* , **45**(1), pp. 95-119.

Eriksen, Thomas H. (1993) *Ethnicity and Nationalism*. London: Pluto Press.

Erlich, Haggai. (1983) *The Struggle over Eritrea, 1962 to 1978: War and Revolution in the Horn of Africa*. Palo Alto (CA): Hoover Press.

ESIS. (2004) "Muhammad Ali Pasha". Egypt State Information Service. Available online: http://www.sis.gov.eg/rulers/html/en01m.htm [accessed 17 February 2007]

ESPAC. (2002) "The Search for Peace in the Sudan: A Chronology of Sudanese Peace Process, 1989-2001". Report, The European-Sudanese Public Affairs Council, London. Available online: http://www.espac.org/pdf/search_for_peace.pdf [accessed 29 August 2008]

Ezza, El-Sadig Yahya Abdallah and Amir Mohammed Salih Libis. (2009) "The Role of Language in Negotiating Power in Sudan". Paper presented at the 8th International Sudan Studies Conference, University of South Africa, 25-28 November.

Fatton, Robert Jr. (1992) *Predatory Rule: State and Civil Society in Africa*. London: Lynne Rienner.

Fawole, W. Alade (2004) "A Continent in Crisis: Internal Conflicts and External Interventions in Africa". *African Affairs*, **103**(411), pp. 297-303.

Fearon, James D. and David D. Laitin. (2000) "Violence and the Social Construction of Ethnic Identity". *International Organization*, **54**(4), pp. 845-77.

Fegley, Randall. (2010) *Beyond Khartoum: A History of Subnational Government in Sudan*. Trenton (NJ): The Red Sea Press.

Fegley, Randall. (2008) "Comparative Perspectives on the Rehabilitation of Ex-Slaves and Former Child Soldiers with Special Reference to Sudan". *African Studies Quarterly*, **10**(1), pp. 35-69.

Fine, Ben. (2001) "Economics Imperialism and Intellectual Progress: The Present as History of Economic Thought?". *History of Economics Review*, **32**(1), pp. 10-36.

Fine, Ben. (1999) "A Question of Economics: Is It Colonising the Social Sciences?". *Economy and Society*, **28**(3), pp. 403-25.

First, Ruth. (1970) *The Barrel of a Gun: Political Power in Africa and the Coup d'État*. London: Allen Lane.

Fluehr-Lobban, Carolyn and Kharissa Rhodes. (eds.) (2004) *Race and Identity in the Nile Valley: Ancient and Modern Perspectives*. Trenton (NJ): Red Sea Press.

Frimpong-Ansah, Jonathan H. (1991) *The Vampire State in Africa: The Political Economy of Decline in Ghana*. London: James Currey.

Frohlich, Norman, Oppenheimer, Joe A., and Oran R. Young. (1971) *Political Leadership and Collective Goods*. Princeton (NJ): Princeton University Press.

Gadir Ali, Ali Abdel. (2000) "The Economics of Conflicts in Africa: An Overview". *Journal of African Economies*, **9**(3), pp. 235-43.

Gadir Ali, Abdel, Ali, Elbadawi, Ibrahim and Atta El-Batahani. (2005) "Sudan's Civil War: Why Has It Prevailed for So Long". *In*: Collier, Paul. *Understanding Civil War: Evidence and Analysis Volume I: Africa.* Herndon (VA): The World Bank, 193-219.

Garang, John. (1987) *John Garang Speaks.* London: Kegan Paul International.

Garnett, John. (2002) "The Causes of War and the Conditions of Peace". *In*: Baylis, John Wirtz, James, Cohen, Eliot and Colin S. Gray. *Strategy in the Contemporary World: An Introduction to Strategic Studies.* Oxford: Oxford University Press, 66-87.

Geffray, Christian. (1990) *La cause des armes au Mozambique: Anthropologie d'une guerre civile.* Paris: Karthala.

Gellner, Ernest. (1983) *Nations and Nationalism.* Ithaca (NY): Cornell University Press.

Gleditsch, Kristian S. (2006) "Transnational Dimensions of Civil War". Manuscript, Division of Social Sciences, University of San Diego. Available online: http://weber.ucsd.edu/~kgledits/papers/transnational.pdf [accessed 23 April 2008]

Graham, Thomas. (1990) *Sudan, 1950-1985: Death of a Dream.* London: Darf.

Gray, Richard. (2002) "Some Reflections on Christian Involvement 1955-1972". *In*: Hasan, Yusuf Fadl and Richard Gray. *Religion and Conflict in Sudan.* Nairobi: Paulines.

Gray, Richard. (1961) *A History of the Southern Sudan 1839-1889.* London: Oxford University Press.

Grey-Johnson, Crispin. (2006) "Beyond Peacekeeing: The Challenge of Post-Conflict Recontruction and Peacebuilding in Africa". *UN Chronicle* XLIII, 1. Available online: http://www.un.org/Pubs/chronicle/2006/issue1/0106p08.htm [accessed 23 April 2008]

Grossman, Hershel. (1995) "Insurrections". *In*: Hartley, Keith and Sandler, Todd. *Handbook of Defense Economics, Vol. 1.* Amsterdam: Elsevier Science B. V.

Grossman, Hershel. (1991) "A General Equilibrium Model of Insurgencies". *American Economic Review*, **81**(4), pp. 912-21.

Grundy, Kenneth W. (1971) *Guerrilla Struggle in Africa: An Analysis and Review*. New York: Grossman.

Gurr, Ted R. (1993) *Minorities at Risk: A Global View of Ethnopolitical Conflicts*. Washington (DC): United States Institute for Peace.

Gurr, Ted R. (1970) *Why Men Rebel*. Princeton: Princeton University Press.

Hagmann, Tobias and Didier Péclard. (eds.) (2011) *Negotiating Statehood: Dynamics of Power and Domination in Africa*. London: Wiley-Blackwell.

Handelman, Howard. (1996) *The Challenge of Third World Development*. Upper Addle River (NJ): Prentice Hall.

Hanes, William Travis (1995) *Imperial Diplomacy in the Era of Decolonization: The Sudan and Anglo-Egyptian Relations, 1955-1956*. Westport (CT): Greenwood Press.

Hardin, Russell. (1982) *Collective Action*. Baltimore (MD): Johns Hopkins University Press.

Hart, Gillian. (2002) *Disabling Globalization: Places of Power in Post-Apartheid South Africa*. Berkeley: University of California Press.

Harvie, C. H. and Kleve, J. G. **(1959)** *The National Income of Sudan, 1955/56*. Khartoum: Department of Statistics, Republic of the Sudan.

Hasan, Yusuf Fadl. (2003) *Studies in Sudanese History*. Khartoum: Sudatek Limited.

Hasan, Yusuf Fadl. (1985) *Kitaab Attabaqaat*. Khartoum: Khartoum University Press.

Heldman, Dan C. (1981) *The USSR and Africa: Foreign Policy under Khrushchev*. New York: Praeger.

Henderson, Errol and Singer, J. David. (2000) "Civil War in the Post-Colonial World, 1946-1992". *Journal of Peace Research*, **37**(3), pp. 275-99.

Henze, Paul. (1991) *The Horn of Africa: From War to Peace*. New York: St. Martin's Press.

Heraclides, Alexis. (1987) "Janus or Sisyphus? The Southern Problem of the Sudan". *The Journal of Modern African Studies*, **25**(2), pp. 213-31.

Herbst, Jeffrey. (2000) "Economic Incentives, Natural Resources and Conflict in Africa". *Journal of African Economies*, **9**(3), pp. 270-94.

Herbst, Jeffrey. (1990) "War and the State in Africa". *International Security*, **14**(4), pp. 117-39.

Heritage. (1987a) "Colonel Dr. John Garang Speaks to Heritage on War and Peace in the Sudan-2". Heritage newspaper, Khartoum, 2 November, p. 4.

Heritage. (1987b) "Colonel Dr. John Garang Speaks to Heritage on War and Peace in the Sudan-2". Heritage newspaper, Khartoum, 9 November, p. 4.

Heritage. (1987c) "Colonel Dr. John Garang Speaks to Heritage on War and Peace in the Sudan-2". Heritage newspaper, Khartoum, 16 November, p. 4.

Hernandez Zubizarreta, Juan. (2009) "El Tribunal Penal Internacional. ¿Justicia Universal en Sudán?". *Pueblos*, 24 March. Available at http://www.revistapueblos.org/spip.php?article1553 [accessed 2 April 2009].

Hill, Richard. (1959) *Egypt in the Sudan, 1820-1881*. London: Oxford University Press.

Hirshleifer, Jack. (1995) "Theorizing about Conflict". *Handbook of Defense Economics, Vol. 1*. Amsterdam: Elsevier Science B. V., 169-189.

Hirshleifer, Jack. (1994) "The Dark Side of the Force". *Economic Inquiry*, 32(1), pp. 1-10.

Hirshleifer, Jack. (1987) "Conflict and Settlement". *In*: Eatwell, John, Milgate Murray and Peter Newman. *The New Palgrave: Dictionary of Economic Thought and Doctrine*. London: Macmillan. Draft available online:http://www.econ.ucla.edu/workingpapers/wp360.pdf [accessed 23 April 2008]

Hobsbawm, Eric J. (1992) *Nations and Nationalism since 1780: Programme, Myth, Reality*. Cambridge (MA): Cambridge University Press.

Hobsbawm, Eric J. and Terence Ranger. (eds.) (1992) *The Invention of Tradition*. Cambridge (MA): Cambridge University Press.

Holt, Peter M. (1961) *A Modern History of the Sudan: From the Funj Sultanate to the Present Day*. London: Weidenfeld and Nicholson.

Holt, Peter M. (1958) *The Mahdist State in Sudan, 1881-1898: A Study of its Origins, Development, and Overthrow*. Oxford: Clarendon.

Holt, Peter M. and Daly, Martin W. (2000) *A History of the Sudan: From the Coming of Islam to the Present Day*. Harlow (UK): Longman.

Homer-Dixon, Thomas F. (1999) *Environment Scarcity and Violence*. Princeton: Princeton University Press.

Homer-Dixon, Thomas F. (1994) "Environmental Scarcities and Violent Conflict: Evidence from Cases". *International Security*, **19**(1), pp. 5-40.

Homer-Dixon, Thomas F. (1991) "On the Threshold: Environmental Changes as Causes of Acute Conflict". *International Security*, **16**(2), pp. 76-116.

Horowitz, David. (1985) *Ethnic Groups in Conflict*. Berkeley: University of California Press.

Howell, John. (1978a) "Horn of Africa: Lessons from the Sudan Conflict". *International Affairs*, **54**(3), pp. 421-36.

Howell, John. (1978b) "Political Leadership and Organisation in the Southern Sudan". Unpublished Ph.D. Dissertation. University of Reading.

Howell, John. (1973) "Politics in the Southern Sudan". *African Affairs*, **72**(287), pp. 163-78.

HRW. (2003) "Sudan, Oil and Human Rights". Report, Human Rights Watch, Brussels.

Humphreys, Macartan. (2003) "Economics and Violent Conflict". Manuscript, Harvard University. Available online: http://www.preventconflict.org/portal/economics [accessed 23 April 2008]

Hunter, Floyd. (1953) *Community Power Structure: A Study of Decision Makers*. Chapel Hill (NC): University of North Carolina Press.

Huntington, Samuel. (1997) *The Clash of Civilizations and the Remaking of World Order*. New York: Simon and Schuster.

Hutchinson, Sharon E. (1996) *Nuer Dilemmas: Coping with Money, War, and the State*. London: University of California Press.

Hyden, Goran. (1983) *No Shortcuts to Progress: African Development in Perspective*. London: Heinemann.

IAO (2004). "Sudan – History". Islam in Africa Organization. Available online: http://www.Islaminafrica.org/sudan-h.htm [accessed 23 April 2008]

Ibrahim, Hassan Ahmed. (2000) "The Strategy, Responses and Legacy of the First Imperialist Era in the Sudan, 1820-1885". Presented in the 5th International Sudan Studies Conference, University of Durham, 30 August-1 September. Available online: http://www.dur.ac.uk/justin.willis/hassanibrahim1.htm [accessed 23 April 2008]

ICG. (2002) "God, Oil, and Country: Changing the Logic of War in Sudan". Report, International Crisis Group, Brussels. Available online: http://

www.crisisgroup.org/home/index.cfm?id=1615&l=1 [accessed 23 April 2008]

Idris, Amir H. (2005) *Conflict and Politics of Identity in Sudan*. New York: Palgrave MacMillan.

Idris, Amir H. (2001) *Sudan's Civil War: Slavery, Race and Formational Identities*. Lewiston (NY): Edwin Mellen Press.

Ignatieff, Michael. (1997) *The Warrior's Honour: Ethnic War and the Modern Conscience*. New York: Henry Holt.

Iyob, Ruth and Khadiagala, Gilbert M. (2006) *Sudan: The Elusive Quest for Peace*. Boulder (CO): Lynne Rienner.

Izzedin, Nejla Abu. (1981) *Nasser of the Arabs*: An *Arab Assessment*. London: Third World Centre.

Jackson, Robert. (1990) *Quasi-States: Sovereignty, International Relations and the Third World*. Cambridge: Cambridge University Press.

Jendia, Catherine. (2002) *The Sudanese Civil Conflict 1969-1985*. Oxford: Peter Lang.

Johnson, Douglas. (2006) "Darfur: Peace, Genocide & Crimes against Humanity in Sudan". *In*: Kaarsholm, Preben. *Violence, Political Culture & Development in Africa*. Oxford: James Currey, 92-104.

Johnson, Douglas. (2003) *The Root Causes of Sudan's Civil Wars*. Oxford: James Currey.

Johnson, Douglas. (2002) "Food Aid, Land Tenure and the Survival of the Subsistence Economy". Presented at "Money Makes the War Go Round: Transforming the Economy of War in Sudan" conference, Brussels, 12-13 June. Available online: www.bicc.de/events/sudanws/10johnson-17june02.pdf [last visited on 23 April 2008]

Johnson, Douglas. (1998) "The Sudan People's Liberation Army and the Problem of Factionalism". *In*: Clapham, Christopher. *African Guerrillas*. Oxford: James Currey, 53-72.

Johnson, Douglas. (1991) "From Military to Tribal Police: Policing the Upper Nile Province of the Sudan". *In*: Anderson, David M. and Killingray, David. *Policing the Empire: Government, Authority, and Control, 1830-1940*. Manchester: Manchester University Press, 151-67.

Johnson, Douglas. (1986) "On the Nilotic Frontier: Imperial Ethiopia in the Southern Sudan, 1898-1936". *In*: Donham, Donald L. and James, Wen-

410

dy. *The Southern Marches of Imperial Ethiopia*. Cambridge: Cambridge University Press, 216-45.

Johnson, Douglas and Gerard Prunier. (1993) "The Foundation and Expansion of the Sudan People's Liberation Army". *In*: Daly, John and Sikainga, Ahmad Alawad. *Civil War in the Sudan*. London: British Academic Press, 117-41.

Jok, Jok Madut. (2007) *Sudan: Race, Religion and Violence*. Oxford: Oneworld.

Jok, Jok Madut. (2001) *War and Slavery in Sudan*. Philadelphia: University of Pennsylvania Press.

Jok, Jok Madut and Sharon E. Hutchinson. (1999) "Sudan's Prolonged Civil War and the Militarization of Nuer and Dinka Identities". *African Studies Review*, **42**(2), pp. 125-45.

Kaarsholm, Preben. (2006) "States of Failure, Societies in Collapse? *Understandings of Violent Conflict in Africa*". *In*: Kaarsholm, Preben. *Violence, Political Culture and Development in Africa*. Oxford: James Currey, 1-24.

Kaldor, Mary. (2009) "New Wars". *The Broker*, **14**(June), pp. 14-7.

Kaldor, Mary. (2003) *Global Civil Society: An Answer to War*. Cambridge: Polity Press.

Kaldor, Mary. (1999) *New and Old Wars: Organized Violence in a Global Era*. Cambridge: Polity Press.

Kalyvas, Stathis N. (2009) "War's Evolution". *The Broker*, **14**(June), pp. 18-20.

Kalyvas, Stathis N. (2006) *The Logic of Violence in Civil War*. Cambridge: Cambridge University Press.

Kaplan, Robert. (2000) *The Coming of Anarchy*. New York: Random House.

Kaplan, Robert. (1994) "The Coming of Anarchy". *Atlantic Monthly*, February, pp. 44-76.

Karsani, Awad al-Sid. (1993) "Beyond Sufism: The Case of Millenial Islam in Sudan". *In*: Brenner, Louis. *Muslim Identity and Social Change in Sub-Saharan Africa*. London: Hurst, 134-53.

Karsani, Awad al-Sid. (1985) "The Majdhubiyya Tariqa: Its Doctrine, Organization, and Politics". *In*: Daly, Martin W. *Al-Majdhubiyya and al-Mikashfiyya: Two Sufi Tariqas in the Sudan*. Khartoum: University of Khartoum Press, 1-97.

Kebbede, Girma. (1999) "Sudan: The North-South Conflict in Historical Perspective". *In*: Kebbede, Girma. *Sudan's Predicament: Civil War, Displacement and Ecological Degradation*. Aldershot: Ashgate, 11-43.

Keen, David. (2001) "Sudan: Conflict and Rationality". *In*: Stewart, Frances, FitzGerald, Valpy, et. al. *War and Underdevelopment Volume II: Country Experiences*. Oxford: Oxford University Press, 220-303.

Keen, David. (1998) "The Economic Functions of Violence in Civil Wars". Adelphi Paper 320. London: International Institute of Strategic Studies.

Khalid, Mansour. (1990) *The Government They Deserve: The Role of the Elite in Sudan's Political Economy*. London: Kegan Paul.

Khalid, Mansour. (1985) *Nimeiri and the Revolution of Dis-May*. London: Kegan Paul International.

Kirkinen, Heikki. (1972) *Kehitysalue – Kehitysmaa: Laulu Kotimaisesta Kolonialismista*. Tampere: Tampereen Kirjapaino.

Knoke, David. (1994) *Political Networks: The Structural Perspective*. Cambridge: Cambridge University Press.

Knoke, David and Jodi Burmeister-May. (1990) "International Relations". *In*: Knoke, David. *Political Networks: The Structural Perspective*. Cambridge: Cambridge University Press, 175-202.

Kok, Peter Nyon. (1996) "Sudan: Between Radical Restructuring and Deconstruction of State Systems". *Review of African Political Economy*, **70**(23), pp. 555-62.

Kok, Peter Nyon. (1992) "Adding Fuel to the Conflict: Oil, War and Peace in the Sudan". *In*: Cliffe, Lionel, Doornbos, Martin, Abdel Ghaffar M. Ahmed, and Markakis, John. *Beyond Conflict in the Horn: The Prospects for Peace, Recovery and Development in Ethiopia, Somalia, Eritrea and Sudan*. London: James Currey, 104-112.

Kopstein, Jeremy and Mark Lichbach. (eds.) (2005) *Comparative Politics: Interests, Identities, and Institutions in a Changing Global Order*. New York: Cambridge University Press.

Korn, David A. (1993) *Assassination in Khartoum*. Bloomington: Indiana University Press.

Kulusika, Simon E. (1998) *Southern Sudan: Political and Economic Power Dilemmas and Options*. London: Minerva Press.

Kuol, Monyluak Alor. (1997) "Administration of Justice in the (SPLA/M) Liberated Areas: Court Cases in War-Torn Southern Sudan". Oxford:

Refugee Studies Programme, February.

Kuran, Timur. (1998a) "Ethnic Dissimilation and Its International Diffusion". *In*: Lake, David A., and Rothchild. Donald. *The International Spread of Ethnic Conflict: Fear, Diffusion, and Escalation.* Princeton: Princeton University Press, 35-60.

Kuran, Timur. (1998b) "Ethnic Norms and Their Transformation through Reputational Cascades". *The Journal of Legal Studies*, **27**(2), pp. 623-59.

Kraushaar, Maren and Daniel Lambach. (2009). "Hybrid Political Orders: The Added Value of a New Concept". Occasional Paper 14, The Australian Centre for Peace and Conflict Studies (ACPACS).

Lagu, Joseph. (1981) *Decentralization: A Necessity for the Southern Provinces of the Sudan.* Khartoum: Samar Printing Press.

Latif Mohammed, Nadir A. (1999) "Economic Implications of Civil Wars in Sub-Saharan Africa and the Economic Policies Necessary for the Successful Transition". *Journal of African Economies* **8**(suppl. 1), pp. 107-148.

Lefevbre, Jeffrey. (1991) *Arms for the Horn: U.S. Security Policy in Ethiopia and Somalia, 1953-1991.* Petersburg (PA): Pittsburg University Press.

Legum, Colin and Bill Lee. (1979) *The Horn of Africa in Continuing Crisis.* New York: Africana Publishing.

Lemarchand, Réne. (2003) "Ethnicity as Myth: The View from Central Africa". *In*: Pumphrey, Carolyn and Schwartz-Barcott, Rye. *Armed Conflict in Africa.* Lanham: Scarecrow, 87-112.

Leonardi, Cherry. (2007) "'Liberation' or Capture: Youth in between 'Hakuma', and 'Home' during Civil War and Its Aftermath in Southern Sudan". *African Affairs*, **106**(424), pp. 391-412.

Lesch, Ann Mosely. (1998) *The Sudan: Contested National Identities.* Bloomington: Indiana University Press.

Lobell, Steven E. and Philip Mauceri. (2004) *Ethnic Conflict and International Politics: Explaining Diffusion and Escalation.* Basingstoke: Palgrave MacMillan.

LOC. (1991) *Country Study: Sudan.* Washington (DC): The Library of Congress.

Lonsdale, John. (1994) "Moral Ethnicity and Political Tribalism". *In*: Kaarsholm, Preben and Hultin, Jan. *Inventions and Boundaries: Historical and Anthropological Approaches to the Study of Ethnicity and National-ism*. Roskilde: International Development Studies, 131-50.

Louis, William Roger. (2006) *Ends of British Imperialism: The Scramble for Empire, Suez, and Decolonization*. London: I. B. Tauris.

Lugard, Frederick D. (1922) *The Dual Mandate in British Tropical Africa*. London: Blackwood.

Lukes, Steven. (2005) *Power: A Radical View*. Basingstoke (UK): Palgrave MacMillan.

Lusk, Gill. (2005) "The Sudan & The Darfur". *Covert Action Quarterly*, Spring. Available at http://www.thirdworldtraveler.com/Genocide/Sudan_Darfur.html [visited 7 October 2009]

Lyons, Roy. (1978) "The USSR, China and the Horn of Africa". *Review of African Political Economy*, 5(12), pp. 5-30.

MacEoin, Dennis and Ahmed Al-Shahi. (1983) *Islam in the Modern World*. New York: Palgrave Macmillan.

MacIver, Robert M. (1947) *The Web of Government*. New York: The Mac-Millan Company.

Madut-Arop, Arop. (2006) *Sudan's Painful Road to Peace: A Full Story of the Founding and the Development of the SPLM/A*. Charleston (SC): BookSurge, LLC.

Majak, Damazo Dut. (1997) "Rape of Nature: The Environmental Destruc-tion and Ethnic Cleansing of the Sudan". *Journal of Developing Societ-ies*, 13(1), pp. 135-49.

Makki, Mohamed Ahmed Hassan. (1989) *Sudan: The Christian Design*. Markfield, Leicester: The Islamic Foundation.

Malwal, Bona. (1985) *The Sudan: A Second Challenge to Nationhood*. New York: Thornton Books.

Mamdani, Mahmood. (1997) *Citizen and Subject: Decentralized Despotism and the Legacy of Late Colonialism*. Delhi: Oxford University Press.

Markakis, John. (1998) *Resource Conflict in the Horn of Africa*. London: Sage.

Mason, T. David. (1989) "Nonelite Response to State Sanctioned Terror". *Western Political Quarterly*, 42(4), pp. 502-534.

Mason, T. David, and Dale A. Krane (1989) "The Political Economy of Death Squads: Toward a Theory of the Impact of State-Sanctioned Terror". *International Studies Quarterly*, **33**(2), pp. 175-198.

Matturi, Kai. (2007) "Understanding the Wars of West Africa through the Prism of Political Economy". Presented in the PSAI Postgraduate Conference, Trinity College, Dublin, 27-28 April.

Mawut, Lazarus Leek. (1983) *Dinka Resistance to Condominium Rule 1902-1932*. Khartoum: University of Khartoum.

Mayall, James. (2005) "The Legacy of Colonialism". *In*: Chesterman, Simon, Ignatieff, Michael and Thakur, Ramesh. *Making the States Work: State Failure and the Crisis of Governance*. Tokyo: United Nations University Press, 36-58.

Mazrui, Ali. (1975) *Soldiers and Kinsmen in Uganda: The Making of a Military Ethnocracy*. Beverly Hills (CA): Sage.

Mazrui, Ali. (1973) "The Black Arabs in Comparative Perspective: The Political Sociology of Race Mixture". *In*: Wai, Dunstan M. *The Southern Sudan: The Problem of National Integration*. London: Frank Cass, 47-81.

McSweeney, Bill. (1999) *Security, Identity and Interests: A Sociology of International Relations*. Cambridge: Cambridge University Press.

Melvill, David. (2002) "Restoring Peace and Democracy in Sudan: Limited Choices for African Leadership", Occasional Paper 34, Institute for Global Dialogue, Pretoria.

Meredith, Martin. (2005) *The State of Africa: A History of Fifty Years of Independence*. London: Simon & Schuster.

Milliken, Jennifer and Keith Krause. (2002) "State Failure, State Collapse, and State Reconstruction". *Development and Change*, **33**(5), pp. 753-74.

Mills, C. Wright. (1956) *The Power Elite*. Oxford: Oxford Press.

Miner, Edward. (2003) "The Historical Background of Missionary Activity in the Sudan". Indiana University Digital Library. Available online: http://www.dlib.indiana.edu/collections/nuer/edward/missionary.html [accessed 23 April 2008]

Mire, Lawrence. (1986) "Al-Zubayr Pasha and the Zariba Based Slave Trade in the Bahr al-Ghazal 1855-1879". *In*: Willis, John R. *Slaves and Slavery in Muslim Africa*. London: Routledge.

Mitchell, J. Clyde. (1956) "The Kalela Dance: Aspects of Social Relationships among Urban Africans in Northern Rhodesia", Paper 27, Rhodes-Livingstone Institute.

Mkandawire, Thandika. (2002) "The Terrible Toll of Post-Colonial 'Rebel Movements' in Africa: Towards an Explanation of the Violence against the Peasantry". *Journal of Modern African Studies*, **40**(2), pp. 181-215.

MLPCJ (1954) "Minutes of the 1954 Liberal Party Conference in Juba". (FO 371/108326; no. 193).

Mohamed Ali, Galal el-Din el-Tayeb. (1989) *Industry and Peripheral Capitalism in the Sudan: A Geographical Analysis*. Khartoum: Khartoum University Press.

Moore, Will H. (1995) "Rational Rebels: Overcoming the Free-Rider Problem". *Political Research Quarterly*, **48**(2), pp. 417-454.

Mueller, John. (2002) "The Remnants of War: Thugs as Residual Combatants". Presented at the International Studies Association Annual Convention, New Orleans, 24-27 March.

Muhammad Ali, Abbas Ibrahim. (1972) *The British, the Slave Trade, and Slavery in the Sudan*. Khartoum: Khartoum University Press.

Munene, Macharia. (2001) "Culture and the Economy: The Creation of Poverty", Presented at the Culture Week Seminar, Kenyatta University, 20 September.

Munene, Macharia. (1995) *The Truman Administration and the Decolonization of Sub-Saharan Africa*. Nairobi: Nairobi University Press.

Murithi, Timothy. (2005) *The African Union: Pan-Africanism, Peacebuilding and Development*. Aldershot: Ashgate.

Murshed, S. Mansoob. (2002) "Conflict, Civil War and Underdevelopment". *Journal of Peace Research*, **39**(4), pp. 387-93.

Musa, Hassan Attiyah. (1988) "Refugees in Southern Sudan". *In*: Arou, Mom, K. N. and Yongo-Bure, Benaiah. *North-South Relations in the Sudan since the Addis Ababa Agreement*. Khartoum: University of Khartoum Press, 456-70.

Musso, Georgio. (2009) "'We Will Revert Back to how We Were': The National Congress Party Face to the Elections and Referendum". Paper presented at the 8th International Sudan Studies Conference, University of South Africa, 25-28 November.

Münkler, Herfried. (2004) *The New Wars*. Cambridge: Polity Press.

Nafziger, E. Wayne, Stewart, Frances, and Raimo Väyrynen. (eds.) (2000) *War, Hunger, and Displacement: The Origins of Humanitarian Emergencies. Volume 1: Analyses*. Oxford: Oxford University Press.

416

New York Times. (1899) "The Khalifa's Position", New York Times, 15 June.

Niblock, Tim. (1987) *Class and Power in Sudan: The Dynamics of Sudanese Politics, 1898-1985.* Albany (NY): State University of New York Press.

Nicolaïdis, Kalypso, Sèbe, Berny, and Gabrielle Maas (eds.) (2015) *Echoes of Empire: Memory, Identity and Colonial Legacies.* I.B. Tauris: London.

Nicoll, Fergus. (2004) *The Sword of the Prophet: The Mahdi of Sudan and the Death of General Gordon.* Phoenix Mill: Sutton Publishing.

Nile Mirror. (1975) "A Colonel and Seven Soldiers Die in Akobo", 14 March.

Noman, Akbar, Botchwey, Kwesi, Stein, Howard and Joseph E. Stiglitz. (2012) *Good Growth and Governance in Africa: Rethinking Development Strategies.* Oxford: Oxford University Press.

Nordstrom, Carolyn. (2004) *Shadows of War: Violence, Power, and International Profiteering in the Twenty-First Century.* Berkeley: University of California Press.

Nordstrom, Carolyn. (2001) "Out of the Shadows". *In*: Callaghy, Thomas, Kassimir, Ronald, and Robert Latham. *Intervention and Transnationalism in Africa.* Cambridge: Cambridge University Press, 216-39.

Nyaba, Peter Adwok. (2000) *The Politics of Liberation in South Sudan: An Insider's View.* Second Edition. Kampala: Fountain Publishers.

Nyombe, Bureng G. V. (2007) *Some Aspects of Bari History: A Comparative Linguistic and Oral Tradition Reconstruction.* Nairobi: University of Nairobi Press.

O'Ballance, Edgar. (2000) *Sudan, Civil War and Terrorism, 1956-99.* New York: St. Martin's Press.

O'Ballance, Edgar. (1977) *The Secret War in the Sudan: 1955-1972.* London: Faber and Faber.

O'Brien, Jay. (1979) *The Political Economy of Development and Underdevelopment: An Introduction.* Khartoum: Khartoum University Press.

O'Fahey, Rex S. (2002) "They are Slaves, but Yet They Go Free". *In*: Fadl and Richard Gray. *Religion and Conflict in Sudan.* Nairobi: Paulines Publications.

O'Fahey, Rex S. (1973) "Slavery and the Slave Trade in Dar Fur". *Journal of African History*, 14(1), pp. 29-43.

O'Fahey, Rex S. and Jay L. Spaulding. (1974) *Kingdoms of the Sudan*. London: Methuen.

O'Neill, Bard E. (1990). *Insurgency & Terrorism: Inside Modern Revolutionary Warfare*. Oxford: Brassey's.

O'Neill, Bard E. (1980) "Insurgency: A Framework for Analysis". *In*: Bard O. Neill, William R. Heaton, and Donald J. Alberts (eds.). *Insurgency in the Modern World*. Boulder: Westview Press, 1-42.

Oduho, Joseph and William Deng. (1963) *The Problem of the Southern Sudan*. London: Oxford University Press.

Olowu, Dele and James S. Wunsch. (eds.) (2003) *Local Governance in Africa: The Challenges of Democratic Decentralization*. Boulder (CO): Lynne Rienner.

Opp, Karl-Dieter. (2009) *Theories of Political Protest and Social Movements: A Multidisciplinary Introduction, Critique, and Synthesis*. Abingdon (UK): Routledge.

Osman, Abdullahi Mohamed. (1985) "The Mikashfiyya: A Sufi Tariqa in the Modern Sudan" *In*: Daly, Martin W. *Al Majdhubiyya and al Mikashfiyya: Two Sufi Tariqas in the Sudan*. Khartoum: University of Khartoum Press, 101-146.

Ottaway, Marina, Herbst, Jeffrey and Greg Mills. (2004) "Africa's Big States: Towards a New Realism". *Policy Outlook*, Carnegie Foundation for International Peace, February. Available online:

http://www.carnegieendowment.org/files/PolicyOutlookOttaway.pdf [accessed 23 April 2008]_

Oxhorn, Philip, Tulchin, Joseph S. and Andrew Selee. (eds.) (2004) *Decentralization, Democratic Governance, and Civil Society in Comparative Perspective: Africa, Asia, and Latin America*. Washington (DC): Woodrow Wilson Center Press.

Pantuliano, Sarah. (2007) "The Land Question: Sudan's Peace Nemesis". HPG Working Paper, Overseas Development Institute, December. Available online: http://www.odi.org.uk/resources/download/3182.pdf [accessed 23 April 2008]_

Paterno, Steve A. (2007). *The REV. Fr. Saturnino Lohure: A Roman Catholic Priest Turned Rebel, the South Sudan Experience*. Frederick (MD): Publishamerica.

Patrick, Stewart M. (2006) "Weak States and Global Threats: Fact or Fiction". *The Washington Quarterly*, Spring, pp. 27-53.

Pearce, Jenny. (2005) "Policy Failure and Petroleum Predation: The Economics of Civil War Debate Viewed 'From the War-Zone'". *Government and Opposition*, **40**(2), pp. 152-80.

Peters, Ralph. (1994) "The New Warrior Class". *Parameters*, **24**(2), pp. 16-26.

Piaget, Jean. (1985) *The Equilibration of Cognitive Structures: The Central Problem of Intellectual Development*. Chicago: University of Chicago Press.

Piaget, Jean. (1971) *Biology and Knowledge*. Chicago: University of Chicago Press.

Pierre, Jon and B. Guy Peters. (2000) *Governance, Politics and the State*. New York (NY): St. Martin's Press.

Poggo, Scopas S. (2008) *The First Sudanese Civil War: Africans, Arabs, and Israelis in the Southern Sudan, 1955-1972*. New York: Palgrave Macmillan.

Popkin, Samuel L. (1979) *The Rational Peasant: The Political Economy of Rural Society in Vietnam*. Berkeley (CA): University of California Press.

Posen, Barry R. (1993) "The Security Dilemma and Ethnic Conflict". *In*: Brown, Michael E. *Ethnic Conflict and International Security*. Princeton: Princeton University of Press, 103-124.

Posner, Daniel. (2005) *Institutions and Ethnic Politics in Africa*. Cambridge: Cambridge University Press.

Prunier, Gérard. (1986) "From Peace to War: The Southern Sudan (1972-1983)". Occasional Paper 3, University of Hull, Department of Sociology and Anthropology.

Prunier, Gérard and Rachel M. Gisselquist. (2003) "The Sudan: A Successfully Failed State". *In*: Rotberg, Robert I. *State Failure and State Weakness in a Time of Terror*. Cambridge (MA): World Peace Foundation, 101-28.

Pumphrey, Carolyn. (2003) "General Introduction". *In*: Pumphrey, Carolyn and Schwartz-Barcott, Rye. *Armed Conflict in Africa*. Lanham (U.S.): Scarecrow, 1-19.

Pumphrey, Carolyn and Rye Schwartz-Barcott. (eds.) (2003) *Armed Conflict in Africa*. Lanham (MD): Scarecrow.

419

Pureza, José M., Duffield, Mark, Woodward, Susan, and David Sogge. (2006) "Peacebuilding and failed States: Some Theoretical Notes". Working Paper 256, Oficina do CES, Centro de Estudos Sociais, University of Coimbra. Available online: http://www.ces.uc.pt/publicacoes/oficina/256/256.pdf [accessed 23 April 2008]

Putnam, Robert D. (1976) *The Comparative Study of Political Elites*. New Jersey: Prentice Hall.

Ranger, Terence. (1992) "The Invention of Tradition in Colonial Africa". *In*: Hobsbawm, Eric and Ranger, Terence. *The Invention of Tradition*. Cambridge: Cambridge University Press, 211-62.

Rapoport, David C. (1996) "Importance of Space in Violent Ethno-Religious Strife". *Nationalism and Ethnic Politics*, **2**(2), pp. 258-85.

RCIDSS. (1956) "Report of the Commission of Inquiry into the Disturbances in the Southern Sudan during August, 1955". Ministry of Interior, Republic of the Sudan: McCorquedale & Co.

Reich, Bernard. (1980) "The Sudan". *In*: Long David E. and Reich, Bernard. *The Government of the Middle East and North Africa*. Boulder: Wesview Press, 353-69.

Reno, William. (2005) "The Politics of Violent Opposition in Collapsing States". *Government and Opposition*, **40**(2), pp. 127-51.

Reno, William. (2004) "Empirical Challenge to Economic Analyses of Conflicts". Presented at "The Economic Analysis of Conflict: Problems and Prospects" conference, Washington (DC), April 19-20.

Reno, William. (2003). "'Resource Wars' in the Shadow of State Collapse". Presented at "Resource Politics and Security in a Global Age" conference, University of Sheffield, June 26-28.

Reno, William (2002). "Economies of War and their Transformation: Sudan and the Variable Impact of Natural Resources on Conflict". Presented at "Money Makes the War Go Round: Transforming the Economy of War in Sudan" conference, Brussels, June 12-13. Available online: http://www.bicc.de/events/sudanws/5reno20august02.pdf [accessed 23 April 2008]

Reno, William. (2001) "How Sovereignty Matters: International Markets and the Political Economy of Local Politics in Weak States". *In*: Callaghy, Thomas, Kassimir, Ronald, and Robert Latham. *Intervention and Transnationalism in Africa*. Cambridge: Cambridge University Press, 197-215.

Reno, William. (1998) *Warlord Politics and African States*. Boulder (CO): Lynne Rienner.

Reno, William. (1997) "War, Market, and the Reconfiguration of West Africa's Weak States". *Comparative Politics*, **29**(4), pp. 493-509.

Reynal-Querol, Marta. (2002) "Ethnicity, Political Systems, and Civil Wars". *Journal of Conflict Resolution*, **46**(1), pp. 29-54.

Richards, Paul. (2007) "Peripheral Wars in Africa: Is General Explanation Possible?". *Studia Africana*, **18**, pp. 8-14.

Richards, Paul. (2005) "New War: An Ethnographic Approach". *In*: Richards, Paul. *No Peace No War: An Anthropology of Contemporary Armed Conflicts*. Oxford: James Currey, 1-21.

Richards, Paul. (1996) *Fighting for the Rainforest: War, Youth and Resources in Sierra Leone*. Oxford: James Currey.

Rist, Gilbert. (1997) *The History of Development: From Western Origins to Global Faith*. Atlantic Highlands (NJ): Zed Books.

RJC. (1947) "Juba Conference 1947". Record of the Juba Conference. EP/SCR/1.A.5/1. Available online:

http://www.gurtong.org/resourcecenter/Documents/Articles/juba_conference_1947.pdf [accessed 23 April 2008]

RMFEP. (1977) The Six-Year Plan of Economic and Social Development: 1977/78-1982/3". Juba: Regional Ministry of Finance and Economic Planning.

Roden, David. (1974) "Regional Inequality and Rebellion in the Sudan". *Geographical Review*, **64**(4), pp. 498-516.

Rogier, Emeric. (2005) "No More Hills Ahead? Sudan's Tortuous Ascent to the Heights of Peace". Security Paper 1, Netherlands Institute of International Relations, Clingendael, The Hague.

Rolandsen, Øystein. (2005) *Guerrilla Government: Political Changes in the Southern Sudan during the 1990s*. Uppsala: Nordic Africa Institute.

Romanucci-Ross, Lola and DeVos, George. (eds.) (1998) *Ethnic Identity: Creation, Conflict, and Accommodation*. London: AltMira Press.

Ross, Michael L. (2004) "How Do Natural Resources Influence Civil War? Evidence from Thirteen Cases". *International Organization*, **58**(1), pp. 35-67.

Ross, Michael L. (2003) "Oil, Drugs, and Diamonds: The Varying Role of Natural Resources in Civil War". *In*: Ballentine, Karen and Sherman, Jake. *The Political Economy of Armed Conflict: Beyond Greed and Grievance*. Boulder: Lynne Rienner, 47-70.

Rotberg, Robert I. (2004) "The Failure and Collapse of Nation-States: Breakdown, Prevention, and Repair". *In*: Rotberg, Robert I. *When States Fail: Causes and Consequences*. Princeton (NJ): Princeton University Press, 1-49.

Rotberg, Robert I. (2003a) "Failed States, Collapsed States, Weak States: Causes and Indicators". *In*: Rotberg, Robert I. *State Failure and State Weakness in a Time of Terror.* Washington (DC): The Brookings Institution, 1-25.

Rotberg, Robert I. (2003b) "Nation-State Failure: A Recurring Phenomenon?", Discussion Paper, NIC 2020 Project. Available online:

http://www.dni.gov/nic/PDF_GIF_2020_Support/2003_11_06_papers/panel2_nov6.pdf [accessed 23 April 2008]

RPRA. (1981) Resolution of the People's Regional Assembly No. 14, 31 March, Juba.

RPS (1978) "Regional Policy Statement". The Regional Ministry of Information and Culture, Juba, June 1978.

Ruay, Deng D. Akol. (1994) *The Politics of Two Sudans: The South and the North 1821-1969*. Motala: Nordic Africa Institute.

Ruiz-Giménez Arrieta, Itziar. (2002) "Los Conflictos Armados del África Subsahariana Contemporánea". *Pueblos* **4**, pp. 31-34.

Ruiz-Giménez Arrieta, Itziar. (2000) "El Colapso del Estado Poscolonial en la Decada de los Noventa". *In*: Peñas, Francisco Javier. *África en el Sistema Internacional: Cinco Siglos de Frontera*. Madrid: Universidad Autónoma de Madrid, 165-207.

Russell, Bertrand. (1962) *Power: A New Social Analysis*. New York: Routledge.

Ryan, Stephen. (1995) *Ethnic Conflict and International Relations*. Aldershot: Dartmouth Publishing Company.

Said, Beshir Mohammed. (1965) *The Sudan: Crossroads of Africa*. London: Dufours.

Salvi, Sergio. (1973) *Le Nazioni Proibite: Guida a Dieci Colonie Interne dell'Europa Occidentale*. Florence: Valletti.

Sanderson, George N. (1985) "The Ghost of Adam Smith: Ideology, Bureaucracy, and the Frustration of Economic Development in the Sudan, 1934-1940". *In*: Daly, Martin W. *Modernization in the Sudan*. New York: Lilian Barber Press.

Sarkesian, Sam C. (1973) "The Southern Sudan: A Reassessment". *African Studies Review*, 16(1), pp. 1-22.

Schaefer, Richard T. (2008) *Racial and Ethnic Groups*. Eleventh Edition. Upper Saddle River (NJ): Prentice Hall.

Sconyers, David. (1978) "British Policy and Mission Education in the Southern Sudan, 1928-1946". Unpublished PhD Thesis, University of Pennsylvania.

Scott, John. (1991) *Social Network Analysis: A Handbook*. London: SAGE.

SEC. (1954) "Final Report on the 1953 Elections". *Sudanese Elections Commission. Government Printer*, Khartoum.

Segal, Ronald. (2002) *Islam's Black Slaves: The Other Black Diaspora*. New York (NY): Farrar, Straus, and Giroux.

Sharkey, Heather J. (2007) "When does Ethnic Identity Turn into Racism". *Chicken Bones: A Journal*. Online at: http://www.nathanieltuner.com/ whendoesethnic identityturnintoracism.htm [accessed 3 April 2009]

Sharkey, Heather J. (2003) *Living with Colonialism: Nationalism and Culture in the Anglo-Egyptian Sudan*. Berkeley: University of California Press.

Sherman, Jake. (2000) "Profit vs. Peace: The Clandestine Diamond Economy of Angola". *Journal of International Affairs*, **53**(2), pp. 699-719.

Sidahmed, Abdel Salam. (1997) *Politics and Islam in Contemporary Sudan*. Richmond: Curzon.

Sidahmed, Abdel Salam and Alsir Sidahmed. (2005) *Sudan*. Abingdon (UK): RoutledgeCurzon.

Sikainga, Ahmad Alawad. (1996) *Slaves into Workers*. Austin: University of Texas Press.

Sikainga, Ahmad Alawad. (1993) "Northern Sudanese Political Parties and the Civil War". *In*: Daly, John and Sikainga, Ahmad Alawad. *Civil War in the Sudan*. London: British Academic Press, 78-96.

Simonse, Simon. (1992) *Kings of Disaster: Dualism, Centralism and the Scapegoat King in Southeastern Sudan*. **Leiden: E.J. Brill.**

Simpson, Morag C. (1981) "Large-scale Mechanised Rain-fed Farming Developments in the Sudan". Presented at Centre of African Studies Seminar, University of Edinburgh, 21-22 November, 1980. Published as part of seminar proceedings in *Post-Independence Sudan*. University of Edinburg: Centre of African Studies, 197-212.

Snow, Donald M. (1996) *Uncivil Wars: International Security and the New Internal Conflicts*. Boulder (CO): Lynne Rienner.

Spaulding, Jay. (2006) "Pastoralism, Slavery, Commerce, Culture and the Fate of the Nubians of Northern and Central Kordofan under Dar Fur rule, ca. 1750-ca. 1850". *International Journal of African Historical Studies*, **39**(3), pp. 393-412.

Spaulding, Jay. (1988) "The Business of Slavery in the Central Anglo-Egyptian Sudan, 1910-1930". *African Economic History*, **17**, pp. 23-44.

Spaulding, Jay. (1985) *The Heroic Age in Sinnar*. East Lansing: Michigan State University.

Spaulding, Jay. (1982) "Slavery, Land Tenure, and Social Class in the Northern Turkish Sudan". *The International Journal of African Historical Studies*, **15**(2), pp. 1-20.

SPLM/A Manifesto. (1983), 31 July.

Sriram, Chandra Lekha and Nielsen, Zoe. (2004) *Exploring Subregional Conflict: Opportunities for Conflict Prevention*. London: Lynne Rienner.

Stewart, Frances. (2001) "Horizontal Inequalities: A Neglected Dimension of Development". CRISE Working Paper 1, Queen Elizabeth House, University of Oxford. Available online: http://www.crise.ox.ac.uk/pubs/workingpaper1.pdf [accessed 23 April 2008]

Stewart, Frances. (2000) "Crisis Prevention: Tackling Horizontal Inequalities". *Oxford Development Studies*, **28**(3), pp. 246-62.

Sørensen, Georg. (1998) *Democracy and Democtratization: Processes and Prospects in a Changing World*. Boulder: Westwood Press.

Taisier, M. Ali and Robert O. Matthews. (1999) *Civil Wars in Africa: Roots and Resolution*. London: McGill-Queen's University Press.

Tajfel, Henri. (1978) "Social Categorization, Social Identity, and Social Comparison". *In*: Tajfel, Henri. *Differentiation between Social Groups*.

London: Academic Press, 61-76.

Tajfel, Henri and John C. Turner (1986) "The Social Identity Theory of Intergroup Behavior" *In*: Austin, William G. and Worchel, Stephen. *Psychology of Intergroup Relations*. Chicago: Nelson-Hall, 7-24.

Tajfel, Henri and John C. Turner. (1979) "An Integrative Theory of Intergroup Conflict". *In*: Austin, William G. and Worchel, Stephen. *The Social Psychology of Intergroup Relations*. Monterey (CA): Brooks and Cole, 33-47.

Taylor, Donald M. and Fathali M. Moghaddam. (1994) *Theories of Intergroup Relations: International Social Psychological Perspectives*. Westport (CT): Praeger.

Thomas, Edward. (2010) *The Kafia Kingi Enclave: People, Politics and History in the North-South Boundary Zone of Western Sudan*. London: Rift Valley Institute.

Thompson, Alex. (2004) *An Introduction to African Politics*. London: Routledge.

Tignor, Robert L. (1987) "The Sudanese Private Sector: an Historical Overview". *The Journal of Modern African Studies*, **25**(2): 179-212.

Tilly, Charles. (1992) *Coercion, Capital and European States, AD 1990-1992*. Cambridge: Blackwell.

Tilly, Charles. (1985) "War Making and State Making as Organized Crime". *In*: Evans, Peter B., Rueschemeyer, Dietrich and Skocpol, Theda. *Bringing the State Back in*. Cambridge: Cambridge University Press, 169-191.

Tilly, Charles. (1978) *From Mobilization to Revolution*. Reading (MA): Addison-Wesley.

Tiyambe Zeleza, Paul. (1993) *A Modern Economic History of Africa Volume I: The Nineteenth Century*. Dakar: Codesria.

Turner, John C. (1990) "Foreword". *In*: Hogg, Michael A. and Dominic Adams. *Social Identifications*. London: Routledge, x-xii.

Turner, John W. (1998) *Continent Ablaze: The Insurgency Wars in Africa 1960 to Present*. London: Arms and Armour.

UCDP. (2008) "Active Conflicts by Conflict Type and Year". Uppsala Conflict Data Program. Uppsala University. Available online:

http://www.pcr.uu.se/research/UCDP/graphs/type_year.gif   [accessed 23 April 2008]

Utas, Mats (2012). "Introduction: Bigmanity and Network Governance in African Conflicts". *In*: Utas, Mats. *African Conflicts and Informal Power: Big Men and Networks*. Zed Books: London, pp. 1-31.

Utas, Mats (ed.) (2012). *African Conflicts and Informal Power: Big Men and Networks*. Zed Books: London.

van de Walle, Nicolas. (2001) *African Economies and the Politics of Permanent Crisis, 1979-1999*. Cambridge: Cambridge University Press.

van Dijk, Teun A. (1993) *Elite discourse and Racism*. London: Sage.

Vandervort, Bruce. (1998) *Wars of Imperial Conquest in Africa, 1830-1914*. London: University College Press.

Veenhoven, Willem A. and Winifred C. Ewing. (1977) *Case Studies on Human Rights and Fundamental Freedoms: A World Survey, Volume 4*. Leiden: Martinus Nijhoff Publishers.

Verney, Peter. (1999) "Raising the Stakes: Oil and Conflict in Sudan", Report, Sudan Update. Available online: http://www.sudanupdate.org/REPORTS/Oil/Oil.pdf [accessed 5 June 2012]

Vlassenroot, Koen and Timothy Raeymaekers. (2004) *Conflict and Social Transformation in Eastern DR Congo*. Gent: Academia Press.

Wai, Dunstan M. (1973) *The Southern Sudan: The Problem of National Integration*, London: Frank Cass.

Wakoson, Elias Nyamlell. (1993) "The Politics of Southern Self-Government 1972-83". *In*: Daly, Martin W. and Sikainga, Ahmad A. *Civil War in the Sudan*. London: British Academic Press, 27-50.

Wakoson, Elias Nyamlell. (1984) "Origins and Development of the Anyanya Movement 1955-1972". *In*: Beshir, Mohammed Omer. *Southern Sudan: Regionalism and Religion*. Khartoum: University of Khartoum Graduate College, 127-204.

Walter, Victor. (1969) *Terror and Resistance: A Study of Political Violence*. Oxford: Oxford University Press.

Walz, Terence. (1978) *Trade between Egypt and Bilad as-Sudan, 1700-1820*. Cairo: Institut Francais d'Archeologie Orientale du Caire.

Warburg, Gabriel. (2003) *Islam, Sectarianism and Politics in Sudan since the Mahdiyya*. Madison: University of Wisconsin Press.

Warburg, Gabriel. (2000) "The Nile Waters, Border Issues and Radical Islam in Egyptian-Sudanese Relations: 1956-1995". *In*: Spaulding, Jay and Stephanie Beswick. *White Nile, Black Blood: War, Leadership, and Ethnicity from Khartoum to Kampala*. Lawrenceville (NJ): The Red Sea Press, 73-90.

Warburg, Gabriel. (1993) "Sudan: Diversity and Conflict in an Unstable State". *Middle Eastern Studies*, **29**(2), 339-54.

Wassara, Samson. (2007) "Traditional Mechanisms of Conflict Resolution in Southern Sudan". Berghof Foundation for Peace Support, Berlin.

Weber, Max. (1968) *Basic Concepts of Sociology: Economy and Society*, Part One, Chapter I. Translated by Guenther Roth and Claus Wittich. Berkeley: University of California Press. Available online:http://www.ne.jp/asahi/moriyuki/abukuma/weber/method/basic/basic_concept_frame.html [accessed 23 April 2008]

Weinstein, Jeremy. (2005) *Inside Rebellion: The Politics of Insurgent Violence*. Cambridge: Cambridge University Press.

Weiss, Holger. (1999) "The 1889-90 Famine and the Mahdiyya in the Sudan: An Attempt to Implement the Principles of an Islamic Economy". Working Paper 4/99, Institute of Development Studies, University of Helsinki.

Whitaker, Jennifer. (1988) *How Can Africa Survive?* NewYork: Harper and Row.

Widatalla, Abdel Latif. (1988) "A History of Oil Exploration in the Sudan Leading to the Present Activities of Chevron in the Interior of the Country". *In*: Arou, Mom, K. N. and Yongo-Bure, Benaiah. *North-South Relations in the Sudan since the Addis Ababa Agreement*. Khartoum: University of Khartoum Press, 420-9.

Woodward, Bob. (1987) *Veil: The Secret Wars of the CIA 1981-87*. New York (NY): Simon and Schuster.

Woodward, Peter. (2006) *US Foreign Policy and the Horn of Africa*. Aldershot (UK): Ashgate.

Woodward, Peter. (2003) *The Horn of Africa: Politics and International Relations*. London: I. B. Tauris.

Woodward, Peter. (2002) "Peace and Elite Non-Oil Economic Interests". Presented at "Money Makes the War Go Round: Transforming the Economy of War in Sudan" conference, Brussels, 12-13 June. Available online:http://www.bicc.de/events/sudanws/7woodward16june02.pdf [accessed 23 April 2008]

Woodward, Peter. (1997) "Sudan: Islamic Radicals in Power". *In*: Esposito, John L. *Political Islam: Revolution, Radicalism, or Reform*. Cairo: American University in Cairo Press, 95-114.

Woodward, Peter. (1995) "Sudan: War Without End". *In*: Furley, Oliver. *Conflict in Africa*. London: Tauris Academic Studies, 92-109.

Woodward, Susan. (2005) "Fragile States: Exploring the Concept". Commentary, FRIDE. Available online: http://www.fride.org/publication/97/fragile-states-exploring-the-concept [accessed 23 April 2008]

World Bank (2008) "Projects & Operations". Available online:http://web.worldbank.org/external/projects/main?pagePK=217672&piPK=95916&theSitePK=40941&menuPK=223661&sortorder=DESC&pagenumber=2&pagesize=50&countrycode=SD&regioncode=1&category=regcountries&sortby=BOARDSORTDATE [accessed 11 August 2008]

World Bank. (2003) "Country Brief – Sudan". Available online: http://www.worldbank.org/afr/sd/sd_ctry_brief.htm [accessed 23 April 2008]

Wright, Deil S. (1978) *Understanding Intergovernmental Relations*. North Scrituate: Duxbury Press.

Ylönen, Aleksi. (2015) "On the Complexity of Analyzing Armed Opposition: Objectives, Labeling, and Reflections on Ethiopia's Somali Region". *Journal of African History, Politics, and Society*, 1, 1, pp. 1-22.

Ylönen, Aleksi. (2009) "On Sources of Political Violence in Africa: The Case of 'Marginalizing State' in Sudan". *Política y Cultura*, 32, Fall, pp. 37-59.

Ylönen, Aleksi. (2008) "Political Marginalization and Economic Exclusion in the Making of Insurgencies in Sudan". *In*: Ström, Kaare and Öberg, Magnus. *Resources, Governance and Civil Conflict*. Milton Park, Abingdon: Routledge, 125-146.

Ylönen, Aleksi. (2005a) "Grievances in the Roots of Insurgencies: Southern Sudan and Darfur". *Peace, Conflict and Development*, 7, pp. 99-134.

Ylönen, Aleksi. (2005b) "The Shadow of Colonialism: Marginalisation, Identities and Conflict in the Sudan". *In*: Cornut-Gentille, Chantal. *Culture and Power: Culture and Society in the Age of Globalisation*. Zaragoza: University of Zaragoza Press, 153-168.

Yohannes, Okbazghi. (1997) *The United States and the Horn of Africa: An Analytical Study of Pattern and Progress*. Oxford: Westview Press.

Yongo-Bure, Benaiah. (1993) "The Underdevelopment of the Southern Sudan since Independence". *In*: Daly, Martin, W. and Sikainga, Ahmad, Alawad. *Civil War in the Sudan*. London: British Academic Press, 51-77.

Yongo-Bure, Benaiah. (1988a) "The First Decade of Development in the Southern Sudan". *In*: Arou, Mom, K. N. and Yongo-Bure, Benaiah. *North-South Relations in the Sudan since the Addis Ababa Agreement*. Khartoum: University of Khartoum Press, 371-407.

Young, William C. (2000) "The Cultural Dimensions of the Sudanese Civil War". *In*: Lacey, Robert Kevin and Coury, Ralph M. *The Arab-African and Islamic Worlds: Interdisciplinary Studies*. Oxford: Peter Lang, 183-99.

Zartman, I. William. (2005) "Need, Creed, and Greed in Intrastate Conflict". *In*: Arnson, Cynthia J. and Zartman, I. William. *Rethinking the Economics of War: The Intersection of Need, Creed, and Greed*. Baltimore: Johns Hopkins University Press, 256-84.

Zartman, I. William. (1995) "Introduction: Posing the Problem of State Collapse". *In*: Zartman, I. William. *Collapsed States: The Disintegration and Restoration of Legitimate Authority*. Boulder: Lynne Rienner, 1-11.

Zartman, I. William. (1985) *Ripe for Resolution: Conflict and Intervention in Africa*. Oxford: Oxford University Press.

Zeidan, David. (1999) "Radical Islam in Egypt: A Comparison of Two Groups". *Middle East Review of International Affairs*, **3**(3) September. Available at: http://meria.idc.ac.il/journal/1999/issue3/jv3n3a1.html [accessed 5 February 2009].

Zubaida, Sami. (2000) "*Trajectories of Political Islam*: Egypt, Iran and Turkey". *The Political Quarterly*, **71**(3), pp. 60-78.

INDEX

E

Economy 2, 11, 74, 75, 78, 88, 91, 99, 101, 116, 125, 129, 178, 197, 214, 228, 233, 236, 252, 259, 261, 291, 296, 299, 300, 301, 318, 319, 320, 321, 322, 352, 366, 369, 373, 374, 381, 392

Egypt 46, 67, 68, 74, 75, 76, 77, 79, 80, 81, 83, 87, 88, 93, 100, 101, 102, 103, 104, 108, 109, 110, 112, 113, 115, 117, 118, 121, 122, 123, 124, 127, 132, 133, 134, 135, 144, 146, 149, 150, 153, 154, 155, 156, 157, 159, 161, 163, 165, 173, 174, 175, 176, 180, 182, 184, 185, 186, 187, 188, 189, 196, 197, 205, 208, 214, 234, 235, 236, 237, 239, 240, 252, 253, 254, 255, 256, 258, 268, 276, 283, 286, 296, 297, 298, 301, 317, 323, 324, 336, 357, 358, 365, 378, 381, 388, 404, 408, 426, 429

Elbadawi, Ibrahim 15, 16, 28, 29, 62, 404, 406

Elite 133, 136, 158, 412, 415, 426, 427

El Obeid 99, 117, 380

Eprile, Cecil 27, 63, 151, 189, 191, 192, 193, 194, 195, 198, 199, 200, 201, 202, 230, 233, 234, 235, 239, 240, 241, 243, 280, 404

Equatoria xii, 39, 72, 73, 83, 85, 93, 94, 103, 111, 118, 124, 128, 143, 147, 150, 153, 159, 166, 168, 169, 170, 171, 174, 177, 179, 180, 186, 190, 191, 200, 216, 217, 218, 221, 225, 227, 230, 238, 241, 245, 247, 257, 260, 265, 271, 283, 303, 309, 310, 311, 325, 328, 330, 332, 333, 334, 343, 351, 353, 355, 369, 372, 373, 375, 376, 378

Eritrea 110, 122, 156, 214, 230, 256, 298, 404, 412

Ethiopia 22, 51, 72, 73, 98, 119, 182, 183, 184, 199, 202, 205, 213, 214, 218, 222, 223, 224, 226, 230, 231, 237, 238, 240, 244, 251, 252, 255, 256, 257, 258, 261, 266, 278, 281, 283, 288, 289, 298, 302, 312, 313, 314, 319, 330, 336, 337, 339, 341, 342, 343, 345, 347, 350, 351, 353, 358, 360, 363, 364, 365, 366, 367, 368, 369, 370, 374, 375, 378, 381, 399, 410, 411, 412, 413, 428

Ethiopian 74, 182, 252, 255, 289, 312, 314, 319, 337, 343, 345, 346, 347, 348, 350, 353, 354, 355, 363, 364, 365, 366, 367, 368, 371, 374, 378

Ethnic 7, 8, 9, 10, 12, 13, 17, 18, 19, 21, 26, 29, 31, 33, 35, 36, 38, 39, 50, 52, 53, 54, 55, 59, 60, 63, 65, 72, 73, 82, 83, 101, 107, 110, 111, 113, 115, 118, 119, 121, 122, 128, 130, 131, 132, 137, 139, 141, 142, 163, 164, 172, 179, 181, 199, 200, 205, 210, 219, 222, 231, 234, 238, 245, 246, 248, 257, 260, 261, 262, 264, 269, 271, 272, 273, 275, 293, 306, 309, 311, 312, 313, 325, 327, 334, 335, 336, 344, 345, 348, 350, 353, 354, 355, 364, 366, 373, 375, 377, 381, 388

Europe 20, 77, 83, 99, 103, 108, 201, 205, 223, 236, 240, 400

Extraversion 5, 33, 49, 51, 86, 101, 116, 122, 223, 254, 283, 296, 359

F

Fashoda 72, 109, 111, 143, 396

Fertit 329, 355, 375

79, 81, 83, 84, 85, 86, 88, 89, 90, 92, 93, 94, 95, 97, 98, 99, 100, 102, 105, 107, 108, 109, 110, 112, 114, 116, 117, 118, 119, 121, 123, 124, 125, 126, 127, 128, 129, 130, 131, 132, 133, 134, 135, 136, 137, 138, 139, 140, 141, 142, 143, 145, 147, 148, 149, 150, 151, 153, 154, 155, 156, 157, 158, 159, 160, 161, 162, 163, 164, 165, 166, 167, 168, 169, 170, 171, 172, 173, 174, 175, 176, 177, 178, 179, 180, 181, 182, 183, 184, 185, 186, 187, 188, 189, 190, 191, 192, 193, 194, 195, 197, 198, 199, 200, 201, 202, 203, 204, 205, 206, 207, 208, 209, 210, 211, 212, 213, 214, 215, 216, 217, 218, 219, 220, 221, 222, 223, 224, 225, 226, 227, 228, 229, 230, 231, 232, 233, 237, 238, 240, 241, 242, 243, 244, 245, 246, 247, 248, 249, 250, 251, 252, 253, 256, 257, 258, 259, 260, 261, 262, 263, 264, 265, 266, 267, 268, 269, 270, 271, 272, 273, 274, 275, 276, 277, 278, 279, 282, 283, 284, 285, 286, 287, 289, 290, 291, 293, 295, 296, 299, 301, 302, 303, 304, 305, 306, 307, 308, 309, 310, 311, 312, 313, 314, 315, 316, 321, 324, 325, 326, 327, 328, 329, 330, 331, 332, 333, 334, 335, 336, 337, 338, 339, 340, 341, 342, 343, 344, 345, 346, 348, 349, 351, 352, 353, 354, 355, 356, 357, 359, 360, 361, 364, 365, 366, 367, 369, 370, 372, 373, 375, 376, 377, 378, 379, 380, 381, 382, 383, 384, 385, 386, 387, 388, 389, 390, 391, 392, 393

Southerners 16, 29, 37, 38, 39, 44, 46, 58, 60, 78, 84, 119, 120, 121, 129, 130, 131, 132, 137, 138, 139, 140, 141, 144, 149, 150, 151, 154, 157, 159, 160, 161, 163, 165, 166, 167, 168, 169, 171, 172, 173, 174, 176, 177, 178, 179, 180, 182, 183, 184, 185, 186, 188, 190, 191, 192, 193, 194, 195, 199, 201, 206, 208, 209, 211, 214, 215, 216, 217, 220, 223, 224, 226, 231, 232, 233, 237, 242, 243, 245, 248, 249, 259, 260, 262, 265, 266, 268, 277, 278, 282, 285, 288, 289, 299, 300, 303, 306, 311, 314, 315, 325, 326, 328, 331, 333, 334, 338, 344, 349, 351, 352, 353, 356, 357, 372, 379, 380, 383

Southern Sudan liberation Movement (SSLM) xii, 219, 220, 221, 222, 223, 224, 225, 226, 241, 242, 244, 248, 250, 251, 260, 265, 271, 277, 284, 335, 377

Southern Sudan Welfare Association (SSWA) xii, 138, 151

Soviet Union xii, 135, 156, 182, 183, 187, 196, 212, 239, 252, 256, 358, 375

Spaulding, Jay 71, 97, 98, 119, 145, 418, 424, 426

State i, iii, ix, xii, 20, 24, 33, 34, 42, 52, 95, 109, 250, 282, 291, 395, 396, 398, 399, 402, 403, 404, 405, 407, 408, 409, 412, 414, 415, 417, 419, 420, 422, 424, 425, 427, 428, 429

Sudan iii, iv, vii, ix, x, xi, xii, xiii, 1, 2, 3, 4, 5, 6, 9, 11, 12, 13, 15, 16, 17, 18, 19, 20, 22, 23, 24, 25, 26, 29, 30, 31, 33, 34, 35, 36, 37, 38, 39, 40, 41, 42, 43, 44, 45, 46, 47, 48, 49, 50, 52, 55, 56, 57, 58, 59, 60, 62, 63, 65, 66, 67, 68, 69, 70, 71, 72, 73, 74, 75, 77, 78, 79, 80, 83, 84, 85, 86, 89, 90, 91, 92, 94, 95, 96, 97, 98, 99, 100, 101, 103, 104, 107, 108, 109, 110, 111, 112, 113, 114, 115, 116, 117, 118, 119, 120, 121, 122, 123, 124, 125, 126, 127, 128, 129, 130, 131, 132, 133, 134,